The
WESTMINSTER
LARGER
CATECHISM

A COMMENTARY

The WESTMINSTER LARGER CATECHISM

A COMMENTARY

JOHANNES G. VOS

Edited by G. I. Williamson

Introduction by W. Robert Godfrey

P&R PUBLISHING

P.O. BOX 817 • PHILLIPSBURG • NEW JERSEY 08865-0817

J. G. Vos's series of 191 lessons on the Larger Catechism appeared in *Blue Banner Faith and Life* (January 1946–July 1949). Used by permission of Crown and Covenant Publications of the Reformed Presbyterian Church of North America.

The introduction by W. Robert Godfrey appeared as "The Westminster Larger Catechism," chapter 6 in *To Glorify and Enjoy God: A Commemoration of the 350th Anniversary of the Westminster Assembly,* ed. John L. Carson and David W. Hall (Edinburgh: Banner of Truth, 1994), 127–42. Used by permission of the Banner of Truth Trust.

The outline by Jeffrey K. Boer was copyrighted by him in 1998. Used by permission.

Page design and typesetting by Lakeside Design Plus

Printed in the United States of America

Library of Congress Cataloging-in-Publication Data

Vos, Johannes Geerhardus.
    The Westminster larger catechism : a commentary / by Johannes G. Vos ; edited by
  G. I. Williamson ; introduction by W. Robert Godfrey.
       p. cm.
    Includes index.
    ISBN-10: 0-87552-514-8 (pbk.)
    ISBN-13: 978-0-87552-514-3 (pbk.)
    1. Westminster Assembly (1643–1652). Larger catechism. 2. Presbyterian Church—Catechisms.
  3. Presbyterian Church—Doctrines. I. Williamson, G. I. (Gerald Irvin), 1925– II. Title.

BX9184.A3 V67 2002

238'.5—dc21   2001036928

Contents

Editor's Preface

I once heard the late Professor John Murray describe the *Blue Banner Faith and Life* magazine as the best periodical of its kind in the world. I became a faithful reader and, in doing so, became aware of the high quality of the work of its editor, the Rev. Johannes Geerhardus Vos. One of the finest things that he wrote for that periodical, in my opinion, was his series of studies on the Larger Catechism of the Westminster Assembly.

Office-bearers in conservative Presbyterian churches such as my own are required to "receive and adopt" this catechism as one of the three documents "containing the system of doctrine taught in the Holy Scriptures." But it is common knowledge that the Larger Catechism has received far less attention than either the Shorter Catechism or the Confession of Faith. One reason for this has been the paucity of good study material expounding it. A reprint of the work by Thomas Ridgeley, originally published in 1731, is the only other study I have seen, and for various reasons it is not nearly as usable as this study by Dr. Vos.

I am therefore most happy that Mrs. Marion Vos—Dr. Vos's widow—encouraged me to edit this work, and that the editorial board of the Reformed Presbyterian Church of North America authorized its publication.

May our sovereign Lord bless this study as a teacher of many who were not present to see it in the original pages of the *Blue Banner Faith and Life*.

An Introduction
to the Westminster Larger Catechism
W. Robert Godfrey

In 1908 B. B. Warfield showed himself a master of understatement when he observed: "In the later history of the Westminster formularies, the Larger Catechism has taken a somewhat secondary place."[1] Compared to the prominence and influence of the Shorter Catechism in Presbyterian circles, the Larger Catechism is a very distant second indeed. At least in the United States the Larger Catechism is seldom mentioned, much less studied, as a living part of the Presbyterian heritage. This situation is not new. From the seventeenth century on, the Shorter Catechism received much more attention than did the Larger. Francis Beattie commented a century ago: "For an exposition of the Larger Catechism alone, Ridgeley's *Body of Divinity* is deserving of notice, when so few treatises deal directly with the Larger Catechism."[2] In fact Thomas Ridgeley's two-volume work printed in 1731–33 seems to be the only major work to focus on the Larger Catechism.

Is such neglect of the Larger Catechism justified? Is there value almost 350 years after the writing of the catechism in renewing our appreciation of it? The answer certainly is yes. The Larger Catechism is a mine of fine gold theologically, historically, and spiritually. This study will delve into this mine by looking briefly at the preparation of the catechism, the purposes it was to fulfill, and the continuing value of the catechism for the church today.

The Larger Catechism's Preparation and Purpose

The catechetical concerns of the Westminster Assembly were grounded in the Solemn League and covenant that England and Scotland had signed in 1643. Article 1 of that covenant declared that we "shall endeavour to bring the Churches of God in the three kingdoms [England, Scotland, and Ireland] to the nearest conjunction and uniformity in religion, confession of faith, form of church-government, directory for worship and catechising; that we, and our posterity after us, may, as brethren, live in faith and love, and the Lord may delight to dwell in the midst of us."[3] Clearly the preparation of a catechism was a significant goal of the alliance.

The responsibility of preparing a catechism was taken very seriously by the Assembly, which appointed a committee to undertake that work.[4] Although much of the committee's work cannot be reconstructed, we do know some of the issues that were debated. The committee proposed a directory of catechizing[5] and discussed a variety of approaches to writing a catechism. Herbert Palmer wrote a draft of a catechism, but even though he had the reputation as the best catechist in England, his draft was not acceptable to the entire committee. The committee also debated whether or not to include an exposition of the Apostles' Creed, which historically had been a central feature of catechisms.[6] Since the creed was not inspired Scripture, the committee ultimately decided not to include such an exposition.

A key breakthrough in the work of the committee came in January 1647 with the decision to write two catechisms instead of one.[7] That decision seemed to clarify and simplify the work of the committee, after which they progressed rapidly. On January 14, 1647, the Assembly had adopted a motion "that the committee for the Catechism do prepare a draught of two Catechisms, one more large and another more brief, in which they are to have an eye to the Confession of Faith, and to the matter of the Catechism already begun."[8] George Gillespie observed that the Larger Catechism would be "for those of understanding" while other Scottish Commissioners referred to it as "one more exact and comprehensive." They acknowledged that it had been "very difficult . . . to dress up milk and meat both in one dish."[9] Clearly the Larger Catechism was intended for the more mature in the faith.

How was this Larger Catechism intended to be used? Certainly it was to help the study and growth of those Christians who were ready for the meaty things of the faith. The General Assembly of the Church of Scotland in approving the Larger Catechism in 1648 called it "a Directory for catechizing such as have made some proficiency in the knowledge of the grounds of religion."[10]

Philip Schaff suggests that the Assembly had another purpose in mind for the Larger Catechism. He wrote that the Assembly prepared "a larger one for the public exposition in the pulpit, according to the custom of the Reformed Churches on the continent."[11] Schaff's suggestion is intriguing, but not one that is supported either by his own footnotes or by other evidence. Schaff may have reasoned that since the general aim of the Assembly was to bring the British churches into conformity with continental Reformed practice, the Assembly would also promote the kind of catechism preaching found in the Genevan, German, and Dutch Reformed churches. Without clear evidence to support it, this reasoning seems to run contrary to other actions of the Assembly. For example, the Assembly's decision not to provide an exposition of the Apostles' Creed in the catechism because it was not inspired by God would make it unlikely that the Assembly would expect an uninspired catechism to be preached in the churches. Also the statement on preaching in the *Directory for the Publick Worship of God* seems to stand against Schaff: "Ordinarily, the subject of his sermon is to be some text of scripture, holding forth some principle or head of religion, or suitable to some special occasion emergent; or he may go on in some chapter, psalm, or book of the holy scripture, as he shall see fit."[12] T. F. Torrance probably expresses better than Schaff the purpose of the catechism for preachers when he writes, *"The Larger Catechism* was designed chiefly as a directory for ministers in their teaching of the reformed faith Sunday by Sunday."[13]

The Larger Catechism's Value

If the purpose of the Larger Catechism was to catechize those already introduced to Christian truth, it must be asked in what ways the catechism can still fulfill that purpose. What is its continuing value for the church today?

First, the value of the catechism should be seen in some of the outstanding summaries of doctrine to be found there. For example, questions 70–77 provide an excellent statement of the Reformation doctrines of justification and sanctification. Question 77 shows the relation of those two truths to each other in a very succinct and powerful way:

Q. *Wherein do justification and sanctification differ?*

A. *Although sanctification be inseparably joined with justification, yet they differ, in that God in justification imputeth the righteousness of Christ; in sanctification his Spirit infuseth grace, and enableth to the exercise thereof; in the former, sin is pardoned; in the other, it is subdued; the one doth equally free all believers from the revenging wrath of God, and that perfectly in this life, that they never fall into condemnation; the other is neither equal in all, nor in this life perfect in any, but growing up to perfection.*

Second, some expositors of the catechism have argued that the Larger Catechism on some doctrinal points is superior to the formulations in the Westminster Confession of Faith. John Murray, for example, maintains that the statement of the covenant of grace in the Larger Catechism, questions 30–32, is superior to chapter 7, section 3 of the Confession. He also states that on the imputation of the guilt of Adam's sin the Larger Catechism, question 22, relates the imputation to the covenant of works more clearly than the Confession of Faith, chapter 6, section 3.[14]

Third, the Larger Catechism provides an especially full and rich exposition of the Ten Commandments. The writing of this section of the catechism has been especially associated with the name of Anthony Tuckney, a noted Puritan moral theologian. Many regard this part of the catechism as an outstanding introduction to Puritan ethical thought.

Not all scholars, however, have regarded this section as a helpful expression of Reformed reflection on the law. Philip Schaff commented: "It serves also in part as a valuable commentary or supplement to the Confession, especially on the ethical part of our religion. But it is over-minute in the specification of what God has commanded and forbidden in the Ten Commandments, and loses itself in the wilderness of details."[15] T. F. Torrance is even more critical. He suggests that Calvin's Genevan Catechism on the law is "more evangelical" while the Larger Catechism is "highly moralistic."[16]

Despite these criticisms other commentators give a much more positive evaluation. Frederick Loetscher, for example, wrote: "Particularly admirable is the exposition of the law. No doubt, there is here a tendency toward excessive elaboration in specifying what is enjoined and what is forbidden by the several Commandments; but no work of the kind offers a more suggestive and helpful treatment of the ethical and social teachings of the New Testament."[17]

Are the criticisms of this section of the catechism justified? One response must be that the Larger Catechism devotes a significantly lower percentage of questions to the law than does the Shorter Catechism (see table 1 at the end of this introduction).[18] If the charge of moralism were true at all, it would be more true of the Shorter Catechism than of the Larger.[19]

More significantly, however, while the exposition of the Ten Commandments in the Larger Catechism is detailed and pointed, it does not fall into trivial or subtle matters. Nor does it take on a legalistic tone. The exposition follows the practice of Calvin in seeing all of man's moral responsibility as summed up in the Ten Commandments. Many of the answers in this section of the catechism are long, but all of the commandments except two are treated in just three or four questions. Not surprisingly the fourth commandment gets longer exposition—seven questions—in view of its importance to Puritans and the controversial nature of sabbatarianism in the seventeenth century. Perhaps it is surprising that eleven questions are devoted to the fifth commandment. Such lengthy treatment probably reflects the unsettled social and political circumstances in England at the time of the Assembly and the need to deal fully with issues of obedience to superiors. The Larger Catechism's exposition of the law is in fact a useful basis for meditation and self-examination as it opens up the meaning of the commandments for the benefit of the believer who seeks to lead a godly life.

David Wells has recently praised the kind of integration of Christian living with Christian theology which is exhibited in the Larger Catechism. Wells wrote that in the past theology had "three essential aspects": "(1) a confession element, (2) reflection on this confession, and (3) the cultivation of a set of virtues that are grounded in the first two elements."[20] He adds, "The third element, the virtues of life, have [sic] not always been seen as central to the work of the theologian *as theologian*. This has at times been a significant weakness in Protestant theology, as compared with Catholic, but Puritanism is a reminder that it need not be excluded from the interests of a genuinely Protestant theology."[21] The discussion of the law in the Larger Catechism seeks to cultivate virtue in a most pointed way and provides a vital encouragement for theologian and believer.

Fourth, the value of the Larger Catechism rests in its presentation of the doctrine of the church. The Larger Catechism develops a full-orbed doctrine of the church—a subject almost entirely absent from the Shorter Catechism. Alexander Mitchell noted about the Shorter Catechism:

> While . . . it is a thoroughly Calvinistic catechism, it has nothing of church censures, church courts, or church officers, as many similar productions have. Nay, it does not even have a definition of the Church, whether visible or invisible, like the Larger Catechism and

the Confession of Faith, but only an incidental reference to it in connection with the answer to the question, To whom is baptism to be administered?[22]

Mitchell saw this as a strength rather than a weakness. He wrote:

> It would seem as if in this their simplest yet noblest symbol they wished, as far as Calvinists could do so, to eliminate from their statements all that was subordinate or unessential—all relating to the mere organisation of Christians as an external community—all in which they differed from sound Protestant Episcopalians on the one hand, and from the less unsound of the sectaries on the other, and to make a supreme effort to provide a worthy catechism in which all the Protestant youth in the country might be trained.[23]

The doctrine of the church, however, cannot be seen as "subordinate or unessential." None of the Westminster divines would have regarded the doctrine of the church as an insignificant matter. The absence of a doctrine of the church in the Shorter Catechism reflects its purpose, which, as Torrance put it, was to aid "the inquirer"[24] with "the appropriation of salvation and with the Christian life."[25] The Assembly intended the Larger Catechism to supplement the Shorter, treating some topics—such as the church—not covered in the Shorter.

The intention that the Larger Catechism supplement the Shorter can be clearly seen by comparing the sections of the two catechisms that occur just before the exposition of the law.[26] Questions 37 and 38 of the Shorter Catechism speak of the benefits derived from the death and resurrection of Christ, whereas questions 82–90 of the Larger Catechism speak of "communion in glory" with Christ rather than benefits. What is striking is that while the Larger Catechism speaks of the communion in glory for "the invisible church," the Shorter Catechism speaks of benefits for "believers." The Shorter Catechism deliberately focuses on individuals while the Larger Catechism focuses much more on the Christian community.

The Larger Catechism's Doctrine of the Church

The decision to eliminate a doctrine of the church from the Shorter Catechism may have made sense in a context where it was assumed that catechumens would move on to the fuller instruction of the Larger Catechism. Where the Larger Catechism no longer functions in that way, however, a very serious omission exists. The doctrine of the church is an integral element of true Calvinism.

Indeed a distinctive doctrine of the church is of the very essence of Calvinism. Calvinism is a form of Christianity that avoids two extremes in its understanding of the church. On the one hand, it rejects a form of sacramental Christianity that sees the offices and sacraments as inevitably or automatically bearing the grace of God. On the other hand, it rejects an interior, mystical form of Christianity that sees the outward means of grace as irrelevant. The institution of the church as the mother of the faithful is essential to genuine Calvinism.

John Calvin makes the centrality of the church very clear in his *Institutes of the Christian Religion.* In broad terms book 1 is about the Father and creation; book 2, the Son and the accomplishment of redemption; book 3, the Holy Spirit and the application of redemption to the individual; and book 4, the Holy Spirit applying redemption through the church. Calvin begins book 4 with these words:

> It is by the faith in the gospel that Christ becomes ours and we are made partakers of the salvation and eternal blessedness brought by him. Since, however, in our ignorance and sloth (to which I add fickleness of disposition) we need outward helps to beget and increase faith within us, and advance to its goal, God has also added these aids that he may provide for our weakness. And in order that the preaching of the gospel might flourish, he deposited this treasure in the church. He instituted "pastors and teachers" [Eph. 4:11] through whose lips he might teach his own; he furnished them with authority; finally, he omitted nothing that might make for holy agreement of faith and for right order.[27]

Indeed book 4 is the longest book of the *Institutes* (more than one-third of the whole work) and is almost entirely devoted to the church and the sacraments.[28]

Calvin's commitment to the centrality of the church is maintained in the various Reformed standards. For example, the Belgic Confession says that the church is necessary to the preservation of true religion.[29] The Westminster Confession of Faith declares that outside the visible church "there is no ordinary possibility of salvation."[30]

A Reformed doctrine of the church is fully developed in the Larger Catechism. The references to the church appear in many different contexts in the Larger Catechism. In discussions of the work of Christ the church is mentioned as the object of his love. Christ is "king of his church" and prophet "to the church." Christ "doth gather and defend his church" and is "the Saviour only of his body the church."[31] The exposition of the law also contains references to the church. The second commandment requires purity in the worship and the government of the church.[32] The fifth commandment requires proper obedience to church authorities.[33] A summary reflection on the law notes that sin is aggravated if committed against church censures.[34] Six questions on the sacraments mention the church, stressing that the sacraments are instituted in and for the church and are administered under the authority of the church.[35] The catechism's section on prayer calls three times for prayer on behalf of the church.[36]

The key element in the Larger Catechism's definition of the church is the distinction made between the visible and invisible church.[37] The visible church is all who profess Christ along with their children. The invisible church is all the elect who do or will enjoy union and communion with him.

This distinction between the visible and invisible church is one expression of the distinction between the outward means through which God ordinarily acts to save and the inward reality of salvation enjoyed by the saved. The visible church has the privilege of God's special protection and "of enjoying the communion of saints, the ordinary means of salvation, and offers of grace by Christ to all the members of it in the ministry of the gospel, testifying, that whosoever believes in him shall be saved, and excluding none that will come unto him."[38] The invisible church includes those who actually share in the salvation held forth in the visible church.

In Reformed theology the "ordinary means of salvation" are a crucial element in God's saving economy. Both the Shorter and Larger Catechisms make this clear. The Shorter Catechism speaks strongly: God requires "the diligent use of all the outward means whereby Christ communicateth to us the benefits of redemption."[39] The Larger Catechism speaks in the same manner, also referring to the outward means as "the ordinary means of salvation."[40]

The Shorter Catechism is relatively brief in its treatment of the means of salvation. It does state the importance of worship and the ordinances in expounding the second commandment.[41] It also lists the Word (especially preaching), the sacraments, and prayer as means.[42] Not surprisingly the Larger Catechism develops these means much more fully in its questions. The Larger Catechism is also more specific about the ordinances of God. In discussing the second commandment, for example, the catechism mentions worship and the ordinances and then specifies: "particularly prayer in the name of Christ; the reading, preaching, and hearing of the Word; the administration and receiving of the sacraments; church government and discipline; the ministry and the maintenance thereof; religious fasting; swearing by the name of God, and vowing unto him."[43]

While both catechisms discuss the outward means of salvation, in the Larger Catechism the means are clearly tied to the church, while in the Shorter Catechism they are not. For example, the role of the ministry is mentioned several times in the Larger Catechism,[44] but is left only implicit in the Shorter Catechism's reference to preaching.[45] The Larger Catechism clearly has a necessary and vital supplement to offer to the Shorter Catechism on the doctrine of the church and the outward means of salvation.

A Mature Summary of the Faith

A final and most important value of the Larger Catechism is that it is a full, balanced, edifying summary of the Christian faith. The Larger Catechism is a useful and worthy aid to the believer as he grows in a knowledge of God's truth. The catechism is not at all difficult to read and understand. In fact, it is simpler in its statements than the Confession. (Compare, for example, the discussion of the decrees of God where the Confession, 3:1, mentions "the liberty or contingency of second causes" and the Larger Catechism, question 12, does not.) The difficulty of using the Larger Catechism is mainly in the length of its sentences, which can be daunting for the contemporary reader. It is in fact easy to understand if taken one clause at a time.

The Westminster Assembly was remarkable in many ways. The standards it produced are one of the great treasures in Christ's church. The Larger Catechism is a crucial part of that treasure, and churches of the Reformed tradition—and especially Presbyterian churches—impoverish themselves if they fail to use it.

As Givens Strickler asked at the celebration of Westminster a century ago, "Why cannot the ministers and officers in our denomination so instruct our people as to these great doctrines, that in every church there shall be a number, at least, who shall know how to maintain them against any of the popular assaults that are so frequently made upon them? We shall never succeed as we may and ought until this is done."[46]

Today the churches face a greater educational task than they have for several centuries. Doctrinal ignorance is widespread. Pastors and teachers are often looking for useful, effective study materials. In response to this need the church must reclaim its great educational resources from the past. The Larger Catechism is a neglected tool the church needs today to help believers develop vital and balanced Christian faith and life.

Table 1. The number of questions given to various subjects in four Reformed catechisms

	Calvin's Genevan Catechism (374 qq.)	Heidelberg Catechism (129 qq.)	Westminster Shorter Catechism (107 qq.)	Westminster Larger Catechism (196 qq.)
On the person and work of Christ	59 (15.8%)	31 (24%)	11 (10.3%)	27 (13.8%)
On the law	102 (27.1%)	24 (18.6%)	43 (40%)	59 (30%)
On prayer	64 (17%)	14 (10.9%)	10 (9.3%)	19 (9.6%)
On the sacraments	78 (20.7%)	17 (13.2%)	7 (6.5%)	17 (8.7%)
Making explicit reference to the Holy Spirit	34 (9.1%)	30 (23.3%)	10 (9.3%)	36 (18.4%)
Using the word *church*	22 (5.9%)	6 (4.7%)	1 (0.9%)	26 (13.2%)

Notes

1. B. B. Warfield, *The Westminster Assembly and Its Work* (New York: Oxford University Press, 1931), 64.

2. Francis R. Beattie, "Introduction," *Memorial Volume of the Westminster Assembly, 1647–1897*, 2d ed. (Richmond, Va.: Presbyterian Committee of Publication, 1897), xxxvi.

3. Cited from *The Confession of Faith* (Glasgow: Free Presbyterian, 1966), 359.

4. For the membership of that committee and the details of how the committee worked and changed, see Alexander F. Mitchell, *The Westminster Assembly: Its History and Standards* (Philadelphia: Presbyterian Board of Publications, 1884), 409ff.; Warfield, *The Westminster Assembly*, 62ff.; and Givens B. Strickler, "The Nature, Value, and Special Utility of Catechisms," *Memorial Volume*, 121ff.

5. Robert Baillie, *The Letters and Journals of Robert Baillie*, ed. David Laing (Edinburgh: Robert Ogle, 1841), 2:148. "As for our Directorie, the matter of Prayer which we gave in, is agreed to in the Committee. Mr. Marshall's part, anent Preaching, and Mr. Palmer's, about Catechizeing, though the one be the best preacher, and the other the best catechist, in England, yet we no wayes like it: so their papers are past in our hands to frame them according to our mind."

6. Mitchell, *The Westminster Assembly*, 416.

7. By April discussion of the Larger Catechism began in the Assembly, and by October the work (except for the Scripture proofs) was completed. For a reconstruction of the original effort to produce a single catechism, see Wayne R. Spear, "The Unfinished Westminster Catechism," appendix A in *To Glorify and Enjoy God: A Commemoration of the 350th Anniversary of the Westminster Assembly*, ed. John L. Carson and David W. Hall (Edinburgh: Banner of Truth, 1994), 259–66.

8. Cited in John Murray, "The Catechisms of the Westminster Assembly," *Presbyterian Guardian*, December 25, 1943, 362.

9. Quotations from Mitchell, *The Westminster Assembly*, 418.

10. Cited from *The Confession of Faith*, 128.

11. Philip Schaff, *Creeds of Christendom*, 3 vols. (Grand Rapids: Baker, 1977), 1:784.

12. Cited from *The Confession of Faith*, 379.

13. Thomas F. Torrance, *The School of Faith* (New York: Harper, 1959), 183. Frederick W. Loetscher makes a similar observation: "[The Larger Catechism is] chiefly designed as an adaptation of the Confession to the didactic functions of the preacher and pastor." "The Westminster Formularies: A Brief Description," in *The Westminster Assembly* (Department of History, Office of the General Assembly of the Presbyterian Church in the U.S.A., 1943), 17.

14. Murray, "The Catechisms of the Westminster Assembly," 363. This portion of Murray's article was reprinted in *Presbyterian Reformed Magazine* 8 (spring 1993): 14.

15. Schaff, *Creeds of Christendom*, 1:786.

16. Torrance, *The School of Faith*, xviii.

17. Loetscher, "The Westminster Formularies," 17.

18. See table 1. While a higher percentage of questions on the law is found in the Shorter Catechism, the amount of space given to the exposition of the law is about 33% in the Shorter and about 35% in the Larger.

19. Torrance does accuse the Shorter Catechism of being moralistic (*The School of Faith*, xvi). But he does not specify the grounds for this charge beyond observing that a substantial proportion of both the Shorter and Larger Catechisms is given to the exposition of the law.

Moralism is usually defined in terms of the way in which the law is related to justification, not in terms of the amount of attention given to it.

20. David Wells, *No Place for Truth* (Grand Rapids: Eerdmans, 1993), 98.

21. Ibid., 99n.4.

22. Mitchell, *The Westminster Assembly*, 432. Others have noticed this as well. In a general way Thomas Ridgeley noted at the beginning of his work on the Larger Catechism: "It is the larger of them that we have attempted to explain and regulate our method by; because it contains several heads of divinity, not touched on in the shorter." Thomas Ridgeley, *A Body of Divinity*, ed. J. M. Wilson (New York: Carter, 1855), 1:2. Torrance notes the absence of any doctrine of the church in the Shorter Catechism. *The School of Faith*, xvi.

23. Mitchell, *The Westminster Assembly*, 432.

24. Torrance, *The School of Faith*, 262.

25. Ibid., xvi.

26. The Larger Catechism is divided into two halves, one on belief (questions 6–90) and one on duty (91–196). The Shorter Catechism is not explicitly divided in this way, but follows the same order as the Larger.

27. John Calvin, *Institutes of the Christian Religion*, ed. J. T. McNeill, trans. Ford Lewis Battles, 2 vols. (Philadelphia: Westminster Press, 1960), 4.1.1.

28. Only the last chapter of book 4 on civil government is not specifically on the church or the sacraments.

29. Belgic Confession, article 30. See table 1 on the church.

30. Westminster Confession of Faith, 25.2.

31. Larger Catechism, questions 42–43, 54, 60.

32. Ibid., question 108.

33. Ibid., question 124.

34. Ibid., question 151.

35. Ibid., questions 162, 164–66, 173, 176.

36. Ibid., questions 183–84, 191.

37. See especially Larger Catechism, questions 61–65.

38. Larger Catechism, question 63.

39. Shorter Catechism, question 85; see also question 88.

40. Larger Catechism, questions 153, 63.

41. Shorter Catechism, question 50.

42. Shorter Catechism, question 88. These three means are then examined in questions 89–107: two questions on the Word, seven on the sacraments, and ten on prayer.

43. Larger Catechism, question 108.

44. Ibid., questions 108, 156, 158, 176, 191.

45. Shorter Catechism, question 89.

46. *Memorial Volume*, 136–37.

An Outline of the Westminster Larger Catechism

Jeffrey K. Boer

1 A. "Man's chief and highest end is to glorify God, and fully to enjoy him forever!" (Larger Catechism, answer 1)
2 A. Then, God's revelation fleshes this out. (2–196)
    1 B. God's general manifestation and special revelation compared (2) (God's general manifestation is not studied any further in the catechism.)
    2 B. Special revelation expounded (3–196)
        1 C. What constitutes God's special revelation? (3–4)
        2 C. What do the Scriptures principally teach? (5–196)
            1 D. What man ought to believe concerning God (6–90)
                1 E. What is God? (7)
                2 E. Persons in the Godhead (8–11)
                3 E. Decrees of God (12–13)
                4 E. Execution of God's decrees (14–90)
                    1 F. God's creation (15–17)
                    2 F. God's providence (18–90)
                        1 G. God's providence toward angels (19)
                        2 G. God's providence toward man (20–90)
                            1 H. God's providence toward man before the fall (20)
                            2 H. The fall of man (21–22)
                            3 H. God's providence toward man after the fall (23–90)
                                1 I. Man's estate after the fall (23–29)
                                  1 J. The sinfulness of man's estate (24–26)
                                  2 J. The misery of man's estate (27–29)
                                      1 K. Punishments of sin in this world (28)
                                      2 K. Punishments of sin in the world to come (29)
                              2 I. God's grace after the fall (30–88)
                                1 J. God's covenant of grace (30–32)
                                2 J. The administration of God's covenant of grace (33–35)
                                      1 K. Old Testament administration (34)
                                      2 K. New Testament administration (35)
                                3 J. The Mediator of the covenant of grace (36–45)
                                    1 K. How Christ the Son of God became man (37)
                                    2 K. Why the Mediator had to be God (38)
                                    3 K. Why the Mediator had to be man (39)
                                    4 K. Why the Mediator had to be both God and man (40)

What Man
Ought to Believe

1

Foundational Doctrines

1. Q. *What is the chief and highest end of man?*

A. *Man's chief and highest end is to glorify God, and fully to enjoy him for ever.*

Scripture References
- Rev. 4:11. All things were created for God's pleasure.
- Rom. 11:36. All things exist for God.
- 1 Cor. 10:31. It is our duty to glorify God in all we do.
- Ps. 73:24–28. God teaches us how to glorify him, and that we shall enjoy him in glory.
- John 17:21–24. Our supreme destiny is the enjoyment of God in glory.

Commentary
1. What is the meaning of the word *end* in this question? It means the purpose for which something exists.

2. Could a consistent evolutionist agree with the catechism's answer to question 1? No. A consistent evolutionist could not agree that man's chief and highest end is to glorify and enjoy God, for he must hold that the human race has evolved from a brute ancestry by a process which originated in blind chance. Therefore he must hold that the human race cannot exist for any purpose outside of itself. There are "theistic evolutionists" who believe that evolution was God's method of creation, but they are not consistent, for creation concerns the origin of things, while evolution starts by assuming that things already exist and seeks to show their development to other forms. The consistent evolutionist cannot believe in creation by the sheer power of God, and therefore he cannot believe that the human race exists not for itself but for God.

3. What is wrong with the following statement: "Man's chief and highest end is to seek happiness"? This statement makes the purpose of human life something within man himself. This cannot be reconciled with the Scripture teaching that all things exist for God because they were created by God for his own glory. To say that man's chief end is to seek happiness is contrary to belief in the God of the Bible. Of course man's real happiness results from his recognizing and seeking his true end, namely, to glorify and enjoy God his Creator.

4. What is wrong with the following statement: "Man's chief and highest end is to seek the greatest good of the greatest number"? This statement involves the same error as the one just discussed, for it makes the purpose of human life something within man himself. The difference is that the present statement makes the happiness or welfare of the human race in general the purpose of human life, whereas the former statement made the happiness of the individual the purpose of human life. Both are contrary to the Bible teaching concerning God the Creator and End of all things. Both are essentially the same as the pagan idea that "man is the measure of all things." Because modern life is largely dominated by this false idea, it is essentially pagan rather than Christian. Even some churches have absorbed this pagan viewpoint and talk about God as "a democratic God."

5. Why does the catechism place glorifying God before enjoying God? Because the most important element in the purpose of human life is glorifying God, while enjoying God is strictly subordinate to glorifying God. In our religious life, we should always place the chief emphasis on glorifying God. The person who does this will truly enjoy God, both here and hereafter. But the person who thinks of enjoying God apart from glorifying God is in danger of supposing that God exists for man instead of man for God. To stress enjoying God more than glorifying God will result in a falsely mystical or emotional type of religion.

6. Why can the human race, or any member of it, never attain true happiness apart from glorifying God? Because true happiness depends on our consciously aiming to serve the purpose for which we were created, namely, to glorify God and enjoy him. Consciously to serve the purpose for which God created him is man's glory, and apart from a conscious conse- cration of himself to that purpose, there can be no real, deep, and satisfying happiness. As Augustine said in his *Confessions,* "Thou hast created us for Thyself, O God, and our heart is restless until it finds repose in Thee."

2. Q. *How doth it appear that there is a God?*

A. *The very light of nature in man, and the works of God, declare plainly that there is a God; but his word and Spirit only do sufficiently and effectually reveal him unto men for their salvation.*

Scripture References

- Rom. 1:19–20. God revealed by the light of nature and by his works.
- Rom. 2:14–16. The law of God revealed in the human heart.
- Ps. 19:1–3. God revealed by the heavens.
- Acts 17:28. Human life totally dependent on God.
- 1 Cor. 2:9–10. God's natural revelation inadequate; not equal to his special revelation by his Spirit.
- 2 Tim. 3:15–17. Holy Scripture a sufficient revelation for salvation.
- Isa. 59:21. God's Word and Spirit given to his covenant people, unlike his natural revelation, which is given to all mankind.

Commentary

1. What is meant by the "light of nature in man"? This means the natural revelation of God in the human heart and mind. This "light of nature" is common to all mankind. The heathen who have never received God's special revelation, the Bible, have a certain knowledge of God by nature, and a certain consciousness of the moral law in their own hearts (Rom. 2:14–16). To believe in God is natural to mankind; only "the fool" says in his heart that there is no God.

2. What is meant by "the works of God"? This expression means the revelation of God in nature outside of human nature. It includes the whole realm of nature, great and small. The starry heavens as observed by the largest telescope, and the tiniest particles of matter that can be photographed by the electron microscope, all disclose the God who is their Creator and Ruler. The works of God also include all living creatures, and all God's works in the course of human history. All bear witness to the invisible God who created, preserves, and controls them all.

3. What message do the light of nature and the works of God bring to mankind? The light of nature and the works of God bring to mankind a message concerning the existence of God, his eternal power and deity (Rom. 1:19–20), his glory (Ps. 19:1), and his moral law (Rom. 2:14–16). This natural revelation of God and of his will is sufficient to leave men without excuse for their sins (Rom. 1:20–21).

4. Why is this message of the light of nature and the works of God inadequate for mankind's spiritual needs? This natural revelation of God and of his will is insufficient for mankind's spiritual needs, in his present fallen and sinful condition, for two reasons. (a) When mankind fell into sin, his spiritual need changed. He now needs more than he did when he was created. Man now needs salvation from sin by divine grace through a Mediator. But the light of nature and the works of God have nothing to say about salvation from sin. They reveal no gospel suited to the sinner's need. (b) Man's fall into sin changed his capacity to receive and understand even the message which the light of nature and the works of God do bring to him. Man's heart and mind became darkened by sin (Rom. 1:21–22). The result of this was that the natural revelation of God was misinterpreted and corrupted into idolatry (Rom. 1:23). This lapse into false religion in turn resulted in terrible moral corruption and degradation (Rom. 1:24–32). But in spite of all this, the natural revelation of God and of his will still leaves men without excuse, because their changed need and their present inability to understand that natural revelation are their own fault. Mankind is responsible not only for falling into sin, but also for all the consequences of falling into sin.

5. What fuller revelation of God and of his will do we have? Besides the natural revelation of God, we have the supernatural revelation of God, which exists today only in the form of the Holy Scriptures of the Old and New Testaments. This supernatural revelation of God is sometimes called his special revelation. It is called supernatural because it was given to man not through the operation of the laws of nature, but by the miraculous working of God the Holy Spirit (2 Peter 1:21).

6. What are the principal differences between God's natural revelation and his revelation in the form of Holy Scripture? (a) The former is given to all men without exception; the latter is limited to those whom the Bible reaches. (b) The former is sufficient to leave men without excuse; the latter is sufficient for salvation. (c) God's revelation in the form of Holy Scripture is clearer and more definite than his natural revelation. (d) God's revelation in the form of Holy Scripture imparts many truths about God and his will which cannot be known from his natural revelation.

7. In order that God's revelation in the form of Holy Scripture may make us wise unto salvation, what is needed besides the Bible itself? For Holy Scripture to make a person wise unto salvation there is required, besides the Bible itself, a true faith (2 Tim. 3:15; Heb. 4:2). This true faith is a gift of God (Eph. 2:8; Acts 16:14), being wrought in the heart of a sinner by the Holy Spirit of God (Eph. 1:17–19). Thus besides the Bible itself is required the illumination of the mind by the Holy Spirit, so that the sinner can understand and appropriate the truth unto his salvation. The Holy Spirit, in his illuminating work, does not reveal any truth in addition to what is revealed in the Bible, but only enables the sinner to see and believe the truth already revealed in the Bible.

3. Q. *What is the word of God?*

A. *The holy scriptures of the Old and New Testaments are the word of God, the only rule of faith and obedience.*

Scripture References
- 2 Tim. 3:16. All Scripture is divinely inspired.
- 2 Peter 1:19–21. The Scriptures not of human origin, but the product of the Holy Spirit.
- Eph. 2:20. The apostles (New Testament) and prophets (Old Testament) form the foundation of the Christian church.

- Rev. 22:18–19. Scripture, being of divine origin, character, and authority, may not be added to or subtracted from.
- Isa. 8:20. Scripture the standard of faith and obedience.
- Luke 16:29–31. No new revelation could supersede Scripture.
- Gal. 1:8–9. Anything contrary to Scripture to be rejected, no matter how appealing it may be.
- 2 Tim. 3:15–17. Scripture a complete and perfect rule of faith and life.

Commentary

1. Why is it proper that the Scriptures be called "holy"? Because they are the revelation of a holy God; because they set forth holy teaching; and because when accepted with true faith they lead to a holy life.

2. In what sense is it true that the Scriptures are the Word of God? The Scriptures are the Word of God in the plain, literal sense of the word *are*. They are the Word of God in written form, without any other limitations whatever. That is to say, the Bible itself, as a book, is the Word of God, and the actual written words of the book are the very words of God.

3. In what sense is it true that the Bible "contains" the Word of God? The Bible "contains" the Word of God in the sense that the Word of God forms the contents of the Bible, just as it is proper to say that the Bible contains two Testaments, or that the Bible contains sixty-six books.

4. In what senses is it not true that the Bible "contains" the Word of God? (a) It is not true that the Bible "contains" the Word of God in the sense that the Word of God forms only a part of the contents of the Bible, the rest being merely the words of men. (b) It is not true that the Bible "contains" the Word of God in the sense that there is a distinction between the actual written words of the Bible, on the one hand, and the Word of God "contained" in them, on the other hand. This distinction, which has been popularized by the Swiss theologian Karl Barth and his followers, cannot be reconciled with the statements of the Bible itself, nor with the doctrine concerning Scripture which is set forth in the Westminster Standards. If the written words of the Bible are not themselves actually the Word of God, then the Bible cannot be infallible.

5. If the Scriptures in their entirety are the Word of God, how can we explain the fact that they contain the words of Satan and of wicked men? The words of Satan and of wicked men are incorporated into the Word of God as quotations, in order that we may learn the lessons that God wants us to learn. The statement "There is no God" is a human falsehood, but the statement "The fool hath said in his heart, 'There is no God'" (Ps. 53:1) is a divine truth. The words "There is no God" are the words of the fool, but the complete sentence, including the words of the fool as a quotation, is the Word of God. "Skin for skin, yea, all that a man hath will he give for his life," was the devil's lie; but the complete sentence, "And Satan answered the Lord, and said, Skin for skin, yea, all that a man hath will he give for his life," is the Word of God, a divinely inspired and infallible record of what Satan said. When we affirm that the Bible in its entirety is the Word of God, this does not mean that any verse or portion of the Bible may be taken out of its context and interpreted as if it stood alone.

6. For what two things are the Scriptures our rule? The Scriptures are our rule for faith and obedience.

7. Why are the Scriptures our only rule of faith and obedience? The Scriptures are our only rule of faith and obedience because as the written Word of God they are unique and infallible, and therefore no other rule of faith and obedience may be placed alongside of them. This principle of course does not rule out such subordinate standards as the Larger Catechism itself, which present not another rule in addition to Scripture, but merely a systematic summary of what Scripture teaches. The Larger Catechism, for example, is a legitimate rule of faith and obedience only because, and only so far as, it is faithful to the teachings of the Scriptures. It possesses no inherent authority of its own.

8. What is wrong with saying that conscience is our guide for faith and conduct? The human conscience cannot tell a person what to believe or how to live. It cannot tell a person what is right and what is wrong. The conscience can only tell a person whether or not he is acting according to what he already believes to be right. If a savage believes it is right to practice cannibalism, his conscience will not reprove him for eating human flesh. If a person somehow believes it is wrong to consult a physician, take medicine, or wear eyeglasses, his conscience will reprove him when he does these things. The conscience can only indicate whether a person's conduct is in accordance with his beliefs; it cannot tell him whether his beliefs are true or not. Therefore the conscience cannot be the rule for faith and life.

9. If we add some other rule along with the Bible, what effect will this have on the authority of the Bible for our faith and life? The inevitable result will be that the Bible will take second place, and something else will become our real authority for faith and life. It is not possible to have two supreme authorities in any field. Nor is it possible to have two equal authorities without making one of them the standard for interpreting the other.

10. What large church makes tradition a rule of faith and conduct along with Scripture? The Roman Catholic Church. The effect, of course, is to make void the Word of God by the tradition of the church. For the Bible is interpreted in accordance with the tradition, not the tradition in accordance with the Bible.

11. How do the followers of Mary Baker Eddy violate the principle that the Scriptures are our only rule of faith and life? By placing Mrs. Eddy's book, *Science and Health with the Key to the Scriptures,* alongside the Bible as an authority, with the inevitable result that Mrs. Eddy's book is their real authority and the Bible is nullified. "Christian Science" cannot stand with the Bible alone as its guidebook; it has to have Mrs. Eddy's writings, which are utterly contrary to the Bible, to prop it up.

12. How do the Friends or Quakers violate the principle that the Scriptures are our only rule of faith and life? By their emphasis on the mystical "inner light" as their guide for faith and life. There are various sects of Quakers; not all are alike. But historically the "Friends" movement has emphasized the "inner light" and has tended to subordinate the Bible to the "inner light."

13. Is the New Testament more fully or more truly the Word of God than the Old Testament? No. The New Testament itself shows that our Lord Jesus Christ and his apostles regarded the Old Testament as the Word of God in the fullest and strictest sense, and taught this high view of the Old Testament consistently.

14. Are the words of Christ, which in some Bibles are printed in red ink, more truly the Word of God than the other parts of the Bible? No. The whole Bible, from Genesis to Revelation, is the Word of Christ. The Old Testament is Christ's Word through Moses and the prophets; the New Testament is Christ's Word through the apostles and evangelists;

included in the New Testament is the record of Christ's sayings during his earthly ministry; but these sayings, although spoken by God more directly than most of the other parts of the Bible, nevertheless are not more truly the Word of God than the other parts of the Scriptures. See 2 Samuel 23:1–2; 1 Corinthians 14:37; Revelation 1:1; 22:16.

15. If we think of our Christian belief as a building, what part of the building would the answer to question 3 of the Larger Catechism be? The foundation, on which all the rest must stand. Sometimes objection has been made to this statement on the ground that the Bible represents Christ as the only legitimate foundation. This objection is without weight, as it seeks to employ a metaphor—the idea of a foundation—without analyzing its meaning. Christ is the foundation of our reconciliation with God, by his blood and righteousness. Christ is the foundation of the church, by his finished work of redemption and his present exaltation in glory. But an acknowledgment that the Scriptures are the Word of God and the only rule of faith and obedience must be the foundation of any legitimate formulation of Christian doctrine.

4. Q. *How doth it appear that the Scriptures are the word of God?*

A. *The scriptures manifest themselves to be the word of God, by their majesty and purity; by the consent of all the parts, and the scope of the whole, which is to give all glory to God; by their light and power to convince and convert sinners, to comfort and build up believers unto salvation; but the Spirit of God bearing witness by and with the scriptures in the heart of man, is alone able fully to persuade it that they are the very word of God.*

Scripture References
- Hos. 8:12; 1 Cor. 2:6–7, 13; Ps. 119:18, 129. The majesty of the Scriptures.
- Pss. 12:6; 119:140. The purity of the Scriptures.
- Acts 10:43; 26:22. The consent of all the parts of the Scripture.
- Rom. 3:19, 27. The scope of the Scriptures as a whole.

- Acts 18:28; Heb. 4:12; James 1:18; Ps. 19:7–9; Rom. 15:4; Acts 20:32; John 20:31. The power of the Scriptures to convert sinners and edify saints.
- John 16:13–14; 1 John 2:20, 27. The witness of the Holy Spirit in the heart.

Commentary

1. What is meant by the "majesty" of the Scriptures? The "majesty" of the Scriptures means their lofty or wonderful character, which lifts them far above all human writings. In the Scriptures are indeed found things which eye hath not seen, nor ear heard, neither have entered into the heart of man, but which God has revealed by his Spirit, who searches all things, even the deep things of God (1 Cor. 2:9–10).

2. What is the position of the Bible among the books of the world? The position of the Bible among the books of the world is altogether unique. It has been translated into more languages than any other book; more copies have been circulated than of any other book. It is recognized as the world's greatest book from the literary point of view. But the Bible is unique especially with respect to its teachings. Among the sacred books of the religions of the world there is none that can compare with the Bible in inherent loftiness or majesty.

3. What is meant by the "purity" of the Scriptures? The "purity" of the Scriptures means their character as the true Word of God, wholly free from all impurities of error and foreign matter.

4. Why can other books not equal the Bible in purity? Because the Bible is the only book whose very words are the product of supernatural inspiration of God, and therefore it is the only book which is infallible and wholly free of errors.

5. Why do we believe that the Scriptures are entirely free from errors? We believe that the Scriptures are entirely free from errors, not because we find no apparent errors in the Bible, for it cannot be denied that a few apparent errors have been pointed out in the Bible, but because the Bible itself claims to be free from errors. Our belief about the Scriptures must not be an inference from facts of our own experience, but a formulation of the teachings of the Scriptures themselves about themselves. If we find some apparent errors in the Bible, that is a matter of our own experience as finders. But if we observe that the Bible represents itself as being free from errors, that is an observation concerning the teaching of the Bible. We must accept the Bible's teaching about hell and other matters. The fact is that the Bible teaches that the Bible is inerrant. Even though we may have some unsolved problems concerning apparent errors in the Bible, still these problems do not justify setting aside the Bible's teaching about itself, unless it can be proved that the Bible really contains errors, and that they exist in the genuine text of the Hebrew or Greek original. If that could be proved, the trustworthiness of the Bible as a teacher of truth on all subjects would thereby be destroyed. If we are to trust the Bible in what it says about God and man, sin and salvation, we must also trust the Bible in what it says about its own infallibility.

6. What is meant by "the consent of all the parts" of the Scriptures? By "the consent of all the parts" of the Scriptures is meant: (a) that there are no real contradictions in the Bible; (b) that all the parts of the Bible form a unity, an organism, a harmonious whole, not merely a collection of separate writings with diverse ideas and viewpoints. This beautiful harmony of the various parts of the Bible is an evidence that back of all the human writers there was a divine Author, the Spirit of God, controlling them all so that a harmonious whole would be produced.

7. How many books are there in the Bible? By how many human writers were these books written? How many centuries did the work of writing require? There are sixty-six books in the Bible. These books were written by about forty different writers. The work of writing required about fourteen centuries, from Moses to the apostle John.

8. How can the absence of contradictions in the Bible be explained? The absence of contradictions in the Bible cannot be explained on the theory that the Bible is merely a collection of human writings. Forty men writing a collection of sixty-six books over a period of 1,400 years could not possibly avoid a vast multitude of contradictions. The absence of contradictions in the Bible can be explained only by the fact that all the human writers were supernaturally controlled by God the Holy Spirit, so that the product is truly the Word of God, and therefore wholly free from errors and contradictions.

9. What is the "scope" of the Bible as a whole? The scope of the Bible as a whole is to give all glory to God. In this the Bible is contrary to the spirit of paganism, ancient and modern, which is to give all glory to man.

10. Why must a book which gives all glory to God be genuine? It must be genuine, that is, it must be what it claims to be, the Word of God, because no one but God could have had a motive for writing it. Wicked men would not write a book which condemns wickedness and gives all glory to a holy, sin-hating God. Good men could not write a book on their own initiative and represent it falsely as the Word of God, for if they did that they would be deceivers, and therefore not good men. For the same reasons neither devils nor holy angels could have written it. Therefore God is the only person who could be the real Author of the Bible.

11. What fruits or results of the Bible show that it is the Word of God? Where the Bible is known and believed, wickedness and crime are curbed, human life and property are secure, education is widespread, institutions of mercy for the care of the sick, unfortunate, and insane are established, and civil liberty is honored and safeguarded.

12. What is the condition of human society in places where the Bible is entirely or practically unknown? "The dark places of the earth are full of the habitations of cruelty" (Ps. 74:20). Where the Bible is unknown or almost unknown, human life is cheap and insecure; dishonesty is almost universal; men live in bondage to superstitions and fears; moral corruption and degradation abound.

13. In addition to the evidences that have been mentioned, what else is needed to give us full conviction, or certainty, that the Bible is God's Word? In addition to the evidences that have been discussed, the almighty work of God the Holy Spirit in our hearts is needed to give us full conviction that the Bible is the Word of God. "But the natural man receiveth not the things of the Spirit of God: for they are foolishness unto him: neither can he know them, because they are spiritually discerned" (1 Cor. 2:14). The evidences that have already been discussed are valid in themselves, and may lead to a conviction of probability that the Bible is the Word of God. But this work of the Holy Spirit bearing witness by and with the Word in the heart results in full conviction or certainty that the Bible is the Word of God.

14. Why do many highly educated and intelligent people refuse to believe that the Bible is God's Word? First Corinthians 2:14, quoted above, provides the answer to this question. These highly educated unbelievers lack the testimony of the Holy Spirit in their hearts. They are what

Paul called "natural" men, that is, not born again. Being spiritually blind, of course they cannot see the light.

15. Why are intelligence and education not enough to enable a person to believe with certainty that the Bible is the Word of God?
Because in the sinful human heart there is strong prejudice against God and the truth of God. The ordinary evidences are sufficient to convince a neutral, unprejudiced inquirer that the Bible is the Word of God. But the fact is that there are no neutral, unprejudiced inquirers. The whole human race has fallen into sin; the human heart has been darkened; the "natural" man is gripped by a tremendous prejudice against accepting the Bible as God's Word. Apart from the special work of the Holy Spirit in men's hearts, there would not be a single true Christian believer in the world. There are of course unconverted people who readily assent to the statement that the Bible is God's Word, by mere custom or tradition rather than by personal conviction. Such people are not really convinced that the Bible is God's Word; they merely have a hearsay or secondhand faith which reflects the true spiritual faith of other persons.

5. Q. *What do the scriptures principally teach?*

A. *The scriptures principally teach, what man is to believe concerning God, and what duty God requires of man.*

Scripture References
- 2 Tim. 1:13. Scripture is sound words to be believed.
- Deut. 10:12–13. What the Lord requires of his people.
- John 20:31. Scripture is to be believed, the way of life.
- 2 Tim. 3:15–17. Scripture a complete and perfect rule of faith and life.

Commentary
1. What are the two principal parts of the teaching of the Bible?
The two principal parts of the Bible's teaching are (a) a message of truth to be believed, and (b) a message of duty to be obeyed.

2. Why is belief mentioned before duty? Belief is mentioned before duty because in the Christian life, as in the natural world, the root must come before the fruit. "As a man thinketh in his heart, so is he." Belief is the root and determiner of life. Therefore the truth to be believed must be set forth before the duties to be performed can be considered.

3. What is wrong with the present-day popular slogan: "Christianity is not a doctrine but a life"? This saying is one of the subtle half-truths of our day. It would be correct to say: "Christianity is not only a doctrine but also a life." It is not a question of "either . . . or" but of "both . . . and." When anyone says that Christianity is not a doctrine but a life, he is setting doctrine and life in opposition to each other. This is a very perverse tendency and is thoroughly characteristic of the antidoctrinal prejudice of our day. Of course according to the Bible Christianity is both a system of doctrine and a life. Moreover the doctrine and the life are organically related, and the life cannot exist and grow apart from the doctrine. After all, roots are important things.

4. Which is more important in the Christian life, belief or conduct? Or should we say that both are equally important? Which is the more important part of a building, the foundation or the roof? No doubt each is equally important for its own proper purpose. Which is more important for an automobile, a motor or four wheels? No doubt each is equally important for its own proper purpose. Our Lord said: "Thou shalt love the Lord thy God with all thy heart, and with all thy soul, and with all thy mind. This is the first and great commandment" (Matt. 22:37–38). Since to love the Lord our God with all the mind is required in the first and great commandment, we may say with confidence that nothing is more important than belief of the truth. Of equal importance in its own sphere is adorning the truth by a godly and consistent life.

We have now studied the first five questions of the catechism, which constitute The Foundation, dealing with the purpose of human life, the existence of God, and the Word of God. Having completed this introductory section, we now come to the first of the two major divisions of the material contained in the Larger Catechism, namely, what man ought to believe concerning God. Questions 6 to 90 deal with this subject, which we shall now proceed to study.

2

God

6. Q. *What do the scriptures make known of God?*

A. *The scriptures make known what God is, the persons in the Godhead, his decrees, and the execution of his decrees.*

Scripture References
- Heb. 11:6; John 4:24. What God is.
- 1 John 5:7; 2 Cor. 13:14. The persons in the Godhead.
- Acts 15:14–15, 18. God's decrees.
- Acts 4:27–28. The execution of God's decrees.

Commentary

1. What are the four parts into which we may divide what the Bible reveals about God? (a) The being of God, or what God is; (b) the persons in the Godhead, or what the Bible reveals about the Father, the Son, and the Holy Spirit; (c) God's decrees, or the plans God made in eternity before the universe existed; (d) the execution of God's decrees, or the carrying out of his plans by creation and providence.

2. How could we divide this information about God into two parts? (a) Information about God himself; (b) information about God's works.

3. Why does the Bible nowhere present an argument to prove that God exists? The Bible does mention the fact that God has revealed himself in the world of nature and in the human heart, and that this natural revelation of God witnesses to his existence (Ps. 19:1; Rom. 1:20). But apart from such references to the revelation of God in nature, the Bible does not attempt to prove the existence of God. Nowhere does the Bible present a formal argument to prove God's existence. Instead, the Bible starts out in its very first verse by assuming the existence of God, and going on to tell about his nature, character, and works. Because of the revelation of God in the world of nature and in the human heart, it is natural for mankind to believe in the existence of God. By starting out by assuming that God exists, the Bible really presents the greatest argument of all for the existence of God. For this assumption of God's existence is the key that unlocks the countless mysteries of nature and of human life. Suppose we make the contrary assumption, that God does not exist—immediately the universe, human life, our own souls, all are buried in unfathomable darkness and mystery. The person who is not willing to start by assuming that God exists has the responsibility of showing that his theory of no God yields a better and more credible explanation of the universe and of human life than that given in the Bible. Of course the atheist and the agnostic are not able to do this. When we follow the Bible and start out by assuming the existence of God as the Bible does, then every fact in the universe becomes an argument for God's existence. For there is not a single fact anywhere that can be better explained by denying God's existence than by assuming God's existence.

4. What does the Bible have to say about the character of atheists?
"The fool hath said in his heart, 'There is no God'" (Ps. 53:1). The person who denies God's existence is a foolish person because he insists on denying the greatest of all facts. We should understand that in the Bible the term "fool" involves the idea of moral perversity as well as that of intellectual weakness. Suppose a person who had lived all his life in the United States were to deny the existence of the U.S. Government, and to claim that he owed no obligation to the government, since he denied its existence. It is obvious that such a person would be regarded not only as lacking common sense but also as incapable of being a good citizen of his country. Yet even more absurd is the attitude of the atheist who owes his very life to God and yet denies that God exists and disclaims all responsibility to God.

7. Q. *What is God?*

A. *God is a Spirit, in and of himself infinite in being, glory, blessedness, and perfection: all-sufficient, eternal, unchangeable, incomprehensible, everywhere present, almighty, knowing all things, most wise, most holy, most just, most merciful and gracious, long-suffering, and abundant in goodness and truth.*

Scripture References
- John 4:24. God is a Spirit.
- Exod. 3:14; Job 11:7–9. God is infinite.
- Acts 7:2. God's glory.
- 1 Tim. 6:15. God's blessedness.
- Matt. 5:48. God's perfection.
- Gen. 17:1. God's sufficiency.
- Mal. 3:6; James 1:17. God is unchangeable.
- Ps. 90:1–2. God is eternal.
- 1 Kings 8:27. God is incomprehensible.
- Ps. 139:7–10. God is everywhere.
- Rev. 4:8. God is almighty.
- Heb. 4:13; Pss. 139:1–4; 147:5. God knows all things.
- Rom. 16:27. God's wisdom.
- Isa. 6:3; Rev. 15:4. God's holiness.
- Deut. 32:4. God's justice.
- Exod. 34:6. God is merciful, etc.

Commentary

1. What is meant by saying that "God is a Spirit"? This means that God is a being who has no material body.

2. Why should we say "God is a Spirit" instead of saying "God is Spirit" as the Christian Scientists do? Two reasons may be given: (a) God is not the only spirit that exists; he is one of a class of beings called "spirits," which includes also the angels and the evil spirits; so we say "God is a Spirit" just as we say "Topeka is a city," implying that it is not the only city in the world, but a member of the class of cities. (b) Because God is a person, we say "God is a Spirit" instead of saying "God is Spirit," for the latter way of speaking seems to imply disbelief in God's individuality and therefore also disbelief in his personality.

3. What false religion in the United States teaches that God has a material body? Mormonism, or the "Church of Jesus Christ of Latter-day Saints."

4. Why is idolatry, or worship of God by images, always wrong and sinful in itself? Since idolatry is plainly forbidden in the Ten Commandments, there can be no doubt as to its sinfulness. The reason back of the second commandment is doubtless the truth that God is pure Spirit, and because God is a pure Spirit, no material object or picture can avoid giving a false idea of God.

5. What is the meaning of the word "infinite"? Literally, it means without limits, or boundless; and therefore it refers to that which cannot be measured.

6. In what four respects is God declared to be infinite? In his being, glory, blessedness, perfection. (Being means existence).

7. Why does the idea of God being infinite baffle our minds? Because we are finite beings, and the finite cannot comprehend the infinite. We cannot know all the truth about God, nor can we fully know any single part or item of the truth about God.

8. If our minds could comprehend God, and understand how he can be infinite, what would this mean? It would mean that we ourselves would be infinite, too, and equal with God.

9. Why do our minds instinctively raise the question, "Who made God?" Because we are created beings and therefore we naturally tend to assume that all other beings must have been created, too. But of course a God who had been made would not really be God at all, but only a creature, and we would have to think of another God who had created him.

10. What do we mean by saying that God is eternal? We mean, first, that God never had a beginning; second, that God will never have an end; and third, that God is above distinctions of time: past, present, and future are all equally present to God; to him one day is as 1,000 years, and 1,000 years as one day.

11. How can we illustrate the idea that God is above distinctions of time? This idea may be illustrated by a circle. The circle has a center and a circumference. The center is equally distant from every point on the circumference. But the points on the circumference are not equally distant from each other. If we think of the circumference of the circle as representing the ages of the world's history, and of the center of the circle as representing God's position in relation to the ages of history, this may help us to realize that all the ages of history—past, present, and future—are equally present to God.

12. What is meant by saying that God is incomprehensible? The catechism uses this word in the sense of 1 Kings 8:27, "Heaven and the heaven of heavens cannot contain thee," meaning that the whole created universe cannot "comprehend" or contain God; although the Bible speaks of God as the one who "filleth all in all," and although God is everywhere in the created universe, still God is so great that the whole universe cannot "contain" him—there is more beyond.

13. If God is unchangeable, why does the Bible speak of God "repenting" or changing his mind, as for example in the case of the city of Nineveh (Jonah 3:10)? God himself never changes; God's creatures change, and the result of this is that the relation between them and God changes. In the case of Nineveh, for example, God did not really change his mind. It was the people of Nineveh who really changed; they turned from their wicked way. God did not change his mind, for the whole series of events, including Jonah's preaching, the Ninevites' turning from their wickedness, and God's "repenting of the evil that he had said he would do," was all a part of God's original plan.

In other words, even before Jonah arrived at Nineveh, God planned and intended to "change his mind" following the Ninevites' change of their conduct. But when God "changes" his mind according to plan, it is clear that he does not really change his mind at all, but only changes his dealings with his creatures.

14. If God is almighty, as the catechism says, then is there anything that God cannot do? The Bible tells us some things that even God cannot do. For one thing, we are told that God cannot lie (Titus 1:2). Also, we are told that God cannot deny himself (2 Tim. 2:13). We may sum up these teachings by saying that God cannot deny his own nature—he cannot deny his moral nature by telling a lie or doing anything unrighteous; and he cannot deny his rational nature by doing anything that contradicts itself. For example, God cannot create a square circle, or make two plus two equal five. Apart from things which would be contrary to his own nature, there is absolutely nothing that God cannot do.

15. What is the importance of the truth that God knows all things? Apart from this truth, the prophecies of the Bible would be impossible. Only because God knows all things can events be foretold, hundreds and thousands of years before they occur. Also there is the practical truth that nothing can be concealed from God, since he sees and knows all things. Because God knows all things, we can be sure that all the wickedness of men will be dealt with in the Day of Judgment.

16. What is the meaning of the statement that God is "most holy"? This means (a) that God is high above all created beings; (b) that God is infinitely removed from all sin and cannot have fellowship with sinful beings unless an atonement has been made for their sin.

17. What is meant by saying that God is "most just"? This means that it is God's nature, or character, to deal with all his rational creatures exactly according to their standing in relation to God's moral law.

18. What is the difference in meaning between "merciful" and "gracious"? The term *grace* means any undeserved favor extended by God to any of his creatures, regardless of whether they are sinful or not. But the term *mercy* means undeserved favor extended to sinful creatures, to those who are not only undeserving, but also ill-deserving. Thus, for example, it was an act of grace on God's part to enter into the covenant of works with Adam, since God was not obliged to do it, even though Adam had not yet sinned. God owed him nothing. But when God established the covenant of grace, this was a much greater act of grace than God's act of establishing the covenant of works, because the covenant of grace meant extending God's favor to sinful creatures; and therefore the covenant of grace shows both the grace and the mercy of God. We may say that God's mercy is his grace extended to sinful creatures.

19. What is meant by saying that God is "long-suffering"? What illustrations of this can be given from the Bible? When we affirm that God is "long-suffering," we mean that God in his mercy often waits long before visiting judgment upon sin, giving the sinner time to repent. The

Bible is full of examples of God's long-suffering character. Revelation 2:21 may be cited, as well as Genesis 15:16. The student will easily be able to think of other examples.

20. What is the meaning of God's goodness? "Goodness" is a more general term than "grace" or "mercy." God's goodness, which is sometimes called "benevolence," is that attribute of God which leads him to provide for the general welfare of all his creatures except those who have been judicially condemned on account of sin. God's goodness, therefore, includes not only angels and men, but also the animal creation. God's goodness is exemplified not only by the plan of salvation, but also by God's works of creation and providence in general. For instance, the fact that millions of tons of coal exist underground, available for the use of mankind, making human life possible in cold climates, shows the goodness of God. For biblical examples of God's goodness to animals, see Jonah 4:11 and Genesis 9:9–10, 16.

21. What is meant by God's attribute of truth? God's truth is an attribute which affects his knowledge, wisdom, justice, and goodness. (a) God's knowledge of all things is perfectly and wholly true and exact. (b) God's wisdom is true because it is wholly unbiased by prejudice or passion. (c) God's justice and goodness are true because they are perfectly true to his own nature or character. Scripture expresses God's attribute of truth by saying: "He abideth faithful; he cannot deny himself" (2 Tim. 2:13). More particularly, God is true in all his revelation to the human race, including the entire Scriptures of the Old and New Testaments, and God is reliable in fulfilling all his promises and covenants.

8. Q. *Are there more Gods than one?*

A. *There is but one only, the living and true God.*

Scripture References
- Deut. 6:4. The unity of God set forth in the Old Testament.
- 1 Cor. 8:4–6. There is only one true God, and all others are false.
- Jer. 10:10–12. The true God is Creator and Ruler over all.

Commentary

1. What do we call the system of religion that believes in only one God? Monotheism.

2. What is the opposite of monotheism? Polytheism, or belief in many gods.

3. What idea of development of religion is commonly held by evolutionists? That religion developed gradually, starting with animism, or belief in spirits; later reaching the stage of polytheism, or belief in many gods; and finally attaining the highest stage, that of monotheism, or belief in only one God.

4. What should we think of this evolution theory of religion? In the first place, it is plainly contrary to the Bible, which represents mankind at the creation as worshiping only one God, and later through the fall and subsequent sinful corruption of the human heart coming to believe in many gods. See Romans 1:21–23. Second, the evolutionary theory of religion is contrary to the known facts of the history of religions. Not only the Bible, but ordinary history, proves that monotheism came first and that it later degenerated into polytheism. In China, for example, the oldest known form of religion was monotheism, which was the religion of the Chinese thousands of years ago; whereas today the Chinese are extreme polytheists, worshiping innumerable gods and spirits.

5. Which of the Ten Commandments forbids the sin of polytheism? The first commandment: "Thou shalt have no other gods before me" (Exod. 20:3).

6. What is the difference between polytheism and idolatry? Polytheism is belief in many gods; idolatry is the worship of any god, true or false, by means of images or pictures. The heathen with their many gods are polytheists; they are also idolaters, for they worship by means of images and pictures. This may take the crude form of actually worshiping the image or picture itself, or the more rational form of worshiping the god or spirit by means of the image or picture; that is, using the idol as an "aid to worship." Those who worship the true God by means of pictures or images are idolaters but not polytheists. The Roman Catholic Church draws a subtle distinction between the worship which is due to God alone and the honor which is given to Mary and the saints. Unquestionably there are multitudes of Roman

Catholics who cannot grasp such a distinction, who give what amounts to divine honor to Mary and the saints, and who are therefore practically polytheists as well as idolaters.

7. What grievous sin involving compromise of monotheism was committed by Christian churches in Japan and Japanese-occupied Asia prior to or during World War II? Under heavy pressure from a totalitarian government, these churches compromised by condoning and practicing polytheism by according divine honor to the sun goddess and the Japanese emperor. In some cases this went so far as putting miniature Shinto shrines in Christian church buildings and bowing toward them just before the beginning of the public worship of God. Since the end of the war, some have publicly repented of their involvement in such practices, but others have not done so.

9. **Q.** *How many persons are there in the Godhead?*

A. *There are three persons in the Godhead, the Father, the Son, and the Holy Ghost; and these three are one true, eternal God, the same in substance, equal in power and glory; although distinguished by their personal properties.*

Scripture References
- Matt. 28:19; 2 Cor. 13:14. Names of three divine persons mentioned together.
- 1 Cor. 8:6. The Father declared to be God.
- John 1:1; 10:30; 1 John 5:20 (last part): The Son declared to be God.
- Acts 5:3–4. The Holy Spirit declared to be God.
- 1 Cor. 8:4; Exod. 20:3. Although there are three persons, yet there is only one God.
- Matt. 11:27; Heb. 1:3. The divine persons the same in substance.
- John 1:18; 15:26. The divine persons differ in their personal properties.

Commentary
1. Why is the doctrine of the Trinity a stumbling block to many people? Because it is a mystery which human reason cannot explain.

2. What system of belief denies the doctrine of the Trinity? Unitarianism, which teaches that there is only one person in the Godhead, the Father, and therefore that the Son and the Holy Spirit are not divine persons.

3. Is the doctrine of the Trinity contrary to reason? No. It is not contrary to reason, but it is above human reason.

4. Does the doctrine of the Trinity contradict itself? No. There is no contradiction involved, although opponents of the doctrine never weary of calling it "contradictory." The doctrine teaches that God is *one* in one sense, and *three* in a different sense. He is *one* in substance and *three* in persons. While we may freely admit that this is a mystery which baffles the human mind, still it does not involve a contradiction. It would be contradictory if we were to affirm that God is both one and three in the same sense, that is, if we were to say that there is only one person in the Godhead and at the same time there are three persons in the Godhead. This would be an absurdity, but no Christian creed sets forth any such view of the matter.

5. What are some of the illustrations that have been proposed to help people to understand the doctrine of the Trinity? The same chemical substance having the various forms of water, ice, and steam; the relations among fire, light, and heat; and many similar comparisons.

6. Why are all these illustrations without value for explaining the Trinity? Because the Trinity is a divine mystery, has no parallels in the natural realm, and has not been revealed in nature, but only in Scripture. Besides, all the illustrations suggested make use of physical distinctions which in the nature of the case cannot represent relations between persons. Moreover, the same substance is water at one time, ice at another time, and steam at still another time, not water, ice, and steam all at the same time; whereas the three persons in the Godhead are the same God yet distinct persons at one and the same time.

7. What phrase in the answer to question 9 is very important as a test of real belief in the doctrine of the Trinity? The phrase "the same in substance." Many people today say that they believe in "the divinity of Christ," for example, but they are not willing to say that Christ is the same in substance with God the Father.

8. What is the practical importance of the doctrine of the Trinity? This is far from being a mere technical theory or abstract doctrine. Christianity stands or falls with the doctrine of the Trinity. The Bible represents the plan of salvation as a compact or covenant among the persons of the Trinity. Where the doctrine of the Trinity is abandoned, the whole Bible teaching about the plan of salvation must go with it.

10. Q. *What are the personal properties of the three persons in the Godhead?*

A. *It is proper to the Father to beget the Son, and to the Son to be begotten of the Father, and to the Holy Ghost to proceed from the Father and the Son from all eternity.*

Scripture References
- Heb. 1:5–6, 8. The Father begets the Son.
- John 1:14, 18; 3:16. The Son is begotten by the Father.
- John 15:26; Gal. 4:6. The Holy Spirit proceeds from the Father and from the Son.
- John 17:5, 24. These personal properties existed from eternity.

Commentary
1. What is the meaning of the word *begets* in speaking of the Trinity? This word is the nearest there is in human language to set forth the relation between God the Father and God the Son.

2. How can it be shown from Hebrews 1:5–8 that the Son is not a created being, but was eternally begotten by the Father? The words "this day" in verse 5 do not imply that before that time the Son did not exist; rather "this day" is the day of eternity, as shown by verse 8, which calls the Son "God" and states that his throne is "for ever and ever." If the Son had ever had a beginning, he would not be called "God."

3. In speaking of the three persons in the Godhead, why do we always name the Father first, the Son second, and the Holy Spirit third? Because the Bible speaks of the Father sending and operating through the Son and the Holy Spirit; also the Bible speaks of the Son as sending and working through the Holy Spirit. In the Bible this order is never reversed;

the Bible never speaks of the Son working through the Father, or of the Holy Spirit sending or working through the Son.

4. What should be our attitude toward the truths of the Trinity? We should accept them with a reverent attitude, realizing that they are divine mysteries far beyond our power to explain or comprehend.

11. Q. *How doth it appear that the Son and the Holy Ghost are God equal with the Father?*

A. *The scriptures manifest that the Son and the Holy Ghost are God equal with the Father, ascribing unto them such names, attributes, works and worship, as are proper to God only.*

Scripture References
- Isa. 6:3–8 compared with John 12:41. Divine names ascribed to the Son.
- Isa. 6:8 with Acts 28:25. Divine names ascribed to the Holy Spirit.
- 1 John 5:20. Divine names ascribed to the Son.
- Acts 5:3–4. Divine names ascribed to the Holy Spirit.
- John 1:1; Isa. 9:6; John 2:24–25. Divine attributes ascribed to the Son.
- 1 Cor. 2:10–11. Divine attributes ascribed to the Holy Spirit.
- John 1:3; Col. 1:16. Divine works ascribed to the Son.
- Gen. 1:2. Divine works ascribed to the Holy Spirit.
- Matt. 28:19; 2 Cor. 13:14. Divine worship ascribed to the Son and to the Holy Spirit.

Commentary
1. According to the Bible, how many Gods are there? Only one. This is the consistent teaching of the entire Bible.

2. How many distinct persons does the Bible speak of as divine? Three: the Father, the Son, and the Holy Spirit.

3. What is the only conclusion that can logically be drawn from these facts? The only conclusion that can logically be drawn from the biblical data is that there is only one God, who exists in three distinct persons, each of which is truly God and equal with the other two.

3

God's Decrees

12. Q. *What are the decrees of God?*

A. *God's decrees are the wise, free, and holy acts of the counsel of his will, whereby, from all eternity, he hath, for his own glory, unchangeably foreordained whatsoever comes to pass in time, especially concerning angels and men.*

Scripture References
- Eph. 1:11. God, who works all things according to the counsel of his own will, predestines men according to his own purpose.
- Rom. 11:33. God's plans and purposes cannot be explained or discovered by men.
- Rom. 9:14–15, 18. God's decrees do not make God the author of sin; God's decrees are according to the counsel of his own will; God's decrees are free from constraint from any source outside of himself.
- Eph. 1:4. God's decrees, including those concerning the eternal destiny of men, were made in eternity, before the creation of the world.
- Rom. 9:22–23. God has predestined some men to wrath and others to glory.
- Ps. 33:11. God's plans and purposes are unchangeable.

Commentary
1. What great truth is set forth in the answer to question 12? The truth that God has an inclusive and exact plan for the universe which he has created.

2. According to the Bible, when was God's plan made? In eternity, or before the creation of the world.

3. What three adjectives are used to describe the character of God's decrees? Wise, free, and holy.

4. What is meant by affirming that God's decrees are "wise"? This means that God's decrees are in perfect harmony with his own perfect wisdom, which directs the use of the right means to attain right ends.

5. What is meant by affirming that God's decrees are "free"? This means that God's decrees are not constrained or influenced by anything outside of God's own nature.

6. What is meant by affirming that God's decrees are "holy"? This means that God's decrees are in perfect harmony with his own perfect holiness, and therefore are utterly free from sin.

7. Should we regard God's decrees as arbitrary decisions, like the heathen ideas of "fate" and "luck?" No. God's decrees are not "arbitrary," for they were framed according to the counsel of his will. Back of God's decrees is the mind and heart of the infinite, personal God; therefore they are totally unlike "fate" or "luck."

8. What is the aim or purpose of God's decrees? The aim or purpose of God's decrees is the manifestation of his own glory.

9. Is it selfish or wrong for God to seek his own glory above all else? No, for God is the Author of all things, and all things exist for his glory. It would be selfish and sinful for human beings to seek their own glory above all else; but since God is the highest being, and there is no being higher than God, it is proper that God should seek his own glory.

10. What is the nature of God's decrees? God's decrees are unchangeable; they cannot be changed; therefore they are certain to be fulfilled (Ps. 33:11).

11. What do God's decrees include? God's decrees are all-inclusive; they include everything that ever happens.

12. Prove from the Bible that God's decrees include what are commonly called accidental or "chance" happenings. Proverbs 16:33; Jonah 1:7; Acts 1:24, 26; 1 Kings 22:28, 34; Mark 14:30.

13. Prove from the Bible that God's decrees include even the sinful acts of men. Genesis 45:5, 8; 50:20; 1 Samuel 2:25; Acts 2:23. In affirming, as the Bible plainly teaches, that God's decrees include even the sinful acts of men, we must carefully guard against two errors: (a) God's decree does not make God the author of sin nor render him responsible for sin; (b) the fact of God's foreordination does not cancel man's responsibility for his own sins. The Bible teaches both God's foreordination and man's responsibility. Therefore we should believe and affirm both although we frankly recognize that we cannot fully harmonize the two. If we give up belief in either God's foreordination or man's responsibility, we immediately become involved in gross errors which contradict the Bible's teaching at many points. It is better and wiser to accept what the Bible teaches in simple faith and confess "a holy ignorance" concerning secret mysteries which have not been revealed, such as the solution of the problem of divine foreordination and human responsibility.

14. What is the difference between foreordination and predestination? Foreordination is a term for all God's decrees concerning anything whatever that comes to pass in the created universe; predestination concerns God's decrees regarding the eternal destiny of angels and men.

15. Why do many people object to the doctrine of God's decrees? Most objections to this doctrine are based not on Scripture, but on human reasoning or philosophy. It is common for those who oppose the doctrine to set up an absurd caricature of it and then demolish it with a great show of indignation. In dealing with a question of this kind no argument that does not take up, thoroughly and in detail, the various Scripture passages on which the doctrine is based can be of any weight against the doctrine of God's decrees. Human opinions, reasonings, and philosophy are of no weight whatever against the statements of God's Word. Some objections urged against predestination or the doctrine of election will be considered in the next lesson.

13. Q. *What hath God especially decreed concerning angels and men?*

A. *God, by an eternal and immutable decree, out of his mere love, for the praise of his glorious grace, to be manifested in due time, hath elected some angels to glory, and in Christ, hath chosen some men to eternal life, and the means thereof: and also, according to his sovereign power, and the unsearchable counsel of his own will (whereby he extendeth or withholdeth favor as he pleaseth), hath passed by and foreordained the rest to dishonor and wrath, to be for their sin inflicted, to the praise of the glory of his justice.*

Scripture References
- 1 Tim. 5:21. Angels elected to eternal glory.
- Eph. 1:4–6; 1 Thess. 2:13–14. Men chosen in Christ to eternal life.
- Rom. 9:17–18, 21–22; Matt. 11:25–26; 2 Tim. 2:20; Jude 4; 1 Peter 2:8. The rest of mankind passed by.

Commentary

1. What is the meaning of the word *immutable*? It means unchangeable.

2. What is the first reason why God elected some of the angels to glory? "Out of his mere love."

3. Why is the word *mere* included in this statement? Because God was under no obligation to elect any of the angels to glory. It was God's love alone that moved him to elect.

4. What is the second reason why God elected some of the angels to glory? To manifest the praise of his glorious grace.

5. What is the difference between God's election of angels to glory and his election of men to eternal life? In the case of men God elected them "in Christ"; that is, to be redeemed from sin through the atonement of Jesus Christ, and to be clothed with Christ's righteousness. But in the case of the angels salvation had nothing to do with it. God simply elected them to glory and then prevented them from ever falling into sin.

6. Besides electing men to eternal life, what has God elected them to? He has also elected them to "the means thereof"; those whom he has chosen for eternal life he has also chosen to receive the means of obtaining eternal life. That is, if God has foreordained that a certain person shall receive eternal life, then he has also foreordained that that person shall hear the gospel, repent of sin, believe in Jesus Christ, etc., so as to make sure of that person's receiving eternal life without fail.

7. What is meant by speaking of God's "sovereign power"? This expression refers to the truth that God is supreme; there is no authority or law higher than God to which God himself is responsible. No one has the right to say to God, "What doest thou?"

8. In the case of those whom God has "passed by," what is the reason for his passing them by and not choosing them to eternal life? The Bible represents this act of "passing by" as grounded in God's sovereignty, that is, it is not based on anything in the character or works or life of the persons involved, but proceeds from God's own supreme authority. This does not mean that God has no reasons for "passing by" those whom he has passed by; it only means that the reasons are God's secret counsel, not revealed to us, and not based on human character, works, or conduct. See Romans 9:13, 15, 20–21.

9. In the case of those whom God has sovereignly "passed by," what is the reason for also ordaining them to dishonor and wrath? The reason for ordaining them to dishonor and wrath is their own sin. Note the words "to be for their sin inflicted." Therefore God's foreordaining some men to eternal punishment is not based on the pure sovereignty of God (as is his act of "passing by" these same persons), but proceeds from God's attribute of perfect justice. They are punished because as sinners they deserve to be punished, not because God has passed them by. In hell the wicked will recognize that they are suffering a deserved punishment and that God has dealt with them strictly according to justice.

10. Suppose some person says: "If I am predestined to receive eternal life, then I will receive it no matter whether I believe in Christ or not. So I need not bother to be a 'Christian.'" How should we answer such a person? The objection raised is based on a misunderstanding of the doctrine of election. God does not elect persons to eternal life apart from the means thereof. When a particular person is elected to eternal life, it is also foreordained that that person shall believe in Christ as his Savior.

11. Suppose some person says: "If God from all eternity has ordained me to dishonor and wrath for my sins, then it is no use for me to believe in Christ, for I cannot be saved no matter how good a Christian I might become. There is no use for me to believe in Christ." How should we answer such an objector? It is no use for us to try to pry into the secret counsel of God and find out by a shortcut whether we are among the elect or not. The secret things belong to God, and the things that are revealed are for us to know. If a person is really dead in earnest about wanting to believe in Christ and be saved, that is a good sign that God has chosen that person to eternal life. The only way we can find out about God's decrees is by actually coming to Christ and receiving, in due course, the assurance of our own salvation. Then, and only then, can we say with confidence that we know ourselves to be of the elect.

12. What special difficulty is involved in this doctrine of election? The difficulty is: How can God's decree of election be harmonized with human free agency? If God has foreordained all that comes to pass, including the eternal destiny of all human beings, how can we ourselves be free agents and how can we be responsible for what we do? We cannot solve this problem, for it is a mystery. We can only affirm that the Bible plainly teaches both God's sovereign foreordination and human freedom and responsibility. To reject either of these Bible truths is to reject the clear teaching of the Word of God and to become involved in even greater theological difficulties.

13. How should we answer the objection "Is it not *unfair* for God to elect one person to eternal life, while he passes by another?" This objection is based on the assumption that God is under an obligation to treat all men with equal favor, and to do for all whatever he does for any. The Bible's answer to this objection is found in Romans 9:20–21. The objection really involves a denial of the sovereignty of God, for it assumes that God is responsible to the human race for his decisions, or else that there is some higher law or power to which God is responsible and by which he must be judged. The truth is that (a) God is sovereign and is responsible to no one but himself for his actions; (b) God is under no obligation to elect anyone to eternal life; it would have been perfectly just for him to leave all mankind to perish in their sins; (c) if God elects some to eternal life, he is under no obligation to elect all; for his electing of some is a matter of grace, and therefore cannot be claimed as a right by any that are "passed by." It is quite true that the Bible represents God as dealing with men unequally, that is, giving to some what he withholds from others; but this is not "unfair" because there is no injustice involved. No one has any basis for a claim that God has treated him unjustly.

14. Q. *How doth God execute his decrees?*

A. *God executeth his decrees in the works of creation and providence according to his infallible foreknowledge, and the free and immutable counsel of his own will.*

Scripture Reference
- Eph. 1:11. (Additional Scripture references will come under the following questions, dealing with God's works of creation and providence. This fourteenth question is of the nature of a summary or outline, dividing God's works into two great parts, namely, creation and providence. The questions which follow deal with these two subjects: 15–17 with creation; and 18–20 with providence.)

Commentary
1. What kind of foreknowledge does God have of all things? Infallible foreknowledge. His foreknowledge is inclusive, exact, and detailed.

2. What is meant by saying that the counsel of God's will is "free"? This means that God acted according to his own nature, without constraint from any source outside himself.

3. What is meant by saying that the counsel of God's will is "immutable"? This means that God's purposes cannot be changed by "chance" or by any of his creatures. What God has decreed will surely come to pass.

4

Creation

15. Q. *What is the work of creation?*

A. *The work of creation is that wherein God did in the beginning, by the word of his power, make of nothing the world, and all things therein, for himself, within the space of six days, and all very good.*

Scripture References
- Gen. 1:1 and also the entire first chapter of Genesis. The account of the work of creation.
- Heb. 11:3. The universe created out of nothing; not formed from preexisting materials.
- Prov. 16:4. God made all things for himself.
- Rev. 4:11. All things created by God, for his own pleasure.

Commentary
1. What truth is implied by the use of the words "in the beginning"? These words imply that the world or the universe is not eternal; it did not always exist; it had a beginning. God, on the other hand, is eternal; God always existed; God never had a beginning.

2. What is the importance of the first three words of the Bible? These words ("In the beginning") prove that the universe had a beginning; therefore the universe did not exist of itself; therefore the universe owes its existence to God; therefore the universe is dependent on God; therefore all attempts of men or nations to live independently of God are foolish, wicked, and doomed to failure in the end.

3. What does the doctrine of creation show about the nature of God? That God is absolutely independent of the world; that God is an almighty being, who possesses infinite supernatural power by which he can do anything which does not contradict his own nature.

4. What was God's aim in the work of creation? God created all things for himself; that is, to manifest his own perfection and glory.

5. What was the character of the created universe as it came from the hand of God? It was "all very good"; that is, it was wholly free from evil of any kind, both moral evil and physical evil. The evil which exists today is therefore abnormal and alien to the universe as God created it.

6. What is the meaning of the phrase "within the space of six days"? The most natural meaning of this phrase is six literal days of twenty-four hours each. However, some orthodox students of the Bible hold that the word *day* is sometimes used to designate a long period of time; one day is said to be with the Lord as a thousand years, and a thousand years as one day, etc. However, the more natural and probable meaning in Genesis 1 is six literal days.

7. When was the world created? We can only say "In the beginning," as the Bible tells us. We are not told when the "beginning" was.

8. What was the origin of the idea that the world was created in the year 4004 B.C.? Archbishop Usher, a scholar of about 300 years ago, made elaborate calculations of the chronology and genealogies of the Bible, and on the basis of these calculations he decided that 4004 B.C. was the time of the creation.

9. What should we think of this idea that the world was created in 4004 B.C.? (a) We can be sure that the world was created at least that long ago, if not longer. (b) Usher's calculation is not a statement of the Word of God, but only a human opinion, which may or may not be reliable. (c) Usher's conclusion is based on the assumption that the genealogies given in the Bible are complete, with no links omitted. But it can be proved by comparison of Scripture with Scripture that in Bible genealogies sometimes generations are omitted; for example, a grandson is spoken of as a son of some person, etc. Therefore it is impossible accurately to calculate the date of the creation of the world from the genealogies.

10. What should we think of the statements of scientists who tell us that the world is millions and even billions of years old? (a) Such statements are only speculations without any real proof. This is shown by the fact that the scientists do not agree among themselves, even as to the approximate age of the world. (b) The idea that the world is millions or billions of years old is usually held by evolutionists who need millions or billions of years to have room for a supposed process of evolution from a single cell to the complex form of life that exists today. These evolutionists do not believe in the Bible account of creation. It is foolish and useless to try to adjust the opinions of such men to the details of the record in Genesis. The real divergence between evolution and creation is not a matter of a few minor details; it concerns the basic conception of the nature and origin of living species. To attempt to reconcile evolution and creation by adjusting details is as futile as it would be to try to reconcile the theory that the world is flat with the fact that the world is round by a compromise between the two.

11. How old is the human race? The Bible does not tell us. But from the genealogies of the Bible it can be proved that the human race is at least 6,000 years old. It may, of course, be older than that. The Bible leaves room for any reasonable antiquity of the human race. Mankind is not millions of years old, but rather a few thousand years old.

12. Why does the Bible not tell us the exact date of the creation and the exact age of the human race? If we really needed to know these things, God would have revealed them in the Bible. Since he has not done so, we can only conclude that these are matters which we do not really need to know. We should always remember that the Bible was not written to satisfy our curiosity, but to show us the way of salvation.

(**Note:** A thorough discussion of the theory of evolution, from the standpoint of orthodox Christianity, would require far more space than could be devoted to this important question in the columns of *Blue Banner Faith and Life*. The reader is referred to the following excellent books on this subject: *Evolution in the Balances*, by Frank E. Allen. New York, Fleming H. Revell Company, 1926; *After Its Kind*, by Byron C. Nelson. Minneapolis, Augsburg Publishing House, 1940.)

16. Q. *How did God create angels?*

A. *God created all the angels spirits, immortal, holy, excelling in knowledge, mighty in power, to execute his commandments, and to praise his name, yet subject to change.*

Scripture References
- Col. 1:16. All the angels created by God.
- Ps. 104:4; Heb. 1:7. The angels are spirits.
- Matt. 22:30. The angels are immortal.
- Jude 6. The angels were created holy.
- 2 Sam. 14:17; Matt. 24:36. The knowledge of the angels.
- 2 Thess. 1:7. The angels' power.
- Ps. 103:20; Heb. 1:14. The functions of the angels.
- 2 Peter 2:4; Jude 6. The angels created subject to change.

Commentary

1. Why is it important to believe that all the angels were created by God? Because of the fact that if any of them were not created by God, they would be divine, existing from eternity as God did.

2. What important difference is there between the angels and human beings? The angels are spirits without any bodies; man on the other hand is a composite being consisting of two elements, body and soul, mysteriously united in a single personality.

3. What other important difference is there between the angels and the human race? The angels are simply a great host of individual beings, not organically related to each other or descended from a common ancestor; whereas the human race is an organic unity, all members of the human race being mutually related by organic ties, and all being the posterity of a single first ancestor, Adam. Adam has no counterpart among the angels.

4. If the angels are pure spirits with no bodies, how could they appear in human form as is related several times in the Bible? The angels are pure spirits and have no bodies of their own. When God sent them, on certain occasions, to appear to men, they appeared in human form. This bodily form was merely assumed for the purpose of appearing to men, and was dropped again when their commission had been carried out.

5. What is wrong with the sentiment expressed in an old hymn which says: "I want to be an angel, and with the angels stand"? This sentiment is based upon a misunderstanding of the Bible teaching about the eternal destiny of the redeemed. We can never be angels, and we would not be satisfied or happy if we could, for the human soul is not complete and self-sufficient apart from the human body. Jesus said that at the resurrection the redeemed will be as the angels in one respect, namely, that they will neither marry nor be given in marriage; but that is very different from affirming that the redeemed will become angels.

6. What wonderful truth did our Savior set forth concerning the work of the angels in connection with little children? See Matthew 18:10.

17. Q. *How did God create man?*

A. *After God had made all other creatures, he created man male and female; formed the body of the man of the dust of the ground, and the woman of the rib of the man, endued them with living, reasonable, and immortal souls; made them after his own image, in knowledge, righteousness and holiness; having the law of God written in their hearts, and power to fulfill it, with dominion over the creatures; yet subject to fall.*

Scripture References
- Gen. 1:27. Mankind created male and female.
- Gen. 2:7. Adam's body made of dust.
- Gen. 2:22. Eve made of Adam's rib.
- Gen. 2:7. Mankind created with living souls.
- Job 35:11. Mankind created with intelligent souls.
- Eccl. 12:7; Matt. 10:28; Luke 23:43. Mankind created with immortal souls.
- Gen. 1:27. Mankind created in God's image.
- Col. 3:10. God's image includes knowledge.
- Eph. 4:24. God's image includes righteousness and holiness.
- Rom. 2:14–15. Mankind created with the moral law written on their hearts.
- Eccl. 7:29. Mankind created with power to fulfill God's law.
- Gen. 1:26; Ps. 8:6–8. Mankind given dominion over the creatures.
- Gen. 3:6; Rom. 5:12. Mankind created subject to the possibility of a fall into sin.

Commentary

1. What is the importance of the fact that Adam's body was made out of dust from the ground? This shows the truth that our physical bodies are composed of the same chemical elements as the ground, a fact which can be demonstrated by chemical analysis.

2. Why did God make Eve from a rib of Adam, instead of making her of dust from the ground as he had made Adam? It was necessary for the organic unity of the human race that Eve's body be derived from that of Adam, not created separately from the lifeless elements. Otherwise it would not be true that God had made of one blood (Acts 17:26) all nations of men. According to God's plan, the human race must have one single origin, not two.

3. Why is it important to believe that mankind were indued (or endowed) with immortal souls at the creation? Because some present-day sects teach that no person has an immortal soul by nature, but only by believing in Christ for salvation. These sects teach this false doctrine as a convenient way of getting rid of the idea of hell. If unbelievers and wicked people do not have immortal souls, then of course they cannot suffer eternal punishment in hell, for if they do not have immortal souls, then death must be the end of their existence. A correct understanding of the Scripture doctrine of the creation of the human race will counteract this dangerous heresy.

4. What common error must be avoided when we say that mankind was created in the image of God? We must guard against the popular error that the image of God consists in a physical resemblance to God. The false religion of Mormonism teaches something like this. Since God is a pure Spirit and has no body, such a thing is of course wholly impossible.

5. If the "image of God" does not involve a physical resemblance to God, then what does it involve? The Bible itself gives the key to the meaning of this expression in Colossians 3:10 and Ephesians 4:21. The "image of God" consists in knowledge, righteousness, and holiness. To state the same truth in a different way, the image of God in man consists in man's rational nature, man's moral nature, and man's spiritual nature. Or we may say that man has a mind, a conscience, and a capacity for knowing and loving God.

6. Does mankind have this "image of God" today? Yes. The "image of God" in man remains, but not perfect as it was at the creation. On the contrary, it is marred and broken because of our fall into sin. Yet the broken fragments remain in every human being even today.

7. What is involved in the statement that mankind was created "with dominion over the creatures"? This divine commission, given to man at the creation, as recorded in Genesis 1:28, includes the whole relationship of mankind to the world of nature, including science, invention, and art. Scientific inventions and discoveries are part of the fulfillment of this commission. See Psalm 8:5–8. We should not think that "the creatures" means only animals, birds, and fishes; really it means all created things in this world below man himself.

8. What one element of total perfection was lacking in the condition of mankind at the creation? As created by God, mankind was "subject to fall," that is, it was possible for the human race to fall into sin. Thus the condition of the human race at the creation was not the highest possible condition. The highest condition will be the state of glory when it will no longer be possible for the redeemed to sin.

9. What serious error, contrary to the doctrine of creation, is prevalent today? The theory of evolution, which denies that mankind was a special creation of God and holds that the human race developed gradually from brute ancestors, that is, from the lower animals.

10. What should we think of the theory of human evolution? (a) Even from the scientific viewpoint it is only a theory, and lacks conclusive proof of its validity. (b) It is clearly contrary to the teaching of the Bible, which unquestionably represents mankind as a special creation of God, wholly apart from the brutes. (c) It is true that the acceptance of evolution as truth often, if not always, leads to a gradual deadening of the conscience and weakening of the sense of moral responsibility. It is entirely true that World War II was, in the deepest sense, a result of widespread acceptance of the doctrine of human evolution as the truth, accompanied by a gradual but very real rejection of the Bible, by highly educated people, as their standard of faith and life. The logic involved in this moral decline is really unavoidable when once the assumption of the truth of human evolution has been made. If we were not created by God, then we are not responsible to God for our beliefs and actions. If we are not responsible to God for our beliefs and actions, then we are responsible only to our fellow man and to ourselves. In that case there is no absolute, permanent moral standard; what is right and wrong changes with the times and the circumstances. From this position it is but a step to the ideology of Nazi Germany and Soviet Russia. The apparently innocent theory of evolution has wrought tremendous havoc in human life. We should always realize that evolution is not merely a biological theory; it is also a philosophy of life held by many.

5

God's Providence

18. Q. *What are God's works of providence?*

A. *God's works of providence are his most holy, wise, and powerful pre-serving and governing all his creatures; ordering them and all their actions, to his own glory.*

Scripture References
- Ps. 145:17. God's providence is holy.
- Ps. 104:24; Isa. 28:29. God's providence is wise.
- Heb. 1:3. God's providence is powerful.
- Matt. 10:29–31. God governs all his creatures.
- Gen. 45:7–8. God controls the actions of his creatures.
- Rom. 11:36; Isa. 63:14. God controls all things for his own glory.

Commentary
1. What is the relation of all created things to God? All created things are always totally dependent on God for their existence. No created thing can ever be independent of God.

2. What religious system denies the doctrine of God's providence? Deism, which holds that God created the universe in the first place, and then left it to work out its own destiny. According to Deism, the universe is like a clock. God made it and wound it up, and since then he has let it alone, and now it is slowly running down in its own way, according to natural laws, and without divine control.

3. Why is the doctrine of Deism a serious error? Because Deism denies that God has anything whatever to do with the world in which we live today. According to Deism, God and the world parted company ages ago, and therefore we cannot come into contact with God. He cannot answer our prayers, nor can we have communion with him.

4. What important and popular organizations of the present day are largely founded on the doctrine of Deism? The Freemasons and some other "fraternal" orders, which speak of God as "the Grand Architect of the Universe," are largely based on the Deistic conception of God.

5. Why should Christian people not join these lodges or "fraternal" orders? There are many good reasons why a Christian should not belong to any secret, oath-bound order; but perhaps the most important reason is that these orders, especially the Masonic order, are founded on the Deistic idea of God, and therefore are really a false religion. The Christian, who holds the Bible doctrine of God, should keep separate from them.

6. What would happen to the whole created universe, including the human race, if God's work of providence were to be withdrawn or suspended for one minute? The entire universe, and the human race, would instantly cease to exist. It is God's providence that sustains the entire created universe in existence from moment to moment.

7. Prove from the Bible that God's providence controls what are commonly regarded as "chance" happenings. Matthew 10:29.

8. Prove from the Bible that the free acts of men are under the control of God's providence. Genesis 45:8.

9. Prove from the Bible that even the sinful acts of men are under the control of God's providence. Acts 2:23.

10. How do the prophecies of the Bible show that God's providence controls all that comes to pass? The Bible contains many prophecies which have already been fulfilled, and others which still await fulfillment in the future. If God's providence did not control all things that come to pass, without exception, predictive prophecy would be impossible. For unless God controls all things, it would be impossible for him to reveal beforehand what is to come to pass, because forces outside of God's control might change everything, so that the prophecy would not be fulfilled. Only a God who controls absolutely everything can really foretell the future with certainty, accuracy, and detail.

11. What is the end or purpose of God's providence? The end or purpose of God's providence is the manifesting of God's own glory.

12. What false idea is common today about the end or purpose of God's providence? Today many people say they want to believe in a "democratic God" who does things, not for his own glory, but for the benefit of the majority of his creatures, or for the greatest good of the greatest number.

13. What should we think of this idea of a "democratic God"? (a) It is contrary to the doctrine of God revealed in the Bible. (b) It is idolatry, for it sets up a god made in man's image as the object of worship. (c) It overlooks the truth that the glory of God includes the welfare of his creatures in general; not the welfare of all of his creatures individually, but of his creatures generally. The non-theistic viewpoint that is dominant in the world today makes the welfare of the creatures, or of humanity, the end or purpose of all things. The theistic viewpoint of the Bible, on the contrary, regards the glory of God as the great end or purpose of all things. According to the Bible, the welfare of the creatures (including humanity) is not the main thing, but rather the by-product of the glorification of God.

14. If God's providence controls the actions of human beings, does not this destroy human free will? No. While it is true, as the Bible clearly teaches, that God's providence controls all the acts of human beings, still that does not destroy human free will (more correctly called free agency) because God does not control the acts of people by forcing them to do something against their will, but by so ordering the facts and circumstances of their lives, and the moral state of their hearts, that they voluntarily, of their own accord, without any constraint, always do exactly what God has foreordained that they are to do.

15. If even the sinful acts of wicked men are controlled by God's providence, does this not make God responsible for their sins? No, because they sin of their own free will, and are not forced to sin by God's providential control. This truth is best understood by considering an actual case, for example, the crucifixion of Christ. See Acts 4:27–28: "For of a truth against thy holy child Jesus, whom thou has anointed, both Herod, and Pontius Pilate, with the Gentiles, and the people of Israel, were gathered together, for to do whatsoever thy hand and thy counsel determined before to be done." Herod, Pilate, etc., all acted according to their own desires and free will; God did not force them to commit this sin; yet when they did commit it of their own accord, it all turned out exactly according to the plan of God. The same principle is illustrated in the history of Joseph's brothers selling him into Egypt. They acted freely, according to their own evil wishes and desires; yet what they did, wicked as it certainly was, turned out to be the exact plan of God.

16. How can it be that God foreordains and controls the sinful acts of men, and yet is not responsible for the sin? This is a mystery which we cannot wholly understand. However, the Bible plainly teaches that it is so.

19. Q. *What is God's providence toward the angels?*

A. *God by his providence permitted some of the angels, willfully and irrecoverably, to fall into sin and damnation, limiting and ordering that, and all their sins, to his own glory; and established the rest in holiness and happiness; employing them all, at his pleasure, in the administrations of his power, mercy, and justice.*

Scripture References
- Jude 6; 2 Peter 2:4. God permitted some of the angels to fall into sin.
- Heb. 2:16. God provided no way of salvation for the angels that sinned.
- John 8:44. These angels sinned willfully.
- Job 1:12; Matt. 8:31. God limited their sins for his own glory.
- 1 Tim. 5:21; Mark 8:38; Heb. 12:22. God established the rest of the angels in holiness and happiness.
- Ps. 104:4; 2 Kings 19:35; Heb. 1:14. God employs the angels as his servants.

Commentary

1. What was the great difference between the fall of the wicked angels into sin, and the fall of the human race into sin? In the case of the human race, the sin of one man brought about the fall of the whole race (Rom. 5:12). In the case of the angels, since they are not a related race, organically connected with each other, but a large number of separate, unrelated individuals, each must have gone through his own probation individually and fallen by his own personal act.

2. What other great difference exists between the fall of the angels and the fall of the human race? Only part of the angels fell into sin; but in the case of the human race, the whole race fell.

3. What special activities of the fallen angels, or demons, took place in connection with the earthly ministry of our Savior? At the time of the earthly ministry of Jesus Christ, when God was most active in executing his plans for the redemption of the human race from sin, Satan and the demons carried on a counteroffensive of desperate activity. Many persons were demon-possessed, that is, demons or fallen angels had entered into them and taken possession of their personalities, using them for wicked purposes. In one case (Matt. 8:31) we read of a great host of demons possessing one man. Christ by his divine power cast out the demons, a sign of the arrival of the kingdom of God.

4. What special activities do the holy angels have in connection with Christian people? Read Hebrews 1:14.

5. What truth does the epistle to the Hebrews teach about the angels in relation to Christ? Read Hebrews 1:4–6. Christ is higher than the angels, for they are only God's servants, whereas Christ is God's Son. When Christ came into the world, the angels worshiped him, indicating that he is higher than they. The angels are created beings; Christ is their divine Creator.

20. Q. *What was the providence of God toward man in the estate in which he was created?*

A. *The providence of God toward man in the estate in which he was created, was the placing him in paradise, appointing him to dress it, giving him liberty to eat of the fruit of the earth; putting the creatures under his dominion, and ordaining marriage for his help; affording him communion with himself; instituting the Sabbath; entering into a covenant of life with him, upon condition of personal, perfect, and perpetual obe-*

dience, of which the tree of life was a pledge; and forbidding to eat of the tree of the knowledge of good and evil, upon the pain of death.

Scripture References

- Gen. 2:8, 15–16. Man placed in paradise, etc.
- Gen. 1:28. The creatures placed under man's dominion.
- Gen. 2:18. Marriage ordained for man's help.
- Gen. 1:28; 3:8. Man originally enjoyed communion with God.
- Gen. 2:3. The Sabbath instituted.
- Gal. 3:12; Rom. 10:5; 5:14. The covenant of works instituted.
- Gen. 2:9. The tree of life.
- Gen. 2:17. The tree of the knowledge of good and evil.

Commentary

1. In what part of the world was "paradise" or the Garden of Eden located? While the exact location cannot be determined, there can be no doubt that it was in the Near East. Many scholars believe it was in Armenia near the sources of the Tigris and Euphrates rivers; others hold that it was probably near the head of the Persian Gulf.

2. Of the four rivers mentioned in Genesis 2:10–14, which are still known by the same names today? The Euphrates. Also the river "Hiddekel" is the same as the Tigris River.

3. Why cannot the other two rivers still be identified with certainty today? Possibly because the great flood in the days of Noah altered the geography of the region.

4. How did God provide for the physical welfare of mankind before the fall? (a) God provided man with a home, the Garden of Eden; (b) he provided man with wholesome work in the garden; (c) he provided food suitable for the human race; (d) he placed the creatures under man's dominion.

5. How did God provide for the social welfare of mankind before the fall? By instituting marriage, thus establishing the home or the family, the fundamental social institution of the human race.

6. How did God provide for the spiritual welfare of the human race before the fall? (a) By affording man communion with God; (b) by instituting the weekly Sabbath; (c) by establishing the covenant of works or covenant of life between God and mankind.

7. Why was this first covenant a covenant of life? Because by it the human race could have attained eternal life, if Adam had obeyed God.

8. Why is this same covenant often called a covenant of works? Because it was a plan by which the human race could attain eternal life by works, that is, by perfect obedience to the will of God.

9. Who were the parties to the covenant of works? The parties were God, who established the covenant, and Adam, the head and representative of the entire human race.

10. What was the condition of the covenant of works? The condition was perfect obedience to God's revealed will.

11. What particular form did this condition take in the covenant of works? It took the form of a command not to eat the fruit of the tree of the knowledge of good and evil.

12. Why did God command Adam and Eve not to eat the fruit of the tree of the knowledge of good and evil? This was a sheer, arbitrary test of obedience to the will of God. The fruit of the tree was good in itself. It was not poisonous or harmful in itself. The only reason why Adam and Eve were not to eat it was just because God had said, "Thou shalt not eat of it." So it was a pure test of obedience to God's will.

13. What kind of fruit was this fruit of the tree of the knowledge of good and evil? We do not know, for the Bible does not tell us. The idea that it was the apple is only a popular legend, without any foundation.

14. What would have been the result if Adam and Eve had obeyed God? The time would have come when they would have received the right to eat the fruit of the tree of life. Then they would have received eternal life, and it would have become impossible for them ever to commit any sin or to die.

15. How long did this test or probation of Adam and Eve in the covenant of works last? It lasted from the time that God gave the command until Adam ate the fruit of the tree.

16. How long would this probation have lasted if Adam and Eve had obeyed God? We do not know, for the Bible does not tell us. However, since it was a test or probation, it could not have lasted forever. The very nature of a probation is temporary, not permanent. There would have

come a time when God would announce that Adam and Eve had passed the
test successfully and had earned the right to eat the fruit of the tree of life.

**17. How long did Adam and Eve live in the Garden of Eden before
they ate the forbidden fruit?** We do not know. The Bible says nothing
whatever on this point. However, the popular idea that it was only a few
days is unfounded. From Genesis 5:3 we know that Adam was 130 years old
when Seth was born. It was entirely possible that Adam and Eve may have
lived in the Garden of Eden for several years.

18. What was the penalty attached to the covenant of works? The
penalty attached to the covenant of works was death.

**19. What was the meaning of death as the penalty of the covenant
of works?** Death must have been meant in the fullest, widest sense, including not only the death of the body, but also spiritual death, or alienation
from God, and eternal death, which the Bible calls "hell" or "the second
death."

**20. If Adam and Eve had obeyed God perfectly, how long would
they have lived?** They and all their descendants would have lived forever
without dying.

21. How can this be proved from the Bible? Romans 5:12.

**22. If death had not entered the world, and the human race con-
tinued to multiply without anyone ever dying, how could the world
hold so many people?** No doubt people would have reached the time
when God would have taken them to heaven without dying, as he took
Enoch and Elijah.

**23. How should we answer the people who say that it was not fair
for God to make Adam the representative of the whole human race?**
We should reply as Paul did in answering a similar objection in Romans
9:20: "Nay but, O man, who art thou that repliest against God? Shall the
thing formed say to him that formed it, why has thou made me thus?" Sinful human beings have no right to decide what was or was not fair for God
to do. God as the Creator of the human race is sovereign and has the right
to do as he pleases with all his creatures.

**24. Why is this doctrine of the covenant of works very important
to us as Christians?** Because it is parallel to the way of salvation through

Jesus Christ. Just as the first Adam brought sin and death, so Christ, the second Adam, brings us righteousness and eternal life. Adam was our representative in the covenant of works; Jesus Christ is our representative in the covenant of grace. Those who reject the doctrine of the covenant of works have no right to claim the blessings of the covenant of grace, for the two are parallel, and stand or fall together, as is proved by Romans 5.

6

The Covenant of Life or Works

21. Q. *Did man continue in that estate wherein God at first created him?*

A. *Our first parents being left to the freedom of their own will, through the temptation of Satan, transgressed the commandment of God in eating the forbidden fruit; and thereby fell from the estate of innocency wherein they were created.*

Scripture References
- Gen. 3:6–8, 13. The historical account of the fall of the human race.
- Eccl. 7:29. Mankind created upright, but later fell into sin.
- 2 Cor. 11:3. The fall took place through the temptation of Satan.
- Rom. 5:12. The fall was a definite event involving one particular agent.
- 1 Tim. 2:14. Eve was deceived, but Adam sinned without being deceived.

Commentary
1. Why was it possible for Adam and Eve to sin against God? God left them to the freedom of their own will, instead of using his almighty power to prevent them from sinning. Since God is almighty, it would certainly have been possible for him to prevent the human race from falling into sin. But God in his wisdom did not choose to prevent the fall. Since God held back his almighty power and left Adam and Eve to their own free will, it was possible for them to choose to commit sin.

2. What was the difference between the sin committed by Adam and the sin committed by Eve? Read 1 Timothy 2:14. Eve was deceived by Satan, and thereupon sinned; Adam was not deceived, but disobeyed God anyway.

3. Which sin was worse, the sin of Adam or the sin of Eve? Undoubtedly Adam's sin was worse than Eve's. It is bad to sin because a person has been deceived by Satan; it is much worse to commit the same sin without having been deceived, that is, fully realizing that it is contrary to God's will.

4. What was the result of our first parents' eating the forbidden fruit? They immediately realized that they had alienated themselves from God. Instead of enjoying communion with God, they became afraid of God and tried to escape from God, because their conscience told them that they had sinned.

5. What great mystery is involved in the Bible account of the fall? The problem of the origin of evil in the human race. Since Adam and Eve were created in a state of knowledge, righteousness, and holiness, there was no evil in their nature to which temptation could appeal. Since they were created in righteousness, evil had to enter their lives from an outside source. But how could temptation to commit sin make a real appeal to a sinless being? What motive could have more influence in a sinless person than the motive to obey God?

6. What should be our attitude toward this mystery? We should accept what the Bible teaches about it in simple faith, and recognize that the psychological problem of the origin of evil in the human race is an insoluble mystery. The information which the Bible provides may be summarized as follows: (a) Our first parents were sinless as they came from the hand of God. (b) Sin entered the human race from an outside source, namely, from the temptation of Satan. (c) Satan tempted Eve through appealing to desires which are not sinful in themselves, but morally indifferent (Gen. 3:6), but which it is sinful to gratify by disobedience to a direct command of God. (d) The temptation came to Adam not directly from Satan, but through Eve, who had already sinned. (e) Although the psychological problem is insoluble, there is not the slightest doubt as to the fact that mankind, although created holy, was tempted by Satan and thereupon fell into an estate of sin.

7. What false interpretation of the Bible account of the fall (Gen. 3) is popular today? The mythical interpretation, which holds that the account of the fall is not a record of historical facts, but a story which grew up in ancient times to explain the presence of sin and death in the world. According to this interpretation, Adam and Eve were not historical persons, nor was there a literal tree of life nor a literal tree of the knowledge of good and evil. It was all the product of poetic fancy, a beautiful story, but not true.

8. What reasons have we for holding that the account of the fall in Genesis 3 is a record of historical facts, to be literally interpreted?
(a) The record itself, being a part of a book of history, is most naturally understood as being historical. (b) Our Lord Jesus Christ regarded it as historical, and Adam and Eve as actual persons, as is shown by Matthew 19:4–6, where he quotes Genesis 2:24 as having actually been spoken by God when he "in the beginning made them male and female." (c) If the account of the fall in Genesis 3 is not literal historical fact, then the apostle Paul's argument in Romans 5:12–21 is meaningless and worthless, for it assumes the historical character of the record of the fall. Since Romans 5:12–21 forms an essential part of the apostle's argument in the entire epistle, we must conclude that since the epistle to the Romans is infallibly inspired Scripture, the record of the fall in Genesis 3 must be a record of historical fact.

22. Q. *Did all mankind fall in that first transgression?*

A. *The covenant being made with Adam as a public person, not for himself only, but for his posterity, all mankind descending from him by ordinary generation, sinned in him, and fell with him in that first transgression.*

Scripture References
- Acts 17:26. The organic unity of the human race; all made "of one blood," therefore all the children of Adam.
- Gen. 2:16–17, compared with Rom. 5:12–21. Adam constituted by God the federal head or representative of the human race, so that his act was determinative for all.
- 1 Cor. 15:21–22. Adam, like Christ, a federal head or "public person."

Commentary

1. To what official position was Adam appointed by God in the covenant of works? God appointed Adam as "head" or representative of the human race to undergo the probation of the covenant of works for the whole human race.

2. What Scripture passage most clearly proves that Adam represented his posterity in the covenant of works? Romans 5:12–21.

3. What is the meaning of the expression "all mankind descending from him by ordinary generation"? This expression means all mankind except Jesus Christ. Jesus Christ descended from Adam, it is true, but not by ordinary generation, for Jesus was born of the Virgin Mary and had no human father. All mankind except Jesus Christ sinned and fell with Adam in his first transgression. The sin of the first Adam brought about the ruin of all mankind except the second Adam.

4. Why is the first transgression of Adam specially mentioned? Because it was only the first transgression of Adam that affected the entire human race as the breach of the covenant of works. Only that first sin of Adam is imputed or reckoned to the whole human race on account of the covenant of works. The rest of Adam's sins, committed in his later life, were committed by him simply as an individual person, not as "head" or representative of the human race. The later sins of Adam have nothing to do with us today; therefore the Bible does not even mention them.

5. How should we answer the person who objects to the Bible teaching that Adam, as the representative of mankind, brought sin and suffering on all of us? Whether we like it or not, the Bible teaches that God deals with humanity on the basis of the principle of representation, both in the covenant of works and in the covenant of grace. The principle of representation functions constantly in ordinary human life, and no one objects to it. The United States Congress declares war, and the life of every individual in the country is affected by it. Parents decide where they will live, and the nationality of their children is determined by it. If it be objected that the people elect their representatives in Congress, whereas we did not choose Adam to be our representative, the answer is: (a) The decisions of lawful representatives are binding whether those represented chose the representatives or not. The acts of Congress affect millions of people who are too young to vote. A child does not choose its own parents, yet its life is largely affected by their actions and decisions. (b) It is true that we did not choose Adam to be our representative, but God chose him; and who could make a wiser, better, or more righteous appointment than God? To object to God's appointment of Adam as our representative in the covenant of works is not only to deny the sovereignty of God, but also to set ourselves up as wiser and more righteous than God.

23. Q. *Into what estate did the fall bring mankind?*

A. *The fall brought mankind into an estate of sin and misery.*

Scripture References
- Rom. 5:12. Death the consequence of sin.
- Rom. 6:23. Death the penalty of sin.
- Rom. 3:23. Sin is universal in the human race.
- Gen. 3:17–19. The curse on the world of nature because of human sin.

Commentary

1. What do we call the estate of mankind before the fall? (a) the estate of innocency; (b) the estate of original righteousness.

2. Why is sin mentioned before misery in describing the estate into which mankind fell? Because sin came first, and misery followed afterward as the result of sin. Sin is the cause of misery; misery is the effect of sin.

3. Which causes the most concern to the human race, misery or sin? Except for Christian people, the human race is very much concerned about its misery or sufferings, and very little concerned about its sins. Even Christian people are often more concerned about the misery of their condition than they are about their sin.

4. What is the basic error of many non-Christian religions, systems of philosophy, and human plans for world betterment? They all try to find a way to relieve the sufferings of humanity, without first providing a way of deliverance from sin, which is the cause of suffering. All human schemes of betterment which are not founded on redemption from sin through Christ are foredoomed to failure. Permanent relief cannot be obtained by treating symptoms only, while ignoring the cause of the trouble.

5. What popular false religion of the present day denies the reality of both sin and misery? Eddyism, or so-called Christian Science.

6. What is the error of the modern scientific view of mankind with respect to the condition of the human race? On the whole, modern scientists regard man as he exists today as normal, and decide what is normal in any particular matter, whether physical or psychological, by taking the average of contemporary human beings. Normal health, normal intelligence, normal growth, etc., are all determined in this way. This attitude of regarding the average of present-day humanity as "normal" is contrary to the Bible teaching about mankind having fallen into a condition of sin and misery. According to the Bible, man was normal in the Garden of Eden, as created by God. Having fallen into sin, man became abnormal, and there is not a single normal human being in the world today. The average of contemporary human beings, in any particular matter, is abnormal, that is, divergent from the perfection of man as created by God. In particular, modern science regards old age and death as normal experiences for human beings, but from the Bible standpoint both of these are strictly abnormal and alien to mankind as created by God.

24. Q. *What is sin?*

A. *Sin is any want of conformity unto, or transgression of any law of God, given as a rule to the reasonable creature.*

Scripture References

- 1 John 3:4. Sin is defined as transgression of the law.
- Gal. 3:10, 12. Want of conformity is sin, as well as positive transgression.
- Rom. 3:20. Sin impressed on the mind and conscience by the law of God.
- Rom. 5:13. Apart from law there could be no sin imputed to men.
- James 4:17. The mere failure to do good is sin.

Commentary

1. Where does the Bible come nearest to giving a formal definition of sin? 1 John 3:4: "Sin is the transgression of the law," or, as translated in the American Standard Version, "sin is lawlessness."

2. What is the difference between sin and crime? Strictly speaking, sin is violation of the law of God; crime is violation of the law of the state. However, many old writers used the words *crime* and *criminal* in the sense of "sin" and "sinful."

3. May the same act be both a crime and a sin? Yes. For example, murder, theft, or perjury.

4. May an act be a sin but not a crime? Yes. For example, to hate one's brother is a sin against God, but not a violation of the law of the state, for the latter has no jurisdiction over men's thoughts.

5. May an act be a crime but not a sin? Yes. For example, in Scotland 250 years ago many covenanters were put in prison or even killed because they assembled to worship God without permission of the king. This was a crime because they violated the law of the state (a wicked and unjust law, in that case), but it was not a sin, because they were obeying God's law in doing it.

6. To what kind of creatures has God given laws? To his reasonable (or rational) creatures, that is, to angels and men.

7. What two kinds of sin does the catechism speak of? (a) Negative sin, or in other words lack of conformity to God's laws; (b) positive sin, or in other words transgression of God's laws.

8. What must a person do to be a sinner? Nothing. Even if there were a person who never transgressed any of God's laws, still that person would be a sinner because he would still be characterized by a sinful lack of conformity to God's holy law.

9. What summary of God's law especially stresses the positive sin of transgression? The Ten Commandments (Exod. 20:1–17), eight of which begin with the words "Thou shalt not . . ."

10. What summary of God's law especially stresses the negative sin of want (or lack) of conformity? The moral law as summarized by Jesus

(Matt. 22:37–39); "Thou shalt love the Lord thy God with all thy heart, and with all thy soul, and with all thy mind. This is the first and great commandment. And the second is like unto it, Thou shalt love thy neighbor as thyself. On these two commandments hang all the law and the prophets."

11. What inadequate definition of sin is often given by those who believe in total sanctification during the present life? They often define sin as "voluntary transgression of known law."

12. Why is this definition of sin inadequate? Because it omits two forms of sin: (a) original sin, or the sin of our nature with which we are born; (b) the negative sin of want (lack) of conformity to God's requirements.

25. Q. *Wherein consists the sinfulness of that estate whereinto man fell?*

A. *The sinfulness of that estate whereinto man fell, consisteth in the guilt of Adam's first sin, the want of that righteousness wherein he was created, and the corruption of his nature, whereby he is utterly indisposed, disabled, and made opposite unto all that is spiritually good, and wholly inclined to all evil, and that continually; which is commonly called original sin, and from which do proceed all actual transgressions.*

Scripture References
- Rom. 5:12, 19. The guilt of Adam's first sin imputed to all mankind.
- Rom. 3:10–19. Mankind universally and totally depraved in sin.
- Eph. 2:1–3. Mankind dead in sin and therefore unable to please God.
- Rom. 5:6. Mankind spiritually without strength and ungodly.
- Rom. 8:7–8. Mankind at enmity with God and cannot please God.
- Gen. 6:5. Mankind sinful in imagination and thoughts as well as in deeds.
- James 1:14–15. Original sin the source of actual transgressions.
- Matt. 15:19. Sinful deeds proceed from a corrupt and sinful heart.

Commentary
1. What are the two principal kinds of sin? (a) Original sin, or the sin of our nature with which we are born; (b) actual transgressions, or the sin of practice that we do ourselves.

2. Why is only the guilt of Adam's first sin imputed to his posterity? Adam acted as our representative only until he broke the covenant of works. After he committed his first sin, he ceased to have any covenant relationship with us that could further affect us. However, he still had (and has) a natural relationship to the human race as the first ancestor of all human beings.

3. What righteousness did mankind lose by the fall? The righteousness in which he was created, or original righteousness.

4. Besides the guilt of Adam's first sin, and the loss of original righteousness, what other evil resulted from the fall? Man's nature was corrupted so that he became depraved in heart and loved sin.

5. What is the extent of the corruption of nature that resulted from the fall? This corruption of nature is complete or total in extent, and is sometimes called "total depravity."

6. Does total depravity of nature mean that an unsaved person cannot do anything good? No. The unsaved person, by God's common grace (or restraining power), can do things that are good within the civil or human sphere. For example, an unsaved person may save another from drowning, at the risk of his own life. But the unsaved person can do nothing that is spiritually good, that is, nothing truly good and pleasing in God's sight. He may do things that are good in themselves, but he never does them with the right motive, namely, to love, serve, and please God; therefore even the "good" works of the unsaved person are spoiled and corrupted by sin.

7. What is the modern attitude toward the doctrine of total depravity? Those who pride themselves on their "modern" spirit ridicule and scoff at this truth of God's Word.

8. What practical lesson may we learn from the doctrines of original sin and total depravity? From these doctrines we should learn that sins in the outward life proceed from the sin in the heart, and therefore learn that reform of the outward life without spiritual cleansing of the heart cannot lead to a truly good life.

9. Is it possible for a person to save himself from his condition of original sin and total depravity? No. Jeremiah 13:23 proves that a change in nature is beyond our own power. Because we are not merely sick, but *dead* in trespasses and sins, we are spiritually helpless and unable to save ourselves (or even to begin to save ourselves). A person may reform his outward life to some extent, but he cannot give himself a new heart; he may be able to change his conduct in some respects, but he cannot raise himself spiritually from the dead (Eph. 2:1–10).

26. Q. *How is original sin conveyed from our first parents unto their posterity?*

A. *Original sin is conveyed from our first parents unto their posterity by natural generation, so as all that proceed from them in that way are conceived and born in sin.*

Scripture References
- Ps. 51:5. We are conceived and born in a sinful condition.
- Job 14:4. Our first parents being sinful, their posterity must be sinful too.
- Job 15:14. All mankind are born with a sinful nature.
- John 3:6. Natural generation produces only sinful human nature; the new birth produces a new nature.

Commentary
1. Besides being our representative in the covenant of works, what other relationship did Adam have to us? Besides the federal or covenant relationship, which came to an end when he committed his first sin, Adam also had a natural relationship to us as our first ancestor. This natural relationship continued through his life.

2. What has been imputed to us because of Adam's covenant relationship to us? The guilt of Adam's first sin has been imputed to all of his posterity (in other words, to all human beings except Jesus Christ).

3. What have we received from Adam by reason of his natural relationship to us? We have derived our physical or bodily life from Adam through our parents and more remote ancestors, who descended from him.

4. What was the effect of Adam's first sin on himself? As a judicial penalty for Adam's violation of the covenant of works, God withdrew from

Adam the life-giving influences of the Holy Spirit. The result was, inevitably, moral and physical death. The moment Adam ate the forbidden fruit he became dead in trespasses and sins; at that same moment the principle of death became operative in his physical body, with the certainty that it would return to dust in the end.

5. How is this effect of Adam's first sin on himself paralleled in his descendants? Every human being is born into the world with the guilt of Adam's first sin reckoned or imputed to him. Therefore, because of the broken covenant of works, every human being comes into existence morally and spiritually dead, because deprived of the life-giving operations of the Holy Spirit. As for our physical body, the principle of death is at work in it when we are born, so that its return to dust, while by God's common grace it may be delayed, yet cannot be permanently prevented.

6. What is the effect of our beginning our existence morally and spiritually dead? The effect of our beginning our existence with a depraved and sinful nature (or morally and spiritually dead) is that personal sin and actual transgressions inevitably follow in the course of time.

7. Is it correct to say that we "inherit" a sinful nature from Adam? It depends on what we mean by the word *inherit*. If we mean that we are born with a sinful nature because of our connection with Adam, our first ancestor, then it is correct to say that we "inherit" a sinful nature from Adam. If we mean that we inherit a sinful nature as we might inherit blonde hair or a tall stature, then it is not correct to say that we "inherit" a sinful nature from Adam. While we must recognize that the problem of the transmission of original sin is a very difficult one, still it seems safe to say that the Bible does not warrant a belief that a sinful nature is transmitted by the mechanism of biological heredity as physical characteristics are transmitted from generation to generation. Sin is a spiritual fact, not a bodily property or characteristic. If original sin were transmitted from parent to child by biological heredity, we would receive it from our immediate parents rather than from Adam. In that case, too, the children of believers would come into the world in a regenerate condition. But as a matter of fact the children of believers are born into the world dead in sin. We may conclude, therefore, (a) that our sinful nature comes to us by reason of our natural birth as descendants of Adam; (b) that it comes to us from Adam, rather than our immediate parents; (c) that we "inherit" a sinful nature from Adam as a man might "inherit" money or property from his father or grandfather, not as a person might "inherit" blue eyes or brown hair from his parents. (For a fuller discussion of this difficult subject the reader is referred to A. A. Hodge's *Commentary on the Confession of Faith,* 151–60.)

8. What system of doctrine denies the Bible's teaching on original sin? The system of doctrine called Pelagianism, after its founder Pelagius, a British monk who lived in the fourth century after Christ. Pelagius denied that we are born with a sinful nature, and taught that infants are born without sin and that they become sinful only by imitating the sins of other persons. Against this heresy of Pelagius, the Bible doctrine of original sin was defended by the great church father Augustine. After a long controversy Pelagianism was condemned as false by the church, and the Bible doctrine was vindicated. During the Middle Ages, however, a modified form of Pelagianism called Semi-Pelagianism became the dominant doctrine in the church.

27. Q. *What misery did the fall bring upon mankind?*

A. *The fall brought upon mankind the loss of communion with God, his displeasure and curse; so as we are by nature children of wrath, bond slaves to Satan, and justly liable to all punishments in this world, and that which is to come.*

Scripture References
- Gen. 3:8–10, 24. By the fall mankind lost communion with God.
- Eph. 2:2–3. By nature we all are the children of wrath.
- 2 Tim. 2:26. By nature we are bond slaves of Satan.
- Gen. 2:17; Lam. 3:39; Rom. 6:23. Because of the fall we are liable to God's punishments in this world.
- Matt. 25:41, 46; Jude 7. Because of the fall we are liable to God's punishments in the world to come.

Commentary
1. What was the first misery which the fall brought upon the human race? The loss of communion with God.

2. How soon after they sinned did Adam and Eve lose communion with God? Immediately after they sinned.

3. How did they know that they had forfeited communion with God? Their own conscience, which had become defiled by sin, caused them to realize that a barrier had come between them and God (Gen. 3:7).

4. Can an unsaved person have communion with God today? Absolutely not. Only through Christ's work of reconciliation can the barrier between God and sinful human beings be removed so that they can have communion with God.

5. How were God's displeasure and curse visited upon Adam and Eve? (a) God sentenced Adam to lifelong labor as the means of existence, until his body would die and be reclaimed by the dust from which it had been taken. (b) God told Eve that her life would be a life of greatly increased suffering. (c) God expelled both Adam and Eve from the Garden of Eden, prevented them from having access to the tree of life, and appointed for them a perpetual conflict with Satan and the kingdom of evil (Gen. 3:15–20, 22–24).

6. How does our experience parallel that of Adam and Eve after they sinned? (a) They lost communion with God; we come into the world alienated from God. (b) The woes pronounced upon Adam and Eve are still the common experience of humanity. (c) They lost their access to the tree of life, although its fruit had been almost within their grasp; we are born into the world far from the tree of life, and no human being can ever receive eternal life except through Jesus Christ. (d) They faced a life of perpetual enmity between themselves and Satan; we too must fight a lifelong battle against Satan and against his allies, the world and the flesh.

7. What is meant by saying that we are by nature children of wrath? This expression, which is taken from Ephesians 2:3, means that we are born into this world with a nature which is sinful and therefore the object of God's wrath, that is, his righteous displeasure against sin.

8. What is meant by saying that unsaved people are bond slaves to Satan? This means that God has justly permitted Satan to have a certain power or dominion over all unsaved people, by reason of which they are not spiritually free, but in bondage to sin and Satan, who tyrannizes over their lives and afflicts them both in soul and in body. Satan's activities are strictly limited by God, however. The believer in Christ, while he may be influenced or tempted by Satan, is no longer a slave of Satan, for he has been liberated by the Son of God (John 8:34–36).

9. What truth is implied by the statement that sinners are justly liable to all punishments in this world and that which is to come? This statement implies the truth that sin involves guilt, for it renders the sinner liable to penalties. Therefore sin is not a mere misfortune or calamity which would call forth the pity of God; nor is it a mere disease which needs to be cured; nor is it a mere moral pollution which needs to be cleansed; it is guilt which deserves punishment and which needs to be forgiven.

10. What is the modern "liberal" attitude toward the doctrines stated in this question of the catechism? The modern "liberal" theology denies every one of the truths set forth in the answer to question 27. (a) Modern "Liberalism" teaches that all men are children of God by nature, and therefore anyone can have communion with God by simply realizing that he is already a child of God. (b) "Liberalism" speaks only of the love of God, and objects to the idea of his displeasure and curse. (c) "Liberalism" follows Pelagius and denies that we are born with a nature that is the object of divine wrath because of its sinfulness. (d) "Liberalism" does not believe in a personal devil, and therefore cannot accept the idea that we are bond slaves to Satan. (e) "Liberalism" defines sin in human and social terms, and therefore rejects the doctrine that sin is guilt before God which deserves divine punishment.

28. Q. *What are the punishments of sin in this world?*

A. *The punishments of sin in this world are either inward, as blindness of mind, a reprobate sense, strong delusions, hardness of heart, horror of conscience, and vile affections; or outward, as the curse of God upon the creatures for our sakes, and all other evils that befall us in our bodies, names, estates, relations, and employments; together with death itself.*

Scripture References
- Eph. 4:18. Blindness of heart and mind as a punishment for sin.
- Rom. 1:28. A reprobate mind a punishment for sin.
- 2 Thess. 2:11. Strong delusions sent by God as punishment for sin.

- Rom. 2:5. Hardness and an impenitent heart.
- Isa. 33:14; Gen. 4:13; Matt. 27:4. Horrors of conscience one of God's ways of punishing sin.
- Rom. 1:26. Sinners punished by being given over to vile passions.
- Gen. 3:17. God's curse upon the world of nature a penalty for human sin.
- Deut. 28:15–68. All calamities, sufferings, and evils are punishments for sin.
- Rom. 6:21, 23. Death itself is the wages, or penalty, of sin.

Commentary

1. What is the spiritual state of unsaved persons? A state of spiritual deadness which the catechism calls "blindness of mind."

2. Is the unsaved person responsible for his own blindness of mind? Yes, for this blindness is itself a punishment for previous sin.

3. What is the meaning of the expression "a reprobate sense"? This expression implies a full and willing abandonment to sin, with little or no restraint.

4. What is meant by "strong delusion"? This expression means a firm, confident belief in something which is not true, but false. For example, the confident faith of the modern world in the evolutionary theory of the origin of the human race is a strong delusion; the Nazi belief (during the Second World War) that the Germans were a "super-race" superior by nature to all other races of men was a strong delusion.

5. How can it be right for God to send people "strong delusions," as 2 Thessalonians 2:11 affirms that he does? (a) The Bible often speaks of God's doing what he does not do himself, but what is done by others. For instance, God withheld the influence of his grace from Pharaoh; the result was that Pharaoh's heart—following its natural inclination—became harder and harder against God; then in the Scripture it says that God hardened Pharaoh's heart. If God leaves people to their own ways, they will choose lies rather than the truth; in this sense it can be said that God sends them "strong delusions." James 1:13–14 teaches that God does not, himself, tempt any man to sin, but that he does permit people to be tempted and enticed by their own lusts. (b) God does not send "strong delusions" to deceive innocent or righteous people such as Adam and Eve were before the fall, but only to deceive those who have already corrupted themselves by choosing sin.

All through the Bible God is seen to punish sin by abandoning the sinner to his sin, which always results in even greater or worse sin.

6. What is meant by "hardness of heart"? This means a condition of moral and spiritual indifference, so that the conscience is no longer sensitive and active, and the person is not affected by calls to repentance nor by the invitations of the gospel. The person who has committed the sin against the Holy Spirit is given over to the most extreme form of hardness of heart.

7. Give some Bible examples of people who were given over to "hardness of heart." (a) Pharaoh: Exodus 14:4, etc. (b) King Saul: 1 Samuel 16:14, etc. (c) Judas Iscariot: John 13:26–27.

8. What is meant by "horror of conscience"? The Bible teaches that there is such a thing as hardened sinners' becoming greatly afraid of the punishments of sin, even though they are quite complacent about the sinfulness of sin. The fact that they have offended against God does not trouble them, but they are terrified at God's judgments, which they know will overtake them. There are accounts of famous infidels being filled with terrors and fear of hell while on their deathbeds.

9. How does Paul in Romans 1:28 explain the presence of vile and gross sins in the world? These "vile affections" are the result of God's abandoning people to their own sinful nature and tendencies, as a punishment for not "liking to retain God in their knowledge."

10. How should we look upon the present condition of the world of nature? The whole world of nature is under a curse of God, as we learn from Genesis 3:17–19 as well as other places in Scripture. Floods, dust storms, calamities of all kinds, as well as bad climates, extremes of weather, thorns and thistles, are all part of this curse. We should realize that the world as created by God was quite different from the world as we know it today. We live in an abnormal world, in the wreckage of a world that has been devastated and cursed by sin. Apart from the testimony of the Bible modern scientific investigation has shown that there was once a warm climate in northern Alaska and other far northern regions. Fossils of palm leaves and other tropical vegetation have been found there in the rocks.

11. In what sense is the curse upon the world of nature a punishment for sin? In the case of unsaved sinners, the curse upon nature is strictly and simply a punishment for sin. In the case of Christian people, the curse upon nature is not strictly a penalty for sin, for they have been delivered from that by Christ's atonement. Rather, in their case, the curse upon nature is to be regarded as a consequence of sin and a part of God's fatherly chastening or discipline by which he prepares us for the life eternal.

12. In what sense is physical death itself a punishment for sin? Death is called "the wages of sin" (Rom. 6:23). Wages means "that which we have earned" or "what we deserve." In the case of the unsaved person, death is simply the wages of sin, a judicial penalty. In the case of the Christian, however, Christ has already suffered death as his substitute. The Christian still has to die, of course, but in the case of the Christian, death is no longer a penalty. It remains an enemy, but it is not a judicial penalty. Rather, to the Christian, death is a change by which God transfers him to the region and the condition of perfect holiness. Thus physical death, to the Christian, is part of God's fatherly discipline. It proceeds not from God's wrath, but from his love in the case of the Christian.

29. Q. *What are the punishments of sin in the world to come?*

A. *The punishments of sin in the world to come, are everlasting separation from the comfortable presence of God, and most grievous torments in soul and body, without intermission, in hell-fire forever.*

Scripture References
- 2 Thess. 1:9. Everlasting separation from the presence of God.
- Mark 9:44–48. Grievous torments in soul and body.
- Luke 16:24. The torment of hell-fire.
- Rev. 14:9–12. The torments of hell without intermission.
- Matt. 5:29–30. Hell involves bodily suffering.
- Matt. 25:41, 46. The punishment of hell equally eternal with the bliss of heaven.

Commentary
1. What three heresies deny the doctrine of eternal punishment for sin? (a) Annihilationism, which teaches that in the case of the unsaved, death

ends their existence, or else that after suffering a certain duration of punishment for sin they will be annihilated and cease to exist. (b) Universalism, which teaches that all human beings will finally be saved. (c) Restorationism, which teaches that after death the wicked will have a "second chance" to accept salvation, and thus will be saved.

2. How can we answer those who say that the word _eternal_ in the New Testament means "age-long" and therefore eternal punishment does not really mean forever? Matthew 25:46 is a text which cannot be explained away: "And these shall go away into everlasting punishment: but the righteous into life eternal." In the Greek of this verse, "everlasting" and "eternal" are exactly the same word. Therefore if the punishment of hell is not really forever, then neither will the blessedness of heaven be forever. The same Greek adjective is used to describe one as the other. It is unfortunate that the King James Version uses two different words, "everlasting" and "eternal." The Revised Version translates the verse as follows: "and these shall go away into eternal punishment, but the righteous into eternal life."

3. What is the main punishment of sin in the world to come? Beyond question the main or chief punishment of sin in the world to come is everlasting separation from the comfortable presence of God. The presence of God is what will make heaven a place of blessedness, and separation from God is what will make hell a place of woe.

4. What parable told by Christ proves that memory of life on earth will continue to exist in hell? The Parable of the Rich Man and Lazarus, Luke 16:19–31, especially verse 25: "But Abraham said, Son remember, that thou in thy life-time receivedst thy good things, and likewise Lazarus evil things: but now he is comforted, and thou art tormented."

5. How can it be proved from Scripture that the punishments of hell include the body as well as the soul? Matthew 5:29–30: "It is profitable for thee that one of thy members should perish, and not that thy whole body should be cast into hell." Revelation 20:13–15: "And the sea gave up the dead which were in it . . . and whosoever was not found written in the book of life was cast into the lake of fire." (The dead in the sea must mean men's bodies, not their souls.) Matthew 10:28: "And fear not them which kill the body, but are not able to kill the soul: but rather fear him which is able to destroy both soul and body in hell."

6. How can we answer the argument that God is too good and loving to send any of his creatures to hell? How do we know whether God is good and loving or not? The only way we know about God's goodness and his love is from the written Word, the Holy Bible. But according to the Bible, love is only one among God's attributes. God is love, but it does not follow that God is nothing but love. The Bible teaches that God is also a God of absolute justice. It is God's attribute of absolute justice that finds expression in the eternal punishment of sinners.

7. How should we answer the person who says that the doctrine of hell is contrary to "the spirit of Christ"? We have no right to define "the spirit of Christ" according to our own imaginations, ideas, or preferences. The only way we can know anything about the teachings of Jesus Christ is from his sayings which are recorded in the New Testament. It has been observed that there is more about hell in the teachings of Jesus than in all the rest of the Bible taken together. The person who claims that "the spirit of Christ" is contrary to the doctrine of hell does not want to take all of the teachings of Christ as his standard (far less is he willing to take the whole Word of God as his guide); he wants to pick and choose among Christ's sayings, taking what appeals to him and omitting the rest. The result of this process is that Christ's teaching is warped and twisted to fit a person's own ideas and prejudices.

8. What feature do many false religions of the present day have in common? The doctrine that there is no hell. There is nothing Satan would rather have men believe than this doctrine that there is no hell.

9. Is it a mistake to urge the fear of hell on people as a motive for believing on Christ as their Savior? Certainly fear of hell is not the only motive nor the highest motive for being a Christian. But the Bible does present this motive over and over again, especially in the teachings of Jesus Christ himself. We conclude that this motive has its place. It is true that we read in 1 John 4:18, "There is no fear in love but perfect love casteth out fear: because fear hath torment; he that feareth is not made perfect in love." But there is a stage in a person's Christian experience where the motive of fear has its place, and the motive may be used by the Holy Spirit to drive an unsaved person to Christ.

7

The Covenant of Grace

30. Q. *Doth God leave all mankind to perish in the estate of sin and misery?*

A. *God doth not leave all men to perish in the estate of sin and misery, into which they fell by the breach of the first covenant, commonly called the Covenant of Works; but of his mere love and mercy delivereth his elect out of it, and bringeth them into an estate of salvation by the second covenant, commonly called the Covenant of Grace.*

Scripture References
- 1 Thess. 5:9. God has appointed his elect to obtain salvation by Christ.
- Gal. 3:10–12. Mankind in sin and misery because of the breach of the covenant of works.
- Titus 3:4–7. The elect are saved from sin by the kindness, love, and mercy of God.
- Gal. 3:21. There is no hope of salvation on the basis of our own works.
- Rom. 3:20–22. Salvation by works being impossible, God has provided another way, by the righteousness of a substitute.

Commentary

1. What two names are given to the first covenant that God made with mankind? (a) The covenant of life; (b) the covenant of works.

2. Why can the same covenant be called both a "covenant of life" and a "covenant of works"? Because the first covenant was an arrangement made by God on the basis of which mankind could gain eternal life by works of obedience to God.

3. Why did God not leave all men to perish in their sin and misery? Because of his mere love and mercy; that is, God was not under any obligation to save any part of the human race; but as a matter of fact, because of his love and mercy, he wished and planned to save some.

4. What part of the human race does God save out of their sin and misery? God saves his elect, that is, those whom he has chosen from all eternity to be the heirs of salvation and eternal life.

5. Is it unfair or unjust for God to save only his elect, and pass by the rest of the human race? No. It is not unfair or unjust because God does not owe salvation to anyone. All have sinned against him, forfeiting all rights, and God owes them nothing but judgment. When God chooses to save some, this is not a matter of obligation, but a free gift. Certainly it is unequal for God to save some and pass by others; but it is not unjust, or unfair, because God is under no obligation to save any of those who have sinned against him.

6. How can we know whether we are among the elect? There is no shortcut to assurance that we are of the elect. We can never find out by trying to pry into God's secret plans and purposes which he has not revealed to us. The only way to find out is to believe on Jesus Christ as our Savior, repent of our sins, and faithfully use the means of grace that God has appointed. In this way, sooner or later, we can come to a full assurance, or certainty, of our personal salvation, from which we can rightly conclude that we are indeed among the elect of God.

7. What is the name of the second covenant which God made with men? The covenant of grace.

31. Q. *With whom was the Covenant of Grace made?*

A. *The Covenant of Grace was made with Christ as the second Adam, and in him with all the elect as his seed.*

Scripture References
- Gal. 3:16. The covenant of grace made with Christ, Abraham's seed.
- Rom. 5:15–21. Christ the second Adam.
- Isa. 53:10–11. The elect, as Christ's "seed," represented by Christ in the covenant of grace.

Commentary

1. Who were the parties of the covenant of works? God was the party who made the covenant; the other party was Adam as the representative of all his descendants, or the whole human race.

2. Why is Christ called "the second Adam"? Because in the covenant of grace, Christ takes the place that Adam had in the covenant of works.

3. Whom did Christ represent in the covenant of grace? He represented "all the elect."

4. Why is it wrong to say that Christ represented the whole human race? (a) Christ's own words contradict such a view of the matter, as we see, for example, in John 17:9: "I pray for them: I pray not for the world, but for them which thou hast given me; for they are thine." Here Christ speaks of a certain body of people as given to him by God the Father; he prayed for them, but he did not pray for the population of the world in general. (b) If Christ in the covenant of grace represented the whole human race, then the whole human race will be saved. But the Bible teaches that only part of the human race will be saved. So if we say that Christ represented everybody, then we will have to say that Christ does not really save anybody, but only gives everybody "a chance" to be saved, and it is "up to each person to take it or leave it." That is a very common belief today, but the Bible is against it. Christ did not suffer and die to give everybody, or anybody, a "chance" to be saved; he suffered and died to accomplish the salvation of the elect.

5. When was the covenant of grace made? It was made in eternity, before the creation of the world, between God the Father and God the Son. Read Ephesians 1:4. The covenant of grace was made before the covenant of works, but it was revealed to mankind after the covenant of works had been broken.

6. When was the covenant of grace first revealed to the human race? Immediately after the fall, in God's words to the serpent—Genesis 3:15—

where God promised that "the seed of the woman," that is, Christ, would finally destroy the serpent, that is, Satan and Satan's kingdom.

How the Covenant of Grace Manifests God's Grace

32. Q. *How is the grace of God manifested in the second covenant?*

A. *The grace of God is manifested in the second covenant, in that he freely provideth and offereth to sinners a Mediator, and life and salvation by him; and requiring faith as the condition to interest them in him, promiseth and giveth his Holy Spirit to all his elect, to work in them that faith, with all other saving graces; and to enable them unto all holy obedience, as the evidence of truth of their faith and thankfulness of God, and as the way which he hath appointed them to salvation.*

Scripture References
- Gen. 3:15. A Redeemer from sin promised.
- Isa. 42:6. Christ promised "for a covenant of the people."
- John 6:27. Christ appointed by God the Father to give men eternal life.
- 1 John 5:11–12. Eternal life given in the Son of God.
- John 3:16. Faith required as the condition of interest in Christ.
- John 1:12. Faith in Christ needed to become children of God.
- Prov. 1:23. God's Holy Spirit promised to his elect.
- 2 Cor. 4:13. Faith wrought in the elect by the Holy Spirit.
- Gal. 5:22–23. Various graces wrought in the elect by the Spirit.
- Ezek. 36:27. The elect enabled unto obedience by the Holy Spirit.
- James 2:18, 22. Good works of the elect an evidence of their faith.
- 2 Cor. 5:14–15. By a good life the elect show their thankfulness to God.
- Eph. 2:10. The Christian's good works foreordained by God, that he should walk in them.

Commentary

1. What is the meaning of the word *grace* when we speak of "the grace of God"? God's grace means his love and favor given to those who deserve his wrath and curse because of sin.

2. How has God offered and provided a Mediator to his people?
God has freely offered and provided a Mediator, that is, as a free gift.

3. What is the meaning of the word *Mediator*? A Mediator is a person
who reconciles two parties who are at enmity with each other.

**4. Why was it necessary for sinners to have a Mediator in order to
be saved?** A Mediator was necessary because sinners could not reconcile
themselves to God.

5. What does Christ, our Mediator, provide? He provides salvation
from sin, and eternal life, to those who receive him.

6. What condition is attached to the covenant of grace? The condition attached to the covenant of grace is faith in Jesus Christ.

7. What is the meaning of the word *interest* in this question? The
word *interest* here means making sure that they will share in the benefits provided by the Mediator.

8. How do we get faith in Jesus Christ? Saving faith in Jesus Christ is a
gift of God. We do not have it of ourselves, or by nature. No one can really
believe on Christ unless God has given him the gift of faith.

9. How does God give us the gift of faith in Jesus Christ? God gives us
the gift of faith in Jesus Christ by the special work of the Holy Spirit in our
hearts.

**10. Since saving faith is a gift of God, do we need to try to believe
on Christ, or should we just wait until God gives us the gift of faith?**
Although it is true that saving faith is a gift of God, and we cannot get it of
ourselves, still it is our duty to strive to believe on Christ. If we really want
to believe on Christ, that is a sign that God is giving us the gift of faith.

**11. What other things does the Holy Spirit work in our hearts and
lives besides faith?** He works "all other saving graces," including repentance and sanctification with all that they include.

12. What is the result of this work of the Holy Spirit in our hearts?
The result of this work of the Holy Spirit in our hearts is that we are made
able to obey the law of God, which we could not do of ourselves because
of our sinful and helpless condition by nature.

13. Why should a Christian want to obey the law of God? A Christian should want to obey the law of God as an evidence of the truth of his faith and thankfulness to God.

14. What other reason is there why a Christian should want to obey the law of God? A Christian should want to obey the law of God because that is "the way which God hath appointed to salvation." This does not mean that obeying God's law is any part of the ground of our salvation, but that being saved from sin unto righteousness, obedience to the law is the way that God has appointed for a saved person to walk in, and the person who is really saved will want to forsake sin and follow righteousness more and more.

The Dispensations of the Covenant of Grace

33. Q. *Was the Covenant of Grace always administered after one and the same manner?*

A. *The Covenant of Grace was not always administered after the same manner, but the administrations of it under the Old Testament were different from those under the New.*

Scripture Reference
- 2 Cor. 3:6–9. The old and new dispensations of the covenant of grace contrasted.

Commentary
1. When did the covenant of works come to an end as a way by which men could attain to eternal life? The covenant of works, as a possible way of attaining eternal life, came to an end when our first parents ate the forbidden fruit. While the covenant of works is still in force today in that unsaved sinners are under the curse of the broken covenant, still no one can attain eternal life by the covenant of works today.

2. When did the covenant of grace begin to operate as the way for sinners to receive eternal life? Immediately after the fall, when our first parents were driven from Eden (Gen. 3:15).

3. Why is it wrong to say that the covenant of grace began when Christ was crucified? Because the Bible clearly teaches that God's people in all ages after the fall were saved by grace and in no other way.

4. What error concerning this question is common today? It is very common today to hold that the Jews were saved by works, but Christians are saved by grace. Those who hold this view say that the covenant of works, as a way of gaining eternal life, did not end until Calvary.

5. Over against this common error, what principle does the catechism set forth? The catechism teaches the unity of the Old Testament and the New Testament in the one covenant of grace. According to the catechism, since Adam's fall there has been only one way of salvation, and that has been by the covenant of grace. It is entirely wrong and harmful to set the Old Testament and the New Testament over against each other as if they taught different ways of salvation. The truth is that both Testaments teach one and the same way of salvation.

6. How can we account for the many obvious differences between the Old Testament and the New Testament? The one way of salvation, or the covenant of grace, was administered in different ways under the two Testaments. We might illustrate this by the history of the United States. Through our national existence we have had one and the same Constitution, but that one Constitution has been administered sometimes by one party and sometimes by another. A Democratic administration differs in some respects from a Republican administration, yet the Constitution that is being administered is one and the same.

34. Q. *How was the Covenant of Grace administered under the Old Testament?*

A. *The Covenant of Grace was administered under the Old Testament, by promises, prophecies, sacrifices, circumcision, the Passover, and other types and ordinances, which did all fore-signify Christ then to come, and were for that time sufficient to build up the elect in faith in the promised Messiah, by whom they then had full remission of sin, and eternal salvation.*

Scripture References

- Rom. 15:8. Christ a minister of the Old Testament dispensation.
- Acts 3:20, 24. Christ the true message of the Old Testament.
- Heb. 10:1. The law had a shadow of the things to come.
- Rom. 4:11. Abraham saved by imputed righteousness received by faith.
- 1 Cor. 5:7. Christ the true meaning of the Passover.
- Heb. 11:13. The Old Testament saints, from "afar off," saw and embraced the promises of the gospel of Christ.
- Gal. 3:7–9, 14. The gospel preached of old unto Abraham; his faith essentially the same as the faith of New Testament believers.

Commentary

1. What is the first recorded promise of a Redeemer in the Old Testament? Genesis 3:15.

2. Give examples of other promises or prophecies of a coming Redeemer. Promises: (a) from the Books of Moses; (b) from the Psalms; (c) from the prophetical books of the Old Testament. Prophecies: (a) Genesis 49:10; Numbers 24:17; Deuteronomy 18:15. (b) Psalms 2, 22, 45, 110. (c) Isaiah 9:6–7; Isaiah 11:1–5; Zechariah 9:9–10; Malachi 3:1. (The student will easily be able to give a great many more such prophecies.)

3. How did the Passover and other sacrifices point forward to Christ? By the slaying of the lamb, and shedding its blood, they taught the people the truth that without shedding of blood there is no remission of sin, and that the coming Redeemer must suffer and die as a substitute for sinners.

4. What is meant by the word *types*? A "type" is a kind of specimen or sample of something, given beforehand, in a smaller way or on a lower plane. Thus we may say that David is a type of Christ the conquering King; Solomon is a type of Christ reigning in eternal peace; Melchizedek is a type of Christ as High Priest; Moses is a type of Christ as Prophet; and so on.

5. What is the difference between a "type" and a "symbol"? A symbol is an arbitrary sign used to denote something else. Thus we say that in the anointing ceremony of the Old Testament, the oil is a symbol of the Holy Spirit; in the Lord's Supper, the bread and wine are symbols of Christ's body and blood; after the flood, the rainbow was a symbol of God's covenant promise; often in the Bible, the number 7 is used as a symbol for perfection, and the number 10 as a symbol for completeness; in Revelation 13 the number 666 is a symbol for the Beast. A type differs from a symbol in that a type is not arbitrarily used to denote something else; there is a real and more or less obvious similarity between the type and the antitype (the fulfillment of the type). Thus there is an obvious resemblance between Melchizedek and Christ, and between Moses and Christ, in the matters typified. But there is no obvious similarity between oil and the Holy Spirit, nor between the rainbow and God's promise not to destroy the earth again by a flood.

6. What was the purpose of the sacrifices, types, ordinances, etc., of the Old Testament? The purpose of all of them was to point forward to Christ, the coming Redeemer. This does not mean that every ordinance, etc., pointed directly to Christ himself. Rather, it means that all the types, ordinances, etc., pointed forward to some aspect of the way of salvation through Christ. For example, the disease of leprosy is plainly treated in the Old Testament as a symbol of sin. Thus the various rules and regulations concerning the disease of leprosy, its uncleanness, etc., were intended to emphasize the vileness and sinfulness of sin, and to show people their need of divine deliverance from it. In this way the rules about leprosy pointed forward to Christ.

7. What was the effectiveness of the Old Testament promises, prophecies, types, sacrifices, and other ordinances? These were sufficient, for that time, to build up the elect in faith in the promised Redeemer. We might compare these Old Testament ordinances to schoolbooks prepared for children. Such books are usually full of pictures, because children readily grasp the meaning of pictures when it is hard for them to understand written descriptions or abstract discussions. But when the child has grown up, the pictures are no longer needed, and ordinary books are then suitable. In the Old Testament period God's people were treated as children, for that was their spiritual condition. God provided "pictures"—that is, the truths of redemption were portrayed before their eyes by a multitude of oft-repeated sacrifices, ordinances, and symbols. These served to prop up their faith, we may say, until the coming of the Redeemer in person. When he came, the "pictures" were no longer needed.

8. What benefits did Old Testament believers receive from Christ?
They had full remission of sin, and eternal life, right then. It is an error to
teach, as some do, that the Old Testament saints did not receive full remission of sin until Christ was crucified. Hebrews 11:39–40 teaches that the
Old Testament saints did not receive the full completion of their redemption, that is, the resurrection of the body, in their own times, for they must
wait for that until the end of the world, when Old and New Testament
believers will receive it together at one and the same time. But in the matter of remission of sins they were not left waiting. They received full remission of sins when they believed. This does not mean that they necessarily
received the same degree of assurance in their own minds as New Testament believers receive. Remission of sins, in God's sight, is one thing; assurance of remission, in the believer's own mind, is another matter.

The New Dispensation of the Covenant of Grace

35. Q. *How is the Covenant of Grace administered under the New*
Testament?

A. *Under the New Testament, when Christ the substance was exhibited,*
the same covenant of grace was and still is to be administered in the
preaching of the word, and the administration of the sacraments of bap-
tism and the Lord's supper; in which grace and salvation are held forth
in more fulness, evidence, and efficacy, to all nations.

Scripture References
- Mark 16:15; Matt. 28:19–20. Under the New Testament, the covenant of
  grace is to be administered throughout all nations, with baptism in the name
  of the Triune God.
- 1 Cor. 11:23–25. The Lord's Supper a New Testament ordinance of the
  covenant of grace.
- 2 Cor. 3:6–9. How the New Testament administration excels the Old Testament administration of the covenant of grace.
- Heb. 8:6, 10–11. The superiority of the New Testament administration over
  the Old Testament administration of the covenant of grace.

Commentary

1. What other name is used for the "New Testament"? The "New Covenant." The same Greek word may be translated either "Testament" or "Covenant," depending on the context in which it is used.

2. What is the relation of the New Testament or New Covenant to the covenant of grace? The "New Testament" or "New Covenant" is the new dispensation of the covenant of grace. It is the second dispensation under which the covenant of grace has been administered. The first dispensation began immediately after our first parents sinned against God, and ended when Christ was crucified. The second dispensation began at Calvary and will continue until the end of the world. It will be terminated by the Judgment Day.

3. What three meanings does the phrase "the New Testament" have? (a) This phrase is used to denote a period of time in sacred history, from the crucifixion of Christ to the Judgment Day or end of the world. This same period of time is sometimes called the age of the gospel. (b) The same phrase is used to denote an arrangement of religious operations and ordinances, under which God administers the covenant of grace. (c) The same phrase, "the New Testament," is used to describe a portion of the Bible, namely, the twenty-seven books written after the coming of Christ, which describe the nature and establishment of "the New Covenant."

4. Why does the catechism speak of Christ as "the substance"? This expression is used in contrast to the promises, prophecies, types, ordinances, etc., by which Christ and his salvation were pictured in the Old Testament period. Christ is the substance, or the reality, while the Old Testament types, sacrifices, etc., were only shadows pointing forward to Christ.

5. What are the main differences between the ordinances of the New Testament and those of the Old Testament? (a) The ordinances of the New Testament are fewer in number than those of the Old Testament. Chiefly they are simply the preaching of the Word, baptism, and the Lord's Supper; whereas in the Old Testament there were a large number of ordinances. (b) The ordinances of the New Testament are simpler in nature than those of the Old Testament. Baptism, the Lord's Supper, and the preaching of the Word are all very simple in their nature, whereas the ordinances of the Old Testament were very complicated, and far more difficult and inconvenient to observe than the ordinances of the New Testament. For

example, think of the elaborate ritual of the Passover; of the complicated
ceremonies of the Day of Atonement; of all the detailed ceremonial laws
concerning uncleanness, concerning foods, concerning sacrifices and offerings. For us who live under the New Testament, God has greatly simplified
the administration of the covenant of grace. (c) The ordinances of the New
Testament are more spiritual than those of the Old Testament. Under the
Old Testament there was much that appealed to the senses of sight and hearing, and even the burning of sweet incense which appealed to the sense of
smell. The tabernacle and later the temple were magnificent and glorious
structures, with a great appeal to the senses. All of this outward display was
well suited to the childish spiritual condition of God's people in those days.
The people of Israel, spiritually considered, were children, and God taught
them, we may say, by "picture books." But under the New Testament the
people of God have come to adult age or maturity, and so God has provided
a more spiritual administration of the covenant of grace. As Jesus said to the
woman at the well of Samaria, "The hour cometh; and now is, when neither in this mountain, nor at Jerusalem, shall ye worship the Father. . . . The
Hour cometh, and now is, when the true worshipers shall worship the Father
in spirit and truth: for the Father seeketh such to worship him" (John 4:21,
23). (d) The ordinances of the New Testament are more effectual than those
of the Old Testament. The ordinances of the Old Testament were effectual,
of course, to worshipers who had faith; but the ordinances of the New Testament are more effectual, for in them "grace and salvation are held forth in
more fulness, evidence, and efficacy." (e) The ordinances of the New Testament are more universal than those of the Old Testament. The ordinances
of the Old Testament were limited to the one nation of Israel; under the
New Testament, the gospel is to be preached, and the covenant of grace
administered, among "all nations," that is, to the human race regardless of
national boundaries.

**6. What is the main point of similarity between the ordinances of
the Old Testament and those of the New Testament?** The main point
of similarity is that both Testaments are dispensations or administrations of
one and the same covenant of grace. Both hold forth one and the same "grace
and salvation." The essential meaning of both is exactly the same; they differ only in external details and appearances; the real meaning and nature of
both is identical. King David worshiped God by types and sacrifices, but he
received exactly the same salvation (although not necessarily the same degree

of assurance and comfort in his own mind) as we receive through the preaching of the Word and the use of baptism and the Lord's Supper.

7. How many dispensations are there in the Bible? The popular *Scofield Reference Bible* teaches that God's dealings with the human race are divided into seven distinct and different dispensations. This is certainly wrong if we define a "dispensation" as the Scofield Bible defines it, as a period of time during which God's dealings with the human race are characterized by some specific principle which was operative only for that time. At most there are three dispensations, one of the covenant of works and two of the covenant of grace. Thus the first dispensation (the covenant of works) was from the creation of man until Adam fell into sin; the second dispensation (the Old Testament) was from the fall of man until the crucifixion of Christ; the third dispensation (the New Testament) is from the crucifixion of Christ until the end of the world.

The Mediator
of the Covenant of Grace

36. Q. *Who is the Mediator of the Covenant of Grace?*

A. *The only Mediator of the Covenant of Grace is the Lord Jesus Christ, who, being the eternal Son of God, of one substance and equal with the Father, in the fulness of time became man, and so was and continues to be God and man, in two entire and distinct natures, and one person, for ever.*

Scripture References
- 1 Tim. 2:5. Christ the only Mediator between God and men.
- John 1:1. The eternal and true deity of Christ.
- John 1:14; 10:30; Phil. 2:6. Christ equal with God the Father.
- Gal. 4:4. In the fullness of time the Son of God became man.
- Luke 1:35; Rom. 9:5; Col. 2:9. Christ's divine and human natures united in one divine person.
- Heb. 7:24–25. Christ will continue as God and man forever.

Commentary
1. How many mediators are there between God and men? There is one only.

2. How does the Roman Catholic Church practically deny this truth of the Bible? By regarding Mary and the saints as mediators, praying to them, and hoping for their intercession with God on behalf of sinners.

3. What is meant by affirming that Christ is the eternal Son of God?
By affirming that Christ is the eternal Son of God, we mean that he has always been the Son of God, the second person of the divine Trinity, from all eternity. He did not become the Son of God when he became man nor at any time in the history of the created universe.

4. What is meant by affirming that Christ is of one substance with the Father? By affirming that Christ is of one substance with the Father, we mean that there is only one God, and Jesus Christ is this one God just as truly as the Father is this one God. As Christians we do not believe in three Gods, but in one God who exists in three persons: the Father, the Son, and the Holy Spirit. Jesus Christ is therefore not like God; he is God, the only God that there is. In him dwells, not a part of the fullness of the Godhead bodily, but all the fullness of the Godhead bodily (Col. 2:9).

5. What is meant by affirming that Christ is equal with the Father? By affirming that Christ is equal with the Father, we mean that so far as his nature is concerned, Christ is not subordinate to the Father in any way. By reason of his self-humiliation, during his life on earth, he was subordinate to the Father in position, for he took upon him the form of a servant. But in nature, even during his life on earth, he was, and is today, fully equal with God the Father.

6. How is the doctrine of the deity of Christ denied today? (a) The doctrine of the deity of Christ is denied by those who say that Christ is divine because all men are divine. If all men are divine, then for Christ to be divine is nothing out of the ordinary. (b) The doctrine of the deity of Christ is denied by those who, while calling Christ "the Son of God," still refuse to say that he is of one substance and equal with the Father. Such people consider it a sin to worship Jesus Christ. (c) The doctrine of the deity of Christ is denied by those who accept his deity only as a "limiting concept"; that is, when they speak of Christ as divine, or call him "the Son of God," they do not mean that this is really the absolute truth about Christ; they only mean that Christ's "deity" is a convenient label for classifying Christ for the time being; in calling Christ "God" they do not mean that he really and truly is God, but only that he is "God" for us human beings—that he may occupy the place of God in our human thinking at the present time. It is obvious that the idea of Christ's deity as a "limiting concept" is something very different from the faith of orthodox historic Christianity in Christ's deity.

7. When did the eternal Son of God become man? At a point in human history called by the Scriptures "the fulness of time" or "the fulness of the time," that is, the time appointed by God in the counsels of eternity, which was also the time when all the age-long preparations for Christ's incarnation had been completed.

8. How long will the Son of God continue to be man? Christ, the eternal Son of God, became man at the time of his incarnation, was man as well as God throughout his life on earth, is man as well as God now in heaven, and will continue to be man as well as God forever, to all eternity. The idea that Christ was human only during his earthly life is contrary to the teachings of the Bible on this subject. Revelation 5:6, for example, teaches that not only Christ's human nature but even the evidences of his crucifixion continue in heaven. Christ's heavenly High Priestly ministry also depends on his possessing a true human nature in heaven: Hebrews 7:25; 5:1–5.

9. What is the importance of the word *entire* in this answer of the catechism? The word *entire* emphasizes the truth that Christ is not only truly but fully God and fully man both on earth and in heaven. There is no element lacking from either his deity or his humanity. With respect to his human nature, Christ possesses both a human body and a human soul, in addition to his divine Spirit. This is often overlooked, and Christ is wrongly represented as composed of a divine Spirit and a human body. Such a Christ would not be fully human. Because of his divine nature, Christ must not be thought of as less than fully God, nor in any sense subordinate to God the Father except positionally, by reason of his voluntarily assumed position of a servant while he was here on earth.

10. What is the importance of the word *distinct* in this answer of the catechism? The word *distinct* teaches the truth that Christ's two natures, divine and human, while they were and are mysteriously united in one divine person, still are not in any way mixed, blended, or confused. Each remains distinct and retains its separate identity. Christ's divine nature always remains his divine nature; his human nature always remains his human nature; these two cannot be mixed in any way. Christ is not a being halfway between God and man; he is a person who is both God and man at the same time; he is as truly God as if he were not man at all; and he is as truly man as if he were not God at all. In the record of our Lord's life on earth, at one point his deity shines forth, as when he said, "Before Abraham was, I am"; at another point his humanity is disclosed, as when he said, "I thirst." But the two are never mixed or confused in any way.

11. What is the importance of the statement that Christ is "one person"? This statement avoids the error of those who have thought of Christ as a divine person united to a human person, so that Christ had a double personality. We should realize that according to the teachings of the Scriptures, Christ, while he possessed two natures, was only one person. It follows from this that Christ, while a human being, is not a human person. From all eternity he has been a divine person. At a certain point in history, this divine person took to himself, not a human person, but a human nature which lacked personality. Christ therefore was and is a divine person with a human nature. We should realize that human nature is that which all members of the human race have in common (namely, a human body and a human soul), whereas personality is that which distinguishes one member of the human race from all others. In the matter of human nature, all human beings are exactly alike. In the matter of personality, of all the people that have ever lived, there have never been two alike; each individual is different from all others. We should always be careful to avoid the common error and popular misconception which regards Christ as a human person. If Christ were a human person, then certainly it would be idolatry to worship him. But because he is a divine person, even though possessed of a human nature, it is not idolatry to worship him as the Christian church always has done.

37. Q. *How did Christ, being the Son of God, become man?*

   A. *Christ the Son of God became man, by taking to himself a true body, and a reasonable soul, being conceived by the power of the Holy Ghost in the womb of the Virgin Mary, of her substance, and born of her, yet without sin.*

Scripture References

- John 1:14. The Son of God became man, with a human body.
- Matt. 26:38. Christ possessed a human soul, capable of sorrow.
- Luke 1:27, 31, 42; Gal. 4:4. Christ born of the Virgin Mary.
- Heb. 4:15; 7:26. Christ was and is without sin.

Commentary

1. What are the parts or elements of which our human nature is composed? Our human nature consists of two parts or elements, namely, body and soul. The body is made of material substance, that is, of chemical elements such as oxygen, hydrogen, calcium, carbon, etc. The soul, which is also called the spirit, is entirely different from the body, because it is not made of material substance. The soul and body are mysteriously joined together in one individual personality. Christ, however, was not a human person; his human body and soul together were united to his divine person.

2. What does the Bible teach about Christ's human body? The Bible teaches that Christ's human body was and is real; it was not a mere illusion or appearance, but a real body made of material substance, just as our body is.

3. What error was held by some people in the ancient church concerning Christ's body? Some people held that Christ's body was not real, but only imaginary, or an illusion. They admitted that he seemed to have a human body, but they denied that it could be real.

4. Besides his human body, what element of human nature did Christ take to himself? As explained in the previous lesson, besides his human body, he took to himself a human soul, without which he could not be a truly human being.

5. What is meant by saying that Christ took to himself a reasonable soul? In this statement the word *reasonable* means rational, or having the power to think and reason.

6. In addition to Christ's human soul, what spiritual nature does he have? In addition to his human soul, he is a divine Spirit, God the Son, the second person of the divine Trinity.

7. In what way was Christ's birth an exception to the ordinary birth of human beings? Christ had no human father. He was miraculously conceived by the power of the Holy Spirit, and born of the Virgin Mary. Thus the Holy Spirit's power wrought a supernatural work, and Jesus, contrary to the laws of nature, was born of a virgin, without a human father.

8. What false belief is very commonly held today concerning Christ's birth? It is very common today to say that Joseph was the real father of Jesus.

9. What should we think of such a belief? To say that Joseph was the real father of Jesus is blasphemous, because (a) it implies that Mary, Jesus' mother, was an immoral person; (b) it implies that the Scripture accounts of the virgin birth of Jesus are false, and therefore that the Word of God is an unreliable mixture of truth and error.

10. How should we answer those who say that the virgin birth of Christ is taught in only two of the four Gospels, and therefore we need not believe it? (a) If it were taught in only one verse of one Gospel, we would be bound to believe it on the authority of God's Word. (b) As a matter of fact Matthew and Luke, the only Gospels that record Jesus' birth, both affirm that he was born of the Virgin Mary. Since the other two Gospels, Mark and John, do not speak of Jesus' birth, infancy, or childhood at all, of course we cannot expect them to present the truth that he was born of the Virgin Mary.

11. Although Jesus partook of human nature the same as our own, composed of body and soul, what great difference existed between his human nature and ours? Our human nature is sinful. We are born in trespasses and sins, with a sinful heart and a tendency to commit sin. But Jesus was born, by the miracle-working power of the Holy Spirit, with a sinless human nature (note Luke 1:35: "that holy thing, which shall be born of thee . . ."). He was born without the stain of original sin, and he never committed actual transgressions.

12. Since Mary, the mother of Jesus, was a sinner like other people, how could Jesus, her Son, be born with a sinless human nature? This was a special miracle, accomplished by the almighty power of God. We cannot doubt that Mary was sinful, although saved by divine grace. By nature she had a sinful heart, as we all do. Only by the supernatural power of God could her child Jesus be born with a perfectly sinless heart and nature.

13. What is the importance of the doctrine of the virgin birth of Jesus today? This doctrine is an outstanding landmark in the controversy between Modernism and orthodox Christianity. Perhaps no other single doctrine of the Christian faith has been subjected to so much ridicule and scoffing. Where the doctrine of the virgin birth of Christ is given up, belief in the full inspiration and authority of the Holy Scriptures goes with it, and it is usually not long until most of the other doctrines of Christianity are given up too.

38. Q. *Why was it requisite that the Mediator should be God?*

A. *It was requisite that the Mediator should be God, that he might sustain and keep the human nature from sinking under the infinite wrath of God, and the power of death; give worth and efficacy to his sufferings, obedience, and intercession; and to satisfy God's justice, procure his favor, purchase a peculiar people, give his Spirit to them, conquer all their enemies, and bring them to everlasting salvation.*

Scripture References

- Acts 2:24–25; Rom. 1:4 compared with Rom. 4:25; Heb. 9:14. The Mediator must be God in order that he might keep the human nature from sinking under the wrath of God and power of death.
- Acts 20:28; Heb. 9:14; 7:25–28. The Mediator must be God in order to give worth and efficacy to his sufferings, obedience, and intercession.
- Rom. 3:24–26. The Mediator must be God in order to satisfy God's justice.
- Eph. 1:6; Matt. 3:17. The Mediator must be God in order to procure God's favor.
- Titus 2:13–14. The Mediator must be God in order to purchase a peculiar people.
- Gal. 4:6. The Mediator must be God in order to give his Spirit to his purchased people.
- Luke 1:68–69, 71, 74. The Mediator must be God in order to conquer all the enemies of his purchased people.
- Heb. 5:8–9; 9:11–15. The Mediator must be God in order to bring his purchased people to everlasting salvation.

Commentary

1. Why could not an ordinary human being, such as Moses, David, or Paul, act as Mediator and save the human race from sin? All ordinary human beings are themselves sinners, and therefore would be disqualified for the work of saving others from sin. Those who are themselves in need of salvation cannot accomplish the salvation of others.

2. Why could not God, by a miracle, provide a sinless human being, such as Adam was before the fall, to act as Mediator and reconcile us to God? Even a sinless human being, if merely human, would not have been able to endure the wrath and curse of God as Christ did. It was necessary that the Mediator be God in order to sustain and support his human nature in its temptations and sufferings.

3. How could Jesus Christ, who was only one person, "give his life a ransom for many" (Mark 10:45) and bear the penalty for the sins of many people? If Jesus Christ had been only a human being—even a sinless human being—at most he could have acted as substitute for only one other person. Then there would have to be as many Saviors as there were sinners. One life could, perhaps, if God were willing to consent to such an arrangement, be substituted for one life. But because Jesus Christ was not only a human being, but also truly divine, it was possible for him to "give his life a ransom for many," becoming the true substitute of all the people of God. His divine nature gave an infinite value to his human nature, so that he could suffer and die for many people at the same time.

4. When Jesus was tempted by the devil, was it possible for him to commit sin? Since Jesus Christ was truly God, we must conclude that it was actually impossible for him to commit sin. Still the Bible teaches that he experienced a real temptation. How the temptation could be real, while at the same time it was impossible for him to commit sin, is a mystery which we cannot hope to understand.

5. How does the fact that Jesus Christ, the Mediator, is truly God guarantee the success of a plan of salvation? If Jesus Christ were only a human being—even a perfect human being—it would have been possible for him to fail in this work, by yielding to temptation and falling into sin. In that case the second Adam would have been a failure just as the first Adam was, by disobeying the will of God. But because Jesus Christ was not only human, but also truly divine, he was and is almighty. Therefore his success is a certainty, since he can neither fail in his work nor fall into sin.

39. Q. *Why was it requisite that the Mediator should be man?*

A. *It was requisite that the Mediator should be man, that he might advance our nature, perform obedience to the law, suffer and make intercession for us in our nature, have a fellow-feeling of our infirmities; that we might receive the adoption of sons, and have comfort and access with boldness unto the throne of grace.*

Scripture References

- Heb. 2:16. Christ took not the nature of angels but human nature.
- Gal. 4:4. The Mediator must be man in order that he might be under the law.
- Heb. 2:14; 7:24–25. The Mediator must be man in order that he might suffer and make intercession for us in our nature.
- Heb. 4:15. The Mediator must be man in order that he might experience a fellow-feeling of our infirmities.
- Gal. 4:5. The Mediator must be man in order that we might receive the adoption of sons.
- Heb. 4:16. The Mediator must be man in order that we might have access to the throne of grace.

Commentary

1. Why could the angel Gabriel or some other angel not have become a Mediator to save the human race from sin? The angels are not members of the human race; they do not possess human nature; therefore none of them could be qualified to become the second Adam to undo the wrong done by the first Adam.

2. Why was it necessary that the Mediator "partake of flesh and blood," that is, possess a human nature? Because to redeem the human race, the Mediator must act as the representative of human beings, and in order to be a representative of human beings, he must first of all be a member of the human race. Even in ordinary human organizations, a person cannot be an officer until he is first a member. Christ could not be a Redeemer of the human race unless he was first of all a member of the human race. Since sin and ruin came by man, redemption must come by man too (1 Cor. 15:21: "For since by man came death, by man came also the resurrection of the dead").

3. Why must the Mediator perform obedience to the law? Adam and all his posterity had broken the law of God and lived in violation of that law. It was necessary that the second Adam keep the law of God perfectly. God himself is not under the law; he is the lawgiver. Jesus Christ had to be truly human so that he could be truly under the law of God, and thus succeed where Adam failed, in meeting the condition of the covenant of works, namely, a perfect obedience to the law of God.

4. Why was it necessary for the Mediator to be truly human in order to be our High Priest? A true priest, according to God's appointment, must be chosen from among men and must be able to sympathize with the sufferings and troubles of human beings because he has experienced suffering and trouble himself. Read Hebrews 5:1–2, and note that these verses do not speak especially concerning Christ; they only set forth the nature of the priestly office in general—the qualifications of any priest. Since Jesus Christ was to be our High Priest, he must meet these qualifications too.

5. But cannot God himself sympathize with our human sufferings? God knows all about our human sufferings, and has pity or compassion on them. We may say that God has sympathy for but not with our human sufferings. The word *sympathize* literally means "to suffer with" someone. Since God is an infinite Being, and suffering implies limitation, God himself, in his own nature, cannot suffer, and therefore he cannot really sympathize with our sufferings. Many people who speak carelessly about God "suffering" should realize that this is contrary to the truth that God is infinite and unchangeable. Suffering by its very nature implies imitation and change; therefore an infinite and unchangeable being cannot suffer. God knows all about our sufferings, for he knows all things, but he cannot experience them in his own nature. The only way that God could experience our human sufferings was by becoming human, as he did. The Son of God, a divine person, took to himself a human nature; and thus God experienced human sufferings, not in his own nature, but in his adopted human nature.

40. Q. *Why was it requisite that the Mediator should be God and man in one person?*

A. *It was requisite that the Mediator, who was to reconcile God and man, should himself be both God and man, and this in one person, that the proper works of each nature might be accepted of God for us, and relied on by us as the works of the whole person.*

Scripture References

- Matt. 1:21, 23. The Mediator both God and man in one person.

- Matt. 3:17; Heb. 9:14. The works of each of the Mediator's two natures accepted by God for us as the works of the whole person.
- 1 Peter 2:6. The Mediator and his work, as a whole, to be relied on by us for our salvation.

Commentary

1. Why could not God provide two Mediators, one divine and the other human, to accomplish the salvation of his people from sin? Because the relation between the works of each of the two natures required that these two natures be united in one person. A divine Mediator could not experience suffering except through a human nature; a human Mediator could not endure the required suffering, except as sustained by a divine nature. Therefore it was necessary, not only that the Mediator be God and that he be man, but that both natures be united in one person that his work might be a unity.

2. What work of Christ's divine nature does Scripture speak of as part of the work accomplishing our salvation? Hebrews 9:14. It was through the eternal Spirit that Christ offered himself a sacrifice to God for our sins. This may be translated "through his eternal Spirit" (see the ARV margin). In any case, the meaning is probably not "through the Holy Spirit," but rather "through his own divine nature"; that is, it was through his divine nature that Christ offered himself as a sacrifice to God for the sins of his people; his divine nature gave value and efficacy to the sacrifice and sufferings of his human nature.

3. What work of Christ's human nature does Scripture speak of as a part of the work of accomplishing our salvation? Scripture speaks of Christ's obedience to the law, and of all his sufferings, and especially his death, all of which were works of his human nature, as essential parts of the work of accomplishing our salvation.

4. How can we explain Scripture texts in which what is proper to one of Christ's natures is referred to the other nature? The unity of Christ's person affords the true explanation of such texts. For example, Acts 20:28: "the church of God, which he hath purchased with his own blood." Here we find blood, which was a part of Christ's human nature, associated with the name *God,* which belongs to his divine nature. And John 6:62: "What and if ye shall see the Son of man ascend up where he was before?"

Here a title associated with Christ's human nature, the title "Son of man," is used in connection with a fact concerning Christ's divine nature, namely, his eternal preexistence in heaven, before his incarnation in this world. In these and many similar Scripture passages the explanation is that the unity of Christ's person permits reference to either of his natures in terms which strictly speaking apply to the other nature.

41. Q. *Why was our Mediator called Jesus?*

A. *Our Mediator was called Jesus, because he saveth his people from their sins.*

Scripture Reference

- Matt. 1:21. The divine command to name the child of Mary "Jesus," and the reason for this name.

Commentary

1. What is the literal meaning of the name *Jesus*? The name *Jesus* is a Greek form corresponding to the Hebrew name *Joshua* or *Jehoshua,* meaning "Jehovah is salvation."

2. Who decided that our Savior should be called "Jesus"? This decision was made by God himself, and was announced to Joseph by an angel of the Lord who appeared to him in a dream.

3. What great truths of our faith are involved in the statement "he shall save his people from their sins"? The following great truths of our faith are involved in this majestic statement revealed to Joseph by an angel of the Lord: (a) Salvation from sin is accomplished by the divinely provided Redeemer, and is not something which we can do ourselves. (b) Our Redeemer actually saves his people from their sins; he does not merely give them "a chance" or "offer" of salvation; he actually saves them, which includes his doing all that is necessary to guarantee that they shall be finally saved. (c) Our Redeemer saves a particular body of human beings, the elect of God, spoken of in this text as "his people." He was not sent into the world to save everybody, nor to try to save everybody but to save "his people."

4. Is "Jesus" a personal name or a title? "Jesus" is a personal name of our Savior.

42. Q. *Why was our Mediator called Christ?*

A. *Our Mediator was called Christ, because he was anointed with the Holy Ghost above measure, and so set apart, and fully furnished with all authority and ability, to execute the offices of prophet, priest, and king of his church, in the estate both of his humiliation and exaltation.*

Scripture References
- John 3:34. The Holy Spirit given to our Savior above measure.
- Ps. 45:7. Our Savior given the Holy Spirit above (more than) his fellows.
- John 6:27. Our Savior "sealed" by God the Father, that is, set apart for his redemptive work.
- Matt. 28:18–20. Our Savior furnished by God the Father with all authority and ability to carry out his appointed work to the end.
- Acts 3:21–22. Our Savior raised up by God the Father to be a prophet.
- Heb. 5:5–7; 4:14–15. Our Savior called by the Father to be a High Priest; and his priestly work for his people.
- Ps. 2:6; Matt. 21:5; Isa. 9:6–7. Our Savior made a king by God the Father, and the glories of his kingly office.
- Phil. 2:8–11. Christ executes his offices both in his estate of humiliation and in his estate of exaltation.

Commentary
1. Is "Christ" a name or a title? "Christ" is not a name, but a title which accompanies the personal name "Jesus." This is brought out by the use of the definite article with "Christ" which occurs in some places, such as Matthew 16:16, "Thou art the Christ, the Son of the living God."

2. What is the literal meaning of the word *Christ*? "Christ" is the English form of the Greek word *Christos*, which means "Anointed." Thus whether we say that Jesus is the Christ, the Messiah, or the Anointed One is a matter of language and not of meaning. These words all mean the same thing. In passages of the Old Testament where the word *anointed* occurs with reference to the coming Redeemer, such as Psalm 2:2, "the rulers take counsel together, against the Lord and against his anointed. . . ," the Hebrew word *Messiah* could equally correctly be translated by the word *Christ,* for the meaning is the same.

3. What is the basic idea involved in the title *Christ?* The basic idea involved in the title *Christ* is the idea of anointing. In the Old Testament period kings and priests were anointed with oil to set them apart to their special offices. This oil of anointing was a symbol of the Holy Spirit who would enter their hearts and equip them with ability and wisdom for their duties as kings or priests. So we see that the idea of anointing in the Old Testament was setting a person apart to a special office, with a symbol of the Holy Spirit's work in that person's life. All the Old Testament kings and priests, however, were only types and shadows pointing forward to Jesus, the true and final king and priest. Jesus is the one who above all others has been anointed by the Holy Spirit to fit him to be our prophet, priest, and king. Instead of being anointed with oil (the symbol), as in the Old Testament period, Jesus received the Holy Spirit in the form of a dove which abode upon him (Matt. 3:16).

4. Why did Jesus receive the Holy Spirit in the form of a dove? While no certain answer can be given to this question, it has been suggested that the form of a dove represented the totality of the Holy Spirit, for Jesus received the Spirit without measure. At Pentecost believers received the Spirit in the form of tongues of fire, something divisible, of which each person present received a share; but in the case of Jesus, the form of a dove may suggest the idea of totality and indivisibility (see Gen. 15:10: "the birds divided he not").

5. When does Christ execute the offices of prophet, priest, and king? Christ, our Savior, executes the offices of prophet, priest, and king both in his estate of humiliation (that is, during his life on earth) and in his estate of exaltation (that is, since his resurrection, and especially in his life of glory in heaven). This means that Christ was a prophet, a priest, and a king when he was on earth, and that he is a prophet, a priest, and a king in heaven today!

43. Q. How doth Christ execute the office of a prophet?

A. Christ executeth the office of a prophet, in his revealing to the church, in all ages, by his Spirit and Word, in divers ways of administration, the whole will of God, in all things concerning their edification and salvation.

Scripture References

- John 1:18. Christ as prophet is the great revealer of the Father.
- 1 Peter 1:10–12. The Spirit of Christ revealed divine truth to the Old Testament prophets.
- Heb. 1:1–2. Christ as prophet brings the final revelation of God to men.
- John 15:15. Christ revealed truth from the Father to the apostles.
- Acts 20:32. The edifying nature of Christ's prophetic work.
- Eph. 4:11–13. Christ's prophetic work edifies or builds up his body, the church.
- John 20:31. Christ's words recorded in Scripture in order that by his work as prophet men might believe and have life.

Commentary

1. What is the true meaning of the word *prophet*? A prophet is God's representative in speaking to men, God's spokesman, God's mouthpiece.

2. Why do we usually think of a prophet as one who foretells the future? Because many of the prophets, especially in the Old Testament, received revelations from God which contained predictions of future events. There are so many predictions of future events in the prophetic books of the Old Testament that we have come to think of a "prophet" as a "predictor of the future." However, many of the messages of the prophets concerned their own times, and a real meaning of the word *prophet* is not a foreteller of the future, but a man who delivers a message from God to the people.

3. In what period of history did Christ execute the office of a prophet? "In all ages."

4. How did Christ execute the office of a prophet during the Old Testament period? During the Old Testament period Christ executed the office of a prophet by his Spirit, revealing his truth through the various prophets, Psalmists, and other writers of the Old Testament Scriptures.

5. How did Christ execute the office of a prophet during his earthly ministry? During his earthly ministry Christ executed the office of a prophet: (a) by preaching to the people of the Jews; (b) by teaching and preaching to his own followers, or disciples, who believed on him; (c) by training and instructing the twelve apostles, who would be his official witnesses after his ascension to heaven.

6. How does Christ execute the office of a prophet today? Christ executes the office of a prophet today: (a) through his written Word, the Holy Bible; (b) by his Holy Spirit, whom he has sent, who illuminates our hearts and minds so that we can receive and understand the truth revealed in the Scriptures.

7. In executing the office of a prophet, what message has Christ revealed to his church? He has revealed a complete message, containing the whole will of God in all things concerning our salvation and our edification.

44. Q. *How doth Christ execute the office of a priest?*

A. *Christ executeth the office of a priest, in his once offering himself a sacrifice without spot to God, to be a reconciliation for the sins of his people; and in making continual intercession for them.*

Scripture References

- Heb. 9:14. Christ executes the office of a priest in offering himself as a sacrifice to God.
- Heb. 9:28. Christ offered himself once for the sins of many.
- Heb. 2:17. Christ offered himself in order to reconcile his people to God.
- Heb. 7:25. Christ as priest makes continual intercession for his people.

Commentary

1. What is the difference between a prophet and a priest? A prophet is God's representative in speaking to men; a priest is men's representative in approaching God.

2. What are the qualifications for the office of priesthood? These are found in Hebrews 5:1–2 and are as follows: (a) The priest must be a member of the human race, that is, chosen from among men. An angel could not act as priest to represent men in approaching God. (b) The priest must be able to sympathize with the ignorant and erring, because he himself "compassed with infirmity." (c) The priest must not take the office on himself, but must be called to it by God, as Aaron was (Heb. 5:4).

3. What are the functions of the office of priesthood? These are also found in Hebrews 5:1–4 and are as follows: (a) A priest must represent men in things pertaining to God. (b) A priest must offer gifts and sacrifices for sins. (c) A priest must make intercession for the people (Heb. 7:25).

4. What book of the Bible most fully discusses Christ's priestly office? While the functions of Christ's priestly office are discussed in many books of the Bible with great fullness, his priestly office as such is discussed most fully in the epistle to the Hebrews. In the Old Testament, Psalm 110:4 is perhaps the most direct statement of Christ's priestly office.

5. How did Christ possess the qualifications for the priestly office? (a) By his incarnation, or taking to himself a human nature, he became a human being; thus becoming a member of the human race, he was qualified to be chosen from among men for the priestly office. (b) Because he was "compassed with infirmity," and underwent the miseries and sufferings of human life as "a man of sorrows . . . acquainted with grief," he was able to sympathize with the ignorant and erring. (c) He did not take the priestly office upon himself, but was called by God, as Aaron had been (Heb. 5:4–5).

6. How does Christ exercise the functions of the priestly office? (a) As the second Adam—the Mediator of the covenant of grace—Christ is the representative of all the elect people of God; thus he acts as the representative of men in things pertaining to God. (b) He laid down his own life on Calvary as a sacrifice for the sins of his people; thus he fulfilled the sacrificial function of the priestly office. (c) He made intercession for his people while still on earth (John 17), and he continues to make intercession for his people as he ministers at the right hand of God the Father in heaven.

7. What is the relative importance of Christ's priestly office? Christ's priestly office is the central and supremely important one of his three offices of prophet, priest, and king. While we must regard the whole of Christ's saving work as a unity, and should realize that no part of it is non-essential, still his work as priest is the very heart and center of his work as our Redeemer!

8. What error concerning Christ's offices is common in modern "Liberalism"? Modern "Liberalism" seeks to retain the doctrine of Christ's kingly office while either abandoning or denaturing the doctrine of his priestly office. Thus widely known and popular "liberal" teachers never weary of speaking about "the kingdom of God," although they either deny or explain away the substitutionary atonement of Christ. Of course these "liberal" teachers put their own ideas into such a term as "the kingdom of God"; they do not mean by such an expression what historic orthodox Christianity has always meant by it. But they try to retain some kind of belief in Christ's kingly office while giving up or bypassing his priestly office. We should realize that Christ's work is a unity and none of his three offices can be retained in our theology without the other two. The Scriptures know only a Christ who is a prophet and a priest and a king. This is the only real Christ; all partial Christs are only the products of human ideas.

45. Q. *How doth Christ execute the office of a king?*

A. *Christ executeth the office of a king, in calling out of the world a people to himself, and giving them officers, laws, and censures, by which he visibly governs them; in bestowing saving grace upon his elect, rewarding their obedience, and correcting them for their sins, preserving and supporting them under all their temptations and sufferings, restraining and overcoming all their enemies, and powerfully ordering all things for his own glory, and their good; and also in taking vengeance on the rest, who know not God, and obey not the gospel.*

Scripture References

- Acts 15:14–16; Isa. 55:4–5; Gen. 49:10; Ps. 110:3. Christ executes the office of a king in calling out of the world a people to himself.
- Eph. 4:11; 1 Cor. 12:28. Christ executes the office of a king in giving his people officers.
- Isa. 33:22. Christ executes the office of a king in giving his people laws.

- Matt. 18:17–18; 1 Cor. 5:4–5. Christ executes the office of a king in giving his people the censures of church discipline.
- Acts 3:31. Christ executes the office of a king in bestowing saving grace on his elect.
- Rev. 22:12; 2:10. Christ executes the office of a king in rewarding his elect for their obedience.
- Rev. 3:19. Christ executes the office of a king in correcting his elect for their sins.
- Isa. 63:9. Christ executes the office of a king in supporting his people in their temptations and sufferings.
- 1 Cor. 15:25; Ps. 110:1–2. Christ executes the office of a king in restraining and overcoming the enemies of his people.
- Rom. 14:10–11. Christ executes the office of a king by powerfully ordering all things for his own glory.
- Rom. 8:28. Christ executes the office of a king by powerfully ordering all things for the good of his elect.
- 2 Thess. 1:8–9; Ps. 2:8–9. Christ executes the office of a king in taking vengeance on his enemies, who know not God and obey not the gospel.

Commentary

1. Into what three spheres does the catechism divide the exercise of Christ's kingly office? The three spheres are: (a) the sphere of the visible church; (b) the sphere of the invisible church; (c) the sphere of the world.

2. Which is the most important of these three spheres in which Christ's kingly office is exercised? The sphere of the invisible church, or the body of the elect, is the most important, for it is for the benefit of the invisible church that Christ exercises his kingly office (a) in the visible church, and (b) in the world or universe.

3. What elements are included in Christ's kingly rule in the visible church? These elements are: (a) calling out of the world a people who shall be members of the visible church; (b) giving them officers, as appointed in the Scriptures, and as realized in actual life; (c) giving them laws and censures, by which he visibly governs them, that is, by means of the structure of church government and discipline.

4. What elements are included in Christ's kingly rule in the invisible church? These elements are: (a) Bestowing saving grace upon his elect, by the work of the Holy Spirit in their hearts and lives, resulting in their being united to Christ in their effectual calling. (b) Rewarding the obedience of his people, both now by his providence, and at the Judgment Day by his supernatural power; and correcting his people for their sins, in his providential discipline during the present life. (c) Preserving and supporting his elect under all their temptations and sufferings, so that they are never overwhelmed with troubles, but are always kept from despair.

5. What elements are included in Christ's kingly rule in the world or the universe? These elements are: (a) Restraining and overcoming all the enemies of his elect. (b) Powerfully ordering all things to his own glory, and his people's good, so that even the evil deeds of the wicked men are made to work out for the true benefit of the elect. (c) Taking vengeance on the wicked, who know not God, nor obey the gospel. This vengeance is partly during the present life, by Christ's providential dispensations; and chiefly at the Judgment Day at the end of the age.

6. In which sphere is Christ's kingly reign over the nations included? Christ's kingly reign over the nations is included in the third sphere, namely, the exercise of his kingly office in the world or universe. ·

7. Is Christ a king today? Certainly Christ is a king today. The Bible teaches that he was a king when on earth, is a king today, and will be a king for ever and ever.

8. Is Christ reigning over the nations of the world today? Yes. While it is true that the nations of the world are living in neglect of, or in rebellion against, Christ's kingly reign, still he is reigning over them and accomplishing his purposes in spite of their neglect and rebellion.

9

The Work of the Mediator

46. Q. *What was the estate of Christ's humiliation?*

A. *The estate of Christ's humiliation was that low condition, wherein he for our sakes, emptying himself of his glory, took upon him the form of a servant, in his conception and birth, life, death, and after his death, until his resurrection.*

Scripture References
- Phil. 2:6–8. Christ's voluntary self-humiliation.
- Luke 1:31. Christ's humiliation in his birth as a human being.
- 2 Cor. 8:9. Christ's self-humiliation in giving up the enjoyment of riches in heaven for a life of poverty on earth.
- Acts 2:24. Christ's resurrection the termination of his humiliation.

Commentary
1. In carrying out the plan of salvation, what kind of condition did Christ take upon himself? A low condition.

2. Why did Christ take on himself a low condition? For our sakes.

3. What was Christ's condition before he came to this world? A state of infinite divine glory, described in the Bible as "being rich."

4. How may the expression "made himself of no reputation" (Phil. 2:7) also be translated? This expression literally means that he "emptied himself."

5. Of what did Christ "empty himself" when he became man? He emptied himself of the enjoyment of his heavenly glory.

6. What serious error has been held concerning Christ's "emptying himself"? Some have held that this expression in the Greek text of Philippians 2:7 means that Christ emptied himself of his deity. According to this interpretation, Christ was divine when he was in heaven, but cast his deity aside, and was only a man when he was on earth. However, since many texts in the New Testament teach that Christ was truly and fully God while he was on earth, the above interpretation cannot be correct. The true meaning is that Christ emptied himself of the enjoyment of his divine glory, taking "the form of a servant" instead. His nature was still the same, but his position was different.

7. What was Christ's position during his earthly life? The "form," position, or status of a servant.

8. What chapter of the Old Testament prophesied that the Redeemer would be "the Servant of the Lord"? Isaiah 53. The whole chapter tells of Christ's estate of humiliation. Verse 11 calls him "my righteous servant."

47. Q. *How did Christ humble himself in his conception and birth?*

A. *Christ humbled himself in his conception and birth, in that, being from all eternity the Son of God, in the bosom of the Father, he was pleased in the fulness of time to become the son of man, made of a woman of low estate, and to be born of her; with divers circumstances of more than ordinary abasement.*

Scripture References
- John 1:14, 18. Christ, who became man, was from all eternity the Son of God.
- Gal. 4:4. Christ, in the fullness of time, became man and was born as an infant.
- Luke 2:7. Our Savior was born of a woman of low estate, and with circumstances of more than ordinary abasement.

Commentary
1. How long had Christ been the Son of God? From all eternity.

2. What is the meaning of the statement that Christ was "in the bosom of the Father"? This means that Christ, the eternal Son, is one God with the Father. The Father and the Son are the same in substance, although they are distinct persons of the Trinity.

3. Why does the catechism say that Christ "was pleased" to become the son of man? This expression conveys the truth that Christ became man voluntarily, of his own free will, not because he was compelled to do so.

4. When did Christ become man? "When the fulness of the time was come" (Gal. 4:4).

5. What is the meaning of the expression, "in the fulness of time"? It means the time appointed by God from all eternity for Christ to be born as a human being; also the time when all the age-long preparations had been completed, and the prophecies were about to be fulfilled.

6. Why is Mary, the mother of Jesus, referred to as "a woman of low estate"? This is based on Mary's own words about herself as found in Luke 1:48. It refers not to her character, but to her economic and social position among the Jews of that day.

7. What "circumstances of more than ordinary abasement" attended the birth and infancy of Jesus Christ? He was born in a stable because there was no room in the inn. It was necessary for him to be taken, suddenly, to a foreign country to escape Herod's plot to murder him.

48. Q. *How did Christ humble himself in his life?*

A. *Christ humbled himself in his life, by subjecting himself to the law, which he perfectly fulfilled; and by conflicting with the indignities of the world, temptations of Satan, and infirmities in his flesh, whether common to the nature of man, or particularly accompanying that his low condition.*

Scripture References
- Gal. 4:4. Christ was born under the law.
- Matt. 5:17; Rom. 5:18. Christ perfectly fulfilled the law of God.

- Ps. 22:6; Heb. 12:2–3. Christ conflicted with the indignities of the world.
- Matt. 4:1–12; Luke 4:13. Christ conflicted with the temptations of Satan.
- Heb. 2:17–18; 4:15; Isa. 52:13–14. Christ conflicted with infirmities in his flesh, either common to humanity or especially involved in his low condition.

Commentary

1. Why was it necessary that our Savior be subject to the law of God? It was necessary that our Savior be subject to the law of God in order that he might fulfill the law as our representative, rendering a perfect obedience to the will of God, which Adam had failed to do in the covenant of works. Christ, the second Adam, had to accomplish this successfully in order that his righteousness could be reckoned to our account.

2. How did our Savior become subject to the law of God? Our Savior became subject to the law of God by his own voluntary decision to become man, according to the stipulated terms of the covenant of grace entered into between him and the Father in eternity before the creation of the world.

3. To what law did our Savior become subject? He became subject to the whole law of God, both the moral law and the ceremonial law.

4. How did Christ fulfill the law of God? Christ fulfilled the law of God perfectly. His obedience to the law was both positive and negative. He never broke any of the law's commands, and he fully performed all that the law required.

5. Why was becoming subject to the law a matter of Christ humbling himself? Because as God he was by nature above the law. By nature he was not under the law, but the Author of the law. In becoming man, he laid aside his heavenly glory, and took the form of a servant, under the law.

6. Why were the indignities of the world a humiliation to our Savior? Because the indignities of the world were contrary to his holy nature, and because they were contrary to the peace, order, and reverence of heaven, whence he had come.

7. Why were the temptations of Satan a humiliation to our Savior? Because it was an insult to his holy character to be tempted by Satan, who is not only deceitful and wicked, but in rebellion against God's authority.

The Lord of glory was approached and tempted by the vilest and most law-less rebel in the universe.

8. What were some of the "infirmities in his flesh" which our Savior suffered during his life on earth? Weariness, hunger, thirst, poverty, "no place to lay his head," being misunderstood and reproached by near relatives, etc.

9. What should be our attitude in view of the way in which our Savior humbled himself during his life on earth? (a) We should be filled with the deepest gratitude to him who endured such afflictions and priva-tions for our sakes. (b) We should resist the temptation to yield to discour-agement and despair when we are faced with troubles and hardships in our earthly pilgrimage, remembering that our Savior, the Lord of glory, endured much more grievous troubles and hardships because of his great love for us.

49. Q. *How did Christ humble himself in his death?*

A. *Christ humbled himself in his death, in that having been betrayed by Judas, forsaken by his disciples, scorned and rejected by the world, con-demned by Pilate, and tormented by his persecutors; having also con-flicted with the terrors of death, and the powers of darkness, felt and borne the weight of God's wrath, he laid down his life an offering for sin, enduring the painful, shameful, and cursed death of the cross.*

Scripture References

- Matt. 27:4. Christ betrayed by Judas.
- Matt. 26:56. Christ forsaken by his disciples.
- Isa. 53:2–3. Christ scorned and rejected by the world (and especially the false church).
- Matt. 27:26–50; John 19:34. Christ condemned by Pilate, and tormented by his persecutors.
- Luke 22:44; Matt. 27:46. Christ's conflict with the terrors of death and the powers of darkness, and his experience of the weight of God's wrath.
- Isa. 53:10. Christ's life laid down by himself as an offering for sin.
- Phil. 2:8; Heb. 12:2; 3:13. The painful, shameful, and cursed death on the cross.

Commentary

1. Why was being betrayed by Judas an especially grievous humiliation for our Savior? Because Judas was not a stranger, or a professed enemy, but a person who had been admitted to special privileges and friendship with Jesus, in the circle of the twelve disciples (Pss. 41:9; 55:12–14).

2. Why was being forsaken by his disciples so hard for Jesus to bear? Because the conduct of the disciples showed that, for the time being at least, they were much more concerned about their personal safety than about loyalty to their Lord. Personal fear was a stronger motive in their minds than love for Christ.

3. Why was being scorned and rejected by the world a humiliation to Christ? Because he was the Creator and Lord of all the world, and the world ought to have received him with reverence and joy. "He came unto his own, and his own received him not" (John 1:11).

4. Why was being condemned by Pilate a special humiliation to Christ? Because his condemnation was contrary to justice. Pilate, the Roman governor, sat as a judge, the official representative of a divine institution in human society, namely, the state. Pilate, who had been appointed to administer justice, condemned Christ unjustly, that is, contrary to the evidence in the case.

5. How was Christ tormented by his persecutors? Read Matthew 27:26–50.

6. When did Jesus engage in conflict with the terrors of death and the powers of darkness? In the Garden of Gethsemane, the night before he was crucified.

7. When did Jesus feel the weight of God's wrath? Jesus felt and bore the weight of God's wrath against human sin the whole of his life on earth, but especially at the end of his earthly life, in the Garden of Gethsemane and most of all during the three hours of darkness while he hung on the cross, from the sixth hour to the ninth hour, ending with his cry, "My God, my God, why hast thou forsaken me?"

8. What was the character of our Savior's death? Our Savior offered his own life as a sacrifice to God to atone for the sins of men. Therefore his death was unique and unlike that of other men. Jesus died, not of sickness, accident, or old age; not simply as a victim of injustice and oppression; not merely as a martyr for a great cause; but as an offering for sin, a substitute for sinners.

9. Why was death by crucifixion a particularly bitter death? Death by crucifixion was a particularly bitter death because it was painful, shameful, and accursed.

10. Why was death by crucifixion a painful death? Because no vital organ of the body was directly injured; therefore the victims of crucifixion often lingered and suffered for many hours and even days before death came; also the loss of blood and exposure to the hot sun would cause extreme exhaustion and thirst.

11. Why was death by crucifixion a shameful and cursed death? In the Roman Empire, death by crucifixion was reserved for slaves and the lowest criminals. Even more important is the fact that God's Word had pronounced this mode of death to be accursed: "He that is hanged is accursed of God" (Deut. 21:23; Gal. 3:13).

12. How did our Savior finally die? Our Savior finally voluntarily laid down his life, at the appointed moment, as we learn from the following facts in the record: (a) "Jesus . . . yielded up the ghost," Matthew 27:50. (b) In John 19:28 we are told that "Jesus knowing that all things were now accomplished saith, I thirst"; that is, he required a drink of water to clear his brain for his final act on the cross, which followed immediately: "When Jesus therefore had received the vinegar, he said, It is finished, and he bowed his head, and gave up the ghost." (c) In John 10:17–18 Jesus said, "I lay down my life, that I might take it again. No man taketh it from me, but I lay it down of myself." (d) Jesus died after being on the cross about six hours. The two thieves were still alive at the end of that time. In Mark 15:44 we read that "Pilate marveled if he were already dead." Thus the evidence indicates that Jesus finally yielded up his life by an act of his own will, and not because the limit of his physical endurance had been reached.

13. What is the importance of the death of Jesus Christ? The death of Jesus Christ is the center of the Bible, the focal point of the world's history, the central fact in the gospel message, and the foundation of our hope for eternal life.

50. Q. *Wherein consisted Christ's humiliation after his death?*

A. *Christ's humiliation after his death consisted in his being buried, and continuing in the state of the dead, and under the power of death till the third day; which hath been otherwise expressed in these words,* He descended into hell.

Scripture References
- 1 Cor. 15:3–4. Christ's burial a necessary fact of the gospel.
- Ps. 16:10 compared with Acts 2:24–31. Christ's continuing in the state of the dead, and under the power of death, until the third day.
- Rom. 6:9; Matt. 12:40. The power of death over Christ's body only temporary, limited to three days.

Commentary

1. Where was Christ's soul (or human spirit) during the time his body was in the tomb? In heaven or paradise, as shown by Luke 23:43.

2. Why was it a humiliation to Christ for his body to be buried and to continue under the power of death for a time? Because "the wages of sin is death" (Rom. 6:23). Christ was "the holy one of God"; he had no personal sin. Death would have had no power over him at all except for the fact that our sins were laid upon him, and he died, and was buried, as our sin-bearing substitute. Because his being buried was a part of the wages of sin, it was an element in our Savior's humiliation.

3. Why could Christ's body be kept under the power of death for a short time only? Because the penalty for sin had been fully paid, and the guilt of his people's sin wholly canceled. If Christ's body had remained permanently under the power of death, it would have indicated that the penalty for sin had not been fully paid.

4. What is meant by the expression in the Apostles' Creed which says, "He descended into hell"? This expression has been understood in various ways. Some hold that Christ literally descended into hell, not the hell of the devil and the wicked angels, but a place where the Old Testament saints were thought to be waiting. There, they say, he preached to those spirits and opened the way for them to enter heaven. This interpretation, which is held by the Roman Catholic Church and by some Protestants, is unsound and is based on a misunderstanding (wrong interpretation) of 1 Peter 3:18–20. Some Protestants hold that the words "He descended into hell" refer to Christ's suffering on the cross, that is, that he descended into hell, not as a place, but as an experience of suffering. While this idea is doctrinally sound, it is historically unwarranted because the word translated "hell" in the Apostles' Creed is not Gehenna (the place of punishment) but Hades (the realm of death). Our catechism teaches that the words "He descended into hell" refer to Christ's being buried, and continuing under the power of death for a time, the word *hell* being understood as "the realm of the power of death."

51. Q. *What was the estate of Christ's exaltation?*

A. *The estate of Christ's exaltation comprehendeth his resurrection, ascension, sitting at the right hand of the Father, and his coming again to judge the world.*

Scripture References
- 1 Cor. 15:4. Christ's resurrection.
- Acts 1:9–11. Christ's ascension to heaven.
- Eph. 1:20. Christ's sitting at the right hand of the Father.
- Acts 1:11; 7:31. Christ's coming again to judge the world.

Commentary
1. What four elements are included in Christ's estate of exaltation? (a) His resurrection. (b) His ascension into heaven. (c) His sitting at the right hand of God the Father. (d) His coming again to judge the world.

2. Which of these four elements are past, which present, and which still future? Two are past: his resurrection and his ascension. One is present: his sitting at the right hand of God the Father. One is still future: his coming again to judge the world.

52. Q. *How was Christ exalted in his resurrection?*

A. *Christ was exalted in his resurrection, in that, not having seen corruption in death, (of which it was not possible for him to be held,) and having the very same body in which he suffered, with the essential properties thereof (but without mortality, and other common infirmities belonging to this life), really united to his soul, he rose again from the dead the third day by his own power; whereby he declared himself to be the Son of God, to have satisfied divine justice, to have vanquished death, and him that had the power of it, and to be Lord of quick and dead: all which he did as a public person, the head of his church, for their justification, quickening in grace, support against enemies, and to assure them of their resurrection from the dead at the Last Day.*

Scripture References

- Acts 2:24, 27. Christ's body was not subject to decay while in the grave.
- Luke 24:39. Christ rose again in the identical (selfsame) body in which he suffered.
- Rom. 6:9; Rev. 1:18. Christ's resurrection body immortal.
- John 10:18. Christ rose again by his own power.
- Rom. 1:4. Christ declared to be the Son of God by his resurrection.
- Rom. 8:34. Christ, by his resurrection, declared to have satisfied God's justice.
- Heb. 2:14. Christ, by his resurrection, declared to have conquered death and Satan, who had the power of death.
- Rom. 14:9. Christ, by his resurrection, shown to be the Lord of the living and dead.
- Eph. 1:20–23; Col. 1:18. Christ, in his resurrection, acted as head of his church.
- Rom. 4:25. Christ raised from the dead for our justification.
- Eph. 2:1, 5–6; Col. 2:12. Christ raised from the dead for his people's quickening in grace.
- 1 Cor. 15:25–27. Christ raised from the dead to conquer his people's enemies.
- 1 Cor. 15:20. Christ raised from the dead to guarantee that his people will rise from the dead also.

Commentary

1. How do we know that Christ's body did not suffer decay while it was in the tomb? Psalm 16:10 compared with Acts 2:27 shows this.

2. Why was it not possible for Christ to be held permanently under the power of death? (a) Because of his deity; being the Son of God, he could not remain under the power of death. (b) Because the penalty for sin had been completely paid and canceled; therefore death had lost its claim on him.

3. With what body did Christ rise again on the third day? With the identical body in which he suffered, but glorified.

4. What is the meaning of the expression "essential properties thereof"? This means the properties or characteristics which identified it as Christ's true human body. See Luke 24:39.

5. What was the difference between Christ's glorified body and his body before he was crucified? His glorified body is "without mortality, and other common infirmities belonging to this life."

6. What was the difference between Christ's resurrection and the miracle of raising Lazarus from the dead, which is recorded in John 11? (a) Christ rose by his own power; Lazarus was raised by the power of another. (b) Christ rose as one immortal, who could never die again; Lazarus was raised as a mortal, and finally did die again. (Tradition says he moved to Cyprus after Christ's ascension, where he later died.)

7. What five great truths were demonstrated by Christ's resurrection? (a) That he is the Son of God. (b) That he had fully satisfied God's justice on account of the sins of his people. (c) That he had conquered death. (d) That he had conquered Satan, the devil. (e) That he is Lord of the living and the dead.

8. What is the meaning of the words *quick* **and** *quickening?* "Quick" is an old word which means "alive" or "living"; "quickening" means "making alive."

9. What is meant by the expression "a public person"? This means someone who acts, not for himself personally, but as an official representative of a body of people. It is the opposite of "a private citizen" or "a private person." Christ's great redemptive acts were of an official nature.

10. As a public person, whom did Christ represent? He represented his people, his church, of which he is the head.

11. What benefits come to the church from Christ's resurrection?
(a) Justification. (b) Quickening in grace. (c) Support against enemies. (d) Assurance of our own resurrection at the Last Day.

53. Q. *How was Christ exalted in his ascension?*

A. *Christ was exalted in his ascension, in that having after his resurrection often appeared unto and conversed with his apostles, speaking to them of the things pertaining to the kingdom of God, and giving them commission to preach the gospel to all nations, forty days after his resurrection, he, in our nature, and as our head, triumphing over enemies, visibly went up into the highest heavens, there to receive gifts for men, to raise up our affections thither, and to prepare a place for us, where he himself is, and shall continue till his second coming at the end of the world.*

Scripture References
- Acts 1:3–4. Christ's appearing to his apostles after his resurrection.
- Matt. 28:19–20. The Great Commission to preach the gospel to all nations.
- Heb. 6:20. Christ ascended to heaven as our head.
- Acts 1:9–11; Eph. 4:10; Ps. 68:18. The record of Christ's ascension: his purpose in ascending to receive gifts for men.
- Col. 3:1–2. Christ's purpose in ascending to raise our affections to heaven.
- John 14:3. Christ has ascended to heaven to prepare a place for his people.
- Acts 3:21. Christ must remain in heaven until his second coming.

Commentary
1. How long was the interval between Christ's resurrection and his ascension? Forty days.

2. How did Christ associate with his disciples during this interval? He did not remain with them constantly, but appeared to them repeatedly.

3. What great command did Christ give to his people during this interval? The Great Commission to preach the gospel to all nations, recorded in Matthew 28:18–20, Mark 16:15–18, Luke 24:47, and Acts 1:8.

4. Why is the phrase "in our nature" used to describe Christ's ascension? Because it was not merely as God that he ascended into heaven, but as a human being, with a human body and a human soul. Christ's *human* nature left this earth and entered the realm within the veil.

5. Why is the phrase "as our head" used to describe Christ's ascension? Because his ascension was an *official* act, in which he functioned as our representative, the second Adam, the head of the *redeemed* human race. In heaven, today, Jesus Christ the God-man is the representative or head of the people of God.

6. How did Christ triumph over enemies in his ascension? His enemies had rejected and crucified him, but now—in spite of their hatred and opposition—he ascended into heaven to be proclaimed King of kings and Lord of lords!

7. How do we know that our Savior ascended *visibly?* Acts 1:9–11: "And when he had spoken these things, *while they beheld,* he was taken up; and a cloud received him *out of their sight.* And, while *they looked steadfastly toward heaven as he went up,* behold, two men stood by them in white apparel; which also said, 'Ye men of Galilee, why stand ye *gazing up into heaven?* This same Jesus, which is taken up from you into heaven, shall so come in like manner *as ye have seen him go into heaven.'* "

8. Why is the *visibility* of Christ's ascension so strongly emphasized in the account in Acts 1:9–11? Undoubtedly the reason for the strong emphasis on visibility is to avoid the idea that Christ's ascension was only a vision or hallucination, or only a *spiritual* ascension. The record leaves no doubt that the disciples were wide awake and actually saw Christ's human form rise up and leave this earth.

9. What is the modern view of Christ's ascension? Modern religious liberalism, since it does not believe in the bodily resurrection of Christ, of course cannot believe in a literal ascension either. Modernism disbelieves both of these great gospel facts, and explains them away as myths or legends.

10. Is it hard to believe that Christ, in his human body, literally ascended from this earth to heaven? It all depends on what kind of Christ we believe in. If Jesus was *merely* a human being, it would be extremely difficult if not impossible to believe that he really ascended to heaven. But if we believe in the Christ of the Scriptures, who came down from heaven in the first place, it is not at all difficult to believe that when his work on earth was accomplished he ascended to heaven again. For if he did not ascend to heaven, then he must still be visibly present somewhere on earth (since he rose from the dead). It is of course perfectly obvious that the risen Christ is not now present in bodily form anywhere in the world; therefore we conclude that the Scripture account of his ascension is entirely reasonable and credible, and the only possible view, once his literal resurrection from the dead is admitted.

11. What is meant by saying that Christ ascended to heaven in order to receive gifts for men? "To receive gifts for men" is an expression taken from Psalm 68:18, and is quoted in Ephesians 4:8. The kind of gifts intended can be discovered from Ephesians 4:11–12, namely, various kinds of official functions in the church, such as the offices of apostles, prophets, evangelists, pastors, and teachers. The purpose of these various gifts is stated in verse 12, namely, "for the perfecting of the saints, for the work of the ministry, for the edifying of the body of Christ."

12. Why should Christ's ascension raise our affections to heaven? The fact that our Savior is in heaven should make us think of heaven and value it more highly than all our possessions in this world. "Where your treasure is, there will your heart be also."

13. What is Christ doing in heaven at this present time? Among other things which the Bible mentions, he is preparing a place for his people in heavenly glory, to be their eternal home. John 14:1–3.

14. How do we know that heaven is a *place* and not just a spiritual *state* or *condition*? Christ's human body is there; therefore it must be a place. Moreover, his own promise in John 14:3 is "to prepare a place for you," and this certainly indicates that heaven is a place. We should resist all tendencies to "spiritualize" or explain away the plain, simple meaning of Christ's promise, and should adhere to the unsophisticated realism of the Scriptures. We do not know *where* heaven is, but we do know that it is a real *place*. The doctrine of the bodily resurrection implies and requires belief in heaven as a place.

54. Q. *How is Christ exalted in his sitting at the right hand of God?*

A. *Christ is exalted in his sitting at the right hand of God, in that as God-man he is advanced to the highest favour with God the Father, with all fulness of joy, glory, and power over all things in heaven and earth; and does gather and defend his church, and subdue their enemies; furnisheth his ministers and people with gifts and graces, and maketh intercession for them.*

Scripture References

- Phil. 2:9. Christ exalted by God the Father.
- Ps. 16:11 compared with Acts 2:28. Christ given all fullness of joy by God the Father.
- John 17:5. Christ given glory by the Father.
- Eph. 1:22; 1 Peter 3:22. Christ given supreme power by God the Father.
- Eph. 4:10–12; Ps. 110:1–2. Christ, at the Father's right hand, gathers and defends his church, subdues their enemies, and furnishes his ministers and people with gifts and graces.
- Rom. 8:34. Christ, at the Father's right hand, makes intercession for his people.

Commentary

1. What is meant by saying that Christ sits at the right hand of God in heaven? This, of course, is figurative language. Since God is a spirit and has no body, he does not have a literal right hand. The meaning is that Christ as Mediator, being God and man in one person, occupies the highest place in heaven next to God the Father. As God, Christ is fully equal to the Father in all things; as God-man, he is exalted to the highest place in heaven next to God.

2. Why was Christ exalted to the right hand of God in heaven? This honor was given him as a reward for his obedience, sufferings, and death, according to the terms of the covenant of grace. Read Philippians 2:8–11.

3. What power does Christ exercise at the right hand of God in heaven? "All power in heaven and on earth" (Matt. 28:18). "He hath put all things under his feet" (1 Cor. 15:27). He has "raised him from the dead, and set him at his own right hand in the heavenly places, far above all principality, and power, and might, and dominion, and every name that is named, not only in this world, but also in that which is to come; and hath put all things under his feet" (Eph. 1:20–22). The power committed to Christ is absolutely universal and includes the entire created universe. First Corinthians 15:27–28 shows that only God the Father is excepted from Christ's dominion.

4. How long will Christ's dominion over the entire created universe continue? It will continue throughout the present age and until Christ's second coming at the end of the age. "For he must reign, till he hath put all enemies under his feet. The last enemy that shall be destroyed is death" (1 Cor. 15:25–26). At that time, when death—the last enemy—has been destroyed by the resurrection of the dead, Christ will give up his mediatorial dominion over the universe, as shown by 1 Corinthians 15:24. "Then cometh the end, when he shall have delivered up the kingdom to God, even the Father; when he shall have put down all rule and all authority and power," and verse 29, which says, "And when all things shall be subdued unto him, then shall the Son also himself be subject unto him that put all things under him, that God may be all in all." However, Christ will never give up his kingly office *as head of the redeemed human race,* as is shown by Luke 1:33: "And he shall reign over the house of Jacob for ever; and of his kingdom there shall be no end."

5. What is the purpose or aim of Christ's dominion over the entire universe? The purpose or aim of Christ's dominion over the entire universe is *the benefit of his church,* as shown by Ephesians 1:22: "And hath put all things under his feet, and gave him to be head over all things to the church." This text is often misunderstood, as if it said "head over all things *in* the church," that is, as if it meant simply that Christ is *head of the church.* But we should note that the text actually says "head over all things *to* (or *for)* the church," that is, *head over the entire universe for the benefit of the church!*

6. How does Christ's universal dominion benefit his church? (a) By gathering his elect into his church. (b) By defending his church against her enemies. (c) By perfecting his church, bestowing gifts and graces on ministers and people. (d) By making intercession for his people.

7. What error is common today concerning Christ's kingly dominion? A very common false teaching asserts that Christ is not a king today, and will not exercise kingly power until after his second coming when, it is alleged, he will reign for a thousand years in Jerusalem. First Corinthians

15:23–28 certainly teaches that Christ is reigning *now* (v. 25), and that his second coming will mark the *end*, not the beginning, of his dominion over the entire universe.

55. Q. *How doth Christ make intercession?*

A. *Christ maketh intercession, by his appearing in our nature continually before the Father in heaven, in the merit of his obedience and sacrifice on earth, declaring his will to have it applied to all believers; answering all accusations against them, and procuring for them quiet of conscience, notwithstanding daily failings, access with boldness to the throne of grace, and acceptance of their persons and services.*

Scripture References

- Heb. 9:12, 24. Christ appears in the presence of God on our behalf.
- Heb. 1:3. Christ's heavenly intercession based on the merit of his sacrifice and obedience on earth.
- John 3:16; 17:9, 20, 24. It is Christ's will that the merit of his obedience and sacrifice be applied to all believers.
- Rom. 8:33–34. Christ in his heavenly intercession answers all accusations against his people.
- Rom. 5:1–2; 1 John 2:1–2. Christ by his heavenly intercession procures quiet of conscience for his people, in spite of their daily failings.
- Eph. 1:6. Christ procures for his people the acceptance of their persons.
- 1 Peter 2:5. Christ procures for his people the acceptance of their services.
- Heb. 7:25. Christ makes intercession for his people continually, saving them "to the uttermost."

Commentary

1. To which of Christ's three offices does his work of intercession belong? To the office of a priest (Heb. 7:24–25).

2. What book of the Bible tells us most about the priesthood of Christ? The epistle to the Hebrews.

3. In what chapter of the Bible is Christ's great "High Priestly prayer" found? John 17.

4. To whom does Christ make intercession for his people? To God the Father.

5. On what basis, or by what right, does Christ intercede for his people? "In the merit of his obedience and sacrifice on earth"; that is, in his heavenly intercession Christ presents his obedience and sacrifice on earth as a sufficient reason why his people's sins should be forgiven, blessings given to them, their services accepted, etc.

6. According to the will and purpose of Christ, to whom is the merit of his obedience and sacrifice applied? To all believers.

7. In the Bible, who is represented as making accusations against God's children? Satan, or the devil. Read Job 1:9–11; 2:4–5; Revelation 12:9–10; and Zechariah 3:1–2.

8. Of what might Satan accuse God's people? Of being unworthy of God's blessings and favor, because of their sins.

9. How can Christ answer Satan's accusations against believers? By showing that, even though God's people are in themselves sinful and unworthy, yet since Christ himself suffered the penalty due for their sins, and also provided a perfect righteousness which is reckoned to their account, Satan has no ground for making charges against them. For every sin that Satan can accuse a Christian of, Christ can say, "My blood was shed to take away that sin." Thus Satan is left without any valid ground for accusing believers.

10. What in the life of Christian people would tend to cause an uneasy conscience? Daily failings in thought, word, and deed.

11. How can we enjoy real peace of conscience in spite of daily failings? "Where sin abounded, grace did much more abound" (Rom. 5:20). Christ's atonement and righteousness, which he pleads on our behalf, are greater than all our sins and failures. Therefore, because of his heavenly intercession, peace of conscience is given to Christian believers. This does not mean that the Christian may be satisfied to commit sin daily; on the contrary, he must fight against it continually. But the Christian can have assurance that his sins are forgiven and cannot bring him into condemnation. "There is therefore now no condemnation to them which are in Christ Jesus" (Rom. 8:1).

12. How can we, with all our sins and failures, have boldness to come to God's throne of grace in prayer? Of ourselves alone we could not have such boldness, for God is holy and we are sinful. But through Christ's heavenly intercession, because he is our Mediator and High Priest, we can come to God in prayer with confidence, as children to a father. Read Hebrews 4:15–16.

13. Why are the services or "good works" of Christ's people acceptable to God? Not because of anything in or of ourselves, for we are sinful by nature; nor because of the quality or character of our "good works," for they are very imperfect and marred by sin; but only because of the heavenly intercession of Christ our Mediator.

56. Q. *How is Christ to be exalted in his coming again to judge the world?*

A. *Christ is to be exalted in his coming again to judge the world, in that he, who was unjustly judged and condemned by wicked men, shall come again at the Last Day in great power, and in the full manifestation of his own glory, and of his Father's, with all his holy angels, with a shout, with the voice of the archangel, and with the trumpet of God, to judge the world in righteousness.*

Scripture References
- Acts 3:14–15. Christ was unjustly judged and condemned by wicked men.
- Matt. 24:30. Christ shall come again visibly with power and glory.
- Luke 9:26; Matt. 25:31. Christ shall come again in his own glory, and the Father's glory, and with all the holy angels.
- 1 Thess. 4:16. Christ shall come with a shout, with the voice of the archangel, and the trumpet of God.
- Acts 17:31. At his second coming, Christ shall judge the world in righteousness.
- Acts 1:10–11. Christ's second coming a definite, visible event.
- Rev. 1:7. When Christ comes, "every eye shall see him."
- Rev. 20:11–12. The great judgment at the Last Day.

Commentary

1. What great event will take place immediately after Christ's second coming? The judgment.

2. When will Christ's second coming take place? At the end of the age, or the Last Day.

3. When will the end of the age, or the Last Day, come? This question cannot really be answered, as the information has not been revealed in the Word of God. Matthew 24:36: "But of *that* day and hour knoweth no man." All attempts to calculate the date of Christ's second coming are useless and unscriptural. We should be on our guard against being deceived by any who claim to know "that day and hour" in advance. At the same time we must remember that Christ's second coming is a definite event which will take place at a definite time, that is, a particular year, month, day, and hour. On a definite day, known only to God, human history will suddenly come to a conclusion with the second coming and the judgment.

4. Can we know whether the second coming of Christ is approaching or drawing near? Yes. Although it is impossible to calculate the date of our Lord's return, still it is possible to know whether that blessed event is drawing near. Certain signs have been prophesied as preceding the Lord's return. The appearance of all these signs will show that his return is near. Matthew 24:33: "So likewise ye, when ye shall see all these things, know that it is near, even at the doors." The American Revised Version translates this verse as follows: "Even so, when ye shall see all these things, know ye that he is nigh, even at the doors."

(Much as I regret the necessity to disagree with Dr. Vos at this point, I consider it my duty to do so. I believe the text quoted above refers strictly and only to events that were certain to take place in the first century, in the time of the apostles. Jesus was speaking to living persons. When he said "ye shall see all these things," he meant those people to whom he was speaking. In contrast to them, and to the time in which they lived—when these things were about to take place [see v. 34]—we live in a time which is better compared with the time of Noah, the thief in the night, or the lightning that shines from the east to the west. All three of these figures are used by Jesus to warn us about "that day" for which there will be no signs. Dr. Vos's next question really shows this. [For more please read my study of New Testament eschatology. GIW])

5. What preparations should we as Christians make for the second coming of Christ? Matthew 24:44: "Therefore be ye also ready; for in such an hour as ye think not the Son of man cometh." Matthew 25:13: "Watch therefore; for ye know neither the day nor the hour wherein the Son of man cometh." Read also Luke 12:35–40.

6. What should be our attitude toward the second coming of Christ and the Day of Judgment? We should look forward to these great redemptive events with eager and joyful anticipation, realizing that they will bring about the completion of our redemption in our complete and permanent deliverance from sin, death, and all their consequences. Titus 2:13: "Looking for that blessed hope, and the glorious appearing of the great God and our Savior Jesus Christ." 1 Peter 1:13: "Wherefore gird up the loins of your mind, be sober, and hope to the end for the grace that is to be brought unto you at the revelation of Jesus Christ." Luke 21:28: "And when these things begin to come to pass, then look up, and lift up your heads; for your redemption draweth nigh." Revelation 22:20: "He which testifieth these things saith, 'Surely I come quickly.' Even so, come, Lord Jesus."

7. What will be the manner of Christ's second coming? Many questions may arise in our minds which cannot be answered. We should always remember that the Bible was given to meet our needs, not to satisfy our curiosity. We should not allow our imagination to wander beyond what is plainly revealed in the Scriptures. Concerning the *manner* of Christ's second coming, the Word of God teaches clearly the following facts: (a) Christ's second coming will be a *personal* coming; Acts 1:11: "This same Jesus." (b) Christ's second coming will be a *visible* coming; Acts 1:11: "In like manner as ye have seen him go into heaven." Revelation 1:7: "Behold, he cometh with clouds, and every eye shall see him." (c) Christ's second coming will be a miraculous or *supernatural* coming, which will crash through the order of nature with the almighty power of God; 1 Corinthians 15:22; 1 Thessalonians 4:16: "For the Lord himself shall descend from heaven *with a shout, with the voice of the archangel, and with the trump of God.*" Matthew 24:27: "*For as the lightning cometh out of the east, and shineth even unto the west, so shall also the coming of the Son of man be.*" (d) Christ's second coming will be a *sudden* coming, at a definite and particular time, which is referred to as that day and hour; see 1 Corinthians 15:52: "in a moment, in the twinkling of an eye," etc.

8. How will Christ judge the world at his second coming? In righteousness, that is, according to the righteous law of God. For the first time in all human history, *absolute justice* is going to be dispensed to the human race.

9. Who will be judged at Christ's second coming? Revelation 20:11–15 shows that the great judgment will include all the dead who have ever lived, and also that all persons then living when Christ returns will be judged.

10. Will Christian people be judged at Christ's second coming? They will be judged, but not condemned. In their case, the sentence will be one of acquittal because of Christ's blood and righteousness which are imputed or reckoned to their account; 2 Corinthians 5:10: "For we must all appear before the judgment seat of Christ"; Romans 14:10: "For we shall all stand before the judgment seat of Christ"; Romans 8:1, "There is therefore now no condemnation to them which are in Christ Jesus."

11. How will the heathen, who lived and died without the light of Scripture, be judged? They will be judged according to the law of nature, which was written in their heart and conscience. Read Romans 2:12–16, where the apostle Paul explains this.

12. What does the Larger Catechism say about a millennium? Nothing whatever. None of the Westminster Standards mentions a "millennium" or thousand-year reign of Christ.

13. What has been the prevalent attitude in orthodox churches, in recent years, toward the doctrine of the second coming of Christ? This doctrine, which beyond question is clearly revealed in the Scripture as one of the great truths of the Christian faith, and which has always been held to be an essential doctrine of Christianity, has been greatly neglected in orthodox churches, so much so that many ministers seldom, if ever, preach on it, and many people know almost nothing about it. The result of this widespread neglect has been that certain denominations and sects have taken up this doctrine and carried it to absurd and fanatical extremes, far beyond what a sober study of the Scriptures would warrant. We should deplore these fanciful studies of "prophecy," but at the same time avoid the opposite extreme of neglecting the doctrine of Christ's second coming until it is practically forgotten. We can believe thoroughly in the real, visible, supernatural second coming of Christ, without accepting the fantastic notions of many so-called experts on prophecy who are popular today.

10

The Benefits of the Mediator's Work

57. Q. *What benefits hath Christ procured by his mediation?*

A. *Christ, by his mediation, hath procured redemption, with all other benefits of the Covenant of Grace.*

Scripture References

- Heb. 9:12. Christ has obtained redemption for his people with his own blood.
- Mark 10:45. Christ's life laid down as a ransom-price.
- 1 Tim. 2:6. Christ gave himself a ransom for all.
- Job 19:25. Long ago Job looked forward to Christ as his Redeemer.
- Rom. 3:24. We are justified on the basis of redemption through Christ.
- 1 Cor. 1:30. Christ is made redemption to his people.
- Eph. 1:7. Redemption is through Christ's blood.
- Col. 1:14. Forgiveness of sins is based on redemption through Christ's blood.
- 2 Cor. 1:20. All benefits of the covenant of grace come to believers through Christ.

Commentary

1. What is the meaning of the word *mediation?* It means to act as a *Mediator,* or go-between, in reconciling parties who were at enmity with each other.

2. What is the basic meaning of the word *redemption?* It means to recover possession by the payment of a purchase or ransom price.

3. To what does the word *redemption* primarily refer in the New Testament? It refers to Christ's reclaiming sinners from sin and death, and gaining salvation and life for them by the payment of his own precious blood as the ransom price for them.

4. What other usage of the word *redemption* is found in the New Testament? It is also used to refer to *the resurrection of the body,* because this is the final installment of the benefits of redemption. See Romans 8:23; Ephesians 1:14; Luke 21:28.

5. Why was it necessary for Christ to pay a ransom price for our redemption? Because the whole human race was guilty before God, and according to God's righteous judgment deserved eternal death.

6. To whom did Christ pay the ransom price? He paid the ransom price *to God.* The notion that the ransom was paid to Satan is a very old error, which reappears from time to time, but has no foundation in the Word of God. Christ came to destroy the works of Satan, it is true, but *not* by paying a ransom price *to* Satan. He destroyed the works of Satan by paying the ransom price to God.

7. If God is love, as the Scripture says, why could he not forgive sinners without the payment of a ransom price? The Bible teaches us that God is love, but it also teaches us that he is a God of righteousness and holiness, and that he cannot deny himself. If God were simply to forgive sin without an atonement, he would deny his own righteousness. The penalty of sin must be borne by a substitute; otherwise God could not forgive our sins.

8. In addition to redemption, or suffering and dying as a ransom for our sins, what other benefits of the covenant of grace has Christ procured for his people? Justification, adoption, and sanctification, and the several benefits which in this life do either accompany or flow from them, including assurance of God's love, peace of conscience, joy in the Holy Ghost, increase of grace, and perseverance therein to the end; also those benefits which come to the believer at death and at the resurrection. See the Shorter Catechism, questions 32, 36–38.

58. Q. *How do we come to be made partakers of the benefits which Christ hath procured?*

A. *We are made partakers of the benefits which Christ hath procured, by the application of them unto us, which is the work especially of God the Holy Ghost.*

Scripture References

- John 1:11–12. Christ's benefits applied to us.
- Titus 3:5–6; John 3:1–10. Regeneration by the Holy Spirit essential to salvation.

Commentary

1. What is the difference between the work of Christ and the work of the Holy Spirit? Christ has *obtained* redemption for us; the Holy Spirit *applies* redemption to us, so that we actually experience the benefits of it.

2. Why is it necessary for the Holy Spirit to apply Christ's redemption to us? Because in ourselves we are so weak and sinful that we could never get the benefit of Christ's redemption if we were left to ourselves; only by the almighty work of the Holy Spirit, changing our hearts and leading us to repent and believe, can we actually receive the benefit of what Christ has done for us.

3. Is it true that in the end our salvation depends entirely on our human free will, by which we either accept the gospel or reject it? This kind of statement is only true if understood properly. We might express the whole matter this way: (a) Our salvation depends on whether we accept or reject the gospel. (b) In accepting or rejecting the gospel, we always act according to our free will. (c) Without the Holy Spirit's work, our free will would lead us to *reject* the gospel. (d) When our hearts are changed by the Holy Spirit, our free will leads us to accept the gospel. (e) Therefore, *in the end*, it depends on the work of the Holy Spirit in our hearts.

4. Is the work of the Holy Spirit, in applying Christ's redemption, subject to human control? No. It is a sovereign work of God. He is the Potter; we are the clay. His work is not subject to our control; but this does not mean that the Holy Spirit does not work in answer to the prayers of Christian people; he does.

59. Q. *Who are made partakers of redemption through Christ?*

A. *Redemption is certainly applied, and effectually communicated, to all those for whom Christ hath purchased it; who are in time by the Holy Ghost enabled to believe in Christ according to the gospel.*

Scripture References

- Eph. 1:13–14; John 6:37, 39; 10:15–16. Redemption effectually communicated to those for whom Christ purchased it.
- Eph. 2:8; 2 Cor. 4:13. Those for whom Christ purchased redemption are in time enabled to believe in him according to the gospel.
- John 17:9. Christ prays for those for whom he purchased redemption.
- Acts 2:47. Those for whom redemption was purchased are in due time added to the church.
- Acts 16:14. For a person to be saved by the gospel, the heart must be "opened" by the Lord.
- Acts 18:9–11. God knows exactly who his elect are, for whom redemption has been purchased, and to whom in due time it is to be applied.

Commentary

1. For whom did Christ purchase redemption? For a body of people described in Scripture by such terms as "his people," "his sheep," "his church," "his body," "the elect," "those whom he foreknew" etc.

2. How many people are included in the body for whom redemption was purchased? "A great multitude, which no man could number, of all nations, and kindreds, and people, and tongues" (Rev. 7:9). Scripture teaches that the elect are: (a) A definite number of particular people, not the entire human race, but a part. (b) A very great number, passing human ability to count. (c) A number unknown to men, but known to God, and determined before the creation of the world.

3. Did not Christ purchase redemption for everyone? Although this is the popular idea today, it is contrary to what the Bible teaches, and it is rightly rejected by our Confession of Faith and catechisms. Instead of this the Bible teaches that Christ purchased redemption for "his own," "his sheep," "his people," etc.

4. How can we explain Scripture texts which say that Christ died for all? When the Bible says, "Christ died for all," this does not mean the entire human race but all believers, or all the elect. Some of the similar texts mean that Christ died for all sorts of sinners, regardless of race or nationality, whether Jews or Gentiles (1 John 2:2). In the Bible such terms as "all," "the world," etc., do not mean *every individual person in the world,* as will easily be seen by consulting Luke 2:1; Acts 19:27; Mark 1:32; Acts 4:21; and John 12:19.

5. Is it right to say, "God gives everybody a *chance* to be saved, and we can take it or leave it"? There is no such thing as *chance* in the plan of salvation revealed in the Bible. Christ's redemption is *certainly and effectually* applied to all those for whom it was intended.

6. How does the Holy Spirit apply Christ's redemption to the elect? By enabling them, at a particular time in their life, to believe in Christ according to the gospel.

60. Q. *Can they who have never heard the gospel, and so know not Jesus Christ, nor believe in him, be saved by their living according to the light of nature?*

A. *They who, having never heard the gospel, know not Jesus Christ, and believe not in him, cannot be saved, be they never so diligent to frame their lives according to the light of nature, or the laws of that religion which they profess; neither is there salvation in any other, but in Christ alone, who is the Savior only of his body the church.*

Scripture References

- Rom. 10:14. The gospel message necessary for salvation.

- 2 Thess. 1:8–9; Eph. 2:12; John 1:10–12. Those who do not know Jesus Christ are under divine condemnation because of their sin.
- John 8:24; Mark 16:16. Faith in Jesus Christ necessary for salvation.
- 1 Cor. 1:20–24. There is no real knowledge of God, or salvation, apart from the preaching of the cross of Christ.
- John 4:22; Rom. 9:31–32; Phil. 3:4–9. Careful living according to the light of nature, or any other religious system which a person may profess, not sufficient for salvation.
- Acts 4:12. There is no salvation except in Christ.
- Eph. 5:23. Christ is the Savior only of his body, the church.

Commentary

1. Why will the heathen, who have never heard the gospel, be condemned at the Judgment Day? Not because of failure to believe in Christ, but simply because of their sins. Read Romans 2:12.

2. Why cannot the heathen be saved by being diligent to frame their lives according to the light of nature? Because the entire human race is in a fallen state, and everyone is born with a sinful heart which inclines him to do evil. Therefore all people have fallen short, even of what they knew to be right by the light of nature. Since the wages of sin is death, those who have sinned are under the sentence of death.

3. Why cannot the heathen be saved by being diligent to frame their lives according to the laws of that religion which they profess? Because the heathen religions are predominantly false. Although they all may contain elements of truth, nevertheless *as systems* they are false. None of them contains the truth which sinners need: the truth about the way of salvation from sin by a divine-human Mediator. Therefore no matter how much zeal the heathen may have for the duties of their own religion, this cannot save them. If Paul's great zeal as a Pharisee could not save him, how much less could the zeal or earnestness of the heathen bring about their salvation.

4. If the heathen are sincere in their heathen belief, will they not be saved because of their sincerity? Modern sentiment inclines people to think this to be true, no doubt, but the verdict of Scripture is to the contrary. Read Acts 4:12. *Sincerity has no value apart from the truth.* The more sincere a person is in a false religion, the more surely he is on the way to ruin. Beyond question the Japanese during World War II sincerely believed that their emperor was divine, but that did not make him divine, nor absolve them from guilt.

5. Is it not unfair for God to condemn those who have never heard the gospel? If God *owed* salvation, or "a chance for salvation," to all human beings, then it would be unjust to condemn those who have never heard the gospel. But God does not owe any such thing to anyone. He is under no obligation to provide salvation, or an offer of salvation, to anyone at all. Therefore no injustice is involved in his saving some and passing others by.

6. But if God condemns those who have never heard the gospel, does not this amount to partiality in dealing with the human race? It certainly does amount to *partiality,* that is, God gives to some what he—in his divine providence—withholds from others. The same is true with respect to God's bestowal of health, intelligence, prosperity, and all the ordinary blessings of life. In his providence God gives to some what he withholds from others; this certainly is partiality. God does not treat all people alike. But this is not injustice, because God owes nobody any blessing at all; nor is it respect of persons, because whatever God's reasons for his actions may be, *they are not based on deference to the character or righteousness of the persons who receive salvation.* Rather, it is a matter of pure, undeserved grace that the elect are saved from sin unto eternal life.

7. What hope is there for the salvation of the heathen? The gospel of Christ, published throughout the whole world by missionaries, is the message of salvation full and free to everyone who believes.

8. Apart from faith in the gospel message, what hope may we have for the salvation of a part of the heathen world? Although it cannot be conclusively proved from the Bible, many orthodox Bible students have held as a matter of opinion the hope that all infants, dying in infancy, are saved. In this connection the reader is referred to the Westminster Confession of Faith, 10.3 (first sentence). It should be carefully noted that the Confession of Faith makes no statement as to whether or not there are any *non-*elect infants who die in infancy. It speaks only of "elect infants dying in infancy." The implied contrast is *not* to "non-elect infants dying in infancy," but rather to "elect infants *not* dying in infancy"; that is, a contrast is implied between *elect infants who die in infancy* and *elect infants who live to grow up to years of discretion.*

9. What further hope may we have for the salvation of some of the heathen? See the Confession of Faith, 10.3 (second sentence), which refers to "other elect persons, who are incapable of being outwardly called by the ministry of the word." This refers to persons born mentally deficient. It is certainly possible that some or even all of such people will be among the saved although they are incapable of coming to understand and believe the gospel.

10. What should we think of the doctrine of Universalism (the belief that all human beings will finally be saved)? (a) It is clearly contradicted by many Scripture texts. (b) It is founded on the false idea that God is nothing but love. (c) It completely cuts the nerve of both foreign missions and evangelism. If everybody is going to be saved in the end anyway, then why preach the gospel, either at home or on the foreign field?

61. Q. *Are all they saved who hear the gospel, and live in the church?*

A. *All that hear the gospel, and live in the visible church, are not saved; but they only who are true members of the church invisible.*

Scripture References
- John 12:38–40; Rom. 9:6; Matt. 7:21; Rom. 11:7. There is a distinction between the external observable body of the people of God, who profess the true religion, and the body of those who truly know God and are really saved.

Commentary
1. Why is hearing the gospel, and membership in the visible church, not sufficient to ensure our salvation? We are saved by means of a personal faith in Jesus Christ as our Savior; but it is possible for a person to hear the gospel and join a church, without having a personal faith in Christ as his Savior.

2. What two classes of people are found in the membership of the visible church? (a) Those who are truly saved because they have a genuine faith in Christ. (b) Those who are not truly saved, because they have only a formal possession of Christianity, without the spiritual power and reality of it.

3. Who can determine with certainty which members of the visible church are really saved and which are merely formal professors of Christianity? Only God can know this with complete certainty. However, it is possible for a person to attain absolute assurance concerning *his own* salvation. We cannot, however, speak with *absolute* certainty about the salvation or non-salvation of other people who make a profession of faith in Christ.

4. What is the ideal condition of the visible church? The ideal condition is a membership which is entirely regenerate (composed of truly saved persons). While this is certainly the ideal, it cannot be attained in this world. Just as there was a Judas among the twelve apostles, so there will always be some unsaved persons in the membership of the visible church in this age. Ministers and elders are not to blame for this unless it is the result of their neglect of their duties. It is their duty to exclude from the visible church such as are ignorant or scandalous, that is, such as do not make a proper profession of faith, or whose lives make it impossible to accept their profession at face value. But apart from the obviously ignorant and scandalous, there are many professing Christians who may be members of the visible church without being truly saved. This is an unavoidable condition, which must be recognized, even though it is to be deplored. The attempt to have an absolutely pure church has always led to even greater evils than it was intended to remedy.

5. Must an applicant for membership in the visible church prove to the officers of the church that he is born again? Certainly not. Church officers are to take an applicant's profession at face value in the absence of evidence that the profession is not credible. It is no duty of ministers and elders to try to examine people's hearts to see if they really are born again. Membership in the visible church is based on *a credible profession of faith and obedience,* not on *demonstration of regeneration.* The acceptance of an applicant for membership is based on *presumption,* not on *proof.* He does not have to *prove* that he is converted. It is *presumed* that he knows what he is talking about and is telling the truth when he makes a profession of faith, unless there is clear evidence which makes such a presumption impossible. (See the Reformed Presbyterian Testimony, 21.2; and 22.1–2, and error 2.)

6. What should be the personal aim of every member of the visible church? Every member of the visible church should make it his aim to attain full assurance that he is not only a member of the visible church, but also truly saved by personal faith in Jesus Christ as his Savior.

62. Q. *What is the visible church?*

A. *The visible church is a society made up of all such as in all ages and places of the world do profess the true religion, and of their children.*

Scripture References

- 1 Cor. 1:2; 12:13; Rom. 15:9–12; Rev. 7:9; Pss. 2:8; 22:27–31; 45:7; Matt. 28:18–20; Isa. 59:21. The visible church consists of those, of all times and places, who profess the true religion.
- 1 Cor. 7:14; Acts 2:39; Rom. 11:16; Gen. 17:7. The children of those who profess the true religion are members of the visible church along with their parents, because they are included with their parents in the covenant promises of God.

Commentary

1. Why is the visible church called "visible"? Because it is possible to see it as an assembly of people. We cannot see how many people in a congregation are born again, or truly saved; but it is possible to see how many are members of that church. It is possible, for example, to see and know that a particular congregation has 100 members, or 450 members. But it is not possible to see how many of them are truly regenerate in heart. That is known only to God.

2. How many visible churches are there in the world? There is only one. But it includes many branches (often called denominations) and is made up of a very large number of particular congregations. We should note that the catechism does not say that "the visible church is an organization," but rather says "the visible church is a society." It is one society, although it includes many particular organizations.

3. What denomination is the true visible church? No one denomination can rightly claim to be *the* true visible church. Every denomination (and congregation) which is loyal to the truth of the gospel according to the Word of God is a *branch* (or part) of the visible church. When any one denomination claims to be *the* true visible church, this necessarily implies that others are false. Such a claim is presumptuous and sinful. We should realize that the true visible church is greater than any one denomination. While we believe that our own denomination holds a broader and more consistent testimony for the truth than others (which is our proper reason for being members of it), we should freely recognize that the visible church includes many branches which hold the gospel with a greater or lesser degree of consistency.

4. What is the scope of the visible church with respect to time? It includes believers of all ages of the world's history, from the time of Adam and Eve to the end of the world. All people of every age who professed faith in the true religion are included in the visible church.

5. What is the scope of the visible church with respect to place? It includes people in all places of the world, wherever the light of the gospel has penetrated the world's darkness and some people have professed the true religion.

6. What makes a person a member of the visible church? A public profession of the true religion, that is, a public profession of faith in Jesus Christ and obedience to him.

7. What is the badge of entrance into the visible church? The sacrament of baptism.

8. What is the highest privilege of membership in a particular congregation of the visible church? Participation in the sacrament of the Lord's Supper.

9. Are there unconverted people or hypocrites in the membership of the visible church? Yes. Nowhere does Scripture promise that there can be such a thing, in this present age, as a perfectly pure visible church, in which no unconverted person holds membership. Even the twelve apostles had a Judas among them. Similarly, it would appear from the book of Acts—and the New Testament Epistles—that there were hypocrites or unconverted persons in the early churches established by the apostles. Some of them were finally suspended or excommunicated by church discipline (see 1 John 2:19).

10. Can we have a perfectly pure church by putting out those members who are not born again? This has been tried at various times by certain sects, and has always proved disastrous. The truth is that only God knows certainly who the regenerate are. A person may attain full assurance of *his own* salvation, but not of the salvation of others. We may be able, in some cases, to say that almost certainly a particular person is born again, or not

born again, but we cannot make absolute statements. Since only God knows
with absolute certainty who the hypocrites are, it is obviously impossible to
purify the church by casting them out. The visible church is not a society of
those who can *prove* that they are born again; it is a society of those who *profess* the true religion and appear to live it as well as profess it.

**11. In addition to those who *profess* the true religion, what other
class of persons is included in the membership of the visible church?**
The infant, or minor, children of those who profess the true religion.

**12. What denominations deny that children of believers are to be
included in the membership of the church?** Baptists, and others who
hold the same doctrine. These hold that children of Christian parents are not
qualified to be members of the visible church until they reach the age of discretion and make their own public profession of faith when they are baptized.

**13. What is the badge or sign that the children of Christian people
are to be members of the visible church?** Baptism, which is also to be
applied to the children of believers.

**14. When children of Christian parents, who have been baptized in
their infancy, reach years of discretion, what is their duty with
respect to membership in the church?** It is their duty to make a public
profession of faith and seek admission to the Lord's Table.

**15. Why is it incorrect to speak of such young people as "joining
the church"?** Because they are already incorporated into the membership
of the church by their baptism.

63. Q. *What are the special privileges of the visible church?*

   A. *The visible church hath the privilege of being under God's special care
   and government; of being protected and preserved in all ages, notwithstanding the opposition of all enemies; and of enjoying the communion
   of saints, the ordinary means of salvation, and offers of grace by Christ
   to all the members of it in the ministry of the gospel, testifying, that*

whosoever believes in him shall be saved, and excluding none that will come unto him.

Scripture References

- Isa. 4:5–6; 1 Tim. 4:10. The visible church is under God's special care and government.
- Ps. 115:1–2; Isa. 31:4–5; Zech. 12:2–9. The visible church is protected and preserved by God in all ages, in spite of the opposition of enemies.
- Acts 2:39, 42. The visible church enjoys the communion of the saints, and the ordinary means of salvation.
- Ps. 147:19–20; Rom. 9:6; Eph. 4:11–12; Mark 16:16. The visible church enjoys the free offer of the gospel.
- John 6:37. The ministry of the gospel, in the visible church, excludes no one willing to come to Christ.

Commentary

1. What is meant by saying that the visible church is "under God's special care and government"? By this we mean that in addition to God's ordinary providence whereby he controls all things that come to pass, God provides for the safety and welfare of his church in a special way, making various circumstances and acts of men work together for the benefit of his church.

2. What promise has our Savior given concerning the protection and permanence of his church? Matthew 16:18: "The gates of hell shall not prevail against it." This implies that there shall be a true visible church of Christ in the world until his second coming.

3. How has this promise of protection and preservation been fulfilled in past ages? We can think of many examples. First, the early church was preserved from the wrath of the Jews, who would have extinguished the light of the gospel if it had been in their power to do so. God used the power of the Roman Empire to protect the early church against Jewish persecution. The destruction of Jerusalem in the year A.D. 70 marked the end of the power of the Jews anywhere in the world to persecute Christianity. This was followed by the Roman persecutions, which lasted for some 250 years, until the Emperor Constantine issued his Edict of Toleration in the year A.D. 313. During these 250 years of persecution, God protected and preserved his church chiefly in three ways: (a) The blood of the martyrs became the seed of the church; the more Christians were killed, the greater the number of Christians became! (b) There were intervals of peace and quiet when the church was free from persecution and could carry on its work without such great hindrance; except for those periods of relief, the church could hardly have survived. (c) In most cases there were places free from persecution to which Christians could flee for refuge. This gave some relief and prevented the complete extinction of Christianity. It would be a long story to tell of God's special care for his church during the Middle Ages, the period of the Reformation, and our own recent twentieth century. In every age God's special providence has been at work for the benefit of the church.

4. How has this promise of special protection and defense been fulfilled in our own time? By the downfall of such totalitarian states as Japan, Germany, and the once mighty Soviet Union, all of which constituted a threat to Christianity as great as that of the ancient Roman Empire, if not even greater!

5. What is meant by saying that the visible church enjoys the communion of the saints? This means that the members of the visible church receive encouragement and spiritual benefit from one another as they have fellowship with one another. It is extremely difficult to live a Christian life in isolation from other Christian people. But with friendship, encouragement, and support from other Christians, it becomes much less difficult.

6. What are "the ordinary means of salvation" which the visible church enjoys? The preaching and teaching of the Word of God; the administration of the sacraments of baptism and the Lord's Supper; church discipline; public worship; and pastoral care in the oversight of the members.

7. What is the chief responsibility of the visible church? The offer of grace by Christ in the ministry of the gospel, which offer is made continually to all members of the visible church, including children who are not yet communicant members, and also made to all adherents and other persons who attend worship services, or otherwise come under the influence of the visible church.

8. How broad is the gospel invitation which is entrusted to the visible church? It is universal; it includes all persons who can be reached with the message; it announces that whosoever believes in Christ shall be saved; it excludes none who desire to come to Christ.

9. Are home and foreign missions properly the work of the visible church, or should they be carried on by voluntary associations outside the church? Certainly home and foreign missions are properly the work of the visible church. In our day a great deal of foreign missionary work is carried on by non-church organizations. The China Inland Mission, with over a thousand missionaries, for example, is not a church but a voluntary association of Christian people. We believe this to be a wrong tendency and that private voluntary associations should not take up the work which God has committed to the church. However, under exceptional circumstances—or when the church neglects or refuses to carry on the divinely mandated missionary task—voluntary associations may rightly undertake the task temporarily.

10. What is the importance of the visible church? Beyond question it is of very great importance. There are three divine institutions in this world: the church, the state, and the family. Each of these is supremely important in its own sphere. We should support the visible church faithfully because it is a divine institution, not merely a human organization.

64. Q. *What is the invisible church?*

A. *The invisible church is the whole number of the elect, that have been, are, or shall be gathered into one under Christ the head.*

Scripture References
- Eph. 1:10, 22–23; John 10:16; 11:52. The invisible church consists of all the elect of God, including all truly saved persons of past, present, and future.
- Acts 18:9–10. Elect persons who have not yet come to Christ are part of the invisible church.
- John 17:20. Christ, in his High Priestly prayer, made intercession for those who would believe in him in the future, thus recognizing them as part of the invisible church.

Commentary

1. Why is the invisible church called this? Because we cannot see exactly who—or how many there are who—are members of it. Only God knows the full number, and their exact identity.

2. When the invisible church is completed, at the end of the age, will the number of its members be great or small? Read Revelation 7:9–10.

3. Where are the members of the invisible church at this present time? Those who have passed away are in heaven with Christ. The ones who are still living are yet in this world.

4. In addition to those in heaven and those now living in this world, what group of persons must be included in the invisible church? Those now living in this world who are not yet Christians, but will believe in Christ before they die; and also those not yet born, who in their own time will believe in Christ and receive salvation.

5. What name is sometimes given to that portion of the invisible church that is now with Christ in heaven? The church triumphant.

6. What name is sometimes given to that portion of the invisible church which is now on earth? The church militant. It is called "militant" because it is engaged in a struggle against the world, the flesh, and the devil.

7. Are Old Testament saints who died in faith, from Abel to the time of Christ, members of the invisible church? Yes. Christ has only one spiritual body, and the redeemed of all ages—both Jews and Gentiles—are members of it.

8. Is it possible for a person to be a member of the invisible church while not a member of a particular branch of the visible church? Yes: it is *possible,* but it is certainly an *irregular* condition. For example, a convict serving a prison term becomes converted while in prison. He is therefore a member of the invisible church, but it might be impossible for him to unite with a particular branch of the visible church (at least for the time being). It is the duty of every Christian, however—unless providentially prevented—to unite with a particular branch of the visible church.

9. Is it possible for a person to be a member of the visible church without being a member of the invisible church? Yes. Unfortunately it *is* possible, and the deplorable fact is that there have been many such, although only God can know infallibly who they are. Beyond question many people have had their names on church membership rolls whose names are not written in the Lamb's book of life.

10. How can we illustrate the relationship between the invisible church and the visible church? One illustration which has been suggested is the analogy of the soul and the body. A more adequate illustration is afforded by drawing a diagram with two circles which partly overlap. One circle stands for the visible church—those who profess faith in Christ. The other circle stands for the invisible church—those who are really redeemed and truly united with Christ. The part where the two circles overlap stands for those who are members of both the visible and invisible church; that is, they are included in *both* circles because they profess faith in Christ and are also truly united to him.

65. Q. *What special benefits do the members of the invisible church enjoy by Christ?*

A. *The members of the invisible church by Christ enjoy union and communion with him in grace and glory.*

Scripture References
- John 17:21; Eph. 2:5–6. The Christian's union and communion with Christ in grace.
- John 17:24. The Christian's union and communion with Christ in glory.

(**Note:** Question 65 is of the nature of a heading or summary of all the questions from 66 to 90. All these questions develop the doctrine which is summarized in 65.)

Commentary
1. Why are the benefits mentioned in this question called "special" benefits? Because they are not given to all members of the visible church, but only to such as are also true members of the invisible church.

2. What two words include all the benefits which believers receive from Christ? *Union* and *communion*. The succeeding questions (66–90) will bring out the difference in meaning between these two words.

3. In what two spheres or states of existence do believers receive benefits from Christ? In the sphere of grace, or the Christian life here on earth; and in the sphere of glory, or the life to come.

66. Q. *What is that union which the elect have with Christ?*

A. *The union which the elect have with Christ is the work of God's grace, whereby they are spiritually and mystically, yet really and inseparably, joined to Christ as their head and husband; which is done in their effectual calling.*

Scripture References

- Eph. 1:22; 2:6–8. The union which the elect have with Christ proceeds wholly from God's grace and is accomplished by his divine power.
- 1 Cor. 6:17; John 10:28. The elect are really and inseparably joined to Christ.
- Eph. 5:23, 30. Christ is the head and husband of the elect.
- 1 Peter 5:10; 1 Cor. 1:9. The elect are united to Christ by their effectual calling.

Commentary

1. What is meant by saying that the union of the elect with Christ "is the work of God's grace"? This means that union with Christ is a gift of God, which is accomplished by the almighty work of his Holy Spirit; it is not something that we can achieve or do for ourselves.

2. What is meant by saying that we are "spiritually and mystically" joined to Christ? This expression guards against the idea that we are literally joined to Christ as if he were an earthly person. The church is the body of Christ, and Christians are the members of Christ, but only in a spiritual sense, not in a physical or material sense of the word.

3. Why does the catechism add the words "yet really and insepa-rably"? Because spiritual relationships, while mysterious and invisible, are yet true and real. We naturally tend to regard that which we cannot see or understand as imaginary or unreal. Our spiritual union with Christ is both invisible and mysterious, but that does not mean that it is unreal. Spiritual things, in their own sphere, are just as real as material things. Moreover, our union with Christ is also unbreakable and permanent. The person who is once truly joined to Christ will always be joined to Christ; therefore the catechism adds the word *inseparably*.

4. What is meant by calling Christ the "head and husband" of the elect? Two figures of speech are involved, both of which are prominent in the New Testament. The first is the figure of the human body. The human body has a head, and also members, such as hands and feet. According to this figure of speech, Christ is the head, and the elect are the members of his spiritual body. The second figure is that of marriage. In this figure Christ is represented as the husband or bridegroom because he provides for, loves, and defends his church. The church, or whole body of the elect, is represented as the bride of Christ, because the church enjoys his protection, provision, and care, and seeks to honor and serve him.

5. How are the elect joined to Christ? By their effectual calling. This is explained in the next lesson.

67. Q. *What is effectual calling?*

A. *Effectual calling is the work of God's almighty power and grace, whereby (out of his free and special love to his elect, and from nothing in them moving him thereunto) he doth, in his accepted time, invite and draw them to Jesus Christ, by his word and Spirit; savingly enlightening their minds, renewing and powerfully determining their wills, so as they (although in themselves dead in sin) are hereby made willing and able freely to answer his call, and to accept and embrace the grace offered and conveyed therein.*

Scripture References

- John 5:25; Eph. 1:18–20; 2 Tim. 1:8–9. Effectual calling is wrought by the grace and almighty power of God.
- Titus 3:4–5; Eph. 2:4–9; Rom. 9:11. Effectual calling proceeds from the free, unmerited love of God to his elect, and does not depend in any sense on their character or works.
- 2 Cor. 5:20 compared with 2 Cor. 6:1–2. Those who are effectually called are united to Christ in God's accepted time.
- John 6:44. The elect are not merely invited or led, but effectively drawn, to Christ.
- 2 Thess. 2:13–14. The elect are united to Christ by the Word and Spirit of God.
- Acts 26:18; 1 Cor. 2:10–12. In effectual calling, the Holy Spirit enlightens the mind so that the person can know and accept the truth.
- Ezek. 11:19; 36:26–27; John 6:45. In effectual calling, the Holy Spirit effectively renews and determines the will so that the person wants to come to Christ.
- Eph. 2:5; Phil. 2:13; Deut. 30:6. In effectual calling, those who of themselves are dead in sin are made both willing and able to respond to the call, so that they actually receive Christ and his salvation.

Commentary

1. In what two ways does God call sinners to come to Christ? First, by the external call of the gospel message, which is addressed to all men indiscriminately. This external calling alone is not sufficient to save men, for it is often resisted and rejected by sinners. Second, by the work of the Holy Spirit in the hearts of men. This work of the Holy Spirit is called effectual calling because it always accomplishes its intended purpose of bringing the person to Christ. When the effectual calling of the Holy Spirit is added to the external call of the gospel message, the person becomes a Christian without fail.

2. Is God's work of effectual calling directed toward all men? No. If it were, all men without exception would be saved. As a matter of fact God's effectual calling is not directed toward everybody, but only toward the elect, whom God has chosen for eternal life.

3. Why does effectual calling always accomplish its intended purpose? Because it is carried out not by limited power, but by God's almighty power.

4. Does God love all men equally and in the same way? No. The Bible speaks of two kinds of divine love. First, there is a general love of God which is bestowed on all men. This general love of God conveys many blessings, but it does not bring about their eternal salvation. Second, there is a special love of God which is not given to all, but is reserved for the elect. This special love of God carries with it the eternal salvation of those on whom it is bestowed. For Scripture proof of the special love of God for the elect, read Romans 9:13, John 17:9, Jeremiah 31:3.

5. Is it not unjust for God to love some people more than others? No. If God were to deal with the human race according to justice alone, all without exception would be condemned. The subject we are considering is not a matter of justice but of mercy. Mercy does not have to be administered equally, or impartially. Since God owes his special, saving love to no one, he is free to give or withhold it as he pleases. See Romans 9:14–18, where the apostle Paul answers this same question, a question which was being asked even in his day.

6. What is meant by saying that God's love is "free"? This means that God loves men of his own free will, and not because he is under any obligation or necessity to do so.

7. What is the reason why God bestows his special, saving love on one person, and withholds it from another person? Doubtless God has a good reason for everything he does, but his reasons are not always revealed to us. We only know that whatever God's reason may be, it is not because one person's works, nature, or character are better than another's. The catechism makes this clear by adding the words "from nothing in them moving him thereunto." This expression rules out also the common error that God's special love is given to particular persons because God knew in advance that they would repent of their sins and believe the gospel. The truth is that the elect repent of their sins and believe the gospel precisely *because the special, saving love of God has been bestowed upon them.*

8. When does God draw the elect to Jesus Christ? "In his accepted time," that is, in the particular time which God has appointed for each person. In some, it may be in their childhood or youth. In some, it may even be in their infancy (see Luke 1:15). In others it may be in mature years, or in old age. In some, it may be just before death, as in the case of the dying thief. But in every case it is during the lifetime on earth of each elect person.

9. How does God invite and draw the elect to Jesus Christ? By his Word and by his Holy Spirit, working together.

10. Why must the minds of sinners be enlightened if they are to come to Christ? Because by nature their minds are darkened and clouded by sin, and therefore they are totally prejudiced against God and the gospel.

11. Why must their wills be renewed and powerfully determined if they are to come to Christ? Because by nature they are dead in sins, and their wills are stubbornly prejudiced and bent against God.

12. Does God, in his work of effectual calling, force the elect to come to Christ whether they want to or not? Certainly not. God deals with the elect as persons, not as if they were sticks or stones. The Holy Spirit so renews and changes their hearts that of their own will they want to come to Christ. If a person really wants to come to Christ with all his heart, that is an evidence that the Holy Spirit has made that person willing by changing his heart.

13. If it were not for the almighty work of the Holy Spirit changing the heart, how many of the elect would come to Christ? None at all, for by nature they are both unwilling and also unable to come.

14. What, in a word, is the difference between the external call of the gospel and the effectual calling of the Holy Spirit? In the external call of the gospel, grace is offered to sinners; in the effectual calling of the Holy Spirit, grace is actually conveyed to sinners so that they respond by accepting the offer. The external call is an offer; the effectual call is an operation.

68. Q. *Are the elect only effectually called?*

A. *All the elect, and they only, are effectually called; although others may be, and often are, outwardly called by the ministry of the word, and have some common operations of the Spirit; who, for their willful neglect and contempt of the grace offered to them, being justly left in their unbelief, do never truly come to Jesus Christ.*

Scripture References

- Acts 13:48. All the elect are effectually called, and eventually believe on Christ.
- Matt. 22:14. Although many are outwardly called by the gospel, only a part of these are effectually called by the Holy Spirit.
- Matt. 7:22; 13:20–21; Heb. 6:4–6. Those who are only outwardly called by the gospel, may and often do share in the common operations of the Spirit.
- John 12:38–40; Acts 28:25–27; John 6:64–65; Ps. 81:11–12. Those who have only the outward call of the gospel and the common operations of the Spirit, and lack the effectual call of the Spirit, inevitably neglect the grace offered to them, are justly left in their unbelief, never truly come to Christ, and so are lost.

Commentary

1. What class of people alone are effectually called by the Holy Spirit? The elect of God.

2. What other names are given in the Bible to this class of people? Christ's "sheep," those whom the Father gave unto Christ, those chosen in Christ before the foundation of the world, those whose names were written in the Lamb's book of life, those predestined to be conformed to the image of God's Son, etc.

3. In addition to the Spirit's work of effectual calling, what other kind of calling takes place? The outward calling of the ministry of the Word, that is, the gospel offer.

4. Which group is the larger, those called by the Holy Spirit, or those outwardly called by the ministry of the Word? Those outwardly called by the ministry of the Word. See Matthew 22:14: "Many are called, but few are chosen." Here the "called" are those outwardly called. The "chosen" are those effectually called by the Holy Spirit.

5. Are the operations of the Holy Spirit in human hearts limited to the elect? No. The saving operations of the Holy Spirit are confined to the elect; but in addition to the Spirit's saving operations, there are the common operations of the Spirit, which may be and often are experienced by others than the elect.

6. What is the nature of the common operations of the Spirit? The common operations of the Spirit may convict of sin, lead to an outward reformation of life of greater or lesser degree, restrain sin and evil, lead sinful people to perform acts of kindness or mercy in the human sphere, and the like. But the common operations of the Spirit fall short of salvation; they do not result in the person's being united to Christ as his Savior in repentance and true faith.

7. Why are the common operations of the Spirit insufficient for salvation? Because unless a person is born again of the Holy Spirit, a person inevitably neglects or misuses the common operations of the Spirit. Nothing short of a new birth will bring about saving faith in Christ.

8. Is it fair for God to give to some people only the common operations of the Spirit, while withholding from them the saving operations of the Holy Spirit? Salvation is a matter of grace, not of debt. God is not obliged to save anyone at all. If he chooses to save some but not all, this does not involve injustice on God's part. Since God owes salvation to nobody, he is perfectly free to bestow it as a free gift on some, while withholding it from others.

69. Q. *What is the communion in grace which the members of the invisible church have with Christ?*

A. *The communion in grace which the members of the invisible church have with Christ, is their partaking of the virtue of his mediation, in their justification, adoption, sanctification, and whatever else, in this life, manifests their union with him.*

Scripture References
- Rom. 8:30. The elect, by the experience of justification, partake of the virtue of Christ's mediation, thus having communion with Christ in grace.
- Eph. 1:5. By the experience of adoption into God's family, the elect partake of the virtue of Christ's mediation, thus having communion with Christ in grace.
- 1 Cor. 1:30. By the experience of sanctification, and other benefits received in this life, the elect partake of the virtue of Christ's mediation, thus having communion with him in grace.

(**Note:** This question is of the nature of a summary of the contents of questions 70–81. Therefore we shall consider it only briefly and then pass on to question 70.)

Commentary

1. What is the meaning of the word *virtue* in this question? It means "power" or "efficacy" in accomplishing an intended purpose.

2. What is the meaning of the word *mediation* in this question? It describes Christ's work of reconciling God and man, who were alienated one from the other by sin. Christ as Mediator brings these two together again.

3. What is the character of Christ's work of mediation? It possesses "virtue" or power to accomplish its intended purpose. Christ's work of mediation is now an accomplished, finished historical fact, although of course the application of it to particular persons is not yet completed, but continues at the present day. The power of Christ's work of mediation will continue forever.

70. Q. *What is justification?*

A. *Justification is an act of God's free grace unto sinners, in which he pardoneth all their sins, accepteth and accounteth their persons righteous in his sight; not for any thing wrought in them, or done by them, but only for the perfect obedience and full satisfaction of Christ, by God imputed to them, and received by faith alone.*

Scripture References

- Rom. 3:22–25; 4:5. Justification is an act of God's free grace unto sinners.
- 2 Cor. 5:19–21; Rom. 3:22–28. In justification, God not only pardons all of a person's sins, but also accepts that person as positively righteous in God's sight.
- Titus 3:5–7; Eph. 1:7. Justification is not based on the character or works of the person justified, nor even on the work of the Holy Spirit in his heart, but is strictly "according to his mercy" and based on Christ's righteousness and "redemption through his blood."

- Rom. 5:17–19; 4:6–8. In justification, the merit of Christ's righteousness and obedience is "imputed" or credited to the account of the person who is justified, who receives this "imputed" righteousness as a free gift of God.
- Acts 10:43; Gal. 2:16; Phil. 3:9. Faith is the means of justification, or the connecting link between the sinner and the righteousness of Christ.

Commentary

1. In what book of the Bible is the doctrine of justification by faith most fully set forth? The epistle to the Romans.

2. In what book of the Bible is the error of justification by works most clearly refuted? In the epistle to the Galatians, which shows that we are justified by faith alone, without the deeds of the law.

3. Does not the epistle of James teach that we are justified by works? Yes. But this is not a contradiction of the teaching of Romans and Galatians. James presents good works as the fruits or evidence of our justification, not as the ground or reason for our justification. We are justified by faith alone, but the kind of faith that justifies is never found alone. We are not saved on the ground of good works, but if really saved, we will not be without them as the fruits of our salvation. (See *Blue Banner Faith and Life,* vol. 1, no. 8 [October–December 1946], 177, col. 2.)

4. What is the meaning of the word *justify* in the New Testament? This is a legal term which means to declare or judicially pronounce a person to be righteous before God, according to the standard of God's moral law.

5. When a person is justified, what becomes of that person's sins? They are freely pardoned or forgiven, being canceled by Christ's atonement.

6. Why would the forgiveness of our sins not be enough to save us and give us eternal life? Because God requires more of us than that we should merely be free of sin. We not only must be without sin, but must also have a positive righteousness, just as if all our life long, without failing for one moment, we had always loved the Lord our God with all our heart, and soul, and mind, and strength, and our neighbor as ourself. If God were merely to pardon our sins, we would still be unsaved because we would lack this positive righteousness without which none can enter heaven or receive eternal life. Suppose a man is arrested and fined for driving an automobile in a reckless manner, and at the same time it is discovered that he does not possess a driver's license. A kind friend may step up and pay the fine, thus canceling that obligation. But paying the fine would not give the person the right to drive an automobile; for that he must have a positive authorization in the form of a driver's license. Similarly, for Christ by his atonement to cancel the guilt of our sins still does not give us the right to enter heaven; for that we must have a positive righteousness credited to our account.

7. In addition to forgiving our sins, what else does God do for us in justification? He accepts and accounts, or regards, our persons as righteous in his sight.

8. What is the only ground of God's act of justification? The only ground is the righteousness of Christ—his "perfect obedience and full satisfaction"—which God "imputes" or reckons to the credit of the sinner. Christ's sufferings and death on the cross cancel the guilt of our sins. The positive righteousness of Christ, by which he actively and perfectly obeyed the whole of God's law throughout his entire earthly life, is the ground or basis for God's accepting our persons as righteous in his sight. Christ not only died for us; he also lived for us a life of perfect, total, blameless obedience to the whole law of God, and without this no human being could possibly receive eternal life.

9. What two false grounds of justification does the catechism reject? (a) "Any thing wrought in them," that is, a change of character wrought in a person by the Spirit of God. Every Christian, of course, has such a change of character, but this is not the ground of his justification before God. (b) "Any thing done by them," that is, good works of any kind, such as are claimed as a ground of salvation by Catholics and others. Thus the catechism rejects, in the first place, the error of Modernism, or salvation by character; and in the second place, the error of Catholicism and all other forms of moralism, namely, salvation by human works.

10. What is the meaning of the word _imputed_ used in connection with justification? This word, which occurs again and again in the apostle Paul's discussion of this subject, means "reckoned" or "accounted." Our sins are reckoned to Christ; Christ's righteousness is reckoned to the Christian, or credited to his account.

11. What part does faith play in connection with our justification? Faith is in no sense the ground or reason for our justification. It is, however, the means or instrument by which we receive the grace of justification. We are justified by means of faith, but on account of the righteousness of Christ.

12. Why does the catechism add the word *alone* **after** *faith?* Because the Roman Catholic Church and some others teach that we are saved by a combination of faith and works. This contradicts the Scripture doctrine that the only ground of justification is the righteousness of Christ, and the only means of justification is personal faith in Jesus Christ.

71. Q. *How is justification an act of God's free grace?*

A. *Although Christ, by his obedience and death, did make a proper, real, and full satisfaction to God's justice in the behalf of them that are justified; yet in as much as God accepteth the satisfaction from a surety, which he might have demanded of them, and did provide this surety, his own only Son, imputing his righteousness to them, and requiring nothing of them for their justification but faith, which also is his gift, their justification is to them of free grace.*

Scripture References

- Rom. 5:8–10, 19. Christ rendered a true satisfaction of God's justice on behalf of those who are justified.
- 1 Tim. 2:5–6; Heb. 10:10; Matt. 20:28; Dan. 9:24–26; Isa. 53:4–6, 10–12; Heb. 7:22; Rom. 8:32; 1 Peter 1:18–19. In the case of those who are justified, God accepts the satisfaction of his divine justice at the hand of a "surety" or substitute, which he might have demanded of each justified person himself. This "surety" is God's own Son, provided as a substitute by God himself.
- 2 Cor. 5:21. Christ's righteousness imputed to the justified person.
- Rom. 3:24–25. The only condition of justification is faith in Christ.
- Eph. 2:8. Faith in Christ is itself a gift of God to the believer.
- Eph. 1:7. Redemption and forgiveness are matters of God's free grace, that is, free, unmerited gifts of God's love.

Commentary

1. What is the meaning of the expression "God's free grace"? This means God's favor bestowed as a free gift on those who are not only undeserving, but also ill-deserving.

2. Why does it seem contradictory to say that justification is an act of God's free grace? It seems contradictory to make this statement, because our justification was purchased by the payment of a price; if purchased and paid for, then how can it be at the same time a free gift? This is the problem that this question of the catechism explains.

3. How can our justification be both a purchase and also a free gift? It was purchased by Jesus Christ; it is a free gift to us. Salvation is free to sinners, but it cost the precious blood of Christ to make it free for us.

4. Why was it necessary that our justification be purchased by Christ? Because the justice of God, which had been violated by human sin, had to be satisfied if sinners were to be justified. God cannot deny himself; because he is absolutely just, he cannot disregard human sin. The sinner cannot be justified unless God's justice has first been satisfied.

5. Was it not unjust for God to take the sins of guilty human beings and lay them on the innocent Christ? This arrangement would have been unjust only if God the Father had compelled Jesus Christ against his will to bear the sins of the elect. This, however, was not the case. Christ was not compelled to suffer and die for sinners; he suffered and died for them voluntarily. Since Christ willingly suffered for our sins, there was no injustice involved in this transaction.

6. What is the meaning of the word *surety?* It means a person who acts as a guarantor or substitute, doing for us what we have failed to do for ourselves, and paying our debt to God's justice, which we could not pay ourselves.

7. Where in the New Testament is Jesus Christ called a "surety"? Hebrews 7:22.

8. How should we answer those who say that a God of love would be willing to forgive sinners without any atonement, and that a God who will not forgive sinners unless his Son is crucified is a harsh and vindictive Being? In the first place, we should remind such people that they have no right to talk about "a God of love" as if God were noth-

ing but love. The God revealed in the Bible is a God of righteousness as well
as a God of love. In the second place, such people are looking at one side of
the matter only. The same God who demanded an atonement also provided
the atonement; the same God who said, "When I see the blood I will pass
over you," also provided the Lamb for the sacrifice. When God gives what
he himself demands, he cannot be accused of being harsh or unloving.

9. What does God require of sinners for their justification? Simply
faith in Jesus Christ as their Savior. The exact meaning of this is explained
in the next question, no. 72.

**10. In addition to giving his Son to die for our sins, what else does
God provide in order that we may be saved?** The faith by which we
believe in Christ is itself a gift of God.

11. Where does the Bible teach that saving faith is a gift of God?
Ephesians 2:8 and Acts 11:18, as well as other places.

12. What do we mean by saying that "faith is a gift of God"? By
this we mean that if God had merely given his Son to die for sinners, and
then left it to men to accept or reject the offer of salvation on a "take it or
leave it" basis, the result would have been that not a single human being
would ever be saved, for all are so enslaved by the power of sin that no one
would believe on Christ. Therefore God in his mercy also changes people's
hearts by the work of his Holy Spirit, so that they become able and willing
to believe on Christ as their Savior.

**13. If faith is a gift of God, does this mean that God makes people
believe in Christ whether they want to or not?** God does not compel
any person to believe in Christ against his will. God changes a person's heart
or nature by his almighty power, with the result that that person voluntarily and gladly accepts Christ.

**14. What has been the history of the doctrine of justification by God's
free grace?** This doctrine is implied and suggested in the Old Testament,
and clearly revealed in the New Testament, especially in the epistles to the
Romans and Galatians. In Acts 15 we read of the apostolic council in
Jerusalem, where the doctrine of justification by free grace prevailed over the
false doctrine which would add works of law-observance as part of the necessary ground of justification. As the centuries passed, the doctrine of justification by free grace was practically forgotten, and its place was taken by the

Roman Catholic system of salvation by grace-plus-works. At the time of the Reformation in the early years of the sixteenth century, the glorious truth of justification by free grace was rediscovered by Martin Luther and widely proclaimed by Luther and the other Reformers. The result was the greatest revival that the church has ever known. In modern Protestantism the doctrine of justification by free grace has been largely abandoned. "Liberalism" or "Modernism" preaches a doctrine of salvation by works or salvation by character. The result is that modern "liberal" Protestantism has already lost its power and is gradually losing most of its influence in the world. Its adherents number many millions of people, but they are only mildly interested in religion.

15. What objection has been raised against the doctrine of justification by free grace? The objection has been raised that if sinners are justified as a free gift of God, regardless of their own works or character, then there remains no motive for righteous or godly living, and we might as well do as we please.

16. How can this objection be answered? First of all, we should realize that this objection is nothing new. People were raising it in the time of the apostle Paul. Romans 6:1: "Shall we continue in sin, that grace may abound?"; Romans 6:15: "Shall we sin, because we are not under the law, but under grace?" To both questions Paul replies in the negative, "God forbid." In the second place, people who raise this objection talk as if justification were the whole of salvation, as if God justified sinners and then did nothing else for them. But we may not look at justification by itself. The person who is justified is also regenerated or born again. He receives a new heart, which will seek after holiness. Gradually he is sanctified by the Holy Spirit, that is, his character is changed and made holy. Justification does not happen alone; it is a link in a chain. The person who has been justified is also in the process of being sanctified, and there are no exceptions to this rule.

17. But if we are not to do good works in order to save our soul, then what is the Christian's motive for practicing righteousness? The right motive for righteous living is devotion and thankfulness to God for creating us and redeeming us from sin as a free gift. We are to practice righteousness, not in order to be saved, but because it is our duty and because we love God.

18. Prove from the Bible that good works are the fruit and not the ground of our salvation. Ephesians 2:8–10: "For by grace are ye saved through faith; and that not of yourselves, it is the gift of God; not of works, lest any man should boast. For we are his workmanship, created in Christ Jesus unto good works, which God hath before ordained, that we should walk in them." Philippians 2:12–13: "Work out your own salvation with fear and trembling: for it is God which worketh in you both to will and to do of his good pleasure." Note that we are not commanded to work for our salvation, but rather to work it out. We receive it as a free gift, and then we are to work out the consequences of it in our lives.

19. Why have many people been bitterly opposed to the doctrine of justification by free grace? Because this doctrine humbles human pride to the dust and gives all the glory and credit for human salvation to God alone. Even faith itself is really God's gift. The result is, as Paul pointed out in Romans 3:27, that "boasting" is excluded. Sinful men would gladly give God part of the credit for salvation, and take part of the credit themselves. But the doctrine of justification by free grace gives all the credit to God alone and none whatever to the sinner. Human pride rises in stubborn rebellion against such a doctrine. Only when a person's heart has been changed by the Holy Spirit can he really accept this doctrine sincerely. Then he will have "a broken and a contrite heart" (Ps. 51:17).

20. Why is a new Reformation needed at the present day? Because in our day the doctrine of justification by free grace is all but forgotten. The majority of the large denominations, although they may have it set forth in their official creeds, as a matter of fact no longer believe or preach it in any pointed or consistent way. In many cases the Protestant churches which claim to hold it yet show but little zeal or enthusiasm for preaching it. It is not an exaggeration to say that the average Protestant church member knows little or nothing of it. Meantime the Roman Catholic Church, which strongly opposes this doctrine, is gaining ground daily.

72. Q. *What is justifying faith?*

A. *Justifying faith is a saving grace, wrought in the heart of a sinner by the Spirit and word of God, whereby he, being convinced of his sin and misery, and of the disability in himself and all other creatures to recover him out of his lost condition, not only assenteth to the truth of the promise of the gospel; but receiveth and resteth upon Christ and his righteousness, therein held forth, for pardon of sin, and for the accepting and accounting of his person righteous in the sight of God for salvation.*

Scripture References

- Heb. 10:39. Justifying faith is a saving grace.
- 2 Cor. 4:13; Eph. 1:17–19. Justifying faith is wrought in the heart of a sinner by the Holy Spirit of God.
- Rom. 10:14, 17. In producing justifying faith, the Holy Spirit uses the Word of God, that is, the gospel message.
- Acts 2:37; 16:30; John 16:8–9; Rom. 5:6; Eph. 2:1; Acts 4:12. The person in whom justifying faith has been wrought is convinced of his own inability to save himself and that none can save him except Christ.
- Eph. 1:13. Assent to the truth of the promise of the gospel is an element in justifying faith.
- John 1:12; Acts 16:31; 10:43. By justifying faith, a person receives and rests upon Christ and his righteousness as the ground of the pardon of sin.
- Phil. 3:9; Acts 15:11. By justifying faith, a person receives and rests upon Christ and his righteousness as the ground of his being accepted and accounted righteous in the sight of God, for salvation.

Commentary

1. What is meant by saying that "justifying faith is a saving grace"? This means that justifying faith brings about a person's eternal salvation. The person who has this kind of faith shall certainly be saved, and receive eternal life.

2. How does a person come to have justifying faith? Not of a person's own human willpower, but as a special gift of God.

3. How does God give a person the gift of justifying faith? He produces this faith in a person's heart by the Word of God and the work of the Holy Spirit.

4. Can either the Word or the Spirit alone produce justifying faith in a person's heart? No. Only by both together can justifying faith be produced. The Word, or gospel, message alone, without the Holy Spirit, may result in a kind of faith, but not justifying faith. Where the Word is not known, as among the heathen who have never heard the name of Christ, the Holy Spirit does not do any saving work (except perhaps in the case of infants dying in infancy, etc.).

5. When God works justifying faith in a sinner's heart, of what four facts does the sinner become convinced? (a) He becomes convinced of his sinful condition. (b) He becomes convinced of his misery. (c) He becomes convinced of his own helplessness to save himself from sin and misery. (d) He becomes convinced of the inability of anyone else except Almighty God to save him from sin and misery.

6. When God works justifying faith in a person's heart, what attitude will that person have to the promise of the gospel? He will give up his natural doubt or unbelief, and gladly recognize that the promise of the gospel is true.

7. When a person denies the truthfulness of God's Word, in whole or in part, what does this show concerning the state of that person's heart? Such unbelief ordinarily indicates that the person does not have saving faith, and is not a child of God. The only exception to this statement would be the case of a person in whose heart justifying faith has been wrought by the Holy Spirit, who yet because of weakness of intellect denies the truthfulness or authority of some portion of the Bible without realizing that this is inconsistent with justifying faith and that it dishonors God.

8. Is it enough for a person to accept the promise of the gospel as true? No. A person may accept the promise of the gospel as true and yet not be a saved Christian. We must also "receive and rest upon Christ and his righteousness," etc.

9. What is meant by "receiving and resting upon Christ and his righteousness"? First of all, this means giving up all hope of being saved in any other way than as a free gift by Christ. We must give up all claim to good works, good character, or whatever it may be that we have been putting our confidence in. Second, we must ask God to save us as a free gift for Christ's sake, because of the merit of Christ's atonement and righteousness. Third, we must count on God doing as he has promised, entrusting ourselves to Christ as our Savior, both for this present life and for eternity.

10. In addition to pardoning sin, what else does God do for the person who has justifying faith? In addition to pardoning the person's sin, God also accepts and accounts the person as righteous. It has been said that *"justified* means just-as-if-I'd," although of course this is not the derivation of the word. But it is true that *justified* means just as if I had always lived a perfect life: not merely just as if I had never committed any sins, but actually just as if I had always loved the Lord my God with all my heart, and with all my soul, and with all my mind, and with all my strength, and my neighbor as myself. Not only does Christ's shed blood take away the guilt of our sins, but the perfect, blameless, righteous life of Jesus Christ, who fulfilled the whole law of God, is "imputed" or placed to the credit of the person who has justifying faith.

11. Besides justifying faith, what other kinds of faith are there? Besides justifying faith, there are also (a) historical faith and (b) temporary faith.

12. What is "historical faith"? This is a mere belief in Jesus Christ as a historical person, just as we believe in George Washington or Abraham Lincoln. The person who has historical faith believes that Jesus Christ lived, said, and did certain things, was crucified—and he may even believe that Jesus rose from the dead and ascended into heaven. But all this is to him merely so much information. He has no personal trust in Christ as his Savior.

13. Can "historical faith" alone save us? No. We read in James 2:19 that the devils have this kind of faith. But it does not save them; it only makes them tremble with fear.

14. What is "temporary faith"? This is a kind of faith which at first resembles true saving faith, but it is only temporary and soon passes away because it has no root in a new heart. We learn of this kind of faith from the Parable of the Sower. Temporary faith often results from "revivals" where there is much excitement and people's emotions are powerfully stirred up. They profess to be "converted," but later return to their former sinful manner of living and lose interest in religion.

15. How can "temporary faith" be distinguished from true justifying faith? The only sure way to distinguish between the two is by the test of time. True faith abides and grows with the passing of time; temporary faith withers and dies. When a person's faith seems to arise largely from emotional excitement, we should realize that it may not be true saving faith, but only temporary.

73. Q. *How doth faith justify a sinner in the sight of God?*

A. *Faith justifies a sinner in the sight of God, not because of those other graces which do always accompany it, or of good works that are the fruits of it, nor as if the grace of faith, or any act thereof, were imputed to him for his justification; but only as it is an instrument by which he receiveth and applieth Christ and his righteousness.*

Scripture References

- Gal. 3:11; Rom. 3:28. Scripture places faith in contrast with "the law" and "deeds"; therefore we are not justified by those graces that accompany faith, or by the good works that are the fruits of faith.
- Rom. 4:5 compared with Rom. 10:10. Believing on Christ for justification is contrasted with working for justification; therefore faith is not a work of the believer, but rather a receiving of Christ's work; and therefore faith itself is not imputed to the believer as the ground of his justification.
- John 1:12; Phil. 3:9; Gal. 2:16. In justification, faith is simply and solely an instrument by which the believer establishes contact with the righteousness of Christ for salvation.

Commentary

1. Is faith the means of our justification, or is it the ground of our justification, or is it both? Faith is the means of our justification, but not the ground. According to the language of Scripture, we are justified by faith or through faith, but not on account of faith.

2. What is the only ground of our justification? The only ground of our justification is the atonement and righteousness of our Savior Jesus Christ. We are saved by grace, through faith, on account of the righteousness of Christ. The source of our salvation is grace, the means of our salvation is faith, and the ground of our salvation is Christ's finished work.

3. Is faith regarded in the Bible as a "good work" of the believer? No. Faith is the Christian's act of believing and trusting Christ as his Savior. But in the Bible this is not regarded as a "work"; on the contrary, it is expressly contrasted with "works," as in Ephesians 2:8–9; "For by grace are ye saved through faith: and that not of yourselves; it is the gift of God; not of works, lest any man should boast." If faith were regarded as a "work," it would leave room for the believer to boast of his faith. But salvation by faith is expressly declared to be "not of works, lest any man should boast." Therefore faith is not regarded as a "work," has no merit attached to it, and cannot be in any sense the ground of our salvation. Note, too, that the catechism, in harmony with the Bible, speaks of "good works" as the fruits of faith; therefore faith itself cannot be a good work of the believer. Rather, faith is a good work of God in the believer.

4. What error is sometimes held concerning the place of faith in our salvation? The error that salvation by faith means eternal life on lower terms than those originally announced in the covenant of works. According to this false teaching, since we as sinners do not have any adequate righteousness, God graciously lowers his requirements, and agrees to accept faith in place of righteousness. This teaching is based on a mistaken interpretation of Romans 4:3, "Abraham believed God, and it was counted unto him for righteousness," which is quoted by Paul from Genesis 15:6. This false teaching interprets this text as follows: "Abraham did not have a perfect righteousness, such as God originally required of men, but he did have faith, and so God graciously accepted faith as a substitute for righteousness." This interpretation would contradict the whole teaching of Romans and Galatians, not to mention other parts of the Bible, concerning the ground of our justification. For example, in Romans 5:12–21 there is an elaborate parallel between Adam and Christ, which teaches that Christ fulfills the covenant of works, and that Christ's righteousness is the ground of our justification. The context in Romans 4 shows that the interpretation of Romans 4:3 cited above is wrong, for in verse 2 and again in verses 4 and 5 it is plainly asserted that Abraham was not justified by works; therefore in Abraham's case faith could not have been regarded as a "work" or substitute for righteousness. By comparison with other parts of the epistle it is evident that the true meaning of Romans 4:3 is as follows: "Abraham believed God, and by means of this faith in God's promises, the perfect righteousness of Christ was imputed to him just as if it were his own personal righteousness." God never accepts anything less than perfect righteousness, but he graciously accepts Christ's righteousness in place of our own.

5. What is meant by saying that faith is "only an instrument"? This means that all the righteousness involved in our salvation and also all the power involved in our salvation are wholly of God; faith is merely a connecting link, a channel, a way of receiving God's grace.

6. What is the error of the Roman Catholic Church concerning faith? The Roman Catholic Church teaches that faith is a grace involving merit, that is to say, a form of "good works." A common Catholic catechism speaks of "faith," "hope," and "charity" as "graces or gifts of God," but adds that "Grace is necessary to salvation, because without grace we can do nothing to merit heaven." This amounts to saying that while we cannot save ourselves without help from God, yet we can save ourselves with help from God. The truth, of course, is that faith is a grace or gift of God by which we receive as a free gift, apart from any merit on our part, the heaven which Christ has merited for us.

7. What is the common error of "liberal" Protestants concerning faith? Modernism or Liberalism tends to regard faith as something valuable for its own sake, something like "morale" or "self-confidence," which keeps a person from discouragement, rather than regarding faith as a connecting link with the righteousness of Christ. Liberalism thinks of faith from the psychological point of view, and regards it as helpful and valuable because of the state of mind which it produces in a person, rather than regarding it from the theological (and scriptural) point of view as having the atonement and righteousness of Christ for its object. According to Liberalism, it is the act and attitude of believing, rather than what or in whom we believe, that is the important thing. Needless to say, this modern "liberal" idea of faith is utterly destructive not only of the doctrine of justification by free grace, but of the whole teaching of the Bible on faith and salvation; that is to say, the "liberal" idea of faith is destructive of Christianity.

74. Q. *What is adoption?*

A. *Adoption is an act of the free grace of God, in and for his only Son Jesus Christ, whereby all those that are justified are received into the number of his children, have his name put upon them, the Spirit of his Son given to them, are under his fatherly care and dispensations, admitted to all the liberties and privileges of the sons of God, made heirs of all the promises, and fellow heirs with Christ in glory.*

Scripture References

- 1 John 3:1. Adoption is an act of God's free grace, that is, an undeserved gift of God's love.
- Eph. 1:5; Gal. 4:4–5. God's act of adoption is "in and for his only Son Jesus Christ."
- John 1:12. All believers in Christ, that is, all justified persons, are also adopted into the number of God's children.
- 2 Cor. 6:18; Rev. 3:12. In adoption, the name of God is put upon the believer.
- Gal. 4:6. In connection with adoption, the Holy Spirit is given to the Christian.
- Ps. 103:13; Prov. 14:28; Matt. 6:32. Those who have been adopted as God's children are under his fatherly care and dispensations.
- Heb. 6:12; Rom. 8:17. Those who have been adopted as God's children are made heirs of all God's promises, and fellow-heirs with Christ in glory.

Commentary

1. What is the difference between justification and adoption? Justification is a change in our legal status; adoption is a change in our personal status. Justification pronounces us to be righteous in God's sight; adoption makes us God's children. Justification makes us citizens of God's kingdom; adoption makes us members of God's family. In justification, God acts as a Judge; in adoption, God acts as a Father.

2. Why is adoption referred to as "an act"? Because it takes place instantaneously at a particular time.

3. Does adoption come before or after justification? In the logical order, as presented in the catechism, justification comes first and adoption follows this. But in Christian experience these two acts of God take place at the same instant of time.

4. Can a person be justified without being adopted, or adopted without being justified? No. These two acts of God always occur together. They can be distinguished, for they differ in meaning one from the other, but they cannot be separated. The person who is justified is also at the same time adopted into the family of God. The person who is truly a child of God, in the religious sense of the term, is also a justified person.

5. Why is the doctrine of adoption often neglected or denied in the present day? Because of the prevalence of the false doctrine of the "universal Fatherhood of God." If God is the Father of everyone, then obviously everyone is already a child of God, and the doctrine of adoption does not make sense. If every person in the world is already a child of God, by nature, then there is no need for adoption into the family of God. Many Christian people fail to realize that this conception of the "universal Fatherhood of God" (in the religious sense) is a false doctrine and without support in the Bible.

6. How can we know by personal experience that we have been adopted as God's children? Galatians 4:6; Romans 8:15–16.

7. What special blessings does adoption involve? (a) A special and intimate relation to God, as his children; (b) the Holy Spirit given to us to dwell in our hearts; (c) a right to all the promises of God in the present life; (d) a title deed to eternal glory as fellow heirs with Christ.

8. How many times can a person be adopted into God's family? Like justification, adoption takes place only once in the life of a person.

9. Can we forfeit or lose our adoption into God's family? No. Once received into God's family, we are his children forever. This privilege cannot be lost.

10. Can we forfeit or lose our own feeling or consciousness that we are God's children? Yes. By falling into sin and grieving the Holy Spirit, we can lose our own assurance or consciousness that we are God's children. This matter is more fully discussed under question 81, "Are all true believers at all times assured of their present being in the estate of grace, and that they shall be saved?" Salvation cannot be lost, but our own assurance of it can be lost to a degree, and for a time. Adoption cannot be lost, but our own enjoyment of it can be forfeited for a time.

11. What special duty does our adoption into God's family impose on us? The duty of living as sons and daughters of the living God. See 2 Corinthians 6:14–18.

75. Q. *What is sanctification?*

A. *Sanctification is a work of God's grace, whereby they whom God hath, before the foundation of the world, chosen to be holy, are in time, through the powerful operation of his Spirit applying the death and resurrection of Christ unto them, renewed in their whole man after the image of God; having the seeds of repentance unto life, and all other saving graces, put into their hearts, and those graces so stirred up, increased, and strengthened, as that they more and more die unto sin, and rise unto newness of life.*

Scripture References

- Eph. 1:4; 1 Cor. 6:11–12; 1 Thess. 2:13. Those whom God from eternity has chosen to be holy are in time sanctified by the powerful operation of his Holy Spirit.
- Rom. 6:4–6. The Holy Spirit applies the death and resurrection of Christ to the believer, that he may be sanctified.
- Eph. 4:23–24. Sanctification involves renewal of the whole man after the image of God.
- Acts 11:18; 1 John 3:9. In sanctification, the "seeds" or roots of repentance and all other saving graces are planted in the believer's heart.
- Jude 20; Heb. 6:11–12; Eph. 3:16–19; Col. 1:10–11. In sanctification, the graces which have been planted in the believer's heart are stirred up, increased, and strengthened.
- Rom. 6:4, 6, 14; Gal. 5:24. Sanctification results in the believer more and more dying unto sin, and living unto righteousness.

Commentary

1. Why is sanctification called a work of God's free grace instead of an act of God's free grace? Because, unlike justification and adoption, sanctification is not an act, but a process. Justification and adoption are instantaneous acts, completed once for all in an instant of time, but sanctification is a lifelong process starting the moment the person is regenerated, and continuing until the moment of death when the soul enters the state of glory.

2. Who will be sanctified? The elect, whom God has chosen from before the creation of the world to be holy, and they only.

3. What is the meaning of the word *sanctify*? It means to make holy.

4. What two kinds of sanctification does the New Testament speak of? (a) It speaks of what may be called a sanctification of position or external privileges. This kind of sanctification is mentioned in 1 Corinthians 7:14. It involves certain spiritual blessings and privileges, but does not necessarily involve the eternal salvation of the person who is thus "sanctified." (b) It speaks of personal sanctification, or the sanctification of a changed and godly character. This personal sanctification is mentioned in 1 Corinthians 6:11. The person who is sanctified in this way is a saved person and heir of eternal life.

5. Which of these two kinds of sanctification is discussed in the question we are studying in the Larger Catechism? The second, or personal sanctification of life and character.

6. What power is involved in the work of sanctification? The almighty power of God the Holy Spirit.

7. What is meant by saying that the Holy Spirit applies the death and resurrection of Christ to those who are being sanctified? This means that those benefits which Christ purchased for the elect by his sufferings and death, and which are guaranteed by his resurrection, are actually bestowed on the Christian by the work of the Holy Spirit. God the Father planned our redemption; God the Son purchased our redemption; God the Holy Spirit applies our redemption so that we actually experience the benefit of it.

8. What is meant by saying that those who are sanctified are "renewed in their whole man"? This means, first of all, that sanctification involves both the body and the soul, as is shown by 1 Thessalonians 5:23. Second, sanctification is not limited to any one function or part of the soul's life, but includes all. It involves the mind, or intellect; the emotions, or feelings; and the will, or power of decision.

9. What is the pattern or ideal according to which the Holy Spirit carries on his work of sanctification? The pattern is "the image of God." Man was created in the image of God, but by his fall into sin, the image of God in man was broken and marred. However, it was not entirely destroyed; the broken fragments of it remain in every human being in the world. By sanctification, the image of God in man is restored. This image of God consists chiefly of knowledge, righteousness, and holiness.

10. What figure of speech does the catechism, following the New Testament, use to describe the process of sanctification? The figure of death and resurrection, or dying unto sin and rising unto newness of life.

11. What lessons concerning the Christian life can we learn from this figure? First, we can learn that we may not tolerate the least sin in our life. We are to die unto sin, to crucify sin. Second, we can learn that our progress in holiness is not something that we can achieve of ourselves; as the dead have no power to raise themselves, so our rising to newness of life depends upon the power of God.

12. What two errors concerning sanctification are common today? (a) The error called antinomianism, which is a denial that the Christian is under obligation to observe the moral law of God. This error of course makes sanctification unnecessary. (b) The error called perfectionism, also called "total sanctification" and "sinless perfection," which teaches that sanctification is not a process but an act which may be completed at a definite time during the course of the present life, after which the person is "totally sanctified."

(**Note:** The question of perfectionism, or "total sanctification," will be further discussed under question 78, "Whence ariseth the imperfection of sanctification in believers?")

13. What attitude should we have toward the matter of sanctification? We should not only seek to understand clearly the Bible doctrine of sanctification, but also seek the reality and power of it in our personal experience.

76. Q. *What is repentance unto life?*

A. *Repentance unto life is a saving grace, wrought in the heart of a sinner by the Spirit and word of God, whereby out of the sight and sense, not only of the danger, but also of the filthiness and odiousness of his sins, and upon the apprehension of God's mercy in Christ to such as are penitent, he so grieves for and hates his sins, as that he turns from them all to God, purposing and endeavoring constantly to walk with him in all the ways of new obedience.*

Scripture References

- 2 Tim. 2:25. Repentance unto life is a saving grace or gift of God.
- Zech. 12:10; Acts 11:18–21. Repentance unto life is wrought in the heart of a sinner by the Holy Spirit and the Word of God.
- Ezek. 18:28–32; Luke 15:17–18; Hos. 2:6–7. In true repentance the sinner is thoroughly aware of the danger of his sins.
- Ezek. 36:31; Isa. 30:22. The sinner who is truly repentant is aware not merely of the danger, but also of the filthiness and odiousness of his sins.
- Joel 2:12–13. In true repentance there is always an apprehension of God's forgiving mercy in Christ to such as are penitent.
- Jer. 31:18–19. The person who is truly repentant has a deep sorrow for sin.
- 2 Cor. 7:11. The person who is truly repentant actually hates his sins.
- Acts 26:18; Ezek. 14:6; 1 Kings 8:47–48. True repentance involves turning from all one's sins unto God.
- Ps. 119:6, 59, 128; Luke 1:6; 2 Kings 23:25. Genuine repentance involves a sincere purpose of new obedience to the will of God.

Commentary

1. Why does the catechism speak of "repentance unto life" instead of speaking simply of "repentance"? Because there is another kind of repentance which is not unto life. We read that Judas "repented himself . . . and hanged himself" (Matt. 27:3–5). This false repentance is also called "the sorrow of the world" (2 Cor. 7:10), in contrast to true repentance or "godly sorrow." There we read that "the sorrow of the world worketh death"; that is to say, it is not "repentance unto life," but "repentance unto death," for the outcome of it is not eternal life but eternal death.

2. Why is repentance unto life called "a saving grace"? It is called "saving" because its outcome is salvation or eternal life; it is called a "grace" because it is something we receive as a gift from God, not something we have naturally of ourselves.

3. According to the teaching of the Bible, who needs to repent? Everyone without exception needs to repent. We should note that the commands to repent in the Bible are universal. John the Baptist and Jesus, for example, in their preaching, said, "Repent ye," without distinguishing between good and bad, religious and indifferent, ignorant and educated, etc. They did not say, "Repent, those of you who have done something that needs to be repented of," nor "Repent, those of you who are sinners," but simply and without qualification, "Repent ye."

4. How is repentance unto life wrought in the heart of a sinner? By the Spirit and the Word of God. Here the term *Word of God* of course means not only the Bible, but the message of saving truth contained in the Bible, that is, the gospel of Jesus Christ, regardless of whether it is read, preached, or proclaimed in some other way. Repentance unto life is not wrought by the Spirit alone without the Word, nor by the Word alone without the Spirit, but by the two together, the Holy Spirit using and applying the truth of the Word. This implies that where the gospel has not been proclaimed, the Holy Spirit does not work in such a way as to bring about people's salvation. He works where the Word has been proclaimed and is known.

5. Is it enough for a person to realize the danger of his sins? No. Fear of God's punishment plays a part, certainly, in bringing people to Christ for salvation, but fear of punishment alone is not enough. The person who is a Christian only because of fear of hell is not really a Christian at all. We must be sorry for our sins, not only for the sufferings and misery that they bring on us. We must turn from sin because sin is wrong, not merely because it is dangerous.

6. In addition to the danger of our sins, what must we realize concerning our sins? We must realize the "filthiness and odiousness" of our sins; that is to say, we must realize that our sins are utterly contrary to the holiness and character of God, and are therefore unclean and to be hated.

7. Why must we also have an apprehension of God's mercy in Christ? Without an apprehension of God's mercy in Christ, repentance would not lead to salvation but to despair, for while realizing that our sins deserve God's wrath and curse for all eternity, we would yet see no way of deliverance from them. It is only when accompanied by faith in Christ as Savior that repentance is a Christian experience. It is reported that a Hindu society in New York City took the Westminster Shorter Catechism definition of "repentance unto life" and changed it to fit their Hindu religion, by omitting the words "and apprehension of the mercy of God in Christ." By this omission, they eliminated everything that is distinctively Christian from the definition. The result was as follows: "Repentance unto life is a saving grace, whereby a sinner, out of a true sense of his sin, doth, with grief and hatred of his sin, turn from it unto God, with full purpose of, and endeavor

after, new obedience." This satisfied the Hindu Society, which shows that
there is no Christianity in it.

8. Is it necessary for a Christian to have deep sorrow for sin? Certainly it is necessary. Sin is not a trifle, nor a slight evil. It is absolutely evil, so that any sin, even the least, deserves God's wrath and curse to all eternity. Even the least sin is a total contradiction of God's holiness. Therefore the Christian, throughout life, must always have deep sorrow for sin.

9. Is repentance an act, a process, or an attitude? Looked at on its human side, repentance is an attitude of heart and mind with respect to God, self, and sin. But repentance unto life is more than an attitude. It is an attitude which results in action, the constant serious effort to live a righteous life.

10. Should we repent once for all when we come to believe on Christ, or should we continue to repent day by day? The crisis of conversion when a person first believes in Christ and turns to God ought to be preeminently a time of repentance. But repentance is not something that can be done once for all. We must continue to have the attitude of repentance day by day throughout our life in this world.

11. How can we test the genuineness of our repentance? It is not safe to rely wholly on our feelings, for they are very deceptive. The only sure test of any religious experience is its fruits. If our repentance leads to "purposing and endeavoring" to live a new and better life, we may believe that it is genuine Christian repentance, or "repentance unto life."

12. Why is there so little true repentance in the present day? There may be several reasons for this condition, but certainly one of the main reasons is that during recent years there has been relatively little preaching of the law of God, the holiness of God, and the wrath of God against human sin. Instead of stressing these subjects, modern Protestantism has shifted its emphasis and proclaims a God who is nothing but love, and who is represented as too kindhearted to punish anyone forever. Sin is represented as an evil, but not a great enough evil to alienate man from God and bring him under the wrath and curse of God. It is no wonder that this shift of emphasis, and these corruptions of the truth, have resulted in the present state of affairs. The unbalanced modern emphasis on the love of God has produced an attitude of complacency and self-righteousness in modern Protestantism. Scripture teaches that Christ came to call, not the righteous, but sinners, to repentance. Those who consider themselves righteous will of course feel no need of repentance. Only by a general return to the whole truth about God and his law can the ground be laid for a real revival of Christian faith and experience.

13. How can it be proved from the Bible that repentance is a gift of God, and not simply an achievement of our human free will? There are texts which speak of repentance as a gift of God, such as Acts 11:18 and 2 Timothy 2:25. Also there are texts which teach the same truth by speaking of repentance as a work of God, such as Jeremiah 31:18–19 and Zechariah 12:10.

14. Can repentance take away the guilt of our sins? No. The guilt of our sins is canceled only by the blood of our Savior Jesus Christ.

15. If repentance cannot cancel our sins, then why must we repent? Christ came to this world, not simply to save us, but to save us from sin. He came not simply to give us eternal life, but to give us eternal righteousness. We cannot accept a part of what Christ offers; we must take all or nothing. If we do not want righteousness, then we cannot have eternal life either. We cannot be saved without being saved from sin. The person who does not repent is the person who wants to hold on to sin. This state of mind is contrary to accepting Christ as our Savior from sin. We cannot have our sins and also have salvation from our sins at the same time, any more than a person could be saved from fire while deliberately remaining in a burning building.

77. Q. *Wherein do justification and sanctification differ?*

A. *Although sanctification be inseparably joined with justification, yet they differ, in that God in justification imputeth the righteousness of Christ; in sanctification his Spirit infuseth grace, and enableth to the exercise thereof; in the former, sin is pardoned; in the other, it is subdued: the one doth equally free all believers from the revenging wrath of God, and that perfectly in this life, that they never fall into condemnation; the other is neither equal in all, nor in this life perfect in any, but growing up to perfection.*

Scripture References

- 1 Cor. 6:11; 1:30. Justification and sanctification are inseparably joined together.
- Rom. 4:6, 8. In justification, God imputes to the sinner the righteousness of Christ.
- Ezek. 36:27. In sanctification, God infuses grace, and enables the Christian to exercise it.
- Rom. 3:24–25. In justification, sin is pardoned.
- Rom. 6:6, 14. In sanctification, sin is subdued.
- Rom. 8:33–34. Justification frees all believers equally, and perfectly in this life, from the wrath of God.
- 1 John 2:12–14; Heb. 5:12–14. Sanctification is not equal in all Christians, but varies according to the progress they have made.
- 1 John 1:8, 10. Sanctification is not perfect in any Christian in this life.
- 2 Cor. 7:1; Phil. 3:12–14. Sanctification is a gradual process which approaches, but does not in this life actually attain, the ideal of moral perfection.

(**Note:** This question of the catechism being a contrast between the two doctrines of justification and sanctification, the following table of resemblances and contrasted points may be helpful in understanding this matter.)

Points in Which Justification and Sanctification Are the Same

1. They are inseparably joined together; there is no justification without sanctification, and no sanctification without justification. The person who has one has the other also.
2. God is the Author and source of both justification and sanctification.
3. Both justification and sanctification proceed from God's grace, or special love and favor to sinners.

Points in Which Justification and Sanctification Differ

Justification is:

1. An act of God's free grace.
2. An act by which God imputes Christ's righteousness.
3. An act in which God pardons sin.
4. Total and equal in all cases.
5. Complete and perfect in this life.
6. A judicial verdict which frees from condemnation and awards eternal life.

Sanctification is:

1. A work of God's free grace.
2. A work by which God infuses grace and power.
3. A work in which God subdues sin.
4. Different in degree in different persons.
5. Incomplete and imperfect in this life.
6. A divinely planted and watered spiritual growth of Christian character.

Commentary

1. What is meant by saying that sanctification is inseparably joined with justification? This means that though these two elements of salvation can be distinguished, they cannot be separated. There is no such thing as justification without sanctification, or sanctification without justification. The person who has been justified is, without exception, being sanctified, and vice versa.

2. Prove from the Bible that justification and sanctification are inseparable. 1 Corinthians 1:30: "But of him are ye in Christ Jesus, who of God is made unto us wisdom, and righteousness, and sanctification, and redemption." Here righteousness (which is the same thing as justification) is linked together with sanctification, and we are told that Christ Jesus is made unto us both righteousness and sanctification. Therefore the person who has Christ has both justification and sanctification. Romans 6:22: "But now being made free from sin, and become servants of God, ye have your fruit unto holiness, and the end everlasting life." Here "being made free from sin," that is, justification, is closely connected with "bringing forth fruit unto holiness," that is, sanctification.

3. What attempts have been made to separate justification and sanctification? (a) People of the Pentecostal persuasion hold that justification is not necessarily accompanied and followed by sanctification. They tend to divide Christians into two classes, namely: (1) those who have only been justified; and (2) those who have been both justified and also sanctified. Those who hold this view also tend to regard sanctification as an act which may be complete in this life.

This same general tendency is manifested by those who attempt to classify Christians into: (1) those who have received the Holy Spirit; and (2) those who are "saved" but have not yet received the Holy Spirit. (See Rom. 8:9:

"Now if any man have not the Spirit of Christ, he is none of his".) (b) Modern "Liberalism" has given up the doctrine of justification by free grace, but seeks to cultivate sanctification apart from justification. Thus the modern liberal preachers no longer believe in or proclaim the truth of justification by the free grace of God, but they never weary of preaching about "character building" and similar subjects. This error is vastly more serious than that of the Pentecostal believers mentioned above. They say that a person may have the foundation of justification without having the house of sanctification built upon it. But the modern liberal preachers say, in effect, that a person may have a wonderful house of sanctification without any real foundation at all underneath it; that is, without any foundation except ordinary, unregenerate human nature.

4. What is the difference in meaning between the terms *impute* and *infuse*? To *impute* is a legal term; it means to reckon something, or charge something to the account of a person. To impute Christ's righteousness to a person means to place Christ's righteousness to the credit of that person. Imputation is a transfer of righteousness or guilt, credit or debit, in God's record books. The term *infuse,* on the other hand, means to pour in: it refers not to a transaction in the record books of God in heaven, but to something that God does in the heart and soul of a person here on earth. It describes, not a change of legal status, but a change of personal character. God imputes to us the righteousness of Christ, but infuses grace and power into our hearts so that we can cultivate our own righteousness. The perfect righteousness of Christ is imputed to the believer while he is still here in this world; but in heavenly glory he shall also be clothed with the perfected righteousness of saints, that is, the personal righteousness of character which is the product of sanctification (see Rev. 19:8).

5. Why did not God provide that sanctification be equal in all believers in this present life? Because God is almighty, of course he could have made sanctification equal in all believers in this present life, but as a matter of fact he did not choose to do so. We are not told why in the Bible. We can only say that God in his sovereignty has done as seemed good in his sight (see Matt. 11:26). We cannot call God to account for his plans and decisions. To do so is a contradiction of the religious relationship between man and God.

6. Why is the distinction between justification and sanctification important for us in our Christian life? This distinction is extremely important for the Christian life, because there is always some tendency to confuse these two things. The person who thinks that justification includes all the sanctification he needs, so that he need not seek personal holiness of character and life, stands in peril because he is not truly justified. On the other hand, the person who thinks that sanctification includes all the justification he needs stands in peril because he is trying to save himself by good works. Thus the distinction between justification and sanctification is extremely important for avoiding the two extremes of antinomianism and legalism. The true believer will avoid both of these extremes, and will realize that justification is the foundation of his salvation, while sanctification is the fruit of his salvation. We should hold and teach the whole Bible truth about both of these great doctrines, noting carefully their similarities and differences, and the relation between the two.

7. Is the difference between justification and sanctification merely a matter of theory or abstract doctrine, or "theological hair-splitting"?
On the contrary, this is a matter of vital importance for the practical life of every Christian. No sincere Christian will regard such matters as mere theories or abstractions. Every true Christian will realize that this distinction is vitally important, and that justification and sanctification are as necessary for the salvation of his soul as air, food, and water are for the life and health of his body.

78. Q. *Whence ariseth the imperfection of sanctification in believers?*

A. *The imperfection of sanctification in believers ariseth from the remnants of sin abiding in every part of them, and the perpetual lustings of the flesh against the spirit; whereby they are often foiled with temptations, and fall into many sins, are hindered in all their spiritual services, and their best works are imperfect and defiled in the sight of God.*

Scripture References

- Rom. 7:18–23; Mark 14:66–72; Gal. 2:11–12. By reason of the sinful corruption of nature, which remains even in believers, they are faced with many temptations and fall into many sins.

- Heb. 12:1. The Christian is hindered in all spiritual exercises by the remnants of sin in his nature.
- Isa. 64:6; Exod. 28:38. Even the Christian's best works are imperfect and defiled by sin in the sight of God.
- 1 John 1:8; James 3:2; 5:16; Phil. 3:12–14; Prov. 24:9; Eccl. 7:20. The imperfection of sanctification in believers is a fact recognized in Scripture.

Commentary

1. If it is true that the Christian has received salvation, then how can the catechism speak about "the imperfection of sanctification in believers"? The term *salvation* in the Bible and in Christian doctrine is not always used in the same sense. It is a complex idea and includes several elements. Sometimes one of these is referred to, and sometimes another. We commonly say that a Christian is a saved person, which is quite true, of course, if rightly understood. But if we wish to speak with precise accuracy, we must say that a Christian is a person who has been saved in one sense, is being saved in another sense, and shall be saved in still another sense. He has been saved from the guilt of sin, is being saved from the power of sin, and shall be saved from the presence of sin. The Christian has received justification, is receiving sanctification, and shall receive glorification. We receive salvation in installments, not all at one time. As the Christian's sanctification is a process which continues throughout his earthly life, it necessarily remains imperfect during this present life.

2. Is our sanctification imperfect because of something outside of us, or because of something inside of us? Our sanctification is imperfect because of something inside of us, namely, the sinful nature which remains with us even after we are born again. It is very common indeed for Christians to blame their sins and failures on something outside of themselves, such as the sinful world, the devil, adverse circumstances, and so forth. But the truth is that our own sinful nature is the real cause of the imperfection of our sanctification.

3. But do not external factors such as the world and the devil lead Christians into sinful compromise with evil? External factors, such as the world, the devil, evil companions, intoxicating liquor, and the like, may be the occasions of our compromising with evil. These external factors take advantage of our sinful nature, and we are seduced into committing actual transgressions. But these external things of themselves could have no power to seduce us into sin if it were not for the sinful nature remaining in us. All these external temptations were faced by our Savior Jesus Christ, yet he never committed the least sin. In his case there was no sinful nature to which the external occasions of temptation could present a powerful appeal. We should guard against the prevalent error of loudly denouncing the world and the devil while saying little or nothing about the sinful corruption of nature which remains in every Christian in the world. Merely condemning the sins of the world will not make Christian people holy or Christlike. More than this is needed. The sin in each person's own heart must be mortified or crucified. When this is done the world and the devil will find much less to appeal to in the Christian's heart.

4. What are some of the names used in the Bible to designate the sinful nature which remains in those who are born again? "The old man" (Rom. 6:6); "the flesh" (Rom. 7:18); "the law of sin which is in my members" (Rom. 7:23); "the stony heart" (Ezek. 36:26); "sin that dwelleth in me" (Rom. 7:17); "the body of this death" (Rom. 7:24).

5. What is the meaning of the word *flesh* in the Bible? This is one of the hardest terms in the Bible to understand, because it is used with at least three different meanings, which are as follows: (a) The term is used in the purely physical sense, as in the expression "flesh and blood." In this sense "flesh" is a certain part of the human body. (b) "Flesh" is also used to mean man in his human weakness, as, for example, in the verse, "All flesh is grass, and all the goodliness thereof is as the flower of the field." (c) The term *flesh* is used to mean the sinful nature of fallen man, which remains even in the Christian, as in the verse, "In me, that is, in my flesh, dwelleth no good thing." We should guard against the extremely common error that the word *flesh* means a part of our human nature. It does not refer to a "lower" nature; it refers to our whole nature as corrupted by sin.

6. What is the most common error in understanding those Bible passages which speak of "the flesh" as something evil? Undoubtedly the most common error in dealing with these passages is to regard "the flesh" as meaning simply the human body. In reality, of course, "the flesh" includes the whole nature of man which has been corrupted by sin, which the catechism recognizes by speaking of "sin abiding in every part of them." Primarily, sin is not a matter of the body but of the soul or spirit, but it involves the whole of our human nature. There is nothing human that has not been corrupted and defiled by our fall into sin.

7. According to the Bible, which is characteristic of the Christian life, peace or conflict? According to the Bible, the Christian life is both a life of peace and a life of conflict. It is a life of peace with God and of conflict with sin. The unsaved person is at war with God and at peace with sin. The Christian is at peace with God and at war with sin.

8. If a person experiences no conflict with sin, what does this indicate concerning his religious experience? A person who experiences no real conflict with sin is in all probability an unsaved sinner, dead in trespasses and sins. A person who experiences but little conflict with sin should examine himself to discover whether he has not grieved the Holy Spirit and so fallen into a condition of spiritual sluggishness and slumber. Such a Christian should heed the warning of Romans 13:11: "It is high time to awake out of sleep; for now is our salvation nearer than when we believed."

9. Should a Christian become discouraged because he has to fight a hard battle against sin? No. While our human weakness naturally leads us to become discouraged by prolonged conflict, it is a fact that a hard battle against sin is a good sign. It shows that we are on the right track, traveling the real highway to heaven, and are experiencing exactly what all of God's saints, even the best and holiest, have had to go through. Instead of becoming discouraged by conflict with sin, we should rather be suspicious and even alarmed if we find that we have little or no conflict with sin.

10. Why is it that prayer and other spiritual duties are often so extremely difficult, even for earnest and faithful Christians? This is undoubtedly a fact of Christian experience, as well as a teaching of God's Word. The reason is that our sinful nature which remains with us fights desperately against those spiritual exercises which tend toward crucifying "the flesh." "For the flesh lusteth against the Spirit, and the Spirit against the flesh: and these are contrary the one to the other; so that ye cannot do the things that ye would" (Gal. 5:17). As the catechism points out, it is true that believers "are hindered in all their spiritual services."

11. What should we think of those evangelists and preachers who represent the Christian life as entirely joyful, pleasant, and easy? Those who speak so have not yet come to grips with the real evil of their own hearts.

12. What is the real character of even the best of our "good works" in God's sight? Even the best of our works are imperfect and defiled in the sight of God, because of the sin remaining in the heart and life of all of us.

13. What great Scripture passage deals with the Christian's warfare against sin? Ephesians 6:10–18, which commands us to "put on the whole armor of God."

14. What part of the "whole armor of God" is the most important of all? "Above all, taking the shield of faith, wherewith ye shall be able to quench all the fiery darts of the wicked (one)" (Eph. 6:16).

79. Q. *May not true believers, by reason of their imperfections, and the many temptations and sins they are overtaken with, fall away from the state of grace?*

A. *True believers, by reason of the unchangeable love of God, and his decree and covenant to give them perseverance, their inseparable union with Christ, his continual intercession for them, and the Spirit and seed of God abiding in them, can neither totally nor finally fall away from the state of grace, but are kept by the power of God through faith unto salvation.*

Scripture References

- Jer. 31:3. The unchangeable love of God for his own.
- 2 Tim. 2:19; Heb. 13:20–21; 2 Sam. 23:5. God's decree and covenant to give his people the grace of perseverance.
- 1 Cor. 1:8–9. The believer's inseparable union with Christ.
- Heb. 7:25; Luke 22:32. Christ's intercession for his own.
- 1 John 3:9; 2:27. The Spirit and seed of God abiding in the Christian.
- Jer. 32:40; John 10:28. The true believer can neither totally nor finally fall away from the state of grace.
- 1 Peter 1:5. The true believer is kept by the power of God through faith unto salvation.

Commentary

1. What class of people does the answer to this question of the catechism discuss? True believers, that is, those who are truly born again, justified, adopted into the family of God, and in the process of being sanctified.

2. What class of people does this answer not discuss? The class commonly called hypocrites, including all who make a profession of Christianity but are not really born again. Some of these may be mere pretenders; others may be self-deceived, thinking they are born again when they really are not; others may know nothing about being born again, but assume that they can be saved by their good works or character. None of these are under discussion in the answer to question 79.

3. Can true believers fall away from the state of grace? No. That is, they cannot totally and finally fall away from the state of grace.

4. Prove from the Bible that true believers cannot totally and finally fall away from the state of grace. John 10:28; Romans 8:35–39, which lists sixteen things which cannot separate the believer from the love of God which is in Christ Jesus our Lord, and then adds "nor any other creature." Those who hold that true believers can fall away from the state of grace and be eternally lost reply that none of the things listed here by the apostle Paul can separate the believer from God's love, but the believer's own free will can do it. By this claim they hold that human free will is not a created thing, for after listing these things the apostle adds "nor any other creature." But we conclude that the believer's free will—being a creature—cannot separate the believer from the saving love of God.

5. What does the catechism imply by the words "neither totally nor finally"? These words imply that true believers may partially and temporarily fall away from the state of grace. As a matter of fact, this partial and temporary falling away is taught in the Bible as a possibility, and it can be observed among Christian people in our own day.

6. Does the fact that true believers cannot perish depend on their own willpower, earnestness, or faithfulness? No. If our eternal salvation depended on ourselves, none of us would be saved.

7. If our eternal security does not depend on our own efforts, then what does it depend on? It depends on the love and power of God.

8. How does the catechism summarize the Bible proofs that true believers cannot perish? The catechism lists five reasons from Scripture, which are as follows: (a) The unchangeable love of God. (b) God's decree and covenant to give them perseverance. (c) Their inseparable union with Christ. (d) Christ's continual intercession for them. (e) The Spirit and seed of God abiding in them.

9. Prove from the Bible that God's love for the elect is eternal and therefore unchangeable. Jeremiah 31:3 speaks of God's loving his people with an everlasting love. If this love is changeable, then it is not really everlasting. If it is really everlasting, then it is unchangeable.

10. What is the nature of God's love for his elect? God's love for his elect is not merely a general love that wishes and hopes for their welfare, but a special, particular love that actually goes into action and infallibly provides for their eternal fellowship with God himself.

11. Give two texts of Scripture which prove that God has promised to keep his elect from falling away from the state of grace. Psalm 138:8 and its New Testament counterpart, Philippians 1:6.

12. Show from Scripture that the believer's union with Christ is an inseparable union, and therefore an eternal union. Romans 8:35–39; Psalms 23:6; 73:24; John 17:24.

13. Give a text from the Gospels and one from the Epistles showing Christ's intercession for his people. John 17:9; Hebrews 7:25.

14. Will Christ ever stop making intercession for his people? No. His intercession will continue until the last of the elect enters the state of eternal glory, for we read in Hebrews 7:25 that "he ever liveth to make intercession for them."

15. How do we know that Christ's intercession for his people will be effective? God the Father will always grant the requests of Jesus Christ, for he is the Father's beloved Son in whom he is well pleased (Matt. 3:17) and everything that he does is always pleasing to the Father (John 8:29).

16. How does the abiding of the Spirit of God in believers prove that they cannot fall away from the state of grace? The Holy Spirit cannot dwell in the heart of an unsaved person (John 14:17), but he dwells in the heart of every believer (John 14:17; Rom. 8:9). Jesus promised that the Holy Spirit would abide forever (John 14:16). If it were possible for a believer to fall away from the state of grace, that would mean that a saved person would become unsaved again. Then the Holy Spirit would have to leave that person, for he cannot dwell in an unsaved person. But Jesus promised that the Holy Spirit would come to believers to abide forever. Therefore the Spirit cannot depart from a true believer's heart; therefore a true believer cannot lose his salvation and become unsaved again.

17. What is meant by the "seed of God" abiding in believers? The "seed of God" means the new, holy nature created in the heart of a person when he is born again by the power of the Holy Spirit.

18. How does the abiding of this new nature or "seed of God" in believers show that they cannot fall away from the state of grace? 1 Peter 1:23: "Being born again, not of corruptible seed, but of incorruptible, by the word of God, which liveth and abideth forever." Here the new nature, or "seed of God," which the Christian receives when he is born again, is affirmed to be incorruptible. If it is incorruptible, then it cannot perish and die, but will live and grow forever. But if it were possible for a believer totally to fall away from the state of grace, then it would be possible for the "seed of God" in that person's heart to perish and die. In that case, the "seed of God" would not be incorruptible, but corruptible. But God's Word plainly says that the "seed of God" in the believer is incorruptible. Therefore the "seed of God" abiding in the believer guarantees that the believer cannot totally fall away from the state of grace and be lost.

19. Should this doctrine of the perseverance of the saints, or the eternal security of the believer in Christ, lead us to indifference or careless living in our Christian life? It has often been made a criticism of this doctrine that it takes away all motive for seeking holiness. This criticism is based on the false notion that Christians seek holiness only because of the fear of hell. Really this criticism is quite without foundation. Christians who believe in this doctrine are just as earnest, faithful, and careful in their Christian life as other Christians who do not accept this doctrine. The truth is that this doctrine, rightly understood, should be, and is, a powerful incentive to patient and faithful Christian service. The Christian who is filled day and night with fears and worries lest he may fall away from the state of grace and perish eternally cannot render the best service to God, because his mind is distracted by his fears. The believer whose mind has been set at rest by the clear teaching of God's Word on this subject will be the better able to devote his life to seeking the kingdom of God and his righteousness. Just as in ordinary human life, so it is true in the spiritual life of the Christian, that security is necessary for normal progress and activity.

80. Q. *Can true believers be infallibly assured that they are in the estate of grace, and that they shall persevere therein unto salvation?*

A. *Such as truly believe in Christ, and endeavor to walk in all good conscience before him, may, without extraordinary revelation, by faith grounded upon the truth of God's promises, and by the Spirit enabling them to discern in themselves those graces to which the promises of life are made, and bearing witness with their spirits that they are the children of God, be infallibly assured that they are in the estate of grace, and shall persevere therein unto salvation.*

Scripture References

- 1 John 2:3. A conscientious endeavor to keep God's commandments is necessary for the attainment of assurance.
- 1 Cor. 2:12; 1 John 3:14, 18, 21, 24; 4:13, 16; Heb. 6:11–12. The attainment of assurance is possible, and depends upon the truth of God's promises and upon the believer's being enabled by the Holy Spirit to discern in himself the graces to which the promises are made.
- Rom. 8:15–16; 1 John 5:10. The testimony of the Holy Spirit in the believer's soul is a factor in the attainment of assurance.
- 1 John 5:13. Full assurance includes assurance of final perseverance unto eternal life.

Commentary

1. What is meant by "assurance of salvation"? By "assurance of salvation" is meant a conviction in the mind of a Christian of the absolute certainty of his present and eternal salvation. Our hearts crave not merely possibility or probability, but full assurance or certainty of our own salvation. The Christian who has full assurance has a conviction of absolute, infallible certainty concerning his own eternal salvation.

2. Do all Christians believe that full assurance is possible? No. Roman Catholics and some Protestants deny the possibility of absolute assurance of salvation. They assert that we can never know, in this life, with infallible certainty, that we are saved and heirs of eternal life. In general, all who deny the doctrine of the perseverance of the saints (or the eternal security of the believer) must also deny the possibility of absolute assurance of final salvation.

3. Why do we hold that those who deny the possibility of assurance are wrong? We hold that those who deny the possibility of assurance are wrong because many passages of Scripture teach us that full assurance, or absolute certainty of salvation, is attainable in this life.

4. Do all people who claim to have assurance of their own salvation have a right to do so? By no means. Many people claim that they are saved when they have no valid basis for such a claim. In particular, there are three classes of people who, if they claim to have assurance, are basing their claim on a foundation of shifting sand: (a) Legalists (also called Moralists), who trust in their own good works, good life, good character, "doing the best they can," etc. (b) Formalists, who put their trust in the observance of external forms, ceremonies, and ordinances, such as church membership, baptism, the Lord's Supper, etc. (c) Emotionalists (including also all Mystics), who trust their own feelings and emotions, who somehow just "feel" they are saved, or who base their assurance on dreams, visions, or special direct revelations from God. All of the above are trusting in what the Scripture calls refuges of lies when they base their conviction of assurance of salvation on such grounds as these. In studying the true scriptural grounds of assurance we shall see the reason why this is so.

5. What false teaching on assurance is very common among earnest Christian people? The teaching on assurance that is generally associated with American "Fundamentalism" is erroneous and very superficial. It is the product of a superficial type of evangelism which says little or nothing about the need for deep repentance for sin, which presents only a partial and inadequate statement of the grounds of assurance, and which almost always tends to confuse salvation itself with the Christian's assurance of salvation. This superficial type of evangelism encourages people to think that when they have written their name in place of "whosoever" in John 3:16 or raised their hand in a meeting to signify their acceptance of Christ as their Savior, they should immediately think of themselves as certainly saved forever. This is a confusion of salvation with assurance, a confusion of faith in Christ with faith that I am in Christ; a confusion of belief of the gospel with belief that I have truly and rightly believed the gospel. It is amazing how dogmatically and confidently people write and speak on this subject, while they yet give no evidence of having studied its problems or being familiar with its history.

6. Are salvation and assurance of salvation the same thing? Certainly not. Salvation and assurance of salvation are two different things, although often confused today as in the past. A person may be really saved, and still not be sure, in his own mind, of his salvation. Such a person is safe, and his safety is sure, but he is not sure about his safety. His salvation is not in doubt, but he may be in doubt about his salvation. Suppose a patient undergoes a surgical operation. When he consents to the operation, he exercises faith in the surgeon. The surgeon does his work skillfully and well; the operation is successful and the patient is on the road to recovery. Hours later he begins to come out of the anesthetic. As his brain clears, he asks whether everything is all right. The surgeon comes and assures him that all is well. He was safe by reason of the surgeon's skillful work, but this fact did not give him assurance of his safety in his own consciousness. That came later, upon appropriate evidence.

7. What is the difference between salvation and assurance? We receive salvation by believing in Christ; we receive assurance by believing that we have believed in Christ aright. In salvation, the object of our faith is Christ. But in the case of assurance, we do not believe directly in Christ; rather, we believe something about ourselves, namely, that we personally have received something from Christ by believing in him. To put it another way, to be saved, we must believe in Christ and what he did *for* us on Calvary long ago; to receive assurance, we must believe not only that Christ has done something *for* us centuries ago, but also that Christ has done and is doing something *in* us right here and now. Confusing salvation with assurance leads many people who no doubt are true Christians to trust in the wrong thing for their assurance of salvation. They base their assurance solely on the promises of the gospel, such as "Whosoever believeth . . . ," etc., and reason thus: "I believe, therefore I am saved." But it must be realized that there is true faith and also counterfeit faith (think of the Parable of the Sower); how do I know that I have believed aright, that my faith is genuine saving faith? It may indeed be genuine saving faith, but we should not rest assured of eternal salvation merely because of a decision made at some time to accept Christ as Savior.

8. What are the grounds of assurance of salvation? These grounds as they are presented in the Bible and summarized in the catechism are three in number, and it should be realized that they work together, not separately, as grounds upon which we have a right to an infallible conviction of our own salvation. These grounds are: (a) the truth of God's promises to believers; (b) the evidence in a person's heart and life of those graces to which the promises are addressed; (c) the testimony of the Holy Spirit, the Spirit of adoption, bearing witness with our spirits that we are the children of God.

9. What is meant by the truth of God's promises to believers as a ground of assurance? The divine truth of the promises of salvation is the foundation upon which assurance must rest. Without it, we could never attain full conviction or certainty. The person who doubts or disbelieves the truth of the Bible can never attain absolute certainty of his own salvation. But a recognition of the divine truth of the promises of salvation alone is not enough to warrant assurance. Many a person believes the Bible from cover to cover, with a technical or "historical" faith, who has no business to feel assured of his own salvation. The divine truth of the Bible, including the promises it contains, alone and by itself, is no proper ground of assurance. The devils also believe, and tremble (James 2:19). To illustrate this: an insurance policy promises to pay the holder $5,000 in the event of the destruction of his property by fire. The policy is genuine, and the company which issued it is financially sound. I may be so convinced of the soundness and reliability of this policy that I neglect even to read the terms and conditions which are printed in rather small type in the policy. Am I not satisfied that the policy is genuine? So I base my assurance solely upon the genuineness of the insurance policy. But one day my property is destroyed by fire. I file a claim. After investigation, the company refuses to pay me anything. The policy was genuine, but it did not apply to my case. I had been using the property for storing gasoline, and there was a clause in the policy stating that if gasoline was stored on the property that would void the policy and release the company from all liability. It was genuine, but it did not apply to my case because I had not complied with the conditions. So a mere acceptance of the promises of God's Word, without evidence of a changed and new life, is not an adequate ground of assurance.

10. What is meant by the evidence in a person's heart and life of those graces to which the promises are addressed? Briefly this means the evidence of a changed and new life, that old things have passed away, and all things have become new (2 Cor. 5:17). Here again, this ground of assurance cannot be taken by itself alone, but must go along with the other two grounds. Whosoever believeth shall not perish, but how do I know that I have believed aright, that my faith is real, that I am not self-deceived? A person might say, "I know just because I know, just as I know that my name is John Doe, or just as I know that I am awake and not asleep." But this will yield only probability and not infallible certainty. There may remain some lingering doubt that my faith is not the real thing, that somehow I am self-hypnotized. The truth is, we know that we have believed aright when we see some of the fruits of salvation in our lives. Christ came to save us from our sins, not in our sins. If we have believed aright, we will be saved not only instantly from their guilt, but also gradually from their power and pollution. Read 1 John 2:3–6; 1 John 3:14. Just what has Christ done for us? Has he forgiven our sins, just that and nothing more? If that is our experience, we have no right to rest assured of our salvation. Good works and a changed life are the fruits of a real salvation, and as such they form a part of the ground of a legitimate assurance of personal salvation. If Christ has really saved a person's soul, he will also, bit by bit, save that person's life—his eyes from tears and his feet from falling. All this enters into the ground of assurance of salvation.

11. What is meant by the testimony of the Holy Spirit as a ground of assurance of salvation? This does not mean some special revelation or strange voice inside of us, or that God will speak to us as he once spoke to Moses and Paul, or as one person might speak to another. If we expect anything like this we will be disappointed. Read 1 John 3:24; 5:10; Romans 8:15–16. God is a person. To know God is a very different thing from merely to know about God. The Holy Spirit, through the experiences of the Christian life, causes the believer really to know God. This personal knowledge of God, by the operation of the Holy Spirit in our hearts, becomes the final, ultimate ground of our infallible assurance of salvation. It serves as a true ground for the hope that maketh not ashamed (Rom. 5:5). "The Holy Spirit is the direct Author of faith in all its degrees, as also of love and hope. Full assurance, therefore, which is the fullness of hope resting on the fullness of faith, is a state of mind which it is the office of the Holy Ghost to induce in our minds in connection with the evidence of our gracious character above stated. In whatever way he works in us to will and to do of his own good pleasure, or sheds abroad the love of God in our hearts, or begets us again to a lively hope, in that way he gives origin to the grace of full assurance—

not as a blind and fortuitous feeling, but as a legitimate and undoubting conclusion from appropriate evidence" (A. A. Hodge, *Commentary on the Confession of Faith,* chap. 18).

12. How can we test the genuineness of our own assurance? Dr.
A. A. Hodge in his *Commentary on the Confession of Faith,* gives four tests by
which true assurance can be distinguished from false or presumptuous assurance. These are: (a) True assurance produces unfeigned humility; false assurance leads to spiritual pride. (b) True assurance results in increased diligence
in the practice of holiness; false assurance leads to slothfulness and self-indulgence. (c) True assurance leads to candid self-examination and a desire to be
searched and corrected by God; false assurance leads to a disposition to be
satisfied with appearance and avoid accurate investigation. (d) True assurance leads to constant aspirations after a more intimate fellowship with God;
false assurance does not.

81. Q. *Are all true believers at all times assured of their present being in
the estate of grace, and that they shall be saved?*

A. *Assurance of grace and salvation not being of the essence of faith, true
believers may wait long before they obtain it; and after the enjoyment
thereof, may have it weakened and intermitted, through manifold dis-
tempers, sins, temptations, and desertions; yet are they never left without such a presence and support of the Spirit of God as keeps them from
sinking into utter despair.*

Scripture References
- Eph. 1:13. Assurance is not essential to faith, and may come afterward.
- Isa. 50:10; Ps. 88. True believers may have to wait long before they attain
  full assurance.
- Pss. 77:1–12; 31:22; 22:1. Even after full assurance has been experienced, it
  is subject to change from various causes.
- 1 John 3:9; Job 13:15; Ps. 73:15, 23; Isa. 54:7–10. True believers are never
  left without any consciousness of the favor of God; they always have such
  a presence and support of the Holy Spirit as to preserve them from utter
  despair.

Commentary

1. What does the catechism mean by saying that assurance is not of the essence of faith? This means that true saving faith in Christ may exist without assurance of salvation in the believer's own mind. A person may have a true faith, and be really saved, without being sure of his salvation in his own consciousness.

2. Do all Christians receive the grace of assurance as soon as they believe in Christ as their Savior? No. There are some Christians who do receive the grace of assurance immediately upon believing in Christ as their Savior. This is often the case with persons who are converted to Christ in a very sudden manner, or who have gone through an intense spiritual struggle before they really came to Christ. The Reformer John Calvin, who was suddenly converted, is an example of this. But most Christians experience a more gradual conversion, and may have true saving faith for some time, even a long time, before they possess full certainty of their salvation in their own minds.

3. Can every Christian attain full assurance of his salvation? Yes. Assurance is possible to attain, and every Christian who uses the appointed means of grace faithfully and patiently waits on God can and will obtain it in the end.

4. After assurance of salvation is once attained, can it be lost? Yes. That is, it may be temporarily "weakened and intermitted" because of a variety of causes, including temptations, the believer's own sins, and providential dispensations of God. This is not only the teaching of Scripture (Pss. 32; 143:1–7; 2 Cor. 7:5), but the common experience of Christian people. For an unchanging and always unclouded consciousness of God's presence and blessing we shall have to wait until we reach heaven; such does not exist on earth. Assurance is not a constant, unchanging quantity; it is real, but it has its ups and downs.

5. Can a true Christian's consciousness of God's presence and favor ever be wholly lost? No. If the believer's consciousness of God's presence and favor could be entirely lost, the believer could only sink into utter despair. But through all the experiences of life the believer is never left without "such a presence and support of the Spirit of God" as will preserve him from despair.

6. How should we seek to maintain a strong and clear assurance of our salvation? Every Christian should earnestly endeavor to attain, and having attained, to retain, a strong and clear assurance of his salvation by a faithful, conscientious use of the means of grace, waiting upon God in Word, sacraments, and prayer.

7. Should we feel discouraged if we do not possess full assurance soon after we believe in Christ? No. We should exercise Christian patience and wait upon God to give us assurance in his own time.

82. Q. *What is the communion in glory which the members of the invisible church have with Christ?*

A. *The communion in glory which the members of the invisible church have with Christ, is in this life, immediately after death, and at last perfected at the resurrection and day of judgment.*

Scripture References

- 2 Cor. 3:18. The believer's communion in glory with Christ in the present life.
- Luke 23:43. The believer's communion in glory with Christ immediately after death.
- 1 Thess. 4:17. The believer's communion in glory with Christ perfected at the resurrection and Day of Judgment.

(**Note:** Question 69 was "What is the communion in grace which the members of the invisible church have with Christ?" Questions 70–81 deal with the communion in grace which they have with Christ. Question 82 introduces the new subject of the communion in glory which they have with Christ. Then questions 83–90 deal with this subject of communion in glory with Christ. The answer to question 82 is a summary of the subject "Communion in glory with Christ." It contains no doctrine which is not more fully stated in the questions which follow. Therefore we shall consider question 82 only very briefly, and then pass on to the questions which follow it.)

Commentary

1. What is the difference between grace and glory? In the Bible, both of these words are used with various meanings. But as used here in the catechism, grace refers to those blessings of salvation which we receive in this present life, while glory refers to those blessings of salvation which we receive chiefly in the life to come.

2. Do the people of God receive glory all at once, or in installments? God's people receive glory, not all at once, but in three stages or installments.

3. What are the three stages in which God's people receive glory? (a) They receive the firstfruits of glory during the present life; (b) they enter the state of glory at their death; (c) they receive the perfection of glory at the resurrection.

83. Q. *What is the communion in glory with Christ which the members of the invisible church enjoy in this life?*

A. *The members of the invisible church have communicated to them in this life the first-fruits of glory with Christ, as they are members of him their head, and so in him are interested in that glory which he is fully possessed of; and, as an earnest thereof, enjoy the sense of God's love, peace of conscience, joy in the Holy Ghost, and hope of glory; as, on the contrary, sense of God's revenging wrath, horror of conscience, and a fearful expectation of judgment, are to the wicked the beginning of their torments which they shall endure after death.*

Scripture References

- Eph. 2:5–6. Believers, because they are members of Christ their head, participate in the glory which Christ possesses in heaven.
- Rom. 5:5 compared with 2 Cor. 1:22. Believers, in this life, enjoy the consciousness of God's love.
- Rom. 5:1–2; 14:17. Peace of conscience, Christian joy, and hope of glory are the believer's portion here on earth.
- Gen. 4:13; Matt. 27:4; Heb. 10:27; Rom. 2:9; Mark 9:44. Just as the believer, in the present life, experiences a foretaste of the glory of heaven, so wicked people, in the present life, experience a foretaste of the miseries of hell.

Commentary

1. What is meant by the expression "the firstfruits of glory"? This means a sample or foretaste of that glory which we shall enjoy to the full in the life to come.

2. What is meant by saying that the members of the invisible church "are interested in that glory" which Christ already fully possesses? Here the word *interested* does not mean that they are eager to learn about it, but rather that they are entitled to a share in the glory which Christ now enjoys in heaven.

3. Why cannot Christian people have the full enjoyment of Christ's glory here and now? This is impossible because of three facts which, in God's providence, continue to exist during the present life: (a) the presence of a sinful nature in the believer; (b) the mortality and weakness of the Christian's physical body; (c) the presence of sin and suffering in the world which surrounds the Christian.

4. When will these three facts, which prevent the full enjoyment of glory here and now, be changed? The presence of the sinful nature in the believer will come to an end at his death. The mortality and weakness of his physical body will end at the resurrection at the Last Day. The sin and suffering in the world which surround the believer here and now will be left behind him at his death, and will be totally abolished at the Judgment Day at the end of the world.

5. What is meant by saying that the believer here and now has "an earnest" of Christ's glory? The expression "an earnest" means a deposit, a token payment, or a payment on account, which is made as evidence of good faith in promising that the balance shall be paid in due time. Glory is our inheritance in the life to come, but we receive a sample of it during this present life as evidence that we shall receive the fullness of it in the future life.

6. What kind of experiences go to make up the "earnest" of glory which God's people receive during the present life? The enjoyment of consciousness of God's love; peace of conscience; joy in the Holy Spirit; the hope (that is, the assurance, or "hope that maketh not ashamed," Rom. 5:5) of the fullness of glory in the future. These experiences enable the believer at times to enjoy a kind of "heaven on earth."

7. How do wicked people receive a sample of their future destiny during the present life? Even before death they experience, more or less, a "sense of God's revenging wrath, horror of conscience, and a fearful expectation of judgment." Sometimes these terrors may be so severe that they can be described as a kind of "hell on earth." The Bible teaches definitely that this is so, and it has often been exemplified by the words and actions of wicked people, especially as they felt the approach of death.

8. Does the believer enjoy this foretaste of glory equally at all times? No. Because of doubts, temptations, the attacks of Satan, and other things, the enjoyment of this foretaste of glory varies from time to time. Sometimes it is very clear, and at other times it is clouded and weak. But the believer is never left entirely without it.

84. Q. *Shall all men die?*

A. *Death being threatened as the wages of sin, it is appointed unto all men once to die; for that all have sinned.*

Scripture References
- Rom. 6:23. Death is the "wages" or penalty of sin.
- Heb. 9:27. God has appointed unto all men once to die.
- Rom. 5:12. Death has passed upon all men, because all have sinned.

Commentary

1. Are there any exceptions to the rule that all men must die? Yes. Enoch and Elijah were translated to the state of glory without dying. Read Genesis 5:24; Hebrews 11:5; 2 Kings 2:11. Also the Bible teaches that all of God's people who are living in the world when Jesus Christ comes again will be translated to the state of glory without dying. Read 1 Corinthians 15:51–52; 1 Thessalonians 4:16–17.

2. Has there ever been an exception to the truth that all men have sinned? Yes, our Savior Jesus Christ lived a blameless, perfect life, wholly without sin. Death would have been unable to claim him, except for the fact that the sins of God's people were laid upon him, and so he voluntarily laid down his life as a sacrifice for others. He came under the curse of God, suffered, and died because of our sins. In him was no sin, but the Lord laid on him the iniquity of us all.

3. Is death to be regarded as a normal or an abnormal experience of human beings? Modern thought, influenced by the evolution theory, holds that death is entirely normal, good, and necessary. It holds that for a human being to die is just as normal and proper as for leaves to drop off trees in the autumn. According to evolution, only by the death of millions of generations of human beings can perfection be attained—if indeed it can ever be attained. But according to the teaching of the Bible, death is strictly abnormal. Men were not created to die; they were created to live. The separation of soul from body and the decay of the body are fearful things because they are contrary to the integrity of our human nature as created by God. Therefore the Bible describes death as "the last enemy," and says that it shall be destroyed. The Bible also says that the devil is the one who has the power of death (Heb. 2:14) and that Christ came to destroy the devil and to "deliver them who through fear of death were all their lifetime subject to bondage" (v. 15).

4. What is proved by the fact that death is universal in the human race? The fact that death is universal proves that sin is universal also. Regardless of the ideas of scientists and philosophers, human beings instinctively recoil from death and realize that death is a fearful thing. The human soul has planted in it an unquenchable thirst for life. Yet in the face of this universal thirst for life, death comes to all. The only adequate explanation is that something is radically wrong with the human race. This the Bible calls sin, and explains the fact of death by the fact of sin (Rom. 5:12; 6:23).

5. Will science ever be able to overcome death? No. By God's common grace, scientific discoveries may be able in some cases to postpone death, but science can never overcome death, because back of the natural causes of death (such as sickness, accident, old age) there is the spiritual cause, namely, sin and God's righteous judgment upon sin.

85. Q. *Death being the wages of sin, why are not the righteous delivered from death, seeing all their sins are forgiven in Christ?*

A. *The righteous shall be delivered from death itself at the Last Day, and even in death are delivered from the sting and curse of it; so that, although they die, yet it is out of God's love, to free them perfectly from sin and misery, and to make them capable of further communion with Christ in glory, which they then enter upon.*

Scripture References

- 1 Cor. 15:26; Heb. 2:15. The righteous shall be delivered from death itself at the Last Day.
- 1 Cor. 15:55–57. Even in death, the righteous are spared the sting and curse of it.
- Isa. 57:1–2; 2 Kings 22:20. In the case of the righteous, death is to be explained by God's love, not by his wrath against sin.
- Rev. 14:13; Eph. 5:27. The death of the Christian serves to free him perfectly from sin and misery.
- Luke 23:43; Phil. 1:23. The Christian's death serves to render him capable of the further communion with Christ, which he then enters upon in the state of glory.

Commentary

1. What is the meaning of the word *wages* in this question? The word *wages* is here used with the meaning of penalty or punishment. Because the sinner deserves death, the Bible speaks of death as the "wages" of sin, for wages are a payment to a person of what he deserves to receive.

2. What is the real problem which this question of the catechism faces? The real problem which this question faces is: Why do Christians have to die? Since death is the penalty for sin, and Christ bore this penalty as the Christian's substitute, it would seem to involve a contradiction to say that the Christian still must die himself.

3. Is it possible to give a complete solution of this problem? No. The catechism presents some truths which shed some light on the problem. But the problem itself cannot be wholly solved. We can only say that God knows what is best for his own glory and the real good of his people. "Even so, Father, for so it seemed good in thy sight." Why does God not take Christian people to heaven without dying, as he took Enoch and Elijah? We do not know. We can only acknowledge the sovereignty of God and affirm that whatever God does is all very good.

4. In what way are the righteous delivered from death, and when? While not delivered from death as an experience, the righteous are delivered from the death of the body as a state or condition. This will take place at the Last Day.

5. What deliverance do the righteous enjoy in the experience of death? In the experience of death, the righteous are delivered from the sting and curse of it.

6. What is meant by the "sting and curse" of death? These terms describe death as the penalty of sin. See 1 Corinthians 15:55–56. The righteous do not have to experience death as the penalty of sin.

7. If death is not the penalty of sin to the righteous, then what is it? To the righteous, death is, first of all, the consequence of sin, that is, an effect of sin on the human personality. In the second place, to the righteous, death is a token of God's love. It brings the Christian benefit rather than harm. This does not mean that the death of the body is not itself a fearful thing, but it means that the result of the death of the body is to bring real benefit to the Christian.

8. How does the death of the body bring benefit to the Christian? The death of the body brings benefit to the Christian by translating him from this environment of sin and misery to the perfect environment of heavenly peace and rest. The Christian, even though justified, adopted, and in process of being sanctified, can never be perfectly happy and blessed in this world because of the presence on every hand, and in his own heart, of sin and suffering. Death removes the Christian from this vale of tears and places him immediately in heavenly glory in the presence of Christ.

9. Why is communion with Christ more perfect in heavenly glory than here on earth? (a) Because the Christian is in the visible presence of Christ in glory. (b) Because the sins and temptations of his own heart and the distractions of earthly life will all have passed away. (c) Because bodily weakness, weariness, infirmity, sickness, and pain will be no more.

86. Q. *What is the communion in glory with Christ, which the members of the invisible church enjoy immediately after death?*

A. *The communion in glory with Christ, which the members of the invisible church enjoy immediately after death, is, in that their souls are then made perfect in holiness, and received into the highest heavens, where they behold the face of God in light and glory, waiting for the full redemption of their bodies, which even in death continue united to Christ, and rest in their graves as in their beds, till at the Last Day they be again united to their souls. Whereas the souls of the wicked are at their death cast into hell, where they remain in torments and utter darkness, and their bodies kept in their graves, as in their prisons, till the resurrection and judgment of the great day.*

Scripture References

- Heb. 12:23. The souls of believers are at their death made perfect in holiness.
- 2 Cor. 5:1, 6, 8; Phil. 1:23 compared with Acts 3:21; Eph. 4:10. The souls of believers are at their death received into the Lord's presence in heaven.
- 1 John 3:2; 1 Cor. 13:12. Believers after their death shall behold the face of God.
- Rom. 8:23; Ps. 16:9. Believers after their death must await the redemption of their bodies.
- 1 Thess. 4:14. The bodies of believers, although buried in the grave, remain united to Christ.
- Isa. 57:2. The bodies of believers rest in their graves as in their beds.
- Job 19:26–27. The bodies of believers shall again be united to their souls.
- Luke 16:23–24; Acts 1:25; Jude 6–7. The souls of the wicked are at their death cast into hell.

Commentary

1. What is the condition of believers in Christ after their death? The condition of believers in Christ after their death is a condition of consciousness, memory, holiness, blessedness, and waiting for the completion of their redemption by the resurrection of their bodies; the condition of their bodies is a condition of rest until the resurrection.

2. When do the souls of believers enter upon this blessed condition? Immediately after their death.

3. What popular false doctrine is rejected by this answer of the catechism? The unscriptural doctrine of "soul sleep," which holds that the souls of Christians at the time of their death pass into unconsciousness, being as if they did not exist, until the resurrection.

4. Give two Scripture passages which prove that the doctrine of "soul sleep" is false. Luke 16:19–31 and Luke 23:39–43.

5. What kind of holiness do believers possess immediately after death? Perfect holiness (a) in extent; (b) in degree; (c) in stability. Never again can they fall short of moral perfection, suffer temptation, or fall into any sin.

6. What will be the chief element in the happiness or blessedness of the souls of believers after their death? The chief element in their blessedness or happiness is their beholding the face of God in light and glory.

7. Where is heaven? This question, which our natural curiosity raises in our minds, cannot be definitely answered. However, the Bible clearly reveals that heaven is the place where God's glory is specially manifested, and it is the place where our Savior Jesus Christ in his glorified human nature now lives.

8. Is the condition of the souls of believers after their death the highest and most blessed condition they are destined to enjoy? No. While the condition of the souls of believers after their death is a condition of perfect holiness, still it is not the highest and most blessed condition they are destined to enjoy. The enjoyment of the supreme blessedness must wait until the resurrection of the body at the Last Day. Therefore the Bible represents the souls of believers in heaven as patiently waiting for the resurrection.

9. When will the resurrection take place? At the time of the second coming of Christ, called in the Bible the "Last Day." This will be a definite time, but it is one of the secret things of God's counsel which have not been revealed to us. Therefore all attempts to predict the time are false and wrong.

10. What is the condition of the bodies of believers after their death? After their death, the bodies of believers rest in their graves as in their beds, and are still united to Christ.

11. What is meant by saying that the bodies of believers are still united to Christ? This means that Christ still regards the human bodies of his people, even though dead and buried, as something exceedingly precious, because he intends to raise them up again at the Last Day. Therefore he does not regard the dead bodies of his people as something worthless, to be discarded because of no more use, but as something valuable, to be watched over until the resurrection. The Bible compares the dead body of the Christian to a seed which has been planted and which will spring forth to new life at the appointed time. See 1 Corinthians 15:36–38.

12. What was the ancient pagan attitude toward the body after death had taken place? The pagan attitude was that the body even in life is the prison of the soul, or a hindrance to the soul, or a burden to the soul, and that death liberates the soul from the body and sets it free for a higher and nobler life; and that the dead body is only worthless matter which must be cast away or discarded because it will only decay and can never live again. This pagan attitude, although characteristic of the ancient world, is quite common in the present day.

13. How does this pagan attitude toward the human body differ from the Christian belief about the body? According to the Word of God, the human body is not something bad; it is not the prison of the soul, but the home of the soul; not a burden to the soul, but an organ of the soul; death by separating soul and body deprives the soul of something which it needs for its highest happiness and self-expression. See the apostle Paul's statements in 2 Corinthians 5:1–4. Especially the Christian attitude toward the body differs from the pagan attitude in that Christianity teaches that the body shall rise again by the power of God, and therefore its real and highest usefulness lies beyond the present life, in the life of eternity; therefore the dead body of a Christian is not something which has no further purpose or function.

14. What should we think of the increasingly prevalent practice of cremation as a substitute for burial? Of course all things are possible to God, who can raise up a body that has been burnt to ashes just as easily as one that has been buried and has returned to dust. But the practice of cremation is fostered by increasing unbelief in the resurrection of the body. It is a part of the modern pagan view of life. The idea back of the practice of cremation is that the dead body is worthless, merely so much lifeless matter which can never again be of use to the person's soul, and therefore is to be destroyed as quickly and as completely as possible.

15. Prove from the Bible that the souls of the wicked are in hell after their death. Luke 16:23–24.

16. What is the doctrine of "spiritualism" or "spiritism"? This is the soul-destroying false doctrine that it is possible for the living to communicate with the dead through a person called a "medium."

17. What is the attitude of the Bible toward "spiritism"? The Bible condemns and forbids "spiritism" in the most emphatic terms. Leviticus 19:31; 20:6, 27; Isaiah 8:19, and other Scriptures referring to "wizards," "witches," "familiar spirits," etc., condemn the practice of "spiritism." These "wizards," etc., were similar to the "mediums" of modern "spiritism."

18. What should we think of the practice of prayers for the dead? Prayers for the dead are unscriptural and wrong. If the dead are in heaven, they do not need our prayers. If they are in hell, our prayers cannot help them. After death there is no more opportunity for repentance or salvation. We should devote our attention rather to praying and working for the salvation of the living, leaving those who have passed away from this earth in the hands of God.

19. What should we think of the Roman Catholic doctrine of purgatory? The Catholic doctrine of purgatory is to the effect that very few Christians are fit to go directly to heaven when they die. The rest must go to purgatory and suffer there until the fires of purgatory have taken away the rest of their sinfulness. This doctrine is utterly contrary to the Scriptures, and makes the cross of Christ of no effect, for it implies that Christ's atonement is not sufficient to take away all a person's sin.

87. Q. *What are we to believe concerning the resurrection?*

A. *We are to believe, that at the Last Day there shall be a general resurrection of the dead, both of the just and unjust: when they that are then found alive shall in a moment be changed; and the self same bodies of the dead which were laid in the grave, being then again united to their souls for ever, shall be raised up by the power of Christ. The bodies of the just, by the Spirit of Christ, and by virtue of his resurrection as their head, shall be raised in power, spiritual, incorruptible, and made like*

to his glorious body; and the bodies of the wicked shall be raised up in
dishonor by him, as an offended judge.

Scripture References

- Acts 24:15. There shall be a general resurrection of the righteous and the wicked.
- 1 Cor. 15:51–53; 1 Thess. 4:15–17. At the time of the resurrection, living Christians shall instantly be changed without dying.
- 1 Cor. 5:53; John 5:28–29. The selfsame bodies that are buried shall rise again.
- 1 Cor. 5:21–23, 42–44. The bodies of the righteous shall be raised incorruptible.
- Phil. 3:21. The bodies of the righteous shall be like Christ's glorious body.
- John 5:27–29; Matt. 25:33; Rev. 20:13. The bodies of the wicked shall be raised by Christ as Judge.

Commentary

1. What is the meaning of the expression "at the Last Day"? This means the time of the second coming of Christ.

2. When will the Last Day come? The time when the Last Day shall come has not been revealed in the Bible. It is one of the secret things which God has reserved to himself. However, the Bible teaches that it will be a definite, particular time. The Bible refers to it as "that day and hour." Although God has not revealed the time, it will certainly be a definite calendar year, month, day, and hour, when the age-long history of this world will suddenly come to a conclusion with the return of Christ in glory upon the clouds of heaven, followed immediately by the resurrection and the judgment.

3. Is it possible that the Last Day may come within our own lifetime? Yes. While we do not believe that a sound interpretation of the Scriptures warrants the popular belief that the second coming of Christ may occur "at any moment," still this does not imply that it could not take place within our lifetime; nor do we have a right to expect that it will surely take place during our lifetime.

4. What attitude does the Bible command us to have toward the second coming of our Lord? "He which testifieth these things saith, Surely I come quickly. Amen. Even so, come, Lord Jesus" (Rev. 22:20).

5. Is it scriptural for a Christian to look forward to the Last Day with eager anticipation? Yes. Read 2 Peter 3:10–14, and note the expression used in verse 12: "Looking for and hasting unto the coming of the day of God. . . ." Also note Titus 2:13, "Looking for that blessed hope, and the glorious appearing of the great God and our Savior Jesus Christ."

6. Will there be more than one resurrection? No. The Scriptures teach that there will be one general resurrection of the dead at the time of Christ's second coming.

7. Prove from the Bible that there will be one single resurrection of both the righteous and the wicked. John 5:28–29: "The hour is coming, in the which all that are in the graves shall hear his voice, and shall come forth; they that have done good unto the resurrection of life; and they that have done evil, unto the resurrection of damnation." Concerning this passage of Scripture, it should be noted that (a) it speaks of "the hour" in the singular: "the hour is coming," not "the hours are coming"; therefore a single, definite time is meant; (b) when that definite time comes, not part, but all that are in the graves shall come forth; (c) those who shall come forth from the graves at that time are expressly stated to include both classes, the righteous and the wicked.

8. What should we think of the doctrine that there will be two resurrections, the first a resurrection of the redeemed and the second, a thousand years later, a resurrection of the wicked dead? This teaching forms a part of the premillennial interpretation of Revelation 20:1–6. This vision, which was revealed to the apostle John on the island of Patmos, is unquestionably filled with symbolic features, such as "the key of the bottomless pit," "a great chain," "a seal," and is therefore somewhat difficult to interpret with certainty. Because of this difficulty of interpretation, there has never been any unanimity in the church, from the post-apostolic age to the present time, concerning the meaning of this vision. This prophetic vision should be interpreted in accordance with the clear teaching of our Lord in John 5:28–29, rather than to start with a theory about the meaning of Revelation 20:1–6 and then interpret John 5:28–29 to fit our theory of the meaning of Revelation 20:1–6. Our Lord's clear teaching in John 5:28–29 rules out the double-resurrection idea. Therefore we believe that "the first resurrection" mentioned in Revelation 20:1–6 is not the resurrection of the body but a spiritual resurrection, possibly being the same as that spoken of by our Lord in John 5:25: "The hour is coming and now is, when the dead shall hear the voice of the Son of God: and they that hear shall live." It should be carefully noted that Revelation 20:4 does not say "they rose from their graves," but only "and they lived. . . ."

9. Will the resurrection body of the redeemed be the same as the present body, or different? Scripture teaches that the identity of the body will be the same, but its qualities will be different. It is the same body that is buried that shall rise again, but it will rise clothed with glory and immortality (1 Cor. 15:37, 42–44).

10. What is meant by saying that the resurrection body will be a "spiritual" body? We must be careful not to misunderstand this word. "Spiritual" is an adjective, not a noun. "A spiritual body" is not the same thing as "a spirit" or "a spirit body." When the New Testament speaks of the resurrection body of the saints as "a spiritual body," this means a body perfectly suited to be the temple of God the Holy Spirit.

11. Prove from the Bible that the resurrection body will not be a mere spirit but will be a tangible, material body. Luke 24:39: "Behold my hands and my feet, that it is I myself: handle me, and see; for a spirit hath not flesh and bones, as ye see me have."

12. Why do many people scoff at the doctrine of the resurrection of the body? This doctrine of God's Word has been made the object of scoffing by unbelievers ever since the Sadducees (Acts 23:8) and the Athenians (Acts 17:32) disbelieved it. Those who regard this doctrine as absurd or impossible do so because they reject the authority of the Scriptures and do not believe in a God who is almighty and can work miracles.

13. Can the resurrection of the body be proved by science or reason? No. The resurrection of the body is a mystery which is revealed only in the written Word of God. Apart from the Scriptures we could not know it. Also we should realize that science and human reason can never disprove the doctrine of the resurrection of the body. We hold this precious truth and promise by faith, on the authority of God's infallible Word, the Holy Bible.

14. Is it proper for the church, in order to avoid offending those who do not believe in the resurrection, to emphasize the immortality of the soul and say little or nothing about the resurrection of the body? No. In the Bible the emphasis is on the resurrection of the body rather than on the immortality of the soul, although of course the Bible plainly teaches both. Romans 8:23: "We ourselves groan within ourselves, waiting for the adoption, to wit, the redemption of our body." We should not trim off one jot or tittle of our faith to suit the ideas or appease the prejudices of modern unbelief. The church should proclaim the whole counsel of God, regardless of consequences, whether men will hear or whether they will forbear.

88. Q. *What shall immediately follow after the resurrection?*

A. *Immediately after the resurrection shall follow the general and final judgment of angels and men; the day and hour whereof no man knoweth, that all may watch and pray, and be ever ready for the coming of the Lord.*

Scripture References

- 2 Peter 2:4; Jude 6. The angels that sinned are to be judged.
- Jude 7, 14–15; Matt. 25:46. Christ is coming again to be the Judge of all.
- Matt. 24:36. The time of the judgment is unknown to men.
- Matt. 24:42–44; Luke 21:35–36. It is our duty to watch and pray and be always ready for Christ's coming.

Commentary

1. How soon after the resurrection of the dead will the judgment take place? Immediately after.

2. Show from the Bible that the resurrection and the judgment are so closely connected that the latter must follow immediately after the former. John 5:27–29. In this portion of Scripture (v. 27) Christ speaks of having received from God the Father authority to execute judgment; (v. 28) he predicts that he will call all that are in the graves to come forth; (v. 30) he states that they shall come forth, some to the resurrection of life, and others to the resurrection of judgment (the word *damnation* in the Authorized Version represents a Greek word which is more accurately translated "judgment"). If the judgment is not to follow immediately after the resurrection, these verses could not connect the two events so closely.

3. What interpretation of prophecy denies that the judgment will take place immediately after the resurrection? The premillennial interpretation of prophecy holds that (a) at the second coming of Christ the redeemed will rise from the dead; (b) this will be followed by a period of a thousand years during which Christ will rule the world from Jerusalem; (c) at the end of the thousand-year kingdom will come "the general and final judgment of angels and men." We believe that this view is based on a misunderstanding of the prophecies of the Bible.

4. What is implied by the use of the expression "the day and hour whereof," in speaking of the Judgment Day? The expression "the day and hour whereof" implies that the judgment will begin at a definite, particular time.

5. Why is it impossible for anyone to know in advance the day and hour of the judgment? It is impossible because this information has not been revealed to men by God. Not only does the Bible not disclose the day and hour, but it is impossible to calculate the day and hour from prophecies in the Bible, in any way whatever.

6. Since we cannot know the day and hour of the judgment in advance, what should be our attitude toward the coming judgment? Realizing the certainty of the judgment, and our own ignorance of the time, we should make adequate preparation, so that if the Judgment Day comes we will be ready for it. The person who is not saved should prepare, first of all, by repenting of sin and believing on Christ as his Savior. The Christian should prepare by daily seriousness and faithfulness in the Christian life; he should "watch and pray, and be ever ready for the coming of the Lord."

7. Is it possible that the second coming of Christ, the resurrection of the dead, and the Judgment Day will come to pass during the lifetime of people now living in the world? Certainly this must be regarded as possible: otherwise the warnings of Matthew 24:42–44 and Luke 21:36 would not apply to the present generation. If it is impossible for the Judgment Day to come during our lifetime, then Christ's words "Therefore be ye also ready" would not apply for us; we do not need to be ready for something which cannot possibly happen to us. We should note that the statement "In such an hour as ye think not the Son of man cometh" refers to the second coming of Christ in glory, not to the death of the Christian as it has often been wrongly interpreted. The content, verses 36–43, shows clearly that the second coming of Christ in glory is the subject that is being discussed.

8. Is it probable that the second coming of Christ, the resurrection of the dead, and the Judgment Day will come to pass during the lifetime of people now living in the world? The Bible affords no basis for answering this question with confidence. Many people in past times have thought that they could answer it confidently, but time has proved them wrong. It is better to refrain from speculations of this kind, and to rest content in the clear teaching of the Bible that it is possible that Christ may come again in our lifetime.

9. What wrong attitudes should be avoided in studying the doctrine of the second coming of Christ and related doctrines? There are two extreme attitudes which should be avoided: (a) Many Christians become so absorbed in these doctrines that they show but little interest in the other teachings of the Bible. This is a fanatical extreme. The second coming of Christ, the resurrection, and the judgment are indeed important doctrines of the Bible, but they are not the only important doctrines of the Bible. (b) There are also many Christians who go to the opposite extreme, and almost totally neglect the doctrines of the second coming of Christ, the resurrection, and the judgment. This also is a harmful extreme. The right view is a balanced one: we should view these doctrines in their proper place in the divinely revealed system of truth, giving them just the degree of emphasis that properly belongs to them, according to the teaching of the Bible.

10. Why do we believe in one single general judgment, instead of two or more? A number of reasons based on the Bible might be given. In Revelation 20:11–15 we see portrayed a general judgment, at which there are present the redeemed, whose names are written in the book of life, and also the wicked, who shall be cast into the lake of fire. The same teaching is set forth in Matthew 25:46. The interpretation that Matthew 25:32 ("And before him shall be gathered all nations . . .") describes a judgment of nations as such, rather than a judgment of individual human beings, is quite unwarranted. The word here translated "nations" is the Greek word *ethnos* (plural *ethne*), which occurs 164 times in the New Testament. It is translated "Gentiles" 93 times; "heathen" 5 times; "nation" or "nations" 64 times; "people" twice. It is quite commonly used to mean the people composing a nation or nations, and has no necessary reference to "states" or nations in their corporate political capacity. It is quite unwarranted to hold that Matthew 25:32 means that before Christ's throne shall be gathered Great Britain, France, Germany, China, the United States of America, Mexico, etc. The meaning is simply that all people, without distinctions of race or nationality, shall be gathered before Christ's judgment throne.

11. Who is to be the Judge of the entire human race? The Lord Jesus Christ (John 5:22, 27).

12. Why is Christ especially qualified to be the Judge of the human race? Because he is both God and man, with these two natures united in one person. Because he is God, he knows all things that ever happened; because he is man, he has experienced temptation and suffering; thus he is eminently qualified to render a just judgment.

89. Q. *What shall be done to the wicked at the day of judgment?*

A. *At the day of judgment, the wicked shall be set on Christ's left hand, and, upon clear evidence, and full conviction of their own consciences, shall have the fearful but just sentence of condemnation pronounced against them; and thereupon shall be cast out from the favorable presence of God, and the glorious fellowship with Christ, his saints, and all his holy angels, into hell, to be punished with unspeakable torments, both of body and soul, with the devil and his angels for ever.*

Scripture References

- Matt. 25:33. The wicked shall be set on Christ's left hand.
- Rom. 2:15–16. The wicked will be convicted by their own consciences.
- Matt. 25:41–43. Christ shall pronounce sentence against the wicked.
- Luke 16:26. The wicked shall be isolated from the presence of God, Christ, the holy angels, and the saints.
- 2 Thess. 1:8–9. The wicked shall be punished with terrible torments forever.
- Matt. 26:24. Those who have been judicially condemned can never to all eternity be restored to the favor of God.
- Matt. 25:46. The punishment of the wicked will be everlasting.

- Matt. 5:29–30. The punishment of hell will involve the body as well as the soul.
- Mark 9:43–48. The sufferings of hell will never come to an end.
- Matt. 10:28. The punishment of hell will involve both body and soul.

Commentary

1. What is the meaning of the prophecy that the wicked shall be set on Christ's left hand, while the righteous are set on his right hand? This teaching of our Lord implies that there is to be a judicial separation of the righteous from the wicked. These two classes of human beings, which have existed side by side during the present life, are to be separated by Christ acting as Judge. The separation will be infallibly accurate, total, and permanent. Never again to all eternity will any of the wicked come into contact with any of the righteous. Never again will it be possible for any communication to take place between the two. Wickedness and wicked men are going to be completely isolated in God's universe.

2. Upon what ground will the wicked be condemned? The wicked will be condemned on account of their own sin (Matt. 25:41–46; Rev. 20:12–13).

3. Will the wicked be condemned because they have not believed on Christ? Those who have heard the gospel and have failed to believe on Christ, being thus guilty of the sin of unbelief, will be condemned on account of this sin as well as on account of all their other sins.

4. Will the wicked be condemned because God has not predestined them to eternal life? Those whom God has "passed by" and not chosen to eternal life will be condemned, but their condemnation will be on account of their own sins, not on account of God's decrees.

5. In the case of the heathen who have never heard the gospel, and are therefore not guilty of the sin of unbelief in Christ, what will be the basis on which they will be judged? They will be judged according to the revelation of God in the light of nature (Rom. 1:20) and the law of God written on the human heart (Rom. 2:14–16), which will convict them as sinners and leave them without excuse.

6. Will the wicked feel themselves unfairly treated at the Judgment Day? No. Even though they do not have the slightest love for God, or thankfulness for any of his mercies, still they will realize in their own consciences that God has treated them strictly according to justice. At the Judgment Day the perfect justice of God will be vindicated before the whole creation, and all will confess that God is just. Those who have spent their lives accusing God of unrighteousness will realize in their own hearts that God is righteous and they themselves are wicked.

7. Prove from the Bible that hell is a place and not merely a state or condition. Matthew 10:28. Since the bodies, as well as the souls, of the wicked will be there, it must be a place.

8. What is the belief of the Universalists? They believe that all human beings, without exception, will finally be saved and enjoy eternal life with God.

9. Can Universalism be reconciled with the statements of the Bible about hell? No. The Bible very plainly teaches that not all, but only part, of the human race will be saved, and the rest will be eternally lost. Jesus spoke of a sin that shall never be forgiven in this world or the world to come (Matt. 12:32). He said concerning Judas Iscariot that it would have been better for him if he had never been born (Matt. 26:24). These and many other texts of Scripture cannot be reconciled with the theory of Universalism.

10. What is the belief of Annihilationists? They believe that the punishments of hell will not be eternal, but only for a period of time, after which the wicked in hell will cease to exist, their personalities having been blotted out or having totally disintegrated, leaving nothing. They also argue that God is too good and loving to punish any of his creatures eternally. They also claim that in the Bible the word *eternal* does not mean really forever, but only age-long, or a long period of time.

11. What Scripture text proves that this doctrine is false? Matthew 25:46. In this text the same Greek word is used for both "everlasting" and "eternal." It is unfortunate that the King James Version uses these two different words, because in the Greek exactly the same word is used in both cases. Therefore if the blessedness of heaven will last forever, the sufferings of hell must last forever too.

12. Is God too good and loving to punish the wicked forever? No. The only way we know of the goodness and love of God is from the Bible. The same Bible which tells us that "God is love" also informs us that "Our God is a consuming fire" (Heb. 12:29). It is wrong to pick and choose among the teachings of the Bible. We must accept all that the Bible teaches, or else reject the Bible as a whole and take the consequences. If we accept what the Bible teaches about God's love, we must also accept what it teaches about God's justice and his wrath against sin (Rom. 1:18).

13. Is it contrary to "the spirit of Christ" to believe in hell? No. The only way we know anything about "the spirit of Christ" is from his teachings and actions recorded in the written Word of God, the Bible. The fact is that Christ's own teachings contain more warnings about eternal punishment than can be found in any other part of the Bible. It was not the apostles, nor the prophets, but Jesus himself who most clearly and emphatically warned men about the worm that dieth not, the fire that is not quenched, the outer darkness, the gnashing of teeth, the God who is able to destroy both soul and body in hell. Those who claim that to believe in hell is contrary to "the spirit of Christ" simply decide for themselves what they would like to believe, and then label their self-made creed "the spirit of Christ." It is really wicked to do this.

14. What Scripture passage proves that there can be no opportunity to repent and be saved in hell? Luke 16:19–31, the Parable of the Rich Man and Lazarus. Note especially verse 23, "And in hell he lifted up his eyes . . . ," and verse 26, "'Between us and you there is a great gulf fixed; so that they which would pass from hence to you cannot; neither can they pass to us, that would come from thence."

15. Is the fear of hell a proper motive for believing on Christ as our Savior? Yes. It is not the highest motive, for we are taught in 1 John 4:18 that the mature Christian, who is "made perfect in love," is beyond the need of being influenced by the motive of fear. But certainly Jesus inculcated the fear of hell (Matt. 10:28; Luke 12:5). We may conclude, therefore, that although it is true that "perfect love casteth out fear," yet those who have not reached that high point of Christian experience, and have not yet attained full assurance or certainty of their own salvation, ought to be influenced by the lower motive of fear of eternal ruin, and "flee from the wrath to come" by repenting of sin, believing on Christ for salvation, and diligently using the means of grace (the Word, the sacraments, and prayer).

90. Q. *What shall be done to the righteous at the day of judgment?*

A. *At the day of judgment, the righteous, being caught up to Christ in the clouds, shall be set on his right hand, and there openly acknowledged and acquitted, shall join with him in the judging of reprobate angels and men, and shall be received into heaven, where they shall be fully and for ever freed from all sin and misery; filled with inconceivable joys, made perfectly holy and happy both in body and soul, in the company of innumerable saints and holy angels, but especially in the immediate vision and fruition of God the Father, of our Lord Jesus Christ, and of the Holy Spirit, to all eternity. And this is the perfect and full communion, which the members of the invisible church shall enjoy with Christ in glory, at the resurrection and day of judgment.*

Scripture References

- 1 Thess. 4:17. The righteous shall be caught up in the clouds to Christ.
- Matt. 25:33. The righteous shall be set on Christ's right hand.
- Matt. 10:32. They shall be openly acknowledged and acquitted.
- 1 Cor. 6:2–3. The redeemed shall join with Christ in the judgment of angels and of the world.
- Matt. 25:34, 46. The righteous shall be received into heaven.
- Eph. 5:27. They shall be fully freed from all sin.
- Rev. 14:13. They shall be fully freed from all misery.
- Ps. 16:11. They shall be filled with joy.
- Heb. 11:22–23. They shall enjoy the company of saints and holy angels.
- 1 John 3:2; 1 Cor. 13:12. They shall have a direct vision of God.
- 1 Thess. 4:17–18. They shall be in the Lord's presence to all eternity.

Commentary

1. What two classes of people will be caught up in the clouds to meet Christ? (a) The dead in Christ, who will rise from their graves as Christ descends from heaven with a shout (1 Thess. 4:16). (b) The living Christians who are in the world at the time of Christ's second coming (1 Thess. 4:17).

2. Why will not the law of gravitation prevent the righteous rising in the air to meet Christ? The rising in the air, on the part of the righteous, will be a miracle wrought by the supernatural power of God. The law of gravity can no more prevent their rising in the air than it could prevent Christ's ascension long ago. The Judgment Day will mark the end of the dominion of natural laws, as we know them now, over God's people. That great day will mark the transition to "the age to come," the day of eternity, in which the supernatural will not be the exception but the rule (Heb. 6:5: "the powers of the age to come").

3. What is the meaning of the statement that the righteous shall be set on Christ's right hand? This statement implies a judicial, total, and permanent separation of the righteous from the wicked. Never again to all eternity can there be the slightest contact or communication between the two classes of human beings, the redeemed and the judicially condemned.

4. What is meant by saying that the righteous shall be "openly acknowledged and acquitted"? This means (a) that the Lord Jesus Christ, acting as Judge, will publicly declare, before the whole universe, that these people, who have been persecuted and reproached because of their faith in him, are his own people, upon whom his special love has been bestowed, and whom he has redeemed from sin to be his spiritual body; (b) that Christ, acting as Judge, will pronounce his people to be not guilty of the slightest sin, and perfectly righteous before the law of God, because he himself has borne the guilt of their sins by his atonement, and because of his own perfect righteousness which has been reckoned (or "imputed") to them just as if it were their own personal righteousness.

5. What is the meaning of the statement that the saints shall join with Christ in judging reprobate angels and men? This truth, which is set forth in 1 Corinthians 6:2–3, does not mean that the saints will have authority of their own to determine the eternal destiny of angels or men, for this solemn function belongs to the Lord Jesus Christ alone. Rather, the meaning is that the saints shall join or concur with Christ in the sentence which he will pronounce upon the wicked angels and men; as Christ pronounces sentence, the saints will give their assent, approving of his judgment as righteous. As Satan and the wicked angels have grievously troubled and afflicted God's people for thousands of years, and as wicked men have oppressed and persecuted and reproached God's children, it is very fitting that the saints, having been vindicated by the great Judge, shall join in the sentence to be pronounced upon the fallen angels and wicked men.

6. What is meant by saying that the righteous shall be received into heaven? This means that the Judgment Day will mark their entrance as total personalities, with both body and soul, into the place, as well as the condition, of total blessedness. The remainder of the answer to question 90 deals with the character of this place and condition of perfect blessedness.

7. Why can we not have perfect blessedness here and now? There are several reasons why the Christian cannot enjoy complete blessedness here and now, such as: (a) He cannot see his Savior face to face here and now. (b) The facts of bodily infirmity, sickness, and pain prevent the enjoyment of total blessedness now. (c) The sinful corruption which remains in the Christian's own heart, here on earth, which necessitates a constant battle against temptation and sin, prevents the enjoyment of total blessedness now. (d) Here on earth the Christian is surrounded by a wicked and miserable environment, and the more holy the Christian becomes, the more he feels distressed by the presence and effects of sin in his surroundings.

8. How will these various factors in our present condition be changed in heaven? (a) We shall see our Savior face to face. (b) Our mortal body, which is afflicted with pain, sickness, weakness, and fatigue, will put on immortality; all sickness, pain, and distress will forever pass away, and what is mortal will be swallowed up of life. (c) The sinful corruption of our own hearts, and the constant conflict against sin and temptation which results from it, will come to an end at the moment of death. (d) The environment of heaven will be perfectly holy; "and there shall in no wise enter into it any thing that defiles, neither whatsoever works abomination or makes a lie; but they which are written in the Lamb's book of life" (Rev. 21:27; see also Rev. 22:15).

9. What will be the chief element in the blessedness of heaven? The chief element in the blessedness of heaven will be "the immediate vision and fruition of God."

10. What is meant by the word *vision* in this statement? It means that the saints shall see God.

11. What is meant by saying that this vision of God will be immediate? The word *immediate* implies that the saints shall see God directly, without anything interposed between them and God. Here on earth we cannot see God directly. We now see only darkly, as in a mirror, but then we shall see "face to face." Here on earth we see God only as he is reflected in his Word, and still more dimly in his works; but in heaven we shall have an immediate or direct vision of God, without the need of his being reflected either in nature or in Scripture. It was this truth that many of the covenanter martyrs had in mind when, in their dying testimonies, they used words similar to those of James Renwick: "Farewell, sweet Bible, and preaching of the gospel. Farewell sun, moon, and stars, and all sublunary things. Farewell conflicts with a body of death. Welcome scaffold for precious Christ. Welcome heavenly Jerusalem. Welcome innumerable company of angels. Welcome General Assembly and Church of the first-born. Welcome, crown of glory, white robes, and song of Moses and the Lamb. And, above all, welcome O thou blessed Trinity and One God! O Eternal One, I commit my soul into Thy eternal rest!"

12. What is meant by the statement that the saints shall enjoy fruition of God? *Fruition* means bearing fruit. The purpose of a fruit tree is to bear fruit. A fruit tree which never bears fruit has no fruition: it has lived without attaining the purpose or goal for which it exists. If we think of a human life as a tree, we may say that the fruit it was intended to bear is the perfect glorifying and enjoying of God. The Christian cannot yield that fruit in this world except in a very imperfect and partial way. But in heaven he will at last attain the goal for which he was created; he will at last yield the real fruit of a perfect glorification and enjoyment of God. This goal is called fruition of God because only in perfect communion with God can this fruit be produced by any human life.

13. What should we think of the popular idea that the saints in heaven will do little or nothing but play on harps? This popular notion is a mere caricature of what the Bible teaches about heaven, based on an absurdly literal interpretation of one or two Scripture passages which are symbolic in character. The Bible warrants believing that the saints in heaven will engage in the most intense activity, out of all comparison with the busiest activity and greatest achievements of their life here on earth. We may be sure that "the life that is life indeed" will not be a life of idleness.

14. Does not the Bible teach that heaven will be a state of perfect rest? How then can it be a state of intense activity? It is true that the Bible teaches that heaven will be a state of perfect rest. The idea of "rest" is really a largely negative idea, meaning freedom from weariness, fatigue, unpleasant or painful toil, etc., all of which evils are solely the result of sin and the curse. It is only because of the presence of sin in the world that rest is incompatible with activity. Before Adam sinned, activity and rest could be simultaneous. But after he sinned, activity became laborious toil because of the curse (Gen. 3:17–19). But in heaven "there shall be no more curse" (Rev. 22:3). Therefore in heaven activity and rest will no longer be contrary to each other; the saints can enjoy the most intense activity, and the most perfect rest, at the same time. Weariness and fatigue will be unknown, for their causes will have been removed forever. (The foregoing is not to be understood as implying that the activity of the saints in heaven will be without pause or intermission, but only that their activity will not cause exhaustion and need for recuperation. Nor should it be supposed that Adam and Eve before the fall were constantly active; certainly God intended the night as a period of rest, even before the fall, and there was the weekly Sabbath as a period of cessation from common activity; but as long as man's life and constitution were normal, that is, sinless, activity was not a destructive force, and rest was not needed to prevent death from exhaustion, as it became necessary after the fall into sin. Adam as created was a perfect, though finite, replica of the Godhead; and as God himself worked and then rested [Gen. 2:1–3] but did not need rest because of exhaustion, so mankind before the fall worked and then rested, following the divine pattern, but not because their work had caused exhaustion.)

15. Where will heaven be? The Bible does not satisfy our curiosity by providing this information for us. However, it definitely teaches that heaven is a place (John 14:1–6).

We have now completed the study of the first ninety questions of the Larger Catechism. It will be recalled that the Larger Catechism consists of 196 questions and answers arranged according to the following plan:

- Nos. 1–5. The Foundation: The purpose of human life, the existence of God, the Word of God
- Nos. 6–90. What Man Ought to Believe Concerning God
- Nos. 91–196. What Duty God Requires of Man

Having completed the first two sections of the catechism, we now proceed to the study of the third section, namely, What the Scriptures Require as the Duty of Man. The following is an outline of the contents of this third section:

- Nos. 91–148. The Moral Law of God, Including an Analysis of the Ten Commandments
- Nos. 149–96. The Way of Escape from God's Wrath and Curse by Reason of Our Transgression of His Law

What Duty God Requires of Man

11

Obedience to God's Revealed Will

Introduction

91. Q. *What is the duty which God requireth of man?*

A. *The duty which God requireth of man is obedience to his revealed will.*

Scripture References
- Rom. 12:1–2. The duty of conformity to the will of God.
- Mic. 6:8. God requires obedience to his revealed will.
- 1 Sam. 15:22. Without sincere obedience to God's will, all worship is vain.
- John 7:17. Willingness to do God's will is the key to knowledge of God's truth.
- James 1:22–25. Hearing the Word of God, without being willing to do God's will, is useless.
- James 4:17. To fail to do God's will, when we know what it is, is sinful.

Commentary

1. Why do we owe a duty to God? Because God is our Creator and we are his creatures, we are under moral obligation to love and serve him. As Christians we are under an added obligation to love and serve God, because he has redeemed us from sin and hell.

221

2. What classes of people deny that human beings owe a duty to God? (a) Atheists, who do not believe that there is a God. (b) Pantheists, who believe that everything is divine, and deny that God is a person except as he attains personality in man. (c) Humanists, who believe that our highest loyalty must be to our fellow men, or to humanity. These usually regard God as someone who exists for the benefit of the human race, or at least that God and man exist for the mutual benefit of each other. They regard religion as a means to an end, for promoting human progress and welfare.

3. Why is it wrong to say that our highest loyalty should be devotion to the welfare of humanity? This humanistic attitude, which is extremely common and popular in the present day, and is taken for granted by the leading newspapers and magazines of America, is really idolatry, for it puts the creature in place of the Creator and amounts to deifying and worshiping mankind.

4. Is it not true that serving our fellow men is a noble way of serving God? It all depends on our motive for serving our fellow men. If our real motive is a desire to serve God, so that we serve our fellow men not just for their own sake, but for God's sake, then we may be truly serving God, provided we act in accordance with his revealed will. But if our motive is merely a desire to help humanity, so that we serve our fellow men for their own sake, then we are idolaters, and we are not truly serving God, even though we may be doing some of the things commanded in God's Word.

5. Do we have a right to choose whether we will obey God's revealed will or not? God does not force or compel anyone to obey his revealed will. He permits free agents to make their own decisions. However, no person has a right to choose to disobey God. To decide against obedience to God's will is to be in rebellion against our Creator.

6. Why does God not consult our wishes before imposing his will on us? We tend to forget that God does not manage the universe according to the principles of democracy. The kingdom of God is not a democracy, but an absolute monarchy; God is sovereign; he has total, absolute, and unchallengeable authority over all his creatures. It is not for us to say whether we like God's commandments and laws; it is for us to obey them whether we like them or not, simply because they are the revelation of God's will. To attempt to place God on the same level with ourselves, as if he were responsible to us, or as if we could criticize or question his requirements, is irreverent, irreligious, and wicked.

92. Q. *What did God at first reveal to man as the rule of his obedience?*

A. *The rule of obedience revealed to Adam in the estate of innocence, and to all mankind in him, besides a special command not to eat of the fruit of the tree of the knowledge of good and evil, was the moral law.*

Scripture References
- Gen. 1:26–27. Mankind created in the image of God, with a moral nature.
- Rom. 2:14–15. The law of God written on the human heart by God's natural revelation.
- Rom. 10:5. The standard of righteousness is the moral law of God.
- Gen. 2:17. God's special command to Adam not to eat the fruit of the tree of the knowledge of good and evil.

Commentary
1. What do we call the condition of the human race before the fall into sin? The estate of innocence.

2. What special command did God give to mankind in the estate of innocence? The command not to eat the fruit of the tree of the knowledge of good and evil. This special command formed the condition of the covenant of works.

3. How was this special command of God given to mankind? This special command of God was given to mankind, not by nature, but by a special revelation or message from God, which Adam and Eve unmistakably recognized as a declaration of the will of God (Gen. 2:16–17; 3:3).

4. Apart from this special command, what rule of obedience did God give to mankind? Apart from the special command which formed the condition of the covenant of works, God gave to mankind the moral law as the rule of obedience.

5. How was the moral law given to mankind in the estate of innocence? The moral law was given to mankind in the estate of innocence by God's natural revelation in the human heart. Mankind as created had the moral law of God written upon their hearts. It was not necessary for God to address Adam and Eve with a special revelation of the moral law, for the moral law was already written by God in their own nature. No special revelation of the moral law was needed so long as mankind had not fallen into sin.

6. Do people have the moral law of God written on their hearts by God's natural revelation today? Yes. The law of God is written by God's natural revelation upon the heart of every human being in the world. But the writing has been terribly darkened and distorted by human sin so that this natural revelation of the will of God is no longer adequate as the guide for human conduct. Since the fall the light of God's special revelation has been necessary. Apart from the light of Holy Scripture, men inevitably change the truth of God into a lie, and worship and serve the creature more than the Creator (Rom. 1:25).

7. Why did God not reveal the Ten Commandments to Adam and Eve? As long as sin had not entered the human race, there was no need for a detailed list of commandments. The simple moral law of God written on the human heart was sufficient, for it told Adam and Eve that their highest obligation was to love God for his own sake, and that their next highest obligation was to love each other for God's sake. Only when sin had entered did specific detailed commandments such as "Thou shalt not steal," "Thou shalt not kill," "Thou shalt not bear false witness against thy neighbor," etc., become necessary. As long as the human race existed in the state of innocence, such specific commandments would have been meaningless as well as unnecessary.

8. What is the popular "modern" view of the moral law? The popular "modern" view of the moral law is not based on the Bible but on human philosophy and scientific theories. According to this popular notion the moral law is not a revelation of the will of God, or an expression of the nature of God. It is thought of as existing of itself, as a part of "the nature of things." Modern thought regards the universe as existing of itself (that is, not created), and the moral law as existing of itself as a part of the universe. According to this view, if there is a God, he too is subject to the moral law, which exists above and beyond him. In accordance with the prevalent idea of human evolution from a brute ancestry, the moral law is not regarded as a revelation of God but as a discovery of man. This theory holds that mankind originated not in the Garden of Eden but in the slime, and that the law originally written on the human heart was not the law of God but the law of the jungle; then through ages amounting to millions of years mankind gradually developed and improved, and discovered more of the true moral law inherent in "the nature of things," until the law of the jungle in the human heart was transformed into the moral law as men recognize it today.

9. What errors are involved in this "modern" view of the moral law? (a) This "modern" view of the moral law regards it not as a revelation of the will of God, and expression of the nature of God, but as something existing of itself as a kind of impersonal force or principle in the universe. (b) This theory holds that mankind originated in the depths and has gradually climbed to the heights, whereas the Bible teaches that mankind originated on the heights and later fell into the depths by disobeying God. (c) This theory holds that the moral law is a human development or discovery, whereas the Bible teaches that the moral law is a divine revelation. In short, modern thought has no room for the three great Bible truths of (a) the creation of the universe by God; (b) the original perfection and subsequent fall of mankind; and (c) the revelation of the moral law as the will of God.

93. Q. *What is the moral law?*

A. *The moral law is the declaration of the will of God to mankind, directing and binding every one to personal, perfect, and perpetual conformity and obedience thereunto, in the frame and disposition of the whole man, soul and body, and in performance of all those duties of holiness and righteousness which he oweth to God and man: promising life upon the fulfilling, and threatening death upon the breach of it.*

Scripture References
- Deut. 5:1–3. God's moral law requires obedience.
- Deut. 5:31–33. God's law is a revelation of God's will.

- Luke 10:26–27. The moral law requires conformity of the whole man to God's will.
- Gal. 3:10. The law of God requires total and perfect obedience.
- 1 Thess. 5:23. God's law is binding on all elements of the human personality.
- Luke 1:75. God's law requires both holiness and righteousness in serving him.
- Acts 24:16. God's law includes duties owed to God and duties owed to men.
- Rom. 10:5; Gal. 3:12. God promises life upon the fulfilling of his law.
- Gal. 3:10; Gen. 3:17–19. Death is the penalty involved in the breach of God's law.

Commentary

1. How does the catechism define the moral law? It defines the moral law as "the declaration of the will of God to mankind." This involves the following Scripture truths: (a) The moral law is not a human discovery, but a divine revelation. (b) The moral law is not a force or principle inherent in the universe, but a revelation of the will of God. (c) God is not simply another name for "the best that is in humanity," but a supreme person, who has a will which he reveals to his creatures.

2. Who is subject to the moral law of God? Every human being that ever lived or ever shall live.

3. Does the moral law of God bind the heathen who know nothing of the Bible? Yes. Apart from the Bible the moral law of God is written on their hearts by God's natural revelation (Rom. 2:14–16).

4. Does God's moral law bind atheists who do not believe in God? Yes. At the Judgment Day they will have to answer for their denial of God's existence as well as for all their other sins. As long as they do not believe in God, even their "good deeds" are really wicked. Their rejection of God cannot cancel the authority of God's law over their lives.

5. Does the moral law of God bind Christians? Certainly it does. Christ saves us unto a life of obedience to God's moral law.

6. Does God's moral law ever change, or is it always the same? Although the real meaning of God's moral law is always the same, we see in the Bible that the particular form in which it was revealed was changed from time to time, chiefly by the addition of more detailed commandments.

7. Does God's moral law change now, in our own time? No. Since the completion of the Bible, the revelation of God's will to mankind is complete and unchangeable and will stand in this fixed form until the end of the world.

8. What attitude do many modern people take toward the idea that God's moral law is fixed and will remain unalterable till the end of the world? Many people who have been influenced by "modern" thought oppose this idea, calling it "narrow" and "static," and saying that it is absurd to suppose that detailed commandments given to men 2,000 or more years ago can be adequate for the needs of humanity in this modern age of scientific progress.

9. How should we answer this objection to the unchangeable character of God's moral law? (a) Those who raise this objection do not think of the moral law as a revelation of God; they regard even the laws in the Bible as products of human experience and progress. If the laws in the Bible are really man-made or man-discovered, then of course we might as well make or discover our own today, instead of depending on the attainments of men who lived ages ago. But if these laws are God-given, then they are equally adapted to the needs of all ages, for God is not limited by the passing of time, and he was able to give laws which would last until the end of the world. (b) When rightly interpreted, according to sound principles of Bible study, the moral law of God as revealed in the Bible is exactly suited to the condition of humanity in the twentieth century and beyond, just as in any other period of human history since the fall.

10. What kind of obedience does God's moral law require of mankind? God's moral law requires absolute obedience, that is, conformity of the whole man to the whole law through his whole life. Thus God's moral law demands absolute perfection in our thoughts, words, and deeds, as well as in the state or disposition of our heart, through our entire life, without falling short even for one instant.

11. Does the moral law of God require us to be good? The moral law of God requires us to be not merely "good," but absolutely good, that is, to be morally perfect. The common manner of speaking about "being good" amounts to a lowering of God's standard. God requires not merely "goodness" but absolute moral perfection.

12. Is not such a standard far too high for the human race? We must freely recognize that the ideal of moral perfection presented in the Bible is not attainable in the present life. The standard is not too high, though. If Adam and Eve had not sinned, all humanity would have attained to this standard of absolute perfection, and the human race would have been very different from what it actually turned out to be. That the standard is too high for fallen man to attain is mankind's own fault by reason of the fall into sin and resultant corruption and inability. God's standard has remained the same ever since the day that he created mankind. It is the human race that has changed. Also we should realize that the fact that the standard is too high for fallen man to attain shows the divine origin of the moral law. A stream cannot rise any higher than its source. If the moral law were the product of man's experience, it would present a standard low enough to be attained by sinful human beings. The absolute moral standard which we find in the Bible must be from God: human beings could never have produced it. Apart from Christ, human thought has never even been able to form an idea of a perfect man in whom no evil whatever exists. The Bible presents an absolute moral standard and portrays Christ as fully emboding that absolute moral perfection in his own character. It is high; we cannot attain unto it; but that very fact shows that it is not man's standard, but God's.

13. What kind of duties does God's moral law obligate us to perform? God's moral law obligates us to perform the duties of holiness and righteousness which we owe to God and man.

14. What is the difference between "duties of holiness" and "duties of righteousness"? While the terms *holiness* and *righteousness* no doubt overlap to some extent, it may be said that "duties of holiness" are religious duties in the strict sense while "duties of righteousness" are moral duties in the strict sense. For example, prayer and reading the Bible are "duties of holiness"; to work industriously six days of the week (Exod. 20:9), avoiding idleness, is a "duty of righteousness."

15. What is the difference between duties owed to God and duties owed to man? Strictly speaking, all duties are owed to God. There is no duty owed to man which is not owed to God also; that is, it is owed to man for God's sake. But some duties are owed to God solely and directly, while other duties are owed to God indirectly, by reason of our relation to our fellow men. For example, to reverence God's name and refrain from taking it in vain is a duty owed directly to God. But to love our neighbor as ourself is a duty owed to God indirectly. In this case our duty to God requires us to love our neighbor and seek his welfare; thus our duty to God involves a subordinate duty to man.

16. What does God promise upon the fulfilling of his moral law? God promises life upon the fulfilling of his moral law; this is of course to be understood in the fullest sense, meaning eternal life.

17. Can eternal life be obtained in any other way than by the fulfilling of God's moral law? Absolutely not. There is and can be no other way. God's standard has never been changed or lowered. Adam and Eve could have obtained eternal life by themselves personally fulfilling God's moral law. If they had done that, we too would thereby have obtained eternal life, and we would have been born into the world unable to commit sin. However, Adam and Eve disobeyed God, and the human race fell into sin, with the result that no one can adequately fulfill God's moral law now. Still God's standard has not been lowered. Eternal life still depends upon absolute obedience to God's moral law. But God himself has provided the second Adam, the Lord Jesus Christ, who perfectly fulfilled God's moral law on our behalf, as our representative, so that "by the obedience of one shall many be made righteous" (Rom. 5:19). We should always be careful to avoid the error that the gospel involves a lowering of the terms on which mankind can obtain eternal life. The gospel does not involve a lowering of the terms; it involves a substitution of the person who complies with the terms: God graciously accepts Christ's fulfillment of the moral law as if it were our own attainment, and imputes or reckons it to our credit.

18. What penalty came upon mankind because of the breach of God's moral law? The penalty of death (Rom. 5:12; 6:23).

19. What is the meaning of "death" as the penalty for breaking the moral law of God? "Death" as "the wages of sin," or the penalty for the breach of God's moral law, means death in the most inclusive sense, including (a) alienation of the person from God's favor; (b) the death of the body, and its return to dust; (c) eternal separation from God's love and favor, called in the Bible "hell" or "the second death."

94. Q. *Is there any use of the moral law to man since the fall?*

A. *Although no man, since the fall, can attain to righteousness and life by the moral law; yet there is great use thereto, as well common to all men, as peculiar either to the unregenerate, or the regenerate.*

Scripture References

- Rom. 8:3; Gal. 2:16. Since the fall, no man can attain righteousness and life by personal obedience to the moral law.
- 1 Tim. 1:8. The law is good in itself, but must be rightly used.

Commentary

1. What popular error concerning the moral law does this question of the catechism guard against? The very common error that sinful human beings can save themselves by their "good works" or "good character," that is, the notion that mankind, since the fall, can attain to righteousness and life by personal obedience to the moral law. The catechism rejects this false idea emphatically. Thus at the very beginning of a long section on the moral law and the Ten Commandments (continuing through question 148), the catechism carefully guards against the idea which the sinful human heart naturally tends to take for granted, that it is possible for sinners adequately to obey the moral law. The moral law, and its expression in the Ten Commandments, has great use to all classes of men; but it is of the utmost importance that we recognize and reject the lie inherent in the Pharisees' system, the belief that the commandments can really be kept. The truth is that unregenerate people cannot keep the moral law at all so as to please God; even their "good works" are sins that need to be repented of; and true believers in Christ, by divine grace, are enabled to keep the moral law only in a partial and inadequate way, so that their "good works" are acceptable to God only by reason of Christ's mediation. It has sometimes been alleged that the Westminster Standards, by their very strong emphasis on the Ten Commandments, encourage the idea of "salvation by works." This charge is utterly unfounded and overlooks the express statements of the Westminster Standards both on the way of salvation and on the moral law.

2. If the moral law is of no use as a way of attaining righteousness and life, then of what use is it? The moral law is affirmed by the catechism to be of great use (a) to mankind in general; (b) to unregenerate sinners; (c) to regenerate persons.

(Questions 95–97 take up these classes in detail.)

95. Q. *Of what use is the moral law to all men?*

A. *The moral law is of use to all men, to inform them of the holy nature and will of God, and of their duty, binding them to walk accordingly; to convince them of their disability to keep it, and of the sinful pollution of their nature, hearts, and lives: to humble them in the sense of their sin and misery, and thereby help them to a clearer sight of the need they have of Christ, and of the perfection of his obedience.*

Scripture References

- Lev. 11:44–45; 20:7–8; Rom. 7:12. The moral law is an expression of the holy nature and will of God.
- Mic. 6:8; James 2:10–11. The moral law serves as a revelation of the duty of all men, as creatures of God, to obey him.
- Ps. 19:11–12; Rom. 3:20; 7:7. The moral law serves to convince men of their sinful and spiritually helpless condition by nature.
- Rom. 3:9, 23. The moral law serves to humble sinners by convincing them of their sin and misery.
- Gal. 3:21–22. The moral law serves to help men to gain a clearer insight into their need of Christ as Savior from sin.
- Rom. 10:4. The moral law serves to give men a high idea of the character and righteousness of Christ, who fulfilled the law perfectly.

Commentary

1. What four uses does the moral law of God have for all men? The moral law of God is of use to all men in the following four ways: (a) as a revelation of truth concerning God; (b) as a revelation of truth concerning man's moral obligation to God; (c) as a means of convincing men of their utterly sinful condition by nature; (d) as a help toward a right estimate of the matchless character of Christ.

2. How is the moral law a revelation of truth concerning God? The moral law is a revelation of truth concerning God because it is an expression of his holy nature and will. This is contrary to the "modern" view of the moral law, which regards it as a force or principle existing of itself in "the nature of things." That which is right is right not because it is right of itself, but because God's own holy nature demands it. We should note that the catechism mentions the nature of God before the will of God. The nature of God determines what is right, and the will of God imposes this on mankind as a moral obligation.

3. How is the moral law a revelation of man's moral obligation to God? As an expression of the will of God, the moral law comes to man with a demand for absolute and total obedience. This demand for obedience is based in the Bible, not on utilitarian considerations such as "the greatest good of the greatest number" or "the welfare of humanity," but upon the Creator-creature relationship which is grounded in the Scripture doctrine of creation. "And God spake all these words, saying, I am the LORD thy God. . . . Thou shalt have no other gods before me," etc. (Exod. 20:1–17). Nothing could be more immoral than the popular modern idea that the moral law is to be obeyed for selfish or utilitarian reasons. The moral law is to be obeyed because it is our duty to obey it in view of the fact that God is our Creator and we are his creatures.

4. How is the moral law of God a means of convincing men of their utterly sinful condition by nature? (a) The moral law of God places before mankind an absolute moral standard. The harder a person tries to conform to this absolute standard, the more he must become convinced in his conscience that he cannot really attain it. Mankind as created by God, in the Garden of Eden, could have attained to this absolute moral standard. Since the fall, the standard has remained the same, but the character of human beings has changed. The attempt of sinners to conform to an absolute moral standard, which could be attained only by sinless human beings, must serve to convince them of their sinful condition because of their inability to live up to the standard. (b) The sinful human heart rebels against the holy requirements of God's moral law; thus the moral law serves to provoke man's sinful, corrupt nature into actual transgressions (Rom. 7:7). The moral law actually makes men worse sinners because their sinful hearts rise in rebellion against it, and the sinful corruption of the heart is translated into sinful practice in the life (Rom. 7:8–11). (c) The moral law of God is calculated to humble men because of their sin and misery; the more keenly they realize their failure and inability really to keep the law, the more they must be humbled because of their sinful condition. Only where the lie that the law can be really obeyed is cherished, as by the Pharisees, can men be blind to their own sinfulness and consequently filled with pride. (d) The moral law of God is calculated to help men to have a sense of need as well as a sense of sin. It is to be a schoolmaster to bring men to Christ. Personal failure to conform to the moral law should convince men of their deep need of a Savior who has kept the law perfectly for them, and who will save them so that in the end they too can conform perfectly to the law.

5. How does the moral law of God help men toward a right estimate of the matchless character of Christ? Christ himself lived under the law (Gal. 4:4). He perfectly fulfilled all the requirements of the moral law of God, conforming totally to the absolute standard which God had set for mankind. If we realize that Christ fulfilled the moral law for sinners, then the deeper insight we have into the real character of the moral law, the greater will be our appreciation of the matchless character of Christ. Those who think of the moral law as a human discovery of a natural force or principle usually also think of Christ as simply "a good man." Those who understand that the moral law is an expression of the absolutely holy nature of God will think of Christ as the one and only absolutely perfect man and also as the God-man. If Christ lived a life on earth of perfect conformity to the absolute standard of God's moral law, then Christ's obedience and righteousness are absolutely perfect in every respect. Christ is absolute moral perfection realized in a human life.

96. **Q.** *What particular use is there of the moral law to unregenerate men?*

A. *The moral law is of use to unregenerate men, to awaken their consciences to flee from wrath to come, and to drive them to Christ; or, upon their continuance in the estate and way of sin, to leave them inexcusable, and under the curse thereof.*

Scripture References
• 1 Tim. 1:9–10. The moral law of God applicable to wicked men.

- Gal. 3:24. The moral law is useful to drive sinners to Christ for salvation.
- Rom. 1:20 compared with Rom. 2:15. The moral law leaves sinners without excuse.

Commentary

1. What is the meaning of the word *unregenerate?* This describes a person who has not been born again, and is therefore a lost, unsaved sinner.

2. What is the ordinary condition of the consciences of unregenerate people? Ordinarily the consciences of unregenerate people are asleep and therefore need to be awakened or aroused.

3. How does the moral law serve to awaken the consciences of unsaved sinners? The moral law declares that the wrath of God is revealed from heaven against all unrighteousness (Rom. 1:18), and so their consciences are stirred up to be afraid of the judgment of God that will come upon them.

4. Does the moral law provide a way of escape from the wrath of God? No. The moral law provides no way of escape. It only pronounces God's judgment on human sin. Because the law itself provides no way of escape from God's wrath, it serves to drive the sinner to Christ, who is the only way of escape.

5. Do all unsaved sinners have a knowledge of the moral law of God? Yes. Not only those who have a knowledge of the Bible, but even those who are entirely ignorant of the Bible, including the heathen, have some knowledge of the moral law of God from God's natural revelation in the human heart.

6. Do all unsaved sinners have an equal knowledge of the moral law of God? No. Those who have only the natural revelation of the moral law have but a very dim and incomplete knowledge of it, yet their knowledge is sufficient to leave them without excuse. Those who have the light of Scripture have a much greater and clearer knowledge of God's moral law.

7. Does the moral law of God awaken the consciences of all sinners. and drive them to Christ for salvation? No. While it is true that all sinners have some knowledge of the moral law of God, yet there are many who never truly come to Christ for salvation.

8. Why does not the moral law drive all sinners to Christ for salvation? The moral law of itself alone is powerless to drive any sinner to Christ for salvation. It is only when the knowledge of the moral law is accompanied by the supernatural work of God the Holy Spirit that the sinner is really driven to Christ (Acts 16:14).

9. Why does the Holy Spirit not open the hearts of all sinners so that all will come to Christ and be saved? The Bible does not give the answer to this question, except to speak of the sovereignty of God, by which he elects and saves whom he will, for his own reasons which he has not revealed to us (Rom. 9:15–18). The Bible plainly teaches that God has chosen some to salvation, and that he saves those whom he has chosen. God's reasons for discriminating between men are among the secret things which he has not revealed to men.

10. What is the effect of the moral law in the case of sinners who never come to Christ? The effect of the moral law in the case of sinners who never come to Christ is "to leave them inexcusable, and under the curse thereof."

11. Is the moral law of any use to enable unregenerate people to live so as to please God? No. Romans 8:8: "They that are in the flesh cannot please God." The expression "they that are in the flesh" means the unregenerate, or those that have not been born again. Such people may learn from the moral law what their duty is, but they are dead in trespasses and sins and therefore they cannot please God. Their hearts are not right with God, and everything they do is done with a wrong and sinful motive.

12. Is the moral law of any use to enable unregenerate people to earn their own salvation? No (Rom. 3:20). No sinner can possibly earn his salvation by his efforts to keep God's law. The harder a sinner tries to keep God's commandments, the more he will realize that he is a breaker of the commandments and therefore a lost, helpless, needy sinner.

13. What is the place of the moral law of God in a scriptural program of evangelism? While the word *evangelism* means "proclamation of the gospel," we should realize that the gospel is meaningless without the law. *Gospel* means "good news": that is, good news of salvation from sin. Sin is the transgression of the law: without conviction of being transgressors of the law, people will feel no need of the gospel; without knowledge of the moral law of God, people will not feel themselves to be transgressors of the law. Therefore no program of evangelism is sound or scriptural which does not emphasize sin as the transgression of God's moral law. Much present-day "evangelism" has little to say about God's law, sin, and repentance; instead, the tendency is to speak only about "accepting Christ." A return to the old emphasis on God's law is urgently needed. Without it, there cannot be a genuine revival of the Christian faith.

97. Q. *What special use is there of the moral law to the regenerate?*

A. *Although they that are regenerate, and believe in Christ, be delivered from the moral law as a covenant of works, so as thereby they are neither justified nor condemned; yet, besides the general uses thereof common to them with all men, it is of special use, to show them how much they are bound to Christ for his fulfilling it, and enduring the curse thereof in their stead, and for their good; and thereby to provoke them to more thankfulness, and to express the same in their greater care to conform themselves hereunto as the rule of their obedience.*

Scripture References

- Rom. 8:14; 7:3–6; Gal. 4:4–5. The regenerate are not under the law as a covenant of works.
- Rom. 3:20; Gal. 5:23; Rom. 8.1. The regenerate are not justified by obedience to, nor condemned because of violation of, the moral law.
- Rom. 7:2, 25; 8:3–4; Gal. 3:13–14. The moral law shows the Christian how much he owes to Christ, who fulfilled the law's requirements for him, and bore its penalty on his behalf.
- Luke 1:68–69, 74–75. The moral law incites the Christian to thankfulness to God for the redemption provided in Christ.
- Rom. 7:22; 12:2; Titus 2:11–14. The moral law is the Christian's standard of obedience, not in order to earn eternal life by obeying it, but in order to express his gratitude to God for the free gift of salvation.

Commentary

1. When a person is "born again," and becomes a Christian, how does his relation to the moral law change? He is instantly and forever delivered from all useless labor of trying to save himself by obedience to the law, and also delivered from the condemning power of the law.

2. When did the covenant of works come to an end? (a) As a way of earning eternal life for all mankind by human obedience to God's law, that is, by Adam's obedience as the representative of mankind, the covenant of works ended when Adam and Eve ate the forbidden fruit in Eden. (b) As the way of earning eternal life for the elect by obedience to God's law on the part of Christ, the divine-human Mediator and second Adam, the covenant of works was incorporated into, and became a part of, the covenant of grace, and so is still in effect today. (c) In the case of those who have not yet come to Christ and received the benefits of the covenant of grace, they are still under the condemnation of the broken covenant of works, and such people often make a desperate and futile attempt to earn eternal life on the basis of the covenant of works, that is, by personal obedience to the moral law.

3. What term describes the type of religion which seeks to earn eternal life by personal obedience to the moral law? Legalism, also called moralism.

4. What sect of the Jews in the time of Christ was dominated by legalism? The Pharisees.

5. What is wrong with legalism? It is "too little, and too late." Too little, because God demands perfect obedience to the moral law, whereas the sinner renders a very imperfect obedience; too late, because the possibility of earning eternal life by law-obedience ceased in Eden ages ago.

6. Are modern Christians ever affected by legalism? It is sad but true that they often are. (a) Where the Bible teaching of salvation by grace is not known or understood, professing Christians are often completely legalistic, frankly trying to earn eternal life by good works. (b) Even those who really know and understand the Bible teaching of salvation by grace often fall unconsciously into a legalistic way of thinking. A person may profess the theology of grace, and yet, without realizing the inconsistency, may be greatly influenced by a legalistic attitude or way of thinking about life and religion.

7. What is the remedy for legalism? (a) A realization of the utter failure and futility of legalism. (b) A deeper understanding and personal experience of the Bible teaching of salvation by grace.

8. Should a Christian be afraid to commit sin? Yes.

9. Should a Christian be afraid to commit sin because of the danger of eternal condemnation? No (1 John 4:18).

10. Then why should a Christian be afraid to commit sin? Because it is right to fear that which is contrary to God's holiness, and which will offend God and hide the light of his countenance from us, even though in the case of the Christian it involves no danger of eternal condemnation.

11. How does the moral law enable the Christian to appreciate Christ? The moral law enables the Christian to appreciate Christ by showing him how much he owes to Christ, that is, how much Christ has done for him in perfectly keeping the whole law and bearing its penalty on the Christian's behalf.

12. How does the moral law provoke the Christian to thankfulness? The moral law provokes the Christian to thankfulness by giving him an appreciation of Christ's work and sufferings on his behalf.

13. Instead of thankfulness, what state of mind does a legalistic type of religion tend to produce? A legalistic type of religion cannot lead to an attitude of real thankfulness to God but on the contrary leads to a self-righteous spiritual pride.

14. How should a Christian express his thankfulness to God? A Christian should express his thankfulness to God not only in words of prayer and praise, but also in taking care to live according to God's moral law as the rule of obedience.

15. Since the Bible teaches that the Christian is not under the law but under grace (Rom. 6:14), how can he be under the moral law as the rule of obedience? The Christian is freed from the penalty of the law, but not from the precept of the law as the standard of right living.

16. Prove from the Bible that the Christian is not freed from the precept of the moral law as the standard of right living. (a) Scripture teaches that Christians may and do commit sin (1 John 1:8; 2:1; James 5:16). But Scripture defines sin as "the transgression of the law" (1 John 3:4). Therefore Scripture teaches that Christians may and do transgress the law. Therefore Christians must be under the precept of the law, for otherwise they could not be said to transgress it. (b) In 1 Corinthians 9:19–21 the apostle Paul expressly denies that he is "without law to God," and affirms on the contrary that he is "under the law to Christ." These words, of course, were written years after he became a Christian. Those modern Christians who claim that faith in Christ has set them free from the precept of the moral law as the standard of right living are claiming something that the apostle Paul did not venture to claim for himself, but rather emphatically disclaimed in the reference quoted above.

98. Q. *Where is the moral law summarily comprehended?*

A. *The moral law is summarily comprehended in the ten commandments, which were delivered by the voice of God upon Mount Sinai, and written by him in two tables of stone; and are recorded in the twentieth chapter of Exodus. The first four commandments containing our duty to God, and the other six our duty to man.*

Scripture References
- Exod. 34:1–4; Deut. 10:4. The Ten Commandments divinely revealed and written by God on two tables of stone.
- Matt. 22:37–40. The moral law summarized by Christ as requiring total love for God, and to love our neighbor as ourself.

Commentary
1. Where in the Bible are the Ten Commandments recorded? Exodus 20:1–17; Deuteronomy 5:6–21.

2. Are the Ten Commandments a complete statement of the moral law of God? The Ten Commandments are not a complete statement in detail of the moral law, but rather a summary of the moral law. Rightly interpreted, they include every moral duty enjoined by God. However, the more detailed statements of God's will are needed for a right interpretation and application of the Ten Commandments. For example, the eighth commandment forbids stealing, but only by a study of other parts of the Bible can we learn what "stealing" includes and frame a correct definition of it.

3. How are the Ten Commandments commonly divided? Following Christ's analysis of the moral law, the Ten Commandments are commonly divided into two "tables," the first four commandments containing our duty to God and the last six our duty to ourselves and to our fellow men.

4. Do not all ten of the commandments deal with our duty to God? Yes. We should not think that the last six commandments are simply a matter between ourselves and our fellow men. They, too, are a matter of our duty to God. The true understanding of the matter is that the first four commandments concern the duty which we owe directly to God, while the last six concern the duty which we owe indirectly to God, that is, the duty which we owe to God in matters involving ourselves and our fellow men.

5. Why do the last six commandments concern our duty to God in connection with our fellow men? Because God, not man, is the Lord of the conscience. God is our Creator; to God we are morally responsible; by God we will be judged at the Last Day. It is only because of our moral responsibility to God that we owe any duties at all to our fellow men. If we ask why we should not steal or commit murder, the answer must be that to steal or commit murder would be a sin against God, because we are responsible to God for our conduct in the social sphere.

6. Are the two tables of the moral law equally important? (a) So far as our obedience to the law is concerned, every one of the Ten Commandments is absolutely important, so that to break any one of them, whether of the first or the second table, is to transgress the whole moral law of God (James 2:10–11). (b) But so far as the logical structure of the Ten Commandments is concerned, it is correct to say that the second table of the law is subordinate to the first table. That is to say, our moral responsibility to God is the basis of our duties to our fellow men. Thus Christ said that the "first and great commandment" is to love God, while to love our neighbor, although it is "like unto" the command to love God, nonetheless is "the second," that is, secondary or subordinate to the first.

7. What wrong views of the Ten Commandments are common today? (a) The view that the Ten Commandments are a code of human laws, composed either by Moses or by other persons among the Jews. (b) The view that the Ten Commandments are the product of human experience, that is, that they are a summary of what people have found to be necessary for the general welfare of mankind. (c) The view that the Ten Commandments were only of temporary significance, having later been superseded by the so-called law of love in the New Testament, or by the evolutionary progress of the human race. All three of these views are wrong. The Ten Commandments are not a code of human laws, but a code of divine laws. They were not composed by Moses or any other human being, but were spoken and written by God himself. They were not of temporary validity, but of permanent validity, and until the end of the world they can never be changed or superseded by any other laws or principles.

99. Q. *What rules are to be observed for the right understanding of the ten commandments?*

A. *For the right understanding of the ten commandments these rules are to be observed: 1. That the law is perfect, and bindeth every one to full conformity in the whole man unto the righteousness thereof, and unto entire obedience for ever; so as to require the utmost perfection of every duty, and to forbid the least degree of every sin.*

Scripture References

- Ps. 19:7. God's law is perfect.
- Matt. 5:21–22, 27–28, 33–34, 37–39, 43–44. God's law requires absolute moral perfection, and cannot tolerate the slightest deviation from perfect and total righteousness.
- Matt. 5:48. God's own perfection demands that man, his creature and image-bearer, be perfect.

Commentary

1. Why do we need rules for the right understanding of the Ten Commandments? Because the Ten Commandments are not a complete application or detailed statement of the moral law, but only a comprehensive summary.

2. How many rules does the catechism present for understanding the Ten Commandments? Eight.

3. From what source are these eight rules derived? From the Bible itself. The rules the catechism presents are a formulation of the Bible's application of the moral law to particular problems and situations.

4. What is meant by saying that God's moral law is perfect? This means that the moral law is a perfect revelation of God's will for man, and that we are bound to fulfill it perfectly.

5. What degree of conformity to righteousness does God's moral law require? Full conformity; therefore partial conformity is worthless in God's sight.

6. What part of our nature is involved in God's requirement of obedience to his moral law? The moral law binds "the whole man," that is, our entire nature, body and soul, including the state of our heart, as well as our thoughts, emotions, words, and deeds.

7. How long will the moral law of God continue to be binding on human beings? Forever; that is, both in this life and in the life to come. However, in the life to come the specific form of the revelation of God's moral law to man will no longer be the Ten Commandments, which are suited to our life in this present world, but a new and more direct revelation of God's will, suited to the life of eternity.

8. Wherein does God's moral law differ from all human laws? Human laws, including all the laws of the various non-Christian religions, are satisfied with a partial, approximate, and imperfect obedience, whereas God's law requires absolute moral perfection and cannot tolerate the slightest degree of any sin.

9. Does God's law, in demanding absolute moral perfection of human beings, demand what is impossible? Yes. No person in the world can meet the demand of God's law for absolute moral perfection.

10. Is God unreasonable in demanding what is impossible for human beings to attain or achieve? No. As created by God, before the fall into sin, man could have attained absolute moral perfection. Man fell into sin by his own fault, and thus moral perfection became impossible. But God could not lower the demands of his law to meet our sinful condition as members of a fallen race. God's law, being the expression of God's own character, is unchangeable. Since our inability to fulfill the law is our own fault, God cannot be expected to lower the demands of the moral law to fit our sinfulness, and there is nothing unreasonable in his demanding what is impossible for us to render.

11. Did any human being ever fulfill the moral law perfectly? Yes. Jesus Christ lived a life of absolute moral perfection in this world for the entire period from his birth to his crucifixion. During this time he never broke any of God's commandments in the slightest degree in thought, word, or deed, and he also perfectly fulfilled the whole positive side of the law, loving God with all his heart and soul and mind and strength, and loving his fellow man with a love second only to his love to his Heavenly Father. In our Lord Jesus Christ we see the absolute moral perfection required by the moral law, not in the abstract, but actually realized in a human life.

99. Q. *(continued) What rules are to be observed for the right understanding of the ten commandments?*

A. *For the right understanding of the ten commandments these rules are to be observed: . . . 2. That it is spiritual, and so reacheth the understanding, will, affections, and all other powers of the soul; as well as words, works, and gestures.*

Scripture References

- Rom. 7:14. The moral law is spiritual in nature.
- Deut. 6:5 compared with Matt. 22:37–39. The moral law requires conformity of all faculties of our mind or soul.

Commentary

1. What is the derivation or original meaning of the word *spirit* in the Bible? The word *spirit* in our English Bible is the translation of a Hebrew word of the Old Testament and a Greek word of the New Testament, both of which primarily mean "wind."

2. Apart from the original meaning of "wind," what meaning does the word *spirit* have in the Bible? The word *spirit* means a self-conscious, active, living being, which may be divine, angelic, demonic, or human. God, the angels, and the demons are pure spirits, having no material bodies. The human spirit is normally united with a material body to form a composite personality of spirit (or soul) and body. However, the human spirit can live apart from a material body, as is the case between death and the resurrection at the Last Day.

3. What is the meaning of the adjective *spiritual* in the Bible? The adjective *spiritual* in the Bible is never used in the popular modern sense of "religious" or "devotional." It is always used in the strict sense of "connected in some way with a spirit." Almost always in the Bible the adjective *spiritual* means "connected with the Holy Spirit of God." Thus in the Bible usage of the word, a "spiritual" man is not just a religious man, but a man in whom the Holy Spirit of God dwells.

4. What is the meaning of the word *spiritual* in question 99 of the catechism? In this question of the catechism the word *spiritual* is used in the sense of "pertaining to the human spirit," or "concerning the spirit of man." Thus the catechism asserts that the moral law of God is spiritual, that is, it concerns not only our outward conduct or actions, but our spiritual life, our thoughts and mental states, our emotions, desires, and the resolutions of our will as well.

5. Are human laws "spiritual"? No. Human laws, that is, laws enacted by the civil government, are not spiritual. They make no claim to govern the spiritual or mental life of the people. Human laws demand outward conformity of conduct only, not conformity of thoughts, desires, beliefs, emotions, etc. For example, the civil government can make a law requiring citizens to pay an income tax, but it has no right to require them to believe in the principle of the income tax, nor to pay it with joy and gladness. The civil government has no jurisdiction over men's mental and spiritual life, but only over outward conduct. Under totalitarian governments the attempt has been made by the state to control people's thoughts, as in Japan where special police bureaus existed for the control of "dangerous thoughts"; but all such attempts are an iniquitous usurpation of the prerogatives of God and are destructive of the liberties of men.

6. How did the Pharisees misunderstand the scope of the moral law of God? They overlooked the spiritual character of the law, and wrongly supposed that it claimed jurisdiction only over their outward conduct. Because of this faulty and partial view of the nature of the moral law, the Pharisees could deceive themselves into thinking that they had attained moral perfection. By a scrupulous observance of the details of the law they thought they had conformed to all its requirements. What they lacked was not outward literal obedience to the precepts and prohibitions of the law, but inward spiritual conformity to its requirements. They cleansed the outside of the cup and platter, while inwardly they were full of wickedness; they worshiped God with their lips, while their heart was far from him.

7. What error concerning the moral law is just the opposite of that of the Pharisees? Just the opposite of the Pharisees' error is the view held by some modern professing Christians who say that inward spiritual conformity to the law is all that is necessary, and we need not bother to conform our outward life and conduct to the literal requirements of the law. Such people say that if we have an attitude of love to God and our neighbor, we need not concern ourselves about such outward details as the literal observance of the Sabbath. They fail to realize that our outward life is the expression of our inward spiritual life, and if the law of God is really engraved upon our hearts it must inevitably come to expression in our outward life and conduct.

8. What is meant by saying that the moral law concerns the understanding? This means that our intellect is subject to the moral law of God, and it is a sin to believe what is false, to reject what is true, or to have our thinking blinded or warped by prejudice. We are responsible for our thinking just as we are for our actions.

9. What is meant by affirming that the moral law concerns the will? This means that our power to make decisions or choices is subject to the moral law of God, and that it is a sin to make a choice contrary to the law of God, to fail to make a choice which is according to the law of God, or to be actuated in our decisions by wrong, sinful motives.

10. What is meant by the statement that the moral law concerns the affections? By "affections" the catechism means what are commonly called "emotions" today, such as love, hatred, anger, joy, sorrow. These emotions are subject to the moral law of God, so that to have wrong feelings or emotions contrary to the requirements of the law is sinful.

11. What are the "other powers of the soul" to which the catechism refers? Possibly the reference is to the memory and also to the artistic sense, which includes the capacity for producing or appreciating beautiful music, pictures, poetry, literature, etc. All these capacities of the human spirit are strictly subject to the moral law of God.

12. In addition to our inward or spiritual life, what activities of human life does the moral law concern? Our words, works, and gestures. That is to say, the moral law concerns every possible way by which our inward or spiritual life finds expression in the external world which is around us. It concerns every possible relation of our spirit to our environment. There is nothing we can possibly do, whether in our inward spiritual life or in our outward conduct, which is not subject to the moral law of God. Truly God's commandment is exceeding broad (Ps. 119:96).

99. Q. *(continued) What rules are to be observed for the right understanding of the ten commandments?*

A. *For the right understanding of the ten commandments these rules are to be observed: . . . 3. That one and the same thing, in divers respects, is required or forbidden in several commandments. 4. That as, where a duty is commanded, the contrary sin is forbidden: and, where a sin is forbidden, the contrary duty is commanded: so, where a promise is annexed, the contrary threatening is included; and, where a threatening is annexed, the contrary promise is included.*

Scripture References

- Col. 3:5. Covetousness is idolatry, hence forbidden in two commandments.
- Amos 8:5. The same sinful desire violated both the fourth and the eighth commandments.
- Prov. 1:19. The same sin may involve both covetousness and murder.
- 1 Tim. 6:10. The love of money also involves many other kinds of sin.
- Isa. 58:13. Negative and positive aspects of Sabbath observance.

- Deut. 6:13 with Matt. 4:9–10. Positive and negative aspects of fearing God.
- Matt. 15:4–6. Positive and negative aspects of the fifth commandment.

Commentary

1. May the same duty be required in more than one of the Ten Commandments? Yes. For example, "six days shalt thou labor and do all thy work" is a part of the fourth commandment, relating to the Sabbath; but the eighth commandment, which forbids stealing, also requires a person to work for his living, for the person who lives without working is really stealing his living from someone else.

2. May the same sin be forbidden by more than one of the Ten Commandments? Yes. For example, to bear false witness in a murder trial, resulting in the death of an innocent person, is a violation of both the sixth and the ninth commandments ("Thou shalt not kill"; "Thou shalt not bear false witness against thy neighbor").

3. What is the reason why the various commandments overlap in this way? Because human life is complex, and every fact of our life is related in some way to all the other facts of our life. Consequently when we look at the facts of our life from the standpoint of God's moral law, we realize that any one fact of our life may be related, in some way or other, to several of the Ten Commandments.

4. Do the Ten Commandments ever contradict each other, so that what is forbidden by one commandment is required by another? No. Because God is the Author of all and they are the expression of one moral law, the Ten Commandments form a harmonious whole. There can be no real contradiction between any of them. If there seem to be contradictions, we may be sure that there is an error in our interpretation of them somewhere. For example, the young man who told his pastor that obedience to the fifth commandment required him to break the fourth commandment (because to honor his father and mother, he must comply with their wishes, and to comply with their wishes he must stay home from church to attend a wedding on the Sabbath day) was mistaken in his interpretation of the fifth commandment. For the command to honor our father and mother requires obedience to parents "in the Lord," that is, in matters not contrary to the law of God. The fifth commandment does not require a person to obey his parents by disobeying a command of God.

5. What is the teaching of the catechism concerning positive and negative aspects of the Ten Commandments? The catechism teaches that in the Ten Commandments, positive and negative elements imply each other, even though only one or the other is expressly stated. Where a duty is commanded, the contrary sin is forbidden; where a sin is forbidden, it is implied that the contrary duty is commanded; and the same principle applies to the matter of threatenings and promises.

6. What do we mean by the negative aspect of the Ten Commandments? Their prohibition of transgression of the law of God, or doing something which God has forbidden.

7. What do we mean by the positive aspect of the Ten Commandments? Their requirement of conformity to the law of God, that is, doing whatever God requires.

8. In the form in which the Ten Commandments are stated, which of these aspects is the more prominent? The negative aspect is the more prominent, as eight of the Ten Commandments begin with the expression "Thou shalt not" or similar words. Eight of the Ten Commandments are negative in form, whereas only two are positive in form (the fourth and fifth).

9. Does this negative emphasis in the form of the commandments mean that God's moral law is negative rather than positive? No. While the form of the Ten Commandments is largely negative, the meaning, as properly interpreted by the catechism, is both negative and positive, with an equal emphasis on both. This interpretation is warranted by comparing the Ten Commandments with Christ's summary of the moral law as requiring us to love the Lord our God with all our heart and soul and mind and strength; this is positive in form.

10. Which of the commandments contain threatenings and promises? The second and third contain threatenings; the fifth contains a promise. In each case, if we interpret the commandments aright, we will realize that both threatening and promise are involved.

99. Q. *(continued) What rules are to be observed for the right understanding of the ten commandments?*

A. *For the right understanding of the ten commandments these rules are to
be observed: . . . 5. That what God forbids, is at no time to be done;
what he commands, is always our duty; and yet every particular duty
is not to be done at all times. 6. That under one sin or duty, all of the
same kind are forbidden or commanded; together with all the causes,
means, occasions, and appearances thereof, and provocations thereunto.*

Scripture References

- Job 13:7–8. We may not do what God forbids, even for a "good" purpose.
- Rom. 3:8. The notion of doing evil that good may come is perverse.
- Job 36:21; Heb. 11:25. We should choose rather to suffer than to commit sin.
- Deut. 4:8–9. What God commands is always our duty.
- Matt. 12:7. Sometimes one duty has priority over another, as mercy over
  sacrifice.
- Eccl. 3:1–8. Every particular duty is not to be done at all times.
- Matt. 5:21–22, 27–28. Under one sin or duty all of the same kind are included.
- Matt. 15:4–6. The command to honor parents, and the prohibition of curs-
  ing parents, is rightly understood to include the duty of providing for the
  support of parents if they are in need.
- Heb. 10:24–25. The duty of provoking one another to love and to good
  works implies that it is wrong for Christian people to forsake assembling
  themselves together, that is, to be neglectful of the regular services of their
  own church.
- 1 Thess. 5:22. The Christian must abstain from every form in which evil appears.
- Jude 23. The Christian is to hate, and abstain from, even the slightest involvement in wickedness.
- Gal. 5:26. The Christian must abstain from provoking and envying other
  Christians, and also from the desire for vain glory, which is the cause of provoking and envying.
- Col. 3:21. Fathers should not provoke their children (by unreasonable
  requirements) lest the children fall into the sins of anger and discouragement; God forbids not only these sins, but the provocations "hereunto."

Commentary

**1. What great principle of ethics does the catechism lay down con-
cerning what God forbids?** That what God forbids is never to be done.

2. What popular notion contradicts this great principle? This great principle is contradicted by the popular notion that whether something is right or wrong depends on the purpose for which it is done. According to this popular notion, it may be right to do something which God forbids, provided we do it for a good purpose. For example, it may be right to tell a lie to save some person's life; or to gain money by gambling in order to donate it to foreign missions; or to maintain a gambling scheme in order to raise money to support the church.

3. Is this popular notion a new idea? No. It is really extremely ancient, and was known in the days of the apostle Paul, who undertook to expose its unsoundness in his epistles (Rom. 3:8).

4. Why is this notion that "the end justifies the means" perverse? This notion is perverse because it breaks down the distinction between right and wrong. To say, "Let us do evil that good may come" amounts to saying, "Let us do right by doing wrong." Such a notion implies that there is no real difference between right and wrong; black and white are mixed into some shade of gray. Throughout the whole Bible the distinction between right and wrong is represented as an absolute one. There is simply no such thing as doing wrong without committing sin, or committing sin without doing wrong.

5. Why is this perverse notion popular in the present day? Partly, no doubt, because it naturally appeals to our sinful human hearts, and is a very convenient and easy doctrine to live by; and partly because the modern world is dominated by a non-Christian philosophy which teaches that right and wrong are not absolute matters, but changing all the time, so that what is right today may be wrong 100 years from now, and vice versa.

6. What is the importance of the principle that what God commands is always our duty? This implies that we are always under the moral government of God, and responsible to him for the state of our hearts and for all our thoughts, words, and deeds; we can never take a vacation from our duty to God; all our life long, every moment, we have a moral obligation to God.

7. Why is not every particular duty to be done at all times? It would of course be not only impossible but absurd to attempt to do every particular duty at all times. God's law, while it does present an ideal so high that we cannot attain it in this present life, still does not present an absurdity. Some duties are specifically limited to certain times, as, for example, Sabbath observance. But even the duties that are not so limited are not to be done all at once. We are to rejoice with them that rejoice, and to weep with them that weep, but not both at the same time.

8. According to the catechism, what are included under each sin or duty mentioned in the Ten Commandments? Under each sin or duty are included all others of the same class. For example, the ninth commandment forbids bearing false witness against our neighbor. While this commandment specifically mentions only this one form of untruthfulness, it is rightly understood to prohibit all forms of untruthfulness. For from other parts of the Bible we learn that all liars shall have their part in the lake of fire (Rev. 21:8; 22:15). That is to say, the Ten Commandments are not to be taken alone, as if they stood by themselves, but must be taken in their context of the whole Bible, and we must take the entire Word of God into account in deciding the true and proper meaning of the Ten Commandments.

9. Why is it correct to say that the causes, means, occasions, appearances, and provocations of or to any sin or duty are included in the meaning of the Ten Commandments? Because God's law is spiritual, and involves thoughts, motives, and intents of the heart as well as outward conduct; and because any particular act in our outward life is not something isolated, by itself, but the product of a complex chain of events and motives. Thus the commandment which forbids the sin of murder is interpreted by Jesus as forbidding the sin of hatred, which is a cause of murder. And the commandment which forbids adultery is interpreted by Jesus as forbidding the sin of lust, which leads to adultery.

10. What danger must we guard against in applying these rules of interpretation to the Ten Commandments? In saying that a certain commandment includes something else, which is not specifically mentioned in that commandment, we must take the greatest care to make sure that we are not reading our own thoughts, preferences, or prejudices into the Ten Commandments. We must take the greatest care that whatever we say is included in a certain commandment is really based on the teaching of God's Word and is not just our own human idea or opinion. For example, it has been claimed that the sixth commandment forbids capital punishment and defensive warfare, but a study of the Bible as a whole shows that such an interpretation is

not legitimate. It has been claimed that the second commandment forbids
honoring the national flag of our country, but this claim is based on a failure
to discriminate between religious worship and civil allegiance. Similarly, to
claim that the sixth commandment forbids eating meat, and requires a vege-
tarian diet, is entirely unwarranted; the person who makes such a claim is
merely reading his own prejudices into the Ten Commandments.

99. Q. *(continued) What rules are to be observed for the right understanding of the ten commandments?*

A. *For the right understanding of the ten commandments these rules are to
be observed: . . . 7. That what is forbidden or commanded to ourselves,
we are bound, according to our places, to endeavor that it may be avoided
or performed by others, according to the duty of their places. 8. That in
what is commanded to others, we are bound, according to our places and
callings, to be helpful to them; and to take heed of partaking with others in what is forbidden them.*

Scripture References
- Exod. 20:10; Lev. 19:17; Gen. 18:19; Josh. 24:15; Deut. 6:6–7. It is our
  duty to encourage righteousness and discourage sin on the part of others.
- 2 Cor. 1:24. We are under obligation to try to help others do right.
- 1 Tim. 5:22; Eph. 5:11. It is our duty to keep ourselves clear of participation in the sins of others.

Commentary
**1. What is the general scope of the last two rules for the right under-
standing of the Ten Commandments?** The general scope of the last two
rules is responsibility for the moral welfare of our neighbor. These two rules
remind us that righteousness, or obedience to God's will, is not merely an
individual matter but involves a concern for others too. While it is of course
true that in the end each individual must give his own account to God, we
must remember that part of that accounting will deal with the effect of our
lives on the moral well-being of other people.

2. Why does the catechism include the phrase "according to our places" in the seventh rule? Because in determining the degree and nature of our responsibility for the moral character and life of others, our own position in human society, and our relationship to others, must be taken into account. Thus, for example, the responsibility of a parent for a child is far greater than that of a child for a parent; yet even a child has a responsibility to endeavor, according to his place, that his parents practice right and avoid wrong. Similarly, a minister or elder has a greater responsibility for influencing the members of the church, by reason of his position of authority, than the members have for influencing their minister and elders toward what is right; yet in each case a certain responsibility exists.

3. Is it right to arrange for someone else to do something that we will not do ourselves because we believe it to be wrong? Certainly not. If a matter is wrong, we must neither do it ourselves nor arrange for anyone else to do it. Yet this principle is frequently violated in practice. A Christian businessman should not keep his store or office open for business on the Sabbath day, and he should also not employ someone else to keep it open for him. If a book or magazine is not fit to read, we ought to refrain not only from reading it ourselves, but also from giving or selling it to others for them to read. It makes no difference whether these other persons are Christians or not. God's moral law is the same for all people; it does not provide one standard of life for Christians and another for non-Christians. God requires absolute moral perfection of everybody, Christian and non-Christian. It is very perverse to say that a Christian, who would not do certain things himself, may engage or employ someone that is not a Christian to do them for him.

4. How are we to endeavor that others practice righteousness and avoid sin? We should endeavor to accomplish this result (a) by showing a good example ourselves; (b) by witnessing to others, or seeking to persuade them, as we have opportunity and as occasion may require; (c) by the exercise of whatever measure of authority God has committed to us. The first two methods may and should be practiced by every Christian; the third is limited to those persons to whom God has committed authority in family, church, and state. Thus any Christian should set a good example of Sabbath observance, for example, and on occasion should seek to persuade others to keep the fourth commandment; but in addition to these ways, a parent has the authority to forbid his children to violate the Sabbath. A civil official should promote honesty by his example and his testimony, but it may also be his duty to exercise his authority by prosecuting those who are guilty of theft. In each case the exercise of authority must be limited by the measure of authority granted by God and the nature of the relation to the persons involved.

5. How should we try to be helpful to others in doing their duty? There are of course many ways of being helpful to others, which change with changing circumstances. We can always be helpful by trying to understand the difficulties and temptations that others must cope with, and maintaining a sympathetic attitude toward them. We should avoid an unduly critical spirit, and even when it is our duty to reprove someone for wrongdoing, we should do it with kindness and Christian love, not in a bitter, harsh, or self-righteous spirit. If someone is facing a hard battle against sin, temptation, and discouragement, we should do what we can, in word and deed, to encourage and help such a person. We should never rejoice in iniquity, or take a secret delight in some other person's wrongdoing. And avoidance of petty gossip about the sins and failures of others will go a long way toward healing the sore spots in the visible church.

6. Why should we "take heed of partaking with others in what is forbidden them"? To participate with others in what is forbidden them is to encourage them in wrongdoing, and thus to incur a share in their guilt, even though the matter in question may be something not forbidden to ourselves. It is wrong, for example, to accept a ride in a stolen automobile if we know that the car is stolen; to accept a ride in a car is not wrong, but in this case we would be participating in the wrongdoing of another person. If a child has been forbidden by his parents to leave home and go to a ball game at a particular time but disobeys his parents and goes to the game, it is wrong for another child, knowing the circumstances, to accompany him, for this would encourage him in his disobedience to parental authority.

12

God's Will with Direct Reference to Himself

100. Q. *What special things are we to consider in the ten commandments?*

A. *We are to consider in the ten commandments, the preface, the substance of the commandments themselves, and several reasons annexed to some of them, the more to enforce them.*

101. Q. *What is the preface to the ten commandments?*

A. *The preface to the ten commandments is contained in these words,* I am the Lord thy God, which have brought thee out of the land of Egypt, out of the house of bondage. *Wherein God manifesteth his sovereignty, as being JEHOVAH, the eternal, immutable, and almighty God; having his being in and of himself, and giving being to all his words and works: and that he is a God in covenant, as with Israel of old, so with all his people; who, as he brought them out of their bondage in Egypt, so he delivereth us from our spiritual thraldom; and that therefore we are bound to take him for our God alone, and to keep all his commandments.*

Scripture References

- Exod. 20:2; Deut. 5:6. The preface to the Ten Commandments.
- Isa. 44:6. The absolute sovereignty of God.

255

- Exod. 3:14. The self-existence of God.
- Exod. 6:3. The revelation of the name *Jehovah*.
- Acts 17:24, 28. God the Creator a Sustainer of all things.
- Gen. 17:7 compared with Rom. 3:29. God in covenant not only with Israel of old, but with believers from the Gentiles also.
- Luke 1:74–75. God redeems his people from spiritual bondage, as well as from human tyranny.
- 1 Peter 1:15–18; Lev. 18:30; 19:37. God's sovereignty and his work of redemption require us to render him total allegiance and absolute obedience.

Commentary

1. Why is the preface to the Ten Commandments important? The preface to the Ten Commandments is important because it is an integral part of the Ten Commandments, and constitutes the foundation of the specific commandments which follow. The preface states the reasons why we are under obligation to obey the commandments; it lays the foundation for moral responsibility in the two facts of (a) God's absolute sovereignty; (b) God's work of redemption.

It is a tragedy that children are often taught the Ten Commandments with the preface omitted, as if it were unimportant. It is deplorable that Sabbath School rooms often have attractively printed wall charts of the Ten Commandments, with the preface omitted. This widespread tendency to disregard the preface to the Ten Commandments is a symptom of the religious declension of our time. The tendency today is to regard morality as grounded in human considerations, such as the welfare of the human race, the safety of society, and similar utilitarian concepts. People whose religious thinking is of this type will consider the preface to the Ten Commandments more or less irrelevant; they will think that we can retain the "values" of the Ten Commandments even if they are detached from the foundation of divine sovereignty and redemption. We should resist this modern tendency, and insist on the God-centered emphasis of the moral law. The preface states the authority back of the moral law: to disregard the preface is to overlook the importance of the source of the law's authority, and inevitably to misunderstand the Ten Commandments.

2. What is meant by the sovereignty of God? By the sovereignty of God is meant the absolute, supreme, and unchallengeable authority and dominion of God over the entire universe. Because God is sovereign he is supreme over all creatures, "and hath most sovereign dominion over them, to do by them, for them, or upon them, whatsoever himself pleaseth" (Confession of Faith, 2.2). No creature may question the righteousness of any act of God; to do so is the height of impiety and irreverence. The sovereignty of God also implies that God is ultimate: there is no principle or law above or beyond God to which God himself is responsible. God is responsible only to himself; his own nature is his only law. There is nothing above or beyond him. God's sovereignty is manifested in a special way in his work of redemption. Redemption from sin is wholly God's work, and its benefits are bestowed wholly according to God's sovereign good pleasure. He saves exactly whom he purposes to save, and does so by his absolute, almighty power.

3. What is the origin of the name *Jehovah*? This divine name, which is usually represented in the Authorized Version by "LORD" (printed in large and small capital letters), is based on the Hebrew consonants JHVH. The Hebrew alphabet consists of consonants only, and the early Hebrew manuscripts of the Old Testament had only consonants. In reading, the correct vowel sounds were supplied by the reader. At a later period a system of writing the vowels was devised by means of "points" written above, beneath, or between the consonants. Just what vowel sounds originally belonged to the divine name JHVH is uncertain. The pronunciation "Jahveh" is thought by many scholars to be correct, but this has not been proved, and it is only a matter of opinion. The Jews considered the divine name JHVH too sacred even to be pronounced, so in reading, whenever they came to JHVH they substituted another word, *Adonai*, meaning "Lord." Then when the vowel "points" were added to the Hebrew text of the Old Testament, the vowels of "Adonai" were inserted with the consonants JHVH, resulting in a hybrid word which is commonly pronounced "Jehovah" in English and European languages. The important thing, of course, is not the pronunciation of the name, but its meaning.

4. What is the meaning of the name *Jehovah*? This name of God was specially revealed in the time of Moses (Exod. 6:2–3). The key to its basic meaning is found in Exodus 3:14–15 and Exodus 33:19. God said to Moses, "I AM THAT I AM," and instructed Moses to tell the people of Israel, "I AM hath sent me unto you." In the next verse (Exod. 3:15) the verb "I AM" is changed to the third person, meaning "HE IS," written by the Hebrew letters JHVH, and translated "LORD" in the Authorized Version. Thus the expression "I AM THAT I AM" gives a key to the meaning of *Jehovah*. It signifies that God is sovereign and self-determined, not limited or influenced by anything outside of himself. Exodus 33:19 further explains the name as signifying God's sovereignty in bestowing salvation upon men: "I will make all my goodness pass before thee, and will proclaim the name of Jehovah before thee: and I will be gracious to whom I will be gracious, and will show mercy on whom I will show mercy" (American Standard Version). Accordingly, we may say that the name *Jehovah* describes God as the God who in his absolute sovereignty and freedom bestows his covenant mercies upon his people, redeeming them from sin by almighty power and drawing them into fellowship with himself.

5. Why does the preface to the Ten Commandments mention God's delivering Israel out of Egypt? Because we must understand that salvation comes first, and keeping God's commandments comes afterward. We cannot really even begin to keep God's holy law until we have been redeemed from Satan's kingdom, just as the people of Israel could not really keep God's law until they were set free from Egyptian bondage. We are not saved because of obedience; we are saved unto obedience. Since Adam fell, redemption has been the basis of obedience. Also God's work of redemption places upon us an added obligation to obey God's law. All men are under obligation to obey God's law, by reason of their relation to him as their Creator; but God's own people are under an added obligation to obey, by reason of their relation to him as their Redeemer.

6. Why did God refer to the land of Egypt as "the house of bondage"? Because the land of Egypt not only was a literal place of bondage to the people of Israel, but also symbolizes the spiritual slavery of sin. Every child of God has been redeemed from a "house of bondage" vastly more powerful, cruel, and tyrannical than the physical bondage of ancient Egypt. This statement in the preface to the Ten Commandments causes us to realizes (a) that as Christians, we have been delivered from bitter slavery; and (b) that this deliverance was not our own achievement, but was accomplished by the sovereign, almighty power of God.

7. What two obligations does God's work of redemption place upon us? (a) The obligation of allegiance, "to take him for our God alone"; (b) the obligation of obedience, "to keep all his commandments." We are to realize that we are not our own, we are bought with a price, the precious blood of Christ, and therefore we must render absolute allegiance and obedience to the God who has redeemed us to himself at infinite cost.

102. Q. *What is the sum of the four commandments which contain our duty to God?*

A. *The sum of the four commandments containing our duty to God, is, to love the Lord our God with all our heart, and with all our soul, and with all our strength, and with all our mind.*

103. Q. *Which is the first commandment?*

A. *The first commandment is,* Thou shalt have no other gods before me.

104. Q. *What are the duties required in the first commandment?*

A. *The duties required in the first commandment are, the knowing and acknowledging of God to be the only true God, and our God; and to worship and glorify him accordingly, by thinking, meditating, remembering, highly esteeming, honoring, adoring, choosing, loving, desiring, fearing of him; believing him; trusting, hoping, desiring, rejoicing in him; being zealous for him; calling upon him, giving all praise and thanks, and yielding all obedience and submission to him with the whole man; being careful in all things to please him, and sorrowful when in anything he is offended; and walking humbly with him.*

Scripture References

- Luke 10:27. Christ's summary of the moral law, showing that love to God is the sum of the first four commandments.
- Exod. 20:3; Deut. 5:7. The first commandment.
- 1 Chron. 28:9; Deut. 26:17; Isa. 43:10; Jer. 14:22. Knowing and acknowledging God to be the only true God, and our God.
- Ps. 95:6–7; Matt. 4:10; Ps. 29:2. Worshiping and glorifying God as the only true God, and our God.

- Mal. 3:16; Eccl. 12:1. We must think about God, and remember him.
- Ps. 71:19. We must have a high idea of God.
- Mal. 1:6. The duty of honoring God.
- Isa. 45:23. The obligation to adore God.
- Josh. 24:15, 22. The duty of choosing God as our God.
- Deut. 6:5; Ps. 73:25; Isa. 8:13. We must love, desire, and fear God.
- Exod. 14:31. The duty of believing God.
- Isa. 26:4; Pss. 130:7; 37:4; 32:11. We must trust, hope, delight, and rejoice in God.
- Rom. 12:11 compared with Num. 25:11. The duty of being zealous for God.
- Phil. 4:6. We are to call upon God with thanksgiving.
- Jer. 7:23. The obligation of total obedience to God.
- James 4:7. The duty of submission to God.
- 1 John 3:22. We are to be careful to please God.
- Jer. 31:18; Ps. 119:136. We are to be sad when we have offended God.
- Mic. 6:8. The duty of walking humbly with God.

Commentary

1. What does it mean to love the Lord our God with all our heart, soul, strength, and mind? This means not merely an emotional attitude toward God, but an all-inclusive practical devotion to God that leads us to honor and obey him in every element, sphere, and relationship of our life. Everything in our life must be determined by our love to God. Thus there can be nothing in our life separate from our religion. We may not draw a boundary line and mark off any sphere or area of life and say that in that area our relation to God does not count. Whatsoever we do, we must do all to the glory of God. The man who thinks he can carry on his business life, or his political life, or his social life, without God is to that extent an irreligious person. The teacher who thinks that his relation to God does not affect his teaching of chemistry, or his interpretation of European history, is to that extent an irreligious person. The consistent Christian will realize that his religion is the ruling principle of all his life, and that there is nothing in life which can be isolated from his relation to God.

2. Why is the first commandment placed first in the Ten Commandments? Because this commandment is the foundation upon which the others depend. Our obligation to God is the source and basis of all other obligations. It is the primary and fundamental obligation of our life.

3. Why are we obliged to acknowledge God as the true God, and our God? Because God is our Creator. It is he that made us, and not we ourselves. Also God is the Redeemer of his people from sin and hell. Therefore every thought of being independent of God is rebellious, irreligious, and wicked.

4. Shall we be dependent on God forever? Yes. To all eternity, the relation between Creator and creature will remain. It can never be changed or pass away. The distinction between Creator and creature is the most fundamental distinction of the Bible. It is assumed or implied in every verse of the whole Bible.

5. How are we to express our dependence upon God? We are to express our dependence on God (a) by a right attitude toward him; (b) by right thoughts about him; (c) by right responses to his revealed will, the Holy Bible.

6. What is a right attitude toward God? A right attitude toward God is a reverent attitude, which realizes and acknowledges the relation between Creator and creature and the infinite difference and distance between the two, and which recognizes that God is an infinite being whom we can never comprehend, but who will always remain mysterious and wonderful to us.

7. What do we mean by right thoughts concerning God? By right thoughts concerning God, we mean thoughts about God which are according to the truth of his revelation of himself in his Word, and which therefore do not come from our own imaginations or desires, but from God's own revelation of himself. Thoughts about God which arise from the opinions, speculations, or philosophy of sin-darkened human minds cannot be right thoughts about God. The only right thoughts about God, on the part of sinful human beings, are those derived from the Bible.

8. What do we mean by right responses to God's revealed will? By right responses to God's revealed will, we mean a conscientious and whole-hearted willing obedience to all that he has commanded, and avoidance of all that he has forbidden, in his Word, so that the Bible is the real guide of our life.

9. What are some of the great truths assumed in this answer of the catechism? (a) The existence of God. (b) The doctrine of creation. (c) The personality of God. (d) Man's moral responsibility to God.

10. How may the duties required in the first commandment be summarized? We may summarize these duties by saying that this commandment requires a devotion to God which shall be supreme, total, and all-inclusive, so that our relation to God is the supreme and all-important fact of our lives. If we regard our relation to God as a side issue or minor detail of our lives, we have not even begun to take the first commandment seriously.

105. Q. *What are the sins forbidden in the first commandment?*

A. *The sins forbidden in the first commandment are, Atheism, in denying or not having a God; Idolatry, in having or worshiping more gods than one, or any with or instead of the true God; the not having and avouching him for God, and our God; the omission or neglect of anything due him, required in this commandment; ignorance, forgetfulness, misapprehensions, false opinions, unworthy and wicked thoughts of him; . . .*

(**Note:** because of the length of the answer to question 105, it will be divided into several parts instead of attempting to deal with it in a single section.)

Scripture References
- Ps. 14:1. The sin of atheism.
- Eph. 2:12. Those who are without God have no hope.
- Jer. 2:27–28 compared with 1 Thess. 1:9. The sin of idolatry contrasted with serving the true God.
- Ps. 81:11. The sin of rejecting God as the object of our supreme devotion.
- Isa. 43:22–24. The sin of neglecting God and the worship he requires.
- Jer. 4:22; Hos. 4:1, 6. The sin of ignorance concerning God and his will.
- Acts 17:23, 29. The sin of misapprehending the nature of God and his will.
- Isa. 40:18. The sin of false opinions concerning God.
- Ps. 50:21. The sin of unworthy and wicked thoughts about God.

Commentary
1. What is the literal meaning of the word *atheism*? *Atheism* literally means "no-God-ism": it designates the teaching or belief that there is no God; hence it signifies the denial of God's existence.

2. What are the three kinds of atheism? (a) Theoretical atheism. (b) Virtual atheism. (c) Practical atheism.

3. What is theoretical atheism? Theoretical atheism is the absolute denial, as a matter of opinion or belief, of the existence of any God or gods.

4. What is virtual atheism? Virtual atheism, which is very common and popular in America today, is the denial of the existence of the God of the Bible, the God who is a Spirit, infinite, eternal, and unchangeable in his being, wisdom, power, holiness, justice, goodness, and truth, in whom there are three persons, the Father, the Son, and the Holy Spirit, the same in substance, equal in power and glory. Since this God of the Bible is the only living and true God, he is the only God that really exists. Therefore to deny the existence of the God of the Bible is virtual atheism. The virtual atheist believes in a god, but not in the God. His "God" is a finite, limited being who is regarded as a necessary implication of the human mind. This "God" is usually regarded as having no absolute, independent existence apart from man and the universe. Just as "husband" and "wife" are correlative terms, which imply each other and depend on each other for their meaning, so the virtual atheist regards "God" and "man," or "God" and "the universe," as correlative terms which imply each other and depend on each other for their meaning. Such a belief differs from bald theoretical atheism in that it is more subtle and does not seem to be so wicked. The virtual atheist may be a very religious person, in his own way. But at bottom his belief is no better than plain theoretical atheism.

5. What is practical atheism? Practical atheism is conducting our lives as if there were no God, even though as a matter of belief we may admit that there is a God.

6. Which form of atheism is most common? Downright theoretical atheism is comparatively rare, and does comparatively little harm because it is honestly and frankly labeled and it is quite easy to recognize as false. Virtual atheism is common among ministers, professors of theology, college and university professors, and especially philosophers. It is held especially by those who pride themselves on being "intellectuals." It is extremely dangerous because it is so subtle and often appears to be very religious. Practical atheism is by far the most common of all forms of atheism. It is the position of plain people who are simply indifferent to God.

7. What is the literal meaning of the word *idolatry*? *Idolatry* literally means the worshiping of images, or of a god or gods by means of images.

8. In what sense does the catechism use the word *idolatry*? This answer of the catechism uses the term *idolatry* in a broad, inclusive sense, making the term include polytheism (belief in more than one God).

9. Why is atheism, in any form, a terrible sin? Because God is the Creator of all men, and the atheist refuses to recognize or worship his Creator. The relation between Creator and creature is the most fundamental relationship in the Bible, and in human life. The person who denies this most fundamental of all relations is a thoroughly perverse and wicked person, for he has gone to the limit in denying the God who gave him life.

10. Why is it a terrible sin to have more gods than one, or to have any other god with or instead of the true God? Because the nature of man's relation to his Creator is such that the true God demands his total, undivided devotion and allegiance. To divide our religious devotion, and give part of it to the true God who created us, and part to some other person or object of worship, is highly insulting to God. God will have all or nothing. To offer him a part of our loyalty and service is to dishonor and offend him.

11. Why is ignorance concerning the true God a great sin? (a) Because only as we have a true knowledge of him can we worship, love, and serve him aright. (b) Because abundant provision has been made, not only in Scripture, but also in the book of nature, for mankind to have a true knowledge of God. The person who is ignorant concerning God has already sinfully disregarded or misused God's revelation of himself, and shows that he does not really want to have a true knowledge of God (Rom. 1:28).

12. Why is forgetfulness of God a great sin? Because our forgetfulness of God indicates that our hearts are hardened by sin and that we do not really care very much about God. We remember what we are really interested in and concerned about. Our forgetfulness of God is a product of our sin-hardened hearts.

13. Why is it sinful to have misapprehensions, false opinions, and unworthy and wicked thoughts about God? Because our mistakes, errors, and false ideas about God do not spring merely from lack of intelligence, but from the fall of the human race into sin, which not only has hardened our hearts and inclined us to all kinds of wickedness, but has also darkened and clouded our minds so that we fail to discern the truth, and fall victims to all kinds of errors. Every false idea or unworthy thought about God arises from sin—not only from our own personal sin, but also from the fall of the human race into sin by Adam's transgression against God.

14. Does not every person have a right to his own opinion about God? When we speak of "rights," we must distinguish between civil rights and moral rights. As to moral rights, the answer to the above question is No. No person has any moral right to believe anything false about God, or to believe otherwise about God than as he is revealed in the Scriptures. As to civil rights, the person who has false ideas about God has a civil right to hold his false beliefs without interference by his fellow citizens or the state; that is, the civil government does not properly have any jurisdiction over people's thoughts and beliefs, and may not persecute or punish any person for his false beliefs or opinions, or even for being an atheist; but such a person will have to give answer to God at the Judgment Day. We believe, however, that the civil magistrate may rightly, for civil reasons, prohibit the public propagation of atheism and of the denial of man's moral responsibility to God. For a civil court to refuse to grant a charter of incorporation to an association the purpose of which is publicly to propagate atheism is no real infringement of civil or religious liberty. The success of such a corporation would result in the destruction of the moral foundations of human society and of the state itself. Civil and religious liberty do not include even the civil right to attempt to destroy the very basis of human civilization.

105. **Q.** *(continued) What are the sins forbidden in the first commandment?*

A. *The sins forbidden in the first commandment are . . . bold and curious searching into his secrets; all profaneness, hatred of God; self-love, self-seeking, and all other inordinate and immoderate setting of our mind, will, or affections upon other things, and taking them off from him in whole or in part; vain credulity, unbelief, heresy, misbelief, distrust, despair; . . .*

Scripture References

- Deut. 29:29. Bold and curious searching into God's secrets.
- Titus 1:16; Heb. 12:16. The sin of profaneness.
- Rom. 1:30. The sin of hating God.
- 2 Tim. 3:2. The sin of inordinate self-love.
- Phil. 2:21. The sin of immoderate self-seeking.
- 1 John 2:15–16. The sin of setting our hearts on created things rather than on God.
- 1 Sam. 2:29; Col. 3:2, 5. Love of the world and earthly things more than God.
- 1 John 4:1. The sin of vain credulity.
- Heb. 3:12. The sin of unbelief.
- Gal. 5:20; Titus 3:10. The sin of heresy.
- Acts 26:9. The sin of misbelief, or sincere belief of what is false.
- Ps. 78:22. The sin of distrust.
- Gen. 4:13. The sin of despair.

Commentary

1. What is meant by "bold and curious searching into [God's] secrets"? This statement, which might easily be misunderstood, does not mean that it is wrong for us to search into the mysteries of God's revelation, whether in nature or in Scripture. What is forbidden is not searching, but bold and curious searching into God's secrets; that is, searching with a wrong attitude (boldness or irreverence), or with a wrong motive (curiosity, rather than a desire to glorify God and benefit mankind). The person who searches into God's secrets with a reverent attitude and a right motive will always realize that he must come to a stopping place where he can proceed no further but is faced with baffling and impenetrable mystery. His aim will be to think God's thoughts after him, that is, to understand what God has revealed for men to understand, not to comprehend God with his human intellect.

2. What is the meaning of "profaneness"? "Profaneness" is not the same as "profanity," which means taking God's name in vain. Profanity is a sin of speech, whereas profaneness is a sin of character, a sin of the whole life. A profane person is one who regards sacred and holy things as if they were ordinary or commonplace. Esau was a profane person because he regarded his birthright as worth no more than an ordinary dinner. Cannibals are profane people because they regard the human body, which is inherently sacred, as having only the value of common food. The heathen who will tear a Bible up and use the paper to make cigarettes or to line shoes are profane people because they have no comprehension of the sacredness of the Word of God, and they treat it as having only the value of the paper it is printed on.

3. How can we explain the fact that unregenerate people really hate God? This fact, which cannot be denied (Rom. 1:30), can only be explained on the basis of the Bible doctrines of original sin and total depravity. The fact that there are people who even boast that they hate God shows the abysmal depths of moral evil to which the human race has sunk through the fall of Adam.

4. Is self-love a sin? Self-love is not a sin unless it is inordinate self-love. The command "Thou shalt love thy neighbor as thyself" implies that self-love is a duty. As self-preservation is the basic instinct of our nature, to love one's self cannot be a sin, but must be a divinely implanted impulse in the human soul. But when self-love gets out of balance, so that a person loves himself more than his neighbor, and especially more than God, then it is inordinate self-love, and therefore sinful. The same is true in the matter of "self-seeking."

5. What is the real nature of the sin of worldliness? Christian people often have very mechanical and superficial ideas of what worldliness is. Worldliness is commonly identified with three or four of its ordinary external manifestations, such as dancing, gambling, card-playing, and the like. But worldliness, in its essence, is really loving and seeking the things of the world more than we love and seek God. It is a matter of "setting our mind, will or affections upon other things" rather than upon God. A person can be a very worldly person without ever indulging in the common forms of worldliness such as dancing and gambling. For example, a great musician who loves his musical art more than he loves God is a worldly person. A famous scientist who is absorbed in his scientific research more than he is in knowing and honoring God is a worldly person.

6. What is the meaning of "vain credulity"? This means a readiness to believe or accept that which is really unworthy of belief or acceptance because it lacks evidence of truth. The common word for it is *gullibility*. The gullible person is ready to believe anything he hears. He is unable to discriminate between what is worthy of belief and what is not. In the religious sphere, the gullible person is greatly influenced by any preacher who presents a message with enthusiasm and eloquence and tells some interesting stories as illustrations. The gullible hearer does not weigh the preacher's statements and compare them with the Scriptures; he just swallows them whole without any accurate or careful thinking. Such people are greatly influenced by the last book or article they have read; soon they will read another book or article, and will change their views accordingly. They follow every changing fad in the realm of religion, and lack discernment and stability.

7. Why is unbelief a dreadful sin? Unbelief is a dreadful sin because we are saved by means of faith, and since unbelief is the opposite of faith, it cuts off the possibility of a person's salvation as long as he continues in his unbelief. Of course there are degrees of unbelief, and even the best Christian has some degree of unbelief. It is only when the person is dominated by unbelief that salvation is out of the question. This condition the Bible describes as having an evil heart of unbelief (Heb. 3:12).

8. What is the meaning of "heresy"? In the Bible the word *heresy* means carrying on propaganda for false doctrine, for example, by forming a sect or party in the church to teach and propagate false doctrines, contrary to what God has revealed in his Word. In modern usage the term *heresy* has come to mean false doctrines, and especially believing and holding false doctrines which are contrary to the essential truths of Christianity. While heresy in this modern sense is certainly sinful, still in the Bible the word includes the idea of forming a party or faction to carry on propaganda for false doctrines.

9. What is misbelief? The term *misbelief* means religious delusion, that is, a firm, confident faith in something which is false or wrong. Paul thought he was doing the will of God in persecuting Christian people. This was misbelief on his part.

10. What is meant by "distrust" and "despair"? These two terms are related to each other. Despair is simply total distrust. Distrust means doubting or disbelieving God's promises, love, and goodness. Despair means disbelieving God's promises, love, and goodness totally, to the limit. Cain gave way to despair, because he said that his punishment was greater than he could bear. He had no faith to ask God to forgive his sin of murdering his brother. Judas gave way to despair when, instead of praying to God for forgiveness, he went and hanged himself. Despair is a common motive for suicide; when a person has come to think that there is no more hope of God's help he may, in his desperate unbelief, seek to "end it all" by taking his own life.

105. Q. *(continued) What are the sins forbidden in the first commandment?*

A. *The sins forbidden in the first commandment are . . . incorrigibleness, and insensibleness under judgments, hardness of heart, pride, presumption, carnal security, tempting of God, using unlawful means, and trusting in lawful means, carnal delights and joys; corrupt, blind, and indiscreet zeal; . . .*

Scripture References

- Jer. 5:3. The sin of being incorrigible.
- Isa. 42:25. Insensibleness under divine judgments.
- Rom. 2:5. The sin of hardness of heart.
- Jer. 13:15; Prov. 16:5, 17; 1 Tim. 6:4. The sin of pride.
- Ps. 19:13; 2 Peter 2:10. The sin of presumption.
- Zeph. 1:12; Rev. 18:8; Isa. 28:15. Carnal security a sin.
- Matt. 4:7. Tempting God a sin.
- Rom. 3:8. The sin of using unlawful means.
- Jer. 17:5. The sin of trusting in lawful means.
- 2 Tim. 3:4. Loving pleasure more than we love God is wicked.
- Gal. 4:17; John 16:2; Rom. 10:2; Luke 9:51, 55. Misguided zeal is sinful.

Commentary

1. What is the meaning of "incorrigibleness"? This word literally means being incapable of being corrected. Both God's goodness and his judgments ought to bring men to repentance, but unless accompanied by the special work of the Holy Spirit, they do not lead to true repentance. There are many people who in time of welfare and prosperity simply ignore or forget God, and then in time of trouble or calamity they become stubborn and defy God in their persistent unbelief. This is the state of incorrigibleness.

2. What is meant by "insensibleness under judgments"? This means failure to recognize God's hand in the troubles and calamities that come upon a person or a nation. Those who attribute all their troubles to "fate" or "chance" or "bad luck," or to the mere operation of natural laws, never see God's hand in what happens to them. They fail to realize that God has foreordained whatsoever comes to pass, and that all things are under God's providential government and all work together in God's moral government of the world. While people are in such a state of mind, no judgments that God might send will make any useful impression on them. A person who is totally blind will not see the brightest light, nor will a person who is totally deaf hear the loudest sound.

3. What do we mean by the expression "hardness of heart"? "Hardness of heart" is an expression used to describe a state of character in which spiritual sensitivity has been largely or entirely lost. When a person is in this condition his conscience functions very little, or not at all. He is indifferent to God, spiritual things, and the eternal salvation of his soul. Both the law and the gospel fail to impress or influence him. Unless God in his special grace and mercy gives such a person a new heart, he cannot be saved.

4. Give a Bible example of a person whose spiritual condition was "hardness of heart." Pharaoh, king of Egypt, in the days of Moses, when in spite of repeated warnings and judgments he would not let God's people go, and even after he had let them go, he changed his mind and pursued after them to the Red Sea.

5. What is pride, and why is it condemned in the Bible as a great sin? Pride is an unjustifiable and falsely high opinion of ourselves, our character, or our achievements. It is the perversion of self-respect, which is legitimate and not sinful. Pride is wicked for two reasons: (a) It is contrary to our position before God as dependent creatures; and (b) it is contrary to our position before God as guilty and helpless sinners. The things people pride themselves on, if they are real, are after all only gifts of God, and therefore they are nothing to be proud of. Thus the apostle Paul in Romans 4:2 informs us that even if Abraham had been justified by works, he would have no ground of glorifying before God. Read 1 Corinthians 4:7 and note the three questions which are asked in this verse, which are calculated to puncture the balloon of human pride. In essence pride amounts to a declaration of independence from God: it rests upon an assumption that we can do something, or be something, or accomplish something good and worthwhile, of ourselves, apart from God and his foreordination and gifts of nature and grace. Therefore pride is based on a lie, which is very offensive to God.

6. What is carnal security, and why is it wrong? Carnal security is an easygoing confidence that everything is going to be all right, when we have no legitimate grounds for such confidence. It is carnal security that leads people to say, "Peace, peace," when there is no peace. Carnal security involves a complacent attitude toward sin and a lukewarm, indifferent attitude toward

God. This is wicked because it dishonors God, whom we ought to seek earnestly and serve faithfully, and it deceives our own selves instead of knowing and facing the real truth about our condition.

7. What is meant by "tempting of God"? The Gospel record of the temptation of our Savior gives the key to the meaning of this expression. It means deliberately or carelessly acting in a wicked or foolish manner and counting on God's goodness and power to keep us out of the trouble that would come upon us because of our actions. For Jesus to have jumped off the pinnacle of the temple, trusting in God to send angels to protect him from bodily injury, would have been to tempt God, which is forbidden in Scripture. For a person to neglect ordinary care and precautions to prevent sickness or accident, and then claim to be trusting in God to keep him safe and in good health, amounts to tempting God, and therefore is wicked.

8. What is meant by "using unlawful means"? This expression means "doing evil that good may come," that is, trying to accomplish a good purpose by doing something that is wrong and sinful. There have always been people who have advocated such a course of conduct.

9. What do we mean by "trusting in lawful means"? By affirming that trusting in lawful means is a sin forbidden in the first commandment, the catechism means that even when we are using means that are lawful and right, we must put our real trust and confidence in God, not in our own methods. It is right to consult a physician and take medicine if we are sick, but we must put our real trust in God, not in the physician or the remedies he may prescribe.

10. What is the meaning of the phrase "carnal delights and joys"? The word *carnal* is derived from a Latin word meaning "flesh," from which our English word *carnival* is also derived. *Carnal* is an adjective and means "pertaining to the flesh." In this statement of the catechism the word *carnal* does not necessarily refer to the body; rather, it refers to "the flesh" as used by the apostle Paul to mean our sinful nature, which he describes by such expressions as "the old man," "the law of sin in our members," "the mind of the flesh," etc. Second Timothy 3:4 shows that it is characteristic of our sinful nature to love pleasure more than we love God. "Carnal delights and joys," therefore, are those delights and joys which appeal especially to our old, sinful nature, but which are far from delightful or joyful to our new nature, which we receive when we are born again of the Holy Spirit.

11. What is "corrupt, blind, and indiscreet zeal," and why is it sinful? The word *zeal* means enthusiasm for something, which leads to vigorous activity for that cause or idea. The Chinese word for zeal is literally "a hot heart," which gives a good idea of the meaning. To have zeal, or to be zealous for God, is good and right. But there are also wrong kinds of zeal, which the catechism describes as "corrupt, blind, and indiscreet zeal." This means that even when we are zealous for the true God and his service, still our zeal may be sinful. Corrupt zeal is zeal that proceeds from our own sinful heart and its desires and impulses, rather than from our new nature and the work of the Holy Spirit in our hearts. When a Christian, in arguing with some person about the truth of the Bible, in his zeal to defend God's Word loses his temper and becomes angry, instead of having a meek and patient spirit, that is an example of corrupt zeal. Blind zeal is a zeal which is not founded on true knowledge. When Paul before his conversion persecuted Christian people, that was an example of blind zeal, as he came to recognize later. The Jews of Paul's day had a zeal for God, but not according to knowledge; therefore it was a blind zeal. Another sinful kind of zeal is indiscreet zeal: this means zeal for something that is true and right, but zeal lacking in wisdom or common sense. For example, to urge Christian people to attend prayer meetings regularly is zeal for something that is right. But if someone insists on having prayer meetings for several hours every day, and tries to persuade his fellow Christians that all their free time must be spent in prayer meetings and nothing else, that is indiscreet zeal, because it is not according to wisdom or common sense. A case was reported in a newspaper of a zealous Christian spoiling the finish of a newly painted automobile which was some other person's property, by writing on it with hard chalk, in large letters, the words "JESUS SAVES"; that was indiscreet zeal, because lacking in wisdom or common sense. All corrupt, blind, or indiscreet zeal is sinful because it proceeds from our own wickedness, ignorance, or foolishness, instead of from the holiness, knowledge, and wisdom which the Holy Spirit imparts to us by his work in our hearts and lives.

105. Q. *(continued) What are the sins forbidden in the first commandment?*

A. *The sins forbidden in the first commandment are . . . lukewarmness, and deadness in the things of God; estranging ourselves, and apostatizing from God; praying, or giving any religious worship, to saints, angels, or any other creatures; all compacts and consulting with the devil, and hearkening to his suggestions; . . .*

Scripture References
- Rev. 3:16. The sin of lukewarmness.
- Rev. 3:1. Deadness in the things of God.
- Ezek. 14:5; Isa. 1:4–5. Estranging ourselves from God.
- Rom. 10:13–14; Hos. 4:12; Acts 10:25–26; Rev. 19:10; Matt. 4:10; Col. 2:18; Rom. 1:25. Religious worship is to be paid to God only and not to any created being.
- Lev. 20:6; 1 Sam. 28:7, 11, compared with 1 Chron. 10:13–14. God has forbidden all attempts to communicate with the dead, or to consult with the devil or evil spirits.
- Acts 5:3. It is wrong to pay heed to the suggestions of Satan.

Commentary

1. What is meant by spiritual "lukewarmness"? Spiritual lukewarmness is a condition of sluggish indifference or complacency about the things of God and the salvation of our souls that leads a person to be satisfied with things as they are and to have no earnest desire to make progress in the Christian life. God's Word teaches us that a condition of spiritual lukewarmness is even more displeasing to God than for a person to be cold in the things of God (Rev. 3:15).

2. Is spiritual lukewarmness a common condition in the present day? No doubt spiritual lukewarmness has always been a common condition, and it is something that every Christian has to fight against continually. However, it may be that spiritual lukewarmness is more prevalent among Christian people in our own day than in former times.

3. What is the remedy for spiritual lukewarmness? Although all kinds of programs and methods have been advocated for dealing with the spiritual and religious lukewarmness of the present day, we may be sure that there is no shortcut by which this condition can be easily or quickly changed. The

only remedy is more of the grace of God in Christian people's lives—more
heed paid to the teachings of the Bible, more repentance and sorrow for sin,
more love to God and man—that is, more of the power of the Holy Spirit
in the lives of Christian people.

4. What is meant by "deadness in the things of God"? We understand lukewarmness to be a sin of Christian people who really are born again
of the Holy Spirit, whereas spiritual deadness is the total lack of spiritual life,
which is the condition of those who have never been born again of the Holy
Spirit. Such people are "dead in trespasses and sins" (Eph. 2:1). This is the
condition of all infidels or unbelievers, and of the non-Christian or heathen
world as a whole. But there are also professing Christians who really lack all
spiritual life. These have only the form of godliness, but lack the power
thereof. They may go through the outward forms and motions of the Christian life, attend church services, and the like, but they do not have the new
life and the power of the Holy Spirit in their hearts. It was such people that
constituted the membership of the church in Sardis, of which Christ said,
"Thou hast a name that thou livest, and art dead" (Rev. 3:1).

5. What is the remedy for spiritual deadness? The only remedy for
spiritual deadness, whether in an individual person's life, or in a church or a
nation, is the old gospel of Jesus Christ, accompanied by the life-giving,
renewing power of the Holy Spirit. Where the gospel message is faithfully
proclaimed, the Holy Spirit will be at work and there will be those who will
pass out of death into life and become "new creatures in Christ Jesus."

**6. What does the catechism mean by "estranging ourselves, and
apostatizing from God"?** This means what is sometimes called "backsliding" or "falling away from God." It is what happens when a professing Christian loses interest in the things of God and gives up even the formal profession of Christianity. Such a person is hardened; he is not concerned about
spiritual things; he fails to make any use of the means of grace (the Bible, the
sacraments, prayer). Ordinarily he will not attend church services or engage
in even the forms of the worship of God. We should realize that a Christian
who has been born again of the Holy Spirit will not totally or permanently
fall away from God. However, even a born-again Christian may fall away
from God to a degree, and for a time, as Peter did when he denied Christ
three times in one night. Another form of "estranging ourselves, and aposta-

tizing from God" is to give up real Christianity and become a member of a false religion or cult. This of course is the height of wickedness.

7. Why is it wrong to give religious worship to saints, angels, or other creatures? It is wrong to give religious worship to saints, angels, or other creatures because: (a) They did not create us and therefore have no claim on our religious devotion. (b) They did not redeem us from sin, and therefore our gratitude for salvation is not due to them, but to God alone. (c) They are not mediators between God and us, for there is only one Mediator, the Lord Jesus Christ. Therefore all religious worship given to saints, angels, or other creatures inevitably detracts from the worship and honor that is due to God alone. No person can worship saints or angels, and still give God the devotion that is due to him.

8. What church sanctions and practices praying to saints and angels? The Roman Catholic Church, which wrongly regards saints and angels as mediators between the worshiper and God.

9. Why is spiritism, or the attempt to communicate with the dead by means of spirit mediums or persons with "familiar spirits," a great sin? God has strictly forbidden this practice in his Word. Those who disregard the Scripture warnings against it will become terribly entangled in the snares of Satan, from which it may be impossible for them ever to escape. This wicked practice is common today, but Christian people should maintain the strictest separation from everything connected with it.

10. Why should Christian people avoid "all compacts and consulting with the devil, and hearkening to his suggestions"? Christian people have been translated from darkness to light, and from the kingdom of Satan to the kingdom of God. Their only attitude toward Satan should be a negative one. The only word a Christian ever ought to say to any suggestion of Satan is the word No. Hearkening to Satan's suggestions began when Eve listened to the serpent and thereupon began to doubt the truth of what God had said. Of course "compacts and consulting with the devil" are wickedly wrong regardless of whether actual contact with Satan is established or not; the mere attempt to do such a thing is giving aid and comfort to God's greatest enemy, and can bring nothing but anguish and woe to human lives.

105. Q. *(continued) What are the sins forbidden in the first commandment?*

A. *The sins forbidden in the first commandment are . . . making men the lords of our faith and conscience; slighting and despising God and his commands; resisting and grieving of his Spirit, discontent and impatience at his dispensations, charging him foolishly for the evils he inflicts on us, and ascribing the praise of any good we either are, have, or can do, to fortune, idols, ourselves, or any other creature.*

Scripture References

- 2 Cor. 1:24; Matt. 23:9. We are not to make men the lords of our faith and conscience.
- Deut. 32:15; 2 Sam. 12:9; Prov. 13:13. The sin of despising God and his commands.
- Acts 7:51; Eph. 4:30. The sins of resisting and grieving the Holy Spirit.
- Ps. 73:2–3, 13–15, 22; Job 1:22. The sins of discontent under God's dispensations and charging God foolishly.
- 1 Sam. 6:7–9. It is wrong to attribute any event of our lives to chance.
- Dan. 5:23. It is wicked to ascribe our success or prosperity to idols or false gods.
- Deut. 8:17; Dan. 4:30. We may not take credit to ourselves for anything good that we are, have or can do.
- Hab. 1:16. We may not regard any creature as the source of any blessing or success that we may enjoy.

Commentary

1. What is meant by "making men the lords of our faith and conscience"? This means making mere human beings our authority in religion, so that we believe and do what they tell us to believe and do, not because of the teachings of God's Word, but merely because of the influence or instruction of men.

2. Why is it wrong to make men the lords of our faith and conscience? Because all merely human authority is fallible and therefore we cannot commit ourselves to it implicitly, to believe and obey what it teaches without question. Only God, whose Word is infallible, can be the Lord of our faith and conscience. We are to commit ourselves to God's Word implicitly, that is, to believe its teachings and obey its commands without question, just because they are from God. But we may not submit thus to any human authority; we must always inquire whether the instructions and commands presented to us are in accord with God's Word or not.

3. What large and influential institution demands that all men everywhere accept its teachings and obey its commands implicitly? The Church of Rome, which claims that its utterances are equivalent to the voice of God and therefore to be accepted without question by all men.

4. Is it a sin for a Protestant to join the Roman Catholic Church? Certainly this is a sin, for the Protestant who does this abandons God's written Word as his supreme authority in religion, and accepts instead the voice of the Roman Church as his supreme authority. He agrees to accept the teachings and obey the commands of the Roman Church implicitly, that is, without raising any questions. This amounts to making men the lords of our faith and conscience.

5. Are members of Protestant churches ever guilty of this sin? Yes. Undoubtedly there are multitudes of careless Protestants who can give no better reason or higher authority for their faith and practice than the customs or teachings of their church, or the statements of their minister. To accept and obey the customs, teachings, and rules of a church, or the statements of a minister, without satisfying ourselves that they are in accordance with the Word of God, is wrong, for it amounts to making churches and ministers the lords of our faith and conscience. It is every Christian's duty to search the Scriptures for himself, to learn whether the statements of his church and minister are true or not.

6. Are there Protestant churches that try to exercise authority over people's faith and conscience? Yes, there are. It is one of the evil signs of our times that some large and influential denominations which formerly regarded God's Word as the only authority over men's faith and conscience now are coming, more or less, to regard the voice of the church as equivalent to the voice of God. Such denominations are coming to demand of their ministers, officers, and people an absolute and unquestioning obedience to the decrees of conferences, General Assemblies, church boards, and agencies, and, it would even appear in some cases, to the utterances and orders of individual men who hold high positions in the denomination's organization. A very large and prominent denomination decided a few years ago that to disobey the command of its church courts was a sin of the same nature as if one were to refuse to partake of the Lord's Supper. This whole tendency is thoroughly perverse and wicked. As the voice of the church becomes more and more important, the Word of God is regarded as less and less important. In reality the voice of the church has weight and authority, to be believed and obeyed, only when it is in accord with the written Word of God.

7. Why is "slighting and despising God and his commands" wicked? Because to slight and despise God and his commands involves contempt for the authority of God, regarding God and his will as less important than our own selfish human desires, the opinions of our fellow men, the commands of the government, etc. To ask God to take second or third place in our thinking or devotion or obedience is an insult to the majesty and authority of God.

8. Why are discontent and impatience under God's dispensations sinful? Because they are the result of unbelief or lack of faith in God's love, God's goodness, God's power, God's promises, etc. The person who gives way to discontent or impatience is no longer willing to take God's Word and God's promises at face value. He feels that God's Word has been contradicted and canceled by God's providential dispensations. As long as we are walking by faith, we will endure hardships and sufferings patiently and will be willing to wait for God to bring us help and relief in his own appointed time.

9. Why is it wrong to charge God foolishly for the evils he inflicts on us? Because the person who dares to charge God foolishly thinks that he can sit in judgment on God and decide whether God is acting rightly or not. This amounts to a claim to be as great and wise as God is, for unless a person is as great and wise as God, how can he decide whether God is doing right or not? All tendencies to charge God foolishly are forbidden by the Word of God. Read Romans 9:19–21.

10. Why is it wrong to ascribe our prosperity or success to "chance" or "fortune"? This is wrong because there really is no such thing as "chance" or "fortune." What men call "chance" is simply that which cannot be humanly calculated or predicted. Every event that men say comes by "chance" really comes by the decree and providence of God. If a coin is tossed in the air, whether it comes up "heads" or "tails" is in every case determined by God. If a man were to find a million dollars in gold and treasure buried on his property, he might regard this discovery as "chance" or "fortune," but in reality it would be the working out of the counsel and providence of God. If we believe that God has foreordained whatsoever comes to pass, and that his providence controls all that happens, then there cannot be such a thing as "chance."

11. Why is it wrong to ascribe our success or prosperity to idols, ourselves, or any other creature? Because the whole created universe, including ourselves, is absolutely dependent on God for its existence and activity. Idols, of course, have no life, nor power to help anyone. But it is equally true that we ourselves, and all other creatures, have no inherent power to accomplish anything. We are totally dependent on God from moment to moment. When we ascribe our success or prosperity to ourselves or to any other creature, we are regarding ourselves as independent of God. This is the great delusion that started when Adam and Eve ate the forbidden fruit in the Garden of Eden. We must always remember that we are created beings and that God is our Creator, on whom we are dependent for our very life and consciousness. This Creator-creature relationship is and always will be the main fact of our existence. To disregard it, even for a moment, is wicked.

106. Q. *What are we especially taught by these words, "before me," in the first commandment?*

A. *These words, "before me," or before my face, in the first commandment, teach us, that God, who seeth all things, taketh special notice of, and is much displeased with, the sin of having any other God: that so it may be an argument to dissuade from it, and to aggravate it as a most impudent provocation: as also to persuade us to do in his sight, whatever we do in his service.*

Scripture References
- Ezek. 8:5–6; Ps. 44:20–21. God sees, and is greatly displeased with, the sin of having any other God.
- 1 Chron. 28:9. Since God sees and knows all things, we should remember this, and realize that we are to live and work "in his sight."
- 1 Kings 18:15. A servant of God who lived and worked as in God's sight.
- Heb. 4:13. All things are seen and known by God.

Commentary

1. In the first commandment ("Thou shalt have no other gods before me"), how may the words "before me" be literally translated from the Hebrew Bible? In the Hebrew the words used mean literally "before my face."

2. What is the meaning of the expression "before my face"? Since God is a Spirit and does not have a body, he does not have a face. In the Bible when we read of God's "face" or "countenance," we should realize that this is a figure of speech. The meaning of it is "in God's presence" or "in God's sight."

3. What part of our lives is passed in God's sight? All of our lives, including all our thoughts, words, and deeds, as well as the inward state of our heart, are always known and observed by God. Hebrews 4:13.

4. Why is it impossible to flee or escape from God's presence? Because God is everywhere, and knows all things. Therefore it is absolutely impossible that anything could ever be concealed from God.

5. Name some Bible characters who attempted to hide or flee from God's presence. Adam and Eve (Gen. 3:8). Jonah (Jonah 1:3).

6. Why did Adam and Eve attempt to hide from the presence of God? Because of their guilty conscience, which was the result of their sin of eating the forbidden fruit.

7. Why did Jonah attempt to flee from the presence of God? Because of his stubborn and disobedient spirit, which made him unwilling to obey the command which he had received from God.

8. What was the result of Adam, Eve, and Jonah's trying to escape from the presence of God? They learned that it is impossible to escape from God's presence, and that wherever people may go, or whatever they may do, God's presence follows them and there is no hiding place from God.

9. How should we answer the person who says that God is too great to care whether we human beings worship him or not, or too great to care whether we worship some other god instead of him? Scripture teaches that as there is nothing too great for God to control, so there is nothing too small for God's interest and attention. God is the Creator and Ruler of all things, both great and small. Moreover the importance of anything, or God's concern about it, does not depend on its size or weight. Human beings are creatures of God, made in his image, subject to his moral law, and the Word of God teaches that every thought, word, and deed is subject to God's judgment.

10. When we read the words "before me" in the first commandment, what should our attitude toward this commandment be? We should pause and consider whether we may in any way, or at any time, be guilty of the sin of having some other god, and realize that this sin is seen and known by the true God; and this should have the effect of persuading us to turn from this sin and repent of it.

11. How does the catechism describe the sin of having another god in the presence of the true God? It describes this sin as "a most impudent provocation" of the true God. Yet we are all guilty of this sin in some form or other. Every Christian is guilty, at least at times, of an idolatrous love of the world. We should realize that this is a most impudent provocation of God our Creator and Redeemer.

12. How should we perform all our service to God, and all the activities of our lives? We should perform all our service to God and all the activities of our lives, "as in his sight," that is, realizing that God sees and observes every detail of our lives. This thought should serve to make us hate and fear sin, and seek to love and serve God conscientiously, moment by moment and day by day.

13. What great Old Testament prophet stated that he stood "in the presence of God"? Elijah (1 Kings 18:15).

107. Q. *Which is the second commandment?*

A. *The second commandment is,* Thou shalt not make unto thee any graven image, or any likeness of any thing that is in heaven above, or that is in the earth beneath, or that is in the water under the earth. Thou shalt not bow down thyself to them, nor serve them: for I the Lord thy God am a jealous God, visiting the iniquity of the fathers upon the children unto the third and fourth generation of them that hate me: and showing mercy unto thousands of them that love me, and keep my commandments.

108. Q. *What are the duties required in the second commandment?*

A. *The duties required in the second commandment are, the receiving, observing, and keeping pure and entire, all such religious worship and ordinances as God hath instituted in his word; particularly prayer and thanksgiving in the name of Christ; the reading, preaching, and hearing of the word; the administration and receiving of the sacraments; church government and discipline; the ministry and maintenance thereof; religious fasting; swearing by the name of God, and vowing unto him: . . .*

Scripture References

- Exod. 20:4–6. The second commandment.
- Deut. 32:46–47; Matt. 18:20; Acts 2:42; 1 Tim. 6:13–14. The duty of receiving, observing, and keeping pure and entire the ordinances of religious worship appointed in Scripture.
- Phil. 4:6; Eph. 5:20. Prayer and thanksgiving in Christ's name is an ordinance appointed in Scripture.
- Deut. 17:18–19; Acts 15:21; 2 Tim. 4:2; James 1:21–22; Acts 10:33. God has appointed the reading, preaching, and hearing of his Word as ordinances of worship.
- Matt. 28:19; 1 Cor. 11:23–30. The sacraments of baptism and the Lord's Supper are appointed ordinances of divine worship.
- Matt. 18:15–17; Matt. 16:19; 1 Cor. 5:1–13; 12:28. Church government and church discipline are appointed in Scripture as divine ordinances.
- Eph. 4:11–12; 1 Tim. 5:17–18; 1 Cor. 9:7–15. The work of the gospel ministry, and its support by the members of the church, are duties appointed by God in his Word.
- Joel 2:12–13; 1 Cor. 7:5. Religious fasting a divine ordinance.
- Isa. 19:21; Ps. 76:11. Making and paying vows to God an ordinance of worship appointed in Scripture.

Commentary

1. What is the general subject of the second commandment? The general subject of the second commandment is religious worship. The commandment deals with this on its negative side, forbidding idolatry or false worship. This of course implies the corresponding duty of observing the true worship of God.

2. With respect to the true worship of God, what three duties are imposed on God's people? (a) To receive the true worship, that is, to recognize it as a binding obligation on the conscience and conduct. (b) To observe the true worship, that is, not merely to believe in it as an article of faith, but actually to practice it in our life. (c) To preserve the true worship, that is, to adhere to it strictly as it is appointed in Scripture, scrupulously avoiding all corruptions or human changes in matters which God has appointed in his Word.

3. Why must we be so careful to receive, observe, and preserve the true worship of God? Because God is jealous concerning his worship, that is, he is not willing to allow us to do as we please in matters of worshiping him. God is sovereign; he is supreme over all; therefore we are bound to obey his will: and he has revealed in the Scripture that it is his will that he be worshiped strictly and only according to his own appointed ordinances and in no other way whatever.

4. How is this obligation commonly disregarded in the present day? In our day and age, with its tremendous emphasis on the dignity and freedom of man, and its corresponding neglect of the majesty and authority of God, the tendency is to hold that men may worship God as they please or, as the saying is, "according to the dictates of their own conscience," and that sincerity is more important than truth or divine appointment. It is quite common today for people to hold that even the false worship of the heathen is acceptable to God provided the worshipers are sincere. This whole notion is of course directly contrary to the statements of the Bible.

5. How is the obligation to maintain purity of worship nullified by the Roman Catholic Church? The Roman Catholic Church, as well as some Protestant bodies, holds that the church is not limited by the Scriptures in matters of worship, but that the church may make decrees concerning ordinances of worship and even add new ordinances not appointed in the Scriptures. This mistaken attitude concerning worship is the explanation of many corruptions of divine worship which exist in the Church of Rome and those bodies which copy "Catholic" forms of worship.

6. How is the obligation to maintain purity of worship disregarded by many Protestant churches? Many Protestant bodies, perhaps most

Protestant bodies, have come to regard divine worship as more or less a matter of indifference, to be determined according to human preference or convenience. It is common to hold that whatever is not forbidden in the Bible is legitimate in worshiping God. This accounts for the introduction of many human corruptions into divine worship.

7. Into what two classifications may the ordinances of divine worship be divided? Into those intended for regular use and those intended for occasional use. Prayer, preaching, and the sacraments, for example, are intended for regular use. Fasting, vowing, and swearing by God's name are for occasional use, that is, to be performed not at any recurring stated time, but when some special occasion calls for them.

8. In what four spheres of human life are ordinances of divine worship to be performed? In the spheres of the individual Christian, the Christian family, the Christian church, and the Christian state or nation.

9. Is every ordinance of divine worship intended for all four of these spheres of human life? No. Some ordinances are limited to the church; others are suitable only for the individual, church, and family. For example, baptism and the Lord's Supper are church ordinances and may not be observed privately in families or voluntary associations. Swearing by the name of God, on the other hand, is an ordinance suitable for a Christian state or nation as well as for a church.

108. Q. *(continued) What are the duties required in the second commandment?*

A. *The duties required in the second commandment are . . . (as also) the disapproving, detesting, opposing, all false worship; and according to each one's place and calling, removing it, and all monuments of idolatry.*

Scripture References
- Acts 17:16–17; Ps. 16:4. The second commandment requires strict separation from and rejection of all forms of worship not appointed in the Scriptures.
- Deut. 7:5; Isa. 30:22. Monuments of idolatry are to be removed.

Commentary

1. What is the Christian's duty with reference to false worship? It is the Christian's duty to disapprove, detest, and oppose all false worship.

2. What is meant by "false worship"? "False worship" means not only worshiping a false god, or practicing the rites of a false religion, but attempting to worship the true God in any other manner than that appointed in his Word, the Holy Bible.

3. How must a Christian disapprove, detest, and oppose false worship? It is a Christian's duty to disapprove, detest, and oppose all false worship not merely by a general or theoretical testimony against it, but by a practical testimony against it, that is, by dissenting and abstaining from participation in it as a matter of conscience as he shall give answer to God at the Judgment Day.

4. Why should a Christian separate from the religious worship of Freemasonry and similar secret "fraternal" orders? It is clear that Freemasonry is essentially a religious institution, and that its religion is different in kind from the Christianity of the Word of God. This being the case, the religious ordinances and ceremonies of Freemasonry must be regarded as false worship, that is, worshiping otherwise than as appointed in God's Word. For a Christian—indeed for any person—to participate in such worship is to violate the second commandment.

5. What is meant by the expression "monuments of idolatry"? This expression means the altars, images, temples, etc., of false religions. Scripture teaches that such "monuments of idolatry" ought to be removed lest they be a temptation to people to use them in religious worship, or a rallying point for a revival and growth of the false religions.

6. How are the "monuments of idolatry" to be removed? The "monuments of idolatry" are to be removed from any nation or social organism, not by indiscriminate action on the part of the public in general, nor by mob violence such as often took place in the days of the Reformation, but in an orderly manner "according to each one's place and calling." That is to say, the work of removing "monuments of idolatry" is to be left in the hands of those persons in family, church, and state who have the legitimate authority to carry out such a task. A private citizen who by reason of his Protestant convictions believes that the Roman Catholic Mass is idolatrous does not have the right to walk into a Roman Catholic church and smash the altar with an ax. The head of a family may remove "monuments of idolatry" from his own house but not from his neighbor's house. In a heathen country, Christian people should hope, pray, and work for the removal of all "monuments of idolatry," but they have no right to undertake the removal by direct action, except where the "monuments of idolatry" exist in their own homes or on their own property. On the other hand, where a family is converted from idolatry to Christianity, it is proper that the "monuments of idolatry" in that household be removed, and other Christians may of course be requested to assist in such an undertaking.

7. How are the elements of false worship to be removed from family, church, and state? In this matter the catechism specifies the same principle as is involved in the removal of "monuments of idolatry," namely, that such elements of false worship are to be removed "according to each one's place and calling," that is to say, every Christian is bound to undertake the removal of false worship according to the measure of authority which God has committed to him, whether in family, church, or state.

8. Does not the principle of religious liberty imply that every person has the right to worship as he pleases, or according to the dictates of his own conscience? This question cannot be clearly and adequately answered unless we first define what we mean by a "right." The word *right* is ambiguous, and its use in this connection leads to confusion and misunderstandings unless it is carefully defined. There is a basic distinction between civil rights and moral rights. A civil right is a right which has validity within the sphere of human society; a moral right is a right which is valid also within the sphere of God's moral law. A millionaire has a civil right to spend his money, after he has paid his taxes, on worldly pleasures for himself and his family, if he desires to do so. The government may not step in and command him to spend his wealth in an unselfish or philanthropic manner. But he has no moral right, before God, to spend his money selfishly. If he does so, the government has no jurisdiction over the matter, but the millionaire will have to give answer to God at the Judgment Day. Similarly in the matter of religious liberty: a person may have a civil right to worship as he pleases, or not at all (provided his manner of worship does not involve gross public blasphemy, or destroy the rights of other persons, or endanger the safety of civil society); and the government may neither forbid false worship nor enforce true worship. But no person has a moral right to worship as he pleases; and those who worship otherwise than as appointed in God's Word will have to give their answer to God at the Judgment Day. God alone is Lord of the conscience, and all such matters are under God's jurisdiction and will finally be adjudicated according to his moral law.

9. Does not the American ideal of "tolerance" imply that one religion, or manner of worship, is as good as another, and that all are equally pleasing to God? Undoubtedly this is the popular American ideal of "tolerance," as inculcated by the motion picture industry, the press, the radio, and the "liberal" churches. These powerful influences are molding public opinion to the idea that all religions and all forms of worship are equally good and valuable if only the worshiper is sincere. Protestantism, Catholicism, and Judaism are to be put on a level and all distinctive features of any of them regarded as unimportant in the interests of "Americanism" and "tolerance." This is one of the most vicious and deplorable tendencies of our day, and we should be awake to its menace. If this emphasis on a false ideal of "tolerance" succeeds, true Bible Christianity will be eliminated as a powerful influence in our country, and the day may even come when orthodox Bible Christians will have to suffer persecution as "enemies of democracy."

109. Q. *What are the sins forbidden in the second commandment?*

A. *The sins forbidden in the second commandment are, all devising, counseling, commanding, using, and any wise approving, any religious worship not instituted by God himself; tolerating a false religion . . .*

Scripture References
- Num. 15:39. God's commandments concerning worship to be observed without changes or additions "after our own heart."
- Deut. 13:6–8. Counseling or urging people to adopt false worship is sin.
- Hos. 5:11; Mic. 6:16. The sin of commanding religious worship not instituted by God.
- 1 Kings 11:33; 12:33. The great sin of practicing worship not instituted by God himself.

- Deut. 12:30–32. It is sinful to approve in any way of worship not instituted by God.
- Deut. 13:6–12; Zech. 13:2–3; Rev. 2:2, 14–15, 20; 17:12, 16–17. It is a sin against God to tolerate a false religion.

Commentary

1. What is the scriptural principle concerning divine worship? The scriptural principle concerning divine worship is that the only right and acceptable way of worshiping God is that appointed by himself, which may not be changed by men.

2. What is the basis of this scriptural principle concerning divine worship? The basis of this principle concerning divine worship is the sovereignty of God in all spheres of life. By the sovereignty of God we mean his supreme and absolute authority, which does not depend on the consent of any created being and cannot be changed or abridged by any created being. God, the almighty Creator, Preserver, and End of all things, is supreme over all, and his revealed will is absolute law concerning all things, and especially concerning that which intimately concerns himself, namely, the matter of how he is to be worshiped by his people.

3. Is the doctrine of the sovereignty of God widely held today? No. Churches which nominally hold this doctrine have largely abandoned it. Modern philosophy since the time of Immanuel Kant has placed great emphasis on the autonomy of man, that is, man's free self-determination. The result of this tendency has been to give up belief in the real sovereignty of God. In some quarters we are hearing today a frank, outspoken demand for a limited God. Some scholars have gone so far as to assert that God does not have any independent existence, but is only an implication of the human mind. Still others say that when God created the universe he limited himself, and is now no longer sovereign, but must adapt himself to the desires and ideas of his creatures. Still others say that God exists for the benefit of the human race, and so they have tried to believe in a "democratic" God. The old-time Bible truth of the absolute, transcendent sovereignty of God is regarded as an outworn curiosity by the prominent leaders of many of the large bodies of present-day Protestantism. However, the real sovereignty of God is still held by many individuals and by some small denominations and a few larger ones.

4. What is the relation between abandonment of belief in the sovereignty of God and the adoption of all kinds of changes and corruptions in divine worship? Undoubtedly when people have given up belief in the sovereignty, or absolute authority, of God, they naturally tend to do as they please, or act according to human feelings, desires, and preferences, with respect to matters of divine worship. When men forsake the sovereign God of the Bible, and put in his place an imaginary God created in their own image, it is no wonder that they also forsake the pure, simple worship appointed in Scripture, and put in its place all kinds of humanly invented rituals and ceremonies, according to the desires of their own hearts.

5. How can we most effectively oppose and counteract corruptions in the worship of God in churches of which we are members or with which we come in contact? Of course, we should oppose all corruptions in the worship of God to the limit of our ability, as opportunities are afforded and as circumstances may require. But merely to witness against or oppose particular details of false worship will accomplish very little unless we also, and first of all, oppose the false principle from which these details of false worship have proceeded, and bear witness to the true principle of divine worship which is taught in the Scriptures. Merely to oppose instrumental music in divine worship, for example, will accomplish little unless we bear emphatic witness to the scriptural principle that God is to be worshiped only as he has appointed in his Word, and not according to human preferences or desires. Unless we can succeed in convincing people of the validity of this principle, our opposition to particular details of false worship will seem to them to be merely a stubborn insistence on our customs of worship over against their customs of worship. To seek reform in particular matters of worship, without gaining acceptance of the underlying principle of worship, is like trying to build a beautiful and substantial house with no foundation under it but sand.

6. How can we most effectively convince people of the validity of this scriptural principle of divine worship? To convince people of the validity of the principle that God is to be worshiped only as appointed in his Word, and not according to human preferences or desires, it is absolutely necessary first of all to convince them of two basic principles which underlie this scriptural principle of worship. These two basic principles are: (a) the full inspiration and authority of the Bible; (b) the absolute sovereignty of God. There was a time years ago when these two basic principles could be taken for granted in all denominations of the Reformed or Calvinistic branch of Protestantism, but they can no longer be taken for granted today, for they are no longer accepted, in their plain and true meaning, by the large and popular denominations which once adhered to them, and which still pay lip-service to them in their official creeds. Unless these two basic principles, the authority of the Bible and the sovereignty of God, are accepted, the scriptural principle of divine worship will be meaningless, and we cannot expect people to accept it. Nothing is more foolish than to expect people who are not willing to accept the scriptural principle of worship to adopt the practical applications of that principle; and nothing could be more futile than attempting to persuade people who do not believe in the real authority of the Bible and the true sovereignty of God to accept the scriptural principle of worship. The foundation must be there or the building will not stand.

7. What is meant by "tolerating a false religion"? The word *tolerating* means "sanctioning or permitting that which is not wholly approved." The catechism teaches that it is a violation of the second commandment, and therefore a sin, to tolerate a false religion. This does not mean that it is the duty of the civil government to prohibit false religions by law, or that Christian people are to destroy the temples and interfere with the meetings of false religions by mob violence. It means, rather, that it is wrong to give a false religion even a limited endorsement by any positive toleration of it, that is, sanctioning or approving of it in any positive way. Simply to let it alone is not necessarily wrong. For a Christian parent to allow his children to attend meetings held by Jehovah's Witnesses is to tolerate a false religion, and therefore wrong. For a Christian church to allow its church building to be used by a Christian Science society for their meetings is to tolerate a false religion, and therefore wrong. For the civil government to enact a law giving legal sanction or recognition to a false religion, or in any way approving of it as a religion, is to tolerate a false religion, and therefore wrong. However, for the civil government to issue a charter of incorporation, dealing only with matters of property, real estate, inheritance, and the like, to an organization connected with a false religion does not involve officially tolerating a false religion since such a charter of incorporation deals only with the civil aspects of a religious organization and does not involve any sanction of its religious features, which in ordinary cases are outside the jurisdiction of the civil government. For the civil government to issue to a Buddhist temple a certificate showing that the fire-prevention regulations have been complied with does not amount to tolerating a false religion, for such a certificate concerns only civil matters; it deals only with those civil aspects of a religious organization which the latter has in common with all other human institutions: it does not deal with it as a religious organization but merely as an organization, regardless of whether it is religious or secular in nature.

109. Q. *(continued) What are the sins forbidden in the second commandment?*

A. *The sins forbidden in the second commandment are . . . the making of any representation of God, of all or of any of the three persons, either inwardly in our mind, or inwardly in any kind of image or likeness of any creature whatsoever; all worshipping of it, or God in it or by it; . . .*

Scripture References

- Deut. 4:15–19; Acts 17:29; Rom. 1:21–25. The sin of making any representation of God.
- Dan. 3:18; Gal. 4:8. To worship any image or likeness of the deity violates the second commandment.
- Exod. 32:5. To worship even the true God by means of any visible representation or image is a violation of the second commandment.

Commentary

1. Why is it wrong to make any representation or picture of God? Because God is a pure Spirit, without bodily form, and any picture or representation which man can make can only give a false idea of the nature of God. This is true, as the catechism intimates, regardless of whether an outward image or likeness is made, or only an inward image in a person's mind. In either case, the attempt to visualize God is sinful and can only falsify or distort the revelation of God presented in the Bible.

2. Is it wrong to make paintings or pictures of our Savior Jesus Christ? According to the Larger Catechism, this is certainly wrong, for the catechism interprets the second commandment as forbidding the making of any representation of any of the three persons of the Trinity, which would certainly include Jesus Christ, the second person of the Trinity, God the Son. While pictures of Jesus are extremely common in the present day, we should realize that in Calvinistic circles this is a relatively modern development. Our forefathers at the time of the Reformation, and for perhaps 300 years afterward, scrupulously refrained, as a matter of principle, from sanctioning or making use of pictures of Jesus Christ. Such pictures are so common in the present day, and so few people have conscientious objections to them, that it is practically impossible to obtain any Sabbath School helps or Bible story material for children that is free of such pictures. The American Bible Society is to be commended for its decision that the figure of the Savior may not appear in Bible motion pictures issued by the Society.

3. What attitude should we adopt in view of the present popularity of pictures of Jesus Christ? The following considerations may be suggested as bearing on this question: (a) The Bible presents no information whatever about the personal appearance of Jesus Christ, but it does teach that we are not to think of him as he may have appeared "in the days of his flesh," but as he is today in heavenly glory, in his estate of exaltation (2 Cor. 5:16). (b) Inasmuch as the Bible presents no data about the personal appearance of our Savior, all artists' pictures of him are wholly imaginary and constitute only the artists' ideas of his character and appearance. (c) Unquestionably pictures of the Savior have been very greatly influenced by the theological viewpoint of the artist. The typical modern picture of Jesus is the product of nineteenth-century "Liberalism" and presents a "gentle Jesus" who emphasized only the love and Fatherhood of God and said little or nothing about sin, judgment, and eternal punishment. (d) Perhaps more people living today have derived their ideas of Jesus Christ from these typically "liberal" pictures of Jesus than have derived their ideas of Jesus from the Bible itself. Such people inevitably think of Jesus as a human person, rather than thinking of him according to the biblical teaching as a divine person with a human nature. The inevitable effect of the popular acceptance of pictures of Jesus is to overemphasize his humanity and to forget or neglect his deity (which of course no picture can portray). (e) In dealing with an evil so widespread and almost universally accepted, we should bear a clear testimony against what we believe to be wrong, but we should not expect any sudden change in Christian sentiment on this question. It will require many years of education in scriptural principles before the churches and their members can be brought back to the high position of the Westminster Assembly on this question. Patience will be required.

4. Are not pictures of Jesus legitimate provided they are not worshiped or used as "aids to worship"? As interpreted by the Westminster Assembly, the second commandment certainly forbids all representations of any of the persons of the Trinity, and this coupled with the truth taught in the Westminster Standards that Christ is a divine person with a human nature taken into union with himself, and not a human person, would imply that it is wrong to make pictures of Jesus Christ for any purpose whatever. Of course, there is a difference between using pictures of Jesus to illustrate children's Bible story books or lessons, and using pictures of Jesus in worship as Roman Catholics use them. Admittedly the former is not an evil in the same class with the latter. In spite of this distinction, however, there are good reasons for holding that our forefathers of the Reformation were right in opposing all pictorial representation of the Savior. We should realize that the popularity—even the almost unchallenged prevalence—of a particular practice does not prove that it is right. To prove that a practice is right we must show that it is in harmony with the commands and principles revealed in the Word of God. Merely showing that a practice is common, is useful, or seems to have good results does not prove it is right.

109. Q. *(continued) What are the sins forbidden in the second commandment?*

A. *The sins forbidden in the second commandment are . . . the making of any representation of feigned deities, and all worship of them, or service belonging to them; all superstitious devices, corrupting the worship of God, adding to it, or taking from it, whether invented and taken up of ourselves, or received by tradition from others, though under the title of antiquity, custom, devotion, good intent, or any other pretense whatsoever; simony; sacrilege; all neglect, contempt, hindering, and opposing the worship and ordinances which God hath appointed.*

Scripture References
- Exod. 32:8. The sin of making a representation of false gods.
- 1 Kings 18:26–28; Isa. 65:11. The sin of worshiping false gods.
- Acts 17:22; Col. 2:21–23. Superstitious practices forbidden by God.

- Mal. 1:7–8, 14. The sin of corrupting God's worship.
- Deut. 4:2. We may not add to, or take anything from, the worship that God has appointed in his Word.
- Ps. 106:39. Changes in divine worship introduced by the worshipers themselves are wrong.
- Matt. 15:9. Changes in divine worship received by tradition from others are wrong.
- 1 Peter 1:18; Jer. 44:17; Isa. 65:3–5; Gal. 1:13–14; 1 Sam. 13:11–12; 15:21. Neither antiquity, custom, devotion, nor good intentions can serve as an excuse for corruptions in divine worship.
- Acts 8:18. The sin of simony.
- Rom. 2:22; Mal. 3:8. The sin of sacrilege.
- Exod. 4:24–25. God is offended by careless neglect of the ordinances of worship which he has appointed.
- Matt. 22:5; Mal. 1:7, 13. The sin of regarding ordinances of divine worship with contempt.
- Matt. 23:13; Acts 13:44–45; 1 Thess. 2:15–16. The sin of hindering and opposing the ordinances of divine worship.

Commentary

1. What is the sin of idolatry? The sin of idolatry, which in its crude or gross form is prevalent in the heathen world, consists in making images or pictures of false divinities, and worshiping these images or pictures, or using them as "aids to worship" in the service of the false gods.

2. How did the sin of idolatry originate in human history? The sin of idolatry originated as a consequence of the fall and resultant depravity of the human race. The apostle Paul gives the explanation of the origin of idolatry in Romans 1:21–23: "Because that, when they knew God, they glorified him not as God, neither were thankful; but became vain in their imaginations, and their foolish heart was darkened. Professing themselves to be wise, they became fools, and changed the glory of the uncorruptible God into an image made like to corruptible man, and to birds, and four-footed beasts, and creeping things."

3. How does this explanation of the origin of idolatry differ from the evolutionary view that is popular today? According to the Bible, mankind originally worshiped the true God, and only after the fall into sin began to worship idols. Thus worship of the true God is more ancient than idolatry. But according to the theory of the development of religion which is popular today, idolatry is more ancient than worship of the true God. According to this theory, religion started from a very primitive animism (worship of spirits), gradually rose to polytheism (belief in many gods, accompanied by idol worship), and finally reached its highest development in monotheism (worship of one God, without idols). This theory of development represents religion as man's search for God. The Bible, on the contrary, describes God's redemption of man, and represents idolatry as a corruption of the original pure worship of the one true God.

4. What is meant by "superstitious devices"? This expression means such things as charms, amulets, "good-luck" symbols, and the like. These vary from such popular superstitions as a horseshoe nailed over a barn door to bring "good luck," to a gold cross worn about a person's neck because of supposed benefits to be derived from it. Also included are all religious figures and medals held to have beneficial powers or effects, "holy water" relics of the saints and martyrs, and so forth. All of these are really superstitious, that is, devoid of such powers as are attributed to them, and therefore to believe in and use them is sinful.

5. Give some examples of "corrupting the worship of God, adding to it, or taking from it." (a) Corrupting the worship of God: administering baptism to infants whose parents are not church members in good standing, that is, are not living as professing Christians before the world. (b) Adding to the worship of God: the five sacraments which the Church of Rome has added to the two appointed in Scripture; the use of salt and oil in addition to water in baptism. (c) Taking from the worship of God: the Romanist practice of denying the cup to lay members in the communion service; administering baptism or the Lord's Supper apart from the preaching of God's Word.

6. What special corruptions of the worship of God have become common, during the past 100 years, in churches of the Reformed or Calvinistic branch of Protestantism? (a) The virtual supplanting of the inspired Psalter by hymns of merely human composition as the matter of praise. (b) The general introduction of instrumental music in divine worship. We should realize that at the Reformation the inspired Psalter formed the praise-book of the Reformed or Calvinistic branch of Protestantism, and that instrumental music was generally rejected as an unscriptural corruption of the worship of God. This position was taken by John Calvin, John Knox, and many other Reformation leaders. Among Presbyterian and Congregational churches of Scottish, English, and Irish origin this pure, simple scriptural worship persisted for about 200 years. After that uninspired hymns and instrumental music began to come in, but these innovations in worship invariably had to contend against strong opposition on the part of multitudes of conscientious Christians. Today the supplanting of the Psalter has become so nearly complete that there are many church members who have never even heard of singing the Psalms exclusively, and without piano or organ music, in the worship of God. Those who still adhere to this "Puritan" principle of worship are regarded as "queer" and "behind the times," but in reality they are only adhering to a principle that was generally accepted by the Calvinistic Reformers and Puritan divines, a principle grounded in the truths of the Reformation as they apply to the worship of God.

(**Note:** For further discussion of this subject, the reader is referred to *Instrumental Music in the Worship of God; Commanded or Not Commanded* by G. I. Williamson.)

7. What is the difference between principles and customs? A principle, in the sphere of religion, is an established law or practice which has been deliberately adopted and is adhered to because of conviction that it is right, that is, in accordance with the revealed will of God. A custom, on the other hand, is merely a long-established usage which is adhered to because it is old and common. A particular practice may be both an application of a principle and at the same time the observance of a custom: thus we read of our Lord that "as his custom was, he went into the synagogue on the Sabbath day" (Luke 4:16); such was Jesus' custom, but it was also a matter of principle. The repeated observance of the sacrament of the Lord's Supper in a Christian congregation is a matter of principle: the use of communion tokens is merely a matter of custom. That Christian people shall assemble on the Sabbath day to worship God is a matter of principle; that the morning service shall be held at eleven o'clock rather than at some other hour is merely a matter of custom.

It is a bad sign of deterioration in any church when principles come to be regarded as if they were mere customs, and when mere customs come to be treated as if they were real principles. We must always distinguish sharply between customs and principles, and we must continually criticize our customs on the basis of our principles. If we find disharmony between the two, loyalty to God's truth requires that our customs, not our principles, be sacrificed for the sake of consistency.

8. Why cannot antiquity or custom justify changes in the worship of God? Because the fact that a practice is old and widespread does not prove that it is right. A particular matter may have been a customary practice for a thousand years, and still be wrong. The real question is not whether a practice is old, nor whether it is popular, but whether it is right, that is, in accordance with a sound understanding of the revealed will of God.

9. Why cannot devotion or good intent justify changes in divine worship? Because what God requires of us is not merely devotion, nor merely good intentions, but obedience to his revealed will. It is common today to hear people say that any form of worship is legitimate if only the worshiper is sincere. In 1 Samuel 15 we read how King Saul, in disobedience to the express command of God, allowed the people to keep the sheep and oxen of the Amalekites "to sacrifice unto the LORD thy God in Gilgal" (v. 21). Thus Saul urged "devotion" and "good intent" as excuses for direct disobedience to God's revealed will. The prophet Samuel, however, rebuked this hypocrisy by saying: "Hast the LORD as great delight in burnt offerings and sacrifices, as in obeying the voice of the LORD? Behold, to obey is better than sacrifice, and to hearken than the fat of rams. For rebellion is as the sin of witchcraft, and stubbornness is as iniquity and idolatry. Because thou hast rejected the word of the LORD, he hath also rejected thee from being king" (vv. 22–23).

10. What is simony, and why is it wrong? Simony is ecclesiastical bribery. The term is derived from the name of Simon the sorcerer, who offered the apostles money for the power to bestow the Holy Spirit on others (Acts 8:9–24). In the history of the church simony came to mean secretly paying money to a bishop or other dignitary, in order to receive in return an appointment to a desirable and profitable "benefice" or position in the church. Simony is wrong because it is a form of bribery, and therefore dishonest; and because it degrades the church of the living God to the level of a corrupt political machine. In choosing men to fill positions in the church, the only legitimate considerations are (a) the qualifications of the candidates for the offices; (b) the lawful call of the people of God. Money, personal prejudices, family relationships should have no influence in determining who shall receive what official position in the church of God.

11. What is the meaning of "sacrilege"? Sacrilege is the sin of treating what is sacred as if it were profane. To make a parody of the 23rd Psalm or any other part of Scripture is sacrilege. To make divine things the butt of a joke is sacrilege. To mimic or parody baptism, the Lord's Supper, or any other ordinance of divine worship is sacrilege, and therefore sinful.

12. What other sins does the second commandment forbid? "All neglect, contempt, hindering, and opposing the worship and ordinances which God hath appointed." These sinful practices have a wide scope, and many illustrations of them could be adduced. A law forbidding free assembly for evangelism and Christian worship, and requiring government permits for these God-ordained activities, such as the "Religious Bodies Law" of Japan before that country's defeat, is a violation of the second commandment. Interrupting a Christian religious service; disorderly and irreverent conduct during divine worship; chewing gum during divine worship; talking, whispering, passing notes unnecessarily, reading books and papers that have no connection with the service—all these practices come under the category of "neglect, contempt, hindering, and opposing the worship and ordinances which God hath appointed." Many church members are guilty of careless and irreverent conduct during divine worship, who probably do not realize that their conduct is sinful and a violation of the Ten Commandments.

110. Q. *What are the reasons annexed to the second commandment, the more to enforce it?*

A. *The reasons annexed to the second commandment, the more to enforce it, contained in these words,* For I the Lord thy God am a jealous God, visiting the iniquity of the fathers upon the children unto the third and fourth generation of them that hate me; and showing mercy unto thousands of them that love me, and keep my commandments; *are, besides God's sovereignty over us, and propriety in us, his fervent zeal for his own worship, and his revengeful indignation against all false worship, as being a spiritual whoredom; accounting the breakers of this commandment such as hate him, and threatening to punish them unto divers generations; and esteeming the observers of* *it such as love him and keep his commandments, and promising mercy to them unto many generations.*

Scripture References

- Ps. 45:11; Rev. 15:3–4. God's sovereignty over us, and his propriety in us.
- Exod. 34:13–14. God's fervent zeal for his own worship.
- 1 Cor. 10:20–22; Jer. 7:18–20; Ezek. 16:26–27; Deut. 32:16–20. God's vengeful indignation against all false worship.
- Hos. 2:2–4. God's threat of punishment to divers generations of those who break the second commandment.
- Deut. 5:29. God's promise of mercy to many generations to those who observe the second commandment.

Commentary

1. What is meant by "God's sovereignty over us, and propriety in us"? God's sovereignty over us is his absolute, unchallengeable authority over our lives. God's propriety in us means that we are God's property, or his possession. Both of these truths form a part of the reason annexed to the second commandment; they are implied in God's describing himself as "the LORD thy God."

2. What is meant by God's "fervent zeal for his own worship"? This expression, which is based on God's revelation of himself as a jealous God, means that God is greatly concerned and desirous, not only that he be worshiped by his rational creatures, but that he be worshiped by them in the particular manner which he has revealed as his will concerning how he is to be worshiped. People often speak as if it made no special difference to God whether people worship him or not, or how they worship him. But God is jealous concerning his own worship; he cannot be indifferent to whether, or how, he is worshiped.

3. What is God's attitude toward all false worship? God's attitude toward all false worship is an attitude of revengeful indignation. This expression of the catechism is abundantly warranted by many passages of Scripture that might be quoted. Large sections of such Old Testament prophets as Isaiah, Jeremiah, and Ezekiel teach precisely this truth of God's revengeful indignation against false worship, and especially against the worship of idols. Nor is this truth limited to the Old Testament, for it is clearly taught in the New. Perhaps the most emphatic statement of God's wrath against false worship

anywhere in the Bible is found in Revelation 14:9–11, where we read that
those guilty of worshiping the Beast and his image, etc., "shall drink of the
wine of the wrath of God, which is poured out without mixture into the cup
of his indignation" and that "the smoke of their torment ascendeth up for
ever and ever: and they have no rest day nor night, who worship the beast
and his image, and whosoever receiveth the mark of his name." If we would
be true to the Bible, we must resolutely resist the modern tendency to tone
down and soft-pedal the Scripture teaching of the wrath of God against sin.

**4. What figure of speech is often used in the Bible to bring out the
hateful wickedness of false worship?** The figure of a wife who is unfaithful to her marriage vows. God is represented as the husband of his people, the
Old Testament nation of Israel, and also the spiritual Israel, which is the Christian church. In this spiritual "marriage" relationship, loyalty required that Israel
worship the true God, with whom she was in covenant, alone. But Israel
proved unfaithful to God's covenant, and turned to worship the divinities of
all the neighboring heathen nations. Time and again in Scripture this involvement in false worship is denounced as spiritual adultery. Hosea 2:2–4 is only
one of many passages of the same nature in the Old Testament prophets. By
this figure of speech, so often and emphatically repeated, God showed how
hateful and displeasing his people's compromise with false worship was to him.

**5. Is it unjust for God to visit the iniquity of the fathers upon the
children, unto the third and fourth generations?** We must keep in
mind that what God here threatens is not merely to visit the iniquity of the
fathers upon the children to the third and fourth generations, but to do so
to the third and fourth generations of them that hate him. The comment of
John Calvin on this phrase (*Institutes,* 2.8.20–21) is most illuminating. Calvin
points out that it is not at all a matter of God's visiting the iniquity of a wicked
man upon righteous children, grandchildren, and great-grandchildren; on
the contrary, it is a case of the children to the third and fourth generations
being themselves also guilty of wickedness before God. "For if the visita-
tion, of which we are treating, be fulfilled, when God removes from the
family of the impious his grace, the light of his truth, and the other means
of salvation, the very circumstance of children blinded and abandoned by
him being found treading in the footsteps of their fathers, is an instance of
their bearing the curse in consequence of the crimes of their parents. But
their being the subjects of temporal miseries and at length of eternal perdi-

tion, are punishments from the righteous judgment of God, not for the sins of others, but on account of their own iniquity."

6. What is the meaning of the promise of God's "showing mercy unto thousands" of those that love him, and keep his commandments? Here the word "thousands" does not mean thousands of people but many generations. "God gives a promise to extend his mercy to a thousand generations; which also frequently occurs in the Scripture, and is inserted in the solemn covenant with the church: 'I will be a God unto thee, and to thy seed after thee' (Gen. 17:7). . . . He also gives us a cursory intimation of the greatness of his mercy, which extends to a thousand generations, while he has assigned only four generations to his vengeance" (Calvin, *Institutes*, as cited above).

7. What should be our attitude to the worship of God, in view of the reasons annexed to the second commandment? Taking to heart the reasons annexed to the second commandment, we should have an attitude of serious concern and of conscientious carefulness with respect to the worship of God and all matters connected with it. We should take great care to participate in the worship of God faithfully, and to avoid all compromise with whatever is contrary to God's revealed will.

111. Q. *Which is the third commandment?*

A. *The third commandment is, Thou shalt not take the name of the Lord thy God in vain: for the Lord will not hold him guiltless that taketh his name in vain.*

112. Q. *What is required in the third commandment?*

A. *The third commandment requires, That the name of God, his titles, attributes, ordinances, the word, sacraments, prayer, oaths, vows, lots, his works, and whatsoever else there is whereby he makes himself known, be holily and reverently used in thought, meditation, word and writing; by a holy profession, and answerable conversation, to the glory of God, and the good of ourselves, and others.*

Scripture References

- Exod. 20:7. The third commandment.
- Matt. 6:9; Deut. 28:58; Pss. 29:2; 68:4; Rev. 15:3–4. The name of God is to be treated with reverence.
- Mal. 1:14; Eccl. 5:1. God's ordinance to be regarded with reverence.
- Ps. 138:2. God's Word to be reverently used.
- 1 Cor. 11:24–29. The sacraments to be carefully observed.
- 1 Tim. 2:8; Jer. 4:2; Eccl. 5:2–6; Acts 1:24, 26. Prayer, oaths, vows, and lots all being ways in which God makes himself known, they are to be used with reverent care.
- Job 36:24. God's self-revelation in his works to be regarded with reverence.
- Mal. 3:16; Ps. 8:1, 3–4, 9; Col. 3:17; Pss. 15:2, 5; 102:18. God's "name" or self-revelation to be used reverently in thought, meditation, speech, and writing.
- 1 Peter 3:15; Mic. 4:5. God's name to be honored by a holy profession.
- Phil. 1:27. God's name to be honored by a consistent life.
- 1 Cor. 10:31. God's name to be honored to the glory of God.
- Jer. 32:39; 1 Peter 2:12. God's name to be honored to the good of ourselves and others.

Commentary

1. What does the third commandment mean by the "name" of God? By the "name" of God, the third commandment means not only the actual word *God,* and other divine names such as *Lord, Jehovah,* etc., but God's self-revelation in its manifold fullness. "Name is often used in Hebrew in the sense of revealed character and essence. God swears by his great name to carry out his purpose (Jer. 44:26), that is, he swears by his attested power to accomplish his word. The name of God which is excellent in all the earth (Psalm 8:1), is that expression of his being which is exhibited in creation and redemption. . . . To know the name of God is to witness the manifestation of those attributes and apprehend that character which the name denotes (Ex. 6:3, with 7; 1 Kings 8:43; Psalm 91:14; Isa. 52:6; 64:2; Jer. 16:21)" (John D. Davis, *A Dictionary of the Bible*).

2. What does the "name" of God include? The "name" of God includes all forms of God's self-revelation, whether his general revelation in nature, or his special revelation which exists today in the form of Holy Scripture (including all ordinances of divine worship appointed in Scripture, such as sacraments, prayer, oaths, vows, etc.).

3. What attitude are we to have toward God's name? A holy and reverent attitude, as we learn also from the first petition of the Lord's Prayer, "Hallowed be thy name."

4. What do we mean by a holy and reverent attitude toward God's name? By a holy and reverent attitude toward God's name we mean, first of all, a sober, serious, respectful attitude that keeps us from treating God's self-revelation lightly or flippantly; second, we mean a worshipful attitude, as we are impressed with the infinite majesty and greatness of God, and filled with awe and wonder as we stand in the presence of the One who is a Spirit infinite, eternal, and unchangeable in his being and attributes.

5. How far should this reverent attitude toward God's name control our consciousness and self-expression? This reverent attitude toward God's self-revelation should completely control our consciousness and self-expression; God requires that his name "be holily and reverently used in thought, meditation, word and writing." That is to say, both in our inner consciousness and in our self-expression in speech and writing, we are to be permeated by an attitude of reverence toward God's name.

6. How is our daily life to be affected by our attitude toward God's name? Our attitude of reverence toward God's self-revelation is to find expression in "a holy profession, and answerable conversation"; that is, in a public profession of faith in the true religion which forms the content of God's "name" or self-revelation, and in a daily walk which is consistent with our profession of faith. Real reverence for God's name requires a true profession of faith and a consistent, godly walk.

7. What should be our aim or purpose in honoring God's name? As the catechism states, the first (and highest) aim in honoring God's name is the glory of God (which is also our chief end in life). Subordinately to this, we should honor God's name for "the good of ourselves, and others." Thus love to God, to ourself, and to our neighbor all require that God's name be honored and regarded with reverence.

8. Who can really honor and revere God's name? Only true Christians can really honor and revere God's name, for only true Christians really know God, and only they really see God's self-revelation, in its true meaning, in nature and in Scripture. A person who is not a Christian may of course be free from the habit of "profane swearing" in the literal sense; he may abstain from "profanity" simply because of his general culture and good taste, and yet, not being a Christian, he can have no real reverence for God in the positive and spiritual sense. To honor God's name, in the true sense, we must be born again and believe on Jesus Christ as our Savior.

113. Q. *What are the sins forbidden in the third commandment?*

A. *The sins forbidden in the third commandment are, the not using of God's name as is required; and the abuse of it in an ignorant, vain, irreverent, profane, superstitious, or wicked mentioning or otherwise using his titles, attributes, ordinances, or works, by blasphemy, perjury; . . .*

Scripture References
- Mal. 2:2. The sin of neglecting to use God's name aright.
- Acts 17:23. Ignorant abuse of God's name.
- Prov. 30:9; Mal. 1:6–7, 12; 3:14. Vain, irreverent, and profane abuse of God's name.
- 1 Sam. 4:3–5; Jer. 7:4–10, 14, 31; Col. 2:20–22. The sin of superstitious misuse of God's name.
- 2 Kings 18:30, 35; Exod. 5:2; Pss. 139:20; 50:16–17; Isa. 5:12. Sinful misuse of God's titles, attributes, ordinances, or works.
- 2 Kings 19:22; Lev. 24:11. The sin of blasphemy.
- Zech. 5:4; 8:17. The sin of perjury.

Commentary
1. What is the meaning of the words *vain* and *vanity* in the Bible?
Various words in the Hebrew Old Testament and the Greek New Testament are translated by "vain" or "vanity" in the English Bible. These do not all have exactly the same meaning. The word for "in vain" in the third commandment means primarily "falsely." It occurs fifty-three times in the Hebrew Old Testament, of which forty-four are translated by "vain" or "vanity." In forbidding us to take God's name in vain, the commandment forbids the use of God's name for anything that is false or wrong.

2. What special kinds of misuse of God's name does the catechism specify as forbidden by the third commandment? Ignorant, vain, irreverent, profane, superstitious, or wicked misuse of God's name, or his self-revelation. Ignorant misuse of God's name means that which arises from the sin-darkened mind of fallen man, apart from the Holy Spirit's work of illumination; because modern man is ignorant of God's self-revelation, he says that God is nothing but love, too kind to punish sinners in hell, etc. This is abuse of God's name. Vain misuse of God's name is that which uses God's name in connection with trivial matters, as when a person takes God's name in vain in connection with a statement that the weather is hot or cool, etc. Irreverent and profane misuse of God's name is similar to this, but even worse, as, for example, using God's name for an oath in connection with something that is sinful or unlawful, such as a conspiracy to commit a crime. Superstitious misuse of God's name is that which uses God's name in connection with superstitious practices of any kind, such as fortune-telling, the attempt to control events by magic, and the like. Wicked misuse of God's name is all use of it which proceeds from a wrong motive, or from a wrong attitude toward God, as when a person who has suffered some calamity curses God. All these forms of abuse of God's self-revelation are more or less common. Even Christian people are tempted to fall into these sins, and must be on guard against them.

3. In addition to the actual names of God, what forms of his self-revelation are we forbidden to misuse or take in vain? His titles, attributes, ordinances, and works; that is, all forms in which God has revealed his nature and character. Many people who do not dare to take the actual name *God* in vain commit virtually the same sin by abusing God's titles and attributes, as by such expressions as "Lord," "goodness!," "gracious!," "mercy!," and the like. Similarly God's self-revelation in his ordinances and works is misused by such profane expressions as "Holy smoke!" (originally, it would seem, a flippant reference to the smoke of incense burned in the temple services), "Jerusalem!" (a profane use of the name of the city where God's presence among his covenant people was especially revealed), "Good grief!" (apparently a careless and irreverent reference to Christ's sufferings in Gethsemane and on the cross). Some of these abuses are so common that even Christian people use them without realizing what they are doing. We should realize that all these and similar expressions are violations of the third commandment, and displeasing to God.

4. What is blasphemy? Blasphemy is name-calling or any kind of wicked language directed against God. For example, to accuse God of wickedness, injustice, or untruth of any kind is blasphemy against God. Under the Old Testament law the sin of blasphemy was punished by death by stoning (Lev. 24:16). This shows how wicked this sin is, and how offensive it is to God.

5. How do people blaspheme God today? God is blasphemed today in many ways. Often severe sufferings or calamities provoke people to blaspheme God. For example, some say that if God is good, he should have prevented World War II; that a good God would have prevented the war if he could; and since the war was not prevented, God must be either not good or else limited in power. Thus to challenge either the goodness or the power of God is blasphemy.

6. What is perjury? Perjury is the sin of making false statements under oath, that is, taking God as a witness that we are speaking the truth, when as a matter of fact we are speaking falsehood. "It is no trifling insult to him, when perjury is committed in his name; and therefore the law calls it a profanation (Lev. 19:12). But what remains to the Lord, when he is despoiled of his truth? He will then cease to be God. But he is certainly despoiled of it, when he is made an abettor and approver of a falsehood. . . . We cannot invoke God to be a witness to our declarations, without imprecating his vengeance upon us if we be guilty of perjury" (John Calvin, *Institutes,* 2.8.24). Perjury is not only a sin against God, but punished by the laws of most countries of the world as a crime.

7. Is perjury a common sin in the present day? Although in the nature of the case it is impossible to obtain any accurate statistics concerning this matter, and although perjury is often a very difficult matter to prove, there is reason to believe that perjury is far from uncommon in present-day law courts, and that it is possible to hire people to swear that the defendant was in a different city at the time the crime was committed, etc. People who go to certain states to obtain divorces will swear in court that they intend to reside permanently in that state, and after obtaining their divorce will go from the courthouse to the railroad station, board a train, and return to their original residence in another state. This lighthearted perjury seems to be regarded as a trifling matter by the public in general. From the Christian viewpoint such a practice is no trifle, but a flagrant and wicked violation of God's law, for which God will hold the violators guilty. A few years ago in one state every applicant for an automobile driver's license was required by law to swear an oath promising, among other things, never to drive faster than thirty miles per hour on the highways of the state. Such a requirement almost amounts to the government itself inviting its citizens to commit perjury. Christian people should oppose all such abuse of the divine ordinance of swearing by the name of God.

113. Q. *(continued) What are the sins forbidden in the third commandment?*

A. *The sins forbidden in the third commandment are . . . all sinful cursing, oaths, vows, and lots; violating of our oaths and vows, if lawful; and fulfilling them if of things unlawful; murmuring and quarreling at, curious prying into, and misapplying of God's decrees and providence; . . .*

Scripture References

- 1 Sam. 17:43; 2 Sam. 16:5; Jer. 5:7; 22:10. Sinful cursing and oaths.
- Deut. 23:18; Acts 23:12–14. Sinful misuse of vows.
- Esther 3:7; 9:24; Ps. 22:18. Sinful misuse of the lot.
- Ps. 24:4; Ezek. 17:16–19. The sin violating lawful oaths and vows.
- Mark 6:26; 1 Sam. 25:22, 32–34. The sin of fulfilling unlawful oaths and vows.
- Rom. 9:14, 19–20. The sin of murmuring and quarreling at God's decrees and providence.
- Deut. 29:29. The sin of curious prying into God's decrees and providence.
- Rom. 3:5–7; 6:1; Eccl. 8:11; 9:3; Ps. 39. The sin of misapplying God's decrees and providence.

Commentary

1. What does the catechism mean by "sinful cursing"? By "sinful cursing" the catechism means sinful cursing directed at some person, as when Goliath cursed David by his gods. Such cursing consists in a wish for calamity or destruction to come upon the person cursed, and the wish is supported by an appeal to God, or to some false divinity. We should realize that a wish for calamity or destruction to come upon some person is not always sinful; it is right to wish for judgment to be visited upon the incorrigible enemies of God, as we learn from the so-called "imprecatory" Psalms as well as from other parts of the Bible. What is sinful is cursing those whom God has not cursed, as King Balak wished Balaam to do (Num. 22:6; 23:8).

2. What is meant by "sinful oaths"? By "sinful oaths," the catechism means what is commonly called "profanity," that is, taking God's name in vain by oaths or "swear words" in our speech, or swearing by the name of false divinities. Obviously this is a terribly common sin, so common that it is little thought of by most people in the present day. Many people are so habituated to profanity in speech that they can hardly speak for two or three minutes without violating the third commandment more than once. Our popular books and magazines abound in profanity today, and those who are represented as "the best people" do not hesitate to "fortify" their speech with a continuous flow of such words as *hell* and *damn,* not to mention their use of the names of God and of the Lord Jesus Christ. Such profanity of speech can be partly explained psychologically, no doubt; but still more basic is the theological explanation, namely, that profanity in speech proceeds from a personality alienated from God and a heart deeply depraved and corrupted by original sin. Christian people should always be on guard against the temptation to compromise with the sinful world's habits of speech.

3. What are minced oaths? A minced oath is a profane oath uttered by a person who hesitates to go quite the whole way in imitating the profane speech of the sinful world. The use of minced oaths is peculiarly a sin of Christian people, who often deceive their own consciences into thinking that they are not doing wrong because they do not exactly duplicate the world's brand of profanity. Some examples of common forms of minced oaths are: "Gosh" (instead of "God"); "darn" (instead of "damn"); "heck" (instead of "hell"); "Gee" (instead of "Jesus"); "Crises" (instead of "Christ"); "the dickens" (instead of "the devil"); "the deuce" (from the Latin *Deus,* meaning "God," used instead of "the devil"). The use of all forms of minced oaths is forbidden, not only by a right understanding of the third commandment, but also by our Lord's command in Matthew 5:34–37: "Swear not at all . . . but let your communication be, Yea, yea; Nay, nay; for whatsoever is more than these cometh of evil."

4. When are vows sinful? Vows are sinful when the thing vowed is forbidden in God's Word, or something that would hinder any duty commanded in his Word, or something not in the person's power to perform, and for which God has not promised any ability. Vows are also sinful if made to any creature, instead of to God; or if made to any false divinity. (See the Westminster Confession of Faith, 22.7.)

5. Give some Bible examples of sinful vows. (a) Jephthah's vow (Judg. 11:30–31). (b) The vow of the Jews who conspired to murder Paul (Acts 23:12–14).

6. When is the use of the lot sinful? "The Lot is a mutual agreement to determine an uncertain event, no other way determinable, by an appeal to the providence of God, on casting or throwing something" (*Buck's Theological Dictionary*). The use of the lot is sinful (a) when it is used for a trivial matter; (b) when used for a matter which could and should be determined in some other way; (c) when used in a light or flippant spirit, without due reverence and faith in God. (For a fuller discussion of this matter, see *Blue Banner Faith and Life*, vol. 1, no. 5 [May 1946], 80.)

7. What is our duty with respect to lawful oaths and vows? It is our duty to fulfill them conscientiously, in the fear of God, in spite of difficulty or personal loss. To fail to do so is to commit a great sin against God.

8. What is our duty with respect to unlawful oaths and vows? If an oath or vow is unlawful, that is, contrary to the moral law of God, then of course it cannot be binding on a person's conscience. God's law does not bind us to break God's law. When a person realizes that he has entangled himself in an unlawful oath or vow, it is not only his right but his God-given duty to repudiate it immediately. A well-known example of a faithful Christian who rightly repudiated unlawful vows is that of the Reformer Martin Luther, who came to realize the unlawful character of the vows he had taken as a Roman Catholic monk, including the vow of perpetual celibacy, and repudiated these unlawful "obligations."

9. What Bible character failed to break an unlawful oath? King Herod, who ordered John the Baptist beheaded (Mark 6:14–29). Herod's oath was an unlawful one; he had no right to promise Herodias's daughter whatever she might ask, to the half of his kingdom. His authority in the kingdom was a sacred trust, a stewardship to be exercised according to law and justice, not given away according to senseless caprice. Having played the fool in swearing such a wicked oath Herod should have confessed his sin and broken the

oath; but this, of course, he was unwilling to do because of the tremendous
"loss of face" that would be involved.

**10. Why is it wrong to murmur and quarrel at God's decrees and
providence?** It is always wrong to murmur and quarrel at God's decrees
and providence (a) because such conduct involves a spirit of rebellion against
the sovereignty of God: the complainer assumes that he is competent to sit
in judgment on God's decrees and acts, and call God to account; (b) because
such conduct involves a lack of faith in God's goodness and love: the complainer is not willing to wait patiently for God to deliver him from hardships, trouble, or poverty; he feels that if God is really a God of goodness
and love, he owes his people immediate deliverance. This implied demand
for immediate help from God is entirely contrary to the attitude of faith,
which is willing to wait patiently for God to provide deliverance in his own
time and way.

**11. What is meant by "curious prying into, and misapplying of
God's decrees and providence"?** Curious prying into God's decrees and
providence is a searching into God's secrets which is motivated by curiosity
rather than by a reverent attitude. The curious prier into God's secrets refuses
to recognize the essential mystery of God and God's works; he wishes to satisfy his sinful curiosity by comprehending God and gaining an exhaustive
understanding of God's works. This is sinful for it implies a denial of the
transcendent mystery and infinitude of God, and seeks to place God on the
same level with humanity.

Misapplying of God's decrees and providence consists in drawing wrong
inferences from them, or using them as excuses for wickedness of any kind.
The person who says: "If God has predestined me to eternal life I am sure
to receive eternal life, so I need not accept Christ nor live a Christian life,"
is guilty of misapplying God's decrees. The person who says: "I know people who work seven days a week, and have become rich; God has prospered
them; this shows that God does not expect people to keep the Sabbath in
our day and age," is guilty of misapplying God's providence. Both in the
case of God's decrees and in the case of his providence, a careful study of the
Bible would expose the sin of misapplication, both in the cases cited above
and in all other instances.

113. Q. *(continued) What are the sins forbidden in the third commandment?*

A. *The sins forbidden in the third commandment are . . . misinterpreting, misapplying, or any way perverting the word, or any part of it, to profane jests, curious or unprofitable questions, vain janglings, or the maintaining of false doctrines; abusing it, the creatures, or any thing contained under the name of God, to charms, or sinful lusts and practices; . . .*

Scripture References

- Matt. 5:21–28. It is sinful to misinterpret any part of God's Word.
- Ezek. 13:22; 2 Peter 3:16; Matt. 22:24–31; Isa. 22:13; Jer. 23:34–38. It is wrong to misapply or pervert God's Word to profane jests, absurdities, or false doctrines.
- 1 Tim. 1:4–7; 6:4–5, 20; 2 Tim. 2:14; Titus 3:9. All misuse of God's Word in support of false doctrines, "strifes of words," "vain babblings," etc., is wicked.
- Deut. 18:10–14; Acts 19:13. All misuse of any form of God's self–revelation in connection with superstitious practices is wrong.
- 2 Tim. 4:3–4; Rom. 13:13–14; 1 Kings 21:9–10; Jude 4. It is wicked to abuse any form of God's self-revelation for sinful lusts and practices.

Commentary

1. Why is it sinful to misinterpret the Bible? Misinterpretation of the Bible is sinful because it proceeds not merely from our limitations as finite human beings, but especially from the corruption of our hearts and darkening of our minds that have resulted from the fall of the human race into sin. We should realize that error, being the opposite of truth, is sinful in itself. It is because of people's sinful hearts and darkened minds that they misinterpret God's Word.

2. What is meant by "misapplying" and "perverting" God's Word? "Misapplying" God's Word includes all use of it apart from its true meaning and proper purpose as the revelation of God's will to man. The person who admires and reads the Bible merely because it is great literature is guilty of misapplying God's Word. The atheist who studies the Bible in order to try to prove it untrue is guilty of misapplying God's Word. Mary Baker Eddy's notorious book, *Science and Health with the Key to the Scriptures*, is an example of misapplying and perverting God's Word in such a way as to make it seem to support the false system of "Christian Science." The person who advocates the teaching of the Bible merely for its moral lessons, apart from its revelation of the way of salvation through Jesus Christ the Mediator, is guilty of misapplying and perverting God's Word; the moral teachings of the Bible are rooted and grounded in the Bible's religious message, and must not be divorced from Christ's work of redemption; to teach the Bible in such a way as to make it seem to have an ethical message apart from Christ's redemption is to misapply and pervert the Word of God, by using it in a way and for a purpose which are alien to its true meaning and purpose.

3. Why is it wrong to use the Bible, or any part of it, for "profane jests"? Because the Bible, as God's Holy Word, is sacred, and must be treated with due reverence. Of course it is true that there is humor in the Bible, and it is not wrong to point it out and appreciate it. But using the Bible for profane jests is something quite different from appreciating the humor in the Bible. What is wrong is to use God's Word as the object of ridicule, so that God's revelation is derided and comes to be regarded with contempt.

4. What is meant by "curious or unprofitable questions" and "vain janglings"? The Jews and others in the time of Christ and the apostles were guilty of just these practices, as is evident from the apostle Paul's warnings in his epistles to Timothy and Titus. Certain types of such misuse of God's Word are mentioned: "fables"; "endless genealogies"; "vain jangling"; "doting about questions and strifes of words"; "perverse disputings"; "profane and vain babblings"; "oppositions of science falsely so-called"; "foolish questions"; "strivings about the law." These various types of misuse of the Scripture may perhaps be summarized as follows: (a) disputes about questions which in the nature of the case cannot be determined with certainty ("fables"); (b) disputes about matters which would be of no value even if they could be definitely decided ("endless genealogies"); (c) merely verbal argumentation, which deals with words alone rather than with the realities that words should stand for ("vain jangling"; "doting about questions and strifes of words"); (d) controversies having to do merely with the concepts of human philosophy, not with the truths revealed in God's Word ("oppositions of science falsely so-called"); (e) disputes about Jewish traditional interpretations of, and additions to, the Old Testament law ("strivings about the law"). All of these forms of abuse of God's Word have their counterparts in the present day. The true servant of God will be careful to avoid all these practices, as also to prevent their occurrence in the church, and to seek to eliminate them if and when they do occur.·

5. Why is "the maintaining of false doctrines" sinful? Because false doctrines are the result of our sin-corrupted hearts and our sin-darkened minds, and our maintaining them involves opposition to the truth of God and shows a total or partial lack of the Holy Spirit's work of illumination. Many people today hesitate to call the maintaining of false doctrines a sin. According to the Bible, however, adherence to doctrinal error, even though sincere, is nevertheless sinful. First Timothy 6:3–5 gives the Holy Spirit's teaching concerning the sinfulness of doctrinal error. Titus 3:10–11 presents the same teaching.

6. What does the catechism mean by "charms"? By "charms" the catechism means the whole array of forbidden practices by which men have sought to gain control of superhuman powers or forces for their own purposes or benefit, including such practices as magic, divination (fortune-telling), attempted contact with the dead through spirit-mediums, use of devices to bring "good luck," etc.

7. How do such practices violate the third commandment? Such practices as those described in the preceding question violate the third commandment because they all involve a misuse of God's self-revelation in one or another of its forms (the Word, the creatures, or any thing contained under the name of God). It is wrong to use God's Word or his self-revelation in his works to try to obtain illicit information (as concerning the future, apart from what is revealed in the prophecies of the Bible), or to attempt to gain control over God's providence (as by the practice of magic, use of "good luck" charms, etc.). All of these practices involve a perversion of religion to magic. Instead of recognizing that man's chief end is to glorify God, they attempt to use God, and his revelation in Word and works, for man's own selfish, sinful purposes. This is really to take God's name in vain, and forbidden by the third commandment.

8. How has God's self-revelation been misused for sinful lusts and practices? All victims of the antinomian heresy (which denies that the Christian is subject to the moral law of God as the rule of his life) inevitably tend toward misusing God's revelation for sinful lusts and practices. Some extreme examples of this could be cited from the history of the church. In the Bible we find a very emphatic condemnation of the sect of the Nicolaitans, which was essentially an antinomian sect (Rev. 2:6, 14–16, 20–23). Similarly, in Paul's epistles (2 Tim. 3:1–9; 4:3–4), 2 Peter 2, and the epistle of Jude, we find strong warnings against, and condemnations of, antinomian tendencies and practices. There have always been some such "ungodly men, turning the grace of our God into lasciviousness, and denying the only Lord God, and our Lord Jesus Christ" (Jude 4). Such wickedness is of course an extreme form of violation of the third commandment, the sin of taking the name of God in vain.

113. Q. *(continued) What are the sins forbidden in the third commandment?*

A. *The sins forbidden in the third commandment are . . . the maligning, scorning, reviling, or any wise opposing of God's truth, grace, and ways; making profession of religion in hypocrisy, or for sinister ends; being ashamed of it, or a shame to it, by unconformable, unwise, unfruitful, and offensive walking, or backsliding from it.*

Scripture References

- Acts 13:45; 1 John 3:12. The sin of the maligning of God's truth, grace, and ways.
- Ps. 1:1; 2 Peter 2:3. The sin of scorning or scoffing at God's truth, grace, and ways.
- 1 Peter 4:4. The sin of reviling God's truth, grace, and ways.
- Acts 4:18; 13:45–46, 50; 19:9; 1 Thess. 2:16; Heb. 10:29. The sin of opposing God's truth, grace, and ways.
- 2 Tim. 3:5; Matt. 6:1–5, 16; 23:14. The sin of a hypocritical or insincere profession of religion.
- Mark 8:38. The sin of being ashamed of Christ and the gospel.
- Ps. 73:14–15; 1 Cor. 6:5–6; Eph. 5:15–17. Being a shame to the gospel by unconformable or unwise walking.
- Isa. 5:4; 2 Peter 1:8–9; Rom. 2:23–24. Being a shame to the gospel by unfruitful and offensive walking.
- Gal. 3:1–3; Heb. 6:6. The sin of being a shame to the gospel by backsliding from our profession of it.

Commentary

1. What is meant by "maligning" God's truth, grace, and ways? To "malign" means falsely and maliciously to speak evil of. The person who maligns God's truth, etc., is not a common unbeliever who merely neglects or rejects the gospel; he is a person (a) who actively opposes the gospel by speaking evil of it; and (b) who in the bottom of his heart knows that the gospel really is true. That there are such maligners of the gospel cannot be denied. Their extreme perversity can be explained only by the scriptural truths of original sin and total depravity. Often persons who for some reason have abandoned the profession of Christianity and have joined some other religion turn out to be very bitter opponents of Christianity. Their very bitterness and the intensity of their opposition may be the result of a desperate struggle to silence a guilty conscience, to silence the voice of God speaking through their conscience and destroying their peace of mind by a haunting conviction that the gospel is true after all.

2. What is "scorning" God's truth, grace, and ways? To scorn is to regard or treat with contempt. Scoffing has much the same meaning except that it includes more of the idea of outward expression of contempt in words of derision. The scorner and the scoffer regard the gospel of Christ not merely as false, but as foolish, ridiculous, unworthy of acceptance by intelligent people, etc. They not merely reject the gospel, but represent it as something mean and unworthy; they belittle God's truth, grace, and ways. Scorners delight to point out what they call the "immoral" portions of the Bible, and to dwell on what they pronounce to be its "incredible" features, such as its miracles. Scorning and scoffing are always signs of a small, single-track, narrow-gauge mind. There are unbelievers who reject Christianity, and yet treat it with respect and dignity; but scorners and scoffers belittle it with contempt and ridicule. At the Judgment Day, of course (if not before), their contempt and ridicule will return upon their own heads.

3. What is "reviling" God's truth, grace, and ways? "Reviling" means denouncing in abusive, scandalous language. It is an extreme form of "name-calling." Reviling is usually directed against the gospel of Christ, not in itself, but in the persons of its adherents, that is, Christian people. This is referred to in the Bible as "the reproach of Christ" (Heb. 11:26). People in heathen countries such as India and China who make a public profession of faith in Christ are called upon to endure reviling for Christ's sake that we in America know but little of. When the devil's kingdom is invaded and some of his victims are translated to the kingdom of God, he becomes angry and stirs up furious and vicious opposition to the gospel. This frequently takes the form of very abusive reviling of Christian people.

4. What are some of the ways in which men oppose God's truth, grace, and ways? In addition to maligning, scorning, and reviling, which we have been considering, there are various other ways in which opposition is made to God's cause in the world. We should realize that genuine opposition is not merely of human origin, but is stirred up by Satan behind the scenes of human life. Satan has two methods of opposing God's truth, grace, and ways, which he has used time and again. The first is persecution. Satan stirs up worldly powers such as kings and governments, or mob violence in some cases, to bring bitter persecution upon the church and its members. Persecution usually checks the spread of the gospel and the growth of the church temporarily. Hypocrites no longer dare to be identified with the church, and so fall away. Missionary work is hindered and blocked by obstacles. But in the end persecution fails. By the power of the Holy Spirit, the church emerges from the fires of persecution stronger than ever; it learns to put its trust in God's Spirit and not in worldly methods. Then Satan tries his second method, which is often much more effective than the first, namely, stirring up heresies and false doctrines within the church itself. These heresies, if tolerated and not challenged, would destroy Christianity as a saving message in the world. The Holy Spirit raises up witnesses for the truth, who challenge the heresy and seek to eliminate it from the church. This often requires many years of intense effort, yet it is absolutely necessary when the truth of God is being opposed within the church itself. Effort which could otherwise be expended on missions, evangelism, etc., must be devoted to preserving the integrity of the church itself as a body that can witness for the truth of the gospel. This necessarily interferes with the normal expansion and growth of the church. Yet Satan's second method of opposing Christianity fails in the end, truth is vindicated in the course of time, and God's cause goes forward in spite of the opposition of Satan and of men.

5. What is meant by "making profession of religion in hypocrisy, or for sinister ends"? "Making profession of religion in hypocrisy" means making profession of it insincerely, with a pretended, not a real, faith. The expression "for sinister ends" describes the motives which actuate the hypocrite. His real motives, which bring him to profess to be a Christian, are not the glory of God or the salvation of his soul, but such improper motives as financial gain, social respectability, and the like. Not every unregenerate church member is a hypocrite. A person may be self-deceived; he may sincerely believe himself to be a true Christian, when as a matter of fact he is an unsaved sinner. The hypocrite is not self-deceived; he knows perfectly well that he is not a real Christian; he is trying to deceive others by putting up the outward appearance of being a Christian. When persecution for Christ's sake comes upon the church, the hypocrites will abandon the profession of Christianity without delay. No real, self-conscious hypocrite will suffer persecution or reproach for the gospel's sake.

6. What makes people ashamed of being known as Christians? Undoubtedly it is fear that makes people ashamed of being known as Christians—fear of reproach, fear of ridicule, fear of contempt, and sometimes fear of suffering or death. This is a sinful, carnal fear which is linked in the Bible with such sins as murder, sorcery, idolatry, and adultery (Rev. 21:8). It is not the mere feeling of fear which is represented as such a terrible sin; rather, it is yielding to fear so that a person's conduct is determined by that fear, and he becomes enslaved to fear.

7. How do professing Christians sometimes become a shame to the gospel of Christ? By "unconformable, unwise, unfruitful and offensive walking, or backsliding from it." It has been well said that Christian people are the only Bible the world will read. The world gets its idea of Christianity largely from observing the lives and conduct of professing Christians. When those who are known as Christians are guilty of scandalous and wicked practices, the gospel appears contemptible in the eyes of the world. Thus professing Christians by their worldly life and conduct may become a shame to the gospel of Christ.

8. What is meant by "backsliding" from the gospel of Christ? This means giving up even the profession of Christianity. The backslider loses interest in the things of God, ceases to attend church services, and hardens his heart in indifference and unbelief. He may still have his name on the membership roll of some church as a member in good standing, not because he shows any interest in the church, but because of the reluctance of church officers to discipline unfaithful members. The backslider, even though he may nominally be a church member, shows no active interest in Christianity; he is complacently indifferent. If he fails to repent before it is too late, he will perish eternally in hell.

Total and permanent backsliding from the gospel of Christ is a sin which is never committed by true believers, who have been born again of the Holy Spirit. Even true believers, though, may be involved in a partial and temporary form of backsliding, losing interest in Christianity and failing to make any active profession of faith for a period of time. For a fuller discussion of these questions, the reader is referred to the Larger Catechism, Q. 79, with its Scripture proofs, and *Blue Banner Faith and Life*, vol. 2, no. 1 (January–March 1947), 42–44.

114. Q. *What reasons are annexed to the third commandment?*

A. *The reasons annexed to the third commandment, in these words,* "The Lord thy God," *and,* "For the Lord will not hold him guiltless that taketh his name in vain," *are, because he is the Lord and our God, therefore his name is not to be profaned, or any way abused by us; especially because he will be so far from acquitting and sparing the transgressors of this commandment, as that he will not suffer them to escape his righteous judgment, albeit many such escape the censures and punishments of men.*

Scripture References
- Lev. 19:12; Ezek. 36:21–23; Deut. 28:58–59; Zech. 5:2–4. Because of the sovereignty, majesty, and holiness of God, his name is not to be profaned or misused.
- 1 Sam. 2:12, 17, 22, 24, compared with 3:13. Those who dishonor the name of God will surely be punished by God, even though they may escape the judgment of men.

Commentary
1. What is meant by affirming that God is the Lord? By affirming that God is the Lord, or Jehovah, is meant that God is sovereign, self-determined, and unlimited by anything outside of himself. (See *Blue Banner Faith and Life,*

vol. 2, no. 3 [July–September 1947], 122.) Thus the term refers to the majesty and authority of God. Because God is what he is, his name must be handled reverently.

2. What is meant by the words "thy God" in the third commandment? This expression implies a special covenant relation between God and his people. Although God's authority is of course universal, and his law ought to be obeyed by all men, those who have been brought into the sphere of God's covenant of grace can call God their God in a special sense, and therefore they are under an added obligation to use God's name in a reverent and right manner. It is wrong for anyone to take God's name in vain; for those living in the sphere of God's covenant, who are called God's people, to do so is a much more wicked sin.

3. How is the sovereignty of God often disregarded or denied today? The sovereignty of God, his majesty, his holiness, his absolute justice—all these truths are denied or obscured by the modern sentimental view of God, which regards him as nothing but love and kindness. Such a view of God represents him as too benevolent to be offended by human sin. Such a God could not be indignant when his name is taken in vain. Very different, of course, is the God revealed in the Bible, who is infinite, eternal, and unchangeable in his being and all his attributes, a God of holiness, justice, and truth as well as of kindness and love toward mankind.

4. How is the special covenant relationship to God, expressed by the words "thy God," often denied or obscured today? This truth is denied or obscured by the popular notions of the universal Fatherhood of God and Brotherhood of man. If all human beings are already the children of God, apart from redemption and adoption, and if all mankind are already brothers in the family of God, then of course the Bible teaching of a special covenant people called out of the world into fellowship with God loses all point and meaning.

5. Why will God not allow those who break this commandment to escape his righteous judgment? It is true, of course, that God will not allow those who break any of the Ten Commandments to escape his righteous judgment. All of the commandments constitute a unity as the law of God. But because this command not to take God's name in vain especially concerns God's own honor and authority, he has added a special warning that he will not hold those guiltless who take his name in vain.

6. Is it a great sin to take God's name in vain? Certainly this is a great sin, although of course there are greater and lesser degrees of taking God's name in vain. The violation of this commandment is commonly regarded as not a sin at all by the world. We should realize that the world's views of right and wrong are far from coinciding with the revelation of God's moral law as we have it in the Bible.

7. Do those who take God's name in vain commonly escape the censures and punishments of men? Yes. It seems that there is no longer any strong public opinion against profane swearing, and many people of education and social standing do not even regard taking God's name in vain as contrary to good taste—to say nothing about regarding it as morally wrong. Popular literature is becoming more and more tolerant of profanity. Magazines which twenty or thirty years ago carefully excluded profanity from their columns allow it to appear freely today. We must face the fact that the Christian veneer of our modern culture has been wearing thin. The general breakdown of faith in the authority of the Bible which has resulted from the spread of "critical" views of the Scriptures is now bearing fruit in a general breakdown in the realm of morals and conduct. The almost unrestrained increase of profane swearing is one symptom of this breakdown. Without a general return to acceptance of the real authority of the Bible, the evil can hardly be remedied.

115. Q. *Which is the fourth commandment?*

A. *The fourth commandment is,* Remember the Sabbath day, to keep it holy. Six days shall thou labor, and do all thy work: but the seventh day is the Sabbath of the Lord thy God: in it thou shall not do any work, thou, nor thy son, nor thy daughter, thy man-servant nor thy maid-servant, nor thy cattle, nor thy stranger that is within thy gates. For in six days the Lord made heaven and earth, the sea, and all that in them is, and rested the seventh day: wherefore the Lord blessed the Sabbath day, and hallowed it.

116. Q. *What is required in the fourth commandment?*

A. *The fourth commandment requireth of all men the sanctifying or keeping holy to God such set times as he hath appointed in his word, expressly one whole day in seven; which was the seventh from the beginning of the world to the resurrection of Christ, and the first day of the week ever since, and so to continue to the end of the world; which is the Christian Sabbath, and in the New Testament called* The Lord's Day.

Scripture References

- Exod. 20:8–11; Deut. 5:12–15. The Sabbath commandment.
- 1 Cor. 16:1–2; Acts 20:7. The first day of the week observed by the apostles and early Christians.
- Matt. 5:17–18. No part of God's law can pass away, until all be fulfilled.
- Isa. 56:2, 4, 6–7. The Old Testament predicts Sabbath observance in the New Testament dispensation.
- Rev. 1:10. The Lord's Day referred to by name.

Commentary

1. Is the Sabbath commandment a moral law or a ceremonial law?
The commandment to observe the weekly Sabbath is a moral law of God.

2. How can it be shown that the Sabbath commandment is a moral rather than a ceremonial law? (a) The fourth commandment itself mentions the fact that the Sabbath originated not at the time of Moses but at the creation of the world. Thus the Sabbath existed thousands of years before God gave the ceremonial law in the time of Moses. (b) The Sabbath commandment is a part of the Ten Commandments, and thus, being found in a context of moral laws, it too must be regarded as a moral law; it would be very strange if the Ten Commandments were composed of nine moral precepts and one ceremonial precept, nine permanent laws and one law of only temporary validity. The Ten Commandments form a unity as a summary of God's moral law, and if the Sabbath commandment were not a moral law, this unity would be broken. (c) Like the rest of the Ten Commandments, the Sabbath commandment was not written on perishable material but upon tablets of stone, indicating its permanent validity. All parts of the ceremonial law passed away at the time of the crucifixion of Christ, and if the Sabbath commandment is a ceremonial law, then it too passed away, and was not permanent, but only of temporary validity. But the fact that it was written on stone by God himself indicates that it was intended to be permanent.

3. On whom is the Sabbath commandment binding? Upon all men without exception. As Jesus said, "the Sabbath was made for man"; he did not say that the Sabbath was made for Israel, but that it was made for man, and not man for the Sabbath. Thus it is not limited to any particular class of men, but is binding upon the human race.

4. What attempts have been made to limit the obligation to observe the Sabbath to certain classes of people? (a) Some have held that the obligation to keep the Sabbath is binding only on the people of Israel or the Jews. (b) Others have maintained that the obligation to observe the Sabbath is binding only on Christians, and that those who do not profess to be Christians need not observe the Sabbath.

5. How can these claims be answered? (a) It has been shown above that the Sabbath commandment is a moral law. But if it is a moral law, it must be binding on all people without exception. (b) If we say that the fourth commandment applies only to Jews, or only to Christians, why not go on and say that the fifth, sixth, and seventh commandments, for example, apply only to Jews, or only to Christians? We must always remember that the Ten Commandments form a unity and may not be arbitrarily broken up. We may not single out one commandment and say that it applies only to a limited group of people, while the rest apply to all mankind. The Ten Commandments must be taken together, and we should realize that while they were originally revealed by God to the people of Israel, they form a summary of God's moral law which is binding on all mankind.

6. What is the principle of the Sabbath? The principle of the Sabbath is the observance as a holy day of one whole day in seven in regular sequence. Whether it is the first day of the week or the seventh day of the week is not a part of the principle of the Sabbath, but a matter determined by other considerations which are set forth in Scripture.

7. How has the principle of the Sabbath sometimes been wrongly stated? It has often been stated that the principle of the Sabbath is that one-seventh of our time must be consecrated to God. This is a very faulty and inaccurate statement of the principle, for it would not require the keeping of a whole day at any time. On such a basis a person might consecrate to

God one hour out of every seven hours, or one year out of every seven years. Or a person might observe the Sabbath on a different day each week. As stated in the preceding question, the correct principle of the Sabbath is the observance of one whole day in seven in regular sequence.

8. Does the fourth commandment require the observance of the seventh day of the week, or Saturday, as the Sabbath? No. It is of course true, as a matter of fact, that the Old Testament Sabbath was on the seventh day of the week, but the fourth commandment does not require this. It commands diligent labor for six days, but does not specify on what day the week is to begin. The fourth commandment requires that the seventh day after six days of labor be observed as the Sabbath, but this does not imply that it must necessarily be on the seventh (or last) day of the week. The requirement of the commandment is met by the Christian practice of working from Monday through Saturday (six days) and then observing the first day of the following week as the Sabbath.

9. Why was the Old Testament Sabbath the seventh day of the week? The Old Testament Sabbath was the seventh (last) day of the week because of God's example and ordinance at the time of the creation (Gen. 2:1–3). Apart from providing an appointed day for rest and worship, the Sabbath served as a reminder of God's work of creation. This truth of creation, of course, implies that all things, including human beings, are absolutely dependent on God for their very existence. It also implies that human beings are morally responsible to God for their lives. Thus the weekly Sabbath, commemorating the creation, was calculated to serve as a continually repeated reminder of man's dependence on God and his moral accountability to God—which is to say that the Sabbath was calculated to serve as a constant reminder of the very foundations of religion and morality.

10. Why is the Christian Sabbath on the first day of the week? The Christian Sabbath, or the Lord's Day, is on the first day of the week in remembrance of Christ's resurrection from the dead. Thus it may be said that the Old Testament Sabbath commemorated God's original creation, while the Christian Sabbath in addition calls attention to God's new creation, his great work of redemption in Jesus Christ.

11. Who changed the day of the Sabbath from the seventh to the first day of the week? Our Lord Jesus Christ, by the accomplishment of his great redemptive work, brought about the close of the Old Testament dispensation and the opening of the New Testament dispensation of the covenant of grace. The change from the seventh to the first day of the week is a part of this change of dispensation. It has been observed that our Savior was crucified on the sixth day of the week, and buried on the evening of the sixth day, and remained in the tomb the whole of the seventh day, and arose from the dead on the first day of the week. Thus Christ buried the Old Testament seventh day Sabbath in the tomb with himself, and left it there, and when he arose he brought with him the New Testament Sabbath, which is to be observed on the first day of the week.

12. Did the Roman Emperor Constantine change the Sabbath from the seventh to the first day of the week? Although this change of day has often been attributed to Constantine, the assertion is false. The Roman Emperor Constantine in the year 321 issued a decree providing for the civil observance of the first day of the week, forbidding courts of justice to hold sessions on that day and commanding the soldiers of the Roman army to abstain from their ordinary military exercises on that day. But the observance of the first day of the week as the Lord's Day goes back far earlier than the time of Constantine, as is evidenced by the New Testament and other early Christian documents.

13. How long is the Sabbath to be observed on the first day of the week? Until the end of the world. This follows from the fact that God's revelation through Christ and the apostles, which we call the New Testament, is God's final word to the human race until the end of the world. Since the completion of the New Testament, God has remained silent and has not spoken directly to the human race, nor can any new revelation be expected until that day when our Lord Jesus Christ shall come again in glory to judge the living and the dead.

14. Will the Sabbath be observed in heaven? While the Bible says nothing directly on this subject, the teachings of Scripture concerning the difference between this present age and the age to come imply that Sabbath observance as we know it will not exist in heaven. Rather, we may say, heaven will be one unending Sabbath. Scripture teaches that there will be no temple in heaven (Rev. 21:22), and of course there will be no need of the Bible in heaven, for the redeemed shall see God's face (Rev. 22:4). There will be no weariness or need of special times of rest in heaven, for in "the life that is life indeed" the most intense activity and the most perfect rest can exist together. It is true that the Sabbath existed before man's fall into sin, and therefore complete deliverance from sin would not mean that the Sabbath must necessarily pass away. Rather, Scripture informs us that "there remaineth therefore a Sabbath rest for the people of God" (Heb. 4:9, ARV), that is, the Sabbath rest of eternity. Thus in eternity the Sabbath which was instituted at the creation will not be abolished, but fulfilled in the eternal Sabbath rest of God's redeemed.

15. What differences exist among Christian people about the obligation of Sabbath observance? As mentioned above under question 3, some hold that the obligation to observe the Sabbath is limited to Jews, or limited to Christians. Those who say that it does not apply to Christians distinguish between the Sabbath and the Lord's Day, and hold that the Lord's Day has no connection with the fourth commandment. There are also great differences about how the Sabbath is to be observed. Obviously the question whether the Sabbath must be observed must be settled before anyone can discuss how it ought to be observed.

16. Is it important for the church to teach the obligation to observe the Sabbath? Certainly this is important. The fact that various differences of opinion about the Sabbath exist among Christian people does not mean that the church may neglect what it regards as the teaching of God's Word on this subject. Nor does the fact that careful Sabbath observance is contrary to the spirit of the present age mean that the church may tolerate disregard of the Sabbath among her members. While recognizing that many earnest Christian people differ from us in their interpretation of the Bible with respect to the Sabbath, we should adhere faithfully, both by profession and by practice, to the obligation of Sabbath observance as set forth in our church standards, which we believe to be an accurate interpretation of the Scriptures.

117. Q. *How is the Sabbath or the Lord's day to be sanctified?*

A. *The Sabbath or Lord's day is to be sanctified by a holy resting all the day, not only from such works as are at all times sinful, but even from such worldly employments and recreations as are on other days lawful;*

and making it our delight to spend the whole time (except so much of it as is to be taken up in works of necessity and mercy) in the public and private exercises of God's worship: and, to that end, we are to prepare our hearts, and with such foresight, diligence and moderation, to dispose and seasonably dispatch our worldly business, that we may be the more free and fit for the duties of that day.

Scripture References

- Exod. 20:8. The Sabbath to be kept as a holy day.
- Exod. 20:10; 16:25–28; Neh. 13:15–22; Jer. 17:21–22. God requires abstinence from ordinary work on the Sabbath day.
- Matt. 12:1–13. Work of necessity may be performed on the Sabbath day.
- John 9:14; Luke 13:14–16. Work of mercy may be performed on the Sabbath day.
- Isa. 58:13–14; Luke 4:16; Acts 20:7; 1 Cor. 16:1–2; Isa. 66:23; Lev. 23:3. The duty of positive observance of the Sabbath day by worship of God.
- Exod. 20:8; Luke 23:54–56; Exod. 16:22–29; Neh. 13:19. The duty of preparing for the Sabbath by arranging our worldly business beforehand.

Commentary

1. What two kinds of Sabbath observance are required by the Scriptures? The Word of God requires both negative and positive observance of the Sabbath.

2. What is meant by negative observance of the Sabbath? Negative observance of the Sabbath means abstaining from those things which ought not be done on that day.

3. What is meant by positive observance of the Sabbath? Positive observance of the Sabbath means doing those things which it is our duty to do on that day.

4. How does the catechism speak of the negative observance of the Sabbath? The catechism affirms that the Sabbath is to be observed by a holy resting (a) from sinful works; (b) from worldly employments; and (c) from worldly recreations.

5. What is meant by a holy resting? This means not merely resting, or abstaining from work, but resting with a religious motive, as an element of obedience and service to God. We are not merely to rest, but to rest as a form of devotion to God.

6. How much of the Sabbath is to be devoted to God by abstinence from work and ordinary recreations? "All the day," that is, the whole of the Sabbath day is to be so devoted to God.

7. Does the Sabbath run from sunset to sunset, or from midnight to midnight? This is a matter which is indifferent in itself. The Jews reckoned their days from sunset to sunset, and their Sabbath accordingly. We count from midnight to midnight. The Sabbath should be reckoned in the customary way of reckoning other days.

8. Besides religious duties, what forms of work are legitimate on the Sabbath? Besides religious duties, works of necessity and works of mercy are legitimate on the Sabbath.

9. What is meant by "works of necessity"? Strictly speaking, works of necessity are works which cannot be avoided, or cannot be postponed until another day. If a house catches fire, the blaze must be extinguished immediately; this is a work of necessity, and does not violate the Sabbath. Domestic animals must be fed and watered; cows must be milked; such tasks are necessary because they cannot be postponed; they do not violate the Sabbath. Even work which might be postponed may properly be performed on the Sabbath, if it results in eliminating other and greater work on the Sabbath day. If fifteen minutes spent repairing an automobile will save two hours of time that would be required to drive to church with a team of horses, or to walk to church, it is legitimate to repair the automobile, because this will result in the least total amount of work on the Sabbath day. There must of course be some allowance for differences of opinion among Christian people about what constitutes a true work of necessity on the Sabbath. Some things are regarded as necessary by conscientious Christians of the present day, which in times past would perhaps not have been considered necessary. The Bible teaches the principle that works of necessity may be done on the Sabbath, and gives some examples of the application of this principle. But the Bible does not provide a ready-made definition of a "work of necessity," such as could be applied to all cases. By inference from the teachings of the Bible we may say that a work of necessity is (a) that which cannot be postponed; or (b) that work which results in eliminating the greatest possible amount of work on the Sabbath day.

10. What is meant by "works of mercy"? This means work done chiefly without any motive of financial gain, but because of sympathy and compassion for human suffering. Physicians and nurses may properly care for the sick on the Sabbath day, and of course they are entitled to compensation for such work, but what makes such work legitimate on the Sabbath is not the element of profit, but the element of relieving suffering. To visit the sick is certainly proper on the Sabbath, provided it is done with a right motive.

11. What should be our principal occupation on the Sabbath? The public and private exercises of God's worship.

12. What are the public exercises of God's worship? These are the services of the church, including the regular services at which the Word of God is preached, and also other church meetings, such as Sabbath Schools, Bible study classes, and prayer meetings.

13. What are the private exercises of God's worship? The private exercises of God's worship are: (a) individual, such as personal Bible reading and prayer; (b) family, including family worship, religious instruction of children, religious conversation, and the like.

14. In order to observe the Sabbath aright, what preparations must we make? (a) We must prepare our hearts, that is, think about the Sabbath and its duties, privileges, and blessings, beforehand, so that we will be in a worshipful frame of mind on the Lord's Day. (b) We must adequately attend to our worldly business beforehand, so that we will be free on the Sabbath day, not only from worldly business itself, but from unnecessary thought and worries about our worldly business. If we have to drive an automobile to attend church services, we should see that it is properly provided with gasoline and oil on Saturday, so that this will not have to be done on the Lord's Day.

118. Q. *Why is the charge of keeping the Sabbath more specially directed to governors of families, and other superiors?*

A. *The charge of keeping the Sabbath is more specially directed to governors of families, and other superiors, because they are bound not only to keep it themselves, but to see that it be observed by all those that are* *under their charge; and because they are prone oft-times to hinder them by employments of their own.*

Scripture References

- Exod. 20:10. The fourth commandment addressed especially to heads of families.
- Josh. 24:15. The responsibility of the head of a family to lead the family in serving the Lord.
- Neh. 13:15, 17. Persons in positions of prominence or authority have an added responsibility to keep the Sabbath day holy.
- Jer. 17:20–22. Kings and civil rulers have a responsibility for the right observance of the Sabbath day.
- Exod. 23:12; Deut. 5:14–15. Servants or employees are entitled to their Sabbath rest, and not to be deprived of it by employers requiring the performance of unnecessary labor.

Commentary

1. On whom is the Sabbath commandment binding? The Sabbath commandment is binding on every individual human being in the world, as well as on all governments, organizations, corporations, or other associations of human beings. There is not a person in the world, individual or collective, who has any right to disregard or violate the command to "remember the Sabbath day, to keep it holy."

2. What class of people are under an added obligation to obey this commandment? "Governors of families, and other superiors," that is, persons whom God has placed in positions of authority in family, church, or state, are under an added obligation to obey this commandment. The general truth that greater authority involves greater responsibility holds true in the matter of Sabbath observance as in other matters.

3. How are heads of families to see that the Sabbath is observed by the members of their families? Heads of families are to see that the Sabbath is observed by the members of their families, first of all, by themselves setting a good example of Sabbath observance, regarding the Sabbath not as a burden but as a delight, and observing it cheerfully and consistently; in the second place, by instructing those under their authority in the obligation and duties of Sabbath observance; in the third place, if necessary, by using their

God-given authority and forbidding worldly activities which would violate the holiness of the Sabbath day.

4. It is possible for heads of families to be too strict in requiring Sabbath observance? It is possible, of course, to be unreasonably strict about the manner of observing the Sabbath. However, it seems probable that in our own time such extreme strictness is very rare. The tendency today is just the opposite, in the direction of toleration of carelessness and disregard for the sanctity of the Sabbath. It would be well if there were a greater degree of strictness about Sabbath observance today. Of course some allowance must be made for little children; they cannot be expected to observe the Sabbath in exactly the way adults should; yet even young children should be made to realize that there is a difference between the Sabbath and other days, and that activities which are proper on ordinary days are wrong on the Sabbath.

5. What kind of activities should be excluded from family life on the Sabbath? While some activities may perhaps be classed as "doubtful," the following are unquestionably wrong on the Sabbath day and should be excluded: studying day-school lessons; reading ordinary books and magazines; reading newspapers; listening to radio broadcasts of any kind (with the exception of orthodox religious broadcasts); playing ordinary games, whether indoors or outdoors; writing ordinary letters to friends or relatives, or other persons; conversations about financial or business matters; ordinary social visiting; common picnicking; attending public amusements or athletic events of whatever type.

6. If all these activities are forbidden on the Sabbath, will not the day prove to be a burden rather than a joy? This depends on whether we love God or not. If our love is for the world and the things of the world, of course any conscientious Sabbath observance will prove to be an unwelcome burden. But if the supreme devotion of our life is our love to God, we will welcome the opportunity and privilege of turning aside from ordinary affairs to devote the Sabbath day to worshiping God and seeking his kingdom and his righteousness in a special way.

7. In addition to religious worship, what activities are proper on the Sabbath day? Besides the duties of religious worship, and works of necessity and mercy, the following forms of activity are certainly proper for the Sabbath day: reading the Bible and orthodox Christian literature; reading and telling Bible stories to the children; playing various Bible games;

writing letters with a view to winning souls for Christ, comforting the afflicted, encouraging weak Christians, etc.; all proper forms of evangelistic activity; listening to orthodox religious broadcasts on the radio.

8. What special responsibility rests upon ministers and other church officers in the matter of Sabbath observance? Ministers and all other church officers should set a good example of consistent and conscientious Sabbath observance before the members of the church, and should bear witness to the teachings of the Bible on this subject as occasion may require.

9. What special responsibility rests upon civil rulers, or state officials, in the matter of Sabbath observance? Government officials should (a) observe the Sabbath carefully themselves, lest they become a scandal to the people; (b) protect the sanctity of the Sabbath by appropriate civil legislation against gross and open violation of the day; (c) oppose and remove all laws and government requirements which interfere with the proper observance of the Sabbath on the part of any of the people.

119. Q. *What are the sins forbidden in the fourth commandment?*

A. *The sins forbidden in the fourth commandment are all omissions of the duties required, all careless, negligent and unprofitable performing of them, and being weary of them; all profaning the day by idleness, and doing that which is in itself sinful, and by all needless works, words, and thoughts, about our worldly employments and recreations.*

Scripture References

- Ezek. 22:26. The omission of a duty is itself a sin.
- Acts 20:7–9. Inattention during divine service may result in falling asleep.
- Ezek. 33:30–32. Careless, negligent, and unprofitable performing of religious duties.
- Amos 8:5. The sin of profaning the Sabbath by being weary of it, and wishing it were past.
- Mal. 1:13. The sin of regarding public divine worship as a weariness.
- Ezek. 23:38. The Sabbath is especially profaned by doing that which is in itself sinful, that is, something which is sinful no matter when it is done.

• Jer. 17:24, 27; Isa. 58:13–14. It is wrong to profane the Sabbath by unnecessary works, words, or thoughts about our ordinary affairs.

Commentary

1. Which of the Ten Commandments forbids the sin of laziness?
The fourth commandment, which commands us to work industriously for six days of every week.

2. Why is "careless, negligent, and unprofitable" performing of Sabbath duties sinful? Because God requires of us not merely formal or technical obedience to his law, but a spiritual devotion and obedience to all his commandments. A merely formal observance of the Sabbath is hypocrisy.

3. Why is it wrong to be weary of the Sabbath, and wish it were past? This attitude of mind is wrong because it is the product of a selfish, worldly heart that finds no joy or satisfaction in the things of God.

4. Why is it wrong to profane the Sabbath day by idleness? This is wrong because God created us active, intelligent beings. A plant or a tree serves to glorify God by simply keeping alive and continuing its normal growth. But human beings are not plants or trees; they are living souls created in the image of God. God, who is himself intensely active, cannot be honored by human idleness, and especially not by idleness on the Sabbath day.

5. Is it wrong to take a nap on the Sabbath afternoon, or to take a walk in the open air? No. Taking a nap or a walk in the open air, provided they are kept within the bounds of reasonable moderation, are to be regarded as works of necessity, and they may be as necessary to bodily health and mental alertness as to eat breakfast, dinner, and supper on the Sabbath day. Reasonable care of our bodies on the Sabbath is not wrong.

6. Is it wrong to enter into an agreement to buy or sell something on the Sabbath day? Certainly this is wrong. There are those who think it would be wrong to buy or sell on the Sabbath, but not wrong to enter into an agreement to buy or sell something, provided the actual transfer of money and property takes place on some other day. Actually, of course, to enter into a contract, whether oral or written, is itself an act of worldly business, and wrong on the Sabbath day.

7. Is it wrong to sit in church and plan out our business for the following week while the sermon is being preached? Of course this practice is sinful, although in its nature it is a secret sin which only God and the one who practices it can know. There is a popular idea that we are not responsible for our thoughts, but the Bible emphatically teaches that we are responsible for our thoughts as well as for our words and our actions. Moreover it is possible by effort and self-discipline to gain control over our thoughts so that they do not wander where we do not want them to go. Of course, the power of the Holy Spirit is needed to do this successfully.

8. What present-day conditions indicate a prevalent disregard for the Sabbath? (a) The obvious and gross commercializing of the Sabbath by the world, including "Sunday" movies, sports, and secular radio broadcasting; (b) the increasing number of Christians who repudiate the very principle of the Sabbath, claiming that it was intended for the Jews only; (c) the general carelessness about the Sabbath even on the part of Christian people who profess to believe in the principle and obligation of the Sabbath. The Sabbath situation at the present time is very bad, and only a genuine revival of true religion, together with sound instruction about the obligation of Sabbath observance, can reclaim the Sabbath and restore it to a place of honor in the modern world. Civil legislation alone cannot accomplish this, although it has its place in preventing gross Sabbath desecration. There must be a real revival of true Christianity, or the Sabbath will be lost beyond recovery.

120. Q. *What are the reasons annexed to the fourth commandment, the more to enforce it?*

A. *The reasons annexed to the fourth commandment, the more to enforce it, are taken from the equity of it, God allowing us six days of seven for our own affairs, and reserving but one for himself, in these words,* Six days shalt thou labor and do all thy work: *from God's challenging a special propriety in that day,* The seventh day is the Sabbath of the Lord thy God: *from the example of God, who in six* days made heaven and earth, the sea, and all that in them is, and rested the seventh day: *and from the blessing which God put upon that day, not only sanctifying it to be a day for his service, but in ordaining it to be a means of blessing to us in our sanctifying it:* Wherefore the Lord blessed the Sabbath day, and hallowed it.

Scripture Reference

- Exod. 20:8–11. (This question being an analysis of the reasons annexed to the fourth commandment, no Scripture references except the commandment itself are required.)

Commentary

1. How many reasons are annexed to the fourth commandment? Four: (a) the equity of God's allowing us six times as much time for our own occupations as we are required to devote to worshiping him; (b) the special claim that God makes to the Sabbath day; (c) the example of God himself in resting on the seventh day, following the six days of creation; (d) the blessing which God has placed upon the Sabbath day.

2. What is meant by the word *equity*? It means reasonableness or fairness in a matter involving two or more parties.

3. How has God shown fairness in the Sabbath commandment? By allowing us six days of the week for our own occupations and enjoyments, and only requiring one day to be devoted solely to him in a special way. Thus God does not require of us something that would be impossible. If we had to spend all seven days in worshiping God, we would have no time for earning a living, nor for the recreation and social life which are necessary for our bodily and mental well-being.

4. If only one day of seven is to be devoted solely to the service of God, may we do as we please on the other six days? Certainly not. We are moral agents and are responsible to God for our words, thoughts, and deeds at all times. But the Sabbath day is reserved solely for the service of God, whereas on the other six days we are to glorify God indirectly by laboring and doing all our work. Our ordinary life and occupations should be directed to the glorifying of God, certainly; but the Sabbath is set apart for glorifying and serving God in a direct and special manner.

5. What is the meaning of the expression "God's challenging a special propriety in that day"? In modern language, this means, "God's claiming that day as his special property."

6. Does God have the right to claim the Sabbath day as His special property? Yes, for he is our Creator and Lord. God is sovereign, and therefore he is free to claim whatever he wishes of any of his creatures.

7. Why is breaking the Sabbath a form of stealing? Because the person who breaks the Sabbath, by taking it for his own use, steals something which belongs especially to God; he appropriates God's property, the Sabbath day.

8. Why did God rest on the seventh day after the six days of creation? Certainly not because God was weary from his task, nor because he needed the rest for himself, for God is almighty, and the work of creation was no effort to him; but in order to give an example, and lay down a religious principle, for the human race to take note of and follow.

9. How does the example of God in resting the seventh day show that the Sabbath is not only for the Jews but for all mankind? It shows that the Sabbath originated at the creation of the world, not merely in the time of Moses when God gave special laws to the people of Israel. The Sabbath was established by God thousands of years before the time of Abraham, who was the first of the people of Israel.

10. What special religious meaning is involved in the example of God's resting on the Sabbath day after his work of creation? See Hebrews 4:9–10. The Sabbath rest into which God then entered became the type or example of the eternal rest of the people of God in heaven.

11. Will the Sabbath rest of God's people in heaven be a condition of idleness? No. Heaven will be a state both of the most perfect rest and also of the most intense activity. Only because of sin is rest incompatible with activity. In heaven there will be no fatigue, no weariness, no need for recuperation of physical or mental powers, because the curse will have been forever abolished. See Revelation 4:8 ("and they rest not day and night . . ."); Revelation 21:25 ("There shall be no night there").

12. What is the blessing which God has placed upon the Sabbath day? In the first place, the Sabbath day is blessed by being set apart as a day for God's service. In the second place, it is an appointed means of blessing to us, and we will find it so if we observe it as God intended, in a reverent, conscientious, and spiritual manner.

121. Q. *Why is the word* **Remember** *set in the beginning of the fourth commandment?*

A. *The word* Remember *is set in the beginning of the fourth commandment, partly, because of the great benefit of remembering it, and being thereby helped in our preparation to keep it, and, in keeping it, better to keep all the rest of the commandments, and to continue a thankful remembrance of the two great benefits of creation and redemption, which contain a short abridgment of religion; and partly, because we are very ready to forget it, for that there is less light of nature for it, and yet it restraineth our natural liberty in things at other times lawful; that it cometh but once in seven days, and many worldly businesses come between, and too often take off our minds from thinking of it, either to prepare for it, or to sanctify it; and that Satan with his instruments much labors to blot out the glory, and even the memory of it, to bring in all irreligion and impiety.*

Scripture References
- Exod. 20:8. The word *Remember* is the first word of the Sabbath commandment.
- Exod. 16:23; Luke 23:54–56 compared with Mark 15:42; Neh. 13:19. To remember the Sabbath day in advance helps us to keep it.
- Ps. 92 (Title, "A Ps. or Song for the Sabbath day"), verses 13–14; Ezek. 20:12, 19–20. Faithful observance of the Sabbath enables us to perform all other religious duties better.
- Gen. 2:2–3; Ps. 118:22–24 compared with Acts 4:10–11; Rev. 1:10. To remember the Sabbath day helps us to think of God's two great works of creation and redemption, which form a summary of religion.
- Ezek. 22:26. By nature we very easily forget the Sabbath.
- Neh. 9:14. There is less light of nature for the Sabbath than for most other of the Ten Commandments; therefore, it is very easy to overlook and dis-

regard the Sabbath. Our knowledge of the Sabbath depends almost entirely on the Bible.

- Exod. 34:21. The Sabbath commandment restrains our natural liberty even in matters which are lawful at other times.
- Deut. 5:14–15; Amos 8:5. Worldly business coming on the weekdays often takes our minds off the Sabbath and keeps us from observing it aright.
- Lam. 1:7; Jer. 17:21–23; Neh. 13:15–23. Satan and his servants try very hard to prevent spiritual Sabbath observance, and to destroy the institution of the Sabbath day.

Commentary

1. How many of the Ten Commandments begin with the word *Remember?* Only one, the fourth or Sabbath commandment.

2. What benefits come from remembering the Sabbath day? We cannot really keep the Sabbath aright unless we remember it beforehand. If we think of it beforehand, and keep it in mind through the week, we will be in a better state of mind to observe the day as it should be observed. If we never give the Sabbath a thought through the week, we will find it very difficult to devote ourselves to the things of God on the Sabbath day.

3. How does keeping the Sabbath help us to perform other religious duties better? A spiritual observance of the Sabbath day helps to keep us in touch with God. When we are really in communion with God, all other religious duties can be performed more earnestly and willingly. But if we neglect the Sabbath, our communion with God will be weakened, and we will be likely also to neglect other duties.

4. What two great works of God does the Sabbath day call to our minds? The works of creation and redemption, which, as the catechism informs us, together "contain a short abridgment of religion." These two works of God, creation and redemption, form the subject matter of the whole Bible. The Bible is the inspired record of God's works of creation and redemption. The Sabbath day calls these two works of God to our minds because God instituted the Sabbath when he finished his work of creation, and our Savior Jesus Christ rose from the dead on the first day of the week, which is the Christian Sabbath.

5. Why is it especially necessary that we remember the Sabbath day? Because we are very likely to forget it. Any Christian can realize this from his own experience, as well as from the Bible. There is no commandment of God that we are more likely to forget than the command to keep the Sabbath day as a holy day.

6. Why is it so easy to forget the Sabbath day? One reason is that the light of nature tells us very little about the Sabbath. By the light of nature we could only know that a portion of our time ought to be devoted to God our Creator. We could not know what portion of our time, nor exactly how it ought to be spent. For this information we are entirely dependent on God's special revelation, the Holy Bible. The light of nature may teach people that it is wrong to commit murder, but the light of nature cannot teach us that one day in seven must be kept holy as a day for worshiping God. Therefore it is much easier to forget the Sabbath commandment than the command not to commit murder.

7. Why do many people consider the Sabbath commandment burdensome and unreasonable? Because the Sabbath commandment restrains our natural liberty in matters which are lawful on other days. To buy, sell, work at our ordinary occupations, engage in sports and other common recreations are not wrong in themselves. These practices are not sinful on other days of the week; they are wrong only on the Sabbath day. But many people are not satisfied with six days of the week for their own business and pleasure; they want all seven. Because the Sabbath interferes with this desire, many people consider it unreasonable and burdensome. And those who have this attitude toward the Sabbath will be inclined to neglect and forget it.

8. How does the fact that the Sabbath comes only once a week make us likely to forget it? If the Sabbath came once every two days, or once every three days, there would not be so many days between Sabbaths, and it would not so easily drop out of our memory. But when there are six days filled with all kinds of business and activity between Sabbaths, it is only natural that we tend to forget the Sabbath. Therefore it was wise of God to use the word *Remember* in the Sabbath commandment.

9. Why does Satan, with his servants, try so hard to break down and destroy the Sabbath day? Satan, with his agents and the citizens of his kingdom, is engaged in an age-long warfare against God and God's kingdom. God's kingdom is a spiritual kingdom, and it is defended and propagated by spiritual weapons and methods. The real extension of God's kingdom depends on people's being converted to Christ, repenting of their sins, and loving and serving God sincerely and loyally. These things depend chiefly upon the preaching of the gospel and the public and private exercises of God's worship, such as Bible study, the sacraments, and prayer. These divine ordinances can find but little time on weekdays; they are largely dependent on the Sabbath day for an adequate amount of time and attention. Satan of course understands this, and he realizes that if he can break down the Sabbath, then the preaching of the gospel and the ordinances of divine worship will be neglected; if the preaching of the gospel and the ordinances of divine worship are neglected, then God's kingdom cannot prosper; if God's kingdom does not prosper, then Satan's kingdom will not be interfered with; and if Satan's kingdom is not interfered with, then Satan will have a clear track to accomplish his wicked purposes in the world. So we see that the Sabbath, far from being an arbitrary or unreasonable command of God, is calculated to accomplish a great purpose and to form a real bulwark against Satan's kingdom and the floods of iniquity. With this thought, we bring our study of the Sabbath to a close.

13

God's Will Expressed in Our Duty to Others

122. Q. *What is the sum of the six commandments which contain our duty to man?*

A. *The sum of the six commandments which contain our duty to man, is, to love our neighbor as ourselves, and to do to others what we would have them to do to us.*

Scripture References
- Matt. 22:39. The second table of the law as summarized by Christ.
- Matt. 7:12. The "Golden Rule" given by Christ as a summary of our duty to our fellow men.

Commentary

1. What part of the Ten Commandments deals with our duty to our fellow men? The last six commandments, beginning with the fifth, which are commonly called "the second table of the law," deal with our duty to our fellow men.

2. What attitude toward our neighbor is required in the second table of the law? An attitude of love to our neighbor; we are to love our neighbor as ourselves.

3. Is it wrong to love ourselves? No. Our Lord's statement implies that to love ourselves is right provided it is kept subordinate to loving God and in balance with loving our neighbor. Self-love is sinful only when it becomes inordinate. A love of self that is subordinate to love for God and coordinate with love for our neighbor is really a duty.

4. What action toward our neighbor is required in the second table of the law? The second table of the law requires that we do to others what we would have them do to us. Thus more than a mere attitude is required. The attitude of love to our neighbor must be translated into action for our neighbor's welfare.

5. When Christ stated the "Golden Rule," was he setting forth something new and previously unknown? No. The meaning and substance of the "Golden Rule" is contained in the Old Testament, as Jesus himself indicated when he added the words: "for this is the law and the prophets."

6. Who is our neighbor? The Parable of the Good Samaritan (Luke 10:25–37) provides the answer to this question. In brief, our neighbor, for practical purposes, is whatever human being it is in our power to help in his time of need. We are to show kindness not only to those we like, or enjoy associating with, but to those who are in need or in trouble, regardless of who they may be, if it is in our power to help them.

7. How is the "Golden Rule" misused in the present day? In the present day there are many who say that the Golden Rule is all the religion they need. This is just another way of saying that they have no consciousness of sin, feel no need of a Savior, and are confident that they can save themselves by their own good life. Such an attitude is the height of spiritual pride, and must be extremely offensive to God, as it despises his free grace in Jesus Christ.

8. Can a person who is not a Christian keep the Golden Rule? Certainly not. We are not really keeping the Golden Rule unless our motive for keeping it is love to God and a desire to do God's will. Those who "keep" the Golden Rule for either selfish or humanitarian reasons are not really keeping the Golden Rule at all. No one can really even begin to keep the Golden Rule until he is born again of the Holy Spirit and a love for God has been implanted in his heart.

123. Q. *Which is the fifth commandment?*

A. *The fifth commandment is,* Honor thy father and thy mother; that thy days may be long upon the land which the Lord thy God giveth thee.

124. Q. *Who are meant by* **father** *and* **mother** *in the fifth commandment?*

A. *By* father *and* mother, *in the fifth commandment, are meant, not only natural parents, but all superiors in age, and gifts; and especially such as, by God's ordinance, are over us in place of authority, whether in family, church, or commonwealth.*

Scripture References

- Prov. 23:22, 25; Eph. 6:1–2. The terms *father* and *mother* in the fifth commandment include our natural parents.
- 1 Tim. 5:1–2. Our superiors in age are included under "father" and "mother" in the fifth commandment.
- Gen. 4:20–22; 45:8. Our superiors in gifts are included under the terms *father* and *mother.*
- 2 Kings 5:13. "Father" and "mother" include all over us in authority in the family.
- 2 Kings 2:12; 13:14; Gal. 4:19. "Father" and "mother" include those in authority over us in the church.
- Isa. 49:23. "Father" and "mother" include those in authority over us in the state.

Commentary

1. What is the obvious primary meaning of "father" and "mother" in the fifth commandment? The obvious primary meaning is our natural parents.

2. Is the meaning of the fifth commandment limited to duties owed to our natural parents? No. The usage of the terms *father* and *mother* in the Bible indicates that the fifth commandment has a wider scope, including the various classes of persons mentioned in the catechism.

3. What is meant by "superiors in age"? This means those who are older than we are.

4. What is meant by "superiors in gifts"? This means those who have been endowed by God with special ability or skill in any particular department of life, or line of human effort.

5. What is the meaning of the expression "God's ordinance"? In this question of the catechism, "God's ordinance" means God's appointments concerning the exercise of authority: thus, for example, it is God's ordinance that the church be governed by ministers and elders chosen by the people but receiving their authority from Christ.

6. In what spheres of life does God's ordinance especially provide for the exercise of authority? God's ordinance especially provides for the exercise of authority in the three divine institutions which exist in the world, namely, the family, the church, and the state.

125. Q. *Why are superiors styled* Father *and* Mother?

A. *Superiors are styled* Father *and* Mother, *both to teach them in all duties toward their inferiors, like natural parents, to express love and tenderness to them, according to their several relations; and to work inferiors to a greater willingness and cheerfulness in performing their duties to their superiors, as to their parents.*

Scripture References
- Eph. 6:4; 2 Cor. 12:14; 1 Thess. 2:7–8, 11; Num. 11:11–12. The obligation of parents to express love and tenderness to their children.
- 1 Cor. 4:14–16; 2 Kings 5:13. Inferiors, regarding their superiors as parents, are to perform their duties with love and cheerfulness.

Commentary
1. What truth concerning positions of authority in human society is taught by this question of the catechism? This question of the catechism teaches us that all positions of authority in human society, whether

in family, church, or state, are in some respect like the position of natural parents in the family and that by reason of this similarity a certain obligation is involved.

2. What obligation rests upon persons occupying positions of authority in family, church, or state? The obligation to exercise their authority with love and tenderness, or consideration, toward those persons who are subject to their authority.

3. Why does the catechism add the phrase "according to their several relations"? This phrase is necessary, because the obligation of an attitude of love and consideration on the part of persons in authority does not cancel all other obligations which may exist in various relationships. The obligation of love and tenderness does not imply that a judge may never sentence a convicted criminal to any punishment, nor does it imply that people shall not be compelled to pay their legal taxes. "Love and tenderness" is not a substitute for the performance of other duties, but rather the attitude with which, and the manner in which, all duties are to be carried out.

4. What obligation rests upon persons who are subject to the authority of others in family, church, or state? The obligation of performing their duties toward those in authority over them, as to their own parents, with willingness and cheerfulness. Thus God's law requires us not merely to obey legitimate authority in family, church, and state, but to do it with a willing and cheerful attitude of mind, because of our devotion to God.

126. Q. *What is the general scope of the fifth commandment?*

A. *The general scope of the fifth commandment is, the performance of those duties which we mutually owe in our several relations, as inferiors, superiors, or equals.*

Scripture References

- Eph. 5:21; 1 Peter 2:17; Rom. 12:10. Various reciprocal obligations in human society.

Commentary

1. What three kinds of relationship are possible between different persons with respect to the degree of their authority? (a) Two persons possessing equal authority may be associated together, as two elders in the same church. (b) A person may possess authority over another person, as a parent over a child, or a government official over a private citizen. (c) A person may be subject to the authority of another person, as a child to a parent, or a citizen to a ruler.

2. What does the fifth commandment require in these various relationships of human society? The fifth commandment requires that all obligations in the sphere of human society, including family, church, and state, be performed properly and with right attitudes. The next six questions of the catechism (127–32) explain this in detail.

127. Q. *What is the honor that inferiors owe to their superiors?*

A. *The honor which inferiors owe to their superiors is, all due reverence in heart, word, and behavior; prayer and thanksgiving for them; imitation of their virtues and graces; willing obedience to their lawful commands and counsels; due submission to their corrections; fidelity to, defence, and maintenance of their persons and authority, according to their several ranks, and the nature of their places; bearing with their infirmities, and covering them in love, that so they may be an honor to them and to their government.*

Scripture References

- Mal. 1:6; Lev. 19:3, 32; Prov. 31:28; 1 Kings 2:19. Superiors to be regarded with due reverence.
- 1 Tim. 2:1–2. The duty of prayer and thanksgiving for those in authority over us.
- Heb. 13:7; Phil. 3:17. We should imitate the virtues and good deeds of those in authority over us.

- Eph. 6:1–2, 5–7; 1 Peter 2:13–14; Rom. 13:15; Heb. 13:17; Prov. 4:3–4; 23:22; Exod. 18:19, 24. The duty of willing obedience to the lawful commands and counsels of those in authority over us.
- Gen. 16:6–9; Heb. 12:9; 1 Peter 2:18–20. The duty of submission to the corrections of those in authority over us.
- Titus 2:9–10; 1 Sam. 26:15–16; 2 Sam. 18:3; Esther 6:2; Matt. 22:21; Rom. 13:6–7; 1 Tim. 5:17–18; Gal. 6:6; Gen. 45:11; 47:12. The duties of loyalty, defense, and support of those in authority over us.
- 1 Peter 2:18; Prov. 23:22. The duty of patience toward the faults of those in positions of authority.
- Ps. 127:3–5; Prov. 31:23. It is God's will that we should be an honor to the government of those in authority over us.

Commentary

1. What attitude should we have toward those in authority over us? We should have an attitude of "due reverence," that is, proper respect, toward them.

2. How is this attitude of proper respect to be shown? The attitude of proper respect toward those in authority over us is to be not merely an attitude of the heart and mind, but also shown by "word and behavior."

3. What duty of religious worship is involved in honoring those in authority over us? The duty of prayer and thanksgiving for them.

4. Are we to follow the example of those in authority over us regardless of their character and actions? No. We are to imitate "their virtues and graces"; that is, we are to follow their example when we find it to be in accordance with the teachings and requirements of God's Word.

5. What should be our attitude toward the commands and counsels of those in authority over us? We should have an attitude of willing obedience to their commands and counsels provided they are lawful, that is, in accordance with the law of God.

6. Is it ever our duty to obey commands which are contrary to the law of God? No. God's law, revealed in the Bible, is the final standard of right and wrong. No command that is contrary to God's law is really binding on a person. It may be our duty to obey commands that are in addition to the law of God, but it can never be our duty to obey any command that is contrary to the law of God. God's law does not require us to break God's law by obeying the laws and commands of men.

7. What attitude should we have to the corrections of those in authority over us? An attitude of "due submission to their corrections"; that is, acknowledging our faults rather than feeling resentful and stubbornly maintaining that we are right, when we are legitimately corrected by those in authority over us.

8. What duties do we owe to the "persons and authority" of those who are set over us by God's providence? Loyalty, defense, and support, the precise nature and degree of these duties being determined by the nature of the relationship in each case. Thus the loyalty which a child owes to a parent is not the same as that which a citizen owes to the state; nor is the defense and support due to a natural parent the same as that due to the state.

9. What should be our attitude toward the faults and failings of those in authority over us? (a) An attitude of patience, "bearing with their infirmities"; (b) an attitude of love, "covering them in love," that is, concealing and disregarding their faults, so far as may legitimately be done. Thus we "may be an honor to them and to their government." This must not be taken to imply that all faults or wrongdoing must be concealed and patiently endured. In some cases a higher loyalty may impose on us the duty of protesting and exposing wrongdoing on the part of someone in authority over us. It may be our duty to report wrongdoing to the constituted authorities of church or state. The catechism, however, speaks of "infirmities," which properly does not mean flagrant wrongdoing, but faults or weaknesses of character such as should be borne with patience and covered by love.

128. Q. *What are the sins of inferiors against their superiors?*

A. *The sins of inferiors against their superiors are, all neglect of the duties required toward them; envying at, contempt of, and rebellion against, their persons and places, in their lawful counsels, commands, and corrections; cursing, mocking, and all such refractory and scandalous carriage, as proves a shame and dishonor to them and their government.*

Scripture References

- Matt. 15:4–6. It is sinful to neglect our duty toward those in authority over us.
- Num. 11:28–29; 1 Sam. 8:7; Isa. 3:5; 2 Sam. 15:1–12. The sins of envy, contempt, and rebellion on the part of those subject to the authority of others.
- Exod. 21:15; 1 Sam. 10:27; 2:25; Deut. 21:18–21. Sinning against the persons and places of those in authority over us, in relation to their lawful counsels, commands, and corrections.
- Prov. 30:11, 17; 19:26. The sins of cursing, mocking, and other scandalous conduct against those in authority over us.

Commentary

1. What sin of neglect of duty toward superiors did Jesus accuse the Pharisees and scribes of? Jesus accused them of encouraging and justifying neglect of support of a needy parent, on the pretext that the money was consecrated to God as an offering (Matt. 15:4–6).

2. What is meant by the sin of envying at the persons and places of those in authority over us? This means feeling resentful that God in his providence has given them something which he has not given to us. Envying is really finding fault with God's providence.

3. What is meant by the sin of contempt of those in authority over us? *Contempt* means looking down on or despising someone, and consequently disregarding his authority, disobeying his commands, etc. The common phrase "contempt of court" illustrates this meaning well.

4. What is meant by the sin of rebellion against those in authority over us? Rebellion is contempt carried to the extreme of a downright repudiation of the authority which we ought to recognize and honor. The person who rises in rebellion against those in authority over him no longer claims or pretends to recognize their authority. Thus Absalom rose in rebellion against David, who was both his father and his lawful king.

5. What kind of counsels, commands, and corrections are to be honored and obeyed? The lawful counsels, commands, and corrections of those properly in authority over us. Thus the commands of a bandit chief need not be honored and obeyed, for he is not properly in authority. Nor are the commands of a government official which are contrary to the law of the land to be obeyed, for such are not lawful commands. Nor are any commands whatever that are contrary to the law of God to be obeyed, for nothing that is contrary to the law of God can be lawful, nor may it be so regarded by those that fear God.

6. What is meant by cursing, mocking, etc.? These terms describe (a) cursing in the strict sense, that is, taking God's name in vain to wish or pray that evil may come upon the person cursed; or any such sinful wish or prayer, even though the name of God is not actually mentioned. (b) Making those in authority over us, their commands, corrections, etc., the butt of laughter, ridicule, sarcasm, or regarding them otherwise than with seriousness and respect. (c) Conduct which speaks louder than words in proclaiming our disregard or contempt of those in authority over us; thus a person may never utter a wrong word, yet may curse and mock his parents, or others in authority over him, by his perverse and incorrigible conduct and manner of life. All these evil tendencies bring shame and dishonor upon those in authority, and upon their government.

129. Q. *What is required of superiors toward their inferiors?*

A. *It is required of superiors, according to that power they receive from God, and that relation wherein they stand, to love, pray for, and bless their inferiors; to instruct, counsel, and admonish them; countenancing, commending and rewarding such as do well, and discountenancing, reproving, and chastising such as do ill; protecting, and providing for them all things necessary for soul and body; and by grave, wise, holy, and exemplary carriage, to procure glory to God, honor to themselves, and so to preserve that authority which God hath put upon them.*

Scripture References

- Col. 3:19; Titus 2:4. 1 Sam. 12:23; Job 1:5; 1 Kings 8:55–56; Heb. 7:7; Gen. 49:28. It is the duty of superiors to love, pray for, and bless those persons under their authority.
- Deut. 6:6–7; Eph. 6:4. It is the duty of superiors to instruct, counsel, and admonish those under their authority.
- 1 Peter 3:7; 2:14; Rom. 13:3; Esther 6:3. The duty of countenancing, commanding, and rewarding such as do well.

- Rom. 13:3–4; Prov. 29:15; 1 Peter 2:14. The duty of discountenancing, reproving, and chastising such as do ill.
- Job 29:12–17; Isa. 1:10, 17; Eph. 6:4; 1 Tim. 5:8. Superiors are bound to protect and provide, spiritually and materially, for those under their authority.
- 1 Tim. 4:12; Titus 2:3–5. Superiors must set a good example to those under their authority, thus glorifying God.
- 1 Kings 3:28; Titus 2:15. By a good example, superiors will gain honor to themselves, and maintain their authority.

Commentary

1. What is the principle set forth in this question of the catechism? The principle set forth in this question of the catechism is that authority involves responsibility. There is no such thing as legitimate authority without a corresponding responsibility; and the greater the authority, the greater the responsibility. Those who have been entrusted with authority in family, church, or state are responsible to God for the right exercise of their authority.

2. Is the responsibility of superiors the same in all cases? No. It varies according to the degree of authority received from God, and according to the nature of the relation involved. Thus the governor of a state has a different responsibility from the mayor of a city; and the responsibility of a parent in the home differs from that of a minister or elder in the church. In each case responsibility exists, for authority always implies responsibility. But the degree and nature of the responsibility vary according to the facts in each case.

3. What attitude ought superiors to have toward those under their authority? An attitude of sincere goodwill, which will find expression in love, prayer, and blessing, that is, a true interest in and earnest effort to procure their welfare.

4. What is the responsibility of superiors concerning the education of those under their authority? "To instruct, counsel, and admonish them"; that is, to inculcate knowledge, advise concerning problems, and warn against evil, as these functions may be required by circumstances and as they are proper to the particular relation involved. A magistrate in the state, a pastor or elder in the church, and a parent in the home all have a responsibility to "instruct, counsel, and admonish," but under different circumstances, and, in part, concerning different matters.

5. What is the responsibility of superiors toward those under their authority who do well? The responsibility of "countenancing, commending and rewarding" them; that is, regarding their actions with approval, commending their actions in words, and rewarding them in a suitable manner, thus encouraging them in their effort to do what is right.

6. What is the responsibility of superiors toward those under their authority who commit wrong? The responsibility of "discountenancing, reproving, and chastising" them; that is, withholding approval of their actions, expressing reproof in words, and, if necessary, correcting them for their wrongdoing by suitable penalties.

7. What protection and provision do superiors owe those under their authority? They owe them whatever protection is required by circumstances, and is in their power to provide, and the provision of "all things necessary for soul and body." Here again the kind and degree of protection and provision vary according to the nature of the relation involved. The state must protect its people against the lawless violence of criminals at home as well as against the hostile acts of foreign foes. The church must protect its members against soul-destroying false doctrines and heresies, and against all forms of propaganda that are contrary to the Word of God. The head of a family must protect its members against whatever is wrong, harmful, or destructive, insofar as it is in his power to do so. With reference to the provision of "all things necessary for soul and body," similar distinctions must be made. The head of a family must provide food, clothing, shelter, medical care, etc., as well as adequate general education and religious nurture, for those under his charge. The responsibility of the church is chiefly in the spiritual sphere, to provide faithful preaching of the Word of God, right administration of the sacraments, and a proper exercise of church discipline without respect of persons. Ordinarily the church is not obligated to provide food, clothing, shelter, etc., for her members, but in cases of real need it is the duty of the church, through the deacons, to provide even these necessities of life to members of the household of faith. As for the state, its obligation consists chiefly in protecting and upholding the freedom and security of the individual, the family, and the church, and in administering public justice, enacting and enforcing just and equitable laws, and providing for the public welfare in times of crisis or emergency. Where parents fail to make adequate provision for the education of their children, the state must undertake this task also, and is responsible to God for the manner in which it is carried out. It is not properly the function of the state to provide food, clothing, shelter, etc., for the people, except under emergency conditions when temporary relief may be imperative. Rather, the function of the state, according to the Bible, is to maintain justice, law, and order in the social and economic spheres so that the citizen can properly provide these material necessities of life for himself and his family.

8. Why should superiors set a good example to persons under their authority? By setting a good example, they will glorify God, obtain honor for themselves, and maintain the authority which God has committed to them. Needless to say, without a consistently good example, persons in positions of authority will not be respected, nor will their instructions, counsels, etc., be heeded and obeyed. The government official who is himself guilty of lawbreaking cannot influence citizens to obey the laws; the minister or elder who is guilty of compromise with the sins of the world cannot have a wholesome influence toward godly living among the members of the church; the parent who lies, swears, and loses his temper cannot really teach his children to be truthful, reverent, and self-controlled. In each case the failure to set a good example may result in contempt for authority on the part of those who are subject to the authority of others in family, church, and state.

130. Q. *What are the sins of superiors?*

A. *The sins of superiors are, besides the neglect of the duties required of them, an inordinate seeking of themselves, their own glory, ease, profit, or pleasure; commanding things unlawful, or not in the power of their inferiors to perform; counselling, encouraging, or favoring them in that which is evil; dissuading, discouraging, or discountenancing them in that which is good; correcting them unduly; careless exposing, or leaving them to wrong, temptation, and danger; provoking them to wrath; or any way dishonoring themselves, or lessening their authority, by an unjust, indiscreet, rigorous, or remiss behavior.*

Scripture References

- Ezek. 34:2–4. Sinful neglect of duty toward those under their authority, on the part of superiors.
- Phil. 2:21; John 5:44; 7:18; Isa. 56:10–11; Deut. 17:17. The sin of selfish attitudes or conduct on the part of superiors.
- Dan. 3:4–6; Acts 4:17–18; Exod. 5:10–18; Matt. 23:2, 4. The sin of persons in authority commanding things that are unlawful, or that are not in the power of those under their authority to perform.
- Matt. 14:8 compared with Mark 6:24; 2 Sam. 13:28; 1 Sam. 3:13. The sins of counseling, encouraging, or favoring inferiors in doing what is wrong.
- John 7:46–49; Col. 3:21; Exod. 5:17. The sin of influencing inferiors against what is good and right.
- 1 Peter 2:18–20; Heb. 12:10; Deut. 25:3. Excessive or immoderate correction of inferiors, even when they are at fault, is wrong.
- Gen. 37:28; 13:12–13; Acts 18:17. The sin of careless exposing of inferiors to wrong, temptation, and danger.
- Eph. 6:4. The sin of provoking inferiors to wrath by unreasonable demands or requirements.
- Gen. 9:21; 1 Kings 12:13–16; 1:6; 1 Sam. 2:29–31. The sinfulness of all conduct which results in the breaking down of respect for authority on the part of inferiors.

Commentary

1. Why is neglect of the duties required of superiors sinful on their part? Because such neglect arises from failure to recognize, or to take seriously, the God-given responsibility which accompanies the authority committed to them. To exercise authority, without recognizing and accepting the corresponding responsibility, is to act irresponsibly and is always sinful (James 4:17).

2. What wrong attitude of heart and mind is the source of much wrongdoing on the part of persons in authority? Selfishness, which if not checked and controlled inevitably leads to the unjust exploitation of persons under the authority of others. Persons who are in positions of authority should realize that this authority has not been committed to them for their own selfish enjoyment, that they have a real duty to those under their authority, and that they are themselves under the moral government of God and must give account to him for their exercise of authority in every case. All selfish use of authority is abuse of authority, and therefore sinful.

3. Give some examples from the Bible of rulers who commanded those under their authority to do things contrary to the law of God. (a) Nebuchadnezzar's command that all the people worship the great golden image (Dan. 3:1–7). (b) Darius's decree forbidding prayer to any god or man for thirty days except to himself (Dan. 6:4–9). (c) Amaziah's command to Amos not to prophesy in Bethel (Amos 7:10–13). (d) Zedekiah's forbidding Jeremiah to prophesy in the Lord's name (Jer. 32:1–5). (e) The Jewish Sanhedrin's command to the apostles not to preach in the name of Jesus (Acts 4:17–18; 5:28, 40).

4. Give some examples from the history of the church of rulers who commanded actions contrary to the law of God. (a) The Roman emperors who persecuted the early Christians, requiring them to render divine honor to the emperor's image, etc. (b) The rulers of Scotland who required the people to renounce the National covenant, Solemn League and covenant, to recognize the king as head of the church, etc. (c) The Japanese government, before that nation's defeat, that required citizens, including Christian people, in Japan, Korea, Manchuria, etc., to bow before Shinto shrines, thus honoring the sun goddess, as a pledge of civil allegiance to the state.

5. Give some examples from the Bible of rulers who demanded of their subjects things impossible for the latter to perform. (a) The Egyptian taskmasters who, in accordance with the orders of Pharaoh, demanded that the people of Israel make bricks without straw being provided for them (Exod. 5:10–18). (b) Nebuchadnezzar's demand that his magicians, etc., declare his forgotten dream, together with the interpretation (Dan. 2:1–13).

6. Why is it especially wrong for superiors to influence those under their authority in favor of what is wrong, or against what is right? This is especially wrong and wicked because to the ordinary influence which one person exerts upon another, there is added the weight of superior authority. It is always wrong to influence another in favor of what is wrong, or against what is right; but when the weight of special authority is added to such influence, the evil is greatly aggravated. Thus for a government official to encourage private citizens in violating the law, or to discourage them in efforts to obey and honor the law, is much more wicked than for a private person to exert similar influence. For a parent to encourage a child to tell lies, or to ridicule a child's effort at honesty, for example, is much worse than for one of the child's playmates to do the same thing. Similarly, for a minister or other church officer to encourage church members to indulge in sinful conduct, or to discourage members who are trying to live a holy and consistent life, is much worse than for a private member of the church to do the same. In the matter of our influence on others, as in other matters, greater authority means added responsibility.

7. Why is undue, excessive, or immoderate correction of inferiors wrong? (a) This is wrong because it is unjust, being out of proportion to the offense or wrongdoing in the case. (b) It is wrong because it counteracts and destroys the proper effect of correction, by producing a feeling of injustice and resentment in the person corrected, instead of leading that person to reformation of conduct.

8. Why is careless exposing of inferiors to wrong, temptation, and danger sinful? Every person has a moral responsibility for his neighbor's welfare, but in the case of persons in positions of authority, this responsibility for the welfare of those under their authority is greatly increased. Careless, heedless, or indifferent exposing of such persons to injustice, or to moral, spiritual, or physical danger, involves a gross disregard and neglect of God-given responsibility for the welfare of those under their authority.

9. Give some Bible examples of careless exposing of inferiors to wrong, temptation, and danger. (a) Lot, who moved nearer and nearer to the wicked city of Sodom, and finally established his residence within that city, regardless of the moral danger to his family (Gen. 13:12–13). (b) Joseph's brothers, who sold him into Egypt, thus not only treating him extremely unjustly, but abandoning him to an environment where he would be faced with temptations to idolatry and immorality (Gen. 37:26–28). (c) Ahab, who married the Baal-worshiping Zidonian princess Jezebel, thus exposing a whole nation to injustice, a bad example, and the temptation to compromise with idolatry (1 Kings 16:29–33).

10. What is meant by provoking inferiors to wrath? This expression, which is derived from Ephesians 6:4, refers to unreasonable requirements, beyond what could properly be expected under the circumstances, or to a harsh, unloving, and unduly critical attitude in connection with requirements which are reasonable and proper in themselves. Extreme strictness about minor matters, expecting children to perform a task as perfectly as adults, threatening punishments out of proportion to the seriousness of the offense are examples of unreasonableness on the part of parents or other persons in authority. Such unreasonableness will naturally have the effect of provoking the persons under authority to wrath and discouragement.

11. Give a Bible example of a person who dishonored himself and lessened his authority by "an unjust, indiscreet, rigorous, or remiss behavior." Nabal, whose very name means "foolish" or "wicked" (1 Sam. 25:25), who although descended from a very godly man (1 Sam. 25:3), possessed of great wealth, and head of a large household, yet was "curlish and evil in his doings," was extremely unreasonable toward David's followers, and had the reputation among his own servants of being "such a son of Belial that a man cannot speak to him" (v. 17). Nabal's unreasonableness, ill temper, intemperance (v. 17), and general folly so undermined his authority and dishonored his own person that even his wife could only call him "this man of Belial" and admit that "folly is with him" (v. 25).

131. Q. *What are the duties of equals?*

A. *The duties of equals are to regard the dignity and worth of each other, in giving honor to go one before another; and to rejoice in each other's gifts and advancement, as their own.*

Scripture References
- 1 Peter 2:17. Our duty to respect and love our fellow men.
- Rom. 12:10. The duty of Christian love and mutual regard.
- Rom. 12:15–16; Phil. 2:3–4. We are to find joy and satisfaction in honor and advancement that come to others, as well as to ourselves.

Commentary
1. What does the catechism mean by the word *equals?* This does not refer to equality of nature, but to equality of position. Two persons may be equal in nature, but unequal in position. A parent and child are equal in nature, but one is in a position of authority over the other. In human society it is inevitable that some persons be unequal in authority. This inequality of position is God's ordinance.

2. What do we mean by persons being equal in authority? By this we mean that they are on the same level of authority, neither possessing authority over the other. For example, in an army, while a general has authority over a private, two privates are equals.

3. What is our general duty toward those who are our equals in human society? We are to regard their "dignity and worth," realizing that like ourselves they are human persons created in the image of God and therefore to be honored and respected because we fear God.

4. What special sins must we avoid if we are to treat our equals with due honor and respect? To treat our equals with due honor and respect, we must especially avoid the sins of selfishness and pride. Everyone by nature tends to think too highly of himself. We tend to magnify our own attainments, and to minimize those of others. We tend to blame others for their faults and failures, while we find plausible excuses for our own. All this comes from sinful human selfishness and pride. Only by the grace of God in our lives can these sins be overcome.

5. What special duty is involved in the command of Romans 12:15–16? The duty of Christian sympathy, that is, being concerned about the affairs and welfare of our neighbor, according to his particular circumstances and needs. We are to rejoice with those who rejoice, and to weep with those who weep; that is, we are to share in or sympathize with the experiences of others.

6. Why should we rejoice in others' attainments and gifts as much as our own? Because God is glorified by these attainments and gifts, regardless of whether they are our own or some other person's. We should regard everything in life, not from a selfish standpoint, but from the standpoint of God's glory.

7. What special sin tends to prevent our rejoicing in other people's gifts and advancement? The sin of envy, which causes us actually to be unhappy over the success attained or honors received by someone else. True Christian love and sympathy for others will overcome the sin of envy in our lives.

132. Q. *What are the sins of equals?*

A. *The sins of equals are, besides the neglect of the duties required, the undervaluing of the worth, envying the gifts, grieving at the advancement of prosperity one of another; and usurping preeminence one over another.*

Scripture References

- Rom. 13:8. The duty of mutual Christian love.
- 2 Tim. 3:3. It is wrong to despise those that are good.
- Acts 7:9; Gal. 5:26. The sin of envy at the gifts of others.
- Num. 12:2; Esther 6:12–13. The wickedness of grieving at the prosperity or success of others.
- 3 John 9; Luke 22:24; 1 Peter 4:15. The sin of usurping preeminence over others.

Commentary

1. Is neglect of mutual Christian love a common sin today? This has probably always been a common sin among Christian people, except during seasons of spiritual revival when Christian people have been strongly drawn together by the powerful work of the Holy Spirit in their hearts. During times of persecution Christian people often find their love for one another greatly increased and deepened. On the other hand, our Savior predicted that a time would come when "because iniquity shall abound, the love of (the) many shall wax cold" (Matt. 24:12). In periods of backsliding, unbelief, or apostasy, as the tide of faith ebbs, so Christian love and sympathy are also diminished, and a callous coldness takes their place. It can hardly be questioned that neglect of Christian love is common in America today.

2. What is the effect of the sin of envy on the envious person? This sin, besides being a grave offense against the law of God, inevitably has a spiritually and psychologically destructive effect upon the person who is guilty of it. The envious person is himself the victim of his own sin, and his personality becomes corroded by envy until he becomes either sour or brittle. Such a person will be suspicious, resentful, easily offended, difficult to deal with, and a "problem" to his friends and associates. The Scripture calls envy "the rottenness of the bones" (Prov. 14:30). The person who tolerates this sin in his life is playing with an acid which, if not checked, will eat away at his personality until his disposition is ruined and he is wholly dominated by envy. Only the almighty power of God can save a person from such a pitiable state of spiritual bondage.

3. What does the catechism mean by "usurping preeminence one over another"? This expression does not refer to that preeminence of one person over another which exists by reason of legitimately acquired authority, such as the authority of a parent over a child or a magistrate over a private citizen. Rather, it refers to the grasping for authority which does not properly belong to a person. Such a person seeks to dominate others with whom he is really on a plane of positional equality. The adjective which describes this trait of character is "domineering," or, in common slang, "bossy." When one member of a congregation tries to have his own way, and dictate to the rest, that is "usurping preeminence." Closely related to this is the sin of meddling in other men's matters, which is forbidden in 1 Peter 4:15: "But let none of you suffer . . . as a busybody in other men's matters." The Greek word translated "busybody in other men's matters" literally means a bishop over others, that is, a self-constituted supervisor of other people's affairs.

133. Q. *What is the reason annexed to the fifth commandment, the more to enforce it?*

A. *The reason annexed to the fifth commandment, in these words,* That thy days may be long upon the land which the Lord thy God giveth thee, *is an express promise of long life and prosperity as far as it shall serve for God's glory and their own good, to all such as keep this commandment.*

Scripture References
- Deut. 5:16. The promise of long life and prosperity to those who obey the fifth commandment.
- 1 Kings 8:25. God's promise to David concerning the perpetual kingship of his descendants.
- Eph. 6:2–3. The promise of the fifth commandment reaffirmed in the New Testament.

Commentary

1. What promise of God is attached to the fifth commandment?
A promise of long life and prosperity to those who faithfully keep this commandment.

2. What is the effect upon human society of obedience to the fifth commandment? The general requirement of the fifth commandment being respect for authority in human society, it is clear that where this commandment is obeyed, conditions which make for long life and prosperity will exist. On the other hand, where respect for legitimate authority is lacking, a greater or less degree of anarchy or lawlessness will prevail in human society, and this will tend toward conditions which shorten life and interfere with prosperity. Thus, in the providence of God, obedience to the fifth commandment will bring about a general increase of length of life and prosperity in society.

3. Do individuals who obey this commandment always live long and attain material prosperity? No. We should carefully note the qualification stated by the catechism: "as far as it shall serve for God's glory and their own good." While it is certainly true, as a general proposition, that obedience to the fifth commandment is followed by long life and prosperity, this does not imply that these blessings are bestowed on every individual who conscientiously obeys this commandment. In a particular case, God's glory and the person's own good may be better served by withholding the blessing of long life, or material prosperity, or both. We must always leave room for the sovereignty and secret counsel of God, in thinking of such promises as this. At the same time we should remember that every child of God has something even better than long life and material prosperity: he has eternal life and a heavenly inheritance, being made a joint-heir with Christ and an inheritor of the kingdom of heaven.

4. Is it right to seek and pray for long life and material prosperity?
Certainly it is right, provided these blessings are not regarded as our chief aim, but are kept in subordination to the kingdom of God and his righteousness, and provided we seek them only in humble submission to the will of God. It is sinful to grasp after long life and prosperity as if they were our chief end. The Christian must always remember that the life that is life indeed is not the present life, but that of eternity; and that the true treasure is not that of this earth, but that of heaven. This does not involve an attitude of contempt for

blessings received here on earth; it only involves a true perspective and a right sense of the relative importance of this life and the life to come.

134. Q. *Which is the sixth commandment?*

A. *The sixth commandment is,* Thou shalt not kill.

135. Q. *What are the duties required in the sixth commandment?*

A. *The duties required in the sixth commandment are, all careful studies, and lawful endeavors, to preserve the life of ourselves and others by resisting all thoughts and purposes, subduing all passions, and avoiding all occasions, temptations and practices, which tend to the unjust taking away the life of any; by just defence thereof against violence, patient bearing of the hand of God, quietness of mind, cheerfulness of spirit . . .*

Scripture References

- Exod. 20:13. The sixth commandment.
- Eph. 5:28–29. The duty of preserving our own life.
- 1 Kings 18:4. The duty of preserving the life of others.
- Jer. 26:15–16; Acts 23:12–27. It is our duty to resist all thoughts and purposes which tend to the unjust destruction of human life.
- Eph. 4:26–27. Passions which tend toward unjust destruction of life are to be subdued.
- 2 Sam. 2:22; Deut. 22:8. Occasions tending to the unjust taking away of life must be avoided.
- Matt. 4:6–7; Prov. 1:10–16. It is our duty to avoid all temptations which tend toward the unjust destruction of life.
- 1 Sam. 24:12; 26:9–11; Gen. 37:21–22. All unjust taking away of the life of any human being is wicked.
- Ps. 82:4; Prov. 24:11–12; 1 Sam. 14:45. The sixth commandment requires a just defense of human life against destruction by violence.
- James 5:7–11; Heb. 12:9. The sixth commandment requires patient submission to the will of God as disclosed by God's providence.
- 1 Thess. 4:11; 1 Peter 3:3–4; Ps. 37:8–11; Prov. 17:22. A serene mental attitude and cheerful spirit are required of us by the sixth commandment.

Commentary

1. What is the meaning of the word *kill* in the sixth commandment?
In the sixth commandment, the word *kill* is used in the sense of "commit murder." The Hebrew text of the commandment is accurately translated "Thou shalt do no murder." The catechism rightly interprets the commandment in this sense, as not forbidding killing as such, but the unjust taking away the life of any person: this is a correct definition of the sin and crime of murder.

2. What general positive duties are required by the sixth commandment? "All careful studies, and lawful endeavors, to preserve the life of ourselves and others."

3. What is meant by "careful studies to preserve the life of ourselves and others"? This includes every form of human research and planning directed toward the preservation of life. For example, it includes such varied matters as scientific investigation of the causes and prevention of diseases, studies of chemistry directed toward discovering drugs which will save life or prevent suffering, plans for preventing traffic accidents on the highways, designing lighthouses by which ships can be warned of dangerous rocks, agricultural research by which the productivity of the soil can be increased, and development of swift and efficient means of communication by which quick relief can be brought to the suffering in time of disaster such as earthquake, fire, or flood.

4. What is meant by "lawful endeavors to preserve the life of ourselves and others"? This means all efforts directly or indirectly aimed at preserving human life, excepting such efforts as may be wrong because forbidden by God's moral law. Thus it is our duty to try to preserve our own and our neighbor's life, but not by telling a lie, or by denying Christ, or by betraying our God-given responsibility to our country. We may not do evil that good may come, even in order to save our own or some other person's life.

5. In addition to the actual, literal crime of murder, what does the sixth commandment require us to avoid? Besides the actual crime of murder, the sixth commandment requires us to avoid, resist, or subdue whatever tends toward the unjust destruction of human life. Thus we are to resist thoughts and purposes, subdue passions, and avoid occasions, temptations, and practices which tend toward such destruction of life. It should be noted that the catechism prudently avoids attempting to present a list of such occasions, temptations, practices, etc. No such list could possibly be complete, adequate, or permanently valid. Some practices, such as dueling, bullfighting, shooting the rapids of the Niagara River in a barrel, clearly and unquestionably tend toward the unjust destruction of human life, and the sixth commandment therefore requires that they be avoided. But there are other practices which might be regarded as doubtful, for example, the attempt to cross the Pacific Ocean in a small sailboat. The catechism lays down the principle, but wisely leaves the precise application of the principle to the sanctified common sense of the Christian.

6. What is included in the just defense of human life against violence? This requirement of the sixth commandment includes the duty of the nation to protect its people against the unjust violence of all enemies, foreign and domestic, as well as the duty of every individual to defend himself and others against violence on the part of lawbreakers of all kinds. Thus the sixth commandment involves the right and duty of defensive warfare and of the power of the police in enforcing law and order, as well as the right and duty of defending oneself and other persons against criminal violence whenever occasion may require.

7. Why does the sixth commandment require "patient bearing of the hand of God"? Patient submission to the will of God, as it is disclosed to us by the events of God's providence, is necessary for our true mental, spiritual, and physical well-being. To be impatient or rebellious against "the hand of God" is essentially self-destructive, for only in submission to God's will, and in harmony with him, can our true destiny be reached and our true welfare secured. This is involved in the basic truth that human beings are creatures of God and their true welfare consists in union and communion with God. When Christian people are impatient and rebellious under God's providential dispensations, they dishonor God and injure themselves. The reprobate in hell will to all eternity continue in total, and totally frustrated, rebellion against God and the will of God. When the Christian gives way to impatience and rebellion against God's will, he is conducting himself, to some extent, like the reprobate in hell.

8. Why are "quietness of mind" and "cheerfulness of spirit" required by the sixth commandment? It is generally known and recognized that a serene mental attitude and cheerful frame of mind tend toward good health and long life. Worry, anxiety, and a pessimistic attitude cause a tremendous amount of needless wear and tear on the human personality. The influence of the mind on the body is well known. It is the Christian's duty to face life serenely and cheerfully, in spite of disappointments, sufferings, and hardships, in order to glorify God in his body and his spirit, which are God's property and are consecrated to God's service.

135. Q. *(continued) What are the duties required in the sixth commandment?*

A. *The duties required in the sixth commandment are . . . a sober use of meat, drink, physic, sleep, labor, and recreations; by charitable thoughts, love, compassion, meekness, gentleness, kindness; peaceable, mild and courteous speeches and behavior; forbearance, readiness to be reconciled, patient bearing and forgiving of injuries, and requiting good for evil; comforting and succoring the distressed, and protecting and defending the innocent.*

Scripture References

- Prov. 25:16, 27; 1 Tim. 5:23. The sixth commandment requires a sober use of meat and drink.
- Isa. 38:21. The sixth commandment requires a proper use of medicine for the relief of suffering and the prolongation of life.
- Ps. 127:2; 2 Thess. 3:10–12; Prov. 16:26; Eccl. 3:4, 11; 5:12. The sixth commandment requires a proper and temperate use of sleep, work, and recreation.
- 1 Sam. 19:4–5; 22:13–14; Rom. 13:10; Luke 10:33–34; Col. 3:12–13; James 3:17; 1 Peter 3:8–11; Prov. 15:1; Judg. 8:1–3. The sixth commandment requires kindness and love in thought, word, and deed.
- Matt. 5:24; Eph. 4:2, 32; Rom. 12:17, 20–21. The sixth commandment requires a patient, forgiving, and unresentful spirit.
- 1 Thess. 5:14; Job 31:19–20; Matt. 25:35–36; Prov. 31:8–9. It is our duty to help and comfort those in distress, and to protect and defend the innocent from injustice.

Commentary

1. What is meant by a sober use of meat, drink, etc.? This means a conscientious, careful, temperate use of these things, such as will not have a harmful effect on our bodily health or mental alertness. We should realize that the Bible represents gluttony as sinful, as well as drunkenness.

2. What is the meaning of the word *physic*? This word in the catechism means what we call "medicine today." It should be understood as including not only drugs but all scientific means and methods used to relieve suffering or prolong life.

3. Is it wrong for a Christian to make use of medicine or other scientific treatment to relieve suffering or cure disease? No. In past times some zealous Christians have maintained that this is wrong, and that a Christian who uses medicine is not really trusting in the power and goodness of God. We should understand that faith in God is not contrary to a use of legitimate means. God has mitigated the curse by placing in the world, for mankind to discover, the means by which human suffering can be alleviated and life prolonged. To refuse to make use of these means because we trust in God involves a mistaken notion of what it means to trust in God. Really our faith in God requires us to use the proper means which his providence has placed at our disposal. What would we think of a farmer who would say: "I will not plow my fields or plant any seed; I will just trust in God to give me a harvest"?

4. What attitude should a Christian have toward sleep, work, and recreation? The catechism presents the teaching of the Bible on this question by stating that the sixth commandment requires "a sober use" of these things. Sleep, work, and recreation are all necessary to human life. Without them we cannot have a healthy body and alert mind. But sleep, work, and recreation must be kept in balance with each other, and a right proportion of time devoted to each, and all three must be subordinated to the great purpose of human life, which is to glorify God and enjoy him. Laziness and slothfulness are sinful, but so is an immoderate and idolatrous addiction to work, as well as the devotion of an excessive amount of time to recreation. Many Christians who would not think of indulging in the common gross forms of intemperance should consider whether they may not be guilty of some of the less obvious forms of intemperance. For a party or social gathering to continue hour after hour until late at night, with the result that those present are tired and unable to work efficiently most of the next day, is a form of sinful intemperance. So is the modern American worship of speed, luxury, and financial success. The Christian should cultivate an attitude of conscientious carefulness about all these matters, realizing that he is a steward of God.

5. Why does the sixth commandment require us to maintain a peaceable and kindly spirit toward others? Because the contrary spirit, that is, an unkind, unreasonable, unloving spirit, will inevitably have a harmful effect both on ourselves and on others. It will disturb our own and our neighbor's peace of mind, and by the influence of the mind on the body, the effect will be to injure, to a greater or lesser degree, our own and our neighbor's bodily health. Anger, stubbornness, a harsh and unfriendly spirit, and similar attitudes cannot but have a harmful effect both on the mind and on the body. This is a form of "killing" which the law of God certainly forbids.

6. What is meant by "forbearance"? This means being willing to suffer some wrong rather than being hasty to stand up for our rights and insist upon justice for ourselves.

7. Why should a Christian have "readiness to be reconciled"? Because by the amazing love and grace of God the Christian has himself been reconciled to God. Therefore he should be willing, and even eager, to be reconciled to his fellow men as far as possible.

8. Why should a Christian patiently bear and forgive injuries? Because God has freely forgiven all his sins. Therefore in gratitude to God the Christian should have a patient and forgiving spirit toward his fellow men.

9. Does the catechism mean that no matter what others may do, we must bear it patiently, without protest or opposition? Certainly not. It may sometimes be our duty, as well as our right, to seek justice from the constituted authorities of church or state. But even when it is a duty to oppose and seek to restrain the actions of others, we are not to hate them, but to maintain a kindly and forgiving spirit toward them. Especially when the rights of God and the truth of God are at stake, it is our duty to stand up courageously for truth and righteousness, without respect of persons. Kindness to men must never induce us to become lukewarm in defense of God's truth.

10. What is the Christian's duty toward the distressed? The Parable of the Good Samaritan, as well as the texts cited by the catechism, teaches us that it is our duty to do what we can to comfort and relieve those in distress, whoever they may be. Our neighbor is the person in need whom we have the power to help. Especially it is our duty to relieve the sufferings and distresses of our fellow Christians, not only in our own church or community, but anywhere in the world.

11. What is the Christian's duty toward the innocent? By "the innocent" the catechism means innocent persons who are in danger of being treated as guilty persons, or who are already suffering as if they were guilty of some wrong. It is always our duty to protect others against injustice so far as it is in our power to do so. This is true in small matters as well as great, in all spheres of human society, including family, church, and state.

136. Q. *What are the sins forbidden in the sixth commandment?*

A. *The sins forbidden in the sixth commandment are, all taking away the life of ourselves, or of others, except in case of public justice, lawful war, or necessary defence; the neglecting or withdrawing the lawful and necessary means of preservation of life; sinful anger, hatred, envy, desire of revenge; all excessive passions, distracting cares; immoderate use of meat, drink, labor, and recreations; provoking words, oppression, quarreling, striking, wounding, and whatsoever else tends to the destruction of the life of any.*

(**Note:** Since a large part of the answer to question 136 covers the same ground as the answer to question 135, we shall limit our discussion of question 136 largely to the questions of the rightfulness of capital punishment, participation in war, and self-defense.)

Scripture References

- Gen. 9:6; Num. 35:31, 33. The death penalty for the crime of murder commanded by God in the Old Testament.
- Rom. 13:4. The death penalty confirmed in the New Testament.
- Jer. 48:10; Deut. 20. War is sometimes legitimate, and under some circumstances it may be our God-given duty to participate in it.
- Exod. 22:2–3. Taking the life of another in necessary self-defense is always lawful.

Commentary

1. Why are many people today opposed to the death penalty for murder? It is clear that there is a great deal of opposition to the death penalty today, and that efforts are constantly being made to have this penalty abolished. The background of this situation is the general weakening and abandonment of faith in the Bible as the inspired Word of God, and, as a result of this, the general abandonment of belief that civil government and jurisprudence is a divinely ordained institution. The prevalent opinion today seems to be that civil jurisprudence is founded on human agreement or custom, and that justice is merely what society has found to be for the general welfare. Thus the death penalty for murder is regarded as merely a human custom which has come down from primitive times. If it is only a human custom, then of course society can change it and substitute some other penalty for it. But if the death penalty for murder is a divine command, and if justice is based on the law of God, then human society has no right to change it.

2. What reason is given for the ordinance of capital punishment in Genesis 9:6? "For in the image of God made he man." That is to say, the death penalty is commanded for the crime of murder, not simply because murder is contrary to the general welfare of the human race, but because murder is an insult to God. Murder affronts God by destroying an image-bearer of God. Thus the murderer commits sacrilege by failing to regard the image of God in man as something sacred. The real dignity and worth of human life consists in man's bearing the divine image. Adam was created a perfect, although finite, copy or replica of the Godhead, and even today, in spite of the fall, the image of God exists in man, although in damaged form. Thus the most heinous element in the sin of murder is its contempt for God in the destruction of a human life which bears his image.

3. Is it right for human lawmakers to abolish the death penalty for murder? No. Where the Word of God provides a positive enactment respecting the duty of the state, as in the case of the penalty for murder, it is obligatory that civil laws be in conformity with the revealed will of God. Genesis 9:6 shows that the death penalty for murder is a divine mandate for the state, and Romans 13:4 shows that this divine requirement of the death penalty has not been repealed, but rather confirmed, by the New Testament revelation.

4. Does the Bible, or the teachings of Jesus, forbid Christians to engage in war? It is generally admitted that the Old Testament does not forbid resort to war upon just and necessary occasion. But those who hold the position commonly called "pacifism" frequently set the New Testament over against the Old, by claiming that the New Testament forbids what the Old sanctioned. In attempting to prove this claim, appeal is usually made to the teachings of Jesus, especially the Sermon on the Mount, and in particular, the "Golden Rule." In this appeal to the teachings of Jesus there are involved two errors: (a) This method of interpretation takes the teachings of Jesus out of their context in the whole Bible of the Old and New Testaments, and interprets them as if they stood by themselves, or even as if they were in opposition to other parts of the Bible. Of course the truth is that the teachings of Jesus are in perfect harmony with the rest of the Bible, and our standard of faith and life is not simply "the teachings of Jesus," but the entire Word of God from Genesis to Revelation. (b) This method does not take all the teachings of Jesus into account, but only certain parts which are regarded as favorable to the pacifist position. These parts, such as the "Golden Rule," are then misinterpreted in the attempt to prove that the use of force to resist evil is always wrong. The first Gentile convert to Christianity, Cornelius, was a professional soldier; there is no indication that the apostles required him to renounce military service in the Roman army. When soldiers came to John the Baptist asking, "What shall we do?" he did not command them to renounce military service and take up some other mode of life, but merely replied, "Do violence to no man, neither accuse any falsely; and be content with your wages" (Luke 3:14); that is, he commanded them to avoid certain temptations to abuse their military position for selfish ends, but said nothing about an obligation to repudiate military service itself. The catechism adopts the principle held by the vast majority of Christian people, namely, that there is such a thing as lawful war. This does not, of course, mean that every war is legitimate, nor that all practices occurring in war can be approved. The catechism is far from sanctioning militarism: it merely affirms that under some circumstances it is not inconsistent with Christian duty to participate in war.

5. Why is it right to defend ourselves against unlawful violence?
Self-defense against unlawful violence is always legitimate. It is more than legitimate: it is a moral obligation. Our life is not our own; it belongs to God, and therefore as stewards of God's possessions we are under obligation to preserve our own life, and the lives of others, from destruction by criminal violence. The principle that necessary self-defense is legitimate is gen-

erally upheld by the civil laws of nations. To claim that the "Golden Rule," or the obligation to love our neighbor, means that it is wrong to kill in an effort at self-defense is to push loving our neighbor to an absurd and fanatical extreme. The Scripture commands a person to love his neighbor as himself: that is, love for one's neighbor is to be kept in balance with a proper love for oneself. The person who will let himself be murdered by a criminal, without attempting self-defense, loves his neighbor too much, and does not love himself enough.

137. Q. *Which is the seventh commandment?*

A. *The seventh commandment is,* Thou shalt not commit adultery.

138. Q. *What are the duties required in the seventh commandment?*

A. *The duties required in the seventh commandment are, chastity in body, mind, affections, words, and behaviour; and the preservation of it in ourselves and others; watchfulness over the eyes and all the senses; temperance, keeping of chaste company, modesty in apparel; marriage by those that have not the gift of continency, conjugal love, and cohabitation; diligent labor in our callings; shunning all occasions of uncleanness, and resisting temptations thereunto.*

139. Q. *What are the sins forbidden in the seventh commandment?*

A. *The sins forbidden in the seventh commandment, besides the neglect of the duties required, are, adultery, fornication, rape, incest, sodomy, and all unnatural lusts; all unclean imaginations, thoughts, purposes and affections; all corrupt or filthy communications, or listening thereunto; wanton looks, impudent or light behaviour, immodest apparel; prohibiting of lawful, and dispensing with unlawful marriages; allowing, tolerating, keeping of stews [brothels], and resorting to them; entangling vows of single life, undue delay of marriage; having more wives or husbands than one at the same time; unjust divorce, or desertion; idleness,* *gluttony, drunkenness, unchaste company; lascivious songs, books, pictures, dancings, stage plays; and all other provocations to, or acts of uncleanness, either in ourselves or others.*

Scripture References

- Exod. 20:14. The seventh commandment.
- 1 Thess. 4:2–8. The duty of purity of heart and life.
- Job 31:1; Matt. 5:28. The seventh commandment requires "watchfulness over the eyes, and all the senses."
- Prov. 2:16–20; 5:8; Gen. 39:10. The duty of avoiding unchaste company.
- 1 Tim. 2:9. The duty of wearing modest and inconspicuous clothing.
- Eph. 5:3–4. The duty of purity in speech and conversation.
- Matt. 15:19. Sins against purity proceed out of the heart.
- 1 Tim. 4:3; Mark 6:18; Mal. 2:11–12. Forbidding lawful marriages, and permitting unlawful ones, are contrary to the seventh commandment.
- Mal. 2:14–15; Matt. 19:5. Monogamy is the divine ordinance of marriage; therefore polygamy is wrong and not sanctioned by God.
- Mal. 2:16; Matt. 5:32. Divorce is contrary to the divine institution of marriage, and never to be permitted except on scriptural grounds.
- Rom. 13:13–14; 1 Peter 4:3. God's Word requires avoidance of all forms of uncleanness, and separation from all occasions and temptations "hereunto."

Commentary

1. What is the relation of the seventh commandment to the sixth? The sixth commandment requires respect for the sanctity of life, whereas the seventh requires respect for the sanctity of sex, by which human life is propagated and continued in the world.

2. What is the general scope of the seventh commandment? "The seventh commandment requireth the preservation of our own and our neighbor's chastity, in heart, speech, and behaviour" (Shorter Catechism, question 71).

3. What is the cause of violation of the seventh commandment? The real, basic cause of the violation of the seventh commandment is spiritual, namely, the corrupt, sinful condition of the human heart (Matt. 15:19).

4. What influence in modern life has contributed greatly to violation of the seventh commandment? Violation of the seventh commandment has been greatly increased by the popular acceptance of a type of psychology which stresses "self-expression," that is, which favors the unrestrained indulgence of natural impulses, regardless of the prohibitions of the law of God and the ordinance of marriage. No doubt many people have carried the implications of this type of psychology much further than the scholars who originally formulated it intended; no doubt, too, this psychology of "self-expression" has been used by many people as a convenient excuse for indulgence in impure lusts. The result has been a general decrease of opposition to the sins of fornication, adultery, unscriptural divorce and remarriage, etc. These sins are nothing new; they have existed since very early times (Gen. 34; 38:15–26), sometimes more, and sometimes less common; but today such is the revolt from the moral law of God that these practices are defended, and declared to be not sinful, by many "respectable" people, and even by many who make a profession of religion. We face today a situation in which many well-educated and respected people regard the expression of the sex instinct not as a moral question subject to the law of God, but merely as a matter of personal preference. Thus there are many today who hold that sexual relations apart from marriage are legitimate, that marriage is not necessarily permanent, etc. There has not in the past been such a justifying of sexual immorality on the part of prominent people in a country enjoying the light of the Christian religion, as exists in America today. The Samaritan woman who had had five husbands and was living with a sixth to whom she was not lawfully married (John 4:17–18) was no doubt regarded as immoral in her day; but in America today there are plenty of people who approach, if they do not equal, that record, and yet are regarded as worthy and respectable citizens. Divorce on unscriptural grounds has become so common that the mass of the people of our country think of it, not as a deep blot on a person's character, but merely as a person's "problem" or piece of "bad luck." To be known as a divorced person (on unscriptural grounds) hardly involves any social stigma in America today. This only shows how far public opinion has moved from the moral standard of the law of God.

It should be added that one of the primary forces presently at work to undermine the law of God is the misuse of television. This is not to say that TV is evil per se. To the contrary it can and ought to be used in a God-honoring way. But the standards that generally prevail with most television programs are now so low that Christians must be very vigilant in regulating its use (GIW).

5. What can be done to remedy the divorce evil in America today?

The divorce situation in America is extremely serious, yet certainly something can be done about it. This is too big a subject to discuss here in any detail. The following possibilities for improvement may be suggested: (a) Civil laws should be brought into harmony with the law of God on the subject of divorce; the many unscriptural grounds on which divorces are granted, such as "incompatibility," "mental cruelty," etc., should be eliminated. Some of them may be justifiable as grounds for judicial separation, but not as grounds for absolute divorce with the right of remarriage. Christian people should seek to have civil laws brought into harmony with the requirements of God's law on this subject. (b) The church should clearly and emphatically proclaim the teachings of God's Word on this subject. Such is the prevalent ignorance of the Scriptures today that there are even church members who do not know what the Bible teaches about marriage and divorce. (c) The church must faithfully enforce its discipline in the case of members who have been divorced without scriptural grounds, and especially in the case of remarriage by either party in such a divorce, or by the guilty party in a divorce granted on scriptural grounds. Those who flagrantly violate the law of God by taking advantage of lax civil legislation certainly have no right to claim the privileges of membership in good standing in the church of Jesus Christ, until they manifest satisfactory evidence of repentance and amendment of their life. (d) The church should exercise much greater care to ensure that the officers of the church really are qualified according to the requirements of 1 Timothy 3 and Titus 1.

6. Are impure books and magazines more common, and more evil, today than in former times? There can be no doubt that, in the United States at least, this is the case. Indecent books and magazines have become commonplace, especially during the years since the First World War. The unclean, subtle suggestiveness of many contemporary books and magazines is extremely offensive. Some well-known popular books and magazines are not fit for the library table of a Christian family. There is at least one widely read women's magazine which abounds in material calculated to break down the Christian standard of sexual morality. It can no longer be taken for granted that because a book or magazine is published by a well-known firm and endorsed by prominent people it must be decent and harmless. In this situation, serious-minded Christian people should be careful about their reading matter, and that of their children.

7. What should be our attitude toward the modern dance? Should Christian people participate in dances? Much could be written on this question. The catechism interprets the seventh commandment as forbidding "lascivious dancings." That the modern dance, in general, comes under this category, can hardly be questioned by anyone who knows the nature of the modern dance and who knows what the word *lascivious* means. Formerly Christian people generally objected to promiscuous dancing because it tended to lead to immorality; today it can plausibly be argued that many dances are inherently immoral, evil not merely in their results, but in themselves; that is, that the act of dancing, as practiced, itself constitutes a sinful indulgence of sexual passion. Needless to say, Christian people should conscientiously abstain from such practices. (The reader is referred to an excellent booklet on this subject, entitled *To Dance or Not to Dance,* by G. Mahler, published by Concordia Publishing House, St. Louis 13, Mo. [Tract No. 141].)

8. What attitude should a Christian take toward the motion picture theater? Of course Christian people should adopt a serious and conscientious attitude toward the motion picture theater as toward all ethical questions. There can be no doubt that many, if not most, commercial motion pictures, as they exist today, are bad in their effect, especially upon young people. For this reason many earnest Christian people feel that they should totally abstain from attending motion picture theaters at all times and under all circumstances. As this decision is conscientiously made, as a matter of Christian duty and devotion to God, it should of course be respected by all Christian people, even by those who may feel unable wholly to agree with it. On the other hand there are many professing Christians who do not seem to have any conscientious scruples whatever about motion pictures, but who attend practically any "show" whenever they feel like doing so. Such an attitude is not compatible with a conscientious Christian life, and cannot be justified. The reputation of the "movies" being what it is, it cannot be taken for granted that a "show" will be fit for Christian people to see. No Christian should have such a heedless, complacent attitude toward the motion picture theater. Apart from these two attitudes there are many truly conscientious Christian people who are quite aware of the general character of modern motion pictures, and who for that reason very seldom go to see them, who yet do not feel that a Christian could never do so without committing sin. It is clear that motion pictures are not necessarily evil: there can be pictures that are clean and wholesome. The conscientious Christian should take the trouble to ascertain the character of the picture before he goes to see it; this can be done in various ways, and should not be neglected. Needless to say, Christian people should always pay heed to the teachings of God's Word about questions of this kind, taking care not to become a stumbling-block to any Christian brother (Rom. 14:4–7, 14–23; 1 Cor. 8:9–13). We must always be willing to deny ourselves some pleasure rather than cause our brother to stumble.

What Dr. Vos says, here, about motion pictures applies with equal—if not greater—force to much of what is now offered in prime-time TV (GIW).

9. What does the catechism mean by "immodest apparel"? The cat-echism states that the seventh commandment forbids "immodest apparel" as sinful. No precise definition of "immodest apparel" can be given; this is a matter for the conscientious decision of every Christian. However, it may be said in general that apparel is immodest if it fails to cover the body decently, that is, if it leaves the body exposed to an extent that is likely to occasion impure thoughts in members of the opposite sex. We should realize that lack of modest apparel is emphatically condemned in the Bible (1 Tim. 2:9; Prov. 7:10, 13). Also the Bible condemns excessively costly, luxurious, or con-spicuous clothing (Isa. 3:16–26; 1 Peter 3:1–4). While religion is primarily a matter of the heart, not of outward clothing, yet vital Christianity will affect even the outward apparel, bringing a person's attire into subjection to the Word of God.

10. Why are vows of perpetual celibacy wrong? Such vows, which the catechism calls "entangling vows of single life," are taken by members of many "religious" orders of the Roman Catholic Church. These vows are sinful because they are vows to do something (a) which is not com-manded in the Word of God, and (b) for the performance of which we have no promise of help from God. Celibacy is not a more holy form of life than marriage. To remain unmarried may be the will of God for a particular per-son's life, but no person has any right to take a vow promising never to marry. According to the Word of God, marriage is the normal life of adult human beings (Gen. 2:18, 24), and therefore celibacy is the exception rather than the rule. In the Middle Ages the Catholic Church reacted strongly against the extreme licentiousness of the Roman Empire, and went to the opposite extreme of setting up asceticism and celibacy as the Christian ideal. Ever since, the Roman Catholic Church has been influenced by this false ideal, and has continued to regard "virginity" or celibacy as a higher and holier estate than marriage.

11. Is it important that the catechism mentions "sodomy, and all unnatural lusts," citing as proof texts Romans 1:24–26 and Leviticus 20:15–16?
It certainly is. Although Dr. Vos did not say anything about this, specifically, when he wrote this material in the late 1940s and early 1950s, it is important to note that the Westminster Assembly displayed its fidelity to Scripture by mentioning even this unpleasant subject. In earlier times—at least in my life-experience—there did not seem to be much need to mention this perversion. Why? Because it was then agreed by most people in our culture that this is a self-evident evil. It was then generally agreed that even our natural biological structure teaches us that it is unnatural (Rom. 1:26–27) for men to have sex with men, and women to have sex with women. Yet, today, even once great Reformed denominations (such as the Reformed churches in the Netherlands) have officially tolerated this evil, allowing even the office-bearers of their churches to practice this perversion. We can be profoundly grateful, therefore, that our Westminster Assembly did not hesitate to speak specifically of this vile sin in explaining the meaning of the seventh commandment (GIW).

140. Q. *Which is the eighth commandment?*

A. *The eighth commandment is,* Thou shalt not steal.

141. Q. *What are the duties required in the eighth commandment?*

A. *The duties required in the eighth commandment are, truth, faithfulness, and justice in contracts and commerce between man and man; rendering to every one his due; restitution of goods unlawfully detained from the right owners thereof; giving and lending freely, according to our abilities, and the necessities of others; moderation of our judgments, wills, and affections concerning worldly goods; a provident care and study to get, keep, use, and dispose those things which are necessary and convenient for the sustentation of our nature, and suitable to our condition; a lawful calling, and diligence in it; frugality; avoiding unnecessary lawsuits, and suretiship, or other like engagements; and an endeavor, by* *all just and lawful means, to procure, preserve, and further the wealth and outward estate of others, as well as our own.*

Scripture References

- Exod. 20:15. The eighth commandment.
- Ps. 15:2, 4; Zech. 7:4, 10; 8:16–17. The eighth commandment requires justice and honesty in business dealings and contracts.
- Rom. 13:7. To fail to render to every man his due is stealing.
- Lev. 6:2–5 compared with Luke 19:8. The duty of restitution of wealth wrongly acquired or retained.
- Luke 6:30, 33; 1 John 3:17; Eph. 4:28; Gal. 6:10. The eighth commandment requires giving and lending as we are able, to help others in their need.
- 1 Tim. 6:6–9; Gal. 6:14. The eighth commandment requires moderation in our attitudes and actions toward worldly wealth.
- 1 Tim. 5:8; Prov. 27:23–27; Eccl. 2:24; 3:12–13; 1 Tim. 6:17–18; Isa. 38:1; Matt. 11:8. The eighth commandment requires industrious efforts to obtain, keep, and use the means of sustaining our life in the situation in which God's providence places us.
- 1 Cor. 7:20; Gen. 2:15; 3:19; Eph. 4:28; Prov. 10:4. It is a duty to have a legitimate occupation, and to work regularly at it.
- John 6:12; Prov. 21:20. Thrift is a Christian duty.
- 1 Cor. 6:1–9. Unnecessary lawsuits are to be avoided.
- Prov. 6:1–6; 11:15. The Christian should avoid the entanglement of suretyship.
- Lev. 25:35; Deut. 22:1–4; Exod. 23:4–5; Gen. 47:14, 20; Phil. 2:4; Matt. 22:39. It is our duty to try, by just and lawful means, to promote the material prosperity both of ourselves and of others.

Commentary

1. What is the general scope of the eighth commandment? The general scope of the eighth commandment is respect for the sanctity of property, just as the sixth enjoins respect for the sanctity of life, and the seventh respect for the sanctity of sex. Property or wealth is created by God and entrusted to man for his use in glorifying and serving God. It is therefore a stewardship committed to man, and for this reason must be respected. Thus the eighth commandment requires not only that we refrain from stealing our neighbor's property, but that we acquire and take care of our own.

2. Does the Bible sanction the private ownership of property? Yes. Private ownership of property, in the sinful state of humanity which has existed since the fall, is necessary for a life that can glorify and enjoy God. Private ownership is not founded on mere human invention or custom, but on the moral law of God. It is definitely sanctioned by the eighth commandment, "Thou shalt not steal," which is meaningless unless there is a divine ordinance of private ownership back of it. Even apart from the Bible, natural revelation teaches all men that stealing is wrong. Those in our day who think that private ownership is evil are profoundly mistaken. The evils they have in mind arise not from private ownership itself, but from abuses of private ownership.

3. What should we think of communism, in the light of the Bible? According to the teachings of the Bible, communism is wrong in principle. It is not merely wrong in some of its features or practices, or because of abuses associated with it, but wrong and wicked in its basic idea. If we could imagine a "perfect" state of communism, in which there would be no tyranny, no concentration camps, no secret police, no propaganda or censorship of information, it would still be inherently sinful and wicked. Capitalism violates the moral law of God by evils and abuses which are associated with it; communism violates God's moral law by its very nature and basic idea. The principle of communism is collective ownership of property enforced by the state. This presupposes that individual private ownership is an evil which can be tolerated on a small scale only, as a concession to human nature. This is contrary to the Bible, which teaches that private ownership is a God-given right. The individual human being, as the image-bearer of God, must have the right of private ownership of property and acquisition of wealth if he is to develop his individual personality as God intends, and to glorify God fully in his relationship to his environment. God's image in man involves the implication that man is to have dominion over the earth (Gen. 1:27–28); but man is essentially an individual, with an individual soul and conscience, individual capacities and abilities, individual hopes and desires. Communism seeks to merge the individual in the mass of humanity, and this involves the sacrifice of essential elements of man's personality as an individual bearer of the divine image and steward of God in holding dominion over a portion of God's creation. For communism assumes that the individual person exists for the sake of the mass, of society; but this is contrary to God's Word, which teaches us that society and all social institutions exist for the sake of the individual, in order that the individual may attain the divine purpose for his life and thus glorify God. It is the individual human person that has an immortal soul, a conscience, and the capacity for communion with God; these will outlast this world, and exist forever; they are what impart real dignity and worth to human life. Any system which regards the individual human being as unimportant and seeks to merge him in the mass for the supposed welfare of "society" is basically wrong and anti-Christian. This applies to compulsory collective ownership of property as well as to other subversions of individual human personality.

4. Did not the early church practice communism, as recorded in Acts 2:44; 4:32–37? It is true that a kind of "communism" existed in the church at Jerusalem, but this was entirely different from communism as it exists today. It should be noted (a) that it was voluntary, not compulsory, as shown by Peter's words to Ananias in Acts 5:4; (b) that it was partial, not total, as shown by the fact that the house of Mary, the mother of John Mark, was not sold (Acts 12:12); (c) that there soon arose a murmuring charge that the rations of food were not being fairly distributed (Acts 6:1); (d) that it was only temporary, and was later discontinued, probably at the time of the great persecution which followed the martyrdom of Stephen, when the Christians were scattered from Jerusalem (Acts 8:1–4); (e) that there is no evidence that any such "communism" was set up in any of the churches established by the apostles, other than the church at Jerusalem. Thus it is clear that the temporary "communism" of the Jerusalem church was not a matter of principle, but of expediency in the face of special existing conditions peculiar to that time and place. It is very foolish, unscriptural, and unhistorical to represent this temporary state of affairs in the Jerusalem church as analogous to modern communism, or as a pattern for Christian people everywhere to imitate.

5. Is socialism contrary to Christianity? The word *socialism* is used with such varying meanings that it is difficult to speak definitely of it unless it is first defined so that it can be known precisely what is meant. Marxian socialism, which is the root of modern communism, is certainly contrary to the Christian religion. Yet there is a limited form of socialism that is not contrary to the teachings of God's Word. For the government to operate the postal service, instead of leaving it to the initiative of private persons or corporations, is a form of socialism; yet it cannot be regarded as sinful for the state to engage in this enterprise. In most countries of the world the railways, telegraphs, and telephone service are operated either chiefly or exclusively by the state. We may consider this wise or unwise, but we can hardly prove that it is contrary to the Bible. However, a line has to be drawn somewhere; it would certainly be wrong for the state to take over and operate all business and commerce. The operation of business by the state should be confined to such activities as the postal service, which are essential to all the people of the country and which for cheapness and efficiency require a nationwide monopoly. The state should maintain conditions in which private business can be carried on, and should regulate private business in the interests of justice, but should not supplant private business by competing with it. God instituted civil government to promote the welfare of men by maintaining justice in human society (Rom. 13:4), not to develop into a colossus of collective enterprise in competition with its own citizens.

6. Why is wastefulness sinful? The catechism says that the eighth commandment enjoins "frugality" as a Christian duty; that is the opposite of wastefulness. The latter is a sin which is especially characteristic of Americans, and from which the Christian people of our country are certainly not free. In China people have to save every chip of wood and wisp of straw carefully, to use for fuel; in America one can look out of a train window and see pile after pile of old railroad ties being burned just to get rid of them. Many other examples of our habitual wastefulness will readily come to mind. This prodigal habit can no doubt be partly explained by the comparative wealth and newness of our country. But that does not excuse wastefulness. Even if there is plenty more available, it is wrong to waste anything that will sustain or enrich human life, or that has cost natural resources and human effort to produce. Our possessions are not ours to use or waste as we please; they are a stewardship entrusted to us by God, for which we will have to give him an account. If we do not become thrifty and economical because of conscientious obedience to God's law, the time may come when we will have to practice economy because of sheer necessity. Equally blameworthy with our national wastefulness is our foolishness as a people in spending vast sums of money on unnecessary luxuries, as well as on various forms of self-indulgence which are injurious to body and soul. Christian people should seriously consider whether they are guilty of a fleshly self-indulgence in their use of the wealth which God has entrusted to them.

142. Q. *What are the sins forbidden in the eighth commandment?*

A. *The sins forbidden in the eighth commandment, besides the neglect of the duties required, are, theft, robbery, manstealing, and receiving any thing that is stolen; fraudulent dealing, false weights and measures, removing land marks, injustice and unfaithfulness in contracts between man and man, or in matters of trust; oppression, extortion, usury, bribery, vexatious lawsuits, unjust enclosures and depopulations; engrossing commodities to enhance the price; unlawful callings, and all other unjust or sinful ways of taking or withholding from our neighbor what belongs to him, or of enriching ourselves; covetousness; inordinate prizing and affecting worldly goods; distrustful and distracting cares and studies in getting, keeping, and using them; envying at the prosperity of others; as likewise idleness, prodigality, wasteful gaming, and all other ways whereby we do unduly prejudice our own outward estate, and defrauding ourselves of the due use and comfort of that estate which God hath given us.*

Scripture References

- James 2:15–16; 1 John 3:17. Neglect of the duties enjoined in the eighth commandment.
- Eph. 4:28; Ps. 62:10; 1 Tim. 1:10. The sinfulness of theft, robbery, and manstealing.
- Prov. 29:24; Ps. 50:18. Knowingly to receive stolen goods is to become a party to the theft.
- 1 Thess. 4:6; Prov. 11:1; 20:10; Amos 8:5. Fraudulent dealing, and the use of false weights and measures, is sinful.
- Deut. 19:14; Prov. 23:10. To remove landmarks by private action is contrary to the eighth commandment, being a form of stealing.
- Ps. 37:21; Luke 16:10–12. Dishonesty, injustice, and unfaithfulness in fulfilling contracts or matters of trust are sinful.
- Lev. 25:17; Matt. 23:25; Ezek. 22:12, 29; Ps. 15:5. All forms of oppression, or taking advantage of the helplessness of others for our own profit, are forbidden.
- Job 15:34; Amos 5:12; 1 Sam. 8:3; Ps. 26:10; Isa. 35:15. Bribery, being essentially dishonest and unjust, is always wrong.
- 1 Cor. 6:6–8; Prov. 3:29–30. Unjust and unnecessary lawsuits constitute a violation of the eighth commandment.

- Isa. 5:3; Mic. 2:2; Prov. 11:26. The attempt to establish monopolies of the means of human subsistence is wicked.
- Acts 19:19, 24–25. All occupations which are in themselves unlawful are contrary to the eighth commandment.
- Job 20:19; James 5:4; Prov. 21:6. All ways of enriching ourselves by taking or withholding from others what is rightly theirs are sinful.
- Luke 12:15; 1 Tim. 6:5; Col. 3:2; Prov. 23:5; Ps. 62:10; Matt. 6:25, 31, 34; Eccl. 5:12. All wrong attitudes toward material wealth are forbidden by the eighth commandment.
- Pss. 73:3; 37:1, 7. It is wrong to envy the material prosperity of others.
- 2 Thess. 3:11; Prov. 18:9; 21:17; 23:20–21; 28:19; Eccl. 4:8; 6:2; 1 Tim. 5:8. All laziness, idleness, wastefulness, and carelessness concerning the acquiring, retaining, and expending of material wealth are sinful.

Commentary

1. What are the common sins which are obviously forbidden by the eighth commandment? Theft, robbery, burglary, larceny, embezzlement, receiving stolen goods, using or tolerating unjust weights and measures, and the like, which are so easily understood and so clearly recognized as wrong that extended comment on them would be superfluous. These sins are shown to be wrong, not only by the Bible, but also by God's natural revelation. Instead of taking time for a detailed discussion of these obvious forms of dishonesty, we shall focus on some of the less easily recognized forms.

2. What is meant by "manstealing"? This includes (a) kidnapping persons to be held for ransom; (b) stealing human beings to be held as slaves, or to be sold into slavery; (c) the wicked modern form of slavery called "forced labor" which has existed in totalitarian countries, especially Soviet Russia, by which vast numbers of human beings, on one pretext or another, are deprived of their liberty and compelled to pass their days in a miserable existence, without comfort or hope, working for the state.

3. How does modern advertising violate the law of God? Modern advertising is so permeated with dishonesty that we may wonder how a Christian can participate in some of its common forms. We listen to a radio broadcast and hear a familiar voice telling us all the reasons why a certain brand of coffee, macaroni, or aspirin is the best on the market, superior to other brands, the most for our money, characterized by "extra" advantages and "special" features, etc., etc., and then two hours later we hear the same familiar voice telling us all the reasons why another brand of coffee, maca-roni, or aspirin is the kind we should buy and use with confidence. Of course the broadcaster is only reading a script prepared for him by the advertisers. But the whole process is so obviously shot through with exaggeration, insin-cerity, and half-truth that the listener becomes hardened to this sort of thing and does not take any of it at face value. The same extravagant type of over-statement is prevalent in magazine and newspaper advertising. In America, it would seem, a thing can hardly be offered to the public as "good" and "worth the price." It must be termed "super," "colossal," "magnificent," "marvelous," etc., etc.

Of course there are advertising claims that are downright false. But what is most common is not outright fraud, but exaggeration, half-truth, and sub-tly misleading statements. All advertising that is calculated to produce any other impression in the public mind than that of strict, objective truth con-cerning the qualities and value of what is offered for sale is dishonest and therefore sinful. When a common brand of aspirin is advertised with the statement, repeated interminably, that "no other brand of aspirin is purer or gives faster relief," the impression is created that this brand is purer or faster than others; whereas the real truth is that aspirin is aspirin, being controlled by the Federal Food and Drug Act, and among legally sold brands of aspirin, one brand is as pure and as speedy as another. No doubt many Christian peo-ple are connected in one way or another with such dishonest advertising practices; they should consider seriously whether their occupation involves violation of the moral law of God.

There is, of course, a legitimate field for advertising. Legitimate advertis-ing (a) will tell the real truth about what is offered for sale, avoiding exag-geration and deception, (b) will not try to create the impression that a prod-uct is better than that offered by competitors, unless it really is as shown by fairly conducted tests; (c) will not put forth imaginary claims which take advantage of the credulity of the public, such as that a brand of toothpaste is better than others because it contains a "special" ingredient (which has a high-sounding name but is unknown to the science of chemistry), or that the flavor of a brand of coffee is enhanced by a "special" secret process, known only to the firm that offers it for sale. Radio, newspaper, and mag-azine advertising is a tremendous business in America today, but it is to be feared that its ethical standards are far from those of the Bible. To judge by present-day advertising we must be a nation of deceivers and deceived, or to state it less nicely, of liars and "suckers." We should think seriously of the relation of this phase of contemporary life to the law of God.

4. What does the catechism mean by "unjust enclosures and depopulations"? By "unjust enclosures" the catechism refers to the practice which at one time existed in England whereby "common" land (owned by the lord of the manor but which other persons had a legal right to use for pasturage) would be "enclosed" or fenced in for purposes of agriculture. Such enclosures would be unjust if the rights of those who were entitled to use the "common" land were disregarded. In the eighteenth and nineteenth centuries laws were enacted providing for "enclosures" on an equitable basis for all parties concerned, when more land was needed to raise crops.

By "depopulations" the catechism means the practice of buying up large tracts of land to form a great estate, and removing the tenants who had been living on it, a form of injustice known in Old Testament times and condemned in Isaiah 5:8 and Micah 2:2.

5. What does the catechism say about monopolies of commodities? The catechism states that "engrossing commodities to enhance the price" is a violation of the eighth commandment, and therefore sinful. Not every form of monopoly is necessarily wrong; some businesses or services are natural monopolies, such as the postal service, and may be best operated either by the state or by private corporations licensed and regulated by the state. What the catechism condemns as sinful are monopolies the purpose of which is to raise prices by "cornering" the total available supply of a product. This practice eliminates competition and prevents the normal functioning of the law of supply and demand; it creates an artificial shortage or disappearance of the product from the market, in order that those who have established the monopoly can name their own price and get it because no one else has the product for sale. Such monopolies of commodities, especially of the necessities of life, are so clearly unjust that they are prohibited by civil legislation in many countries.

The principle laid down by the catechism does not imply that patent laws, by which invention is encouraged by the state guaranteeing the inventor a monopoly of the manufacture and sale of his own invention for a limited period of years, are wrong. However, the common practice by which large corporations purchase patent rights from inventors, not in order to manufacture the article and offer it to the public, but in order to prevent it from being manufactured and sold by anyone, is quite another matter. It may well be that this latter practice is essentially immoral and contrary to the eighth commandment; certainly it frustrates the legitimate purpose of the patent laws, which is to promote progress and encourage invention. When corporations take advantage of these laws to prevent progress, and to keep the public from enjoying the fruits of new inventions, it may be that Christian principles require a revision of the patent laws.

6. What is "wasteful gaming" and why is it wrong? By "wasteful gaming" the catechism denotes all forms of gambling, which are inherently sinful because they involve an attempt to gain wealth without rendering an equivalent value in return. If the gambler wins, he is a thief; if he loses, he is a waster of his Lord's property. The fact that gambling involves an implied agreement to transfer money or property one way or the other as determined by the "chance" fall of dice, etc., does not make it legitimate. A contract to do something sinful is itself sinful. It has been well said that gambling stands in the same relation to stealing as dueling does to murder. Gambling includes "slot machines," raffles, "punch boards," betting, lotteries, games of chance played for money or prizes, various forms of "pools," etc. All of these are essentially immoral, and Christian people should leave them all strictly alone. Gambling is not only a sinful vice, but a fever which grows on a person until he cannot let it alone. The only safe and right course is to have nothing whatever to do with gambling in any form. Of course churches and civic organizations that sponsor any kind of gambling scheme are beneath contempt.

143. Q. *Which is the ninth commandment?*

A. *The ninth commandment is,* Thou shalt not bear false witness against thy neighbor.

144. Q. *What are the duties required in the ninth commandment?*

A. *The duties required in the ninth commandment, are, the preserving and promoting of truth between man and man, and the good name of our neighbor, as well as our own; appearing and standing for the truth; and from the heart, sincerely, freely, clearly, and fully, speaking the truth, and only the truth, in matters of judgment and justice, and in all other things whatsoever; a charitable esteem of our neighbors; loving, desiring, and rejoicing in their good name; sorrowing for, and covering of their infirmities; freely acknowledging of their gifts and graces, defending their innocency; a ready receiving of a good report, and unwillingness to admit of an evil report, concerning them; discouraging tale-bearers, flatterers, and slanderers; love and care of our own good name, and defending it when need requireth; keeping of lawful promises; studying and practicing of whatsoever things are true, honest, lovely, and of good report.*

Scripture References

- Exod. 20:16. The ninth commandment.
- Zech. 8:16. The duty of maintaining truth between man and man.
- 3 John 12. Preserving the good name of our neighbor.
- Prov. 31:8–9; Ps. 15:2; 2 Chron. 19:9; 1 Sam. 19:4–5; Josh. 7:19; 2 Sam. 14:18–20; Lev. 19:15; Prov. 14:5, 25; 2 Cor. 1:17–18; Eph. 5:25. The duty of speaking the truth in all matters, and especially in matters of public justice.
- Heb. 6:9; 1 Cor. 13:7; Rom. 1:8; 2 John 4; 3 John 3–4. The duty of a charitableness toward others, and concern for their good name.
- 2 Cor. 2:4; 12:21; Prov. 17:9; 1 Peter 4:8. It is our duty to be sorry about, and seek to cover, the infirmities of others.
- 1 Cor. 1:4–7; 2 Tim. 1:4–5; 1 Sam. 22:14; 1 Cor. 13:6–7; Ps. 15:3; Prov. 25:23. The duty of maintaining a right attitude toward the good qualities of others, defending them against injustice, and being unwilling to believe an evil report about them.
- Prov. 26:24–25; Ps. 101:5. Both flatterers and slanderers are to be discouraged as dealers in untruth.
- Prov. 22:1; John 8:49. It is a duty to defend our own good name in case of need.
- Ps. 15:4. Lawful promises must be kept.
- Phil. 4:8. It is our duty to study and practice whatsoever things are true, honest, lovely, and of good report.

Commentary

1. What is the general scope of the ninth commandment? The general scope of the ninth commandment is the sanctity of truth and honesty in human society, and the duty of maintaining our own and our neighbor's good name.

2. Why is truth to be regarded as sacred? Truth is to be regarded as sacred because it is an attribute of God, that is, it is a feature of the character of God. God is infinite, eternal, and unchangeable in his truth. We are told in the Bible that God cannot lie (Titus 1:2). God is called the "Lord God of truth" (Ps. 31:5). Similarly, we read that "God is light, and in him is no darkness at all" (1 John 1:5). Because the Scripture is from God, Jesus could say, "Thy word is truth" (John 17:17). The Scripture is "truth," but Jesus Christ himself is not merely truth but "THE truth" (John 14:6), that is, he is the absolute, ultimate, eternal Truth in person. Because God is infinite, eternal, and unchangeable in his truth, truth must be regarded as sacred by all his rational creatures (angels and men).

3. How can we explain the prevalence of untruth in the world? We cannot understand the prevalence of untruth in the world without believing in a personal devil as set forth in the Bible. Just as God is the source of truth, so Satan is the source of untruth, the father of lies (John 8:44). Untruth entered the human race when Eve listened to Satan and believed the devil's lie rather than the truth of God. Satan is described in the Bible as the one who deceives the whole world (Rev. 12:9). Satan is also called "the god of this world" (2 Cor. 4:4) and "the prince of this world" (John 14:30) who has nothing in Christ. Satan has a kingdom which he seeks to extend and propagate, a kingdom of untruth. Those who are dominated by untruth are citizens of Satan's kingdom; Christian people who deal in untruth are handling the weapons of Satan's kingdom.

4. What modern system of philosophy violates the sacredness of truth? The philosophy called "pragmatism," which teaches that the important question is not whether something is true, but whether it works. According to pragmatism, success is the test of truth. Something is to be accepted if it "works"; we are not to measure things by an absolute standard of truth such as the Bible. This notion has had a tremendous influence in American life, and even the religious life of our country has been greatly affected by it. It has done incalculable harm in breaking down and undermining people's sense of the sacredness of truth and their belief in the existence of such a thing as absolute, unchanging truth. Today many people have come to think that truth changes with the times. Many who perhaps have never heard the word *pragmatism* are under the influence of this philosophy. Those who say that the Westminster Standards were true for the seventeenth century but are not suitable for the twentieth century, for example, have suffered from this spiritual blight. The aversion to doctrine and the depreciating of the importance of sound doctrine which are so common in contemporary American church life have resulted largely from this influence. Many people who demand that religion have "a practical emphasis" mean by that, that they want the church to have a program of action without a solid foundation of truth underneath it. We should not hesitate to say that the modern demand for practical action, when coupled with indifference to or impatience of truth, is thoroughly perverse and wicked. Nothing can be really practical unless it is founded on absolute, unchanging truth.

5. What change must take place in our lives before we can really know and love the truth of God? By nature we are all deeply prejudiced against the truth, and inclined to doubt or deny the truth, as well as to speak untruth or lies. This state of affairs is to be explained in part by the deceptive activities of Satan, and in part by our spiritual blindness as those who are dead in trespasses and sins (Eph. 2:1). Because of this, we need to be regenerated or "born again" by the almighty power of God the Holy Spirit. This experience of the new birth opens the eyes of the heart and enables a person really to see and appreciate the truth of God. It is followed by the process of sanctification, one effect of which is to work in the person a hatred of untruth and a love for honesty and truthfulness in his daily life and conversation. Without the Holy Spirit's work of regeneration and sanctification, we would remain the victims and the agents of untruth forever.

(**Note:** Inasmuch as question 145 covers much the same ground as question 144, but is somewhat more complete, we shall limit our discussion of question 144 to the foregoing questions dealing with the general principles of truthfulness, and shall leave the details of obedience to the ninth commandment to be discussed under question 145, in the lessons that follow.)

145. Q. *What are the sins forbidden in the ninth commandment?*

A. *The sins forbidden in the ninth commandment are, all prejudicing the truth, and the good name of our neighbors, as well as our own, especially* *in public judicature; giving false evidence, suborning false witnesses, wittingly appearing and pleading for an evil cause, out-facing and over-bearing the truth, passing unjust sentence, calling evil good and good evil; rewarding the wicked according to the work of the righteous, and the righteous according to the work of the wicked . . .*

Scripture References

- 1 Sam. 17:28; 2 Sam. 1:9–10, 15–16; 16:3. The sin of prejudicing the truth and the good name of ourselves or others.
- Lev. 19:15; Hab. 1:4. The great sin of prejudicing the truth in matters of public justice.
- Prov. 6:16, 19; 19:5; Acts 6:13. The sin of giving false evidence, or arranging for it to be given by others.
- Jer. 9:3, 5; Acts 24:2, 5; Pss. 12:3–4; 52:1–4. The great wickedness of knowingly opposing the truth.
- Prov. 17:15; 1 Kings 21:9–14. The sin of passing unjust sentence, of delivering an unjust verdict, in the administration of justice.
- Isa. 5:20–23; Prov. 17:15; Amos 5:7. All breaking down of the absolute distinction between right and wrong is morally perverse.

Commentary

1. What is the general scope of the sins forbidden by the ninth commandment? The general scope of the sins forbidden by the ninth commandment is whatever is contrary to the truth and to the good name of any person. That is, the ninth commandment forbids all conduct which in any way, whether by word, by deed, or by sinful silence, interferes with the maintaining of truth between man and man, and with the preservation of the good name which any person justly possesses.

2. Why is it a sin to act in such a way as to injure our own good name? We are to love our neighbor as ourself, which implies that a proper love of self is a divinely imposed duty. As each individual bears in himself the image of God and was created to glorify God, the legitimate good name of each person must be preserved, including one's own good name. This obligation must, however, be kept in balance with a conscientious concern for the good name of our neighbor, and must be subordinated to a supreme zeal for the honor and glory of God.

3. What special form of falsehood is especially wicked? Opposing the truth, by word, deed, or silence, in matters of "public judicature," that is, in the administration of justice in the courts of the state or of the church.

4. Why is "giving false evidence" sin? Giving false evidence in court, and especially giving false evidence under oath, or perjury, is sinful because it is contrary to the nature of God, who is Truth; because it is contrary to love for our neighbor, in taking away his rights; because it reduces the divinely ordained administration of justice to a mockery; and because it proceeds from the moral corruption of human hearts depraved by the fall of the race into sin.

5. What is meant by "suborning false witnesses"? This expression means to engage, employ, or arrange for persons to appear in a court of justice to give false evidence in order that guilty persons may escape punishment, or innocent persons suffer punishment, or in order that a civil lawsuit may be decided in a manner contrary to what the true facts would require.

6. Is "suborning false witnesses" a common sin today? While there is of course no way of obtaining any exact statistics concerning such a matter, it seems probable that giving false evidence for money is far from uncommon in America in the present day. One form of this is the false "alibi," where a person is paid money to swear that the person on trial was in another city at the time when the crime was committed, etc.

7. Why is "wittingly appearing and pleading for an evil cause" wrong? Because it is sinful to try to make the guilty appear to be innocent, or to try to make wrong appear to be right. If a lawyer knows that his client has committed a crime, he may not try to prove the man innocent. In such a case, the lawyer must insist that his client enter a plea of guilty. The lawyer has the duty, however, to see that even a guilty person is not deprived of the protection and civil rights which the law guarantees. He may not try to make the guilty appear to be innocent, but he is bound to endeavor that the guilty shall not be punished beyond what the law requires.

8. What is meant by "out-facing and over-bearing the truth"? These expressions mean a stubborn, persistent, perverse effort to oppose and defeat what a person knows, in his heart and conscience, is really the truth. Such stubborn opposition to the truth often arises from deep prejudice against the person or institution that is standing up for the truth. Those who have left a strict and faithful church to join one that is more "inclusive" will often argue stubbornly against the doctrines and principles of the denomination of which they formerly were members. In such cases it is evident that they are not so much zealous for the truth, as prejudiced against a particular denomination and its creed. Stubborn opposition to the truth may also arise from envy. Because of a secret envy of the gifts, talents, or attainments of persons who are standing up for the truth, others may obstinately and persistently oppose not only the persons, but also the truth they are maintaining. All such conduct is "out-facing and over-bearing the truth" and is very wicked and displeasing to God.

9. Why is calling evil good and good evil a special sin? Calling evil good and good evil, and its practical application in treating the wicked as if they were righteous and the righteous as if they were wicked, is heinously sinful because it amounts to breaking down or denying the distinction between right and wrong. The distinction between right and wrong is absolute and unchangeable, because it proceeds from the nature of God himself. Whatever breaks down the distinction between right and wrong is a practical denial of the righteous character of God. We may never forget that God is absolutely good and hates evil.

145. Q. *(continued) What are the sins forbidden in the ninth commandment?*

A. *The sins forbidden in the ninth commandment are . . . forgery, concealing the truth, undue silence in a just cause, and holding our peace when iniquity calleth for either a reproof from ourselves, or complaint to others; speaking the truth unseasonably, or maliciously to a wrong end, or perverting it to a wrong meaning, or in doubtful and equivocal expressions, to the prejudice of truth or justice; . . .*

Scripture References
- Job 13:4; Ps. 119:69; Luke 16:5–7; 19:8. The sin of forgery.
- Lev. 5:1; Deut. 13:8; Acts 5:3–9; 2 Tim. 4:16. Concealing the truth, and undue silence in a just cause.

- 1 Kings 1:6; Lev. 19:17. Remaining silent when it is our duty to speak.
- Isa. 59:4. Remaining silent when it is our duty to complain to the constituted authorities of church or state.
- Prov. 29:11. Speaking the truth unseasonably.
- 1 Sam. 22:9–10, compared with Ps. 52:1–5. Speaking the truth maliciously to a wrong end.
- Ps. 56:5; John 2:19 compared with Matt. 26:60–61. Perverting the truth to a wrong meaning.
- Gen. 3:5; 26:7, 9. Using doubtful or equivocal expressions, to the prejudice of truth or justice.

Commentary

1. What is the meaning of "forgery"? In the Bible and the catechism this word has a somewhat broader meaning than in our common usage today. It refers not only to the falsifying of written documents, but to any use of falsehood in legal charges, contracts, etc.

2. Why is concealing the truth a sin? Concealing the truth is really the same thing as telling a lie. It is done with the intention of deceiving some person, and is therefore the acting of a lie.

3. Is concealing the truth always a sin? No. Sometimes it may be our duty to conceal a matter from those who have no right to know it. Concealing the truth is a sin when we conceal a matter from those who have a right to know it. For example, to keep vital military information from falling into the hands of the enemies of our country is not wrong; rather, it is our duty.

4. What is meant by "undue silence in a just cause"? This means remaining silent, for private or selfish reasons, fear of reproach, etc., when it is our duty to speak in the interests of truth and justice. For example, it may be our duty to testify as a witness in a lawsuit or court trial; by our refusal or reluctance to do so, justice may be perverted, the innocent suffer punishment, or the guilty escape.

5. Why is it wrong to be unduly silent in a just cause? Because "no man liveth unto himself"; we have a moral responsibility to God and a duty to our neighbor and to human society, to see that truth and justice prevail, so far as it is in our power to do so. Our personal feelings or convenience must not be allowed to stand in the way of the vindication of truth and justice.

6. Do we have a right to remain silent when iniquity calls for a reproof, or for complaint to those who have authority to act? No. Although the easy thing is to keep still and say nothing, this is not doing our duty to God and our neighbor. We are to bear witness against wrongdoing as occasion may require, even though it is difficult.

7. What is meant by "speaking the truth unseasonably," and why is it wrong to do so? "Speaking the truth unseasonably" means speaking the truth at the wrong time, when wisdom or common sense would lead us to wait until a more suitable time. If someone is rushing to catch a train, we should not choose that particular time to talk to him about the salvation of his soul. It would be more tactful and sensible to choose a more suitable time, when the person concerned would be able to give his attention to the matter.

8. What is meant by "speaking the truth maliciously, to a wrong end"? This means speaking the truth with a wrong motive, and for a wrong purpose. Even though what we say may be strictly true, it may be wrong to say it. For instance, if we speak the truth with the intention of injuring some person's reputation, or of stirring up someone to become angry against someone else, such speaking of the truth is wrong.

9. Why is it wrong to pervert the truth "to a wrong meaning or in doubtful and equivocal expressions," etc.? These are wrong because all of them are only ways of deceiving people. Intentionally to use expressions that can be understood in two different ways, in order to deceive some other person, is just as wicked as telling an outright lie. For example, the minister who was reported to have said, "I believe in the divinity of Christ," and then later explained to someone else that he believed in the divinity of Christ because he believed in the divinity of all human beings, was guilty of the sin of breaking the ninth commandment.

10. What is the essential nature of a lie? The real, essential nature of a lie is the intention to deceive some person. Even though what we say may be itself true, if our intention is to deceive others we are really liars in God's sight.

145. Q. *(continued) What are the sins forbidden in the ninth commandment?*

A. *The sins forbidden in the ninth commandment are . . . speaking untruth, lying, slandering, backbiting, detracting, talebearing, whispering, scoffing, reviling, rash, harsh, and partial censuring; misconstructing intentions, words, and actions; flattering, vainglorious boasting, thinking or speaking too highly or too meanly of ourselves or others; . . .*

Scripture References

- Isa. 59:13; Lev. 19:11; Col. 3:9. The sin of speaking untruth.
- Pss. 15:3; 50:20. The sins of slander and backbiting.
- James 4:11; Jer. 38:4. The sin of "detracting," or unjustly speaking evil of another.
- Lev. 19:16; Rom. 1:29–30. Talebearing and whispering condemned as sinful by God's Word.
- Gen. 21:9; Gal. 4:29; 1 Cor. 6:10. The sins of scoffing and reviling.
- Matt. 7:1; Acts 28:4; Gen. 38:24; Rom. 2:1. The sins of rash, harsh, and partial censuring of others.
- Neh. 6:6–8; Rom. 3:8; Pss. 69:10; 1 Sam. 1:13–15; 2 Sam. 10:3. It is sinful to misrepresent the intentions, words, and actions of others.
- Ps. 12:2–3. The sin of flattery.
- 2 Tim. 3:2. The sin of vainglorious boasting.
- Luke 18:9–11; Rom. 12:16; 1 Cor. 4:6; Acts 12:22; Exod. 4:10–14. It is wrong to think or speak too highly, or not highly enough, of ourselves or others.

Commentary

1. Why is it wrong to speak untruth, or tell a lie? It is wrong to speak untruth, or tell a lie, because this is contrary to the character of God, who is Truth. Satan is called in the Bible the father of lies: and the person who tells a lie is using Satan's method instead of doing what is pleasing to God. Beside being an affront to God's holiness, the telling of a lie breaks down the very foundations of human society. It destroys the world's currency of truth by introducing the counterfeit coin of falsehood. If everyone told lies all the time, human society could not exist, for it would be impossible ever to believe anyone. It is only because of the general prevalence of truth-telling that human society can function at all. The liar is a "chiseler" who takes advantage of human society's general reputation for truthfulness, by telling a lie for his own selfish purposes.

2. What are "slandering" and "backbiting"? "Slandering" is injuring someone by maliciously uttering a false report about that person. "Backbiting" is an aggravated form of slandering which consists in secretly uttering a false report about some person, behind that person's back. Slandering and backbiting are sinful not only because they involve untruthfulness, but also because they are contrary to a proper love for our neighbor, and concern for his good name.

3. What does the catechism mean by "detracting"? The common word used for this today is *disparaging*. It means speaking evil of a person in order to detract from that person's influence or good reputation; to depreciate a person.

4. What is meant by "talebearing" and "whispering"? "Talebearing," as used in the catechism means much the same as the word *gossip* today: a sinful spreading about of reports of the sins and failings of other people, because we derive some personal satisfaction by dwelling on the faults of others. "Whispering" is the most contemptible form of talebearing or gossip; it means circulating stories or rumors about some person secretly, in such a way that it is difficult or impossible to trace the rumors to their source and correct them. In past times banks and business firms have been ruined by whispering campaigns conducted against them by unscrupulous persons.

5. Is it always wrong to tell what we know about wrongdoing committed by other persons? No. It may be our duty to report wrongdoing to the proper authorities. If we know that a child is stealing or destroying property, it is our duty to inform the child's parents. In the case of serious wrongdoing by members of the church, it may be our duty to report the matter to the officers of the church who have authority to deal with the offender. If the law of the land has been broken, and it is a matter of some importance (as where a crime has been committed), it is our duty to report it to the constituted authorities of the government. Reporting a matter to persons in authority is not to be regarded as "talebearing" or "whispering." In such a case, the motive involved is not gossip, or a sinful delight in telling of other persons' faults, but a proper desire that wrongdoing may be stopped and that justice may be performed.

6. What are "scoffing" and "reviling," and why are they sinful?
"Scoffing" as used by the catechism means mocking or ridiculing persons as a way of injuring them or making them unhappy. "Reviling" is what is commonly called "name-calling" today; it means to oppose and injure persons by calling them hard and evil names, contrary to truth, justice, and love for our neighbor. When Christian people are laughed at because of their Christian faith and profession, that is "scoffing"; when they are called hypocrites, that is "reviling." Scoffing and reviling are always wrong because they are contrary to truth and to love for our neighbor.

7. What does the catechism mean by "rash, harsh, and partial censuring"? By "censuring" is meant finding fault with, or passing judgment upon, some other person because of that person's speech or conduct. "Rash" censuring means passing judgment when it is not our duty to do so; "harsh" censuring means going beyond what the evidence warrants, or "jumping to conclusions" in passing judgment on another; "partial" censuring means passing judgment unfairly or showing partiality, by being prejudiced in favor of, or against, some person. All these forms of fault-finding or passing judgment are sinful because contrary to justice and to love for one's neighbor.

8. Why is misrepresenting the intentions, words, and actions of others a violation of the ninth commandment? Because intentionally or knowingly to represent the intentions, words, and actions of others is the same as telling lies about them. This is quite a common sin, but Christian people should be ashamed to be guilty of such conduct. If some person is prominent in some good cause, we have no right to accuse him of selfish ambition. If someone opposes a particular method of accomplishing some good purpose, we should not jump to the conclusion that he is opposed to the good purpose and in favor of the corresponding evil. This principle is often sadly disregarded, and sincere Christian people are accused of being in favor of various forms of evil because they do not agree wholly with others as to the methods which should be used in combating the evils.

9. Why are "flattering" and "vainglorious boasting" wrong? "Flattering" means praising some other person too highly, in order to please that person and gain some favor from him. "Vainglorious boasting" means praising our own selves too highly, beyond what truth and justice warrant. Both of these practices are sinful because they are forms of dealing in untruth, instead of depending on the strict truth for accomplishing our purposes.

10. Why is it wrong to think or speak too highly or too meanly of ourselves or others? All such thinking and speaking is wrong because it is not according to the truth of the matter. We have a duty to others; we have a duty to ourselves also. In both cases it is wrong to have or express an opinion that is either too high or too low. Some Christians have a false humility; they are always speaking evil of themselves, and representing themselves as extremely unworthy. This is wrong, because it disparages the graces and gifts of God which have been given to them. In all cases we should make it our aim to think and speak according to the real truth of the matter.

145. Q. *(continued) What are the sins forbidden in the ninth commandment?*

A. *The sins forbidden in the ninth commandment are . . . denying the gifts and graces of God; aggravating smaller faults; hiding, excusing, or extenuating of sins, when called to a free confession; unnecessary discovering of infirmities; raising false rumors, receiving and countenancing evil reports, and stopping our ears against just defence; . . .*

Scripture References
- Job 4:6; 27:5–6. The sin of denying the gifts and graces of God.
- Matt. 7:3–5. It is wrong to aggravate smaller faults of others.
- Prov. 28:13; 30:20; Gen. 3:12–13; 4:9; Jer. 2:35; 2 Kings 5:25. The sin of hiding or trying to excuse our sins, when we should confess them.
- Gen. 9:22; Prov. 25:9–10. It is wrong unnecessarily to tell the faults or failings of others.
- Exod. 23:1. The sin of raising false rumors.
- Prov. 29:12. The sin of listening to and countenancing evil reports.
- Acts 7:56–57; Job 31:13–14. The sin of refusing to pay attention to the just defense of any person.

Commentary

1. What is meant by "denying the gifts and graces of God"? This expression means being stubbornly unwilling to recognize as true and real God's gifts and graces, whether given to ourselves or to others. Sometimes when it is reported that a certain person has made a profession of the Christian faith, others are very reluctant to believe that that person is sincere, or really converted. When God called Moses to deliver his people from Egypt, Moses was very reluctant to comply, and denied that he had the qualifications needed for the task that God was imposing on him; this amounted to a denial of the gifts and graces of God which had been given to him (Exod. 4:10–13).

2. What is meant by "aggravating smaller faults," and why is it wrong? This means to represent small faults or failings of others as more serious and more important than they really are. We are not to call black white, or white black; we must not speak of people's faults as if they were virtues, or as if they were not faults at all. But it is wrong to represent people's little faults as if they were great and serious matters. Our Lord's words in Matthew 7:3–5 should serve to remind us that we all have serious faults of our own, which should have our attention before we undertake to correct the smaller faults in the lives of others.

3. Why do people frequently try to hide or excuse their sins, when they ought to confess them freely? Ever since Adam and Eve tried to evade responsibility for what they had done, people's sinful nature has led them to try to make excuses for themselves instead of honestly confessing their sins. The sinful corruption of our hearts results in our being filled with pride or "vanity," and the result of this is that we are stubbornly unwilling to confess our sins or admit our faults. Only the real work of the Holy Spirit can soften our hard and stubborn hearts so that our pride gives way to a true Christian humility, and we become willing to confess our wrongdoing, not only to God, but to others whom we may have wronged in some way.

4. Why is "unnecessary discovering of infirmities" wrong? By "unnecessary discovering of infirmities" the catechism means what we commonly call gossip about other people's faults and failings. People indulge in such gossip because it gives them a comfortable, self-righteous feeling to dwell on the misdeeds of other people. This habit is wrong, first, because it proceeds from a self-righteous pride; second, because it is contrary to a right love for our neighbor, which should make us feel sad when he has done something wrong; third, because it tends toward injustice to the person who has done wrong, for as the story is passed on from person to person it grows and is exaggerated until the wrongdoing may be reported in a manner out of all proportion to the real facts of the case.

5. How can we avoid involvement in the sin of raising false rumors? Deliberately starting a false rumor in order to injure some person, or to accomplish some unjust purpose, is so baldly and plainly wicked that it should hardly be necessary to warn Christian people against it. But it is very easy to help a false rumor along after it has once been started by some person. This sin of contributing to the prevalence of a false rumor may be committed either knowingly or unknowingly; we may or may not realize that the rumor is false. Before we help to circulate a story which may do harm or deprive some person of justice, we should take the trouble to find out whether it is really true or not (and even if it is true, we should not repeat it unnecessarily). A tremendous amount of harm has been done by well-meaning people who were ready to believe and repeat whatever they might happen to hear to the discredit of some person. This careless habit is contrary both to justice and to love for our neighbor.

6. How do people sin by "receiving and countenancing evil reports"? By this expression the catechism does not mean that receiving and countenancing evil reports is always wrong. There are those whose official duties involve receiving evil reports, and countenancing them at least temporarily. For example, a prosecuting attorney is bound by his oath of office to do so. It is his duty to listen to such reports, and investigate them in the light of the available evidence, in order that justice may prevail. What is wrong is for persons who have no official responsibility in such matters to welcome and eagerly listen to evil reports about other people. This is a form of the sin of rejoicing in iniquity which the apostle Paul declares to be contrary to Christian love (1 Cor. 13:6).

7. What induces people to stop their ears against just defense? Blind, violent prejudice is the force at work in cases of this kind. This is well exemplified by the attitude of the rulers of the Jews when Stephen presented his defense (Acts 7:57). Similarly the Jewish multitude at Pilate's judgment hall refused to listen to a just defense of Jesus, and demanded that he be crucified (Matt 27:22–24). So also the mob in the theater at Ephesus refused to listen to the defense of Alexander, and drowned his voice out with their shouting about the goddess Diana (Acts 19:33–34). Again as Paul sought to make his defense on the stairs of the castle in Jerusalem, the multitude refused to listen to the end of his speech, and violently put a stop to his discourse (Acts 22:22–23). All of these cases were instances of the operation of extreme prejudice. Such violent prejudice is not merely the result of ignorance, or misunderstanding, but arises from the deep wickedness and ingrained depravity of the sinful human heart.

145. **Q.** *(continued) What are the sins forbidden in the ninth commandment?*

A. *The sins forbidden in the ninth commandment are . . . evil suspicion; envying or grieving at the deserved credit of any, endeavoring or desiring to impair it, rejoicing in their disgrace and infamy; scornful contempt, fond admiration; breach of lawful promises; neglecting such things as are of good report, and practicing or not avoiding ourselves, or not hindering what we can in others, such things as procure an ill name.*

Scripture References

- 1 Cor. 13:5; 1 Tim. 6:4. The sin of harboring evil suspicions concerning others.
- Num. 11:29; Matt. 21:15. The sin of envying the deserved credit of others.
- Ezra 4:12–13. Seeking to damage the good reputation of others.
- Jer. 48:27; 1 Cor. 13:6. The sin of being glad of the sins or disgrace of others.
- Ps. 35:15–16, 21; Matt. 27:28–29. The sin of scornful contempt.
- Jude 18; Acts 12:22. The sins of fond admiration and flattery.
- Rom. 1:31; 2 Tim. 3:3. The sin of breaking lawful promises or vows.
- 1 Sam. 2:24; 2 Sam. 13:12–13; Prov. 5:8–9; 6:33. The sins of neglecting such things as are of good report, and involvement in such things as procure a bad reputation.

Commentary

1. What is meant by "evil suspicion"? This expression does not mean a legitimate suspicion, which is supported by reasonable evidence, but rather an improper suspicion, which is not based on evidence but arises from "wishful thinking" or our too-great readiness to believe something bad about others. Because of our sinful hearts we are too ready to put the worst interpretation on other people's conduct, when perhaps the actual facts of the matter could be explained in a more charitable way.

2. What is meant by "envying or grieving at the deserved credit of any," and why is this wrong? Envying means being highly displeased when someone else receives some honor, praise, or recognition that we would like to have ourselves, but which has not been given to us. Such envy results in nursing a secret grudge or dislike against the person whose success is envied. It is sinful because it is a proud and selfish dissatisfaction with the providence of God.

3. Why is it wrong to wish or attempt to injure the honor or good reputation of others? This common practice is wrong (a) because it is contrary to truth, and therefore displeasing to God, whose nature is truth; (b) because it is contrary to love to our neighbor, whose true honor and welfare should be an occasion of rejoicing to us, as if it were our own honor and welfare.

4. How do Christian people commit the sin of rejoicing in iniquity? Many Christian people who would no doubt be ashamed openly to rejoice in iniquity practiced by others yet commit this sin in other ways. Some gossip about sins committed by others, claiming to be highly scandalized by the wrong that has been done, yet obviously taking a great satisfaction in telling about it. Others who are ashamed to do this openly will take a secret satisfaction in their hearts, rejoicing in the sins and shame of others.

5. What is "scornful contempt"? This means treating or regarding others, in word, thought, or deed, in a way which ignores their natural human dignity as people created in the image of God. When such contempt is directed against those who are our Christian brethren and fellow members of the household of God, it is a greatly aggravated sin. Our Savior was treated with scornful contempt when he was mocked and derided by the Roman soldiers and the scribes and Pharisees and priests at the cross.

6. What is "fond admiration"? This expression means a blind, foolish devotion to some person, so that we praise and honor that person extravagantly, beyond what he really deserves, and regardless of the real facts of that person's life. Fond admiration is an attitude of the mind, which leads to the sin of flattery, or expressing of foolish and extravagant praise of some person.

7. Why is it wrong to break our lawful vows and promises? We are morally responsible to God for our actions, and God requires of us that lawful vows and promises be sacredly kept. The godly man is described in the Bible as the man who swears to his own hurt, and changes not; that is, the man who stands by his word even when he finds that it will cause him some financial or other loss to do so. His contracts are fulfilled even when he suffers a loss by doing so.

8. What is our duty with respect to the good name, or good reputation, of ourselves and others? (a) We are to attend to and practice such things as result in a good reputation; (b) we are to avoid whatever results in a bad reputation. Thus we have a duty, both for ourselves and for others, to seek to have a good name, and to seek to avoid its opposite. "A good name is rather to be chosen than great riches."

146. Q. *Which is the tenth commandment?*

A. *The tenth commandment is,* Thou shalt not covet thy neighbor's house, thou shalt not covet thy neighbor's wife, nor his manservant, nor his maid-servant, nor his ox, nor his ass, nor any thing that is thy neighbor's.

147. Q. *What are the duties required in the tenth commandment?*

A. *The duties required in the tenth commandment are, such a full contentment with our own condition, and such a charitable frame of the whole soul toward our neighbor, as that all our inward motions and affections touching him, tend unto, and further all that good which is his.*

Scripture References
- Exod. 20:17. The tenth commandment.
- Phil. 4:11; Heb. 13:5; 1 Tim. 6:6. The Christian duty of contentment.
- Job 31:29; Rom. 12:15; Ps. 122:7–9; 1 Tim. 1:5; Esther 10:3; 1 Cor. 13:4–7. The duty of a right attitude toward our neighbor and all that is his.

Commentary

1. What is meant by "contentment"? Contentment, as the word is used in the catechism, means willingness to accept that condition in which God's providence has placed us, without murmuring or complaining, or being envious at the blessings or prosperity of others.

2. Why are communists particularly opposed to the tenth commandment? Communism opposes the tenth commandment with the slogan "Religion is the opium of the people"; that is, communism holds that Christianity, by this commandment and similar statements of God's Word, teaches people that it is their duty to be patient and contented with their situation in life, whereas communism would have the people improve their condition by violent revolution, the poor taking possession of the wealth of the rich, etc. According to Christianity, contentment is a virtue; according to communist doctrine, it is a vice.

3. Does the Christian duty of contentment imply that it is wrong to try to improve our condition in life? No. It is our duty to be content with our condition in life, as long as by God's providence it remains our condition. This does not imply that it is wrong to try to change or improve our condition, so long as we use right and lawful means and methods for doing so. The duty of contentment must not be made an excuse for laziness, lack of ambition, or neglect of industrious work. We may seek to improve our condition and increase our worldly wealth by all right and lawful means, but while we are doing this we must always maintain a Christian spirit of contentment with what we have at the moment. That is to say, we may never make the increase of wealth our main concern in life, or regard it as the real object of our hopes. Even while we are working to improve our condition, we must always regard God and God's kingdom as our true riches.

4. Is it true that "Religion is the opium of the people"? No doubt there have been some very corrupt and degenerate forms of Christianity that have tended to destroy people's ambition and make them satisfied to live in misery and wretched poverty without trying to do anything to change such conditions. But this is not true of real Christianity, and especially not of Protestant Christianity in its most consistent form (Calvinism, or the Reformed Faith). Everywhere that the Calvinistic system of doctrine has been accepted and taken seriously, it has stirred people up to vigorous activity in all spheres of life, and has tended to increase the material prosperity of the people in general. There have been three striking examples of this in three regions of the world which naturally are far from rich in wealth or material resources. The first is the little country of Holland, which is so situated that constant effort is required to hold the land against the encroachments of the ocean. The second is Scotland, largely a country of rocky hills, very poorly suited to agriculture, and apparently unable to support a large population. The third example is New England, a region of stony hillsides and very cold winters. In all three of these regions the Calvinistic form of Christianity was generally accepted and became the prevailing religion; and all three, in spite of their natural handicaps, became world-famous for their advancement and prosperity. In each case, Christianity led to honest government, initiative, hard work, and thrift, which greatly improved the condition of the people.

5. What attitude toward our neighbor is required by the tenth commandment? The tenth commandment requires "a charitable frame of the whole soul toward our neighbor," which means that we are to love our neighbor in such a way that we will be glad and thankful for his true welfare and prosperity, as if it were our own.

6. Is it easy to have such an attitude of love toward our neighbor? No. Our natural sinful hearts are extremely selfish, and they tend toward envy and covetousness at the welfare and prosperity of others. Only by the grace of God in our hearts, by the power of the Holy Spirit, can we really even begin to love our neighbor as ourself.

7. What is meant by "our inward motions and affections" with regard to our neighbor? By "our inward motions and affections" the catechism means the thoughts, desires, and motives of our hearts, which spring from our character, and which determine our outward life and conduct. Thus the tenth commandment requires that we shall have right thoughts, desires, and motives concerning our neighbor, and all that is his.

8. Why must our lives "tend unto, and further" the welfare of our neighbor? Because God has placed us in human society as members of it; it is his plan and purpose that human beings be dependent on one another for their welfare. There is a true sense in which we are our brother's keeper, and therefore our lives must be so directed that they will tend toward the prosperity and welfare of others as well as toward our own.

9. What is the relation of the tenth commandment to the right of owning private property? Clearly the tenth commandment, in speaking of our neighbor's possessions, sanctions the right of private ownership of property. In consistent communism there would be no private property; everything would be owned by the state, or by the people in general, collectively, and people would only borrow and use what belonged to the public. Of course such extreme communism has never actually been practiced, for human nature demands the private ownership of at least some few possessions. Communism, however, denies the principle of the right of private ownership, and allows people to have a few possessions merely as a matter of privilege or concession, not as an inherent human right. Under a truly consistent communist system it would be impossible to speak of coveting "any thing that is thy neighbor's," for all property would be collectively owned. The tenth commandment in forbidding coveting "any thing that is thy neighbor's" implies the truth that private ownership of property is a divinely sanctioned human right. This is implied, also, in the truth that man was created in the image of God.

148. Q. *What are the sins forbidden in the tenth commandment?*

A. *The sins forbidden in the tenth commandment are, discontentment with our own estate, envying, and grieving at the good of our neighbor, together with all inordinate motions and affections to any thing that is his.*

Scripture References
- 1 Kings 21:4; Esther 5:13; 1 Cor. 10:10. The sin of discontentment with our own estate.
- Gal. 5:26; James 3:14–16. The sin of envy.
- Ps. 112:9–10; Neh. 2:10. It is wrong to grieve at the good of others.
- Rom. 7:7–8; 13:9; Col. 3:5; Deut. 5:21. The sin of having a wrong attitude toward anything that is our neighbor's.

Commentary
1. Why it is sinful to be discontented? A spirit of discontent is sinful because it involves dissatisfaction with God's providence. The discontented

person really feels that God is not treating him right. Thus discontent amounts to finding fault with God. Therefore discontent is really a form of irreverence, and unbelief in the goodness and love of God.

2. What is envying, and why is it wrong? Envying means selfish and unfriendly grudging in view of what another possesses or enjoys. It means that if we do not have the same blessings as our neighbor, we are not willing for him to have them either; if our neighbor has blessings that God has not given to us, we sinfully wish that our neighbor did not have these good things either. Envying is wrong because it proceeds from sinful selfishness. The person who is really unselfish cannot be envious at the same time.

3. What causes people to grieve at the good of their neighbors? It is people's sinful hearts that cause them to grieve at the good of others. We should rejoice in all blessings, whether material or spiritual, enjoyed by others; but because of our sinful hearts, we sometimes take more satisfaction in the knowledge that our neighbor has committed some sin, or suffered some loss, than in thinking of the blessings that God has bestowed on him.

4. How do wrong attitudes of the mind violate the tenth commandment? The tenth commandment is violated by "all inordinate motions and affections" to anything that is our neighbor's. That is, not only wrong actions, but wrong attitudes of the mind are sinful and contrary to this commandment. It is wrong to desire that which is the property of others. This commandment especially emphasizes the truth that it is not only outward actions that are sinful, but also even thoughts, desires, motives, and mental attitudes.

5. What Bible characters violated this commandment in a specially wicked manner? (a) Ahab, who coveted Naboth's vineyard. (b) Haman, who coveted worldly honor and therefore was grieved at Mordecai.

Note that in each case the sin of coveting led on to other forms of sin.

149. Q. *Is any man able perfectly to keep the commandments of God?*

A. *No man is able either of himself, or by any grace received in this life, perfectly to keep the commandments of God; but doth daily break them in thought, word and deed.*

Scripture References

- James 3:12; John 15:5; Rom. 7:3. No human being has power of himself perfectly to keep the commandments of God.
- Eccl. 7:20; 1 John 1:8, 10; Gal. 5:17; Rom. 7:18–19. No human being can keep the commandments of God perfectly, even by the grace of God and help of the Holy Spirit, during this present life.
- Gen. 6:5; 8:21; Rom. 3:9–19; James 3:2–13. Every person in the world breaks God's commandments daily in thought, word, and deed.

Commentary

1. Why is it true that no human being has power of himself perfectly to keep the commandments of God? This statement is true because all human beings are born with a sinful "heart" or nature, which results in their committing all kinds of sins constantly. Every person comes into this world with a nature depraved and corrupted with original sin. This original sin inevitably determines the moral quality of a person's life and actions. Even in the person who is born again of the Holy Spirit, this corruption of original sin is in this life not eradicated, but only subdued.

2. Is this truth of "original sin" generally accepted in the present day? No. While the doctrines of original sin and total depravity are taught in God's Word with unmistakable clearness, these truths are extremely unpopular in the present day. Many people become angry and indignant when these truths are taught and preached. The popular idea today is that there is much good in every person—enough good to overcome the evil. This optimistic view of human nature is not derived from the Bible but from the philosophy of evolution which is prevalent today, with its belief in boundless progress and betterment by human development and achievement. Modern thought is rather optimistic about human nature; the Bible on the contrary is distinctly pessimistic about the natural moral condition of the human heart.

3. What do we call the belief of those who say that by the grace of God, or the power of the Holy Spirit, it is possible in this life perfectly to keep the commandments of God? This mistaken belief is called perfectionism, or "sinless perfection." It arises from a failure to grasp the real nature and scope of God's requirements. The person who really understands the spiritual nature and comprehensive character of the moral law of God cannot be a perfectionist. Only the person who has a very partial and inadequate idea of what God's law requires of human beings can imagine that it is possible, even by God's grace, in this life perfectly to keep all the commandments of God. God requires of us, not merely that we shall "be good," but that we shall be morally perfect. What God requires of us is not mere sincerity, earnestness, or relative "goodness," but absolute moral perfection. The requirement of God's moral law has never been changed. It cannot be changed because the moral law is an expression of the character of God himself, and God of course is unchangeable. Mankind was created in the image of God, and God requires absolute moral perfection of those created in his image. Any deviation from absolute perfection is sin.

4. Did any person in the Bible claim to have attained absolute moral perfection in the present life? No. The best and holiest of God's saints all confessed that they still committed sin. For example, many of David's Psalms contain confessions of sin. The apostle Paul, long after his conversion, experienced a constant conflict with sin. Peter, long after he was filled with the Holy Spirit, had to be publicly rebuked for his unchristian and inconsistent conduct (Gal. 2:11–14). We search the pages of Scripture in vain for a perfect human being in this present life, with only a single exception, our Lord Jesus Christ, who lived a life of absolute moral perfection in this world.

14

Our Lost Condition

150. Q. *Are all transgressions of the law of God equally heinous in themselves, and in the sight of God?*

A. *All transgressions of the law of God are not equally heinous; but some sins in themselves, and by reason of several aggravations, are more heinous in the sight of God than others.*

Scripture References
- John 19:11; Ezek. 8:6, 13, 15. There are degrees of sinfulness in various actions which are contrary to God's law.
- 1 John 5:16. Sin "not unto death" and sin "unto death."
- Ps. 78:17, 32, 56. Sin rendered more heinous in God's sight by reason of various aggravating factors.

Commentary

1. What is the meaning of the word *heinous?* This word means "extremely wicked," "atrocious."

2. Are all sins *heinous,* or very wicked, in God's sight? Yes. There is no such thing as a sin that does not matter. Even the littlest sin is a sin against the infinite and holy God, and therefore even the smallest sin is infinitely evil. It has been stated that it is a great sin to love a little sin. This true statement brings out the inherent sinfulness of sin. There is no such thing as a sin that does not count against a person, or a sin that can be disregarded.

3. Are all sins *equally* wicked in God's sight? No. Although even the least sin is an offense against the holy God, and therefore absolutely evil, still, as the catechism teaches, some sins are in themselves more wicked than others, and some sins by reason of aggravating factors are more wicked in God's sight than others.

4. What is meant by the statement that some sins in themselves are more heinous in the sight of God than others? This statement means that apart from any special circumstances, some sins are more heinous than others. Thus, for example, the sin of murder is more heinous than the sin of theft; the sin of theft is more heinous than the sin of idleness or laziness.

5. How does the Roman Catholic Church misuse the Bible teaching that some sins are more heinous than others? The Roman Catholic Church teaches a false distinction between "mortal sin" and "venial sin." According to the Roman Catholic doctrine, "mortal sin" is "a grievous offense against the law of God" which "brings everlasting death and damnation on the soul," whereas "venial sin" is "a slight offense against the law of God," which only lessens the love of God in our heart, makes us less worthy of God's help, and weakens our power to resist "mortal sin."

6. Why is this Roman Catholic doctrine false? This doctrine is false because the Bible teaches that every sin, even the least, deserves God's everlasting punishment. According to the Bible, the wages of sin is death (Rom. 8:23), a general statement which includes every kind of sin. The Roman Catholic Church is wrong in teaching that some sins are only "a slight offense against the law of God." And since no sinner is worthy of God's help at all, it is wrong to speak of venial sins as making us "less worthy of God's help."

7. What common popular error gives a wrong idea of the seriousness of sin? The common popular idea is that many of what are called "little sins" are only of trifling importance and that God is too generous and kindhearted to hold them against a person. People tend to think that those sins that are commonly committed in "polite society" or among respectable people are unimportant and need not be repented of. Such sins as conventional untruthfulness, or telling "white lies," a mild or occasional use of profanity, occasionally losing one's temper, slight dishonesty or injustice in business transactions, forgetting to express thanks to God before eating our meals, are frequently regarded as mere trifles and of no real importance. Many people think they are not really sinners because they are not guilty of gross open sins such as literal murder or theft; some consider themselves "good Christians" just because they are not guilty of specially wicked sins beyond the average of their neighbors. There are those who claim that they have no real sins, though they admit that they have a few "faults" and "shortcomings." We should realize that the world's standard of sin and righteousness, and God's standard, are very different.

8. What is the meaning of the "sin unto death" and the "sin not unto death" in 1 John 5:16? The "sin unto death" is commonly understood to mean a form of sin which inevitably results in eternal death because it cuts off the possibility of repentance; that is, a deliberate, definite, and long-continued rejection of the gospel of Christ, which finally results in the Holy Spirit ceasing to plead with the person, and abandoning him to his own sinful hardness of heart. For such a person, we are not commanded even to pray. This "sin unto death" cannot be committed by a true, born-again Christian, but it may be committed by nominal Christians who have never really been born again. The "sin not unto death" is understood to mean any sin short of deliberate and permanent rejection of Christ; that is, any sin that a true Christian can commit. We are commanded to pray for those who "sin a sin which is not unto death"—that is, for our Christian brethren—and we are promised that God will answer our prayers for such persons by giving life, that is, by bringing the persons back to a spiritual state.

151. Q. *What are those aggravations that make some sins more heinous than others?*

A. *Sins receive their aggravations, 1. From the persons offending: if they be of riper age, greater experience of grace, eminent for profession, gifts, place, office, guides to others, and whose example is likely to be followed by others. . . .*

Scripture References

- Jer. 2:8. Sin is aggravated when committed by those who have a special responsibility for exemplary and godly living.

- Job 32:7, 9; Eccl. 4:13. Persons of riper age have a greater responsibility; hence when they commit sin it is more serious than the same sin committed by younger persons.
- 1 Kings 11:4, 9. Sin is aggravated when committed by persons who have had greater experience, and more blessings of God's grace than others.
- 2 Sam. 12:14; 1 Cor. 5:1. When those who make a public profession of the Christian faith commit sin, it is more serious than the same sin when committed by persons who make no such profession.
- James 4:17; Luke 12:47–48. Greater privileges involve greater responsibility, hence aggravate the sins committed by such persons.
- Jer. 5:4–5. Persons who occupy places of prominence in society are under an added obligation to do right, and when they commit sin their prominence constitutes an aggravation.
- 2 Sam. 12:7–9; Ezek. 8:11–12. Persons who hold office in church or state have an added responsibility for godly living, and when they are involved in wrongdoing their official position aggravates their sin.
- Rom. 2:17–24. Those who are, or claim to be, guides to others are under an added obligation to live righteously themselves, and when they sin it is an aggravated sin.
- Gal. 2:11–14. Those whose example is likely to be followed by others, when they are involved in wrongdoing, are guilty of aggravated sin.

Commentary

1. What is the meaning of the word *aggravations* in this question of the catechism? In this question, the word *aggravations* means anything that makes a matter heavier or more serious. An aggravation of a sin is any factor or circumstance that makes that sin more serious or wicked.

2. What general truth is taught by the first part of the answer to question 151? The first part of the answer to question 151 teaches the general truth that the same sin committed by different persons involves different degrees of guilt according to the special responsibilities of the persons concerned. Sin always involves guilt, but various factors and circumstances may increase the guilt in the case of particular persons.

3. Why are sins aggravated when committed by persons of riper age? Persons of more mature years have had a longer opportunity to learn the will of God and to experience his grace and salvation and learn to overcome temptation. It is natural to expect that aged persons will have greater wisdom and experience and better judgment than young people can be expected to have. Accordingly when people of advanced age fall into sin, it is an aggravated transgression.

4. Why does a greater measure of experience or grace increase the guilt of a person's sin? Because the person with greater experience of grace is sinning against light and conscience more than other people. The greater our experience of the grace of God, the less excuse we have for falling into sin. Experience of grace means progress in holiness: when a person who has made great progress in holiness falls into sin, he falls from a height previously attained, and this increases the guilt of his fall.

5. Why are persons who are "eminent for profession" especially guilty when they commit sin? Because the person who is eminent for profession, if he commits sin, is guilty not only of breaking God's commandments, but also of inconsistency; that is, his conduct is at variance, not only with God's law, but even with his own claims. Of course, sin is sin, no matter who commits it; but when people who are publicly known as Christians and church members are involved in sin and scandal, their very profession of faith increases their guilt before God.

6. What is meant by "gifts" and "place" aggravating a person's sins? By "gifts" the catechism means such blessings of God as knowledge of the Bible, the law of God, and the gospel of Christ, opportunities for learning the Word of God, etc. It was a sin for the Egyptians and Babylonians to worship idols, but it was a much greater sin for the people of Israel to worship idols, because they had been favored with much greater gifts of light and knowledge by God.

By "place" the catechism means one's standing or position in human society. The more prominent a person is, the greater his responsibility, and the more aggravated his transgressions. This is because all persons who are prominent in society inevitably have a greater influence on others than those who are obscure or practically unknown. When a person who is prominent before the public obtains an unscriptural divorce, the news of this is spread from coast to coast, whereas a similar action on the part of an obscure person would attract very little attention.

7. How does official position in church or state affect a person's responsibility for doing right? Those in official positions, whether in church or state, are looked up to by ordinary citizens or church members and are expected to set a good example of righteous conduct. When they fail to do so, their guilt is aggravated by their official position. Years ago an ex-president of the United States visited Europe, and shocked and scandalized the Christian people of Holland by traveling on trains on the Sabbath day. Many American tourists in Holland had committed the same sin, but when a former president of the United States did it, it was particularly offensive, and of course involved aggravated guilt. Similarly, when a minister, elder, or deacon in the church is involved in wrongdoing, this is more serious than the same sin committed by an ordinary church member would be.

8. How does responsibility for the moral welfare of others affect the seriousness of a person's sins? As members of human society, and especially as Christians, we have a responsibility for the moral welfare of our neighbor. Our responsibility for our sins is measured not only by the actual sins themselves, but also by their influence on other people. Therefore those who are in positions of leadership, who are guides to others, and whose example is likely to be followed by others have an added responsibility, and when they commit sin it is aggravated transgression. Thus, for example, a schoolteacher's example is likely to be followed by the pupils; older children's actions are likely to be imitated by younger children; what church members see their church officers doing they naturally tend to think will be all right for them to copy themselves, etc. Persons whose sinful conduct leads others into sin clearly have a double sin to account for—their own sin, and the sin of their neighbor whom they have led astray.

151. Q. *(continued) What are those aggravations that make some sins more heinous than others?*

A. *Sins receive their aggravations. . . . 2. From the parties offended; if immediately against God, his attributes, and worship; against Christ, and his grace; the Holy Spirit, his witness, and workings, against superiors, men of eminency, and such as we stand especially related and engaged unto; against any of the saints, particularly weak brethren, the souls of them, or any other, and the common good of all or many. . . .*

Scripture References

- Matt. 21:38–39. An example of the wickedness of a sin increased by reason of the position of the person injured by the sin.
- 1 Sam. 2:25; Acts 5:4; Ps. 51:4; Rom. 2:4; Mal. 1:8, 14. The guilt of a sin is increased when it is committed directly against God and his attributes and worship.
- Heb. 2:2–3; 12:25. Those who sin against the Lord Jesus Christ and his grace are guilty of aggravated transgression.
- Heb. 10:29; 6:4–6; Matt. 12:31–32; Eph. 4:30. Those who sin against the Holy Spirit and his witness and workings are guilty of sin of aggravated seriousness.
- Jude 8; Num. 12:8–9; Isa. 3:5. It is especially offensive to God when offenses are committed against persons who should be specially honored and respected for any reason.
- Prov. 30:17; 2 Cor. 12:15; Ps. 55:12–15. To sin against those to whom we are closely related, or especially obligated, is to be guilty of aggravated sin.
- Zeph. 2:8–11; Matt. 18:6; 1 Cor. 6:8; Rev. 17:6. Any offense against Christian people is an aggravated offense in God's sight.
- 1 Cor. 8:11–12; Rom. 14:13, 15, 21. It is our duty to be especially considerate concerning weak brethren, and therefore any offense which injures them is an aggravated sin against God.
- Ezek. 13:19; 1 Cor. 8:12; Rev. 18:12–13; Matt. 23:15. Any offense which imperils the souls of others, or works against their salvation, is especially heinous in God's sight.
- 1 Thess. 2:15–16; Josh. 22.20. A sin which involves others, or which interferes with the true welfare of all or many, is an aggravated transgression.

Commentary

1. Can we sin against men, or only against God? Strictly speaking, we can sin only against God, our Creator and Judge, to whom we are morally responsible. We injure our fellow men, but in doing so we sin against God. Therefore David, who had grievously injured Uriah and Bathsheba, nevertheless said in his prayer to God, "Against thee, thee only, have I sinned." Strictly speaking, we cannot injure God, and we cannot sin against men. But in our common speech we often say that we have sinned against men, and the Bible itself uses such language sometimes. This is of course perfectly proper, provided we understand that in the strict sense of the words we sin only against God, and injure only our fellow men. Our moral responsibility is solely to God.

2. What part of the Ten Commandments deals with sins committed directly against God? The first "table" of the law, or the first four commandments.

3. Why are sins committed directly against God especially heinous? Because of the infinite majesty and holiness of God, against whom such sins offend, and because our highest obligation is to love the Lord our God with all our heart, soul, mind, and strength. Thus the person who sins directly against God disregards and violates his highest obligation.

4. In what ways do men sin directly against God? Men sin directly against God by violating the commandments of the first table of the law. Particularly flagrant are such sins as atheism, idolatry, taking God's name in vain, and Sabbath-breaking. All those, in their many forms, are sins directly against God; some are sins directly against God himself as a person; others are sins directly against God as revealed in his worship, ordinances, etc.

5. Why are sins against Christ, and his grace, especially heinous in God's sight? (a) Because Christ is himself truly God, just as the Father is, and therefore to sin against Christ is the same as to sin against God. (b) Because Christ's grace is the gift of God's love to lost and guilty sinners, and the person who sins against Christ's grace is sinning against the love and mercy of God, which should lead him to repentance.

6. Give a Bible instance of someone who sinned against the Holy Spirit. Ananias: Acts 5:3 ("to lie to the Holy Ghost") and verse 4 ("Thou hast not lied unto men, but unto God").

7. Why is sinning against the witness and workings of the Holy Spirit especially heinous in God's sight? Because the Holy Spirit is given by God's love and grace to dwell and work in the hearts of his people. Those who sin against the inward witness and workings of the Holy Spirit are treating this gracious gift of God with contempt. Not every sin against the inward work of the Holy Spirit is the "unpardonable" sin mentioned in the Bible. But every person who resists or despises the inward work of the Holy Spirit is guilty of aggravated sin.

8. Why are offenses against "superiors" and "men of eminency" especially serious? We are under special obligations to treat some persons with honor and respect. For example, children are commanded to honor their parents, and it is the duty of citizens to honor those in positions of authority in the state. Similarly, in God's Word it is commanded that aged people be treated with honor and respect. Where there is a special obligation to honor and respect, any offense that is committed must be regarded as an aggravated offense. Thus, while it is wrong to slander any person, it is an aggravated offense to slander the president of our country, or any other public official.

9. Why is it a heinous sin to injure "such as we stand especially related and engaged unto"? The closer the relationship to any person, the greater our obligation to treat that person with justice and love. This is true regardless of whether the relationship is a blood relationship, or a social connection of some other kind. It is our duty to treat all our fellow men with justice and love, but especially those who, in God's providence, are closely connected with us in some way or other. This truth is often forgotten and disregarded. People often treat outsiders better than they treat their own family. But it ought not to be so. One's own family, one's own relations, one's own employer, employees, etc., have a special claim on one's consideration. An injury done to such is an aggravated offense in God's sight.

10. What should we think of offenses committed against our fellow Christians? Offenses committed against our fellow Christians are especially grievous in God's sight. This does not mean merely members of our own church, but "any of the saints," as the catechism rightly affirms. That is, all Christian people are our brethren in Christ and have a special claim on our consideration; an offense against any of them involves one member of the body of Christ injuring another member of the body of Christ. One of Satan's most effective ways of hindering God's cause in the world is by stirring up quarrels and trouble between Christian people. In the Bible this is called "discord among brethren," and we are told that sowing discord among brethren is one of the things that God hates (Prov. 6:19).

11. What is meant by "weak brethren"? Romans 14 gives the key to the meaning of this expression. Briefly, a "weak brother" is a true Christian whose knowledge is defective, and whose faith, although real, is yet weak and wavering. He may have scruples of conscience about matters which are not really wrong at all, and he may be easily scandalized and discouraged by seeing other Christians doing things which he considers wrong. The "weak brother" has a really hard time to keep on going forward in the Christian life. Such people should have special consideration on the part of other Christians, but this does not mean that the scruples of the weak brother are to be imposed on other Christians as necessary rules of conduct, or that the weak brother is to be allowed to dominate the church and dictate to its officers and members. The weak brother's scruples constitute an infirmity to be tolerated, not a platform to be propagated by the church as a whole. But we should be careful to avoid offending against weak brethren, that is, shocking and scandalizing them needlessly by conduct which they consider wrong, even though it may not really be wrong in itself. Such disregard of the problems and difficulties of weak brethren is a heinous sin against Christ (1 Cor. 8:12).

12. Why is it an aggravated sin to offend against "the common good of all or many"? We are all members of human society, and as Christians we are all members of the body of Christ, the church. If each individual person could live out his life alone on an isolated island as Robinson Crusoe did for several years, he would have only God and himself to think of in connection with his moral life. But we cannot live like Robinson Crusoe. We are members of society, and as such we are mutually dependent. Therefore we must realize that any sin we commit may involve three parties—God, ourself, and our neighbor (or society in general). Obviously, the more people affected or injured by our conduct, the greater will be our guilt before God. Thus a person whose criminal negligence results in a train being wrecked, a hotel destroyed by fire, or a great forest fire started is much more guilty than one whose carelessness has endangered only his own life or his own property.

151. Q. *(continued) What are those aggravations that make some sins more heinous than others?*

     A. *Sins receive their aggravations. . . . 3. From the nature and quality of the offence: if it be against the express letter of the law, break many commandments, contain in it many sins; if not only conceived in the heart, but breaks forth in words and actions, scandalize others, and admit of no reparation; . . .*

Scripture References

- Prov. 6:30–33. The seriousness of a sin depends, in part, on the nature and quality of the offense committed.
- Ezra 9:10–12; 1 Kings 11:9–10. Offenses against the express letter of God's law are especially heinous, since they violate a direct command of God.
- Col. 3:5; 1 Tim. 6:10; Prov. 5:8–12; Josh. 7:21. An offense which involves breaking several of the commandments, or committing many sins, is especially displeasing to God.
- James 1:14–15; Matt. 5:22; Mic. 2:1. When sin not only is conceived in the heart, but breaks forth into words and actions, it is of aggravated seriousness.
- Matt. 18:7; Rom. 2:23–24. A sin which scandalizes others is an aggravated offense in God's sight.
- 2 Sam. 12:7–10. A sin which admits of no reparation is especially heinous in God's sight.

Commentary

1. What is meant by "the nature and quality of the offence"? This expression means the inherent character of an offense, considered apart from all questions of persons and circumstances. Thus murder is a more heinous sin than theft, entirely regardless of who the murderer or thief may be, who may be the victims of the crimes, the time, place, etc. No matter who does it, or when or where or why, murder is in itself more wicked than theft.

2. What is meant by "the express letter of the law"? This means the actual words of the law of God as given in the Scripture. Thus to steal is against the express letter of the law, for God's law commands, in so many words, "Thou shalt not steal." But to participate in a raffle or a lottery, although sinful, is not against the express letter of the law. It requires a process of logical reasoning based on the law of God in the Bible to prove that raffles and lotteries are sinful.

3. Give some examples of offenses which involve breaking many commandments, or committing many sins. (a) The Bible teaches that covetousness is idolatry. Thus the person who covets also commits idolatry, by setting his heart on worldly possessions. (b) Sabbath-breaking also involves the sins of theft, irreverence, and taking God's name in vain. The person who breaks the Sabbath in doing so violates the second, third, fourth, and eighth commandments.

4. Where do all sins originate? In the "heart" or innermost character of a person. (Read Mark 7:21–23.) Sin proceeds from the heart, and finally finds expression in the outward conduct (words and deeds) of the person.

5. Which is more wicked, to harbor sin in the heart, or to express it in actual conduct? To express the sin in actual conduct is much more wicked, although we should not forget that even to conceive a sin in the heart is sinful in God's sight. But the sin which is expressed in actual conduct is even more wicked, because it is a fuller development of rebellion against God. Read James 1:14–15, and note how these verses teach this very truth.

6. Why is a sin which has the effect of scandalizing others especially grievous in God's sight? Because such a sin concerns not merely two, but three parties, namely, oneself, one's neighbor, and God. A sin which does not affect other persons, or a secret sin known only to the sinner and God, is sinful and offensive to God; much more offensive is the sin which scandalizes others, or tempts others to sin too. Thus Eve's sin of eating the forbidden fruit had the effect of leading Adam to commit sin too; this multiplied its seriousness in God's sight.

7. What is meant by an offense which admits of no reparation? So far as our relation to God is concerned, no sin that a person commits admits of any reparation. We are all guilty before God, and only the shed blood of Jesus Christ can take away the guilt of our sin. But in our relation to our fellow men some sins admit of reparation, and others do not. For example, the sin of theft admits of reparation; a person who has stolen a sum of money from his neighbor can pay the money back. But the sins of murder and adultery do not admit of reparation; when once the wrong is done to our neighbor, there is no way by which it can be undone. The sin of bearing false witness against our neighbor may or may not admit of reparation. Thus, for example, if a person were to bear false witness in court, and then during the same session of the court confess this sin and retract the false statement, the harm done would be largely undone. But if the retraction were made years later, it would be too late to undo the wrong done.

151. Q. *(continued) What are those aggravations that make some sins more heinous than others?*

A. *Sins receive their aggravations, . . . 3. From the nature and quality of the offence: . . . if against means, mercies, judgments, light of nature, conviction of conscience, public or private admonition, censures of the church, civil punishments; and our prayers, purposes, promises, vows, covenants, and engagements to God or men: . . .*

Scripture References

- Matt. 11:21–24; John 15:22. Sins are aggravated when committed in spite of means used by God which should restrain sin.
- Isa. 1:3; Deut. 32:6. Sins committed in spite of God's special mercies are aggravated transgressions.
- Amos 4:8–11; Jer. 5:3. To sin against God's judgments is to commit aggravated sin.
- Rom. 1:26–27; 1 Cor. 11:14–15. It is especially sinful to do what nature, even apart from Scripture, shows to be wrong.
- Rom. 13:2; Dan. 5:22; Titus 3:10–11. Those who sin in spite of the conviction of their own conscience commit aggravated transgression.
- Prov. 29:1. Sin is aggravated by being committed in spite of warning or reproof.
- Titus 3:10; Matt. 18:17. Sin is aggravated by being committed in spite of the censures of church discipline.
- Prov. 27:22; 23:35. Those who disregard civil penalties become guilty of aggravated transgression.
- Ps. 78:34–37; Jer. 2:20; 42:5–6, 20–21; Eccl. 5:4–6; Prov. 2:17; 20:25; Lev. 26:25; Ezek. 17:18–19. Sins committed in spite of our own promises, vows, covenants, etc., are aggravated transgressions.

Commentary

1. What is meant by sins committed against means? As used in the catechism, this expression means sins committed in spite of special acts of God which should have the effect of restraining people's sinning. In Bible times such special acts of God often took the form of miracles; in our own day they may take the form of special and remarkable workings of God's providence, which should have the effect of making us stop and abstain from sin.

2. How do people sin against God's mercies? All human beings sin against God's mercies continually, inasmuch as the very continuance of our existence depends on the free mercy of God. "It is of the LORD's mercies that we are not consumed, because his compassions fail not. They are new every morning: great is thy faithfulness" (Lam. 3:22–23). Christian people especially sin against God's mercies, since Christian people have received the special mercy of God in his salvation. There are also cases where people sin against particular special mercies and blessings which they have received from God; for example, where a person is by God's mercy delivered from danger of death, or from serious illness, and then instead of turning to God in repentance and faith, simply forgets God and lives a selfish, worldly life. Clearly all sinning against God's mercies amounts to aggravated transgression.

3. What is meant by sinning against God's judgments? In the case of those who are not God's children, God's judgments are sent both to punish them for their sins and to warn them against continuing in sin. In the case of God's own children, his judgments are for the purpose of chastening, that is, to bring about their sanctification and prevent their being condemned with the world (1 Cor. 11:32). In either case, God's judgments should have the effect of leading a person to repentance and submission and obedience to God. In the book of Revelation we read symbolic descriptions of many terrible judgments of God upon an unbelieving and Christ-rejecting world, several times with the added statement that these judgments did not bring about repentance (Rev. 9:20–21; 16:9, 11). Such continued sinning in spite of divine judgments greatly increases people's guilt before God.

4. What is meant by the "light of nature," and how do people sin against it? By the expression "light of nature" the catechism means that elementary knowledge of God and of moral obligation which men have from the general revelation of God in the world of nature and the human heart and conscience, apart from God's special revelation in Scripture. The light of nature is not sufficient for salvation, but it is sufficient to teach men that there is a God, that it is their duty to worship and honor him, and that certain things are wrong. Thus the light of nature leaves men without excuse (Rom. 1:20). The light of nature, apart from Scripture, is in no sense adequate as a rule of conduct for sinners, but it does teach men that certain sins, such as murder, atheism, and dishonesty, are wrong. When people commit sins which not only the Bible, but even the light of nature shows to be sinful, they are guilty of aggravated transgression. The person who sins against the light of nature sins against the law of God written in the constitution of his own being (Rom. 2:14–16), and thus violates not only God's revelation but his own psychical makeup.

5. How do people sin against "conviction of conscience"? Conscience is that moral thermometer within our soul that registers disapproval when we act contrary to what we believe to be right, and approval when our action is in harmony with what we believe to be right. Conscience cannot tell us what is right and what is wrong; it can only tell us whether we are acting according to what we believe to be right or wrong in any case. A person's conscience needs to be enlightened by the moral law revealed in Scripture. But it is always wrong to act against conscience; that is, it is always a sin to drive past the red light of conscience and do something which we believe to be wrong. There is a general operation of conscience, caused by the general operation of the Holy Spirit, in all human beings except those who have committed the "unpardonable" sin and have been abandoned by God to the most extreme moral and spiritual hardening. Apart from such exceptional cases, every person has some conviction of conscience, or sense of right and wrong. To disregard this is to commit aggravated sin. The Christian, by the special grace and operation of the Holy Spirit (through the new birth and sanctification), has a quickened or highly sensitized conscience, which functions far more quickly and accurately than the conscience of the non-Christian person. Yet even Christian people, because of their indwelling sinful nature, often act against conviction of conscience. In the case of the Christian, acting against conscience is even more heinous than in the case of the non-Christian person.

6. Why does sinning against "public or private admonition, censures of the church, civil punishments" involve increased guilt before God? Because all these admonitions, censures, and punishments are ways by which God shows his displeasure against sin and warns men to turn from it and practice righteousness. The church and the state are both divine institutions, and as God's servants each in its own sphere and manner are to warn against wrongdoing and to encourage men in well doing. The person who goes on in a course of sinful conduct in spite of one or more of these forms of warning and reproof is hardening himself in sin and rebellion against God. The more warnings he disregards, the greater his guilt.

7. Why does acting contrary to our own prayers, purposes, promises, vows, etc., involve aggravated sin before God? Our own prayers, purposes, promises, vows, etc., are an abomination to God unless they are sincere; that is, unless we really mean them from the bottom of our heart and intend, by God's help, to live according to them for all time to come. If our prayers, etc., are not sincere, then they are hypocritical and God will not accept them (Ps. 68:18). If they are sincere, but at a later time we act contrary to them, this indicates backsliding or falling from a spiritual to a more or less carnal state. To allow ourselves to slip or retreat from high ground already attained in our Christian life must always be very displeasing to God and an offense against his holiness, and involves increased guilt which can only be cleansed away by the blood of Jesus Christ.

151. **Q.** *(continued) What are those aggravations that make some sins more heinous than others?*

A. *Sins receive their aggravations, . . . 3. From the nature and quality of the offence: . . . if done deliberately, willfully, presumptuously, impudently, boastingly, maliciously, frequently, obstinately, with delight, continuance, or relapsing after repentance. . . .*

Scripture References
- Ps. 36:4; Jer. 6:16; Num. 15:30; Exod. 21:24. Deliberate, willful, and presumptuous sinning.
- Jer. 3:3; Prov. 7:13. Impudent sinning.
- Ps. 52:1. Boastful sinning.
- 3 John 10. Malicious sinning.
- Num. 14:22; Zech. 7:11–12; Prov. 2:14; Isa. 57:17. The wickedness of a person's sin is increased by stubbornness, persistence, delight, and various other characteristics.

Commentary
1. What is meant by sinning "deliberately, willfully, presumptuously"? These three adverbs are closely related in their meaning in connection with sin. To sin deliberately is to sin after some consideration of the matter in one's mind. To sin willfully is to sin with the attitude of being bent on having one's own way, no matter whether it is right or wrong. To sin

presumptuously is to sin intentionally, counting on God's grace to bestow forgiveness for our sin afterwards. Deliberate, willful, and presumptuous sinning is to be contrasted with unintentional sinning, sinning resulting from weakness or sudden temptation rather than from a set purpose to sin, and sin resulting from ignorance or a faulty understanding of the requirements of God's law. Clearly all deliberate, presumptuous, and willful sinning is heinous and highly offensive to God.

2. What special form of willful sinning is common in the present day? Unwillingness to submit our judgments, opinions, and practices to the authority of the Holy Scripture, which is the special revelation of God's truth and will. There are those who frankly admit that the Bible requires the singing of the inspired Psalms exclusively, and without instrumental music, in the worship of God, who yet say, "I like hymns and instrumental music and I intend to have them." Some who would not say this in words say it by their actions, even contradicting their own voluntary profession by their inconsistent practices. Similarly there are persons who are violently opposed to the Calvinistic doctrine of predestination or election, who yet do not venture to deny that it is taught in the Scriptures. It is one thing to fail to grasp or understand the teaching of the Scriptures about some matter; it is quite a different thing to refuse to submit ourselves to a doctrine or principle which we admit to be scriptural. Willful rejection of a teaching of God's Word, understood and admitted to be such, is one of the most awful sins that a person can commit.

3. Give some Bible examples of godly people who sinned deliberately, willfully, or presumptuously. (a) David's sin in numbering the people of Israel, even after Joab had tried to dissuade him from it (2 Sam. 21:1–14). (b) Peter's sin of dissimulation, for which Paul rebuked him to his face (Gal. 2:11–14).

4. What is meant by sinning "impudently, boastingly, maliciously"? To sin impudently is to sin boldly, without any feeling of shame because of our sin. The person who sins impudently makes no attempt to conceal his sin; he does not care who knows about it. The person who sins boastingly goes one step even beyond this; he is even proud of his sinning, and brags about it to others; his glory is in his shame (Phil. 3:19). When Claverhouse shot the covenanter martyr John Brown and then on being asked "How will you answer for this morning's work?" replied, "To man I can be answerable, and as for God I will take him into my own hands!," he sinned impudently and boastingly.

To sin maliciously is to sin with spite or enmity against God or God's people. When officials of the Roman Empire were not satisfied with taking the lives of Christian people, but did it in the most cruel and inhuman ways that could be invented, by lingering, excruciating tortures, they were guilty of sinning maliciously against God.

5. What makes people sin "frequently, obstinately, with delight, continuance"? It is the perverse, wicked stubbornness and hardness of the human heart that brings about such inveterate sinning. It can only be explained by the Bible doctrines of original sin and total depravity. According to God's Word, sin is not a superficial defect in human nature, but a deeply rooted, all-pervasive moral corruption. The heart is deceitful above all things, and desperately wicked. Thus there are people who actually sin not with regret or remorse, but with pleasure and delight (Rom. 1:32). Indeed it is really true of all unconverted people that they love sin (2 Tim. 3:4), and only the common grace of God restrains this natural love of sin from finding its fullest expression in outward deeds of iniquity and abomination.

6. Why does relapsing after repentance aggravate the seriousness of a person's sin? Relapsing after repentance is particularly offensive to God because it involves a fall from a degree of separation from sin previously attained. This is peculiarly a sin of Christian people, for the person who is not a Christian never really repents in the true sense of the word. The non-Christian may experience a kind of natural regret for sin and a resolution to "turn over a new leaf," but as he has not been born again this "repentance" is not real "repentance unto life." Christian people experience true repentance unto life, and yet often fall back into various sins of which they had once truly repented before God. In their case this lapse will be only temporary and will be followed ultimately by new repentance and restoration to a spiritual state. But even a temporary lapse into our old sins grieves the Holy Spirit and displeases God. The only way of preventing it is by constant self-distrust, spiritual watchfulness, and prayer.

151. Q. *(continued) What are those aggravations that make some sins more heinous than others?*

A. *Sins receive their aggravations, . . . 4. From circumstances of time and place: if on the Lord's day, or other times of divine worship; or immediately before or after these, or other helps to prevent or remedy such miscarriages; if in public, or in the presence of others, who are thereby likely to be provoked or defiled.*

Scripture References

- 2 Kings 5:26; Jer. 7:10; Isa. 28:10. Sins aggravated by circumstances of time and place.
- Ezek. 23:37–39; Isa. 58:3–5; Num. 25:6–7. Sins aggravated by being committed on the Lord's Day, or other times of divine worship.
- 1 Cor. 11:20–21; Jer. 7:8–10; Prov. 7:14–15; John 13:27, 30. The guilt of sins increased by their being committed immediately before or after divine worship.
- Ezra 9:13–14. Sin aggravated by commission directly after experiencing God's chastisements.
- 2 Sam. 16:22; 1 Sam. 2:22–24. Sin rendered more heinous by reason of its being committed publicly, or in such a manner as to scandalize others.

Commentary

1. Why may circumstances of time and place increase the guilt of people's sins? There are certain circumstances of time and place which are calculated to impress upon our minds the seriousness of our duty to God and the requirements of his moral law. When these circumstances of time and place are disregarded, and sin committed in spite of them, the sin is flagrant and the guilt aggravated. For Judas to betray Christ would have been wrong at any time, but when it was done so soon after the observance of the Passover and the institution of the Lord's Supper, Judas's guilt was greatly increased.

2. Why does a sin committed on the Lord's Day, or other appointed time of divine worship, or immediately before or after such occasions, involve aggravated guilt? Because such a sin involves not only the guilt of the sin in itself, but the added guilt of profanation of the Lord's Day or other ordinances of divine worship. In Matthew 12:9–14 we read that the Pharisees held a meeting on the Sabbath, the purpose of which was to devise a plan for killing Jesus. A meeting the purpose of which is a conspiracy to commit murder is unlawful regardless of time or place; but when it was held on the Sabbath day, the Pharisees' guilt was greatly increased.

3. How is guilt increased by disregard of recently experienced special providences of God? The special providences of God which enter our lives are intended to make us "stand in awe, and sin not" (Ps. 4:4), that is, they should lead us to stop and think about our moral condition and our relation to God. When we disregard such special providences, we inevitably harden our own hearts and increase the guilt of our sin. To deny Christ is a great sin at any time; when Peter committed it three times in succession, all within a few hours after he had been specially warned by the Lord concerning that very matter, it was an even more serious sin.

4. Why are sins committed publicly, or in such a way as to have a bad influence on others, especially wicked in God's sight? There is a true sense in which each of us is his brother's keeper. We have a moral responsibility for our neighbor as well as for ourselves. A sin committed privately, or known only to a few persons, is wrong and offensive to God; one committed publicly must inevitably have a bad effect on many persons, and so involves added guilt before God. For a person to use the golden and silver vessels of God's holy temple for drinking wine would be sinful even if done with the utmost privacy; when King Belshazzar did it publicly, in the presence of a thousand of his lords, accompanied by his princes, wives, and concubines, the guilt was necessarily aggravated (Dan. 5:1–4, 23). It would be easy to think of many forms of sin whose guilt is aggravated by commission in a public manner.

152. Q. *What doth every sin deserve at the hands of God?*

A. *Every sin, even the least, being against the sovereignty, goodness, and holiness of God, and against his righteous law, deserveth his wrath and curse, both in this life, and that which is to come; and cannot be expiated but by the blood of Christ.*

Scripture References

- James 2:10–11; Exod. 20:1–2; Hab. 1:13; Lev. 10:3; 11:44–45. Every sin is committed against the sovereignty, goodness, and holiness of God.
- 1 John 3:4; Rom. 7:12. Every sin is a violation of God's righteous law.
- Eph. 5:6; Gal. 3:10. Every sin deserves God's wrath and curse.
- Lam. 3:39; Deut. 28:15–19; Matt. 25:41. All sin deserves not only temporal but eternal punishment.
- Heb. 9:22; 1 Peter 1:18–19. No sin can be canceled except by the blood of Christ.

Commentary

1. How evil is sin? The catechism asserts, and the Scripture references prove, that sin is absolutely evil; that is, that sin possesses an absolute character, and even the least sin shares in that absolute character as a repudiation of the authority of God. Some sins are more heinous than others, but even the least sin is a total rejection of God's authority over us. This principle is well illustrated by the first sin committed by any human being, the sin of Adam and Eve in eating the forbidden fruit. In itself what can seem to us a slight and apparently unimportant action, the eating of the fruit nevertheless involved a total rejection of God's authority over the human race. It involved believing Satan's lie in preference to God's truth, and trusting human reason rather than God's revelation. The same is true, essentially, of every sin; every sin involves believing a lie rather than the truth, and following our own reason or desires rather than the revealed will of God. Thus every sin is absolutely evil, and deserves God's wrath and curse both here and hereafter.

2. How can a finite being, such as man, commit a sin which is absolutely or infinitely evil? Sin is infinitely evil because it is committed against God, who is infinitely perfect. We must always guard against the modern humanistic way of thinking about sin, which tends to regard sin primarily in relation to its effects on human beings. The primary fact about sin is that it is an offense against God. Since God is infinite, eternal, and unchangeable in his sovereignty, goodness, and holiness, every sin, even though committed by a finite creature such as man, is infinitely evil.

3. What does the character of God's law show about the wages of sin? God's law is a perfect law, and it demands perfect righteousness of human beings. The moral law of God does not require of us mere "goodness," but absolute moral perfection. Any deviation, even the slightest, from absolute moral perfection is sin. Since this is true, even the slightest deviation from absolute moral perfection deserves the penalty of the broken law; that is, the penalty of death in its widest sense, physical, spiritual, and eternal.

4. What is meant by the "wrath and curse" of God? God's wrath is his righteous indignation and displeasure against sin and sinners; it is the opposite of love and grace, and means that God cannot regard sinners with favor or complacency (except on the basis of an atonement provided to take away their sin). God's curse is the expression of his wrath in the form of a penalty. God's wrath is an attitude toward sinners; God's curse is the attitude carried into action against them. Thus every sin deserves God's indignation and punishment in this life and the life to come. Read Romans 1:18; Ephesians 2:3.

5. Why does every sin deserve the wrath and curse of God eternally? Because every sin is a sin against the eternal God. Many people have stumbled over this truth, objecting that it cannot be just for God to punish temporal sin with eternal penalties. But whether men like this doctrine or not, the Bible definitely teaches it. Even though sin is committed in time, it is committed against the God who is above and beyond time, and thus incurs his wrath and curse beyond the limits of time, that is, beyond the present earthly life. Moreover it is the nature of sin, once started, to go on without ceasing (unless the person is redeemed by Christ). The person who is guilty of sin not only cannot remove the guilt of that sin, but goes on and on in rebellion against God, always becoming more and more guilty and more and more evil. Thus in the nature of the case sin deserves eternal punishment.

6. How alone can sin be expiated or canceled? Sin can be expiated or canceled in no other way than by the blood of Christ, who suffered and died as the divinely provided substitute for guilty sinners. Every human being deserves God's eternal wrath and curse; that all do not actually suffer his wrath and curse to all eternity is due only to the free grace and mercy of God in giving his Son to bear the penalty of the broken law as a substitute. This implies, of course, that all attempted human ways of dealing with sin are wrong and useless. The person who tries to take away his own sin by moral reform, good resolutions, "turning over a new leaf," performing good works, acts of charity, religious observances, forms and ceremonies, church membership, prayer, ascetic practices, or any other way whatever is a miserable, self-deceived sinner on the road to eternal frustration in hell. Only the precious blood of Christ, the Lamb of God, can take away the guilt of human sin. There is no other way.

15

Repentance, Faith, and Use of the Word

153. Q. *What doth God require of us that we may escape his wrath and curse due to us by reason of the transgression of the law?*

A. *That we may escape the wrath and curse of God due to us by reason of the transgression of the law, he requireth of us repentance toward God, and faith toward our Lord Jesus Christ, and the diligent use of the outward means whereby Christ communicates to us the benefits of his meditation.*

Scripture References

- Acts 20:21; Matt. 3:7–8; Luke 13:3, 5; Acts 16:30–31; John 3:16, 18. That we may escape God's wrath and curse, he requires of us true repentance accompanied by faith in Jesus Christ as our Savior.
- Prov. 2:1–5; 8:33–36. Besides the spiritual attitudes of repentance and faith, God requires us to use diligently the outward means by which the benefits of Christ's saving work are communicated to us.

Commentary

1. Why did God provide a way by which human beings could escape his wrath and curse for their sin? Because of God's great love, which led him, even in eternity before the creation of the world, to decree a plan of salvation by means of which his elect would in due time be redeemed and saved from their sin.

431

2. When was the way of escape from God's wrath and curse first revealed to the human race? Immediately after the fall, when God promised that at some future day the seed of the woman (Jesus Christ) would crush the head of the serpent (Satan, and so also Satan's kingdom) (Gen. 3:15).

3. How are we to take advantage of the way of escape from his wrath and curse which God has provided? We are to take advantage of this way of escape by complying with God's revealed requirements concerning it, which are outlined in the catechism as including (a) repentance toward God; (b) faith in Jesus Christ; (c) diligent use of appointed outward means.

4. Why is repentance necessary for escape from God's wrath and curse? To escape from God's wrath and curse means to be saved from sin. We cannot be saved from sin without recognizing the awful evil of our sin, hating it with our whole soul, and earnestly desiring to be delivered not only from its guilt but also from its power. That is to say, we cannot be saved from sin while we still desire and intend to continue in sin. If we are to escape God's wrath and curse, we must turn from our sins to God.

5. What is meant by "faith toward our Lord Jesus Christ," and why is it necessary for salvation from God's wrath and curse? By "faith toward our Lord Jesus Christ," the catechism means true, saving faith in Christ; that is, (a) Jesus Christ being regarded as the object, and not merely the example, of our faith; we are to have faith *in* Christ. (b) Our faith is to be faith in the real Christ, as he is revealed to us in the Scriptures; that is, we are to have faith in him as our Redeemer, prophet, priest, and king, the one and only Mediator between God and ourselves, and only way of salvation. (c) We are to put our trust and confidence for salvation and eternal life wholly and only in Christ, not at all in ourselves or anything we can do.

6. Why is diligent use of the outward means of grace necessary if we are to escape God's wrath and curse for our sin? God has chosen to appoint these outward means of grace (the Word, the sacraments, and prayer) as instruments by which the benefits of Christ's saving work are communicated to us. These means of themselves cannot save us; it is only Christ that can save us; but he makes use of these appointed means. Therefore if we would have Christ and make sure of an interest in him, we must be diligent in our use of the appointed means. The false tendency called "mysticism" despises and neglects the use of these outward means of grace, and is therefore contrary to the Scriptures and spiritually dangerous. Of course God could have made a plan to save sinners without the use of outward means of grace; but he has not chosen to do so, and so we must avail ourselves of the means which God has provided.

154. Q. *What are the outward means whereby Christ communicates to us the benefits of his mediation?*

A. *The outward and ordinary means whereby Christ communicates to his church the benefits of his mediation, are all his ordinances, especially the word, sacraments, and prayer; all which are made effectual to the elect for their salvation.*

Scripture References

- Matt. 28:19–20. The preaching of the gospel, and the sacrament of baptism, appointed by Christ as means of salvation.
- Acts 2:42, 46–47. The word and the sacrament of the Lord's Supper are means of grace, used by God for the salvation of his elect.
- Eph. 6:17–18. The Word of God and prayer are appointed means of grace.

Commentary

1. Why does the catechism speak of "outward and ordinary means" used by Christ for the salvation of his people? These means—the Word, sacraments, and prayer—are called "outward" to distinguish them from the inward work of the Holy Spirit by which we are born again, sanctified, etc. These means are called "ordinary" because in ordinary cases the Holy Spirit makes use of them to bring about a person's salvation, although in special cases (infants dying in infancy; persons mentally incapable of using means) the Holy Spirit may bring about a person's salvation entirely by his inward Word, apart from any use of outward means.

2. Are means of grace, such as the Word, sacraments, and prayer, necessary for salvation? As explained in the previous question, these means of grace are necessary in ordinary cases. They are the appointed way by which the Holy Spirit does his work. Therefore these appointed means of grace ought to be used with earnestness and in faith, if we would make sure of our salvation. However, the saving grace of God is not absolutely tied to these outward means, as if the Holy Spirit could not work without them. We should avoid the error of Romanism, on the one hand, which regards salvation as absolutely dependent on sacraments, and the error of Mysticism, on the other hand, which regards the sacraments and other outward means as unnecessary and without value. Our catechism sets forth the exact truth as presented in the Bible, namely, that the Word, sacraments, and prayer are "the outward and ordinary means" by which God's elect are brought to salvation.

3. What benefits come to us by the use of the Word, sacraments, and prayer? The benefits of Christ's mediation; that is, all the benefits and blessings which Christ purchased for his people through his perfect life and his sufferings and death on the cross. These benefits include the sum total of all that is good and valuable, for all eternity. We are made "heirs of God, and joint heirs with Christ" (Rom. 8:16–17).

4. What does the catechism mean by "the word"? By "the word" the catechism means the Holy Bible, the written Word of God, and the message of truth about God, man, and salvation which the Bible presents and which is usually conveyed by preaching. Of course a person can be saved without having actually read the Bible itself, provided certain truths of the Bible have become known to him. But it would hardly be possible to overrate the importance of the Bible itself as a book. All real knowledge of the way of salvation can be traced back to the written Word of God.

5. What does the catechism mean by "sacraments"? By "sacraments" the catechism means baptism and the Lord's Supper. These only were appointed by Christ, and therefore these are the only true sacraments. Those added by the Church of Rome are not sacraments. Part of them (such as marriage and ordination) are divine ordinances; part of them (such as penance and extreme unction) are human inventions or corruptions of the worship of God. But only baptism and the Lord's Supper are sacraments.

6. What does the catechism mean by "prayer"? By "prayer" the catechism means *Christian prayer*. There are two things necessary to make a prayer a Christian prayer: (a) It must be a prayer addressed to the true God, the God revealed in the Bible; (b) it must be a prayer in the name of Jesus Christ, who is the only real way of approach to the throne of God. Thus prayers to the gods of the heathen religions, and prayers to the Virgin Mary, the saints and angels, etc., are both useless and wrong; and any prayer which attempts to reach God's presence directly without faith in Christ as Mediator is not a Christian prayer.

7. To whom are the means of grace made effectual for salvation? To the elect of God (Acts 2:47). Those whom God has foreordained to eternal life he will, sooner or later, bring out of their sin into a state of salvation. In ordinary cases, this is accomplished by means of the Word, sacraments, and prayer. The fact that a person is really in earnest about using these means of grace is a sign that the Holy Spirit is working in that person toward bringing about his salvation.

8. Since the Holy Spirit makes these means of grace effectual for the salvation of the elect, is it necessary for us to make any effort ourselves to use the means of grace? Yes. The Bible commands us to use the means of grace diligently. We are not to wait for some special impulse, but to avail ourselves of the appointed means of grace immediately, without delay, and continuously. It is true that a harvest of grain depends on rain and sunlight, which only God can provide; but that is no excuse for neglecting to plant the seed, which God expects men to do. Faith in the Holy Spirit and his work is no excuse for spiritual laziness, or neglect of the use of appointed means.

155. Q. *How is the word made effectual to salvation?*

A. *The Spirit of God maketh the reading but especially the preaching of the word an effectual means of enlightening, convincing and humbling sinners; of driving them out of themselves, and drawing them unto Christ; of conforming them to his image, and subduing them to his will; of strengthening them against temptations and corruptions; of building them up in grace, and establishing their hearts in holiness and comfort through faith unto salvation.*

Scripture References

* Neh. 8:8; Acts 26:18; Ps. 19:8. The Word of God is used by the Holy Spirit for enlightening sinners, that is, imparting to them a knowledge of the truth.

- 1 Cor. 14:24–25; 2 Chron. 34:18–19, 26–28. The Spirit uses the Word for convincing and humbling sinners.
- Acts 2:37, 41; 8:27–39. The Word is used by the Spirit to drive sinners out of themselves, and draw them to Christ.
- 2 Cor. 3:18. The Spirit uses the Word as a means for conforming God's children to the image of Christ.
- 2 Cor. 10:4–6; Rom. 6:17. Believers are to be subdued to Christ's will by the power of the Spirit, who works through the Word.
- Matt. 4:4, 7, 10; Eph. 6:16–17; Ps. 19:11. By means of the Word believers are strengthened to overcome Satan.
- 1 Cor. 10:11. By means of the Word of God, the Holy Spirit strengthens God's people against temptations and corruptions.
- Acts 20:32; 2 Tim. 3:15–17; 1 Thess. 2:2, 10–11, 13; Rom 1:16; 10:13–17; 15:4; 16:25. Through the whole course of the believer's life, until he finally enters the state of glory, the Holy Spirit uses the Word as a means for his spiritual development and progress.

Commentary

1. What do the first five words of the answer to question 155 teach us? The first five words are: "The Spirit of God maketh . . ." These words teach us that the Bible or the Word of God does not have any *inherent* power of its own, apart from the inward work of the Holy Spirit in a person's heart, to accomplish anything toward a person's salvation. It is of course not impossible for the Spirit, in special cases, to work apart from the Word (see the Confession of Faith, 10.3). But the Word by itself alone, without the inward, saving work of the Holy Spirit, can *never* bring about any step in the salvation of a person. The Spirit is not helpless without the Word, but the Word is useless for salvation without the Spirit.

2. Can the Bible accomplish any good apart from the special work of the Holy Spirit? Yes. Apart from the saving work of the Holy Spirit, the Bible may, by God's common grace (His grace which is not limited to the elect, but is given to the elect and the reprobate in common), have the effect of restraining sin, stirring up people's consciences to a certain extent, and promoting what is called "civic righteousness," that is, ordinary virtues in the sphere of human society. For example, a man might read the Ten Commandments, and as a result decide not to commit a murder or theft that he had been planning. This would not contribute anything to his salvation, but it would make the world a more tolerable place to live in.

3. If the Word of God by itself alone cannot accomplish anything toward the salvation of human beings, is there any use in publishing and circulating the Scriptures far and wide as is done by the American Bible Society and similar organizations? Yes. Circulating the Scriptures is scattering the seed. It is true that apart from the saving work of the Holy Spirit the seed can never spring to life and lead to salvation, but we can never know when and where the Holy Spirit will use Scripture portions that have been circulated to bring about the salvation of souls. Men have been converted to Christ by reading Bibles placed in hotel rooms by the Gideons, and by reading small portions of the Bible printed on thin, cheap paper and circulated on foreign mission fields.

4. What two methods of using the Word of God does the Holy Spirit make use of to bring about the salvation of sinners? (a) The reading of the Word. (b) The preaching of the Word.

5. Which of these two methods is especially used by the Spirit? The preaching of the Word is the method especially used by the Spirit, although of course the Spirit uses both methods, sometimes in combination and sometimes separately. We see this illustrated in the account of Philip and the Ethiopian (Acts 8:27–39). The Ethiopian had been reading the Scripture, and had no doubt gotten some light from it, but he was still in a confused state of mind, as his question addressed to Philip revealed. When Philip sat down in the chariot with him and "preached unto him Jesus," his confusion was cleared away, and the Holy Spirit used the Word for his salvation.

6. Why is the special work of the Holy Spirit absolutely necessary if the Word of God is to lead to a person's salvation? Because by nature we are alienated from God and dead in trespasses and sins (Eph. 2:1). Because of our natural corruption and total spiritual deadness or helplessness, the life-giving and life-sustaining work of the Holy Spirit must accompany the Word if salvation is to result.

7. In what experiences of the Christian life does the Holy Spirit make use of the Word to bring about a person's salvation? The Spirit uses the Word as a means of grace in every stage and phase of the process of salvation, from the new birth to the believer's entrance upon the state of glory at death. The believer's soul being at death "made perfect in holiness" is of course accomplished solely by the almighty power of the Holy Spirit, apart from the Word. So also the final stage of salvation, the resurrection of the body at the Last Day, will be accomplished directly by the Holy Spirit apart from the use of the Word as a means (Rom. 8:11). It is true that we read, "The Lord himself shall descend from heaven with a shout . . . and the dead in Christ shall rise first" (1 Thess. 4:18), but this "shout" is not the use of the Word (Scripture) as a means, but a *new* Word of Jesus Christ at his second coming, at which the dead shall rise. Therefore those final stages of the process of salvation which take place after death are accomplished apart from the use of Scripture as a means. But for every part of the saving process in this life, from beginning to end, the Spirit's ordinary way of working is by the use of the Word as a means of grace. Regeneration, or the new birth, is a supernatural act of the Holy Spirit wrought directly in the human soul, not by the use of means but by the direct, creative power of God. In this experience the human soul is as passive as it was in its own creation. However, Regeneration is always accompanied by the Holy Spirit's use of the Word as a means of grace, by which the person is convicted of his sins, given an understanding of the way of salvation, etc. There are two exceptions to this use of the Word by the Holy Spirit to accompany the act of regeneration, namely, (a) infants, who because of their immaturity are incapable of knowledge of the truth; and (b) the insane and mentally deficient, who by reason of their mental abnormality are incapable of knowledge of the truth. See the Confession of Faith, 10.3. John the Baptist was filled with the Holy Spirit even before he was born (Luke 1:15); in such a case regeneration clearly must have taken place without being accompanied by the use of the Word by the Holy Spirit.

156. Q. *Is the word of God to be read by all?*

A. *Although all are not to be permitted to read the word publicly to the congregation, yet all sorts of people are bound to read it apart by themselves, and with their families: to which end the holy scriptures are to be translated out of the original into vulgar languages.*

Scripture References
- Deut. 31:9–13; Neh. 8:2–3; 8:3–5. Reading the Word of God publicly to the congregation is a duty of those especially called as ministers of the Word.

- Deut. 17:19; Rev. 1:3; John 5:39; Isa. 34:16. All classes of people are bound to read the Word of God privately.
- Deut. 8:6–9; Gen. 18:17, 19; Ps. 78:5–7. The duty of reading the Word of God in the family.
- 1 Cor. 14:6, 9–12, 15–16, 24, 27–28. As the Scripture would be useless in an unknown language, we infer that it is to be translated into the various languages in common use by the people of the world.

Commentary

1. Why are not all Christian people "to be permitted to read the word publicly to the congregation"? Reading the Scripture "publicly to the congregation" is a part of conducting the public worship of God, and therefore it is to be done only by those who have been properly called to that office in the church. Of course in the absence of an ordained minister or licentiate, the elders of the church may properly appoint some person to read the Scripture and conduct a prayer meeting or "fellowship meeting." What the catechism denies is that any private Christian may lawfully take it upon himself to conduct public worship, without being appointed to do so by those whose office it is to rule the house of God.

2. What classes of people are under obligation to read the Scriptures privately? All classes of people, everywhere in the world where the Scriptures have been circulated. To read the Bible is a duty not only of Christians or church members, but of all people whatever who are old enough to be able to read.

3. If a person has never learned to read, is it his duty to read the Bible? Yes. A person who has never learned to read should realize that it is his Christian duty to learn to read, so that he may read and study the Word of God. The fact that God has given us His Word in written form implies that it is the duty of all people to learn to read, that they may read the Scripture. Modern experience on many foreign mission fields proves that there are practically no people who cannot learn to read. It is worthy of note, too, that the spread of the gospel in mission lands is accompanied and followed by a remarkable increase of literacy, or the ability to read and write. Even many persons past middle age have learned to read a script as difficult as that of China, that they might read the Bible for themselves. On many mission fields it is considered a shame for a church member to be unable to read.

4. Why do we believe that the Word of God is to be read in the family circle? As the family is the basic unit of human society, so too the family is the basic unit in God's covenant of grace. It is through the Christian family that the body of God's covenant people is perpetuated from generation to generation. Parents together with their children are participants in this covenant of grace. Therefore the Christian family is a covenant institution and has covenant obligations as well as covenant promises and covenant blessings. Among these obligations is the obligation to maintain family worship. Of course family worship could be carried on without the actual reading of the written Bible, as was no doubt often necessary before the invention of the art of printing. But since in the providence of God the Word is available to all in printed form, it is obvious that family worship is greatly facilitated, and also rendered more effective, by the reading of the printed Bible. (See also *Blue Banner Faith and Life,* vol. 1, no. 7 [July–September 1946], 138–39: "Is the practice of family worship commanded in the Bible, and if so, where?")

5. What is the meaning of the expression "vulgar languages"? This expression, which might easily be misunderstood, means simply the ordinary living languages in common use by the peoples of the world. The word *vulgar* has come to have the meaning of "lacking in refinement or good taste," but in the catechism it simply means "ordinary" or "common." English, French, German, Chinese, etc., are "vulgar languages" in the sense intended by the catechism.

6. Why must the Bible be translated into modern languages? The Old Testament was written in the Hebrew language, which at the time of the writing was the common language of the covenant people of God; and the New Testament was written in Greek, which at the time of writing was the language most widely known in the Roman world. Today these languages are known only to the comparatively few who have made a special effort to learn them. The Bible is a message for all mankind, and the gospel which it contains is to be proclaimed to all nations. The Great Commission cannot be carried out adequately without translating the Bible into the various languages of the world. This work of Scripture translation has been going on since very early times, but by far the greatest progress has been made during the past 100 years. Today the Word of God, in whole or in part, speaks to men in more than 1,000 languages and dialects. This great achievement has been accomplished by the toil of multitudes of missionaries working in cooperation with the great Bible societies of the world. Today the Bible is diffused through the world as never before.

157. Q. How is the word of God to be read?

A. *The holy scriptures are to be read with a high and reverent esteem of them; with a firm persuasion that they are the very word of God, and that he only can enable us to understand them; with desire to know, believe, and obey the will of God revealed in them; with diligence, and attention to the matter and scope of them; with meditation, application, self-denial, and prayer.*

Scripture References

- Ps. 19:10; Neh. 8:3–10; Exod. 24:7; 2 Chron. 34:27; Isa. 66:2. We are to read the Scriptures with a high and reverent esteem of them.
- 2 Peter 1:19–21. We are to read the Scriptures with a firm faith that they really are the Word of God.
- Luke 24:45; 2 Cor. 3:13–16. In reading the Bible, we are to realize that only God can enable us really to understand it.
- Deut. 17:19–20. We are to read the Bible with a real desire to know and obey the will of God revealed in it.
- Acts 17:11. The Word of God is to be read with diligence.
- Acts 8:30, 34; Luke 10:26–28. We are to pay attention to "the matter and scope" of the Scriptures, that we may grasp their true meaning.
- Pss. 1:2; 119:97. The Word of God is to be read with meditation.
- 2 Chron. 34:21. In reading the Word of God, we are to apply it to our own selves, that is, to seek to discern its bearing on our own lives and needs.
- Prov. 3:5; Deut. 33:3. We are to read the Word of God with self-denial; that is, we are to be willing to give up our own opinions, preferences, and prejudices, and to accept and obey the will of God instead of our own ideas.
- Prov. 2:1–6; Ps. 119:18; Neh. 7:6, 8. The reading of the Word of God is to be accompanied with prayer.

Commentary

1. What is meant by reading the Scriptures "with a high and reverent esteem of them"? This means that in reading the Bible we should do so with an attitude different from that which we would have toward any other book. The Bible is the only source of saving truth; all other religious books, insofar as they present the truth, are based on the Bible. The Bible is the standard by which all other books are to be judged; in reading them, we are always to do so with an attitude of reserve and caution, accepting their statements only insofar as we find them to be in accordance with the teachings of the Bible. We may never commit ourselves implicitly, or without reservation, to any book but the Bible. In reading the Bible, on the other hand, we are to commit ourselves to it implicitly, without any reservation whatsoever. Many people who have the outward appearance of reverence and piety in their handling of the Bible are in point of fact extremely irreverent in their attitude toward it. A minister once said, "We must not accept all the teachings of Jesus, but only those of his teachings which we find to be true." Such an attitude toward the Bible is blasphemously irreverent; it amounts to placing our own human reason above the Word of God, and accepting only those teachings of God's Word which agree with our own reason. We may never regard the Bible as a mixture of truth and error: we may never try to decide what teachings of the Bible are true. We are to accept all the teachings of the Bible as true, and to judge and measure the teachings of all other books, and the opinions and judgments of human reason, by the Scriptures. We may of course have doubts or difficulties in ascertaining what is the true meaning of a text or portion of Scripture: but we must always commit ourselves without reserve to the true meaning, whatever it may be. That is to say, our attitude toward the Bible must always be a wholly *receptive* attitude, never a hesitant or *critical* attitude.

2. Are we to regard the Scriptures as the word of men, or the Word of God? We are to realize, of course, that every word in the Scriptures was written by men. At the same time we are to understand that the real Author of the Bible is God the Holy Spirit. Consequently we are to read the Bible with a firm conviction that it is "the very Word of God." The fact that a particular portion of the Bible was penned by Moses, Isaiah, or Paul is a minor, secondary consideration; the important thing is that God is the real Author of it and that it is really the Word of God.

3. How does modern religious "Liberalism" undermine people's faith that the Scriptures are the very Word of God? Modern religious "Liberalism" does not believe that the Bible as a whole, in the entirety of its content and teachings, is the Word of God. It holds that the Bible is a human book which, however, "contains" the Word of God; that is, the Bible is partly the Word of God and partly the word of man. Since the human mind must decide which statements of the Bible are the Word of God and which are only the word of man, this viewpoint really amounts to enthroning the human faculty of reason as the real authority for faith and life. If we must pick and choose among the contents of the Bible, accepting one statement and rejecting another, then obviously the Bible is no longer our real standard. Only when we accept all that the Bible teaches, without question, as the Word of God do we really regard the Bible as our standard.

4. What currently popular religious viewpoint subtly destroys the authority of the Bible as the Word of God? The comparatively recent brand of theology called "Barthianism," which has been developed by the Swiss theologians Karl Barth and Emil Brunner and their many disciples. This "new" theology is also called "the theology of crisis," "neo-orthodoxy," and "the dialectical theology." It denies that the Bible, as a written book, is really the Word of God. At the same time the Barthian theology teaches that any statement of the Bible may *become* the Word of God to a person when it grips that person's conscience and comes home to that person as a revelation of God's will. This makes the authority of the Bible depend, not on the fact that the Bible itself, as a book, is the inspired Word of God, but on human experience in connection with the Bible. Barthianism adheres to the "higher critical" theories about the Bible; it holds that many statements of the Bible are not true in their common, plain meaning: and yet it tries to hold on to the Bible as an instrument by means of which the Word of God takes hold of people. In spite of its current popularity, "neo-orthodoxy" must be adjudged to be extremely dangerous and unsound.

5. Why is it true that only God can enable us to understand the Scriptures aright? Because the human mind is darkened and clouded by sin, so that it is not a reliable judge of truth and error. The fall of the human race into sin resulted not only in a perversion of the moral sense, so that men love sin rather than righteousness, but also in a darkening of the mind or intellect, so that men love falsehood rather than truth. The human race is deeply prejudiced against the truth of God and in favor of sinful error. "Their foolish heart was darkened" (Rom. 1:21); "they did not like to retain God in their knowledge" (Rom. 1:28). Only by the regenerating and illuminating work of the Holy Spirit can this natural sinful darkness of the human mind be taken away, so that a person becomes spiritually discerning and receptive of the truth. While regeneration is an act which is complete in an instant of time, the Spirit's work of illuminating the minds of God's people is a gradual process which must continue through our whole earthly life. We must always seek the illumination of the Holy Spirit to understand the Scriptures.

6. What should be our motive in reading and studying the Bible? In reading and studying the Bible we should have a practical motive, namely, a desire "to know, believe, and obey the will of God" which the Bible makes known to us. Many people study the Bible with wrong or inadequate motives. Some study the Bible merely as literature; others merely as history. There have even been those who studied the Bible in order to contradict its teachings and argue against the Christian religion. Still others have studied the Bible with a kind of idle curiosity, or with some fanatical idea or fad; for example, there have been those who have studied the Bible merely to tabulate its teachings about baptism, or about hell, or about the powers of magistrates: such people have a kind of "collectors" interest in some one line or element of the Bible's teaching, but they have no intention whatever of applying the teachings of the Bible to their own personal condition as lost sinners in need of salvation. They collect items from the Bible as a person might collect antique furniture or porcelain ware. All such study of the Bible is inadequate and wrong. No person studies the Bible aright unless he has studied it first of all as a message from God concerning the salvation of his own soul. We may properly study the Bible as literature, as history, etc., but only after we have paid heed to the Bible as God's Word revealing the way of salvation to lost and guilty sinners. For those who reject or neglect the great message of the Bible, the gospel of Jesus Christ, to play with the Bible as literature, etc., must be an abomination in the sight of God. What would we think of a guilty, convicted criminal who, when offered a free pardon, would pay no attention to this offer, but merely write an essay on the literary form and style of the message by which the offer was conveyed?

7. Why must we read and study the Bible "with diligence"? The Bible is a big book and contains many things that are hard to understand. It contains not only milk for babes but strong meat for mature Christians. We will never gain an adequate understanding of the Bible by reading it for five minutes a day. No one would expect to gain a grasp of chemistry or mathematics by occasional slight exposure, without any conscious effort, to these sciences; why should anyone expect to understand the Bible without any effort or hard work? It is a tragedy that many professing Christians and church members are so spiritually and intellectually lazy that they remain spiritual "babes" all their life and have to be fed with carefully prepared "milk"; anything like the "strong meat" of which the Bible speaks (Heb. 5:11–14) they immediately protest against as "too deep." Instead of regarding the Bible as "too deep," or wishing that God had given us a shallower Bible, we should pray with the Psalmist, "Open thou mine eyes, that I may behold wondrous things out of thy law" (Ps. 119:18). And we cannot pray that prayer sincerely if we are too lazy or indifferent to study the Bible seriously. God will not open our eyes to behold wonderful things in his Word if we are neglectful or indifferent in reading His Word.

8. Why must we pay attention to the "matter and scope" of the Scriptures? In studying the Bible, we must make use of all the intelligence that God has given us. Piety is not contrary to a right use of the faculty of reason. In studying any text or portion of the Bible, we should always note not only what is said, but who the speaker is, the occasion and circumstances, and the relation of the statement to other statements before or after it, and to the chapter and book as a whole. In the Bible we read these words: "There is no God." We cannot grasp the true import of this statement unless we note the fact that it is reported as a sentiment of "the fool": "The fool hath said in his heart, There is no God" (Ps. 53:1), and that in the remainder of the verse people who cherish such sentiments are declared to be "corrupt" and to "have done abominable iniquity." Similarly we read; "Skin for skin; yea, all that a man hath will he give for his life" (Job 2:4). Quoted by itself, out of its context, this verse would be very misleading; it is only when we note that Satan, the father of lies, is reported as having made this statement that we can discern its true import.

9. What is meant by "meditation," and why is it necessary in connection with reading the Bible? "Meditation" means thinking carefully and seriously, for a greater or less length of time, about the meaning of something. "Meditation" does not mean, as many people wrongly suppose, a mere idle wandering of the thoughts or vague daydreaming. It is definite; it calls for effort. Meditation is necessary in connection with Bible reading because we cannot expect to gain the real riches of its truth by a hasty skimming of its surface. It is true in Bible study as in all other fields that serious thinking requires time. The Bible is not a modern supermarket with its wares all packaged and arranged on shelves ready to be checked out with the least possible effort; the Bible is a gold mine that has to be methodically and patiently worked if we are to gain possession of its treasures. We have more and better helps for Bible study today than ever before, but the haste and complexity of modern life, with its many activities which make demands on people's time, have resulted in many Christians who have only an elementary and superficial knowledge of the Bible, and who live from one year to the next with virtually no real increase in their understanding of Bible truth. There is no shortcut to success in Bible study: meditation is needed, and that takes time.

10. Why must we study the Bible with "application"? The Bible is not a merely theoretical or abstract message, but a personal message suited to the needs of those who read it. A person might study geometry or astronomy out of sheer intellectual interest and curiosity, without any intention to make any practical application of these sciences to his own life. But to study the Bible in such a way as that would be to miss the real meaning and importance of the Bible. Unless we apply its teachings to ourselves personally, our Bible study not only will do us no good, but will actually add to our guilt at the Judgment Day.

11. Why does the catechism speak of "self-denial" in connection with Bible study? Presumably the catechism does not here refer to that self-denial which a person must practice in order to have sufficient free time for adequate Bible study. The Scripture references which are cited indicate that the meaning is that we must deny ourselves by giving up our own prejudices, preferences, and special ideas, and accepting the teachings of the Word of God as our standard for faith and life. We are to accept *all* the teachings of the Bible, not merely those which commend themselves to us as reasonable, desirable, or helpful. We are to deny ourselves by surrendering our own reason as our supreme standard of truth, and becoming as little children, accepting God's Word on God's authority.

12. What is the place of prayer in relation to Bible study? Clearly prayer has an important place in connection with Bible study. If a real understanding of the Bible is dependent on the inward illumination of the Holy Spirit, it follows that we must pray for the continuance and increase of this illuminating work in our hearts and minds. But the place of prayer in connection with Bible study has sometimes been sadly misunderstood. A person will say, "I know that such-and-such is the true interpretation of this text, because I got it in answer to prayer." We have no warrant for expecting the Holy Spirit to reveal the true interpretation of any text of Scripture to us miraculously, without study on our part, in answer to prayer. Prayer is not a substitute for dictionaries and commentaries and other reference books. We are rather to pray that in our diligent use of the best available helps, the Holy Spirit will bless and guide us into the real truth. To claim that an interpretation is true because a person just somehow "got it in answer to prayer" is foolishness. If it is really true we will be able to set forth substantial reasons why it is true, and why other interpretations are false. Obviously the fact that Mr. A. "got it in answer to prayer" will not carry any weight with Mr. B. When prayer becomes a substitute for thinking and study, it is not the kind of prayer that is pleasing to God.

158. Q. *By whom is the word of God to be preached?*

A. *The word of God is to be preached only by such as are sufficiently gifted, and also duly approved and called to that office.*

Scripture References

- 1 Tim. 3:2, 6; Eph. 4:8–11; Hos. 4:6; Mal. 2:7; 2 Cor. 3:6. Those who preach the Word of God publicly must be possessed of certain qualifications, which are set forth in the Bible.
- Jer. 14:15; Rom. 10:15; Heb. 5:4; 1 Cor. 12:28–29; 1 Tim. 3:10; 4:14; 5:22. The Word of God is to be preached publicly only by those who have been lawfully called to the office of the ministry of the Word.

Commentary

1. With what kind of preaching of the Word does this question of the catechism especially deal? With public preaching of the Word in a congregation of Christ's church. This may be inferred from the words "publicly to the congregation" in the answer to question 156. A person who is not an ordained minister or licentiate may witness for Christ privately or publicly as opportunity is afforded, but the official public preaching of the Word in the church is to be done only by those duly set apart for that work.

2. Why is the official preaching of the Word to be done only by "such as are sufficiently gifted"? It is clear that the preaching of the Word is a work of very great importance. For it to be done adequately, proper qualifications are necessary. There are spiritual qualifications, intellectual qualifications, and educational qualifications which must be insisted upon if the church is to have an adequate ministry. A man who is not a born-again and consistent Christian clearly is not fit to preach the Word of God to others; he would only be a blind leader of the blind. A man who cannot think straight, who is unable to detect a fallacy in an unsound argument, will be likely to be led astray by false teachings himself, and to lead others astray in turn. A man who lacks adequate general and theological education will ordinarily not be able to do justice to the great work of preaching the Word of God, and will be in danger of preaching an unbalanced or one-sided message. When God calls a man to the work of the ministry, he also equips him with the necessary abilities and qualifications that he may execute the work adequately.

3. Why does our church, along with most Protestant churches, require a full college and seminary education for the office of the ministry? The more important a work is, the more important it is that those who must do that work have adequate training. There have always been those who have thought that it is more or less a waste of time to spend seven years in college and seminary in preparation for the work of the ministry. In many denominations today there is a constant pressure to relax such requirements and admit men to the ministry who have had less than a full college and seminary course. Some consider college subjects such as philosophy, European history, and literature as useless for the ministry, and as a waste of time which could be spent on "winning souls." Similarly there are those who think that a short course on "the English Bible" together with such practical subjects as public speaking and pastoral work should be sufficient, and that extended study of Hebrew, Greek, church history, and systematic theology is a waste of time.

No person who needed to have an operation performed would willingly go to a surgeon who had obtained his training by a shortcut. The state rightly insists that those whose decisions and actions involve the life and death of their fellow men be thoroughly trained for their work. How much more important it is that ministers of the gospel, whose work may affect the eternal destiny of human beings, be thoroughly educated for their appointed task. Considering the length of time required for training for the medical and other learned professions, four years of college and three years of seminary work are not too much for ministerial training.

The minister who lacks college training will hardly be able to understand the modern world in which he must deliver his message. The study of philosophy, history, and other academic subjects is far from a waste of time; such study gives the background of modern thought and enables the minister to proclaim the whole counsel of God in a way that will really come to grips with the present-day situation. Similarly the study of Greek, Hebrew, systematic theology, church history, etc., is anything but a waste of time; such study enables the minister to have a thorough firsthand knowledge of the Bible and its teachings, and to preach a scriptural, consistent, and integrated message.

The modern trend toward cutting down on "theoretical" studies in preparation for the ministry, and increasing "practical" studies, is deplorable and should be resisted. There are in America two kinds of theological seminaries and Bible institutes. In one kind, the aim is to equip the student with a certain amount of prepared material, which he can go out and preach. In the other kind, the aim is to place the tools of Bible study and theological research in the student's hands, and to train him in their proper use. He can then go out and preach, and will never run out of material to the end of his life. We believe the latter is the proper and only adequate type of training for the work of the ministry.

The foregoing must not be taken to mean that there can never be any exceptions to such rules. Clearly some of our Lord's disciples had but little formal education, yet they became effective ministers of the Word. They, however, had the priceless advantage of three years of association with Jesus and personal instruction from him. God sometimes calls to the office of the ministry a man who has had little formal education, and in such exceptional cases, where the divine call is evident, the church should not hesitate to ordain the candidate to the ministry. Such cases will, however, be quite rare, especially in times when there are normal opportunities for gaining an education. The exception should not be allowed to become the rule.

4. What is meant by being "duly approved and called" to the work of the ministry? There is a divine call to the work of the ministry, and there is a call of the church. We should always remember that the ministry is not a profession, but an office. A person may not simply decide to become a minister, as he would decide to become a lawyer or to go into some line of business. He must have some reason to believe that he is called by God to the ministry. This does not mean a special revelation from heaven, such as a dream or vision, but a consciousness that one possesses some measure of the requisite qualifications, together with an earnest desire to preach the gospel, a willingness to make sacrifices for the cause of Christ, and a readiness to endeavor to gain the necessary preparation. Those whom God calls to the ministry he will lead into it in his own way.

The call of the church consists, first, in authenticating the call of God by "duly approving" of the candidate, his religious convictions, his general ability, and his academic and theological preparation. This "approving" is ordinarily divided into various stages; first, the candidate is received under the care of a presbytery as a student for the ministry; then, after partial preparation he is licensed to preach; finally, after full preparation and a call from a congregation or mission board, he is ordained to the office of the ministry.

The formal call of the church consists of a call by a congregation upon the candidate to become their pastor, or the call of a mission board or other agency of the visible church to engage in home or foreign missionary work or some other phase of the work of the ministry. In every case there ought to be a definite call, either to the pastorate of a congregation or to some other specific field of work, before a man is ordained to the office of the ministry.

5. Why must a man be duly called by God and the church before entering upon the office of the ministry? Even the Lord Jesus Christ did not make himself a High Priest, but was called of God to that office, as Aaron had been (Heb. 5:4–5). While there are today many "free-lance" and independent preachers and missionaries, this is a wrong tendency and ought to be discountenanced. Many of these independent preachers and missionaries may indeed have been called of God, and may be doing a good work in preaching Christ and him crucified; but there is a certain contempt and neglect of the visible church as a divine institution involved in their attitude, which cannot be endorsed. The call of God and the call of the church are not contrary to each other; every true church is an instrument of God in training and ordaining men to the office of the ministry. Some who claim a superior kind of piety hold that the call of God is sufficient, and that they do not need the call and ordination of the church. Such disregard of the visible church is not scriptural and should be discountenanced.

159. Q. *How is the word of God to be preached by those that are called hereunto?*

A. *They that are called to labor in the ministry of the word, are to preach sound doctrine, diligently, in season and out of season; plainly, not in the enticing words of man's wisdom, but in demonstration of the Spirit, and of power; . . .*

Scripture References

- Titus 2:1, 8. The duty of preaching sound doctrine.
- Acts 18:25; 2 Tim. 4:2. The duty of preaching the Word diligently and persistently.
- 1 Cor. 14:19; 2:4. The Word of God to be preached plainly, with dependence not on human cleverness, but on the power of the Holy Spirit.

Commentary

1. What is meant by "sound doctrine"? The expression "sound doctrine" means *true* doctrine, or doctrine that is in accordance with the truth revealed in the Bible.

2. Why is the preaching of sound doctrine important? The preaching of sound doctrine is important because it is only through knowledge of the truth revealed in the Bible that we can come into real contact with Christ and experience salvation through him. If pure food and medicine are necessary for our bodily health, how much more important is pure spiritual food for the life and nourishment and healing of our souls!

3. How can ministers make sure of preaching sound doctrine? The only way to make sure of preaching sound doctrine is by a steadfast loyalty to the written Word of God, the Holy Bible, and an unceasing effort to grasp its real meaning. Only by continuous and careful Bible study can sound, true doctrine be maintained.

4. Why is it necessary that the Word of God be preached diligently? What God commands is to be done diligently. The preaching of the Word is commanded by God, as an appointed means of the salvation of souls and extension of his kingdom. This work, being of such great importance, should of course be carried on with diligence and continuous earnest effort.

5. What is meant by preaching the Word "in season and out of season"? This expression means that preaching the Word is not to be limited to formal occasions such as the regular services of the church, but is also to be done informally, whenever opportunity offers and occasion demands. The minister is to be a witness for the truth at all times, not only in the regular church services.

6. What is meant by preaching the Word of God "plainly"? This means making the meaning plain and clear to those who hear. The preacher should not aim at being regarded as "deep," but at being understood by his hearers. It is wrong to smooth over unpleasant truths or duties for fear of offending the hearers. The minister of Christ must make the truth clear and plain, whether men will hear or whether they will forbear. His aim must not be to please his hearers, but to please God.

7. On what should ministers rely for the effectiveness of their messages? They should rely, not on "enticing words of man's wisdom," but on the "demonstration of the Spirit, and of power." That is, the minister is not to place his trust in his own ability as an orator or public speaker, nor to depend on the psychological influence of his own manner of presenting the message, but to depend on the Holy Spirit blessing the message and applying it to the hearts of the hearers. The minister's reliance is to be placed, not in psychology or "salesmanship," but in the work of the Holy Spirit that accompanies and follows his preaching. This does not mean that the message should not be presented in an interesting and attractive way, but that dependence must not be placed on the human factor, but on the divine.

159. Q. *(continued) How is the word of God to be preached by those that are called thereunto?*

    A. *They that are called to labor in the ministry of the word, are to preach . . . faithfully, making known the whole counsel of God; wisely, applying themselves to the necessities and capacities of the hearers; zealously, with fervent love to God and the souls of his people; sincerely, aiming at his glory, and their conversion, edification, and salvation.*

Scripture References

- Jer. 23:28; 1 Cor. 4:1–2; Acts 20:27. The Word of God to be preached faithfully, honestly, and fully.
- Col. 1:28; 2 Tim. 2:15; 1 Cor. 3:2; Heb. 5:12–14; Luke 12:42. The Word to be preached in a wise manner, taking account of the capacities and spiritual state of the hearers.
- Acts 18:25; 2 Cor. 12:15; 5:13–14; Phil. 1:15–17; Col. 4:12. The duty of preaching the Word of God zealously, with fervent love to God and the souls of his people.
- 2 Cor. 2:17; 4:2; 12:19; 1 Thess. 2:4–6; John 7:18; 1 Cor. 9:19–22; Eph. 4:12; 1 Tim. 4:16; Acts 26:16–18. The duty of preaching the Word of God sincerely, with right motives, namely, God's glory and the true spiritual welfare of his people.

Commentary

1. Why must ministers preach the Word of God faithfully, honestly, and fully? Because it is not their own message, but God's message, that they are handling. A minister is an ambassador; therefore he has no right to tamper with the message entrusted to him. It must be delivered accurately and in full.

2. What is meant by the expression "the whole counsel of God"? This expression, which is taken from the apostle Paul's words in Acts 20:27, means the entire revealed truth and will of God. Ministers are to preach the whole truth of the Bible. They have no right to preach a limited, deformed, or partial message.

3. How are ministers to preach "the whole counsel of God"? It is of course impossible to preach the whole counsel of God all at one time. Ministers can proclaim only a small part of the counsel of God in any one sermon or address. To attempt too much at one time would only result in confusion and spiritual indigestion on the part of the hearers. But ministers must make it their aim to preach, in due time, all that God has revealed in his Word, omitting nothing of the system of divinely revealed truth.

4. Are all truths of the Bible equally important? No. All are equally true, but all are not equally important. The most important ones are the ones which receive the most emphasis in the Bible itself. While aiming at proclaiming the whole counsel of God, a minister must take care to place the chief emphasis on the most important truths or doctrines, which are given the most prominence in the Bible itself, or which are most in need of emphasis because most neglected or denied in the present day. No minister should indulge in fads or hobbies, specializing in certain truths to the neglect of all others.

5. What temptation to deviate from preaching the whole counsel of God must be faced and resisted by ministers? The temptation to say little about, or remain silent about, those truths of the Bible which are commonly regarded as "unpopular," while emphasizing and saying much about those truths which are commonly called "popular." Thus a minister may face the temptation to say little or nothing about sin, death, and eternal punishment, while preaching much on the love of God, the teachings of Jesus about love to our neighbor, and the like. Ministers have no right to "soft-pedal" part of God's message because it may be distasteful to their hearers. As servants of God they must preach the whole truth without "trimming" it to suit human prejudices.

6. Why must ministers take "the necessities and capacities of the hearers" into consideration in their preaching? Because if they fail to do this, their preaching will be largely ineffective and useless. The truth of God is always the same, but it must be preached in a somewhat different manner to different groups of people. The manner or method of preaching that would be suited to an audience of non-Christians on a foreign mission field would be different from that suited to a congregation of Christian believers in the same country, and the latter again would be somewhat different from that suited to a congregation of Christian believers in America. The minister may not deviate from the truth of God, but he must try to present the truth of God in such a way that his hearers, whoever they may be, will really "get the point."

7. What is meant by preaching the Word of God "zealously"? This does not necessarily mean an emotional pitch of excitement, but rather a deep spiritual attitude, which the catechism describes as "with fervent love to God and the souls of his people." That is, a minister of Christ is to preach the gospel earnestly, regarding it as an extremely important matter, not something trifling or indifferent. The minister's motive should not be popularity or applause, but devotion to God and desire for the spiritual welfare of his people.

8. What is meant by preaching the Word of God "sincerely"? This word means without presence or hypocrisy; that is, really and honestly meaning what one says.

9. What is to be the chief aim in preaching the Word of God? The chief aim is to be the glory of God.

10. What is to be the subordinate aim in preaching the Word of God? The subordinate aim in preaching the Word of God is to be the accomplishment of God's purpose in the conversion, edification, and final salvation of his people.

160. Q. *What is required of those that hear the word preached?*

A. *It is required of those that hear the word preached, that they attend upon it with diligence, preparation, and prayer; examine what they hear by the scriptures; receive the truth with faith, love, meekness, and readiness of mind, as the word of God: meditate, and confer of it; hide it in their hearts, and bring forth the fruit of it in their lives.*

Scripture References
- Prov. 8:34; 1 Peter 2:1–2; Luke 8:18; Ps. 119:18; Eph. 6:18–19. We are to attend upon the preached gospel with diligence, preparation, and prayer.
- Acts 17:11. The preached message to be tested by the Scriptures.
- Heb. 4:2; 2 Thess. 2:10; James 1:21; Acts 17:11. Hearers of the preached Word are to receive the truth with faith, love, meekness, and readiness of mind.
- 1 Thess. 2:13. The truth is to be received, not as a mere matter of human opinion, but as the Word of God, having divine authority.
- Luke 9:44; Heb. 2:1; Luke 24:14; Deut. 6:6–7; Mal. 3:16. Hearers of the preached Word are to meditate and confer concerning it.
- Prov. 2:1; Ps. 119:11. The Word to be hidden in the heart.
- Luke 8:15; James 1:25. The Word to be fruitful in the life.

Commentary

1. What is our first duty in connection with the preached gospel? Our first duty in connection with the preached gospel is to hear it. This implies regular attendance upon the ordinances of divine worship. In an age when iniquity abounds, and the love of many has waxed cold, there are many church members who attend the services of their church only occasionally.

Some think that if they attend half of the regular services of their own church they have done very well. We should conscientiously attend *all* the regular public preaching services of our own church unless prevented by circumstances beyond our control. "Not forsaking the assembling of ourselves together, as the manner of some is" (Heb. 10:25).

2. Does regular church attendance fulfill our duty in connection with the preached gospel? Certainly not. Regular church attendance is only the first step. The catechism not only affirms that we must "attend upon" the preached Word, but goes on to state *how* we must attend upon it. This answer of the catechism sets forth a very high ideal for Christian people's response to the preached Word, but it is an eminently scriptural ideal. We should certainly avoid the mistaken idea that occupying a seat in the house of worship on the Sabbath day fulfills our duty or even confers a favor on God. It is possible to attend church services regularly and yet get no benefits whatever, because we do not pay attention to the service or take the message seriously.

3. What are some of the practices that we should avoid during church services? We should avoid coming late, sleeping, talking or whispering unnecessarily, reading books or papers that have nothing to do with the service, thinking over our worldly affairs and planning our business for the following week, and all other conduct which will distract ourselves or others from paying reverent attention to the service.

4. What is the remedy for habitual sleeping during church services? Sleeping during church services is sometimes blamed on the preacher, but where one or two members fall asleep and all the rest have no difficulty in staying awake it is probably not the preacher's fault. Sleepiness during church services may be caused by poor ventilation of the building. Janitors often fail to realize this; it should be tactfully explained to them that fresh air is necessary for mental alertness, and a building which has been closed for several days needs to be thoroughly aired out before the service begins. In other cases sleeping in church may be caused by keeping late hours on Saturday evening—something which every conscientious Christian will try to avoid. In some cases it may really be the minister's fault; he should try to make his sermons interesting and to deliver them in an effective manner so as to hold the congregation's attention.

5. What kind of preparation should we make to hear the Word preached? We should take care of our ordinary business, except for real works of necessity, on Saturday, so that our minds will be free to think about God and his Word on the Sabbath day. We should endeavor to dismiss all worldly business and pleasures from our thoughts so that we will be receptive to God's Word. We should conscientiously avoid reading "Sunday" newspapers and listening to secular radio broadcasts on the Lord's Day. No minister can preach effectively if the people come to church with their minds full of thoughts about movies, radio, baseball, politics, business, and other worldly affairs. Nor can the people pay attention to the preaching of the Word if their minds are occupied with picnics, auto trips, or other recreations planned for the Sabbath afternoon or evening. The Lord's Day should be entirely consecrated to the service of God, if we are really to honor God and get blessing from his Word.

6. What should we pray for in connection with the preaching of the Word? We should pray that the Holy Spirit will bestow spiritual gifts upon the minister, so that he may expound the Scriptures truly and effectively. We should also pray that we and others may be given the grace of the Spirit to receive the Word, that the Holy Spirit will accompany and follow the preaching with his gracious working, so that sinners will be converted to Christ and the saints built up in their Christian faith and experience.

7. Is it the duty of Christian people to believe and accept whatever their minister preaches? Certainly not. They are to "examine what they hear by the Scriptures"; that is, they are to test and judge the content of the message by the Word of God which is the infallible rule of faith and life. No real minister of Christ will want his hearers to accept anything just because he says it is true; he will want them to accept the truth because God says it is true, and because they find that it is taught in God's Word. The minister is not only to preach the truths of God's Word, but to show the people where and how God's Word teaches those truths. The people are to believe the truth, not on their minister's authority, but on the authority of God speaking in his Word.

8. What attitude should we have to the truth of God as it is preached to us? We should "receive the truth with faith, love, meekness, and readiness of mind, as the word of God." That is, we should have a *receptive* attitude toward the truth, not an attitude of stubborn resistance to it. Such a

receptive attitude can exist only by the special work of the Holy Spirit in a
person's heart and mind. By nature we all have a stubborn, perverse prejudice against the truth and a tendency to resist and argue against the truth.
Many can testify that when they were really converted to Christ, their opposition to the truth of God ceased, and they became meek and receptive in
their attitude. Sometimes professing Christians manifest a spirit of violent
rebellion against such doctrines as original sin, total depravity and inability,
predestination, and eternal punishment. The fact that these doctrines are
taught very plainly in the Bible, which they usually do not attempt to deny,
seems to carry no weight with such objectors, but rather to increase their
opposition. With respect to the doctrines mentioned above, and all other
doctrines, the only question that really matters is *are these doctrines scriptural?*
If they are taught in God's Word, that should settle the matter for every
Christian believer. Whether we like these doctrines or not is irrelevant. We
are to receive the truths of God's Word with "readiness of mind," on God's
authority, whether we like them or not.

**9. Why should we meditate and confer concerning the preached
Word?** We should meditate on it because only by spending time in serious
thinking can we really grasp the truth in its relation to our own lives and
problems. We should confer concerning it with our fellow Christians because
this will tend greatly to increase the effectiveness of the message. Conversation on divine truth among Christian people is greatly neglected in the present day. We are so busy with a multitude of interests and activities that we
seem to have little opportunity for fellowship and conference with other
Christians. A person who likes to talk about religion today is likely to be
regarded as something of a "crank" or fanatic. Of course those who feel they
must always be talking about religion and nothing else will come to be
regarded as a nuisance and will bring reproach on the church. "To every
thing there is a season, and a time to every purpose under the heaven" (Eccl.
3:1). To confer concerning divine truth seasonably and profitably is an art
that should be cultivated by the Lord's children.

10. Why must we hide the Word of God in our hearts? To hide the
Word in our hearts means more than merely memorizing portions of Scripture, although that is a very profitable pursuit. It means to retain the truth
in our mind and keep on thinking it over and reflecting on its relation to
every sphere of our life. This is the opposite of the "in one ear and out the
other" manner of receiving the truth of God. If we really believe and receive

the truth, it will remain in our hearts and we will reap benefits at future times as well as right away.

11. Why must we bring forth the fruit of the Word of God in our lives? Because the Word of God is an intensely practical message. We should beware of being like the character named "Talkative" in Bunyan's *Pilgrim's Progress,* who had the Bible and Christian doctrine at the tip of his tongue and could speak fluently on all religious subjects, but was a complete stranger to the power of godliness in his own personal and family life. "By their fruits ye shall know them." The Word of God is a message of salvation, godly living, and Christian self-denial or being crucified with Christ. If a person is a stranger to these experiences, he is not bringing forth the fruit of the Word of God in his life, and his habitual hearing of the preached gospel will only add to his condemnation at the Judgment Day.

16

Use of the Sacraments

161. Q. *How do the sacraments become effectual means of salvation?*

A. *The sacraments become effectual means of salvation, not by any power in themselves, or any virtue derived from the piety or intention of him by whom they are administered, but only by the working of the Holy Ghost, and the blessing of Christ, by whom they are instituted.*

Scripture References

- 1 Peter 3:21; Acts 8:13 compared with Acts 8:23; 1 Cor. 3:6–7; 12:13. The efficacy of the sacraments depends entirely on the working of the Holy Spirit and the blessing of Christ, not on any inherent power or on any power derived from the minister who administers them.

Commentary

1. What does the Roman Catholic Church teach concerning the efficacy of the sacraments? The Roman Catholic Church teaches that grace is contained in the sacraments themselves, and that this grace is conferred on every recipient of the sacraments who does not positively resist it. This grace is said to be bestowed as an *opus operatum* (that is, as a "work wrought" or an "operation performed") upon every recipient who does not positively resist. A person may be ignorant of the truth about God and the way of salvation; he may even be unconscious because of sickness or accident; even so, it is held, baptism will of itself confer on him the grace of regeneration. According to this teaching, faith is not necessary; the sacrament works of itself, just as a red-hot piece of iron will burn a person, whether he believes it will or not (Council of Trent, Session 7, Canons 6 and 8).

The Roman Catholic Church also holds that the efficacy of the sacraments depends on the secret intention of the administrator at the moment of administering the sacrament. The priest must, at the moment of performing the actions and pronouncing the words, have in his mind the intention of doing what the church intends to do in that sacrament. In other words, the priest might say all the prescribed words and perform all the required actions, yet if he does not have in his heart and mind the secret intention of conveying grace through that sacrament, the recipient does not really receive any grace at all, and the sacrament is null and void (Council of Trent, Session 7, Canon 11). If the administering priest has the right intention, the sacrament conveys grace to the recipient automatically unless the recipient positively resists it.

2. Do the sacraments have any power in themselves? No. Our catechism rightly rejects the Roman Catholic view of the efficacy of the sacraments, by saying that the sacraments do not become effectual means of salvation by any power in themselves. The Roman Catholic view is untrue and without support in the Bible. Note Acts 8:13, 23, where it is stated that Simon the Sorcerer "was baptized" and then soon afterwards the apostle Peter said to him "thou art in the gall of bitterness, and in the bond of iniquity." If baptism of itself confers regeneration, as an *opus operatum,* Simon would have been regenerated by his baptism: he would have been a new creature in Christ Jesus; but as a matter of fact he was still in the bond of iniquity. Clearly baptism did not convey any grace to Simon the Sorcerer. The whole idea that the sacraments of themselves confer grace is contrary to the Bible's emphasis on faith as necessary for salvation.

3. Is this false view of the sacraments limited to Roman Catholics? No. There are many Protestants who have a mistaken and unscriptural view of the efficacy of the sacraments. Many who have never really repented of their sins and who have no clear faith in Jesus Christ as their Savior cherish the idea that to be baptized, or to "take communion," will of itself confer some spiritual benefit on them. Some go so far as to suppose that participation in the sacraments will get an ungodly person into heaven when he dies. Others think that "taking communion" will somehow make up for their sins and give them standing with God. The notion that baptism of itself removes a person's sins is quite common among uninstructed Protestants. Sometimes parents who make no Christian profession and are not living as Christians will ask a minister to baptize their children, and will be offended when he declines to do so. We should always remember that the sacraments do not work of themselves, and are without value apart from faith in Jesus Christ.

4. Does the efficacy of the sacraments depend on the piety or moral character of the minister? No. On this point the Church of Rome is in agreement with orthodox Protestantism. The validity and efficacy of the sacraments are not dependent on the piety, spiritual life, or moral character of the person who administers them. Of course every minister should be a truly pious man and of moral character beyond reproach. But the spiritual state of the minister does not alter the efficacy of the sacraments. If a minister is proved to be an ungodly and wicked man, this does not mean that the people he has baptized were not really baptized, or that those who sat at the communion table under his ministry did not really partake of the Lord's Supper. It is a terrible thing for a minister to be an unconverted person, but it does not limit the efficacy of the sacraments administered by him.

5. Does the intention of the minister determine the efficacy of the sacraments? No. So long as the sacraments are administered substantially in accordance with Christ's institution, the personal intentions of the minister have no effect upon their efficacy. Suppose an unconverted man were to go into the ministry with wrong motives, regarding the ministry simply as an occupation or means of livelihood, and administering the Lord's Supper not because of real faith in Christ and obedience to him but merely because the rules of the church required it. Such a minister would be a hireling, not a true servant of Christ, and his intention would be merely to comply with the formal requirements of his occupation. Although such a minister would be unworthy and his motives wrong, still his wrong intentions, and lack of the right intention, would not affect the validity or efficacy of the sacrament. Those communicants who partook of the sacrament with true repentance and faith in Christ would receive the real benefit and blessing of the Lord's Supper, in spite of the minister's wrong intentions or motives.

6. On what does the efficacy of the sacraments really depend? The efficacy of the sacraments really depends entirely upon the working of the Holy Spirit, and the blessing of Christ who instituted the sacraments. As the sacraments were not invented by man, but instituted by the Lord Jesus Christ as means of grace, we can be sure that God will accompany them with the gracious working of the Holy Spirit in the case of every person who partakes of them with a true faith, according to Christ's appointment. The Holy Spirit, whom Christ has sent, takes of the things of Christ and shows them unto his people. It is His purpose to work through and with the sacraments. Thus the sacraments which have no inherent power are yet, by the Holy Spirit's working, real means of grace to God's children.

7. Is it possible to underrate the importance of the sacraments? Yes, and many do so. While avoiding the error of the Church of Rome, which teaches that the sacraments have an inherent power, we must avoid going to the opposite extreme and holding that the sacraments are not real means of grace. There have been many, and are many today, who look upon baptism as simply a rite or ceremony of dedication of a child or adult person to God, and on the Lord's Supper as merely a memorial service to symbolize the truths of redemption and to remember Christ. Such a view of the sacraments is not in harmony with orthodox Calvinism or the Reformed Faith set forth in our church standards. Baptism is more than a rite of dedication; the Lord's Supper is more than a symbolic portrayal and memorial service. Both sacraments are real means of grace, although they have no inherent power.

162. Q. *What is a sacrament?*

A. *A sacrament is a holy ordinance instituted by Christ in his Church, to signify, seal, and exhibit unto those that are within the covenant of grace, the benefits of his mediation; to strengthen and increase their faith, and all other graces: to oblige them to obedience; to testify and cherish their love and communion one with another; and to distinguish them from these that are without.*

Scripture References
- Gen. 17:7, 10; Exod. 12; Matt. 28:19; 26:26–28. The sacraments are holy ordinances instituted by Christ in his church, that is, in and for the visible body of the covenant people of God.
- Rom. 4:11; 1 Cor. 11:24–25. The sacraments are intended to signify, seal, and exhibit the benefits of Christ's work of redemption.

- Rom. 15:8; Exod. 12:48. The sacraments are not intended for the world but for those within the sphere of the covenant of grace.
- Acts 2:38; 1 Cor. 10:16. The benefits of Christ's mediation constitute the meaning of the sacraments.
- Rom. 4:11; Gal. 3:27. The sacraments are intended to increase believers' faith, and all other graces.
- Rom. 6:3–4; 1 Cor. 10:21. Participation in the sacraments involves a pledge or covenant of obedience to Christ.
- Eph. 4:2–5; 1 Cor. 12:13. The sacraments are a bond of unity among Christian people.
- Eph. 2:11–12; Gen. 34:14. Participation in the sacraments is a badge of separation from the world on the part of Christian people.

Commentary

1. How does the Shorter Catechism define a sacrament? "A sacrament is a holy ordinance instituted by Christ, wherein, by sensible signs, Christ, and the benefits of the new covenant, are represented, sealed, and applied to believers" (S.C. 92). This is somewhat briefer than the Larger Catechism's definition, and it gives only what is essential to a correct definition of a sacrament. The Larger Catechism's answer is more detailed, and describes the nature and purpose of the sacraments more fully. We may analyze the Shorter Catechism's statement as follows: (a) A sacrament is a holy ordinance; it belongs to the classification of things called "holy ordinances"; some holy ordinances are sacraments; others are not; but every sacrament is a holy ordinance. (b) A sacrament is something instituted by Christ; that is, of course, by Christ during his life on earth. Thus marriage, while a holy ordinance, is not a sacrament, for it was not instituted by Christ during his earthly life; but baptism and the Lord's Supper were so instituted; therefore they are sacraments. (c) A sacrament involves the use of "sensible signs," that is, material elements such as water, bread, wine, and certain actions by which these elements are used. (d) A sacrament, with its "sensible signs," is for the purpose of portraying, sealing, and applying Christ and his redemption. (e) A sacrament is for believers (not for the world).

2. What is the original meaning of the word *sacrament?* The word *sacrament* does not occur in the Bible. It is derived from the Latin word *sacramentum,* which meant a pledge or an oath, especially a military oath of allegiance. In the early church the Latin *sacramentum* came into use as a translation of the Greek word *mysterion* ("mystery"). This word occurs twenty-seven times in the Greek New Testament; in Jerome's Latin version, the Vulgate, eight of these are translated by *sacramentum* (Eph. 1:9; 3:3, 9; 5:32; Col. 1:27; 1 Tim. 3:16; Rev. 1:20; 17:7). The Greek word *mysterion* means something which remains unknown until it is revealed; thus it came to be used for various Christian doctrines and ordinances, including baptism and the Lord's Supper, and so the Latin *sacramentum* came into use for the same things. Some have objected to the word *sacrament* because it does not occur in the Bible. This is foolish, for many necessary religious terms in common use are not found in the Bible; the word *Trinity* is an example; so are the words *attribute, infallible, supernatural,* and many others. These words do not occur in the Bible, but the ideas they stand for do, and the words are necessary as handles for the ideas. We cannot find out what a sacrament is by studying the history of the word *sacrament,* but we can properly use the word *sacrament* to designate a certain class of ordinances which we find in the Bible. The important thing is not that we should use only Bible words, but that the ideas we have in mind should be those intended by God in his Word.

3. For what body of people did Christ institute the sacraments? For his church, the body of people included in the sphere of the covenant of grace. Since the sacraments involve the use of external elements and actions, they have been entrusted to the visible church, that is, the church as a visible institution. We should always remember that baptism and the Lord's Supper are *church* ordinances. They are intended only for those who are members of the church, and except in extraordinary circumstances they should never be administered except in a congregation of Christ's church. To administer either sacrament to those outside the sphere of the covenant of grace is wrong. Private baptism and private communion are irregular and should be avoided. The idea that any company or association of Christian people may properly administer the Lord's Supper is also wrong. The sacraments pertain to the visible church as an institution; they are not to be individualized by private observance, nor divested of their ecclesiastical character by administration in voluntary associations or groups of Christian people. They are for the church only.

4. What is meant by the word *signify*? In this connection, "signify" means to be a sign of something, that is, to portray or represent something. Thus the sacraments are to signify the benefits of Christ's mediation unto those that are within the covenant of grace. In the Lord's Supper the bread signifies the body of Christ and the wine signifies his blood. The Lord's Supper as a whole signifies the believer's participation in the benefits of Christ's redemption. Spiritual realities are represented by material elements and external actions.

5. What is meant by the word *seal*? The word *seal* is here used in the sense of "to pledge," "to guarantee," or "legally to certify." The catechism states that the sacraments were instituted by Christ to seal the benefits of his mediation to those that are within the covenant of grace; that is, to guarantee, or legally to certify, these benefits to those persons. This does not mean that baptism and the Lord's Supper of themselves, as mere outward ordinances, can guarantee anything to their recipients, but it means that when the sacraments are *rightly used, with true faith in Christ,* they function as "seals" or divinely given certificates of the benefits of Christ's redemption. The person who, with true faith, makes a right use of the sacrament, is to regard them as seals of the covenant of grace—as God's guarantee of the fulfillment of all the covenant promises.

6. What is meant by the word *exhibit*? We would naturally suppose that the word *exhibit* here means "to show forth" or "to display," but that is not the meaning intended in the catechism nor in the Confession of Faith. Writing of the use of the same word in the Confession of Faith (27.3; 28.6), Dr. A. A. Hodge says: "The old English word 'exhibit,' there used, does not mean to *show forth;* but in the sense of the Latin *exhibere,* from which it is derived, *to administer,* to apply" (*Commentary on the Confession of Faith,* 451). In support of the explanation, Dr. Hodge points out that while the Larger Catechism says "to signify, seal, and exhibit," the Shorter Catechism in the corresponding place (question 92) says "represented, sealed, and applied." Thus "exhibit" must be understood in the sense of "apply." Here again we must realize that, as in the case of the verb *seal,* this "applying" must be understood to exist only when there is a right use of the sacraments, with true faith. Apart from real faith in Christ, the sacraments do not apply any spiritual benefits to those who receive them.

7. To whom are the sacraments intended "to signify, seal, and exhibit" Christ's benefits? "Unto those that are within the covenant of Grace," that is, to believers in Jesus Christ and to their children.

8. What are the benefits of Christ's mediation? These benefits include all that Christ has done, is doing, and will do in the future for his people. They include his work as our Redeemer in his three offices of Prophet,

Priest, and King. In short, the entire plan of salvation is embraced within their scope, from God's decree to redeem his elect, made before the creation of the world (Eph. 1:4), to the final glorification of the elect, and their enjoyment of eternal life in the kingdom of glory (Rom. 8:30). All this is included in the benefits of Christ's mediation which are signified, sealed, and exhibited by the sacraments.

9. What practical purposes do the sacraments serve in the life of believers? The sacraments serve "to strengthen and increase their faith, and all other graces," and also "to oblige them to obedience." That is, the sacraments when rightly used serve to strengthen and build up believers in all phases of their Christian life, thus making them better and more consistent Christians; and they also serve as pledges on the believer's part of obedience to the requirements of God's covenant of grace.

10. What function do the sacraments perform in human society as a whole? In addition to their other uses and functions, the sacraments serve "to distinguish" the people of God "from those that are without." That is, they serve as badges or emblems or evidences of membership in the covenant people of God. They mark off those that are within the covenant of grace from the population of the world in general. Baptism is the mark of church membership as such; a baptized person is rightly regarded as a member of Christ's church unless and until he has repudiated his baptism by long-continued neglect of the means of grace or has been excommunicated because of heinous sin. This function of baptism has been greatly obscured by the abuse of the sacrament which has become terribly common in American Protestantism, by which many churches will baptize any infants whatever, regardless of whether the parents are church members or not, and apart from any proper understanding and acceptance of the obligations of the covenant of grace. In large sections of American Protestantism baptism has come to be regarded merely as a ceremony for attaching a name to an infant and in some vague manner dedicating the infant to God. When we speak of baptism serving as a mark to distinguish the church from the world, we mean baptism strictly as set forth in the Bible and our church standards, not the modern American free and easy perversion of the sacrament.

While baptism is the mark of church membership as such, the Lord's Supper is the mark of *communicant* church membership, that is, of church membership as involving a voluntary personal profession of faith in Jesus Christ and obedience to him. As in the case of baptism, the true function of the

Lord's Supper has been greatly obscured by the extreme form of "open communion" which is practiced in many churches today, by which the decision whether to partake is left entirely to the individual, and by which virtually all who may wish to come are invited, even though they may have only a vague, sentimental attachment to Jesus, and may not be members in good standing of any truly evangelical church. This practice breaks down the distinction between the church and the world which the Lord's Supper is intended to maintain. Of course not all churches that practice "open communion" have this extreme form of it; some limit the invitation to members in good standing in evangelical denominations or churches; this, however, is not "open communion" in the strict sense but a form of "restricted communion."

163. Q. *What are the parts of a sacrament?*

A. *The parts of a sacrament are two: the one an outward and sensible sign, used according to Christ's own appointment; the other an inward and spiritual grace thereby signified.*

164. Q. *How many sacraments hath Christ instituted in his church under the New Testament?*

A. *Under the New Testament Christ hath instituted in his church only two sacraments, baptism and the Lord's Supper.*

Scripture References
- Matt. 3:11; 1 Peter 3:21; Rom. 2:28–29. The sacraments are not mere external signs or ceremonies, but involve also inward spiritual realities.
- Matt. 28:19; 1 Cor. 11:20, 23; Matt. 26:26–28. Baptism and the Lord's Supper are the only appointed New Testament sacraments.

Commentary
1. What is meant by saying that "the parts of a sacrament are two"?
This statement means that when a sacrament is rightly used, with true faith in Jesus Christ, it involves two parts, namely, an outward, sensible sign, and

an inward, spiritual grace. Those who use the sacraments wrongly, without true faith in Jesus Christ, do not really participate in *the sacraments;* they only participate in the outward forms or ritual of the sacraments, not in the spiritual realities of the sacraments.

2. What is meant by "an outward and sensible sign"? By an "outward" sign the catechism means a sign that exists in the external, material world—the realm of matter, having physical and chemical properties, existing in the dimensions of time and space. The sacramental elements (water, bread, wine), and their accompanying actions, are "outward" in this sense.

By a "sensible" sign the catechism means a sign that can be perceived by the senses, such as sight, taste, touch. The sacramental elements can be seen, touched, tasted; the sacramental actions can be perceived by the sense of sight. Thus the sacraments involve "sensible" signs.

3. In the outward part of the sacraments, what is necessary besides the actual material elements (water, bread, wine)? Besides these actual material elements, it is necessary that they be "used according to Christ's own appointment"; that is, in the manner appointed by Christ in the Scripture, with the proper actions, and with words which are truly in harmony with the institution of Christ. Thus in the sacrament of baptism, it is necessary that water be applied to the person baptized; but this is not sufficient; it must be applied in the name of the Triune God: the Father, Son, and Holy Spirit. In the Lord's Supper, it is not sufficient that bread and wine be passed to the communicants and partaken of by them; Christ's appointment must be followed in taking the elements, giving thanks for them, breaking the bread, giving the bread and wine to the communicants with the words of institution.

4. What is meant by "an inward and spiritual grace"? In this expression, "inward" is in contrast to "outward," "spiritual" is in contrast to "sensible," and "grace" is the counterpart of "sign." The word *grace* here means a saving work of God for and in the believer, which is also a gift of God to the believer. This grace is the counterpart of the external "sign"; the grace is what the sign stands for; the grace is the real thing, the reason for which the sign exists. The external sign may be regarded as a signboard pointing to the grace. This grace is called "inward" because it does not exist in the physical or material world, but in the realm of the "heart," the spirit, the realm of personality; it exists in what we commonly call the "soul." This grace is called "spiritual" because it does not affect the bodily senses, such as sight, taste, touch, or hearing, but the human spirit or soul; so far as it can be consciously perceived by the subject, it is perceived not by the senses but by spiritual discernment (1 Cor. 2:9–16).

5. What is the connection between the "outward and sensible sign" and the "inward and spiritual grace"? "There is in every sacrament a spiritual relation, or sacramental union, between the sign and the thing signified; whence it comes to pass that the names and effects of the one are attributed to the other" (Confession of Faith, 27.2). The Roman Catholic Church teaches that in the case of the Lord's Supper, at least, the sign is literally identical with the thing signified; the bread really is the actual body of Christ, and the wine really is the actual blood of Christ. Some Protestant churches have a doctrine of the Lord's Supper which approaches this Roman Catholic teaching. We believe, on the other hand, that the bread and wine only represent the body and blood of Christ. The bond of connection, or sacramental union, between the "outward and sensible sign" and the "inward and spiritual grace," then, is a symbolical and therefore a representative connection; the bread and wine symbolize, and therefore represent, the body and blood of Christ. In addition to this symbolic connection, there is what may be called an instrumental connection between the sign and the grace. That is to say, by Christ's appointment, when the outward sign is rightly used, with true faith, the spiritual grace which it stands for is actually given or conveyed to the recipient. God by his Holy Spirit bestows the grace on the person who uses the outward sign aright, so in this sense we may affirm that there is an instrumental connection between the sign and the grace. The grace is conveyed not by the sacrament of itself, but by the Holy Spirit; but inasmuch as the sacrament is a divinely appointed means of grace, the Holy Spirit honors it by bestowing the grace where the sacrament is used aright.

6. How many sacraments are there under the New Testament? Only two, namely, baptism and the Lord's Supper. These alone meet the requirements of the correct and scriptural definition of a sacrament which is set forth in the catechism (question 162). That is, these two divine ordinances, baptism and the Lord's Supper, are clearly in a class by themselves, having certain characteristics which no other divine ordinances possess, and therefore they are set apart from the rest and the term "sacraments" is reserved to these alone. This question of the catechism (question 164) is especially directed against the Roman Catholic doctrine that there are seven sacraments (baptism, confirmation, holy Eucharist, penance, extreme unction, holy orders, and matrimony). Part of these are essentially divine ordinances but not sacraments; others are not even divine ordinances, but have their roots in human tradition. Only two of this list of seven can really claim to be sacraments in the scriptural and theologically correct sense of the term.

165. Q. *What is baptism?*

A. *Baptism is a sacrament of the New Testament, wherein Christ hath ordained the washing with water in the name of the Father, and of the Son, and of the Holy Ghost, to be a sign and seal of ingrafting into himself, of remission of sins by his blood, and regeneration by his Spirit; of adoption and resurrection unto everlasting life; and whereby the parties baptized are solemnly admitted into the visible church, and enter into an open and professed engagement to be wholly and only the Lord's.*

Scripture References
- Matt. 28:19. The sacrament of baptism instituted by Christ.
- Gal. 3:27. Baptism is a sign and seal of union with Christ.
- Mark 1:4; Rev. 1:5. Baptism represents remission of sins by Christ's blood.
- Titus 3:5; Eph. 5:26. Baptism represents generation or the new birth.
- Gal. 3:26–27. Baptism represents adoption into the family of God.
- 1 Cor. 15:29; Rom. 6:3–5. Baptism stands for the resurrection unto everlasting life.
- 1 Cor. 12:13. Baptism is the rite of formal initiation into the visible church.
- Rom. 8:4. Baptism involves "an open and professed engagement to be wholly and only the Lord's."

Commentary

1. What action constitutes baptism? Baptism is constituted by a washing of the person with water in the name of the Father, and of the Son, and of the Holy Spirit, by a minister of Christ.

2. What is the proper mode of baptism? The mode of baptism is a matter of indifference. That is, the quantity of water to be used and the manner in which it is to be applied are not matters which have been appointed in the Scripture. In the history of the church there have been three modes of baptism, namely, effusion (pouring), sprinkling, and immersion. Any one of these constitutes a valid administration of baptism. The Confession of Faith states: "Dipping of the person into the water is not necessary; but baptism is rightly administered by pouring or sprinkling water upon the person" (28.3). It should be noted that the Confession does not say that immersion is wrong, but only that it is not necessary; nor does it say that sprinkling is the only right mode of baptism, but only that by sprinkling or pouring baptism is "rightly administered," that is, that either of these modes, equally with immersion, constitutes a valid administration of the sacrament.

3. Is it true that the Greek word translated "baptize" in the New Testament literally means "to immerse"? Certainly not. In its New Testament usage, the Greek verb *baptizo* literally means "to wash," as will be seen by looking up Mark 7:4 and Luke 11:38, in both of which texts this verb is used, and where the idea of "immersion" would obviously be out of place. The Greek noun *baptismos* literally means "washing," as is evident from Mark 7:4, 8 and Hebrews 9:10. To suppose that tables were cleansed by immersion is absurd. Yet the Greek text of Mark 7:4 speaks of the "baptism" of tables. The confident claim of Baptists that *baptizo* and *baptismos* in their New Testament usage mean "to immerse" and "immersion" will not stand the test of a careful scrutiny of the passages in the New Testament where these words occur.

4. What is the essential meaning of baptism? Essentially baptism signifies union with Christ, and consequently it signifies, in a general way, all the benefits which Christ brings to his people. There are also certain of Christ's benefits which are represented by baptism in a more particular and direct way, especially the washing away of our sins and the new birth by the power of the Holy Spirit.

5. What is the meaning of "ingrafting" in Christ? This phase means being brought into vital union with Christ, so that the person is a member of the spiritual body of which Christ is the head, a branch of the true vine, a partaker of the spiritual life and power of Christ. As a twig is grafted into a tree, and thereafter exists in vital union with the tree, receiving its nourishment and strength from the tree, so the believer is grafted into Christ, and thereafter lives in union with him, receiving his spiritual nourishment and strength from Christ.

6. What is the connection between baptism and the forgiveness of sins? Baptism is a sign and seal to the believer of the remission of his sins by the blood of Christ. Just as in ordinary life water is used to cleanse away dirt, so in the plan of salvation the blood of Christ cleanses away the sins of his people. This is of course a figure of speech; the "blood" of Christ means his death, at which his blood was shed; when the Bible says that the blood of Christ cleanses away our sins, the meaning is that God forgives our sins, and sanctifies our hearts, on the basis of Christ's atonement. These are transactions that take place in the spiritual realm; baptism is the outward sign and seal of them. There may be forgiveness of sins without baptism; there also may be (outward) baptism without the forgiveness of sins; but where baptism is rightly used it seals, and thus involves, the forgiveness of sins.

7. What is the relation between baptism and the new birth? Roman Catholics and some Protestants hold that baptism itself confers regeneration or the new birth, so that the two are virtually identical, and whoever is baptized is also regenerated. The great majority of Protestants reject this teaching as an error. It is a confusion of the sign with the thing signified. If baptism is a sign and seal of regeneration, then it cannot be identified with regeneration. Titus 3:5 is relevant in this connection; note that it does not speak of "the regeneration of washing," but of "the washing of regeneration," which is a very different thing. We are not regenerated by washing (baptism), but we are washed (spiritually cleansed) by regeneration (the new birth).

8. How is baptism a sign and seal of adoption into God's family? Galatians 3:26–27 provides the answer to this question. To be baptized, in the true sense and use of baptism, involves union with Christ and faith in Christ. By faith in Christ the believer is adopted into God's family. Thus baptism is a sign and seal of adoption.

9. How is baptism a sign and seal of the resurrection unto everlasting life? The catechism cites 1 Corinthians 15:29 and Romans 6:3–5 in support of this proposition. The former of these texts is a very difficult one, and apparently refers to an (unauthorized) custom in the Corinthian church of being baptized for the dead. The text does not sanction this custom, but recognizes it as existing, and the apostle then argues that if there is no resurrection, such baptism would be meaningless. From the apostle's argument we may properly infer that the baptism of any person would be useless and meaningless if there were no resurrection of the body. Thus baptism implies election unto everlasting life. Romans 6:3–5 specifically links the two ideas of baptism and the resurrection: the believer who is united to Christ in baptism shall also be united with Christ in his resurrection. The Baptist view that the basic meaning of baptism is identification with Christ in his burial and resurrection and that this requires immersion as the mode of baptism is without foundation. Romans 6:3–5 has nothing to do with the *mode* of baptism, which is not there under discussion; the subject under discussion is sanctification, not baptism; baptism is introduced into the argument to prove a point about sanctification. It is quite true, of course, that union with Christ in his death and resurrection is represented by baptism, but this is just part of what baptism represents, and it implies nothing concerning the mode of baptism; it does not imply that the act of baptism is intended directly to portray burial and resurrection by immersion under water and rising out of it.

10. What is the connection between baptism and church membership? The catechism states that by baptism "the parties baptized are solemnly admitted into the visible church." It is clear that baptism is a badge, sign, or emblem of membership in the visible church. A question arises, however, as to the precise function of baptism in this connection. Are people baptized because they are church members, or are they church members because they are baptized? Question 165 of the catechism and the similar statement of the Confession of Faith (28.1) seem at first sight to imply that people are church members because they are baptized. On the other hand, the Westminster Standards uniformly teach that the sacraments are for those who already are church members (Larger Catechism, 162; Confession of Faith, 27.1). While there has apparently always been some confusion on this point, it appears that the view that people are baptized because they are already church members is sound, and held by the most eminent writers on Reformed theology. The key to the difficulty may be found in the word *solemnly,* which is apparently used by the catechism in the sense of "formally" or "publicly." That is, those persons who are already in God's sight members of the visible church by reason of their covenant standing (in the case of infants) or by reason of their own profession of faith in Christ and obedience to him (in the case of adults) are formally and publicly *rec-*

ognized as members "solemnly admitted into the visible church"—by the sacrament of baptism. We might say that by baptism the persons baptized (whether adults or infants) are publicly recognized, not only as members of the visible church in general, but also as members of a particular branch and congregation of the visible church.

11. What engagement or promise on the human side is involved in baptism? "An open and professed engagement to be wholly and only the Lord's." In the case of adults being baptized, this engagement is entered into by them personally. In the case of infants, it is entered into by the parents on behalf of the children, as their proper representatives. The fact that baptism involves obligations on our part, as well as grace on God's part, is often insufficiently emphasized. We should always remember that baptism involves solemn vows on our part, as well as blessings on God's part.

166. Q. *Unto whom is baptism to be administered?*

A. *Baptism is not to be administered to any that are out of the visible church, till they profess their faith in Christ, and obedience to him, but infants descended from parents, either both or but one of them professing faith in Christ, and obedience to him, are, in that respect, within the covenant, and to be baptized.*

Scripture References

- Acts 2:38; 8:36–37. For adults to be baptized, a personal profession of faith in Christ is required.
- Gen. 17:7–9 compared with Gal. 3:9, 14; Col. 2:11–12; Acts 2:38–39; Rom. 4:11–12. God's covenant with Abraham includes all believers in Christ, together with their children.
- 1 Cor. 7:14. One Christian parent is sufficient to give children a "holy" or covenant status, even though the other parent may be an unbeliever.
- Matt. 28:19. All nations to be baptized.
- Luke 18:15–16. Infants brought to Jesus, with his approval, to be blessed by him.
- Rom. 11:16. The "holy" or covenant standing passes from parent to child, from "root" to "branches."

Commentary

1. What class of persons can rightly be baptized? Only those who are members of the visible church can rightly receive the sacrament of baptism.

2. Into what two classes are members of the visible church divided? The visible church is composed of two classes of people, namely, (a) those who have made a personal profession of faith in Christ and obedience to him; and (b) their infant children, that is, their children who have not yet made a personal profession of faith.

3. How does a person of adult age, or one who has reached the age of responsibility, become a member of the visible church? Persons formerly outside of the church become members of the church by making a public profession of faith in Christ and obedience to him. Upon making such a profession, they are admitted to membership and are thereupon baptized, and their names added to the roll of the particular congregation in which the sacrament is administered. Their baptism is both a token of their formal admission to the membership of the church, and a privilege which belongs to them as members.

4. How do the infants of Christian parents become members of the church? The infants of one or both Christian parents are born into the church, and thus are members from birth, just as children born in the United States are American citizens from birth. The infants of Christian parents are baptized because they are members of the church from birth. They are not made members by being baptized; on the contrary, they are baptized because they are already members from birth.

5. Why are the children of Christian parents members of the church from birth? They are members of the church from birth because of God's covenant with their parents, which is a continuation of God's covenant made with Abraham, which included his children after him as well as Abraham himself. However, the children of Christian parents do not have all the privileges of church membership until they themselves make a personal profession of faith in Christ, and obedience to him, and are thereupon admitted to the Lord's Supper.

6. Is it correct to speak of Christian young people, children of church members, who have themselves been baptized as infants, "joining the church" when they make a profession of faith and are admit-

ted to the Lord's Supper? No. A person cannot "join" anything if he is already a member of it. The children of Christian parents are *already* church members from their birth, in evidence of which they are baptized. To speak of such young people "joining the church" is wrong, for it implies that previously they were not members, and that in their case baptism was not a sign of church membership. We do not speak of a person "joining" the United States, or becoming an American citizen, when he reaches his twenty-first birthday; he was an American citizen the day he was born, even though unable to express personal allegiance to his country. The common manner of speaking of Christian young people "joining the church" is contrary to the scriptural doctrines of the covenant of grace, of the church, and of baptism. This prevalent manner of speaking betrays an individualistic, baptistic ideology which is contrary to the ideology of the covenant of grace which is set forth in our church standards and which we believe to be scriptural. In denominations where this individualistic ideology is prevalent it will probably require an entire generation—perhaps two generations—of continuous, faithful preaching and teaching of the doctrine of the covenant of grace, and its implications, before the people can be brought to the point where they will no longer speak of the children of Christian parents "joining the church." Here is a real challenge for all ministers and members who take the doctrine of the covenant of grace seriously.

7. Do all churches believe that the infants of Christian parents ought to be baptized? No. The Baptists and others of similar faith teach that only those who can make a personal profession of faith are to be baptized. This belief, however, has never been held by more than a minority of the Christian people of the world. The vast majority of professing Christians have believed in infant baptism.

8. What objections are commonly urged against the practice of infant baptism? It is commonly objected by Baptists and some others: (a) that there is no command in the New Testament to baptize infants; (b) that there is no example of infants being baptized; (c) that infants cannot understand the meaning of baptism and therefore it cannot benefit them; (d) that most of those baptized in infancy grow up to be ungodly, or in later life turn out to be merely nominal Christians; (e) that infant baptism is a Roman Catholic superstition.

9. How can we answer the objection that there is in the New Testament no command to baptize infants? We reply that no command is needed. Infant baptism is based on God's covenant with Abraham. Infants received the sign of the covenant (circumcision) in Old Testament times; therefore they are to receive the sign of the same covenant also in New Testament times (baptism). We would not expect to find a definite command to baptize infants. On the contrary, we would expect that, if the Baptist position were correct, there would be a definite command *not* to baptize infants, as this would be a change from the Old Testament practice.

10. Is it true that there is in the New Testament no example of infants being baptized? It is true that there is no positive proof that infants were baptized, or that they were not baptized, one way or the other. Similarly there is no positive proof in the New Testament that women partook of the Lord's Supper. But a number of New Testament passages are best explained on the presumption that infants were baptized. For example, the Philippian jailer "was baptized, he and all his" (Acts 16:33); Paul baptized "the household of Stephanas" (1 Cor. 1:16); Cornelius was baptized together with "his kinsmen and near friends" (Acts 10:24, 48). Can we suppose that in all these various family groups there were only adults, with no infants or young children?

11. How can we answer the objection that infants cannot understand the meaning of baptism, and therefore it cannot benefit them? Jesus took young children in his arms and blessed them, upon their parents' request. The Greek word means "babies," not children of eight or nine years old. This was not baptism, but it has something to do with the question of infant baptism. Clearly these children were too young to understand who Jesus was, or what he was doing. Yet Jesus did not hesitate to take them in his arms, and bless them. Who shall say that this was a useless act, or could not bring benefit to the children? As elsewhere in the Bible, the parents' faith was accepted on behalf of the children (compare Mark 9:24–27).

12. Is it true that most of those baptized as infants grow up to be either ungodly or merely nominal Christians? This has often been asserted, but never proved. There are no accurate statistics to prove any such claim. Such evidence as exists proves nothing one way or the other. Many people who are baptized in adolescence or adult life also later turn out to be either ungodly or merely nominal Christians. It has never yet been proved that churches which reject infant baptism are more pure than those which practice it. Nor has it ever been proved that those baptized as adults tend, as a class, to be more faithful and consistent Christians than those baptized in their infancy.

13. Is infant baptism a Roman Catholic superstition? Of course the fact that the Roman Catholic Church practices infant baptism does not prove that infant baptism is wrong. The Roman Church also accepts the doctrine of the Trinity, the deity of Christ, and many other truths of Christianity; we do not reject these because the Church of Rome teaches them. As a matter of fact the practice of infant baptism existed, and can be proved to have existed, in the church long before the appearance of the characteristic Romish errors and superstitions.

167. Q. *How is our baptism to be improved by us?*

A. *The needful but much neglected duty of improving our baptism, is to be performed by us all our life long, especially in the time of temptation, and when we are present at the administration of it to others; by serious and thankful consideration of the nature of it, and of the ends for which Christ instituted it, the privileges and benefits conferred and sealed thereby, and our solemn vows made therein; by being humbled for our sinful defilement, our falling short of, and walking contrary to, the grace of baptism, and our engagements; by growing up to assurance of pardon of sin, and of all other blessings sealed to us in that sacrament; by drawing strength from the death and resurrection of Christ, into whom we are baptized, for the mortifying of sin, and quickening of grace; and by endeavoring to live by faith, to have our conversation in holiness and righteousness, as those that have therein given up their names to Christ; and to walk in brotherly love, as being baptized by the same Spirit into one body.*

Scripture References

- Col. 2:11–12; Rom. 6:4, 6, 11. We are to improve our baptism throughout life, and especially in time of temptation to sin.
- Rom. 6:3–5. We are to think seriously of the meaning of our baptism, and its implications for our lives.

- 1 Cor. 1:11–13; Rom. 6:2–3. We are to be humbled for our failure to live according to the implications of our baptism, and our own vows.
- Rom. 4:11–12; 1 Peter 3:21. It is our duty to attain in actual experience the blessings sealed to us in our baptism.
- Rom. 6:3–5; Gal. 3:26–27; Rom. 6:22; Acts 2:38. Rightly to improve our baptism involves a serious effort to trust Christ fully and lead a genuinely righteous and holy life.
- 1 Cor. 12:13, 25–27. Improving our baptism involves a realization of our unity with our fellow Christians, and an effort to walk in brotherly love with them, since all have been baptized by the same Spirit into one body.

Commentary

1. What does the catechism mean by "improving our baptism"? By "improving" our baptism, the catechism means using it to good purpose in our daily life; thus it means experiencing its meaning, and working out its implications, in actual life. Baptism is (a) a sacrament; (b) a doctrine; (c) an obligation to progressive Christian experience and service. We are to receive the sacrament, by being baptized; to believe and understand the doctrine, that is, the nature and meaning of baptism; and to live out the implications as growing Christians. This question of the catechism is intended to guard against the all-too-prevalent tendency to regard baptism as a mere rite or ceremony, something to be attended to and then forgotten. That this tendency was common 300 years ago when the catechism was written is shown by the reference to improving our baptism as a "much neglected duty." The situation is still the same today.

2. Is the efficacy of baptism limited to the time at which it is administered? Certainly not. Baptism is a sign and seal of salvation from sin, and its efficacy continues as long as there remains any sin, or effects of sin, to be saved from. A mistaken notion that the efficacy of baptism is tied to the time of administration of it is the reason for some people's opposition to the baptism of the infants of believers. Since many of the things that baptism stands for or implies cannot be experienced by infants (such as repentance, faith, conscious assurance of salvation, etc.), some people hold that there is no use or meaning in the baptism of infants. But they are greatly mistaken. The efficacy of baptism covers the person's whole life subsequent to his baptism; those baptized as infants are to repent, believe, attain assurance, seek sanctification, etc., when they reach an age at which these experiences are psychologically possible for them. We are born into this world only once, but we celebrate our birthday year after year throughout life; we are baptized only once, but are to remember our baptism and experience its meaning, and work out its implications, year after year throughout life.

3. At what times ought we especially to improve our baptism? In times when we are confronted with temptation, when the recollection of our baptism should serve as a reminder that we are of the covenant people of God and must live accordingly and not compromise with sin as ungodly and worldly people do; and when we are present at the administration of baptism to others, when the meaning of baptism, and the vows connected with it, should become especially real and vivid to our minds and hearts. On such occasions we should remember that we, too, have received this same sacrament, with the same meaning, and that we, too, are bound by the same solemn covenant vows.

4. Do we ever really fulfill our duty in improving our baptism? No, for even the most faithful Christians break the law of God daily in thought, word, and deed. Therefore in thinking of our baptism and what it should mean in our life, we are always to be humbled because of our past unfaithfulness and failures in living up to our solemn vows. Some people who are not very earnest about seeking holiness yet have a very complacent feeling about their own baptism, sometimes even counting on baptism to get them into heaven when they die. Such is a wrong attitude. The more fully we appreciate the real meaning of our baptism, the farther will spiritual complacency be from our hearts; instead, we will have a real humility because of our personal failure to attain what was our duty to attain.

5. What ways of improving our baptism does the catechism specify? The catechism specifies a number of Christian experiences and duties, such as being humbled for our sins, growing up to assurance of salvation, drawing strength from Christ for mortifying sin and quickening of grace, etc. These various experiences and duties, taken together, mean a continuous, serious undertaking to live a faithful, consistent Christian life, according to the teachings of the Word of God, all along the line. As baptism stands for salvation from sin, improving our baptism involves taking salvation from sin seriously, in actual living experience. This in turn involves experiencing the reality of, and living out the implications of, effectual calling, justification, adoption, sanctification, and the several benefits which in this life do either accompany or flow from them. That is, improving our baptism means walking steadily forward in the highway of God's salvation, according to God's Word.

6. What does improving our baptism imply concerning Christian unity? By the baptism of the Holy Spirit all Christians are baptized into the invisible church; by the sacrament of baptism, all Christians are publicly recognized as members of the visible church of Christ. This implies the duty of cultivating unity and brotherly love with those who participate in the same baptism and are members of the same body. We should cultivate unity and love with all faithful Christians, and especially with those who are fellow members with us of the same branch of the visible church.

168. Q. *What is the Lord's Supper?*

A. *The Lord's Supper is a sacrament of the New Testament, wherein, by giving and receiving bread and wine according to the appointment of Jesus Christ, his death is showed forth; and they that worthily communicate feed upon his body and blood, to their spiritual nourishment and growth in grace; have their union and communion with him confirmed; testify and renew their thankfulness, and engagement to God, and their mutual love and fellowship each with other, as members of the same mystical body.*

Scripture References
- Luke 22:20. The Lord's Supper is a sacrament of the New Testament.
- Matt. 26:26–28; 1 Cor. 11:23–26. The Lord's Supper is constituted by giving and receiving bread and wine according to the appointment of Christ.
- 1 Cor. 10:16. The right use of the Lord's Supper confirms the believer's union and communion with Christ.
- 1 Cor. 11:24. Partaking of the Lord's Supper involves thankfulness to God for his grace.
- 1 Cor. 10:14–16, 21. The Lord's Supper involves a renewal of our covenant vows of love and obedience to God.
- 1 Cor. 10:17. By partaking of the Lord's Supper, believers show and renew their mutual love and fellowship as members of Christ's spiritual body, the church.

Commentary

1. What is meant by saying that "the Lord's Supper is a sacrament of the New Testament"? In this statement, the phrase "the New Testament" does not refer to the New Testament as a book, or portion of the Bible, but to the New Testament (or New Covenant) as a dispensation of the covenant of grace. The Greek word translated "Testament" in Luke 22:20 usually means "covenant" in its New Testament usage, and it is so translated in this verse in the American Revised Version. The covenant of grace constitutes God's plan and arrangements for the salvation of his people. The old dispensation of the covenant of grace was from Moses to Christ, and is called "the Old Testament" or "the Old Covenant." The new dispensation of the covenant of grace is from the crucifixion of Christ to the end of the world, and is called "the New Testament" or "the New Covenant." Circumcision and the Passover were sacraments of "the Old Covenant" or "the Old Testament"; baptism and the Lord's Supper are the sacraments of "the New Covenant" or "the New Testament."

2. What constitutes the Lord's Supper? The Lord's Supper is constituted by giving and receiving bread and wine according to the appointment of Jesus Christ. What is meant by "the appointment of Jesus Christ" is explained in the next question of the catechism (question 169). There may be many circumstances (such as time, place, frequency, and the like) which may vary greatly without interfering with the essential character of the Lord's Supper. On the other hand, those matters which are included in Christ's appointment are essential elements of the Lord's Supper, which may not be changed or omitted. Any substantial deviation from Christ's appointment would involve the danger of destroying the essential character of the ordinance as the Lord's Supper. Thus the Roman Catholic Mass is not really the Lord's Supper because the communicants receive only the bread or wafer and not the wine, which is reserved for the priest alone. This is a substantial deviation from Christ's appointment. Similarly, to omit any of the sacramental actions, such as the breaking of the bread, is a deviation from Christ's appointment, although less serious than the Roman Catholic practice referred to above.

3. What is the essential meaning of the Lord's Supper? By the Lord's Supper, the death of Jesus Christ is showed forth. This means, of course, that the Lord's Supper portrays the doctrine of the substitutionary atonement, by which Christ died for the sins of his people. We might say that in the Lord's

Supper the atonement of Christ is acted out in a pageant. There is a possible reference to this in Galatians 3:1, where Paul tells the Galatian Christians that Jesus Christ had been "evidently set forth" (that is, *visibly* set forth) before their eyes, and even crucified among them. Our Lord's own words ("This is my body, which is given for you"; "This is my blood . . . which is shed for many, for the remission of sins") make it unmistakably clear that the doctrine of the substitutionary atonement is the basic meaning of the Lord's Supper. This is not all that the Lord's Supper means, but it is the basic meaning of the sacrament, and without this basic truth, the other things which it represents are meaningless. Therefore persons who have no knowledge of the doctrine of the substitutionary atonement cannot rightly partake of the Lord's Supper. Similarly, those who, under the influence of modern theology, have denied or explained away the substitutionary atonement of Christ cannot rightly partake of the Lord's Supper, and for them to go through the motions of it is both blasphemy and a meaningless mockery. Those who do not believe that Christ died for our sins, in the honest, historic meaning of the words, are not Christians and have no right to the Lord's Supper, since they reject its central truth.

4. What is the purpose of the Lord's Supper? In brief, the purpose of the Lord's Supper is the spiritual edification of the Lord's people. This means that rightly partaking of the Lord's Supper will strengthen, encourage, and spiritually build up Christians along the whole line of their Christian faith, life, and work. The catechism elaborates this by stating that those who rightly partake of the Lord's Supper (a) are confirmed in their spiritual relation to Christ their Savior; (b) are renewed and strengthened in their resolve to live a life of thankfulness and obedience to God; and (c) testify and renew their love and fellowship for their fellow believers. Thus the right use of the Lord's Supper encourages and builds up the Christian in relation to his Savior, in relation to his God, and in relation to his brethren.

5. What is the relation of the Lord's Supper to the second coming of Christ? "For as oft as ye eat this bread, and drink this cup, ye do show the Lord's death *till he come*" (1 Cor. 11:26). The Lord's Supper points forward to the second coming of Christ. The Christian's partaking of the Lord's Supper thus involves a profession of faith in the second coming of Christ. The Lord's Supper shows that human history will not go on and on forever; it will come to a sudden termination at the second coming of Christ. The Lord's Supper is full of meaning with respect to the Christian philosophy of history. In this it parallels the Sabbath, which originated at the creation, and shall be consummated in eternity (Gen. 2:2–3; Heb. 4:1–10). The Lord's Supper bridges the gap from the first coming of Christ to his second coming, from the crucifixion to the Judgment Day. By portraying the Lord's death, it points us backward to Calvary; by the command to observe it "till he come," it points us forward to the Last Day. The three great focal points of history, according to the Bible, are (a) the creation of the universe; (b) the crucifixion of Christ; (c) the "Day of the Lord," that is, the Last Day, or the day of Christ's second coming. The Sabbath, which originated prior to sin and apart from redemption, links the first and last of these points together; it spans the course of history from the original creation to the eternal consummation. The Lord's Supper, which was instituted after man sinned, and as a part of the scheme of redemption, spans the course of *Christian* history from the cross to the "great white throne."

169. Q. *How hath Christ appointed bread and wine to be given and received in the sacrament of the Lord's Supper?*

A. *Christ hath appointed the ministers of his word, in the administration of this sacrament of the Lord's Supper, to set apart the bread and wine from common use, by the word of institution, thanksgiving and prayer; to take and break the bread, and to give both the bread and the wine to the communicants: who are, by the same appointment, to take and eat the bread, and to drink the wine, in thankful remembrance that the body of Christ was broken and given, and his blood shed, for them.*

Scripture References

• 1 Cor. 11:23–24; Matt. 26:26–28; Mark 14:22–25; Luke 22:17–20. The institution of the sacrament of the Lord's Supper by Jesus Christ.

Commentary

1. Where in the New Testament is the record of Christ's institution of the Lord's Supper found? In the three Synoptic Gospels (Matthew,

Mark, and Luke), and in Paul's first epistle to the Corinthians, chapter 11. The latter is the fullest account of the institution of the Lord's Supper.

2. Why is it important that Christ's appointment be exactly followed in the administration of the Lord's Supper? The headship of Christ over the church requires this. The church is subject to Christ, and must obey his instructions and conform to his will in all things (Eph. 5:23–24). The Lord's Supper is *the Lord's* supper; therefore the church has no right to change or modify it. It did not originate in custom or tradition, but from a specific command of the Lord Jesus Christ. The church has no right to alter it, to add to it, or to subtract from it.

3. Whom has Christ appointed to administer the Lord's Supper? Christ has appointed "the ministers of his word" to administer the Lord's Supper. While this truth is not stated in the biblical accounts of the institution of the Lord's Supper, it follows from other portions of the Scripture which speak of officers being ordained to have charge of the work and worship of the visible church. Ministers of Christ are called "stewards of the mysteries of God" (1 Cor. 4:1–2; Titus 1:7). The word *steward* means a person officially entrusted with the oversight, care, or administration of something. As the sacraments are certainly part of "the mysteries of God," it follows that they have been committed to the stewardship of the ministers of Christ. The same truth follows by analogy from the Old Testament, in which the sacrifices, ritual, tabernacle, and its contents and worship were entrusted to the priests and Levites. While there is of course a true sense in which every Christian is a priest of God, yet so far as official responsibility for the preaching of the Word and administration of the sacraments is concerned, the ministers of Christ are the New Testament counterpart of the priests and Levites of the Old Testament.

Some people believe that any Christian may administer baptism and the Lord's Supper. This, however, is contrary to good order in the church. The church is a visible body and as such must necessarily have leadership in its official functions. Good order requires that such authority be in the hands of those who have been duly chosen, examined, and set apart for the exercise of it, and who accordingly can be held responsible for the rightful use of it. That such is indeed the will of Christ is shown by the considerations adduced in the preceding paragraph. The admonition of Paul "Let all things be done decently and in order" (1 Cor. 14:40) applies to the administration of the sacraments as well as to the matters with which the apostle was immediately concerned in that context.

4. What are the elements used in the Lord's Supper? The sacramental elements used in the Lord's Supper are two in number, namely, bread and wine. These elements serve a symbolical purpose. The bread represents Christ's body; the wine represents his blood. Taken together, the bread and wine represent his human nature, which he took to himself when he "was made flesh, and dwelt among us" (John 1:14) by being born as a human child in Bethlehem.

5. What sacramental actions are involved in the Lord's Supper? There are six sacramental actions involved in the Lord's Supper. Four of them were performed by Jesus (taking the bread and the cup, giving thanks, breaking the bread, giving the bread and the cup to the disciples). Two sacramental actions were performed by the disciples (taking the bread and the cup; eating the bread and drinking the wine). These six sacramental actions, taken together in their true meaning, portray or act out the atonement of Christ and a sinner's receiving him by faith.

6. What is the meaning of the four sacramental actions performed by Jesus? The meaning of the four sacramental actions performed by Jesus, and by his ministers in his name, is as follows: (a) He *took* the bread and the cup from the table where the Passover meal had been partaken of, signifying his taking a human nature (body and soul) when he was born into this world in Bethlehem. (b) He *blessed,* or gave thanks for, the bread and the wine, setting them apart from ordinary uses for a special religious purpose. This action signifies our Savior's being set apart for his special work as the Redeemer of men, when he was baptized by John at the Jordan River at the age of thirty years. Jesus had previously been known as a carpenter, but now he was solemnly set apart for his special work, which he followed exclusively from that day until his crucifixion. (c) He *broke* the bread, an action which signifies the breaking of his own body by being nailed to the cross, and by the spear of the Roman soldier which was thrust into his side after his death. This sacramental action reminds us that we are not saved by Jesus' teachings, or by his life alone, but preeminently by his death on the cross. (d) He *gave* the bread and wine to the disciples, signifying the gift of Christ to sinful men by the infinite grace of God (John 3:16) and the preaching of the gospel in which this divine gift of the Savior is offered to sinners.

7. What is the meaning of the two sacramental actions performed by the disciples? The meaning of the two sacramental actions performed by the disciples, and by communicants today, is as follows: (a) They *took* the bread and the cup, signifying taking Jesus as Savior by believing on him. Christ's incarnation, baptism, and atonement, and the preaching of the gospel, must be followed by personal faith in Jesus Christ on the part of sinners. This personal faith in Christ for salvation is signified by taking the bread and the cup. (b) They *ate* the bread and *drank* the wine, signifying dependence on Christ for spiritual life and growth. As our bodily life is dependent on daily food and drink, without which we could not have bodily life and health, so our spiritual life is dependent on Christ, and apart from him we cannot have spiritual life and health. Partaking of the elements of bread and wine signifies our continued dependence on Christ, by our spiritual union with him, for our growth in grace unto the perfection which shall be ours in the state of glory (Eph. 4:13).

170. Q. *How do they that worthily communicate in the Lord's Supper feed upon the body and blood of Christ therein?*

A. *As the body and blood of Christ are not corporally or carnally present in, with, or under the bread and wine in the Lord's Supper, and yet are spiritually present to the faith of the receiver, no less truly and really than the elements themselves are to their outward senses; so they that worthily communicate in the sacrament of the Lord's Supper, do therein feed upon the body and blood of Christ, not after a corporal and carnal, but in a spiritual manner; yet truly and really while by faith they receive and apply unto themselves Christ crucified, and all the benefits of his death.*

Scripture References

- Acts 3:21. Christ's human nature is now in heaven, and must remain there until the end of the world; therefore his body and blood "are not corporally or carnally present in, with, or under the bread and wine in the Lord's Supper."
- Matt. 26:26, 28. Christ's body and blood are spiritually present to the faith of the person who receives the Lord's Supper, just as the bread and wine are present to their outward senses.

- 1 Cor. 11:24–29. Those who rightly partake of the Lord's Supper feed upon Christ's body and blood, not in a physical sense, but spiritually, and yet truly and really.
- 1 Cor. 10:16. Those who rightly partake of the Lord's Supper by faith receive and apply to themselves Christ crucified, and all the benefits of his atonement.

Commentary

1. What are the principal views concerning the presence of the body and blood of Christ in the Lord's Supper? There are three principal views concerning the presence of the body and blood of Christ in the Lord's Supper, namely, (a) the Roman Catholic doctrine; (b) the Lutheran doctrine; and (c) the Reformed doctrine. These three are united in affirming that in the Lord's Supper believers receive and feed upon the body and blood of Christ. They differ as to the mode of Christ's presence in the sacrament and the mode of the believer's feeding upon his body and blood.

2. What is the Roman Catholic doctrine concerning the presence of the body and blood of Christ in the Lord's Supper? The Roman Catholic doctrine, called "transubstantiation," was officially adopted as a doctrine by the Fourth Lateran Council, A.D. 1215, and authoritatively defined by the Council of Trent, A.D. 1545–63, as follows: "If any one shall say that, in the Holy Sacrament of the Eucharist, there remains, together with the Body and Blood of our Lord Jesus Christ, the substance of the Bread and Wine, and shall deny that wonderful and singular conversion of the whole substance of the Bread into (His) Body and of the Wine into (His) Blood, the species only of the Bread and Wine remaining—which conversion the Catholic Church most fittingly calls Transubstantiation—let him be anathema." (The word *species* is here used to mean "outward appearance," while *substance* is used to mean "reality"). Thus the Roman Catholic Church teaches that the bread and wine are miraculously changed into the literal body and blood of Christ, only the outward appearance of bread and wine remaining. This doctrine has the corollary of the idea of the Mass as a *sacrifice* in which Christ is offered up anew for the sins of men. A common Roman Catholic catechism speaks of the Mass as the unbloody sacrifice of the body and blood of Christ, and adds that the Mass is the same sacrifice as that of the cross, though without real shedding of blood or real death, since of course Christ can die no more.

3. How can the Roman Catholic doctrine of transubstantiation be shown to be false? A. A. Hodge (*Outlines of Theology*) presents the following points as an argument against the Romish doctrine: (a) By analogy of the Scripture use of language, the word *is* in the statement "This is my body" must be understood to mean "represents"; see Genesis 41:26–27; Exodus 12:11; Daniel 7:24; Revelation 1:20. (b) Paul refers to one of the elements as "bread," even after it has been consecrated in the Lord's Supper: 1 Corinthians 10:16; 11:26–28. (c) Even Roman Catholics hold that in every sacrament there is *a sign* and *a thing signified*. The doctrine of transubstantiation confuses, and indeed identifies, the sign with the thing signified, by holding that the bread and wine become the literal body and blood of Christ; thus the doctrine is contrary to the proper definition of a sacrament, held even by the Church of Rome itself. (d) If transubstantiation were true, it would mean that we could no longer believe the testimony of our senses, which tell us that bread is bread and not flesh, and that wine is wine and not blood. No miracle recorded in the Bible ever involved such a contradiction of the senses, which are God-given and reliable within their proper sphere. (e) Transubstantiation is also contrary to reason, because it teaches that Christ's human body, while wholly present in heaven, may yet be present at many different places on earth at the same time. Also it is contrary to reason in maintaining that the body and blood of Christ are present without their sensible qualities, while the sensible qualities of bread and wine are present without the substance of bread and wine, since qualities can have no existence apart from the substance of which they are qualities. (f) The doctrine of transubstantiation is part and parcel of an anti-Christian system of priestcraft, which regards the Mass as a sacrifice, and virtually puts the priest and his work in the place of Christ and his work as the object of people's faith. For all the above reasons, we may rightly conclude that the doctrine of transubstantiation is false, unscriptural, and religiously harmful.

4. What is the historic Lutheran doctrine concerning the presence of the body and blood of Christ in the Lord's Supper? Following the teaching of the Reformer Martin Luther, orthodox Lutheranism teaches that "the Sacrament of the Altar" is "the true body and blood of our Lord Jesus Christ under the bread and wine, for us Christians to eat and to drink, instituted by Christ Himself" (Luther's Small Catechism). This is quite different from the Roman Catholic doctrine of transubstantiation, for the Lutheran doctrine denies that the bread and wine are changed into the body and blood of Christ. Orthodox Lutheranism does, however, hold to a real bodily and local presence of the body and blood of Christ in the sacrament. This is coupled with a doctrine of the ubiquity of the glorified body of Christ. While we believe that these elements of the historic Lutheran doctrine of the Lord's Supper are erroneous, we should realize that it is both ignorant and unfair to say, as some do, that the Lutheran doctrine is almost the same as that of the Church of Rome.

5. What is the historic Reformed doctrine concerning the presence of the body and blood of Christ in the Lord's Supper? The orthodox Reformed doctrine is set forth in question 170 of the catechism. This doctrine affirms that in the Lord's Supper true believers "truly and really" feed upon "the body and blood of Christ, not after a corporal and carnal, but in a spiritual manner." The Reformed doctrine expressly denies that the body and blood of Christ are "corporally or carnally present in, with, or under the bread and wine in the Lord's Supper," thus rejecting both the Roman Catholic and the Lutheran doctrines. Yet the body and blood of Christ are held to be "spiritually present to the faith of the receiver, no less truly and really than the elements themselves are to their outward senses."

A. A. Hodge (*Outline of Theology*) summarizes the doctrine of the historic Reformed creeds as follows: "All the Reformed agree as to the following particulars: 1st. This eating was not with the mouth in any manner. 2d. It was only by the soul that they were received. 3d. It was by faith, which is declared to be the hand and mouth of the soul. 4th. It was by or through the power of the Holy Ghost. But this receiving Christ's body is not confined to the Lord's Supper; it takes place whenever faith in him is exercised."

6. If a person who is not a true believer partakes of the sacramental elements, does he receive and feed upon the body and blood of Christ? No, for such a person lacks the faith by which alone Christ and his benefits can be received by any human being. Such a partaker would receive only bread and wine, and his partaking of the elements would be presumptuous and sinful.

7. What is meant by "worthily communicat[ing] in the sacrament of the Lord's Supper"? We should note carefully that "worthily" is an adverb, not an adjective. This adverb, which is taken from Paul's words in 1 Corinthians 11:27, describes the manner of partaking of the sacrament, not the character of the person who partakes. It does not mean that a person must be *worthy* of partaking of the Lord's Supper. Since all human beings are sinners, and can only be saved by the free mercy of God, of course none can ever be worthy of partaking of the Lord's Supper; to speak of being worthy is the same as to speak of *deserving grace,* a contradiction in terms: if we deserve it, then it is not grace; if it is grace, then it is something we do not deserve. The adverb *unworthily* is translated in the American Revised Version as "in an unworthy manner," which brings out the meaning clearly. To partake in an unworthy manner would be to partake without true faith in Christ, or while cherishing unrepented sin in our hearts, or without a proper understanding of the meaning of the Lord's Supper.

We should realize, too, that the word translated "damnation" in 1 Corinthians 11:29 does not necessarily mean eternal damnation. The Greek word is *krima,* which means "judgment." This word is translated "judgment" thirteen times in the King James Version of the New Testament. The American Revision translates it by "judgment" in 1 Corinthians 11:29. The nature of the divine judgment in question is indicated by the next verse (30): "For this cause many are weak and sickly among you, and many sleep." (See *Blue Banner Faith and Life,* vol. 3 [April–June 1948], 92–93.)

171. Q. *How are they that receive the sacrament of the Lord's Supper to prepare themselves before they come unto it?*

A. *They that receive the sacrament of the Lord's Supper are, before they come, to prepare themselves thereunto, by examining themselves of their being in Christ, of their sins and wants; of the truth and measure of their knowledge, faith, repentance; love to God and the brethren, charity to all men, forgiving those that have done them wrong; of their desires after Christ, and of their new obedience; and by renewing the exercise of these graces, by serious meditation, and fervent prayer.*

Scripture References

- 1 Cor. 11:28. Self-examination is required before partaking of the Lord's Supper.
- 2 Cor. 13:5. A Christian should examine himself as to the reality of his faith and experience.

- 1 Cor. 5:7; Exod. 12:15. Separation from sin is required as a preparation for receiving the Lord's Supper.
- 1 Cor. 11:29; 2 Cor. 13:5; Matt. 26:28; Zech. 12:10; 1 Cor. 11:31; 10:16–17; Acts 2:46–47; 1 Cor. 5:8; 11:18, 20; Matt. 5:23–24. In preparing to partake of the Lord's Supper, it is our duty to examine ourselves concerning the "truth and measure" of our knowledge, faith, repentance, and consistency of Christian living.
- Isa. 55:1; John 7:37; 1 Cor. 5:7–8; 11:24–28; Heb. 10:21–22, 24; Ps. 26:6; 2 Chron. 30:18–19; Matt. 26:26. We are to examine ourselves as to our desires after Christ, and our new obedience to him; we are to seek the renewal of all Christian graces, and to engage in serious meditation and prayer for divine grace.

Commentary

1. Why is special preparation necessary before partaking of the Lord's Supper? Because of the importance of the Lord's Supper, the solemn nature of the sacrament, and the danger of incurring divine judgments if we partake in an unworthy manner. Proper preparation is required, not only by these considerations, but by the specific command of the Word of God (1 Cor. 11:28). In the face of this express command, it is definitely wrong and sinful to partake of the Lord's Supper without proper preparation.

2. What is the purpose of such special preparation for the Lord's Supper? The purpose of such special preparation is that we may partake of the sacrament aright, to our strengthening, encouragement, and growth in grace, not to judgment or being chastened of the Lord. The purpose of self-examination is not to discourage us and frighten us away from the Lord's table, but that we may approach the Lord's table aright and receive a blessing. Note 1 Corinthians 11:28: "But let a man examine himself, *and so let him eat of that bread, and drink of that cup.*" The apostle does not say, "Let a man examine himself, and refrain from eating of that bread." The outcome of self-examination ought to be repentance and confession of sin, renewed faith and love toward our Savior, and then receiving his blessing at the communion table. The "communion season" is the divinely appointed time for taking an inventory of our spiritual state, measuring ourselves by the divine standard, repenting of and forsaking what is contrary to God's will, and resolving by God's grace to live a life that will be pleasing to Him.

3. Why does the church have special services in preparation for the Lord's Supper? What is their purpose, and do they fulfill that purpose? The purpose of special preparatory services before the Lord's Supper is obedience to the command of 1 Corinthians 11:28, 31. Every individual Christian should examine himself and make his own preparation individually, but for our greater encouragement and assistance it is eminently proper to have special services of the church before the Lord's Supper is administered. Such services are to impress upon us the wickedness of our sins, our great need of God's grace, and the urgent duty of hearty repentance, so that we may not add sin to sin by partaking in an unworthy manner. While of course there is always room for improvement, and a danger of formalism, yet many can testify that such preparatory services have been a blessing to them and have been used by the Holy Spirit to bring them closer to the Lord. The general abandonment of such preparatory services in many denominations that formerly maintained them is one of the signs of the spiritual decadence of modern Protestantism.

4. What should we say to a church member who is unwilling to partake of the Lord's Supper because he "feels he is not good enough"? Such a state of mind reveals a pitiable condition of spiritual bondage. It is the outcome of a legalistic view of salvation (salvation by works or character) plus a fear of incurring the divine judgment mentioned in 1 Corinthians 11:29–32. Such a church member should be kindly and patiently instructed so that he may come to understand that no person in the world is "good enough" to deserve any of God's blessings, and that salvation and everything the Lord's Supper stands for is the free gift of God's unmerited grace to sinners. Such a person should be encouraged to cast himself on the free mercy of God in Christ, and then to partake of the Lord's Supper after the proper preparation. See also the discussion of the next question of the catechism (question 172).

Sometimes the statement that a person does not feel himself "good enough" to partake of the Lord's Supper may be a mere excuse offered by nominal church members who are living in sin and have no intention or desire of taking Jesus Christ and the Lord's Supper seriously. We should be very careful never to encourage such to partake of the sacrament while in their carnal condition, for they will be in peril of incurring divine judgments if they partake. What such people need is to be born again of the Holy Spirit, honestly to repent of their sins, sincerely to believe in Christ as their Savior, and only then—after due preparation—to partake of the Lord's Supper.

Besides the legalists and the nominal church members already discussed, there are some true Christians who may be described as victims of a morbidly active conscience. Such people fully realize that we are saved by grace, not by works, and they are far removed from the nominal church members who carelessly continue in sin. Filled with doubts and scruples, they find the approach of the communion season an occasion of distress rather than of joy. We should endeavor to help such Christians by sympathy and encouragement rather than by reproaches or harsh criticism. Such morbidly introspective souls should be encouraged to look outward rather than inward— to Christ and his redemption rather than always to be thinking only about their own doubts and weaknesses. They are like the diffident Mr. Fearing, in the second part of Bunyan's *Pilgrim's Progress,* of whom Greatheart said, "He had, I think, a Slough of Despond in his mind, a slough that he carried everywhere with him, or else he could never have been as he was." Mr. Fearing was always pessimistic about himself, yet "he was a man that had the root of the matter in him," and finally crossed the last river triumphantly, "not much above wetshod," saying, "I shall, I shall." (See also next lesson, on question 172 of the catechism.)

5. What is the most important element in preparation for the Lord's Supper? Personal faith in Christ and him crucified as our only Savior, accompanied by sincere repentance for sin.

172. **Q.** *May one who doubteth of his being in Christ, or of his due preparation, come to the Lord's Supper?*

A. *One who doubteth of his being in Christ, or of his due preparation to the sacrament of the Lord's Supper, may have true interest in Christ, though he be not yet assured thereof; and in God's account hath it, if he be duly affected with the apprehension of the want of it, and unfeignedly desires to be found in Christ, and to depart from iniquity: in which case (because promises are made, and this sacrament is appointed, for the relief even of weak and doubting Christians) he is to* *bewail his unbelief, and labor to have his doubts resolved; and, so doing, he may and ought to come to the Lord's Supper, that he may be further strengthened.*

Scripture References

- Isa. 50:10; 1 John 5:13; Pss. 88:1–18; 77:1–12. Jonah 2:4, 7. Assurance not being of the essence of salvation, a person may possess the fact of salvation without having attained the consciousness of salvation.
- Isa. 54:7–10; Matt. 5:3–4; Pss. 31:22; 73:13, 22–23; Phil. 3:8–9; Pss. 10:17; 42:1–2, 5, 11; 2 Tim. 2:19; Isa. 50:10; Ps. 66:18–20. A deep concern about one's personal salvation, coupled with an earnest desire to be found in Christ and to depart from iniquity, is an evidence of being in the state of grace, even though subjective assurance may be absent or defective.
- Isa. 40:11, 29, 31; Matt. 11:28; 12:20; 26:28. Divine promises are made, and the Lord's Supper provided, for the spiritual help even of weak and doubting Christians.
- Mark 9:24; Acts 2:37; 16:30; Rom. 4:10; 1 Cor. 11:28. The person who is troubled with doubts about his own salvation, or proper preparation for the Lord's Supper, after doing what he can to remove the difficulty, ought to come to the Lord's Supper, for his spiritual benefit.

Commentary

1. With what class of persons is this question of the catechism concerned? With diffident Christians, that is, with Christians who hesitate to partake of the Lord's Supper because of doubts in their mind, either concerning the fact of their salvation or concerning their proper preparation for the sacrament. This question does not concern those who make no profession of faith in Christ, nor those who, while making a profession, live careless lives of easy compromise with sin. It is concerned only with the spiritual problem of the person who is in earnest about the salvation of his soul, who believes in Christ, but who has doubt about his own spiritual state.

2. What is the difference between salvation and assurance of salvation? Salvation is a matter of a person's relation to God; assurance of salvation is a matter of a person's feeling sure, in his own mind, about his relation to God. Many popular Fundamentalist Bible teachers confuse these two things, saying that if a person is saved he will always know it, and that if a person has accepted Christ and yet lacks assurance of salvation he simply does not believe God's Word. This teaching is oversimplified and erroneous, and has caused an untold amount of mental and spiritual anguish. Following the definite teaching of the Bible, our catechism and the rest of the Westminster Standards teach that there is a distinction between salvation itself, on the one hand, and mental assurance of salvation on the other. To deny or ignore that distinction is to open the door to serious theological errors.

For a fuller discussion of the distinction between salvation and assurance, the student is referred to Lessons 66 and 67 of this course, on questions 80–81 of the Larger Catechism. Briefly, possession of something is one thing, and knowledge or certainty in one's own mind of the possession is something else. A person might have a million dollars in the bank, and yet not know about it, or not feel certain that the money is really his. Similarly, a person may be really born again by the power of the Holy Spirit, and yet not enjoy certainty concerning this spiritual change. The Holy Spirit's work is much deeper than our consciousness. Salvation, once a person really has it, is permanent and cannot be lost, but a person's certainty of it in his own consciousness is often obscured and interfered with by temptations, lapses into sin, or lack of understanding of the truths that are involved.

To upbraid a person who is struggling with spiritual doubts by telling him that he "doesn't believe John 3:16," etc., not only is heartlessly unkind, but reveals ignorance of the nature of such a person's real problem. A statement made in jest may well be repeated here: It is amazing how dogmatically and confidently people write and speak on this subject (of assurance), while they yet give no evidence of having studied its problems or being familiar with its history. Some of these Bible teachers who are so positive that salvation and assurance are inseparable should read up on the subject in a standard orthodox work on systematic theology such as that of Charles Hodge. This matter is not by any means "as simple as A. B. C."

3. Why should lack of assurance not keep a person from partaking of the Lord's Supper? We are not saved by assurance, but by faith in Christ as our Redeemer. That is to say, we are saved by believing *in Christ,* not by believing that we are saved. It is a fine and comforting thing to be able honestly to believe that we are saved, but the really important thing is to believe on Jesus Christ as our Savior. The person who confesses himself a lost sinner, sincerely intends and wants to believe in Christ as his only Redeemer, and is really trying to depart from iniquity is a Christian and ought to partake of the Lord's Supper, even though he may have some doubts about his salvation, or about his proper preparation for the sacrament.

When the Passover was observed by the people of Israel in Egypt, every family that had killed the lamb and put the blood on the lintel and side posts of their house door was *safe* from the plague that destroyed the firstborn of the Egyptians. Suppose two families lived side by side. Both have killed the lamb and put the blood on the door. One family is rejoicing in the conscious certainty of safety from the destroying plague; the other family is troubled by doubts and worries, questioning and worrying about whether they will really be spared or not. Which of these families is the safer? The answer is: *Both are alike safe,* though one has assurance, the other has doubts. For God had not said, "When I see a house where the people have no doubts or worries, I will pass over you." What God had said was: "When I see *the blood* I will pass over you" (Exod. 12:13). The person who is putting his faith in *the blood,* whatever doubts about himself he may have, is saved in God's sight, belongs with the covenant people of God, and ought to partake of the Lord's Supper.

4. How should a diffident Christian prepare for the Lord's Supper?
Besides the self-examination which every Christian should engage in before partaking of the Lord's Supper, the diffident Christian should "bewail his unbelief, and labor to have his doubts resolved," and thereupon come to the Lord's table expecting a blessing. Lack of assurance is not to be complacently tolerated; we are always to strive to attain and retain the full conscious assurance of our personal salvation. Doubts may be unavoidable, for the time being, but we are never to regard them as legitimate tenants of our mind. Just as it is wrong to tell a diffident Christian "you don't believe John 3:16," so it is also very wrong to tell a person who is struggling with spiritual doubts: "Forget it: just ignore your doubts and problems; pay no attention to them and they will pass." Spiritual doubts are very real to the person who has them. They cannot be disposed of by a wave of the hand and a pat on the back. Such a person should face his own troubles frankly and seek relief. Study of God's Word, prayer, and conference with godly, experienced Christians will help. And as the catechism rightly affirms, the Lord's Supper itself is intended for the spiritual help of weak and doubting Christians.

173. Q. *May any who profess the faith, and desire to come to the Lord's Supper, be kept from it?*

A. *Such as are found to be ignorant or scandalous, notwithstanding their profession of the faith, and desire to come to the Lord's Supper, may and ought to be kept from that sacrament, by the power which Christ hath left in his church, until they receive instruction, and manifest their reformation.*

Scripture References

- 1 Cor. 11:27–34, compared with the following Scriptures: Matt. 7:6; 1 Cor. 5:1–13; Jude 23; 1 Tim. 5:22. Christ has committed to his church authority to exclude from its membership ignorant and scandalous persons, and this power must be understood to include the right and duty of keeping such persons from the Lord's Supper.
- 2 Cor. 2:7; 2 Tim. 2:24–26. When his ignorance has been overcome, or scandalous living corrected, the person who had been excluded is to be admitted to the fellowship and privileges of the visible church.

Commentary

1. Is the Lord's Supper intended for the unconverted? No, for such persons lack saving faith in Christ, without which the sacrament cannot benefit them. Weak and doubting Christians may and ought, after due preparation, to partake of the Lord's Supper. But persons who are really not Christians at all, or who are only hypocrites, can receive no benefit from the Lord's Supper and have no right to partake of it.

2. Is the church to decide what persons are converted, and have saving faith in Christ? Certainly not. Only God can see people's hearts, to be able to know with certainty what their spiritual condition is. Church officers and church courts cannot see people's hearts, and they have no business to pronounce judgment on whether people are, or are not, truly saved Christians. At various times and in various sects and denominations the attempt has been made to have a perfectly pure church by excluding all persons adjudged to be unregenerate. This attempt has always failed in practice, and must always fail, for church officers cannot see the heart. All such attempts to pronounce on people's spiritual condition, or their relation to God, are bound to produce evils even greater than ones they are intended to remedy.

There have always been some unregenerate people in the visible church; ministers and elders are not to blame for this unless they have been negligent in their legitimate duties.

3. If the church is not to decide what persons are converted, how can there be any church discipline? The true idea of church discipline is based on evaluation of people's *profession* and *practice,* not on an attempted decision as to whether they are converted or not. The church has no business to try to examine people's hearts, and pronounce judgment on their relation to God; but the church, through its proper officers, does have the function of evaluating people's profession of faith and their manner of life. If a person applies for membership in a congregation, the session is not to try to decide whether he is born again or not, nor to ask him to prove that he is converted, nor to ask him to narrate his religious experience so that the officers of the congregation can decide whether he is saved or not. To attempt to exercise such functions would be to invade the realm which belongs to God alone. The officers of the congregation are, on the other hand, to inquire as to the applicant's profession of faith and manner of life; and having done this, it is further their function to decide whether his profession of faith and manner of life are compatible with membership in the church. The applicant does not have to prove that he is saved. His profession is to be taken at face value unless contradicted by his manner of life.

4. What classes of people are to be excluded from the Lord's Supper? "Such as are found to be ignorant or scandalous." By "ignorant" the catechism means persons who do not make a proper profession of faith. A profession of faith of an ignorant person is inadequate for admission to church membership or to the Lord's Supper. This inadequacy may be the result of lack of information, or it may be the result of false doctrines held by the applicant. Thus an applicant who did not know that Christ died on the cross to save sinners, or who did not know that salvation is by free grace and not by works, would have an inadequate profession because of lack of information. On the other hand, an applicant who professed belief in the universal Fatherhood of God and brotherhood of man would have an inadequate profession because of false doctrine. Both kinds of ignorance—mere lack of knowledge and actual profession of error—constitute a legitimate ground for exclusion from the Lord's Supper, or from church membership (Titus 3:10).

By "scandalous" the catechism means persons whose profession cannot be taken at face value because it is contradicted by their manner of life. "Scandal" does not mean any sin or fault whatever, but only such sinful conduct as would nullify the person's profession and render it improper to admit him to the Lord's Supper, or to the membership of the church. Such scandal might take many different forms, and the circumstances would have to be taken into account to arrive at a just decision concerning it.

The catechism wisely refrains from attempting to provide a ready-made definition of either ignorance or scandal. It lays down the principle—which is undoubtedly scriptural and therefore valid—and wisely leaves the precise application of the principle to the church courts before which such matters properly come for decision. The decision as to whether a particular applicant is ignorant or scandalous (in a way which would exclude him from church membership or from the Lord's Supper) must be made by the church officers whose duty it is to pass on his application. In the course of time every denomination acquires a body of precedents from decisions of such cases which have the effect of church law in deciding similar cases. Thus a denomination may have a settled church law or rule that professional gamblers cannot be admitted to church membership or to the Lord's Supper. Or a denomination may have a church law that members of oath-bound secret societies must be excluded. In each case the denomination has applied the principle set forth in the catechism, that the ignorant or scandalous are not to be admitted.

5. What is the position of the catechism concerning the question of open, close (often called "closed"), or restricted communion? This question, in the form in which it exists today, is not directly answered by the catechism, or any of the Westminster Standards, because the problems created by denominationalism were not then in view. The purpose of the Westminster Assembly of Divines was to lay the foundation for a "covenanted uniformity in religion" in the churches of Scotland, England, and Ireland. It was contemplated that there would be but one national church in each kingdom, of which all faithful Christians would be members. Therefore the Westminster Assembly, while stating that the ignorant or scandalous are not to be admitted to the Lord's Supper, did not take up the question of whether members of one denomination should be admitted to the sacrament in congregations of another denomination. This is a question which has arisen, for the most part, since the time of the Westminster Assembly.

However, the statements of the catechism do have some relation to the question of open, close, or restricted communion. Open communion means that all persons who wish to come are admitted to the Lord's Supper. (The invitation is usually to "all members of evangelical churches" or "all who are the Lord's," etc., but all who wish to partake are admitted without any investigation of their faith or life.) Restricted communion means that members of other denominations may be admitted to the Lord's Supper after they have met with the officers of the congregation and have satisfied them concerning their faith and life. (There are various degrees of "restricted communion," some broader, some more narrow, in various denominations.) Close communion means that only members of the denomination that is administering the sacrament, or of closely allied denominations officially recognized as of virtually identical faith, are admitted to the Lord's Supper. The question of who is to be admitted to the Lord's Supper has been greatly confused by the assumption that the only alternatives are "open" or "close" communion. This is untrue. "Restricted" communion is also a possibility that must be considered.

It should be said at once that the catechism is clearly opposed to open communion. Open communion leaves no opportunity for the exclusion of "such as are found to be ignorant or scandalous"; it takes the whole question of whether people are ignorant or scandalous out of the hands of the church, and leaves everything up to the individual would-be communicant. This is contrary to the biblical teaching that the church may and should exclude the ignorant and scandalous, and in practice it involves the danger of a breakdown in church discipline and profanation of the sacrament.

As for restricted and close communion, the catechism *at least* requires the practice of restricted communion, and there is nothing said which is contrary to the practice of close communion on a denominational basis.

6. Does the practice of close communion deprive Christian people of their right to partake of the Lord's Supper? There can be no real privilege or "right" without the existence of a corresponding obligation or responsibility. The "right" to participate in the sacraments in a particular denomination of the visible church implies the corresponding obligation of submission to the spiritual oversight and church discipline of the courts of that denomination. Where a person is not subject to the jurisdiction of a denomination, he cannot claim any "rights" in that denomination. It is no doubt true that every faithful Christian, by the grace of God, has a right to partake of the Lord's Supper, but not in a church whose doctrines he does not accept and to whose discipline he is unwilling to subject himself. Every faithful Christian, by God's grace, has a right to partake of the Lord's Supper in the church of which he is a member, whose doctrines he has professed to accept, and to whose discipline he is subject in the Lord. To claim such a "right" to partake of the sacrament in some other denomination amounts to asking that denomination to deal with non-members on a different basis from that on which it deals with its own membership. A denomination sets up certain standards of faith and life, which it believes to be scriptural, and then states that those who fail to come up to those standards are either ignorant or scandalous. Those of its own members who fail to measure up to those standards are excluded from the Lord's Supper by church discipline. But no church can exercise church discipline in the case of persons who are not subject to its jurisdiction. Therefore a denomination may officially decide that the only way it can make sure of excluding the ignorant and the scandalous from the Lord's Supper is by limiting participation to persons subject to its own jurisdiction and members of closely allied denominations which maintain virtually identical standards of faith and life. Only by mutual agreement on what constitutes ignorance and scandal can church discipline be maintained and the purity of the church be safeguarded.

7. How can we answer the argument for open communion that "it is the Lord's Supper, and all who are the Lord's should be invited to it"? This argument is based on an unconscious confusion of the visible with the invisible church. According to the teaching of the Bible, it is not all members of the invisible church (all who are born again), but all who are living orderly as members of the visible church (with a proper profession of faith and a corresponding life) that are entitled to the privileges of the visible church, including the Lord's Supper. The apostle Paul directed that a certain member of the Corinthian church, who was guilty of scandal, be excluded from church fellowship (1 Cor. 5:13). This was actually done. The excluded member, although guilty of scandal, was presumably a Christian, as indicated by the fact that Paul later directed that he be restored to church privileges (2 Cor. 2:5–8). Because it is the Lord's Supper, it must be administered in accordance with the rules of the Lord's house (the visible church) as these are set forth in the Bible. Of course each denomination must search the Scriptures and decide for itself what the rules of the Lord's house are, and then administer the Lord's Supper accordingly. It is altogether unreasonable to expect that the Lord's Supper shall be administered in denomination A according to the rules of the Lord's house as these are understood in denomination B. Each denomination is responsible to the Lord for its own interpretation of the Bible and for carrying out that interpretation in actual practice, including the administration of the sacraments.

174. Q. *What is required of them that receive the sacrament of the Lord's Supper in the time of the administration of it?*

A. *It is required of them that receive the sacrament of the Lord's Supper, that, during the time of the administration of it, with all holy reverence and attention they wait upon God in that ordinance, diligently observe the sacramental elements and actions, heedfully discern the Lord's body, and affectionately meditate on his death and sufferings, and thereby stir up themselves to a vigorous exercise of their graces; in judging themselves, and sorrowing for sin; in earnest hungering and thirsting after Christ, feeding on him by faith, receiving of his fulness, trusting in his merits, rejoicing in his love, giving thanks for his grace; in renewing of their covenant with God, and love to all the saints.*

Scripture References

- Lev. 10:3; Heb. 12:38; Ps. 5:7; 1 Cor. 11:17, 26–27. At the time of administration of the Lord's Supper, communicants are to wait upon God in that ordinance with all holy reverence and attention.
- Exod. 24:8 compared with Matt. 26:28. At the administration of the Lord's Supper, the sacramental elements and actions are to be diligently observed.
- 1 Cor. 11:29. Communicants should "heedfully discern the Lord's body," that is, realize the relation of the sacrament to Christ's person and work.
- Luke 22:19; 1 Cor. 11:26; 10:3–5, 11, 14. Communicants are to meditate on Christ's sufferings and death, to stir themselves up to a vigorous exercise of their graces.
- 1 Cor. 11:31; Zech. 12:10. Communicants are to judge themselves for their own sins, and feel sorrow for the same.
- Rev. 22:17; John 6:35; 1:16; Phil. 3:9; Ps. 63:4–5; 2 Chron. 30:21; Ps. 22:26. At the administration of the Lord's Supper, communicants are to hunger and thirst after Christ, and feed on him by faith.

• Jer. 50:5; Ps. 50:5; Acts 2:42. The administration of the Lord's Supper is to be preeminently a time of renewing our covenant with God, and love to his people.

Commentary

1. What is the most obvious duty of communicants at the time of the administration of the Lord's Supper? Their most obvious duty is "with all holy reverence and attention [to] wait upon God in that ordinance." Reverence and attention are duties in connection with every divine service, but especially in connection with the Lord's Supper, which is a very solemn and sacred service because it commemorates the sufferings and death of our Lord. All irreverent or inattentive conduct at such a time must be very displeasing to God. Unnecessary talking or whispering, reading books or papers not connected with the service, falling asleep, daydreaming about our worldly affairs, turning around to stare at people coming in late—all these and other forms of conduct that are contrary to reverent attention should be strictly avoided. We cannot expect a blessing from the sacrament unless we are willing to devote our undivided attention to it.

2. Why should communicants "diligently observe the sacramental elements and actions"? Because these elements and actions are all essential to the meaning of the sacrament. The Lord's Supper is a visible, tangible portrayal, by symbolic elements and actions, of Christ's redemption and the way of salvation. To receive the full impression that the sacrament is intended to produce upon our minds and hearts, we must attend carefully to every detail of the ordinance. The Lord's Supper does not produce spiritual results automatically, as the Church of Rome wrongly teaches by its doctrine of an *opus operatum,* but by the truth which the sacrament presents, which the communicant grasps by faith, and which the Holy Spirit applies to his heart and life. Each of the sacramental elements and actions especially presents some phase of that truth.

3. What is meant by "discern[ing] the Lord's body"? The word *discerning* in the Greek text of 1 Corinthians 11:29 means literally "distinguishing" or "discriminating"; "to distinguish or separate a person or thing from the rest" (Thayer's Lexicon). Thus "discerning" in this verse means *realizing* that the sacramental elements represent Christ's human nature, or *appreciating* them as symbols of his body and blood. A person who saw in the sacrament only bread and wine, and who failed to see Christ and his redemption set forth in it, would fail to discern the Lord's body. In order truly to discern the Lord's body, there is required, first, a measure of doctrinal knowledge; and in the second place, personal trust in Christ as one's Savior.

4. Why should communicants affectionately meditate on Christ's death and sufferings? Christ's death and sufferings should be the principal object of our thoughts at the communion table, because his death and sufferings constitute the meaning of the Lord's Supper. We should *affectionately* meditate on them because the infinite love of our Lord calls for a cordial response of love or affection on our part. The more we realize what our redemption cost our Savior in shame and suffering, the more we will feel moved to love him in return. Our attitude toward Christ and his sufferings and death is never to be a sentimental one. Many people who are not really Christians feel a kind of sentimental admiration for Jesus while they do not regard him as a living person today nor as the only Redeemer of men. Such a sentimental attachment to Jesus does not differ essentially from the attitude people may have toward Florence Nightingale or Abraham Lincoln. The Christian's devotion to Christ, on the other hand, is to be a devotion to him *crucified and risen from the dead, the living Lord*—a devotion which stirs them up to "a vigorous exercise of their graces" and thus affects the whole course of their lives.

5. Why should communicants judge themselves, and sorrow for their sins? It was because of the sins of his people that Jesus suffered and died on the cross. There can be no adequate appreciation of Christ's sufferings and death unless a person judges himself and sorrows for his sins. While our thoughts at the communion table are to be mainly on Christ's sufferings and death, we are to realize at the same time that it was our sins that he suffered and died to atone for; therefore we should judge ourselves and feel deep sorrow for our sin.

6. What special spiritual attitudes should Christians have at the communion table? (a) An attitude of earnest desire for communion with Christ ("hungering and thirsting after Christ"); (b) an attitude of personal faith in him as Redeemer ("feeding on him by faith, receiving of his fulness, trusting in his merits"); (c) an attitude of spiritual joy ("rejoicing in his love"); (d) an attitude of thankfulness for his grace ("giving thanks for his grace"); (e) an attitude of sincere purpose to live in covenant with God and in love to his people ("renewing of their covenant with God, and love to all the saints").

175. Q. *What is the duty of Christians, after they have received the sacrament of the Lord's Supper?*

A. *The duty of Christians, after they have received the sacrament of the Lord's Supper, is seriously to consider how they have behaved themselves therein, and with what success; if they find quickening and comfort, to bless God for it, beg the continuance of it, watch against relapses, fulfill their vows, and encourage themselves to a frequent attendance on that ordinance: but if they find no present benefit, more exactly to review their preparation to, and carriage at the sacrament; in both which, if they can approve themselves to God and their own consciences, they are to wait for the fruit of it in due time; but, if they see that they have failed in either, they are to be humbled, and to attend upon it afterward with more care and diligence.*

Scripture References

- Lev. 10:3; Heb. 12:28; Ps. 5:7; 1 Cor. 11:17, 26–27. After receiving the Lord's Supper, Christians are to consider how they have acted, and what benefit they have received.
- 2 Chron. 30:21–26; Acts 2:42, 46–47; Ps. 36:10; Song 3:4; 1 Chron. 29:18; 1 Cor. 10:3–5, 12; Ps. 50:14; 1 Cor. 11:25–26. Those who find that they have received benefit from the Lord's Supper are to thank God for it, seek to conserve the benefit for the future, fulfill their vows, and look forward to partaking of the Lord's Supper often.
- Song 5:1–6; Pss. 123:1–2; 42:5, 8; 43:3–5. In case no immediate spiritual benefit is experienced after partaking of the Lord's Supper, communicants are to consider whether this may be their own fault, and if they conscientiously decide that it is not, they are to expect the benefit in due time.
- 2 Chron. 30:18–19; Isa. 1:16, 18; 2 Cor. 7:11; 1 Chron. 15:12–14. Communicants who find that failure to receive benefit from the Lord's Supper is their own fault are to be humbled in their hearts, and to exercise more care and diligence in the future.

Commentary

1. Does the Christian's duty in connection with the Lord's Supper end when the administration of the sacrament is completed? No. Since the Lord's Supper is intended to bring real spiritual benefit to Christian people, it is their duty to consider seriously how they have conducted themselves prior to and at the sacrament, and what benefit they have received. To drop the matter from our thoughts as soon as the actual communion service is dismissed would be to lose a part of the spiritual profit that we should receive from the sacrament.

2. Is the spiritual benefit of the Lord's Supper always experienced at the time when the sacrament is received or immediately afterwards? No. While it is undoubtedly true that most serious Christians consciously experience benefit at the time and immediately afterwards, this is not always nor necessarily the case. Sometimes God in his wisdom withholds the blessing, or the consciousness of the blessing, for a time.

As in the case of baptism, the benefits of the Lord's Supper are not tied or limited to the time of administration.

3. When benefit is experienced, what attitudes should this produce in the communicant? (a) An attitude of thankfulness to God; (b) a prayerful desire that the blessing may be continued; (c) a careful avoidance of pride or overconfidence which would occasion a relapse into sin; (d) a sincere purpose of paying his vows to God; (e) a desire to partake of the Lord's Supper often. The danger of spiritual pride or overconfidence is especially to be guarded against. The Christian who has experienced spiritual blessings and benefits is always in danger of becoming overconfident and starting to trust in himself instead of in Christ. This will lead to a humiliating fall into sin unless carefully guarded against.

4. When no immediate benefit is experienced from the Lord's Supper, what should a Christian do about the matter? He should realize that the failure to experience spiritual benefit may be his own fault, and therefore he should review his preparation for, and conduct at, the sacrament. If he finds himself to be at fault in either of these matters, he is "to be humbled, and to attend upon it afterward with more care and diligence." That is to say, lack of proper preparation for the Lord's Supper and improper partaking of the sacrament, are sins, and should be repented of the same as any other sins.

5. What should be the attitude of a Christian who is not conscious of benefit received from the Lord's Supper, but does not find this to have been caused by his own faults? Such a Christian should "wait for the fruit of it in due time"; that is, his attitude toward God in connection with this matter should be an attitude of faith, confidently expecting a blessing, and an attitude of patience, being willing for the blessing to be deferred if that is God's holy will. There are many examples in the Bible of saints whose blessings were deferred, either to develop their faith or because of some secret purpose of God. Impatience is always contrary to faith.

176. Q. *Wherein do the sacraments of baptism and the Lord's Supper agree?*

A. *The sacraments of baptism and the Lord's Supper agree, in that the author of both is God; the spiritual part of both is Christ and his benefits; both are seals of the same covenant, are to be dispensed by ministers of the gospel, and by none other; and to be continued in the church of Christ until His second coming.*

177. Q. *Wherein do the sacraments of baptism and the Lord's Supper differ?*

A. *The sacraments of baptism and the Lord's Supper differ, in that baptism is to be administered but once, with water, to be a sign and seal of our regeneration and ingrafting into Christ, and that even to infants; whereas the Lord's Supper is to be administered often, in the elements of bread and wine, to represent and exhibit Christ as spiritual nourishment to the soul, and to confirm our continuance and growth in him, and that only to such as are of years and ability to examine themselves.*

Scripture References

- Matt. 28:19; 1 Cor. 11:23. God is the author of both baptism and the Lord's Supper.
- Rom. 6:3–4; 1 Cor. 10:16. The spiritual part of both sacraments is Christ and his benefits.

- Rom. 4:11 compared with Col. 2:12; Matt. 26:27–28. Both sacraments are seals of the same covenant.
- John 1:33; Matt. 28:19; 1 Cor. 11:23; 4:1; Heb. 5:4. Both sacraments are to be dispensed only by ministers of the gospel.
- Matt. 28:19–20; 1 Cor. 11:26. Both sacraments are to be continued in the church until Christ's second coming.
- Matt. 3:11; Titus 3:5; Gal. 3:27. Baptism is to be administered with water, as a sign and seal of the new birth and union with Christ; and since it represents the beginning of the Christian life, it is to be administered only once to any person.
- Gen. 17:7, 9; Acts 2:38–39; 1 Cor. 7:14. Baptism is to be administered to the infants of believers.
- 1 Cor. 11:23–26. The Lord's Supper is to be administered repeatedly, with bread and wine, to represent Christ as spiritual nourishment to the soul.
- 1 Cor. 10:16. The Lord's Supper is to confirm our continuance and growth in Christ.
- 1 Cor. 11:28–29. Unlike baptism, the Lord's Supper is to be administered only to persons of years and ability to examine themselves.

Commentary

1. How many points of agreement are there between baptism and the Lord's Supper? The catechism enumerates five points of agreement, as follows: (a) The author of both sacraments is God. The catechism might have added that both were instituted by the Lord Jesus Christ during his life on earth. (b) The spiritual part of both sacraments is Christ and his benefits; that is, Christ and his redemption is what is represented, sealed, and applied by both baptism and the Lord's Supper. (c) Both sacraments are seals of the same divine covenant, the covenant of grace, which provides for the eternal salvation of God's elect. (d) As ordinances of the visible church, both sacraments are to be administered only by the ministers of the gospel, to whom the mysteries of God have been entrusted. (e) Both sacraments are permanent in nature, to be continued in the church until Christ's second coming at the Last Day. Thus it appears that in everything which constitutes them *sacraments,* baptism and the Lord's Supper are in agreement. That which constitutes them sacraments, they have in common.

2. What difference exists in the outward material part of the two sacraments? The material element of baptism is water, whereas the material elements of the Lord's Supper are bread and wine.

3. What difference exists between baptism and the Lord's Supper as to the spiritual reality signified and sealed by the sacraments? While the spiritual reality signified and sealed by the two sacraments is basically the same, namely, Christ and his redemption and benefits, there is a difference in that baptism is a sign and seal of the *beginning* of the Christian life (the new birth by the Holy Spirit, remission of sins through Christ's blood, union with Christ), whereas the Lord's Supper is a sign and seal of the *continuance* of the Christian life (feeding upon Christ for spiritual nourishment and growth in grace). The one is a sign and seal of spiritual *birth*, the other a sign and seal of spiritual *growth*, both being based on Christ's redemption.

4. Why is baptism to be administered only once to any person, while every Christian is to partake of the Lord's Supper repeatedly? This is because of the difference in the spiritual reality signified and sealed by the two sacraments. Baptism is a sign and seal of spiritual birth, and just as a person can have only one natural birth into this world, so he can be born again of the Holy Spirit only once. Since baptism is a sign and seal of this, a person is to be baptized only once. The Lord's Supper, on the other hand, is a sign and seal of spiritual growth by faith in Christ. Birth is an event, but growth is a process capable of exercising faith. It has been held by some that for these very reasons baptism also ought to be withheld from infants, namely, because they are not capable of faith or of self-examination. In answer to this argument, it may be said that baptism is the New Testament counterpart of circumcision, and under the Old Testament infants were circumcised by God's command, even though they were incapable of exercising faith. Therefore if their incapacity to exercise faith did not prevent infants from being circumcised under the Old Testament, it should not prevent infants from being baptized under the New Testament. It is eminently appropriate that infants should receive the sacrament which is a sign and seal of spiritual *birth* (which occurs prior to and is the source of conscious faith and obedience), while it would be highly inappropriate for them to receive the sacrament which is a sign and seal of feeding on Christ for spiritual *growth* (which occurs subsequent to and is dependent upon the conscious exercise of faith). The contention that those who practice infant baptism should also permit infant communion is entirely without weight, as it overlooks the distinction between the spiritual realities signified and sealed by the two sacraments.

17

Use of Prayer

The Nature of Christian Prayer

178. Q. *What is prayer?*

A. *Prayer is an offering up of our desires unto God, in the name of Christ, by the help of his Spirit; with confession of our sins, and thankful acknowledgment of his mercies.*

Scripture References

- Ps. 62:8. We are to offer up our desires unto God.
- John 16:23. Prayer is to be offered in the name of Christ.
- Rom. 8:26. We are to pray by the help of the Holy Spirit.
- Ps. 32:5–6; Dan. 9:4. In prayer, we are to confess our sins.
- Phil. 4:6. In prayer, we are to thank God for his mercies.

Commentary

1. What kind of prayer is defined in this question and answer of the catechism? In this statement the catechism gives a definition of true prayer, or Christian prayer; that is, prayer offered to God according to his revealed will by a person who has been reconciled to him through the redemptive work of Christ.

2. Besides Christian prayer, what other kinds of prayer are there? Prayer is practically universal in the human race. Even atheists have been known to pray when thoroughly alarmed or in deep trouble. All the non-Christian religious systems involve the practice of some kind of prayer. Non-Christian prayer, however, is not addressed to the true God but to some false divinity or misrepresentation of God. The only true God is the Triune God of the Scriptures, Father, Son, and Holy Spirit; all others are false and have no real existence. Non-Christian prayer, moreover, does not approach God through Christ as Mediator. It is not offered in the name of Christ but simply in the name of the person praying, or perhaps in the name of some other mediator than Christ. Thus non-Christian prayer lacks the guarantee of acceptance with God (John 14:6). That God in his great mercy may sometimes hear and answer the prayers of non-Christians, in spite of their spiritual ignorance and lack of a Mediator, we should not deny. But such prayers differ essentially from Christian prayer, as explained above.

3. Why should we offer up our desires unto God? We are God's creatures, and it is our nature to be dependent upon him for the supply of our needs, physical, mental, social, and spiritual. Even before the human race fell into sin, man was dependent on God and there was need for prayer. The fall into sin greatly increased our need and our dependence upon God. Since no human being is able to face life by his own abilities and power, prayer is necessary if we are truly to glorify and enjoy God.

4. What kind of desires are we to offer to God in prayer? In prayer, we are to offer to God only lawful desires, that is, desires that are in harmony with the moral law of God and that are offered in submission to the secret will of God. See the Shorter Catechism, question 98 ("for things agreeable to his will"), and the Larger Catechism, question 184 ("For what things are we to pray?"). We may not pray for just anything we might please; we must pray according to the Word of God and in submission to the will of God.

5. Why must we pray only in the name of Christ? Because we are sinners, and only through Christ can we be reconciled to God and have access to his holy presence. Even a Christian sins against God daily in thought, word, and deed, and his very prayers are stained by elements of sin. Therefore it is only through Christ's mediation, on the basis of his blood and righteousness, that we and our prayers can be acceptable to God.

6. Why must we pray only by the help of the Holy Spirit? Romans 8:26 gives the key to the answer to this question. In the first place, we are too ignorant to pray without the help of the Holy Spirit. We do not know how to pray as we ought, nor what to pray for. We are also hindered by infirmities; that is, we are too weak and lacking in spiritual power to pray adequately. Instead of being filled with earnestness and zeal in approaching God in prayer, how often we are cold or lukewarm, and our minds distracted with all kinds of wandering thoughts! How often we consider prayer a burdensome duty rather than a real privilege! Clearly there can be no real prayer apart from the help of the Holy Spirit.

7. Why must we confess our sins in praying to God? Over and over again the Bible stresses the truth that to approach God acceptably in prayer we must confess our sins. "If I regard iniquity in my heart, the Lord will not hear me" (Ps. 66:18). Because of God's holiness and absolute intolerance of even the least sin, we cannot have company with God unless we sincerely desire to part company with sin. The person who approaches God in prayer without feeling his own sinfulness and without confession of sin is a proud and self-righteous Pharisee rather than a Christian.

8. Why should we include thanksgiving for God's mercies in our prayers? We are debtors to God for everything in life except our own sinfulness. Life itself and all the things that make the continuance of life possible and pleasant are gifts of God's kindness and love. Besides the natural blessings of life, such as rain and sunshine, food and clothing, peace and plenty, a Christian is under a far greater obligation to render thanksgiving to God by reason of the great blessings of God's gracious salvation. The Christian has had his soul delivered from eternal death, his eyes from tears, and his feet from falling. He has been rescued from the horrible pit and miry clay and has been set firmly upon that great Rock, Christ Jesus. Redeemed from Satan's kingdom, he has been made a citizen of the kingdom of heaven and an heir of all things. Surely the Christian has abundant reason for thankfulness to God. Accordingly, the Word of God teaches us that even in times of affliction, we are to remember to give thanks to God: "Pray without ceasing. In every thing give thanks: for this is the will of God in Christ Jesus concerning you" (1 Thess. 5:17–18).

To Whom Are We to Pray?

179. Q. *Are we to pray unto God only?*

A. *God only being able to search the hearts, hear the requests, pardon the sins, and fulfill the desires of all; and only to be believed in, and worshipped with religious worship; prayer, which is a special part thereof, is to be made by all to Him alone, and to none other.*

Scripture References

- 1 Kings 8:39; Acts 1:24; Rom. 8:27. God alone knows the hearts of all human beings.
- Ps. 65:2. God is the one who is able to hear our prayers.
- Mic. 7:18. God is the one who is able to pardon our sins.
- Ps. 145:18–19. God is the one who is able to fulfill the desires of all who call upon him.
- Rom. 10:14; Matt. 4:4–10; Acts 10:25–26; Rev. 22:8–9. God alone is to be believed in and worshiped with religious faith and worship.
- 1 Cor. 1:2. Prayer is a special part of religious worship.
- Exod. 20:3–5; Ps. 50:15. Men are to pray to God alone.

Commentary

1. What large and influential religious body teaches that it is right to pray to others besides God? The Roman Catholic Church, which teaches that it is proper to pray to the Virgin Mary, the saints, and the angels, as well as to God.

2. Why does the Church of Rome teach that it is proper to pray to Mary, the saints, and angels, as well as to God? Because of a correct feeling of the need of a mediator in approaching the holy God, together with a failure to realize that Christ is the one and only Mediator between God and men, who alone can give us access to the Father's presence and acceptance with him. The Church of Rome does indeed regard Christ as a Mediator between God and men, but goes beyond this and regards Mary, the saints, and the angels as mediators between us and Christ.

This false teaching results in an adoration of Mary, the saints, and angels, which virtually amounts to idolatry. A common Roman Catholic catechism contains an appendix with nineteen hymns, of which six are addressed to Mary, two to Joseph the husband of Mary, and the remaining eleven, so far as they are addressed to anyone in particular, are addressed to God the Father, Jesus Christ, or the Holy Spirit. The same catechism states that we know that the saints hear our prayers, because they are with God, and God will make our prayers known to them! To say the least, this seems a roundabout way of reaching God with our prayers.

3. Why is God the only one who is able to hear our prayers? Only God is omniscient; therefore only God is able to search and know the hearts of men. Only God is omnipresent; therefore only God is able to hear the prayers of his creatures wherever they may be. Apart from the question of power to *answer* prayers, only God has the certain, sure power to *hear* our prayers, discern the desires of our hearts, and understand what our real needs are.

4. Why is God the only one who is able to pardon people's sins? People's moral responsibility is to God, who is their Creator and Judge. The Jews were entirely correct in their belief that none can forgive sins, but God only. God is the person whom our sins have offended, and only the offended party can forgive the sins. Our repentance and prayer for forgiveness are to be directed to God, not to some third party. We live in a day when many people think of sin only in terms of its effects on human society; we should remember that the effects on human society are only a side issue or by-product of sin; the real and great evil is the offense committed against God; only God can forgive that.

5. Why is God alone able to fulfill the desires? Because God alone is omnipotent, that is, only God has absolute and unlimited power. Nothing is too hard for the Lord. With God there is no such thing as impossibility. We are to pray only to him who really has the power to answer our prayers. God is almighty; he is in complete control of all that comes to pass, in accordance with his own great eternal plan; therefore our prayers must be addressed to him alone.

6. What does the catechism mean by saying that God only is to be believed in? By this statement the catechism means that God only is to be believed in as the object of religious faith. We believe in the sun, moon, and stars; we believe in angels and devils; we believe in ourselves and the human race, that is, we believe that all of these exist, and we believe certain things about them. But we do not believe in them as objects of religious faith, but only as objects of general knowledge, and sometimes as objects of general or non-religious faith. If we mail a letter at the post office, we have faith in the postal service; we believe that it is reliable and will deliver the letter to the addressee in due time. That is general faith, but not religious faith.

As for God, not only do we believe that he exists, that he is almighty, infinite, eternal, unchangeable, etc., but we believe *in* him with religious faith; that is, we take him as *our* God, and entrust ourselves to him for time and eternity, and confess that our destiny is in his hands, and that our chief end is to glorify and enjoy him.

7. Why is God alone to be worshiped with religious worship? This follows from the great truth that God alone is God. Religious worship, by definition, is that which is due to him who is the object of our religious faith. If we believe that there is only one God, it follows that this one God alone is to receive religious worship or devotion.

8. What king in the Bible tried to usurp God's prerogative of alone receiving religious worship? Darius (Dan. 6:6–9).

9. Is it everyone's duty to pray to God? Yes. Only the Christian can pray acceptably, for only the Christian has the help of the Holy Spirit in prayer. Yet it is everyone's duty to pray. The prayers of non-Christians, who try to approach God without coming through Christ as their Mediator, cannot be pleasing to God; yet for them to neglect to pray is even more sinful and displeasing to God.

180. Q. *What is it to pray in the name of Christ?*

A. *To pray in the name of Christ is, in obedience to his command, and in confidence on his promises, to ask mercy for his sake; not by bare mentioning of his name, but by drawing our encouragement to pray, and our boldness, strength, and hope of acceptance in prayer, from Christ and his mediation.*

Scripture References

• John 14:13–14; 16:24; Dan. 9:17. We are to pray in the name of Christ, asking mercy for his sake.

- Matt. 7:21. A merely formal mentioning of Christ's name in prayer is not what is meant by praying in Christ's name.
- Heb. 4:14–16; 1 John 5:13–15. We are to pray through Christ as our Mediator, by whom we have access to God's presence and acceptance with him.

Commentary

1. How is Christian prayer distinguished from all other kinds of prayer? Christian prayer is distinguished from all other kinds of prayer in that it is addressed to the true God, who is revealed in the Bible, through the God-man Jesus Christ as Mediator. All non-Christian prayer either is addressed to a non-existent false god, or attempts to approach the true God directly, without a mediator, or attempts to approach the true God through some other mediator than Jesus Christ.

2. Is it proper to mention the name of Jesus Christ in our prayers? Certainly it is proper, and we should always remember to do so; but we should realize that praying in the name of Christ means something more than merely mentioning his name in some form of words at the end of our prayer.

3. Did God's people in Old Testament times pray in the name of Christ? Yes, insofar as they prayed with faith in the coming of the promised Redeemer, and with an obedient observance of the appointed sacrifices which pointed forward to him. The pious Israelite of Old Testament times approached God in prayer on the basis of the covenant of grace as truly as we do today; his prayers were offered to God on the basis of the redemptive work of the coming Messiah. This does not imply that all Old Testament saints understood this truth with equal clearness, but only that they had some understanding of it. And in God's sight their prayers were acceptable because of the future mediatorial work of Christ.

4. What is meant by asking mercy for Christ's sake? To ask God for mercy for Christ's sake means to ask God to deal with us in love and favor, in spite of our great sins, because of what Jesus Christ has done for us. Because of Christ's perfect life of righteousness, which is reckoned to our account as if it were ours, and because of his shed blood which cleanses away our sins, God can receive us as his children and treat us with love and kindness instead of in wrath and judgment. To ask mercy for Christ's sake, then, means to ask God for mercy on the basis of Christ's work as our Savior.

5. What wrong attitude of mind and heart prevents people from really praying in the name of Christ? The attitude of self-confidence or self-righteousness, which causes people to put their trust in themselves, their own righteousness or good life, works, or character, so that they really trust in themselves rather than in Christ. Such people may mention the name of Christ in their prayers, but they are really praying in their own name, not in Christ's name, for they really think that they can stand on their own feet before God, and they do not realize their need of Christ's redemption.

6. What character in one of Jesus' parables prayed a self-righteous prayer? The Pharisee in the Parable of the Pharisee and the Publican, who publicly thanked God that he was so much better than other people, always performed his religious duties, and so forth (Luke 18:9–14).

7. Why do we need encouragement to pray? We need encouragement to pray because the sinful corruption of our hearts has inclined us to discouragement and spiritual sluggishness. Our knowledge and experience of Christ and his salvation should encourage us to engage in prayer in spite of our natural lack of inclination to it.

8. What is meant by drawing our boldness, strength, and hope of acceptance in prayer from Christ and his mediation? We could never have any real boldness or confidence in approaching God in prayer except for our faith in Christ as our Redeemer, for our hearts would always be filled with doubts and fears, wondering whether God would hear and accept our prayers or not. The person who is not a Christian may sometimes pray, and under stress of great affliction is likely to try to pray, but he can never enjoy any real boldness or confidence in prayer, because he does not know Christ, and consequently he does not have any certainty of acceptance with God. This lack of faith in Christ's mediation must always leave his mind in a cloud of doubt and uncertainty; he can never be sure that his prayers will be accepted and answered. This feeling of doubt and uncertainty must always have the effect of preventing a person from praying with his whole heart. It is only when we have, through Christ, the assurance of being accepted with God that we can really pour out our heart to God in prayer.

9. Why does the catechism specially mention Christ's mediation? There are multitudes of people who have only a vague, sentimental attachment to Jesus, thinking of him as a great teacher, a great leader, a great ideal of humanity, and the like. Such people are not really Christians, and their prayers, although they may mention the name of Christ, are not really Christian prayers. We are not saved by Christ's teaching, but by his work—his blood and righteousness. Without faith in Christ's work of mediation, there can be no truly saving Christian faith. A sentimental admiration of Jesus as a human being is not sufficient, and does not constitute Christian faith.

181. Q. *Why are we to pray in the name of Christ?*

A. *The sinfulness of man, and his distance from God by reason thereof, being so great, as that we can have no access unto his presence without a mediator; and there being none in heaven or earth appointed to, or fit for, that glorious work but Christ alone, we are to pray in no other name but his only.*

Scripture References

- John 14:6; Isa. 59:2; Eph. 3:12. Man's sinfulness has separated him so far from God that he can have no access to God's holy presence except through a mediator.
- John 6:27; Heb. 7:25–27; 1 Tim. 2:5; Acts 4:12. Christ, and he alone, is qualified for the work of a Mediator between God and man.
- Col. 3:17; Heb. 13:15. We are to pray only in the name of Christ.

Commentary

1. What is the reason for the distance which separates man from God? There are two reasons for the distance which separates man from God: (a) God is the infinite Creator, whereas man is a finite creature; (b) God is absolutely holy, whereas man is guilty and corrupted in sin.

2. When God created mankind, what was the reason for the distance which separated man from God? At the creation of the human race, man was separated from God, his Creator, only by reason of the fact that he was a creature. This distance between Creator and creature was so great that man could not fully glorify and enjoy God except by God's bridging the chasm between himself and mankind, which he did by the establishment of the covenant of works. As long as the human race had not yet fallen into sin, a *covenant* was necessary for fully glorifying and enjoying God, but a *Mediator* was not necessary.

When the covenant of works was broken by Adam's disobedience, the distance between God and man was increased by the fact of human sinfulness. Therefore from that time on human beings could not have fellowship with God without *both a covenant and a Mediator* (see the Confession of Faith, 7.1).

3. Why is a Mediator needed for sinful human beings to have access to God's presence? Because absolute holiness is one of God's attributes, and this means that God is and must be infinitely removed from all that is sinful. The Bible teaches that God cannot deny himself. If sinful human beings could, without a mediator, have access to the presence of the holy God, that would amount to God's denying himself; that is, it would mean that God would deny or disregard his own holiness, which is inseparable from himself. If it were possible for human beings to come into God's presence without a mediator, it would bring them instantly under judgment and condemnation by reason of the intensity of God's wrath against sin.

4. Why is none but Christ qualified to be the Mediator between God and man? For a full answer to this question the student is referred to *Blue Banner Faith and Life,* vol. 1, no. 7 (July–September 1946), 125–27. The Mediator must be God, he must also be man, and he must be God and man in one person. Clearly none but Jesus Christ possesses these qualifications. Angels could not serve as mediators, for they are neither God nor man. God the Father could not serve in this capacity, for he is only God and not man. No human being except Christ could serve, for others are only man and not God. Moreover, all human beings except Jesus Christ are sinners, and therefore they are themselves in need of someone to be their mediator; therefore they could not serve as mediators for others.

5. Why can we not pray in the name of the Virgin Mary or the saints? Because neither the Virgin Mary nor any of the saints possesses the qualifications for the work of mediation between God and ourselves. As a matter of fact, Mary and the saints themselves were saved and reconciled to God only through the mediatorial work of the Lord Jesus Christ. We may and should honor Mary and the saints for their faithful service, witnessing, and suffering for the cause of Christ, but we may not give them any of the honor that belongs to Christ alone. They are of the company of the saved, but they are not co-saviors with Christ.

6. Why does the catechism refer to the work of mediation between God and man as "that glorious work"? Because the work of mediation manifests the glory of God in the salvation of man, and has its consummation in the eternal glory of the redeemed.

7. How does this answer of the catechism contradict modern "liberal" views of Jesus Christ? In this answer the catechism sets forth the absolute uniqueness of Jesus Christ. He is represented as the only possible Savior of the human race. There neither is, nor ever can be, anyone alongside of him. But the popular modern "liberal" view of Jesus Christ regards him as essentially only human, the same as other men, differing from others only in degree, not in nature. Modernists may regard Jesus as the best man that ever lived, but according to their belief the human race, by its evolutionary progress, may someday produce a more perfect individual than Jesus Christ. The thorough Modernist, insofar as he believes in Jesus Christ at all, believes in him as "a" Savior, not as *the one and only* Savior of the human race.

8. How is the command to pray in the name of Christ most commonly violated? This command is most commonly violated by people ignorantly supposing that they can approach God's presence directly, without Christ as their Mediator. This is extremely common among those who have not been instructed in the truths of the Christian faith. Such people have no genuine consciousness of sin nor of their need for a mediator. They will address God as "Father," which they have no right to do apart from faith in Christ, and will then close their prayer by simply saying "Amen," without so much as mentioning the name of Jesus Christ. This amounts to people praying *in their own name*. The person who tries to approach God without a Mediator is trying to pray in his own name.

182. Q. *How doth the Spirit help us to pray?*

A. *We not knowing what to pray for as we ought, the Spirit helpeth our infirmities, by enabling us to understand both for whom, and what, and how prayer is to be made; and by working and quickening in our hearts (although not in all persons, nor at all times, in the same measure) those* *apprehensions, affections, and graces which are requisite for the right performance of that duty.*

Scripture References

- Rom. 8:26–27. The Holy Spirit helps us to pray aright.
- Ps. 10:17. God prepares the hearts of his people, that they may pray aright.
- Zech. 12:10. God imparts to his people the desire and ability to pray by bestowing his Holy Spirit upon them.
- Eph. 6:18; Jude 20. We are to pray in the Spirit.

Commentary

1. Why do we need the help of the Holy Spirit to pray? We need the help of the Holy Spirit because of our spiritual ignorance, by reason of which we do not know what we should pray for, nor how to pray aright; and because of our spiritual weakness and sluggishness, by reason of which we feel disinclined to pray, and tend to engage in prayer in a formal and perfunctory manner, rather than in an earnest and spiritual manner.

2. How does the Holy Spirit remedy our spiritual ignorance? The Holy Spirit remedies our spiritual ignorance, not by revealing to us any truth apart from or in addition to the Bible, but by opening our spiritual eyes so that we can discern the true meaning of what is already revealed in the Bible, and thus be enabled to know the will of God concerning prayer.

3. Does the Holy Spirit reveal to us that God has chosen a particular person for eternal life, and therefore we should pray for the salvation of that individual with assured confidence that our petition will be granted? No. Only God knows who the elect are, and neither through prayer nor through any other shortcut can this information be obtained in advance of the actual salvation of elect persons. We have no right to say positively that a particular person must be one of those whom God has chosen for eternal life because the Holy Spirit has "laid it on our heart" to pray for that person's salvation.

It is true that the Holy Spirit, by his own mysterious working, may stir up one or more of God's children to pray long and earnestly for the salvation of a particular unsaved person. In such a case we may be justified in cherishing a probable hope that that person will eventually come to Christ in repentance and faith. But we are not warranted in asserting this in advance of the person's actual experience of salvation. All such praying must always be done in humble submission to the sovereignty and secret counsel of God. We are to pray for the salvation of God's elect, and we are to pray that *if* a particular person is one of the elect he will come to Christ and be saved.

God's decree of election was completed from all eternity, before the creation of the world; it cannot be changed or set aside by our praying. Even if the person we pray for is never saved, such prayers are not wasted or useless. They will be for the honor and glory of God at the Judgment Day, and will leave the unsaved sinner even more without excuse than he otherwise would be.

In this connection the history of the conversion of Augustine of Hippo is most interesting. It is related in his *Confessions,* especially 3.19–21 and 8.25–30. Augustine's mother Monica prayed for his salvation continually for many years, until he was finally converted to Christ at the age of thirty-two years.

4. Why do we need the Holy Spirit's "working and quickening in our hearts" in order to pray as we should? *Quickening* means "life-giving" or "stimulation." We need the Holy Spirit's working and quickening in our hearts in order to pray as we should, because even those who have been born again are of themselves very sluggish and spiritually lukewarm, and apart from the special help of the Holy Spirit they would never pray as they should. By the special work of the Holy Spirit in the Christian's heart, this sinful sluggishness and indifference are in a measure overcome, so that real prayer becomes possible.

5. Does the Holy Spirit always work uniformly in helping Christian people to pray? No. Every real Christian receives the help of the Holy Spirit for prayer, but this work of the Spirit is "not in all persons, nor at all times, in the same measure." That is, some persons receive more of this help than others; and the same person receives more help at one time than at another.

The reasons for this lack of uniformity in the working of the Holy Spirit are reserved to the secret counsel of God. We may be sure that there is a wise purpose behind it, but what that purpose is has not been revealed to us. It may be that in some cases the Holy Spirit largely withdraws his inward working for a time in order that we may be humbled and made to realize our dependence upon him, and our helplessness of ourselves.

6. What is the meaning of "apprehensions" in this answer of the catechism? Here the word *apprehensions* means "items of knowledge," that is, items of truth which the Holy Spirit enables us to grasp and understand in order that we may pray aright.

7. What is the meaning of "affections"? "Affections" here are feelings and desires which the Holy Spirit stirs up in our hearts that we may pray aright, such as love for God, thankfulness to him, a desire that his name may be glorified and his will done, etc.

8. What is meant by "graces" in this connection? By "graces" the catechism here means the spiritual qualifications which we must have, apart from right apprehensions and affections, in order to pray in a manner pleasing to God. Such "graces" are humility, self-denial, faith in God's promises, and persistence which enables us to overcome obstacles and keep on praying even when our sinful flesh would rather incline us in some other direction. These "graces" are definitely the work of the Holy Spirit in our hearts; we do not have them of ourselves, and we cannot get them by human planning, good resolutions, or willpower.

9. What should be our attitude toward "prayer books" and written forms of prayer? The Reformed Presbyterian Testimony speaks as follows on this matter: "Public prayer is to accompany the word preached: written *forms* of prayer, whether read or repeated, are not authorized in the Scriptures—are not calculated to exercise the mind in the graces of the Holy Spirit—are not adapted to the varieties of the state of the Church and its members, and are not to be used in approaching the throne of grace" (24).

Certainly we may learn something of value by reading and studying the prayers of eminent Christians of past times; but we should not depend on them in our own approach to the throne of grace. Rather, we should seek the grace of the Holy Spirit that we may frame acceptable and fervent prayers in our own words. We must always be on our guard against the tendency to religious formalism.

183. Q. *For whom are we to pray?*

A. *We are to pray for the whole church of Christ upon earth; for magistrates, and ministers; for ourselves, our brethren, yea, our enemies; and for all sorts of men living, or that shall live hereafter; . . .*

Scripture References

- Eph. 6:18; Ps. 28:9. We are to pray for the whole church of Christ on earth.
- 1 Tim. 2:1–2; Col. 4:3. We are to pray for all who occupy positions of authority in church and state.
- Gen. 32:11; Isa. 38:1–5. It is proper to pray ourselves.
- James 5:16; Gen. 20:7, 17; Job 42:7–8; Matt. 5:44. We are to pray for our brethren, our friends, and even our enemies.
- 1 Tim. 2:1–2; John 17:20; 2 Sam. 7:29. We are to pray for all sorts of men living, or that shall live in the future.

Commentary

1. Why must we pray for the whole church of Christ on earth? We must pray for the whole church of Christ on earth because of the spiritual unity of the church as one body under Christ the head. Our prayers are not to be limited to our own congregation nor even to our own denomination; they are to include all branches of the church of Christ. This does not mean, of course, that we are to pray in detail for all branches of the church; but it does mean that we are not to limit our intercessions to that branch of the church of which we ourselves are members. We are to pray for Christ's church and kingdom as a whole; we are not to be nearsighted or denominationally minded in the matter of intercessory prayer. We should of course pray especially for our own denomination, for which we have a special concern and responsibility; but this should never exclude the larger outlook of pleading with God for the whole church of Christ in all the world.

2. Why are we commanded to pray for magistrates? We are commanded to pray for magistrates and ministers, that is, for persons in positions of authority in both state and church, because both the state and the church are divine institutions for the accomplishment of God's purposes in the world, and both need his help and blessing for the proper accomplishment of their tasks. Magistrates and ministers need wisdom, courage, honesty, and integrity as well as other gifts of God's common and special grace; therefore Christian people should pray for them.

3. Is it right to pray for ourselves? Certainly it is right. To pray for ourselves is not the same thing as to pray selfishly. We may pray unselfishly for ourselves. The person who prays a selfish prayer sins in doing so, and will not receive any blessing from God in answer to his prayer (James 4:3). But there is a right way of praying for ourselves, as is exemplified many times in the Bible. (a) We may pray for legitimate temporal blessings for ourselves, such as health or healing, food, clothing, material prosperity, success in business, etc., and God will give us these blessings, in answer to our prayers, so far as is in accordance with his glory and our own true welfare. (b) We ought always to pray for spiritual blessings for ourselves, and when we do so sincerely and humbly we may be confident that God will answer our prayers, either by granting our requests, or in some other way that is even better, according to his own wisdom and love.

4. Why are we commanded to pray for our enemies? It is sad but true that it is impossible to go through life and do our duty without incurring the enmity of some people, that is, without having some enemies. The best and holiest of God's saints have found this to be true; think, for example, of David, Elijah, Paul, Martin Luther, John Knox, Andrew Melville, and James Renwick. In the present sinful state of the world it is also inevitable that nations sometimes be at enmity one with another. We should note that the Bible does not say that we should not have any enemies, but that we should love and pray for our enemies; this implies that we cannot avoid having them.

Even those who may unavoidably be our enemies are still human beings created in the image of God, and like ourselves they are sinners such as Christ died to redeem. Even though they are our enemies, they are not beyond the power of Christ to save. Therefore we should pray for them. This does not mean to pray that they will succeed in wrongdoing, but to pray for their true welfare.

5. Does the duty of praying for our enemies imply that we should not resist them? By no means. We are to pray for our enemies, but at the same time it is also our duty to defend ourselves, our families, and our country against injustice and violence. To pray for our enemies means chiefly to pray for their repentance, conversion to Christ, and salvation. It may also be our God-given duty to resist their aggressions or injustice. If possible this is to be done by appeal to law; but if this is not possible, it may be our real duty to resist violence by force. If a criminal breaks into our house and threatens to murder our family, we should not hesitate to try to overpower him, or if necessary even to shoot him. Similarly it may be our duty to use force in resisting the public enemies, domestic or foreign, of our country; but even so we are not to hate them, but to pray that God will have mercy on them and save them from their sins.

6. Why are we to pray "for all sorts of men living, or that shall live hereafter"? All human beings, both those living today and those yet to be born, are created in the image of God and for the purpose of glorifying God. Also many of those living today and those who shall live in the future are the elect of God, for whom Christ died, who shall in time be saved and become heirs of eternal glory. We are to pray that God will be glorified in them and that his elect, down to the end of time, will be gathered into one in Christ.

183. Q. *(continued) For whom are we to pray?*

A. *We are to pray . . . but not for the dead, nor for those that are known to have sinned the sin unto death.*

Scripture References
- 2 Sam. 12:21–23. We are not to pray for the dead.
- 1 John 5:16. We are not commanded to pray for those who have sinned "a sin unto death."

Commentary
1. Why is it wrong to pray for the dead? Briefly, it is wrong to pray for the dead because the redeemed are with Christ in heaven, where they no longer need our prayers, and the lost are in hell, where our prayers can no longer avail to help them. As the souls of believers are at their death made perfect in holiness (Heb. 12:23) and are enjoying perfect rest and peace with Christ in heaven while they wait for the resurrection of their bodies and the Judgment Day (Rev. 6:11; 14:13), it is clear that they do not need our prayers; there is no blessing we could ask God to give them that they do not already have. As for the lost, Scripture teaches with the utmost plainness that death is the end of all opportunity for repentance, conversion, and salvation; after death there is "a great gulf fixed" and there remains no possibility of the lost ever being reconciled to God (Luke 16:24–26; Rev. 22:11).

2. Why does the Roman Catholic Church sanction prayers for the dead? The Roman Catholic Church sanctions prayers for the dead because of its unscriptural belief in purgatory as "the state in which those suffer for a time who die guilty of venial sins, or without having satisfied for the punishment due to their sins." The Roman Church teaches that the prayers of living believers can help the souls in purgatory. If the whole idea of purgatory is unscriptural, as we believe it to be, then of course prayers for the souls in purgatory are also excluded.

3. Are there Protestants who believe in praying for the dead? There are some Protestants who believe in praying for the dead. This is not because they believe in purgatory, but because of a lack of faith in the scriptural teaching that death is the end of all opportunity for salvation. Those who do not believe in heaven and hell as absolutely separate destinies, but simply believe in "the other world," will naturally not see any reason why they should not pray for the dead. Also those who believe that after death there will be a "second chance" for salvation may tend to believe that it is right to pray for the dead. As we believe that all these teachings are wrong and contrary to the Bible, we reject the idea of praying for the dead in all its forms.

4. Do we find any examples of prayers for the dead in the Bible? No. There is not a single instance of such in the Word of God.

5. What is meant by "the sin unto death"? This expression, which is taken from 1 John 5:16, is usually understood to be equivalent to the "unpardonable sin" or the "sin against the Holy Spirit" mentioned in Matthew 12:31–32; Mark 3:29. This sin is unpardonable, not because it is too great to be forgiven, but because in its nature it inevitably cuts off the possibility of repentance and saving faith, and therefore of salvation.

It is understood to be a stubborn, permanent, and complete resistance to the pleadings of the Holy Spirit which finally results in the Holy Spirit abandoning the person to his own sin, and totally ceasing to influence that person. Since true repentance is the gift of God, and comes by the working of the Holy Spirit in a person's heart, it is no longer possible when the Holy Spirit has finally abandoned a person. Such a person becomes utterly "hardened," and no longer shows the slightest interest in spiritual things or the salvation of his soul.

Since the salvation of such a person is impossible, because not in accordance with the purpose of God, it is clearly wrong to pray for such a person. We should not pray for a person who is known to have sinned the sin unto death, any more than we should pray to God for those who have died in sin.

However, we should be extremely cautious about saying that any particular individual has sinned the sin unto death. It is improbable that this is a common sin. We should note the exact words of 1 John 5:16: "There is a sin unto death: I do not say that he shall pray for it." The text does not say: "I say that he shall *not* pray for it"; it simply refrains from commanding us to pray for such a person: "I do not say that he *shall* pray for it." If there is any reasonable doubt as to whether the person has committed "the sin unto death," we may properly pray for such a person that if it is God's purpose, God in his mercy will save him from sin and eternal death.

184. Q. *For what things are we to pray?*

A. *We are to pray for all things tending to the glory of God, the welfare of the Church, our own or others' good, but not for anything that is unlawful.*

Scripture References

- Matt. 6:9. In our prayers, we are to think first of what will tend to glorify God.
- Pss. 51:18; 122:6. We are to pray for the welfare of the church.
- Matt. 7:11. We are to pray for whatever will be for our own good.
- Ps. 125:4. We are to pray for what will be for the good of others.
- 1 John 5:14; Ps. 66:18. We are not to pray for anything unlawful, or contrary to the will of God.

Commentary

1. What is the most important consideration in deciding what things to pray for? The most important consideration must be the glory of God. The preface to the Lord's Prayer teaches us this, as well as many other parts of the Bible. Our chief end is to glorify God and enjoy him. We are not to think first of our own needs, problems, and desires, but of God and his honor and glory.

2. How can we know what things tend to the glory of God? There is only one way to learn what things tend to the glory of God, and that is by studying the Bible, which is the revealed will of God. Apart from the light of Scripture, men have always gone astray and thought that many things would glorify God which are really contrary to God's will and even hateful to God. Jephthah thought he was glorifying God by offering his daughter to God as a burnt offering (Judg. 11:29–40). This, however, was contrary to the will of God, and it was Jephthah's ignorance of the Scripture (the law of God in the Books of Moses) which allowed him to go so far astray. In the Middle Ages and the period of the Reformation, the Inquisition took the lives of countless faithful, God-fearing Christians, and all in the name of the glory of God. When men deviate from the written Word, they will commit all kinds of errors in the name of the divine glory. We cannot pray aright unless we also study the Bible aright.

3. Why must we pray for the welfare of the church? The church is not a mere human organization; it is the house of God, a divine institution, the body of which Christ is the head. The true welfare of God's people, and even the peace and prosperity of the nations of the world, really depends on the spiritual welfare and security of the church. This of course does not mean merely one denomination, but the whole visible church of God on earth. The Bible teaches that God deals with the nations in accordance with their treatment of his covenant people, his church. God said to Abraham: "I will bless them that bless thee, and curse him that curseth thee; and in thee shall all families of the earth be blessed" (Gen. 12:3). Much later God spoke through the prophet Jeremiah and predicted the destruction of the Babylonian Empire by the Medes and Persians because of Babylon's cruel treatment of God's covenant people. "Thou art my battle-ax and weapons of war; for with thee I will break in pieces the nations, and with thee will I destroy kingdoms; and with thee will I break in pieces the horse and his rider; with thee also will I break in pieces man and woman, and with thee will I break in pieces old and young; and with thee will I break in pieces the young man and the maid; I will also break in pieces with thee the shepherd and his flock; and with thee will I break in pieces the husbandman and his yoke of oxen; and with thee will I break in pieces captains and rulers. And I will render unto Babylon and to all the inhabitants of Chaldea all their evil that they have done in Zion in your sight, saith the LORD" (Jer. 51:20–24). This remarkable statement does not mean that the church is to attack the nations and their people with force of arms; it means, rather, that because of their persecution, oppression, and mistreatment of Zion (the church), God in his providence will bring about the judgment and destruction of the nations. From this it follows that the true welfare and prosperity of the church are very closely related to the peace and prosperity of the nations of the world. It is still true that God will bless them that bless Zion, and curse them that curse Zion.

4. How do we know what things are for our own good? In some matters, we can be sure that certain things are for our own good, because they are so revealed in Scripture. For such blessings we can always pray with the fullest confidence. For example, we know that it is always for our own good to "depart from evil, and do good, seek peace and pursue it" (Ps. 34:14). It is always for our own good to "draw near unto God" (Ps. 73:28). It is always for our own good that we be sanctified and made holy and Christ-like in our character. In all matters which are thus revealed in the Bible, we are to pray confidently.

There are, however, other matters concerning which we have no positive revelation in the Bible. Business and financial prosperity, bodily healing, success in any particular undertaking—such things as these may or may not be for our true welfare. God has not revealed in his Word whether it is for his glory and our own good, in any particular case, that we receive such blessings as these. In such matters we are always to pray in submission to the will of God, saying as our Savior did in the Garden of Gethsemane, "Not my will, but thine, be done." These blessings will be given to us *if* they are in accordance with God's will, and they are in accordance with God's will *if* they will best serve to promote his glory and our own good. But only God knows *whether* they will do so; consequently we must pray in humble submission to God's will. The promoters of the present-day "divine healing" movement tell us that we are to pray for healing *because* it is God's will; this is unscriptural. Rather, we are to pray for healing *if* it is God's will.

5. What is meant by praying for the good of others? By praying for others' good we mean, first of all, praying for their salvation, in submission to the sovereignty and secret counsel of God. In the second place, we mean praying for temporal blessings to be bestowed on others, insofar as God will be truly glorified in bestowing them.

6. Why is it wrong to pray for anything that is unlawful? In the Bible, the distinction between right and wrong is an absolute one. Right is always right and wrong is always wrong. Anything that tends to obliterate or obscure this absolute distinction between right and wrong is wicked and displeasing to God. Consequently the Bible teaches that we may not "do evil that good may come"; that is, we may not try to accomplish good by doing something that is wrong. For example, we may not tell a lie to further a good cause. Similarly, we may not pray that we will win money in a lottery in order to contribute it to the church or to foreign missions. We may not pray that anything which is dishonest or morally wrong will be blessed with success or prosperity.

There have been people who have conceived the idea that God's glory may require some utilization of evil on the part of God's people. A group of gangsters about to rob a bank would have no warrant for praying for God's blessing on their efforts. This is of course an extreme case, but the principle is valid in all cases. We may never seek God's blessing upon evil or wrongdoing. "If I regard iniquity in my heart, the Lord will not hear me" (Ps. 66:18). God in his divine sovereignty can permit evil to exist and he can turn it to His own glory, but this does not mean that God ever approves of evil; he always hates it because it is contrary to his nature, and his people are always to hate evil and to abstain from it.

185. Q. *How are we to pray?*

A. *We are to pray with an awful apprehension of the majesty of God, and deep sense of our own unworthiness, necessities, and sins; with penitent, thankful, and enlarged hearts; with understanding, faith, sincerity, fervency, love, and perseverance, waiting upon him, with humble submission to his will.*

Scripture References

- Eccl. 5:1–2. In prayer we are to realize and remember the majesty of God.
- Gen. 18:27; 32:10. We are to pray with a sense of our own unworthiness in God's sight.
- Luke 15:17–19. We are to pray with a sense of personal need.

- Luke 13:13–14. We are to pray with a sense of personal sin.
- Pss. 51:17; 32:5–6; 38:18. We are to pray with a spirit of repentance.
- Phil. 4:6. We are to pray with an attitude of thankfulness to God.
- 1 Sam. 1:15; 2:1. We are to pray with enlarged hearts, having a deep desire to receive blessings from God.
- 1 Cor. 14:15. We are to pray with understanding, or intelligently.
- Mark 11:24; James 1:6. We are to pray with faith in God and his promises.
- Ps. 145:18; 17:1; James 5:16; 1 Tim. 2:8. We are to pray with sincerity, fervency, and love to God.
- Eph. 6:18; Mic. 7:7. We are to pray perseveringly, waiting on God to answer in his own time.
- Matt. 26:39; 1 John 5:14–15. We are to pray with humble submission to God's will.

Commentary

1. What is meant by "an awful apprehension of the majesty of God"? In this expression, the word *awful* means "having reverential fear"; compare Hebrews 12:28–29: "let us have grace, whereby we may serve God acceptably with reverence and godly fear [ARV: reverence and awe]: for our God is a consuming fire." The word *apprehension* means "realization." "The majesty of God" means God's absolute and infinite greatness, by which he is far above and beyond all created beings. We might paraphrase the catechism's statement as follows: "We are to pray with a reverential realization of God's absolute, infinite greatness and separation from all created beings."

2. Why should we pray "with an awful apprehension of the majesty of God"? Because of who and what God is, as he is revealed to us in the Bible. God and man are not equals. We could not approach God with acceptance at all if God had not opened the way for us by condescending to establish his covenant with us. Even before the human race fell into sin, when Adam and Eve lived in their original righteousness in the Garden of Eden, they could not have enjoyed communion with God if God had not taken the initiative in bridging the chasm between Creator and creature by establishing the covenant of works (see the Confession of Faith, 7.1). If this was true even before the human race fell into sin, how much more true it is today, when we are separated from God not merely by our finitude as creatures, but also by our sinfulness as members of a fallen and corrupted race.

3. Is a reverent realization of the majesty of God often lacking in present-day prayers? Yes. Even those who give evidence of being true children of God often fail to approach God in prayer with proper reverence. Even public prayers are sometimes offensively familiar in addressing God. This wrong attitude is doubtless a product of the one-sided emphasis on the love of God which has become more or less prevalent in modern Protestantism. Modern religion in stressing the love of God has failed to remember that love is only one aspect of God's being. We must never forget the majesty, holiness, and justice of God. We should always remember that God is not a casual acquaintance to whom we may speak in any manner we please; God is the infinite, eternal, unchangeable Creator and Ruler of the universe.

4. Why has modern religion tended to emphasize only the love of God, while forgetting His majesty and holiness? Because the modern view of life is man-centered, not God-centered. This perverse man-centered view of life has even invaded many churches and the religious life of their members. The result has been a tendency to cling to those aspects of the Christian doctrine of God which are regarded as useful to mankind, while forgetting and neglecting those aspects which do not appear to have a value for mankind. Sinful men can see how the love of God can benefit mankind, so they stress the love of God; they cannot see how the majesty of God can benefit mankind, so they neglect the majesty of God. The result is a one-sided idea of God and a lack of reverence in addressing God.

5. What does the catechism mean by a "deep sense of our own unworthiness"? This expression means a true consciousness of the fact that God owes us nothing; we have no valid claims on God's goodness and mercy. Even if we were not sinners, it would still be true that we would be *unworthy* of God's blessings. God did not make the covenant of works with Adam because he had to; it was an unmerited act of grace and condescension on God's part. Still more are we unworthy of God's blessings by reason of our sinfulness; as sinners we are not only undeserving, but actually ill-deserving. When we approach God in prayer, we must realize this. The person who thinks that God owes him something, that he has some rights that God is obligated to respect and pay attention to, cannot pray aright.

6. What is meant by a "deep sense of our own necessities"? This means a true consciousness of our condition of personal need. Unless we have a true consciousness of our need, prayer is foolishness. If we have no sense of need, how can we sincerely ask God for anything? The Pharisee's prayer is an example of a "prayer" lacking the consciousness of need; he asked nothing of God; he only congratulated himself on his own attainments (Luke 18:11–12).

7. Why must we pray with a "deep sense of our own sins"? Our guilty, sinful condition is real. If we do not have a full realization of it, our entire approach to God will be on the wrong basis. We can never approach God aright in prayer unless at the same time we recognize the real truth about ourselves. The person who lacks a deep sense of his own sinfulness will inevitably pray a self-righteous prayer which can only be an abomination to God. The person who prays lacking this deep consciousness of personal sin only deceives himself. Such prayer cannot be acceptable to God.

8. Why must we pray with "penitent, thankful, and enlarged hearts"? We must pray with penitent hearts because God's mercy is promised to those who not only confess their sins, but sincerely desire to forsake them. To pray with an impenitent heart—a heart that proposes to keep on sinning—is to add presumption to all our other sins (Pss. 19:13; 68:18).

We must pray with thankful hearts because we have received many blessings from God; to fail to feel thankful for these would be to add the sin of ingratitude to our other sins.

By "enlarged hearts" the catechism means hearts with a deep longing and desire to receive God's blessings and experience communion with him. We are not to pray as if we had only a slight desire for God and his blessings, but with an intense, earnest longing for nearness to God and blessings from him. Only such an attitude in prayer can be acceptable to God.

9. What is meant by praying "with understanding"? As used in the catechism, this expression means praying with an intelligent insight into God's revelation in his Word, and our own personal needs, as well as the needs of others. There is such a thing as foolish prayer, and even wicked prayer. Some people try to make prayer a substitute for Bible study and for the functioning of their own intelligence and conscience. Faced with a choice between right and wrong, they will try to evade the issue by "making it a matter of prayer." When prayer is regarded as a substitute for obedience to the revealed will of God, it is not prayer that God will accept. When God commanded Abraham to offer his son, Isaac as a sacrifice, Abraham did not say, "I will pray about this for a few days to ask God's guidance as to what

I should do." He obeyed the will of God which had already been revealed to him. When people "pray" to get "guidance" as to whether they should obey the Ten Commandments or not, they are on dangerous ground. Such praying is both stupid and wicked.

10. Why is faith necessary for right prayer? The Bible states that without faith it is impossible to please God (Heb. 11:6). God has been pleased to make faith the instrument of our salvation and the means by which we are to get blessings from him. When the catechism speaks of faith in this connection, of course it means faith in the true God and his Word and promises. Only such a faith has any value whatever in prayer. In our day the word *faith* is often used to describe such human attitudes as optimism, self-confidence, confidence in our fellow men, etc. Such is not religious faith in the Bible sense. Only God can properly be the object of religious faith.

11. Why must we pray with sincerity, fervency, and love to God? If we do not pray thus, our prayers will not be real prayers; they will merely be hypocritical and mechanical pronouncing of words. Only if we are dead in earnest can we really pray.

12. What should be our expectation as to God's time and way of answering our prayers? We should expect and believe that God will answer our prayers in his own appointed time and way according to his holy will. That is, in all our praying we must be careful to maintain an attitude of submission to the sovereignty of God. We may never presume to dictate to God as to when and how our prayers are to be answered. If God in his sovereignty chooses to delay the answer to our prayers, we are not to become discouraged and give up praying; we are to exercise Christian patience, and keep on praying with "perseverance, waiting upon him." Luke 18:1–8 is very instructive in this connection.

If God does not answer our prayers in the way we desired, we should realize that this is not unkindness or lack of love on God's part, but because to grant our requests as we asked would not really be for God's glory and our own good. God may answer our prayer by withholding what we have asked him for, either for a time or permanently. The apostle Paul prayed three times that his "thorn in the flesh" might depart from him, but God did not grant this request; instead, he said to Paul, "My grace is sufficient for thee: for my strength is made perfect in weakness" (2 Cor. 12:7–9). Paul then understood that God had a purpose in permitting his servant to continue to suffer from this "thorn in the flesh"; it was to keep him from becoming proud and self confident (v. 7).

186. Q. *What rule hath God given for our direction in the duty of prayer?*

A. *The whole word of God is of use to direct us in the duty of prayer; but the special rule of direction is that form of prayer which our Savior Jesus Christ taught his disciples, commonly called "The Lord's Prayer."*

Scripture References

- 1 John 5:14. The whole Word of God is of use to direct us in the duty of prayer.
- Matt. 6:9–13; Luke 11:2–4. The prayer Christ taught his disciples, commonly called "The Lord's Prayer."

Commentary

1. Why do we need a rule for our direction in the duty of prayer? We need a rule for our direction in the duty of prayer because the fall of the human race into sin has so affected our hearts and minds that we could never pray aright without a God-given rule. In order to pray aright, we need to know the truth about God, about ourselves, and about how we can be reconciled to God; besides this, we need special knowledge about prayer, without which our prayer would inevitably be ignorant and wrong.

2. What is the source of the knowledge we need to pray aright? The Holy Bible, the written Word of God, is the only adequate source of this knowledge. God's revelation in nature is not sufficient to guide us in prayer, nor is it suited to our need as sinful human beings. The heathen, who do not have the light of Scripture, but only the light of nature, invariably pray ignorantly and wrongly.

3. In what three ways does the Bible serve our rule for direction in prayer? The contents of the Bible, as our rule for direction in prayer, may be divided into three classifications, as follows: (a) The teachings of the Bible in general; that is, the sum total of what the Bible teaches about God, man, salvation, and duty. Since these teachings concern our relation to God, they have a bearing on the subject of prayer. (b) The teachings of the Bible on the specific subject of prayer. There are many portions of the Old Testament and especially of the New Testament that deal directly with the special subject of prayer. From these we are to learn how we should pray. (c) The form of prayer which Christ taught his disciples, commonly called "The Lord's Prayer." In this model prayer we have the Bible's teachings on the subject of prayer presented in concrete form; this is a prayer that embodies what the Bible teaches about prayer.

4. Is the prayer commonly called "The Lord's Prayer" really the Lord's prayer? Of course not. It is the prayer that our Lord taught his disciples. It neither was nor could be our Lord's own prayer. Jesus Christ could not have used this form of prayer as his own personal prayer, for it contains a petition for forgiveness, which implies a consciousness of guilt and sinfulness which he did not have. The New Testament records certain prayers that Jesus actually prayed. The longest is in John 17; it should be noted that it reveals no consciousness of sin, and contains no petition for forgiveness. The prayer commonly called "The Lord's Prayer" has been called by this name so long that it would be very difficult to change its name now. We may continue to call it by that name, but at the same time we should realize that Jesus himself never prayed this prayer.

5. Where in the Bible is the Lord's Prayer found? In Matthew 6:9–13, and in a slightly different form in Luke 11:2–4.

6. How can we account for the differences between the form of the Lord's Prayer in Matthew and the form of it in Luke? Probably Jesus taught this prayer to his disciples on more than one occasion. The record given in Luke may be, and probably is, a record of a different occasion from that recorded in Matthew. Thus the two forms are to be regarded as equally correct.

There is a question about the textual genuineness of the conclusion of the Lord's Prayer in Matthew ("For thine is the kingdom, and the power, and the glory, for ever. Amen."). Some of the most important Greek manuscripts lack these words, while others vary in the wording of the conclusion. This problem must also be taken into consideration in comparing the form of the prayer in Matthew with that in Luke. The conclusion of the prayer is not given in Luke.

187. Q. *How is the Lord's prayer to be used?*

A. *The Lord's prayer is not only for direction, as a pattern, according to which we are to make our prayers; but may also be used as a prayer, so that it be done with understanding, faith, reverence, and other graces necessary to the right performance of the duty of prayer.*

Scripture References

- Matt. 6:9. The Lord's Prayer is to be used as a pattern or model for making our own prayers.
- Luke 11:2. The Lord's Prayer may properly be used as a prayer.
- 1 Cor. 14:15. The Lord's Prayer is to be used with understanding.
- Heb. 11:6. The Lord's Prayer is to be used with faith.

Commentary

1. How can we use the Lord's Prayer as a pattern or model for making our own prayers? We can use the Lord's Prayer as a pattern or model for making our own prayers by noting its characteristics and its contents, and framing our own petitions accordingly. We should note, first, the reverence of the Lord's Prayer; it is free from the objectionable familiarity with God which is common in modern prayers; it addresses God as "Father," but immediately adds "which art in heaven" so that the greatness and majesty of God are stressed.

In the second place, we should note the simplicity and directness, as well as the brevity, of the Lord's Prayer. Here is no flowery language, no display of oratory, no long, involved sentences. It is simple, short, to the point; we will realize the propriety of this when we consider that God knows our desires and our needs even before we present them to him.

In the third place, we should note the God-centered character of the Lord's Prayer. It does not start with ourselves and our needs, but with God, His name, His kingdom, His will. Only after these have been considered are our needs mentioned; clearly the Lord's Prayer is formed on the plan of "God First."

Finally, we should note that the Lord's Prayer includes our material needs as well as our spiritual needs, and that it does not commit the error, common in many modern prayers, of failing to ask for forgiveness of sins. In all these various respects the Lord's Prayer is to serve as a pattern or model according to which we can frame our own prayers in a manner that will be acceptable to God.

2. How may the Lord's Prayer properly be used as a prayer? The Lord's Prayer may properly be used as a prayer, either by itself or in connection with a prayer framed by ourselves, with the provisions laid down by the catechism, "that it be done with understanding, faith, reverence, and other graces necessary to the right performance of the duty of prayer." That is, we are always to guard against and avoid the danger of a merely mechanical and formal use of the Lord's Prayer.

3. How has the Lord's Prayer sometimes been misused? The Lord's Prayer has been misused, as suggested in the previous question, by being used in a merely mechanical and formal manner. Those who have thought that there is merit in repeating the words of the Lord's Prayer over and over, fifty or a hundred times, do not have the slightest understanding of its real nature and proper use. Many who avoid this extreme error yet use the Lord's Prayer in a mechanical or irreverent manner, by repeating its words hastily and without thinking of their meaning and importance.

4. What objections have been raised to the use of the Lord's Prayer as a prayer? Some Protestant Christians have been opposed to the use of the Lord's Prayer as a prayer on the ground that it is liable to mechanical and formalistic abuse. They cite the words of Jesus in Matthew 6:9 ("After this manner therefore pray ye") and say that this shows that the Lord's Prayer is intended to be used as a pattern for prayer, not as a prayer in itself. Such people fail to note that Jesus' words in Luke 11:2 ("When ye pray, say, Our Father," etc.) fully warrant the use of the Lord's Prayer as a prayer. The fact that something is liable to abuse does not constitute an argument against its proper and legitimate use.

More important is the objection raised by a certain type of the teaching called Modern Dispensationalism, exemplified by the notes in the *Scofield Reference Bible*. This teaches that the Lord's Prayer, used as a form of prayer, belongs exclusively to the old dispensation (the dispensation of law, before the crucifixion of Christ), and is on legal ground and not suited to the New Testament people of God (*Scofield Reference Bible*, 1002, 1089–90). The *Scofield Bible* adds that the Lord's Prayer is not a prayer in the name of Christ, and that it makes our forgiveness of others the condition of God forgiving us, which, it is said, is characteristic of "law" in contrast to "grace" (p. 1090).

Accordingly, those Dispensationalists who follow this teaching of the *Scofield Reference Bible* refuse to use the Lord's Prayer as a form of prayer.

5. How can this dispensational objection to the use of the Lord's Prayer as a prayer be answered? (a) It is based on the error that the period from Moses to Christ was an era of law rather than an era of grace. The truth is that the covenant of works, or opportunity of gaining eternal life by legal obedience to God's will, came to an end when Adam and Eve sinned. Salvation by divine grace was announced in Genesis 3:15 and has been the only basis of approach to God ever since then. The period from Moses to Christ was not a period of approaching and serving God on a "legal" basis. It was a period of divine grace and redemption, followed by obedience to God's commandments as the fruit of salvation and as a token of gratitude to God. See the preface to the Ten Commandments (Exod. 20:1–2), which shows that obedience to the commandments is based on prior redemption, that is, on grace. Therefore the Lord's Prayer, even though given by Jesus before he was crucified, is not to be regarded as "legal" or connected with the idea of salvation by works. (b) Even though it is true that the Lord's Prayer is not formally a prayer in the name of Christ, yet it really is a prayer in the name of Christ. It addresses God as "our Father." How can anyone call God "Father" except through Christ, on the basis of Christ's redemption? See John 14:6: "No man cometh unto the Father, but by me." (c) It is not true that the Lord's Prayer makes our forgiveness of others the condition of God's forgiving us. "Forgive us our debts *as* we forgive our debtors" is not the same thing as saying, "Forgive us our debts *because* we forgive our debtors." The catechism in question 194 gives the correct interpretation of the clause, which will be discussed in a subsequent lesson.

(**Note:** The teaching of the *Scofield Reference Bible* on the subject of "law" and "grace" in the period from Moses to the crucifixion of Christ is very difficult to ascertain with accuracy, and appears to be inconsistent with itself. It is stated that at Sinai Israel "rashly" accepted the law, and even that Israel exchanged grace for law [p. 20n.1]. Yet Dr. Scofield freely recognizes that there was grace and redemption in the period from Moses to Christ; for instance, he calls Exodus "the book of redemption," states that this redemption is wholly of God, by the blood of Christ, etc. [p. 88n.1]. The result of this apparent inconsistency has been great confusion in the minds of many Christian people.)

For an explanation of the function of the law in the period from Moses to Christ that is self-consistent and in line with the theology of the Westminster Standards, see Geerhardus Vos, *Biblical Theology: Old and New Testaments* (Grand Rapids: Eerdmans, 1948), 141–45.

188. Q. *Of how many parts does the Lord's prayer consist?*

A. *The Lord's prayer consists of three parts: a preface, petitions, and a conclusion.*

189. Q. *What doth the preface of the Lord's prayer teach us?*

A. *The preface of the Lord's prayer (contained in these words,* Our Father which art in heaven) *teacheth us, when we pray, to draw near to God with confidence of his fatherly goodness, and our interest therein; with reverence, and all other child-like dispositions, heavenly affections, and due apprehensions of his sovereign power, majesty, and gracious condescension: as also, to pray with and for others.*

Scripture References

- Matt. 6:9. The preface of the Lord's Prayer.
- Luke 11:13; Rom. 8:15. We are to approach God with confidence in his fatherly goodness.
- Isa. 64:9. We are to approach God with a reverent attitude, as his children.
- Ps. 123:1; Lam. 3:41. We are to pray with heavenly affections.
- Isa. 63:15–16; Neh. 1:4–6. We are to pray realizing God's sovereign power, majesty, and gracious condescension.
- Acts 12:5; Matt. 18:19; James 5:16–18. We are to pray with and for others.

Commentary

1. How is the Lord's Prayer divided? The Lord's Prayer is made up of a preface ("Our Father which art in heaven"), six petitions, and a conclusion ("For thine is the kingdom, and the power, and the glory, for ever. Amen.").

2. What lessons can we learn from this division of the Lord's Prayer?
From this division of the Lord's Prayer, we can learn that our own prayers
should be similarly composed. There should be order and progress in our
prayers; they should not have everything thrown together and mixed up
without order or arrangement. First of all, every prayer should have an introduction or "preface," recognizing God's infinite majesty and greatness; we
should not rush into God's holy presence and begin to talk about our personal needs, without first addressing him in a reverent and worthy manner.
Second, the petitions of our prayers ought to be properly arranged. Those
dealing with God, his honor and glory, his kingdom, etc., should come first,
and those dealing with ourselves, our needs and desires, etc., should come
afterwards. Third, our prayers should have a fitting conclusion.

**3. What two main ideas are taught in the preface of the Lord's
Prayer?** (a) The truth that God is the Father of his people; (b) the truth that
God and his people are not equals, for God exists far above His people, in
the majesty and glory of heaven.

4. Who can rightly call God "Father"? Only Christian people, who
have been reconciled to God through the work of the Lord Jesus Christ
(John 14:6: "no man cometh unto the Father, but by me"). No person who
is not a believing Christian has any right to use the Lord's Prayer. To encourage those who do not believe in Jesus Christ as their Savior to use the Lord's
Prayer is to encourage them in a sinful delusion, making them think that
they are the children of God when really they are not.

5. Are not all human beings the children of God? It is quite true that
all human beings are children of God in the *natural* sense, because they are
God's creatures and he is their Creator. The Bible sometimes speaks of people as children of God in this natural sense (Acts 17:28–29). But most places
in the Bible which speak of God being a Father of people, or of people being
children of God, use the terms *Father* and *children* not in the natural sense but
in the *religious* sense; they mean that there is a special religious relationship
between God and certain people.

It is in this religious sense that the term *Father* is used in the Lord's Prayer.
In the religious sense, it is not true that all people are children of God. Jesus
told some of the Jews that they were not children of God but children of
the devil (John 8:42–44). See also 1 John 3:10; 5:18–19, where we are taught
that some people are children of God, while the rest are children of the devil.

6. What attitude should Christian people have toward their heavenly Father? An attitude of confidence in his fatherly goodness, and their interest therein. By "interest" the catechism means their *share* of the benefits of God's goodness. We are to realize that our heavenly Father loves us and cares for us, and that it is not a vain or useless thing to approach his throne in prayer. Such an attitude of confidence in God as our Father comes from the special work of the Holy Spirit in our hearts (Rom. 8:15).

7. Why should we draw near to God with reverence? Because the fact that God is our Father does not mean that God and we ourselves are on a plane of equality, nor that we can approach God just as we please, or just as we would talk with an earthly friend. The Fatherhood of God does not cancel the majesty, glory, and sovereignty of God; it does not mean that we can approach God with careless familiarity. The casualness and near-flippancy of some modern prayers is extremely irreverent, and very offensive. The Fatherhood and love of God make a poor excuse for irreverence in prayer.

8. What is meant by "heavenly affections"? The Scripture verses cited by the catechism show that this expression is used in the sense of *heavenward* affections, that is, affections directed toward heaven, where God dwells in light and glory. That is, in prayer we are to separate our thoughts for a time from their common preoccupation with our own earthly concerns, and to think of heaven, of the greatness, glory, power, and wisdom of God, and to concentrate our thoughts and desires on God and heaven.

9. What is meant by "due apprehensions of his sovereign power, majesty, and gracious condescension"? By "due apprehensions" the catechism means realizing and feeling these truths as we should, and acting accordingly. The person who refers to God as a "pal" lacks a due apprehension of the majesty, power, and gracious condescension of God.

By God's majesty, the catechism means his infinite, absolute greatness above all created beings. By his power it means his almighty power, by which he can do anything which is not contrary to his own nature. By God's gracious condescension the catechism means God's voluntarily doing for his people what he is not under any obligation or necessity to do. God did not have to send his Son into the world to die for sinners; he did this because he *chose* to do it; therefore it was an act of "gracious condescension" on God's part, something to which his creatures had no claim whatever. In approaching God in prayer, we must keep these truths about God in mind, if we would pray aright.

10. What can we learn from the plural pronoun *our* in the expression "Our Father which art in heaven"? From this plural pronoun we can learn that we are to pray with and for others. Prayer is not only an individual matter; there is also such a thing as joint or united prayer, as well as intercessory prayer. Each individual Christian is part of a great organism, the invisible church, or body of Christ; each Christian is related to the other members of this spiritual organism; each must have a concern for the welfare of the others. God's relation to us as Father is something which we share with all other Christian people; therefore we should pray with and for others, as occasion may require and as opportunity may exist.

190. Q. *What do we pray for in the first petition?*

A. *In the first petition (which is, Hallowed be thy name), acknowledging the utter inability and indisposition that is in ourselves and all men to honor God aright, we pray, that God would by his grace enable and incline us and others to know, to acknowledge, and highly to esteem him, his titles, attributes, ordinances, word, works, and whatsoever he is pleased to make himself known by; and to glorify him in thought, word and deed; that he would prevent and remove atheism, ignorance, idolatry, profaneness, and whatsoever is dishonorable to him; and by his overruling providence, direct and dispose of all things to his own glory.*

Scripture References

- Matt. 6:9; Luke 11:2. The first petition of the Lord's Prayer.
- 2 Cor. 3:5; Ps. 51:15. No man of himself can honor God aright.
- Ps. 67:2–3. We are to pray that God would enable and incline men to know and praise him.
- Pss. 8:1–9; 83:18; 86:10–15; 138:1–3; 145:1–10; 147:19–20; 2 Cor. 2:14–15; 2 Thess. 3:1. We are to pray that God would enable and incline men to know, acknowledge, and highly value all the ways by which he makes himself known.

- Pss. 19:14; 103:1; Phil. 1:9, 11. We are to pray that God would enable and incline us and others to glorify him in thought, word, and deed.
- 2 Kings 19:15–16; Pss. 67:1–4; 74:18, 22–23; 97:7; Eph. 1:17–18. We are to pray that God would prevent and remove whatever dishonors him.
- 2 Chron. 20:5–6, 10–12; Pss. 83:1–5, 13–18; 140:4, 8. We are to pray that God, by his providence, would direct and dispose of all things to his own glory.

Commentary

1. What is the meaning of the word *hallowed* in the Lord's Prayer? It means "regarded and treated as holy." For God's name to be hallowed means for all God's revelation of himself to be regarded and treated as holy. God's "name" does not mean merely the divine names such as "God," "Lord," "Jehovah," etc., but all by which God makes himself known. This includes his names in the narrower sense, and it also includes his titles, attributes, ordinances, Word, works, etc. All these constitute God's revelation of himself; therefore they are to be regarded and treated as holy.

2. Whose duty is it to hallow God's name? To hallow God's name is the duty of all his rational creatures, that is, angels and men, but especially it is the duty of his saints, whom he has redeemed from sin and death. All rational creatures are bound to hallow God's name because he is their Creator; but the redeemed have an added obligation to hallow his name, because besides being their Creator, God is also their Redeemer. They have been bought with a price, to serve and honor God.

3. Which of God's rational creatures are able to hallow his name aright? The angels that have never sinned and the saints that have departed this life and entered the state of glory are able to hallow God's name aright, for they have no sinful nature which could prevent them from doing so. The angels that have fallen into sin can never hallow God's name, nor will they ever have the slightest desire to do so. Of human beings in this world, those who have not been born again cannot hallow God's name, nor do they have any real desire to do so for God's sake. Only the saints, who have been born again by the power of the Holy Spirit, can hallow God's name, and they only imperfectly, because their remaining corruption of nature causes them to fall into many temptations and sins, and renders even their best service partial and imperfect.

The catechism speaks of "the utter inability and indisposition that is in ourselves and all men to honor God aright." This teaching of human sin-

fulness and inability is an unpopular teaching, but still it is true. Even real
Christians have neither the ability nor the inclination, of themselves, to honor
God as he should be honored; and even the work of the Holy Spirit in the
heart does not in the present life remove this "inability and indisposition"
wholly, but only partially.

**4. What do we mean by praying "that God would, by his grace,
enable and incline" us to honor him aright?** In this sentence, God's
grace means the special, powerful work of the Holy Spirit in our hearts, by
which our natural "utter inability and indisposition" is overcome. This takes
place, first, through the new birth, or regeneration, and second, through the
process of sanctification by which Christians are made more and more holy
in heart and life. Following the Bible, the catechism teaches that both the
desire and the power to please God come from the work of the Holy Spirit
in our hearts (Phil. 2:13).

5. How do Christian people fail to hallow God's name? Of course all
Christian people fail to hallow God's name perfectly; only the saints and angels
in heaven can really do that. But many Christian people are habitually or
occasionally involved in grossly irreverent failure to hallow God's name.

This includes all violations of the first four commandments, especially
such sins as profane swearing and cursing, use of minced oaths ("Gosh,"
"Gee," "Heck," "Darn," "Jeepers," "Cripes," "Dickens," etc.), profane use
of God's attributes ("Goodness," "Mercy," "Gracious," etc.), neglect and
misuse of God's ordinances (such as family worship, church services, baptism, the Lord's Supper, church discipline, official positions in church and
civil government), neglect and misuse of God's Word (failure to read and
study it, failure to take it seriously, misinterpreting it, using it for a wrong
purpose, criticizing or ridiculing it, failure to believe its statements and obey
its commands).

It also includes misuse of God's works in the realm of nature (regarding
nature as existing and functioning of itself by impersonal natural law, trying
to interpret and understand nature by human science without taking God
into account, attempting to maintain an educational system which is '"neutral" toward God and Christianity, interpreting human history otherwise
than as the working out of the eternal plan of God for human redemption).

Clearly many—indeed all—Christian people are involved in at least part
of these ways of failing to hallow God's name. Hallowing God's name
involves more than a few minutes morning and evening and some time on

the Sabbath devoted to religious worship; it really includes all our life, in thought, word, and deed. By all we do or leave undone, by all we think or leave unthought, we either hallow or fail to hallow God's name. It is a matter not only of religious worship in the narrow sense, but of our whole philosophy of life in the broadest sense.

6. What specially hinders the hallowing of God's name? All forms of sin hinder the hallowing of God's name, but some kinds of sin hinder it more than others. The catechism mentions atheism, ignorance, idolatry, and profaneness as especially hindering the hallowing of God's name. Atheism in its various forms is the denial of, or failure to believe in and worship, the true God who is revealed in the Bible. Ignorance is a lack of knowledge of the true God and His will, which makes it impossible to hallow his name. Idolatry consists in giving to any other the honor which belongs to God alone. Profaneness consists in regarding and treating what is holy as if it were common or ordinary; it is a life and attitude lacking in faith, reverence, and the fear of God. All these in their various forms constitute obstacles to the proper hallowing of God's name; therefore when we pray "Hallowed be thy name," we are praying that these various forms of sin may be prevented and removed.

7. What should be the Christian's attitude toward the world's failure to hallow God's name? The Christian should always be on guard against falling into a complacent agreement with or indifference to the world's failure to hallow God's name. Christian people must always stir themselves up to remember that they are radically different from worldly people and must never assent to the world's easy bypassing of God. Through the whole range of life in all its realms and in every fact, every experience, and every detail of life, the Christian must always take God into account. There is no place in a Chritian's life where God does not matter, there is no place where God's name need not be hallowed. Christians are to glorify God—hallow his name—in their every thought, word, and deed; they may never copy the world in regarding God as irrelevant, and leaving him out of consideration (Ps. 10:4).

8. How does God hallow his own name? God hallows his own name—regards and treats it as holy—by his providence which controls all things that come to pass. God's providence is all-inclusive; from the fall of a sparrow to the rise of an empire, it embraces all that occurs in the universe. God controls and directs all things so that they work out for his own glory. Thus God perfectly hallows his own name; by his providence he displays his own nature and perfections. When we pray "Hallowed be thy name," we pray that God, by his providence, would order all events in such a way that his own glory will be manifested.

191. Q. *What do we pray for in the second petition?*

A. *In the second petition (which is,* Thy kingdom come*), acknowledging ourselves and all mankind to be by nature under the dominion of sin and Satan, we pray, that the kingdom of sin and Satan may be destroyed, the gospel propagated throughout the world, the Jews called, the fulness of the Gentiles brought in; . . .*

Scripture References

- Eph. 2:2–3. All mankind are by nature under Satan's dominion.
- Ps. 68:1, 18; Rev. 12:10–11; Deut. 33:27; 1 John 3:8. Satan's kingdom is to be destroyed, for which we should pray.
- 2 Thess. 3:1. We are to pray for the propagation of the gospel.
- Rom. 10:1. We are to pray for the salvation of the Jews.
- John 17:9, 20; Rom. 11:25–26; Ps. 67:1–7; Matt. 28:18–20. We should pray for the salvation of God's elect among the Gentiles.

Commentary

1. What is the spiritual condition of the human race apart from Christ and his salvation? The spiritual condition of the human race apart from Christ and his salvation is a condition not only of guilt but also of bondage or slavery to the power of sin. The human race and all members of it are not only guilty before God but also enslaved to the power of evil. Because people are slaves to sin, they are not free to do good. They must be set free by the redemption of Christ, the Son of God, before they can love and serve God.

2. Why does the catechism say that "by nature" we are enslaved to sin? The catechism uses this expression, "by nature," to show that our sinfulness is not merely a matter of bad habits, or the result of our environment, but part of *our nature.* We are born with a sinful nature, and from the beginning of our life we are slaves to sin, until Christ sets us free from its power. The expression "by nature" is taken from the exact words of the Bible (Eph. 2:3).

3. What is the kingdom of Satan? The "kingdom of Satan" is the sum total of everything in the universe that is contrary to the will of God. Satan, the chief of the fallen angels, became king of the kingdom of evil when he fell from his original holiness. The catechism rightly speaks not only of "the kingdom of sin" but of "the kingdom of Satan," because sin is not a natural force such as gravity or electricity; sin is committed by persons, and the kingdom of sin is a kingdom of sinful persons—evil spirits and human beings—under the control of the supremely evil person called Satan. The kingdom of sin is a real kingdom with a real king, Satan or the devil. Every attempt to tone down or explain away the objective reality and personality of the devil is contrary to the Bible.

4. How can Satan exercise power as a king? Satan can exercise power as a king only by the permission of God. The Bible teaches that all Satan's activities are strictly controlled by God. This is shown very clearly by the first two chapters of the book of Job, as well as by other parts of the Bible. God in his wisdom has permitted Satan to have certain power and to do certain things, but Satan cannot go beyond what God has permitted. This is also clearly shown by the power of Christ to cast out devils, as recorded in the Gospels. Satan's kingdom is temporary only and is doomed to total destruction (Rev. 12:12).

5. How is Satan's kingdom destroyed? Satan's kingdom is destroyed by the work of Christ, the Son of God, who came to destroy the works of the devil (1 John 3:8). Worldly, mechanical, or merely human methods cannot accomplish anything toward destroying Satan's kingdom. Satan's kingdom is partly destroyed by the work of God's Holy Spirit, through the Word of God, in the conversion of sinners and the sanctification of believers. It will be completely and forever destroyed at the second coming of Jesus Christ (2 Thess. 2:8). Many people are deceived into thinking that the general progress of human civilization, general education and culture, science and invention, and economic and social progress and organization can restrain or destroy Satan's kingdom. All these can fit in with Satan's kingdom as much as with God's kingdom. Only the gospel of Christ, by the power of the Holy Spirit, really destroys Satan's kingdom.

6. How should we pray that Satan's kingdom may be destroyed? We should pray this prayer sincerely, with true faith. This means that we will not be satisfied merely to pray. We will also do what we can to bring about the destruction of Satan's kingdom, whenever we have an opportunity. If our faith is real, it will be accompanied by works.

7. Why must we pray for the gospel to be propagated throughout the world? It is through the preaching of the gospel that God's elect are brought to salvation (Rom. 10:13–15). Since this is a matter of such great importance, with so many obstacles in the way, and involving such great difficulties, it calls for earnest prayer. It is God's will that the gospel of Christ be preached to all nations. Some countries are shut against the gospel today. We should pray that God would cause the doors that are shut to be opened, so that the gospel of Christ can enter and salvation be offered to the people of those countries. Some countries, such as Turkey and Russia, are almost locked tight against the gospel of Christ. In other countries, such as Spain and Mexico, there are various restrictions and hindrances to the preaching of the gospel. Read Revelation 3:7–8 and note that Christ has the power to open doors so that the gospel can enter in and have a clear track to go ahead.

8. What does the catechism mean by prayer that the Jews may be called? By the word *called* the catechism here means effectually called, that is, converted to Christ. The catechism cites Romans 10:1, where Paul said that his prayer was for the salvation of Israel. The eleventh chapter of Romans predicts that at some future time there will be a great movement of the Jews to believe on Christ (Rom. 11:13–27). This does not mean that every Jew in the world will be converted to Christ, but that there will be a great increase in the number of Jews that believe in Christ, at some time before the second coming of Christ. Paul tells us that the spiritual blindness of the Jews, which prevents them from seeing that Jesus is the Messiah, is only temporary, "until the fulness of the Gentiles be come in" (Rom. 11:25). This shows that after "the fulness of the Gentiles" has "come in," the blindness of the Jews will be taken away, and large numbers of them will be converted to Christ. There are some Jews being converted to Christ all the time; we should pray for the hastening of the time when many of them will turn to Jesus Christ.

It is very important that a clear distinction be made between the return of many Jews to the land of Palestine and the return of many Jews to the God of the Bible. It is true, of course, that in God's providence there is again—after nearly 2,000 years—a Jewish state in Palestine. It is for this reason that many Fundamentalist Christians refer to the Jews as "God's people" and their return to the land as a fulfillment of Bible prophecies. But it is not true that Jews who still reject Jesus as the promised Mes-

siah are God's people. No, the true Israel of God is the Christian church. It is that people who believe in Jesus as the Christ of God. In the early days of the church's history it was predominantly Jewish (as the book of Acts shows). Into that Jewish church the Gentiles were engrafted, becoming "fellow citizens with the saints and members of the household of God" (Eph. 2:19). It is only when the Jews—whether individually or en masse—return to the Messiah of God that we can rightly speak of them as "the people of God" (GIW).

9. Why should we pray that the fullness of Gentiles will be brought in? The expression "the fulness of the Gentiles brought in" means the salvation of the great company of God's elect of all nations throughout the world, except the Jews. We should pray for the accomplishment of this work of God for three reasons: (a) God is glorified in the salvation of people of every race and nation. (b) The sooner "the fulness of the Gentiles" is brought in, the sooner the Jews will have their blindness removed and will turn to Christ. (c) The sooner all God's elect, both Jews and Gentiles, are saved, the sooner Christ will come to deliver his people from all sin and suffering, and give them eternal glory.

191. Q. *(continued) What do we pray for in the second petition?*

A. *In the second petition (which is,* Thy kingdom come) . . . *we pray, that . . . the church [may be] furnished with all gospel officers and ordinances, purged from corruption, countenanced and maintained by the civil magistrate: that the ordinances of Christ may be purely dispensed, and made effectual to the converting of those that are yet in their sins, and the confirming, comforting, and building up of those that are already converted: that Christ would rule in our hearts here, and hasten the time of his second coming, and our reigning with him for ever: and that he would be pleased so to exercise the kingdom of his power in all the world, as may best conduce to these ends.*

Scripture References

- Matt. 9:38; 2 Thess. 3:1. We are to pray that the church may be furnished with all gospel officers and ordinances.

- Mal. 1:11; Zeph. 3:9. We are to pray that the church may be purified from corruption.
- 1 Tim. 2:1–2. We are to pray that the church may be countenanced and maintained by the civil magistrate.
- Acts 4:29–30; Eph. 6:18–19; Rom. 15:29–30, 32. We are to pray that the church may be purified from corruption.
- 2 Thess. 1:11; 2:16–17. We are to pray that the ordinances of Christ may be purely dispensed and made effectual for their intended purposes.
- Eph. 3:14–20. We are to pray that Christ would reign in our hearts while we are in this present world.
- Rev. 22:20. We are to pray that Christ would hasten his second coming, and our reigning with him forever.
- Isa. 64:1–2; Rev. 4:8–11. We are to pray that Christ would so exercise his kingdom of power in the world, as may best further the kingdom of grace and hasten the kingdom of glory.

Commentary

1. Why should we pray that the church may be furnished with all gospel officers and ordinances? (a) These gospel officers and ordinances, so far as they are genuine and truly spiritual and beneficial, rather than merely mechanical and formal, are gifts of God and are dependent for their effectiveness on the special work of the Holy Spirit. It is the Holy Spirit that calls men to be ministers of the gospel; it is the Holy Spirit that provides and equips pastors, elders, and deacons for the church; it is the Holy Spirit that provides and makes effective such church ordinances as the preaching of the gospel, the administration of the sacraments, the exercise of church discipline. (b) If we are really sincere in praying that the church may be furnished with all gospel officers and ordinances, we will not be content to pray and do nothing more; we will be inclined to do what we can about it. For example, we will encourage young men to enter the gospel ministry; we will contribute liberally to the support of Christian education and church ordinances; we will attend upon the ordinances of the gospel, and will encourage and support those church officers who are charged with the administration and work of the church.

2. Why does the church need to be purged from corruption? Of course the church *ought* not to need to be purified from corruption. But the fact is that it always *does* need to be purified from corruption. This is not merely sometimes the case; it is always the case. There are always retrograde tendencies at work, which cause corruption in the doctrine, worship, government, and discipline of the church. These retrograde tendencies never cease to operate, and must always be vigilantly guarded against and counteracted.

The reformation of the church is not to be regarded as a once-for-all act; it must be a continuous process. We should both pray and work for it. In this connection the letters to the seven churches, in Revelation 2 and 3, are most instructive. Nothing is more dangerously insidious than the comfortable belief that our own branch of the visible church is safe and secure from all inroads of corruption. "Let him that thinketh he standeth take heed lest he fall" (1 Cor. 10:12). Whole denominations have succumbed to the deadly virus of modern unbelief and have become apostate from the truth, so they have ceased to be witnesses for the gospel of Christ, while their ministers and members reassured each other by saying, "The church is basically sound." See the Confession of Faith, 25.5; Reformed Presbyterian Testimony, 21.6. It is highly presumptuous to assert that a particular denomination is so sound that there not only is not, but never will be, any Modernism in it. Yet this statement has been heard in a church court. We should always be on our guard against the leaven of corruption; we should always pray that the church may be kept from it, and purified of it.

3. How is the church to be countenanced and maintained by the civil magistrate? (a) When the catechism was written, 350 years ago, the prevailing idea on this question was that there was to be an official or established church, which would not only be recognized by the civil government as the true visible church of Jesus Christ, but also be supported financially from the national treasury. We no longer accept this view of the relation between church and state. (b) Neither do we accept the extreme view sometimes called Voluntaryism, to the effect that the state has nothing to do with religion and need not recognize or countenance the church in any way. "Church and State are two distinct and separate institutions. The Christian religion should be the religion of both. . . . Each has its own sphere, and its own functions to perform. Neither should invade the territory of the other. Where their duties coincide, as for example in the suppression of profanity, they should cooperate; yet always in such a way as not to mar their integrity as separate institutions . . ." (Reformed Presbyterian Testimony, 29.7). Thus our standards teach an absolute separateness of *jurisdiction* of church and state, but the duty of friendly cooperation in matters in which their duties coincide. (c) The church should be countenanced and maintained by the civil magistrate, by being protected in the security and enjoyment of its rights and freedom; also it is proper for the state to "countenance and maintain" the church by remission of taxes on church property, etc. (d) Our standards do *not* teach that both true and false churches are to be countenanced and maintained by the state. At this point the teaching of the Westminster Standards differs from the prevalent American view of the relation between the state and religious associations and institutions. Under the Constitution and laws of the United States a Buddhist temple, a Unitarian church, a Jewish synagogue, and a Mohammedan mosque enjoy identical and equal rights and privileges with the most evangelical and orthodox Protestant Christian churches. There is not only no discrimination between Christian denominations; there is not even any discrimination between Christianity and other religions, so far as the state is concerned. This state of affairs is obviously not what the Westminster divines had in mind in saying that the church should be "countenanced and maintained" by the civil magistrate. It is obvious that they meant that the *true* church should be countenanced and maintained by the civil magistrate. This of course raises difficult and serious problems, which we cannot discuss further here. We may accept as sound, however, the principle that a truly Christian nation would at least guarantee the freedom and security of the true church of Jesus Christ in all its denominational branches.

4. What is meant by saying that the ordinances of Christ should be purely dispensed, and why should we pray for this? (a) The ordinances of Christ are chiefly the preaching of the Word of God, the administration of the sacraments, the government of the church, and the exercise of church discipline. (b) These ordinances are purely dispensed when they are dispensed according to Christ's appointment in his Word, the Holy Bible, without human corruptions, additions, or subtractions. (c) This pure dispensing of Christ's ordinances depends on the church's membership really wanting it, which in turn depends on the special work of the Holy Spirit in their hearts. Therefore we should pray that the Holy Spirit will so work in people's hearts that they will love, adhere to, preserve, and defend the pure dispensation of Christ's ordinances. When this special work of the Holy Spirit is partly or wholly withdrawn, the membership and leadership of the churches will soon introduce changes in Christ's ordinances, not according to Scripture, but according to the whims and fancies of their own hearts and the changing demands of "popularity."

5. Why should we pray that Christ's ordinances may be made effective for their intended purposes? Unless made effective by the special work of the Holy Spirit, these ordinances will be mere forms without spiritual fruitfulness. Paul may plant, and Apollos water, but only God can give the increase (1 Cor. 3:6). We are not to put our trust in ecclesiastical mechanics, but in the life-giving power of the Holy Spirit's work.

6. What three forms or phases of Christ's kingdom are dealt with in the last part of this answer of the catechism? (a) Christ's present spiritual kingdom in the hearts of his people, called "the kingdom of grace" in the Shorter Catechism (S.C. 102). (b) Christ's eternal reign in glory, which will begin at his second coming, called "the kingdom of glory" in the Shorter Catechism (S.C. 102). (c) Christ's kingdom of power in the world, by which at the present time he has all power in heaven and in earth, even over his enemies.

To disregard any of these forms or phases of Christ's kingdom is sure to result in an erroneous, unbalanced, one-sided view of Christ's kingly office. Such error is extremely common at the present day. One Christian will emphasize Christ's present spiritual kingdom, another his eternal kingdom of glory, and still another his present reign of power over the universe. Only by believing in and emphasizing all three together, in their mutual relations, can we really grasp the scope of Christ's kingship and hold a truly scriptural view.

In the second petition of the Lord's Prayer we rightly pray for all three phases of his kingdom: the kingdom of grace, the kingdom of glory, and the kingdom of power. We pray for the extension and continuance of the kingdom of grace, the hastening of the kingdom of glory, and the success of the kingdom of power for its appointed ends. Note that the kingdom of power is not an end in itself, but a means to the furtherance of the kingdom of grace and the hastening of the kingdom of glory. In this statement of the matter the catechism is eminently scriptural.

7. Is it proper to pray that Christ's second coming may be hastened? Certainly, and we should be sure to do so. See Revelation 22:20; the Confession of Faith, 33.3. Of course we should not wish for Christ's second coming to take place before the appointed time, when all of God's elect will have been brought to the saving knowledge of Christ. But we should wish and pray that the appointed time may be hastened. The spirit that would prefer to postpone the kingdom of glory in order to afford greater scope for the plans, programs, and activities of the church during this present age is alien to the philosophy of history taught in the Scriptures. According to the Bible the present world is a preparation for the eternal kingdom of God; the eternal may not be subordinated to the temporal. We are not only to desire our Lord's second coming, but to pray that it may take place quickly.

192. Q. *What do we pray for in the third petition?*

A. *In the third petition (which is,* Thy will be done in earth as it is in heaven*), acknowledging, that by nature we and all men are not only utterly unable and unwilling to know and do the will of God, but prone to rebel against his word, to repine and murmur against his providence, and wholly inclined to do the will of the flesh, and of the devil: we pray that God would by his Spirit take away from ourselves and others all blindness, weakness, indisposedness, and perverseness of heart; and by his grace make us able and willing to know, do, and submit to his will in all things, with the like humility, cheerfulness, faithfulness, diligence, zeal, sincerity, and constancy as the angels do in heaven.*

Scripture References

- Matt. 6:10. The third petition of the Lord's Prayer.
- Rom. 7:18; Job 21:14; 1 Cor. 2:14. Man's natural inability and unwillingness to know and do the will of God.
- Rom. 8:7; Exod. 17:7; Num. 14:2; Eph. 2:2. Man's natural tendency to rebel against God's Word and providence, and to serve self and Satan.
- Eph. 1:17–18; 3:16; Matt. 26:20, 41; Jer. 31:18–19. We are to pray that God, by his Spirit, would take away from us and others whatever is contrary to knowing and doing his will.
- Ps. 119:1, 8, 35–36; Acts 21:14. We are to pray that God, by his grace, would make us able and willing to know, do, and submit to his will.
- Mic. 6:8; Ps. 100:2; Job 1:21; 2 Sam. 15:25–26; Isa. 38:3; Ps. 119:4–5; Rom. 12:11; Ps. 119:80, 112; Isa. 6:2–3; Ps. 103:20–21; Matt. 18:10. We are to pray that God would make us able and willing to know, do, and submit to his will as truly and fully as the angels do in heaven.

Commentary

1. In what two senses does the Bible speak the will of God? (a) The Bible speaks of the revealed will of God, which is the rule of duty which he has given to the human race (e.g., John 7:17). (b) The Bible also speaks of the secret will of God, that is, God's counsel or decrees, by which he has foreordained whatsoever comes to pass (e.g., 1 Peter 4:19).

The revealed will of God is also called his preceptive will, and is the standard of man's moral obligation. The secret will of God is also called his decretive will; it is not a rule of human duty, and cannot be known by man except as it unfolds in the events of God's providence; however, some parts of the secret will of God have been revealed in the prophecies of the Bible.

2. In what sense does the Lord's Prayer speak of the will of God? As interpreted by the catechism, the third petition of the Lord's Prayer refers both to the revealed will of God and to the secret will of God. We are to know and do the revealed will of God; we are to submit cheerfully to the secret will of God, that is, to the events of God's providence. Thus the revealed will of God requires us to obey the Ten Commandments, to love God and our neighbor, etc., while submission to the secret will of God means that we will endure suffering, disappointments, hardships, bereavements, etc., patiently and without murmuring or rebelling against God.

3. Why are men by nature unwilling and unable to know and do the will of God? Because of the sinful state of the human mind and heart which is the result of the fall of the race into sin. The fall into sin has darkened the human mind, so that apart from the new birth it cannot see and know the truth (Rom. 1:18–22: 1 Cor. 2:14), and it has also corrupted the human heart, so that men are inclined toward wickedness and opposed to righteousness (Rom. 1:28–32; Eph. 2:2–3). The new birth by the power of the Holy Spirit is God's remedy for this natural darkness of the sinful human mind and depravity of the sinful human heart. Men can never really know the will of God by human reason, science, or philosophy, nor can they ever really do the will of God until their hearts have been renewed by the life-giving work of the Holy Spirit. Thus when we pray "Thy will be done," this implies, first of all, a prayer for the special work of the Holy Spirit in human minds and hearts.

4. Why do people murmur and rebel against God's providence? There can be no doubt that murmuring and rebelling against God's providence is a very common sin even among Christian people. A very common form is complaining about the weather. It is strange but true that most people will ascribe their successful and pleasant experiences to "chance," "luck," or their own prudence and industry, etc., but when things turn against them, they will blame the situation on God and murmur and rebel against God. Men who never think to thank God for seasons of good weather will curse God if there is a storm or tornado that causes them suffering and loss.

This perverse murmuring and complaining against God's providence arises from the natural sinfulness of the human heart. People wrongly suppose that God *owes* them happiness, prosperity, good health, and other blessings, and that if any of these are taken away from them, God is cheating them of their just rights. While a Christian will of course realize that all such attitudes are wicked, he will also realize that such thoughts do arise in his own heart, and will be humbled because of them.

5. How is God's will done in heaven? God's will is done in heaven by the holy angels and by the saints that have departed this life and been made perfect in holiness (Heb. 12:23). It is clear that in heaven God's will is done perfectly, as the catechism explains. To do the will of God perfectly means not only to do exactly what God requires, but to do it with perfect attitudes and motives ("humility, cheerfulness, faithfulness, diligence, zeal, sincerity, and constancy"). In heaven God's will is done perfectly because in heaven there is no sin or temptation to interfere with the perfect doing of God's will. It is a wonderful thought for the Christian that such a heaven is his sure destiny. The Christian is destined to be perfect and to be presented faultless before God's throne (Jude 24). The thought of our destiny of physical, mental, moral, and spiritual perfection should be a strong encouragement to us as Christians in our conflicts with evil here on earth.

6. Is it possible for us to do God's will on earth as perfectly as the angels do in heaven? No. It is our duty to do God's will, here and now, as perfectly as the angels do it in heaven; that simply means that what God requires of us is perfect conformity to His revealed will. This perfect conformity would have been possible for the human race in this present world—indeed, it would have been actually attained—if Adam had not disobeyed God by eating the forbidden fruit. Adam's act of disobedience plunged the human race into sin and misery, and made perfect conformity to God's will in this life impossible.

Even born-again Christians, who are being sanctified by the Holy Spirit, can conform to God's will in this life only in part. Yet perfect conformity to God's will is always the ideal toward which we are to strive. It is not only our destiny in the life to come; it is also our duty in the present life; therefore we must always press on and strive toward a greater and greater attainment of it. "Brethren, I count not myself to have apprehended; but this one thing I do, forgetting those things which are behind, and reaching forth unto those things which are before, I press toward the mark for the prize of the high calling of God in Christ Jesus" (Phil. 3:13–14).

193. Q. *What do we pray for in the fourth petition?*

A. *In the fourth petition (which is, Give us this day our daily bread), acknowledging that in Adam, and by our own sin, we have forfeited our right to all the outward blessings of this life, and deserve to be wholly deprived of them by God, and to have them cursed to us in the use of them; and that neither they of themselves are able to sustain us, nor we to merit, or by our own industry to procure them; but prone to desire, get, and use them unlawfully: we pray for ourselves and others, that both they and we, waiting upon the providence of God from day to day in the use of lawful means, may, of his free gift, and as to his fatherly wisdom shall seem best, enjoy a competent portion of them; and have the same continued and blessed unto us in our holy and comfortable use of them; and to be kept from all things that are contrary to our temporal support and comfort.*

Scripture References

- Gen. 2:17; 3:17; Rom. 8:20–22; Jer. 5:25; Deut. 28:15–17. In Adam, and by our own sin, we have forfeited the right to all blessings of this life.
- Deut. 8:3. Outward blessings, of themselves, cannot sustain our life.
- Gen. 32:10; Deut. 8:17–18. We can neither earn God's blessings nor obtain them by our own efforts.
- Jer. 6:13; Mark 7:21–22; Hos. 12:7; James 4:3. Because of our sinful hearts, we tend to desire, get, and use the outward blessings of life unlawfully.
- Gen. 43:12–14; 28:29; Eph. 4:28; 2 Thess. 3:11–12; Phil. 4:6. We are to pray that, in subordination to the law and will of God, we may enjoy a suitable portion of the outward blessings of this life.
- 1 Tim. 4:3–5; 6:6–8. We are to pray that God will bless us in our legitimate use of earthly blessings.

• Prov. 30:8–9. We are to pray that we may be preserved from all that is contrary to our true welfare in this present life.

Commentary

1. Is it true that all men have an inalienable right to life, liberty, and the pursuit of happiness? This is only true within the limited sphere of civil society. Human beings have a civil right to life, liberty, and the pursuit of happiness without unjust interference on the part of their fellow men. Even within the sphere of human society the right of life or liberty may be taken away as a judicial penalty for the commission of crime. A man who has committed murder no longer has a right to life and liberty.

When we speak of man's relation to God, it is definitely *not* true that all men have a right to life, liberty, and the pursuit of happiness. Whatever rights human beings might have had, have been forfeited by sin; first by Adam's sin, which is imputed to all mankind; and then by each person's own sin, so that no human being has any rights which he can claim over against God. Man has no rights which God is bound to respect.

2. If God were to treat the human race with strict justice, apart from any way of salvation, what would be the result? Human life would immediately become impossible, for all the common blessings such as rain and sunshine, food and clothing, homes and comforts, would be taken away; health would turn to sickness, and life to death. The human race has forfeited its claim to all these blessings. Only the *grace and mercy* of God cause sinful human beings to continue to receive and enjoy earthly blessings.

3. Is it true that God owes every man a life of happiness and prosperity? No. What God owes every man is simply justice. In the case of fallen, sinful humanity, justice would mean God's wrath, curse, and condemnation. Those who think God owes them something better than this fail to realize the meaning of God's righteousness and their own sinfulness. We should be deeply thankful that God deals with us on the basis of grace as well as justice.

4. Why cannot earthly blessings of themselves sustain our life? We are not independent of God; our life is in his hands moment by moment. The real usefulness of all earthly things depends upon the providence of God. Food cannot give life to the starving, nor medicine health to the sick, except by the working of God's providence. It is only because God's providence is at work that bread is more nourishing than stones. We tend to forget that we are dependent on God's providence every moment of our lives; we tend to place our faith in things rather than in the God who gives us the things. This becomes a form of idolatry, and even Christian people are often guilty of it. We should use the earthly things, and place our faith in God who gave them and who alone can bless them to our use.

5. Why can we not procure what we need by our own efforts? Human independence is a vain delusion that is flattering to our sinful hearts. We cannot procure what we need by our own efforts because, in the first place, our efforts are always dependent on the providence of God. Our breathing, the beating of our heart, the functioning of our nervous system and muscles, our power to think and make decisions—all these depend continuously on the providence of God. We cannot do anything independently of God; in him we live, and move, and have our being.

In the second place, the whole world of nature is constantly dependent on the providence of God. A man may plant wheat, but if God does not provide rain and sunlight, there will be no harvest. Or if there is rain and sunlight, in the providence of God a hailstorm may ruin everything. Men may build ships, and storms which only God controls may wreck them on their first voyage. It is evident that we must recognize that in every detail of our lives we are completely dependent on God.

6. Why do we tend to desire, get, and use earthly blessings unlawfully? Because of our sinful hearts, which cause us to commit sin in thought, word, and deed every day of our lives. Even born-again Christians are not perfectly sanctified in this life, and must always contend against the sinful lusts and temptations which lurk in their hearts and which if unchecked will lead them into gross sins.

7. What is meant by "waiting upon the providence of God from day to day in the use of lawful means"? This expression of the catechism is a beautiful gem of scriptural teaching. It means, in the first place, that we are to put our trust, not in our own powers or actions, but in the providence of God, that is, in God, whose providence controls our lives. We are to wait upon the providence of God from day to day, realizing that God will give us blessings according to his holy will in his own appointed time; therefore we are to avoid both unbelief and impatience. We will not demand blessings immediately when God in his wisdom sees fit to postpone them.

In the second place, while placing our trust in God, we will not be lazy or inactive, but still will make use of means. If we are sick, we will trust in God to make us well if it is his will to do so, but we will also avail ourselves of the best possible medical treatment. If we are waiting on God for a harvest, we will also take pains to cultivate the soil and plant the seed. We will not expect God's providence to eliminate our own toil and efforts.

In the third place, we will take care to use only *lawful* means. We will not take matters in our own hands by breaking the moral law of God. We will try to promote our business interests by intelligence and honest work, but not by use of dishonesty, untruth, or theft, or by injustice to anyone.

8. Why are earthly blessings a free gift to God's children? They are a free gift because we can never earn or deserve them. Earthly blessings were purchased for God's children by the Lord Jesus Christ (Reformed Presbyterian Testimony, 10.5 and error 6). Christ earned them, so they could be given to us as a free gift.

9. Is it right to pray for earthly blessings such as financial prosperity for ourselves and others? Certainly this is right, and we ought to do it, but always in subordination to the will of God "as to his fatherly wisdom shall seem best." We may pray for financial prosperity and similar earthly blessings, provided we pray that *if* it is God's will he will give them to us. We have no way of knowing in advance whether or not such will be his will.

10. What does the catechism mean by "a competent portion" of earthly blessings? By this expression the catechism means such a supply of earthly blessings as shall be for our true temporal and spiritual welfare. If God were to make all his children millionaires, this probably would not be for the true welfare of most of them. On the other hand, in most cases dire poverty would not be for their true welfare, either. In most cases God provides his people with a moderate portion of this world's goods, from which we may conclude that he deems this to be best for them. We should not cherish an ambition to "get rich," far less to "get rich quickly." The Christian ideal is a moderate, suitable portion of earthly prosperity. God gives some people great wealth, but we should not seek it.

11. Why should we pray for contentment in the use of God's blessings? If we do not have contentment, we cannot really enjoy and appreciate the blessings of God. The lack of a spirit of contentment will turn all blessings into temptations or curses. Contentment is an attitude of mind which God can work in us by his Holy Spirit. We should seek this blessing from him. "Be content with such things as ye have" (Heb. 13:5); "I have learned, in whatsoever state I am, therewith to be content" (Phil. 4:11); "Godliness with contentment is great gain" (1 Tim. 6:6).

194. Q. *What do we pray for in the fifth petition?*

A. *In the fifth petition (which is, Forgive us our debts, as we forgive our debtors), acknowledging, that we and all others are guilty both of original and actual sin, and thereby become debtors to the justice of God; and that neither we, nor any other creature, can make the least satisfaction for that debt; . . .*

Scripture References

- Matt. 6:12; Luke 11:4. The fifth petition of the Lord's Prayer.
- Rom. 3:9–22; Matt. 18:24–25; Pss. 130:3–4; 51:5; 1 John 1:8, 10. We and all mankind are guilty before God, and wholly unable to satisfy his justice.

Commentary

1. What is the meaning of the word *debts* in the Lord's Prayer? The word *debts* in the Lord's Prayer (Matt. 6:12) is used with the meaning of "sins," as shown by the parallel passage Luke 11:4. The meaning, therefore, is not commercial debts (which could be satisfied by a money payment) but penal debts—that is, obligation to suffer punishment according to the justice of God by reason of want of conformity unto, or transgression of, the law of God. (The Greek word used in Matt. 6:12 is correctly translated "debts" in both the Authorized and Revised Versions, and therefore "debts" is preferable to "trespasses," which is used by some churches. The word *debts* brings out more clearly the truth that we are debtors to the justice of God.)

2. What aspect of sin does this petition of the Lord's Prayer concern? It concerns the guilt of sin, which is the basic aspect of sin in the Bible. In addition to involving guilt, sin also involves pollution or uncleanness, bondage or helplessness, and misery or unhappiness. Sin condemns, defiles, enslaves, and renders miserable. But the basic, all-important truth about sin is that it condemns, it involves guilt, it brings a person under the judgment and punishment of God.

3. How is this emphasis on the guilt of sin neglected today? In the present day it is popular to soft-pedal the guilt of sin and to place the main emphasis on the misery—personal and social—which sin produces. The guilt of sin is an unpopular idea today; the man-centered religion of recent decades has tried to avoid this idea or explain it away. Sin is regarded as a misfortune or calamity, rather than as something deserving blame and punishment. Consequently, many modern people regard themselves as quite righteous; or if they think of themselves as sinners, they feel that they are to be pitied and consoled rather than judged and condemned.

4. What mistaken idea about guilt is common today? Today it is very common to confuse *the feeling of guilt* with *the fact of guilt*. Popular notions of psychiatry have led many people to suppose that there is nothing to guilt beyond the feeling of guilt, and that if they can manage somehow to get rid of that troublesome feeling of guilt, they will have nothing to fear.

The legitimate practice of psychiatry deals with neurotic or mentally abnormal individuals only. Such persons may have an abnormal feeling or "complex" of guilt which destroys their happiness and usefulness, and which is entirely different from their real guilt before God. It may be possible to relieve such an abnormal feeling of guilt by psychiatric methods. But real guilt before God cannot be affected one whit by psychiatry. Guilt remains guilt, regardless of whether we are obsessed by it or unconscious of it.

Real guilt is not a mere subjective feeling, but an objective fact concerning a person's relation to God. A person may be so hardened in sin that he is entirely unconscious of his guilt, and vainly imagines himself to be a righteous person on the road to heaven. By the special work of the Holy Spirit a sinner is brought under conviction of sin and then realizes himself to be guilty before God and deserving of eternal punishment in hell. Imaginary guilt or the mere feeling of guilt may be removed by psychiatry, but real guilt can only be removed by the blood of Jesus Christ, the sinner's substitute.

5. Of what forms of sin is every person guilty? Every person is guilty of both original and actual sin. (The term *actual* as used in this connection does not mean "real," for original sin is just as real as actual sin. Rather, the term *actual* means "pertaining to one's acts," in contrast to original sin, which is the state in which we are born.)

Infants, of course, are guilty only of original sin; all others are guilty of both original and actual sin. Original sin includes: (a) the guilt of Adam's first sin; (b) the lack of that original righteousness in which the human race was created; (c) the moral corruption of our whole nature. On these three counts every individual is guilty before God, quite apart from any personal actions of his own; every individual is born into this world with guilt charged against him on these three counts. Actual sin is the product, in a person's life and activity, of original sin; it includes all the sins of omission and commission which occur in the course of a person's life, as distinguished from the sin with which a person is born.

Many people today deny that original sin involves guilt. Some try to limit the scope of sin by defining it as "voluntary transgression of known law," etc. Such a definition is unbiblical because far too narrow. According to the Bible "all unrighteousness is sin" (1 John 5:17) and "the wages of sin is death" (Rom. 6:23). David confessed that he was born in sin (Ps. 51:5); therefore according to Romans 6:23, when he was born he deserved death.

Many people especially rebel against the doctrine that newborn infants are guilty before God by reason of original sin. Against the teaching of the Scriptures they place their unrealistic and sentimental ideas of the "innocence" and "purity" of infancy. The Bible, however, definitely teaches that infants are guilty before God (Rom. 5:14), as witnessed by the fact that they are subject to death, which is the wages of sin.

6. What can we do to take away our guilt before God? Absolutely nothing; "neither we, nor any other creature, can make the least satisfaction for that debt." Suppose that we could start tomorrow morning and live an absolutely perfect life all our days—that would be no more than our duty, and could not avail to cancel the guilt of any of our past sins. Of course, no one can start to live a perfect life anyway. We are morally bankrupt, totally debtors to the righteous judgment of God, and unable of ourselves to pay any part of the debt. Our guilt before God can be taken away only by the redemption of Jesus Christ.

194. Q. *(continued) What do we pray for the fifth petition?*

A. *In the fifth petition (which is,* Forgive us our debts, as we forgive our debtors*) . . . we pray for ourselves and others, that God of his free grace would, through the obedience and satisfaction of Christ, apprehended and applied by faith, acquit us both from the guilt and punishment of sin, accept us in his Beloved, continue his favor and grace to us, pardon our daily failings, and fill us with peace and joy, in giving us daily more and more assurance of forgiveness; . . .*

Scripture References

- Rom. 3:24–26; Heb. 9:22. We pray that God would, through Christ's redemption, acquit us from the guilt and penalty of sin.
- Eph. 1:6–7. We pray that God would accept us in his Beloved Son, Jesus Christ.
- 2 Peter 1:2; Hos. 14:2; Jer. 14:7. We pray that God would continue his grace toward us, and pardon our daily failings.
- Rom. 15:13; Ps. 51:7–12. We pray that God would fill us with peace and joy, by a daily increasing assurance of his forgiveness.

Commentary

1. What is meant by God's free grace? This means the undeserved love and favor of God given to sinners by God's own good pleasure. This free grace of God is the source of our salvation. It is the ultimate reason why some are saved from sin and inherit eternal life. Thus it is also the true basis of the forgiveness of our sins. We are to come to God praying for forgiveness, not on the basis of our own character, good works, good resolutions, nor even on the basis of our own faith, but only on the basis of God's own free grace.

2. How is God's free grace given to sinners? "Through the obedience and satisfaction of Christ," that is, through the finished work of Christ in the plan of redemption. This finished work of Christ is "apprehended and applied by faith"; that is, the Holy Spirit works faith in a sinner's heart, enabling and disposing him to believe on Jesus Christ; thus Christ's finished work is apprehended by the sinner, grasped, taken hold of, appropriated, and applied to his guilty condition by the work of the Holy Spirit. The free grace of God is the *source* of forgiveness, the finished work of Christ is the *ground* of forgiveness, and faith is the *means* by which forgiveness is obtained.

3. Why does the catechism mention both obedience and the satisfaction of Christ? Because both are essential to his saving work for sinners. By the "obedience" of Christ is here meant what is sometimes called his active obedience—his lifelong perfect keeping of the law of God, by which he achieved a perfect righteousness which can be imputed or credited to sinners. By the "satisfaction" of Christ is meant what is sometimes called his passive obedience—his sufferings and death by which he offered a sacrifice to atone for the sins of his people so that they could be forgiven and their sins canceled. Christ both lived for his people (to give them righteousness) and died for them (to cancel their guilt).

Many present-day Christians fail to realize the importance of the active obedience of Christ. Christ had to live a perfect life under the law in order to save his people; not only must a perfect righteousness be imputed to them, but only a perfect life would meet the requirements for the sacrifice required to atone for sin. An imperfect life could not be offered to God in sacrifice for the sins of others.

4. Why does the catechism speak of God's acquitting us "both from the guilt and punishment of sin"? It is very important that the distinction and relation between these two be grasped. Guilt means debt to God's justice, and involves obligation to suffer punishment. Christ's redemption saves us from both the guilt and the punishment. Our guilt was laid upon him, and he suffered the punishment in our place on Calvary. Unregenerate people almost always think of salvation as deliverance from the punishment of sin; the true Christian realizes that it is first of all a matter of deliverance from the guilt of sin. Many people are afraid of going to hell, who are not at all concerned about the fact that they are guilty before God. Almost everybody wants to be saved from hell, but only the born-again Christian wants to be saved from his guilt. True Christian repentance is being sorry for the guilt of sin; false repentance is sorry only about the penalty of sin.

5. Why must we pray to God to pardon our daily failings? When a person truly believes on Christ he is instantly justified for all eternity; the guilt of all his sins, past, present, and future, is wholly canceled and he is declared to be a righteous person by reason of Christ's blood and righteousness. So far as the judicial punishment of sin is concerned, the believer is justified once and for all. "There is therefore now no condemnation to them which are in Christ Jesus" (Rom. 8:1).

Yet the justified person still can and daily does commit sin in thought, word, and deed, by omission and by commission. These "daily failings" cannot cancel his standing as a justified person; they cannot bring him into condemnation. But they can offend his heavenly Father, and cause him to withdraw the light of his countenance from the person's soul for a time. They cannot destroy the believer's union with God, but they can interrupt and weaken his communion with God. Therefore the believer is daily to confess his sins and to pray for God's pardon for his daily failings.

6. What effect does the forgiveness of sin produce in a person's consciousness? The forgiveness of sin results in an experience of peace and joy and an increased assurance of forgiveness and salvation. This peace, joy, and assurance are wrought in the heart by the Holy Spirit. Since they are not given to all persons in equal measure, nor to the same person at all times in the same degree, it is proper that we should pray for the bestowal and increase of these blessings in our hearts.

194. Q. *(continued) What do we pray for in the fifth petition?*

A. *In the fifth petition (which is,* Forgive us our debts as we forgive our debtors*), . . . we pray . . . that God of his free grace would . . . acquit us both from the guilt and punishment of sin, etc. . . . which we are the rather imboldened to ask, and encouraged to expect, when we have this testimony in ourselves, that we from the heart forgive others their offences.*

Scripture References
- Luke 11:4; Matt. 6:14–15; 18:35. Our heavenly Father requires of his children a sincere readiness to forgive others their offences against them.

Commentary
1. Why is the phrase "as we forgive our debtors" of special importance at the present time? This phrase is of special importance at the present time because a certain type of the teaching called "Modern Dispensationalism" uses this phrase as the basis of a claim that the Lord's Prayer is "on

legal ground" and not suited to "the dispensation of grace" or "the age of the Church." This peculiar teaching is especially prominent in the notes of the popular *Scofield Reference Bible,* which states in a note on Matthew 6:12 ("as we forgive our debtors") that this is "legal ground" in contrast to Ephesians 4:32 ("which is grace"). The *Scofield Bible* adds (p. 1002), "Under law forgiveness is continued upon a like spirit in us; under grace we are forgiven for Christ's sake, and exhorted to forgive because we have been forgiven." On pages 1089–90 the *Scofield Bible* informs us that "Used as a form, the Lord's prayer is, dispensationally, upon legal, not church ground . . . it makes human forgiveness, as under law it must, the condition of divine forgiveness; an order which grace exactly reverses (cf. Eph. 4:32)." Because of this dispensationalist teaching about the Lord's Prayer, some ministers have become so convinced that it is not a suitable prayer for Christians to use that they are unwilling to have it used in the public worship of the church.

2. How can this dispensationalist error concerning the Lord's Prayer be answered? See the comments on question 187 of the Larger Catechism. The dispensationalist error concerning the Lord's Prayer, as exemplified by the *Scofield Reference Bible,* is open to criticism on two counts. First, it is based on a mistaken notion of the character of the period from Moses to Christ, namely, that that period was an era of law in contrast to grace. Second, it is based on a misunderstanding of the meaning of the fifth petition of the Lord's Prayer. We shall consider each of these matters in the following questions.

3. Was the period from Moses to Christ an era of law in contrast to grace? Certainly not. This is one of the outstanding errors of Modern Dispensationalism. It was an era of law, certainly, but not of law in contrast to grace, nor law in place of grace. In the period from Moses to Christ, the law was subsidiary to the system of grace. "Wherefore then serveth the law? It was added because of transgressions, till the seed should come to whom the promise was made; and it was ordained by angels in the hands of a mediator" (Gal. 3:19); "by the law is the knowledge of sin" (Rom. 3:20); "the law entered, that the offense might abound" (Rom. 5:20); "the law was our schoolmaster to bring us unto Christ, that we might be justified by faith" (Gal. 3:24). All these and many other Scriptures that might be cited show that the function of the law, in the period from Moses to Christ, was not to serve as an alternative to the system of grace, but as a subsidiary to the system of grace, to convince people of their utter sinfulness and their need of divine redemption.

The period from Moses to Christ was not "legal ground" in the sense affirmed by the *Scofield Reference Bible* (which on p. 20 actually affirms that at Sinai the people of Israel "rashly accepted the law" and "exchanged grace for law"). Since this dispensationalist teaching is certainly erroneous, and greatly misunderstands the essential character of the period from Moses to Christ, it must also be erroneous to say that the Lord's Prayer is "on legal ground."

Modern Dispensationalism confuses the unscriptural, legalistic Judaism of the scribes and Pharisees with the pure, gracious, divinely revealed religion of the Old Testament. Judaism and the real religion of the Old Testament cannot be equated in this way, for the former is a legalistic perversion of the latter. (See Geerhardus Vos, *Biblical Theology: Old and New Testaments* [Grand Rapids: Eerdmans, 1948], 141–45.)

4. How does Dispensationalism misunderstand the fifth petition of the Lord's Prayer? Modern Dispensationalism, as exemplified by the *Scofield Reference Bible,* sees a conflict between Matthew 6:12 ("Forgive us our debts, as we forgive our debtors") and Ephesians 4:32 ("Forgiving one another, even as God for Christ's sake hath forgiven you"). The former of these texts is said to be forgiveness "under law," and the latter is said to be forgiveness "under grace." It is stated that "Under law forgiveness is conditioned upon a like spirit in us; under grace we are forgiven for Christ's sake, and exhorted to forgive because we have been forgiven" (*Scofield Reference Bible,* 1002).

We should realize that there is no real conflict between these two texts. They merely present different aspects or phases of the same matter. From Adam and Eve to the end of time, no human being ever was, ever will be, or ever could be forgiven by God except *for* Christ's *sake,* and on the basis of Christ's blood and righteousness. Forgiveness is the very essence of *grace,* and it is simply meaningless to talk about "forgiveness under law" and "forgiveness under grace." *All* forgiveness is under grace; otherwise it would not be forgiveness. If we earn it by obeying the law, then it is wages, not forgiveness. All the Old Testament saints were forgiven *by the grace of God,* on the basis of the blood and righteousness of Christ, through faith in the promised Messiah, as evidenced by their obedient compliance with the ordinance of sacrifice. In their case, no less than in the case of Christians of the present day, willingness to forgive others was the fruit and product of God's having first graciously forgiven them their sins.

Those who hold that God did not forgive the Old Testament saints until he saw in their hearts a spirit of forgiveness of others, not only grossly misread the Old Testament, but virtually deny the doctrine of the total depravity of fallen man. If man is wholly sinful, as the Bible certainly teaches, how can he do good until his heart is renewed by the Holy Spirit? How can he begin to love and forgive his fellow man *until he has been reconciled to God and given a new heart?* And what does being reconciled to God mean, if not divine forgiveness of a person's sins? Nobody ever really loved or forgave his fellow man, in the Bible sense of the words, until he was first by grace reconciled to God, that is, forgiven by God. "Do men gather grapes of thorns, or figs of thistles?" (Matt. 7:16). Does a selfish, hateful, unregenerate heart that is at enmity with God love and forgive others? Not until divine grace works a change and the person is renewed and forgiven.

On the other hand, it is as true today as it was in Old Testament times that God requires his people to have a loving and forgiving spirit toward others. We are not merely "exhorted" to forgive because we have been forgiven; we are *commanded* to forgive, as a matter of duty. If we are not willing to forgive others, we should question the reality of our own Christian experience. If our life does not produce the *fruits* of salvation, what ground have we for assurance that we are saved? Genuine love of the brethren is an evidence that a person is truly saved: "We know that we have passed from death unto life, because we love the brethren. He that loveth not his brother abideth in death" (1 John 3:14). The person who is unwilling to forgive his brother abides in death; that is, the person who does not love his brother is unsaved. Therefore the Bible teaches that the person who is unwilling to forgive his brother is himself unforgiven by God. Forgiving our brother is of course not the *ground* of God's forgiving us; rather, it is the *evidence* that God *has forgiven us.* Where there is the real root, there will also be the fruit; if there is no fruit, then the real root is absent.

Looked at from one point of view, our forgiving others is a moral duty which is enjoined upon us. Looked at from another point of view, our forgiving others is a fruit and evidence of the grace of God in our lives. There is no real conflict between the two. It is only by grace that any sinner is ever enabled to do his duty; the fact that we do our duty (forgive others) is an evidence of God's grace in us. Since forgiving others is the fruit of a person himself being forgiven by God, it could never have been the "condition" of being forgiven by God (as Dispensationalists hold that it was "under the law"). If we want to use the word *condition* at all in this connection, we should only say that our willingness to forgive others is the condition of our *assurance* that God has forgiven us; and this was as true in Old Testament times as today.

5. What is the true interpretation of the phrase "as we forgive our debtors"? The true meaning of this expression is that given by the catechism, namely, that we are "imboldened to ask" and "encouraged to expect" that God will forgive our sins, "when we have this testimony in ourselves, that we from the heart forgive others their offences."

Our readiness to forgive others is an evidence of the gracious working of God's Holy Spirit in our hearts; it is, therefore, an evidence that we have been reconciled to God and that we have a true, saving faith in Jesus Christ. When we are privileged to have this boldness and assurance, we can come to God as children to a Father, confessing our daily sins with full confidence that they will be forgiven—that he will treat us as his children and not as his enemies.

195. Q. *What do we pray for in the sixth petition?*

A. *In the sixth petition (which is, And lead us not into temptation, but deliver us from evil), acknowledging, that the most wise, righteous, and gracious God, for divers holy and just ends, may so order things, that we may be assaulted, foiled, and for a time led captive by temptations; . . .*

Scripture References
- Matt. 6:13; Luke 11:4. The sixth petition of the Lord's Prayer.
- 2 Chron. 32:31; Judg. 2:21–22; Deut. 4:34; 7:19; Job 1:12; 2:6; Acts 20:19; James 1:2–3; Heb. 11:37. For his own wise and holy purposes, God sometimes permits his children to be tempted by evil, and even to yield to temptation for a time.

Commentary
1. What great problem is involved in the subject of temptation? The problem of the relation of God to evil. This problem, we must at once con-

fess, cannot be wholly solved. The Bible does not reveal the solution of it, except in part; and our finite and sin-clouded minds are unable to give a full and final answer to the question: How can a good God permit evil to originate and exist in his creation?

We can only accept what the Bible tells us concerning this subject with childlike faith and humility, and frankly confess that "we know in part" only, and that the full solution is one of the secret things which God has reserved to himself. Those who attempt fully to rationalize this problem run a terrible risk of falling into skepticism.

2. What wrong solutions of this problem have been attempted? (a) The theory of dualism, which holds that good and evil, or God and Satan, are both eternal, so that from all eternity they have confronted each other and have been in conflict with each other. This theory cannot be accepted because it is contrary to the plain teaching of the Bible that in the beginning there was only God, and that evil originated in the universe subsequently to God's work of creation. Only God has existed from all eternity; Satan had a beginning. (b) The theory of a limited God, who would like to prevent and restrain evil in the universe, but finds that he lacks the power to do so. According to this theory God is doing the best he can, but his power is limited in various ways (such as by the laws of nature, or by the free will of his creatures) and therefore it is not possible for him to cope adequately with the forces of evil. This theory cannot be accepted because it is contrary to the clear teaching of the Bible that God is Almighty; he is infinite in his being and all his attributes, and nothing that he chooses to do is too hard for him to accomplish. Moreover, this theory of a limited God fails to explain how evil originated.

3. What light does the Bible shed on the problem of the relation of God to evil? While the Bible does not provide a complete solution, it does give some truths which shed light on the problem and guard us against jumping to erroneous conclusions. What the Bible teaches on the subject may be summarized as follows: (a) Only God has existed eternally; all that exists except God owes its existence to his work of creation (Gen. 1:1). (b) When the created universe came from the hand of God, it was wholly good, that is, free from both physical and moral evil (Gen. 1:31). (c) Evil originated subsequently to the creation, beginning with the fall of certain of the angels "from their first estate," that is, from holiness (2 Peter 2:4; Jude 6). (d) Satan, the chief of the fallen angels, introduced evil into the human race by seducing Eve to commit sin (Gen. 3:1–6). (e) Through the sin of Adam, sin and death became universal in the human race (Rom. 5:12). (f) The fall of the angels and the temptation and fall of the human race, were permitted by God, and also foreordained by God (Eph. 1:11; Pss. 33:11; 115:3; Dan. 4:35). (g) The responsibility for the origin and continuance of evil rests wholly upon the fallen angels and human beings, not at all upon God (Ps. 25:8; 1 John 1:5). (h) God's reason for permitting evil was his own purpose to order it to his own glory in the end (Rom. 11:32; Job 1:12; 2:6; 42:10–17).

4. What aspects of this problem does the Bible leave unexplained?
(a) How evil could originate in beings wholly good, as Satan and all the angels were when they were created. (b) How Satan could succeed in leading our first parents into sin, when there was no evil in their nature to which he could appeal. (c) How God could permit and foreordain evil without himself becoming responsible for its sinfulness.

These are mysteries which baffle our minds. We simply do not know the answers. Yet we dare not attempt to deny the facts. Those who attempt to solve the problem by denying these three facts only plunge into heresies which are totally destructive of Christianity. There is a point at which a reverent ignorance, rather than irreverent speculation and theorizing, becomes us.

5. Is it right to blame our temptations on God? Certainly not (James 1:13–14). God does not himself tempt any person. To blame our temptations on God is wicked and irreverent. Yet it is also wrong to suppose that God has nothing whatever to do with the temptations that we experience. While God does not himself tempt us, it is true all the same that God, for his own purposes, "may so order things" that we are tempted. We should never fall into the atheistic notion that "things" exist or occur apart from the foreordination and providential control of God. When we meet with temptation, we should realize two things: (a) It is not God that is tempting me, but Satan or my sinful heart, or both. (b) Yet this temptation has been foreordained by God as part of his plan, and it is God that has permitted this temptation to come to me, for his own wise purposes.

195. Q. *(continued) What do we pray for in the sixth petition?*

A. *In the sixth petition (which is, And lead us not into temptation, but deliver us from evil), acknowledging . . . that Satan, the world, and the flesh, are ready powerfully to draw us aside, and ensnare us . . .*

Scripture References
- 1 Chron. 21:1; Job 1:6–12; 2:1–7; Zech. 3:1. Satan is our adversary.
- Mark 4:15; Luke 22:31; 2 Cor. 2:11; 12:7. The assaults of Satan come upon God's children.
- Luke 21:34; Mark 4:19; James 4:4; 1 John 2:15–17; Rev. 18:4. The world, as Satan's ally, is ready to draw the Christian into sin.
- James 1:14; Gal. 5:17; Rom. 7:18; 8:12–13. The flesh, or our sin-corrupted nature, as Satan's ally, is ready to lead us into sin.

Commentary

1. Who is Satan? Satan is the chief of the fallen angels. The name *Satan* means "adversary" or "one who opposes." Satan is described in the Bible as "the prince of the power of the air" and "the spirit that now worketh in the children of disobedience." He is also described as the one "which deceiveth the whole world" (Eph. 2:2; Rev. 12:9). According to the Bible Satan is very crafty, intelligent, and powerful, yet always strictly under the control of God (Job 1:12; 2:6; Matt. 4:10–11).

2. What false belief concerning Satan is common today? The notion that Satan has no real, personal existence, but is merely a personification of the forces of evil in the universe and in the human soul. Modern "liberal" theology tends to deny the existence of an objective, personal devil. Satan is said to be just a name for the sinful tendencies and desires of our hearts. The people described in the New Testament as possessed by demons are said to have been simply mentally ill. Such an attitude toward Satan must be highly satisfactory to Satan himself, as he can do his work all the better when his objective existence is denied.

The Bible, however, speaks of Satan and the evil spirits with the utmost realism. Satan is described as a definite person, not a mere personification of an idea. Demon possession is spoken of as objectively real and is carefully distinguished from ordinary insanity and bodily sickness (Matt. 4:24). Christian theology cannot be maintained without belief in a personal devil, any more than it can be maintained without belief in a personal God. Moreover the authority and trustworthiness of Jesus Christ are at stake in this matter. It is clear that Jesus believed in Satan as a real, individual, personal spirit. If we are disciples of Jesus, we must accept his teaching on this as on all other matters.

3. What allies does Satan have in his effort to lead us into sin? Satan, of course, has a great host of fallen angels, or evil spirits, through which he can act and work. Unlike God, Satan is a finite being and therefore cannot be present everywhere at once; but aided by the host of demons he can have his work carried on at many places and in many people simultaneously. Apart from the demons, Satan has two great allies in this world, namely, "the world" and "the flesh." Through these he is able, within the limits of God's permission, to accomplish many of his purposes.

4. What is meant by "the world" as an ally of Satan? The term *world* is used in the Bible with various meanings. It is used in a good sense, meaning the world as God's creation and property (Ps. 24:1; 1 Cor. 3:22; 7:31). It is also used in a bad sense, meaning Satan's kingdom in the world, the sum total of all in the world that is against God (1 John 2:15–17). Even those things in the world which are themselves legitimate and innocent, such as science, art, literature, athletic sports, social fellowship, become allies of Satan when we become too firmly attached to them, and love them more than we love God.

Then, too, there is that world which is always Satan's ally, the world of sinful pride, lusts, and pleasures. Satan is very intelligent, and he knows just how to appeal to a person to try to draw him away from God. One person he will tempt with intoxicating liquor, gambling, nightclubs, and the like; another he will seek to lead to an idolatrous supreme devotion to music or painting; another he will persuade to make science his god, so that he will not worship the living and true God. In each case Satan seeks to use "the world" as his ally.

5. What is meant by "the flesh" as an ally of Satan? When the phrase "the flesh" is used in the Bible in a bad sense, it does *not* mean the human body, as many have wrongly supposed, but the whole sinful nature of fallen man. Paul said that a Christian, in whom the Spirit of God dwells, is "not in the flesh" (Rom. 8:9). Manifestly, a Christian is still *in the body* until his death; therefore "the flesh" cannot mean "the body." The Christian is "not in the flesh," but some of "the flesh" remains in the Christian throughout the present life.

This remaining corruption, or sinful nature in the Christian, gives Satan something to appeal to in seeking to tempt the Christian to sin. "The flesh"— the remaining sinful corruption of nature—is the occasion of innumerable failures and falls on the part of Christians. If it were not for our remaining sinful natures, the temptations of Satan would not be so serious. It is because there remains within us something akin to Satan and utterly contrary to God (Rom. 8:8–9) that satanic temptations are so insidious and so often successful. The Christian cannot take any real comfort from his own strength of character or willpower, but only from the realization that God's power is limitless and God's covenant promises cannot fail. "If God be for us, who can be against us?" (Rom. 8:31). The Christian will not place confidence in his own constancy, but in the fact that the Almighty God is *for* him.

6. Why do Christians often experience a desperate struggle with temptation, while unsaved people seem to enjoy untroubled calm?
It is strictly true that Christians often experience a desperate struggle with temptation. As the catechism says, "Satan, the world, and the flesh, are ready *powerfully* to draw us aside, and ensnare us." By being born again, the Christian has a new spiritual life from God. This new life is utterly contrary to "the flesh" or the old sinful nature. Therefore these two clash in a desperate encounter, the one against the other, and the Christian's soul becomes a battlefield (Gal. 5:17) as one temptation after another has to be faced.

In the case of the unsaved person, on the other hand, the sinful nature or "the flesh" has the field to itself. Special temptation is unnecessary in such a case; Satan is already in control of the person's life. It is when Satan's dominion is challenged by the work of the Holy Spirit that a real struggle between "the flesh" and "the Spirit" takes place.

195. Q. *(continued) What do we pray for in the sixth petition?*

A. *In the sixth petition (which is, And lead us not into temptation, but deliver us from evil), acknowledging . . . that we, even after the pardon of our sins, by reason of our corruption, weakness, and want of watchfulness, are not only subject to be tempted, and forward to expose ourselves unto temptations, but also of ourselves unable and unwilling* *to resist them, to recover out of them, and to improve them; and worthy to be left under the power of them; . . .*

Scripture References

- Gal. 5:17; Matt. 26:41, 69–72; Gal 2:11–14; 2 Chron. 18:3 compared with 2 Chron. 19:2. Because of their remaining corruption of nature, etc., even true Christians are not only subject to temptation, but sometimes actually reckless in exposing themselves to temptation.
- Rom. 7:23–24; 1 Chron. 21:1–4; 2 Chron. 16:7–10. We are unable of ourselves to resist, recover out of, and improve our temptations.
- Ps. 81:11–12. We justly deserve to be under the power of our temptations.

Commentary

1. What class of people is the catechism dealing with in the portion quoted above? With Christian people, believers in Jesus Christ, as shown by the fact that it says "even after the pardon of our sins." Of course people who are not Christians also suffer temptation, are unable of themselves to resist and overcome it, etc. But the catechism is here dealing with the special subject of the effect of temptation on Christian believers. It is here counteracting the errors of those who claim that Christian people can, in this life, attain a spiritual state where temptation can no longer affect them, where "the flesh" will no longer lust against the Spirit, and where spiritual conflict against sin need no longer be engaged in. We should realize that a daily battle against sin and temptation is not characteristic of people's experience before they are born again, but is precisely the experience of born-again Christian people, and is so represented in the Bible.

2. What reasons does the catechism assign the Christian being subject to temptation? "Corruption, weakness, and want of watchfulness." These three reasons really all amount to the same thing: the Christian's remaining corruption of nature, "the flesh" which remains in him even after he is born again and is in process of being sanctified. It is because of this corruption of nature that the Christian is spiritually weak; it is because of this corruption of nature that he is prone to be careless instead of watchful. Bodily or physical weakness is of course a factor in our readiness to yield to temptation, and Satan is very subtle in taking advantage of weakness, sickness, or bodily fatigue in order to seduce the soul. Physical weakness alone, however, could not account for our readiness to yield to temptation; it is only a subordinate accessory to the spiritual factors.

3. Is it too strong to say that Christians are forward to expose themselves to temptations? According to some modern teachings about sanctification, this expression is too strong, but not according to a sound interpretation of the biblical data. Of course Christians are not *always* forward to expose themselves to temptations, but only sometimes. We very easily become proud and confident of our own ability to stand upright and resist evil, and then we are very likely to become careless and even foolhardy with reference to temptation, and too often the outcome is a humiliating lapse into sin from which we are later recovered by the grace of God.

4. What is meant by improving our temptations? To improve our temptations means to benefit from them in some way, as by learning the lessons that they can teach us, being humbled by them, resolving to be more watchful in the future, and praying to God for increased grace to resist the devil. Every temptation that comes to a child of God is permitted in the wisdom and love of God for a good purpose. We are to discern, so far as possible, what that purpose is, and to learn the spiritual lessons involved accordingly.

5. Why are we of ourselves unable to resist, recover out of, and improve our temptations? Because of our remaining sinfulness or corruption of nature, by reason of which our mind is still partly clouded and our will still partly paralyzed. We should realize that we are absolutely dependent on the grace of God for every phase and factor of our salvation, our faith, and our life. Not only are we dependent on the power of God for being born again and believing on Christ at the beginning of our Christian life; we are also dependent on the power and help of God moment by moment and day by day to the end of our earthly pilgrimage. By the special help of the Holy Spirit and the intercession of Jesus Christ our Mediator we are enabled more and more to gain the victory over temptation, to live a holy life, and thus to glorify God.

6. Why does the catechism add that we are worthy to be left under the power of our temptations? In order that we may realize that all our progress in the Christian life is wholly a matter of grace. God often punishes wicked people for their sins by abandoning them to their own sinfulness. That he does not do so in the case of Christian people is not because they are themselves worthy of the special, powerful work of the Holy Spirit in their hearts, but wholly because of the free love and mercy of God.

195. Q. *(continued). What do we pray for in the sixth petition?*

A. *In the sixth petition (which is,* And lead us not into temptation, but deliver us from evil*), . . . we pray that God would so overrule the world and all in it, subdue the flesh, and restrain Satan, order all things, bestow and bless the means of grace, and quicken us to watchfulness in the use of them, that we and all his people may by his providence be kept from being tempted to sin; . . .*

Scripture References

- John 17:15; Pss. 51:10; 119:133; 2 Cor. 12:7–8; 1 Cor. 10:12–13. We pray that God would overrule the world, subdue the flesh, restrain Satan, and order all things so that we may be kept from being tempted.
- Heb. 13:20–21; Matt. 26:41; Ps. 19:13. We pray that God would bless the means of grace, enable us to use them aright, etc., that we may be kept from temptation to sin.

Commentary

1. How does God overrule the world for the benefit of his people?
God overrules the world by his providential control which makes all things—even the acts of Satan and of wicked men—work together for his own glory and the eventual good of his people. The background of this truth is, of course, the Calvinistic (that is to say, the biblical) view of the absolute sovereignty of God. If God is not absolutely sovereign, then he does not really control all that comes to pass, and he cannot make *all things* to work together for good for his people.

Only a God who is absolutely in control of the entire created universe can make all things turn out according to his own predetermined purpose. If some things are beyond the control of God, then there is no telling what unexpected factors may disrupt his plans and ruin everything. As a matter of fact, of course, the Bible emphatically teaches the absolute sovereignty of

God over the entire created universe, including the devil and all his works (Ps. 115:3; Eph. 1:11; Acts 4:27–28; Rom. 8:28).

Back of every fact in the universe is the eternal plan of God, not a mere general plan, but a specific plan that provides in the minutest details for the time, place, causes, effects, and relationships of every individual fact. This eternal plan or counsel of God is put into effect by his works of creation and providence. All that ever takes place—from the fall of a sparrow to the rise of an empire, from the melting of a particular snowflake to the growth of a civilization, from the growth of a particular blade of grass to the formation of a spiral nebula—takes place in exact accordance with the plan and providence of God, and each individual fact fits perfectly into its specific place in the plan. Therefore it is not vain or foolish for us to pray that God would overrule the world and all in it for his glory and our spiritual welfare.

2. Can we always see how God overrules the world for the benefit of his people? No. Sometimes we can see remarkable instances of such overruling, which we call "special providences." The famous Spanish Armada, which was sent to attack and destroy the Protestant nation of England was destroyed by an unexpected storm. There have been many instances, great and small, of such remarkable overruling of the world by God. But often we cannot see how the world is overruled for good. We must believe, on the authority of God's Word, that he will overrule all things for his glory and our good, even when we cannot see how things will work out to make this come true.

3. How does God "subdue the flesh" in the Christian? God does not totally remove or eradicate "the flesh" from the Christian until death, when the souls of believers are made perfect in holiness, and do immediately pass into glory. But God subdues the flesh—limits its activity, and keeps it under control—by the regenerating and sanctifying work of the Holy Spirit. This is a supernatural work of the Holy Spirit, which imparts to the person a new heart, or a new nature, and then after that enables that new nature more and more to become the controlling factor in the person's life. Sometimes after a building has caught fire, we hear an announcement that the fire has been brought under control. This means that while the fire has not yet been put out, but is still burning, yet it is being prevented from spreading and destroying without limit. The remaining corruption in the Christian, called "the flesh," is like a fire that has not been entirely extinguished, but has been brought under control. The new nature more and more gains the ascendancy over it.

4. How does God restrain Satan? The book of Job gives an instance of God restraining Satan (1:12; 2:6). God restrains Satan, according to his own wise plan, by his almighty power, which even Satan is compelled to recognize and obey. Satan is a finite, created spirit, and as such is totally subject to the control of God.

5. How does God use the means of grace to keep his people from being overcome by temptation? The means of grace are the Word, the sacraments, and prayer. These are the appointed means for the conversion and sanctification of sinners. God first of all makes these means available for his elect. They are brought into contact with the visible church, which proclaims the gospel and dispenses the sacraments. Second, the Holy Spirit inclines the heart to use these means of grace, and to use them aright. Third, the Holy Spirit accompanies the right use of the means of grace by his own almighty, supernatural working in the person's soul, so that they are made effectual to their intended purpose. The right use of the means of grace thus accompanied by the inward work of the Holy Spirit keeps the Christian in a spiritual state in which temptation cannot easily appeal to him, or gain a lodgment in his heart.

195. Q. *(continued) What do we pray for in the sixth petition?*

A. *In the sixth petition (which is, And lead us not into temptation, but deliver us from evil), . . . we pray . . . that we and all his people may by his providence be kept from being tempted to sin; or, if tempted, that by his Spirit we may be powerfully supported and enabled to stand in the hour of temptation; or, when fallen, raised again and recovered out of it, and have a sanctified use and improvement thereof; that our sanctification and salvation may be perfected, Satan trodden under our feet, and we fully freed from sin, temptation, and all evil, for ever.*

Scripture References
- Eph. 3:14–17; 1 Thess. 3:13; Jude 24. We pray that God by his Holy Spirit would support us and keep us from falling when we are tempted.

- Ps. 51:12; 1 Peter 5:8–10; 2 Cor. 13:7, 9. We pray that when we have yielded to temptation, God would raise us up again and that our experience might be used for our sanctification.
- Rom. 16:20; Zech. 3:2; Luke 22:31–32. We pray that God would give us victory over the assaults of Satan.
- John 17:15; 1 Thess. 5:23. In the sixth petition of the Lord's Prayer we also pray for our final and complete redemption from all sin and evil.

Commentary

1. Why does God not always keep us from being tempted, or keep us from falling when we are tempted? God, who is almighty, could of course keep us entirely isolated from all Satan's temptations, if it were his purpose to do so. He could also keep us from falling into sin when we are tempted. But such is not always his purpose. For his own wise and proper reasons, God sometimes allows his children to be tempted, and even to fall under the assaults of temptation. One reason for this is easy to discern: that we should not become too proud and self-confident by constant freedom from conflict with sin, or by constant success in striving against it. God allows his children to suffer temptation, and sometimes to fall under it, to keep them humble. But there may be many other special reasons known to God.

2. Give an example from the Bible of a person who was enabled to resist and overcome temptation. (a) Joseph (Gen. 39:9). (b) Micaiah (2 Chron. 18:12–13). (c) Daniel (Dan. 6:10).

3. Give an example from the Bible of a person who was tempted and fell into sin, but was later recovered out of it by the grace of God. (a) David (2 Sam. 12:13). (b) Jonah (Jonah 1). (c) Peter (Mark 14:66–72).

4. What state of mind is likely to result when a Christian yields to temptation and falls into sin? Yielding to temptation and falling into sin will interrupt the Christian's spiritual joy and peace, and produce a troubled, uneasy conscience. His assurance of salvation may be diminished or even destroyed for the time being. Under such circumstances the Christian may become very discouraged spiritually, and may become very formal or neglectful in his use of the means of grace. For all this there is only one remedy: hearty repentance, confession of sin, and prayer for the restoration of the light of God's countenance upon the soul. "Let us therefore come boldly unto the throne of grace, that we may obtain mercy, and find grace to help in time of need" (Heb. 4:16).

5. When will our sanctification and salvation be perfected? Not until we enter the state of glory will we be made perfect in holiness. However, we are to experience a constant progress toward the ideal of perfection throughout our Christian life. Clearly a faithful resistance to temptation, and a "sanctified use and improvement thereof" when we have suffered temptation or have yielded to it, will deepen the quality of our spiritual life and increase our progress in holiness. We should never tolerate the idea that because perfect holiness cannot be attained in this life, therefore we need not resist sin and strive for holiness. We are constantly to advance toward the goal, even though we know we cannot actually attain it in this present life.

6. What is meant by Satan being trodden underfoot? This expression, which is taken from Romans 16:20, refers to special and significant victories given to the saints by the grace of God, whereby Satan is remarkably defeated and his evil designs frustrated. Sometimes after a long and weary conflict with temptation and suffering, God shows his favor by giving his children special and noteworthy victories over the devil and his works. Persecutors of the saints may be cut off by death or otherwise, obstacles to Christian profession and practice may be removed, closed doors may be opened, burdens or handicaps may be removed, etc. Acts 16 narrates how Satan was trodden under the feet of the saints of Philippi, a city where he had previously had the field pretty much to himself.

7. Why should we have confidence in praying that we shall be "fully freed from sin, temptation, and all evil, for ever"? Because God is a covenant-keeping God and completes the good work which he has begun in the Christian. "The LORD will perfect that which concerneth me: thy mercy, O LORD, endureth for ever: forsake not the works of thine own hands" (Ps. 138:8). "Being confident of this very thing, that he which hath begun a good work in you will perform it until the day of Jesus Christ" (Phil. 1:6).

196. Q. *What doth the conclusion of the Lord's Prayer teach us?*

A. *The conclusion of the Lord's Prayer (which is,* For thine is the kingdom, and the power, and the glory, for ever, Amen*), teacheth us to enforce our petitions with arguments, which are to be taken, not from any worthiness in ourselves, or in any other creature, but from God; and with our prayers to join praises, ascribing to God alone eternal sovereignty, omnipotency, and glorious excellency; in regard whereof, as he is able and willing to help us, so we by faith are emboldened to plead with him that he would, and quietly to rely upon him, that he will fulfil our requests. And, to testify this our desire and assurance, we say,* Amen.

Scripture References

• Matt. 6:13. The conclusion of the Lord's Prayer.
• Rom. 15:30. It is proper in prayer to enforce our petitions with arguments.
• Dan. 9:4, 7–9, 16–19. Our arguments in prayer are to be based on God, not on ourselves or other creatures.
• Phil. 4:6; 1 Chron. 29:10–13. To our prayers we are to join praises, ascribing glory to God.
• Eph. 3:20–21; Luke 11:13. God is both able and willing to help us.
• 2 Chron. 20:6, 11; 14:11. By faith we are encouraged to plead with God to help us, and to trust him to answer our prayers.
• 1 Cor. 14:16; Rev. 22:20–21. In testimony of our desire and assurance of answer from God, we say "Amen" at the conclusion of our prayers.

Commentary

1. What special difficulty is involved in the conclusion of the Lord's Prayer? There is a serious question as to whether the conclusion of the Lord's Prayer forms a part of the genuine text of the Scriptures. The Lord's Prayer is found in Matthew 6:9–13 and Luke 11:2–4. The conclusion ("For thine is the kingdom, and the power, and the glory, for ever. Amen.") is not found in Luke, and in Matthew it does not occur in the most authentic and reliable manuscripts. The King James Version includes the conclusion in Matthew 6:13, but the American Revised Version (1901) omits it from the text, and states in the margin: "Many authorities, some ancient, but with variations, add 'For thine is the kingdom, and the power, and the glory, for ever. Amen.' "

Alford's *Greek Testament* states that the conclusion "must on every ground of sound criticism be omitted. Had it formed part of the original text, it is absolutely inconceivable that all the ancient authorities should with one consent have omitted it," and adds: "We find absolutely no trace of it in early times, in any family of manuscripts or in any expositions." Jamieson, Fausset, and Brown's *Commentary on the Whole Bible* states of the conclusion of the Lord's Prayer: "If any reliance is to be placed on external evidence, this doxology, we think, can hardly be considered part of the original text. . . . On a review of the evidence, the strong probability, we think, is that it was no part of the original text."

We should realize that our authority is not the King James Version, but the *genuine* text of the Bible in the original Hebrew and Greek (Confession of Faith, 1.8). While the evidence indicates that the conclusion of the Lord's Prayer is not a genuine part of the text of the Bible, nevertheless the ideas expressed in the conclusion are all true and scriptural, as the texts cited by the catechism demonstrate. Everything in the conclusion can be found taught somewhere in the Bible. Therefore we shall study the conclusion along the lines suggested by the catechism.

2. Is it proper to enforce our petitions with arguments as we plead with God in prayer? Certainly it is, and this practice is exemplified by many prayers in the Bible. We have only to think of the prayers of Moses, of David, of Daniel, and of other Old Testament saints to realize that this is true.

3. What kind of arguments should we use to enforce our petitions in pleading with God? Our arguments should not be based on ourselves, our own character, earnestness, faith, good works, good intentions, or anything else whatsoever about ourselves or other creatures, but on God, his love and mercy, his covenant and promises, his mighty deeds for his people in past times, the honor of his name in the world, etc.

4. Why should we join praises with our petitions? We should join praises with our petitions, ascribing glory to God, because praise is an essential element in prayer. God is supremely worthy to be praised. Man can fulfill no higher or nobler purpose than to praise God. As Augustine said in the beginning of his *Confessions,* "Thou awakest us to delight in Thy praise; for Thou madest us for Thyself, and our heart is restless, until it reposes in Thee."

5. What is the meaning of the word *Amen?* The word *Amen* comes from a Hebrew word meaning "firm," "faithful," "truly." In the Greek New Tes-

tament the word occurs 150 times, of which the King James Version translates 50 by "amen" and 100 by "verily." In the discourses of Jesus recorded
in the Gospels, the word *Verily* or the expression "Verily, verily . . . " occur
frequently. In each case the Greek word is "Amen," meaning "truly."

6. Why do we close our prayers with "Amen"? As the word *Amen*
means "truly," we close our prayers with this word to show our sincere, real
desire and confidence that God will hear and answer our prayers. As the catechism points out, God is the one who is able to help us, because he possesses eternal sovereignty ("the kingdom"), omnipotency ("the power"), and
glorious excellency ("the glory"), and therefore, when we have pleaded with
him to help us according to our need, we are "quietly to rely upon him, that
he will fulfill our requests."

The "Amen" at the end of our prayer is like the signature at the close of
a letter, a token or evidence of our sincere belief and desire. At the same
time it forms a fitting and properly solemn conclusion for our prayers, and
is therefore an indication of reverence.

Index of Scripture

Johannes G. Vos (1903–1983) taught in Geneva College's department of biblical literature, religious education, and philosophy from 1954 to 1978, chairing the department for nineteen of those years. He edited *Blue Banner Faith and Life,* a quarterly journal, from 1945 to 1974, and he wrote most of the articles.

Before joining Geneva's faculty he devoted twenty-four years to serving as pastor of two Reformed Presbyterian churches and as missionary to Manchuria, where he first pastored a small group of believers, then taught at and administered Newchang Bible Seminary.

Vos wrote several books, including *Christian Introduction to Religions of the World, Covenant of Grace, Hebrews, Old Testament History, Philippians,* and *The Scottish Covenanters.* He contributed to *Biblical Expositor* (the Song of Solomon) and *Zondervan Pictorial Encyclopedia of the Bible.* And he edited several works of Geerhardus Vos (his father): *The Self-Disclosure of Jesus, The Teaching of the Epistle to the Hebrews,* and *Biblical Theology: Old and New Testaments.*

J. G. Vos graduated from Princeton University in 1925 with an A.B. degree (Phi Beta Kappa) and, three years later, from Princeton Theological Seminary with a Th.B. In 1938 Westminster Theological Seminary awarded him a Th.M.

He was honored in 1978 with the publication of *The Book of Books: Essays on the Scriptures in Honor of Johannes G. Vos,* edited by John H. White.

G. I. Williamson is a semiretired minister in the Orthodox Presbyterian Church and editor of *Ordained Servant.* He has written several books, including *The Westminster Confession of Faith: For Study Classes* and *The Shorter Catechism: For Study Classes.*